ACCOUNTING SIMPLIFIED

Visit the *Accounting Simplified* Companion Website at **www.pearsoned.co.uk/fortes** to find valuable **student** learning material including:

- Additional practice exam questions with hints and tips to help you complete them
- The latest advice from chief examiners on how to do well in your exams

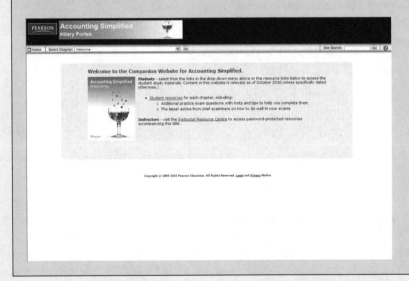

PEARSON

We work with leading authors to develop the strongest
educational materials in accounting, bringing cutting-edge
thinking and best learning practice to a global market.

Under a range of well-known imprints, including
Financial Times Prentice Hall, we craft high-quality print
and electronic publications which help readers to
understand and apply their content, whether studying
or at work.

To find out more about the complete range of our
publishing, please visit us on the World Wide Web at:
www.pearsoned.co.uk

ACCOUNTING SIMPLIFIED

Dr Hilary J Fortes

Financial Times
Prentice Hall
is an imprint of

Harlow, England • London • New York • Boston • San Francisco • Toronto • Sydney • Singapore • Hong Kong
Tokyo • Seoul • Taipei • New Delhi • Cape Town • Madrid • Mexico City • Amsterdam • Munich • Paris • Milan

Pearson Education Limited
Edinburgh Gate
Harlow
Essex CM20 2JE
England

and Associated Companies throughout the world

Visit us on the World Wide Web at:
www.pearsoned.co.uk

First published 2011

ISBN: 978-0-273-73446-8

British Library Cataloguing-in-Publication Data
A catalogue record for this book is available from the British Library

Library of Congress Cataloging-in-Publication Data
Fortes, Hilary Jack.
  Accounting simplified / Hilary Fortes.
    p. cm.
  ISBN 978-0-273-73446-8 (pbk.)
  1. Accounting. I. Title.
  HF5636.F67 2011
  657—dc22

                                                              2010030668

10 9 8 7 6 5 4 3 2 1
15 14 13 12 11

Typeset in 9.5/12.5pt Stone Serif by 35
Printed by Ashford Colour Press Ltd., Gosport

Contents

Contents

Supporting resources
Visit **www.pearsoned.co.uk/fortes** to find valuable online resources

Companion Website for students
■ Additional practice exam questions with hints and tips to help students complete them
■ The latest advice from chief examiners on how to do well in exams

For instructors
■ Downloadable PowerPoint slides for use in lessons and lectures
■ Downloadable Teaching Guide including templates for common accounting reports

Also: The Companion Website provides the following features:

■ Search tool to help locate specific items of content
■ Online help and support to assist with website usage and troubleshooting

For more information please contact your local Pearson Education sales representativeor visit **www.pearsoned.co.uk/fortes**

Preface

This book is intended as an introductory text for students taking a course in accounting or business studies. As such the focus is on the traditional handwritten form of accounting entry and does not attempt to link this with computerised accounting. The opening chapters are designed to acquaint students with the basics of accounting before going on to the more complex situations of double entry and the preparation of accounts.

As most courses also incorporate an obligatory knowledge of management accounting, this has been covered to a limited extent in the final chapters of this book.

The aim of this book is to give an in-depth detailed introduction to financial accounting. While there is, of necessity, some theory, the emphasis is on the application of accounting methods. Each element is important and must be studied, preferably in the order in which it is written.

The book follows widely practised teaching methods. Each chapter is specific to a topic. The order of presentation is significant as it leads to a logical flow from chapter to chapter.

Every chapter has a number of worked examples to help illustrate a particular topic. In addition, self-tests are interspersed with the text to add to the information being delivered. These self-tests are accompanied by suggested solutions. It cannot be overemphasised how important it is for the student to attempt all the questions and check them, only after completion, with the suggested solutions.

Needless to say, this is the first edition of this textbook and there are possibly some errors and omissions. The author would be grateful for any suggestions and comments from the users of this book.

I wish you all happy studies and good luck in your future careers.

Dr Hilary J Fortes
August 2010

Acknowledgements

Author's acknowledgements

In writing a book such as this I hope that my beliefs in 'practice making perfect' will prove invaluable to the many students sitting examinations conducted by a diverse range of examining bodies. I consider that only by working through many examples can students perfect their knowledge of the subject. I have coupled this with comments of chief examiners and subject examiners on many exam papers in the belief that these comments from authoritative persons will help in the study of the subject.

I believe the experience I gained in the many years teaching at various universities both here and abroad has been of immense value. I learnt much – both from colleagues and students. Added to this, I have gained great insight into student examination problems through marking students' work in examinations, be they A levels, university modules or for professional bodies.

It is always difficult to know who to thank and mention by name and who will accept a general thank you. I believe that I am not able to thank the many people and friends who have encouraged me to write this book without being accused of omitting others. So I take the safe route and say 'thank you' to all.

But this would be unfair to one person who has spent considerable time and given me substantial input into the presentation, layout and content of this work. This person is Laurie Lerner who acted as consultant to this project. Laurie is responsible for examining in this subject and has devoted a great deal of time in helping students develop their knowledge of the subject. His constant feedback was greatly appreciated and vastly beneficial to the final content of the work.

I am extremely grateful to the many examining bodies who have agreed to my using these reports together with past examination papers. I wish to acknowledge the permission to use past examination papers granted by the Assessment and Qualifications Alliance (AQA), the Association of Business Executives (ABE), the Association of Chartered Certified Accountants (ACCA) and the Oxford Cambridge and RSA Examination Board (OCR).

I am also grateful to Arriva plc and Tate & Lyle plc for permission to use extracts from their annual reports.

Over the years I have accumulated a great deal of material from the many institutions with which I have been associated. Unfortunately, with the passage of time, identities of the originators of such material has been lost. I hope that they will excuse my using their material without proper acknowledgment.

Finally I thank my wife, Marigold, for her tolerance and understanding of the many hours, days and weeks that I sat at my computer oblivious to all around me.

To you the reader I say thank you. I trust you will find this book of immense use to you and that it will help you succeed in your tasks ahead. I would welcome any comments from you about the book.

Hilary J Fortes
August 2010

Publisher's acknowledgements

We are grateful to the following for permission to reproduce copyright material:

Figures

Figure 29.2 from Annual Report, Arriva Plc, http://www.arriva.co.uk.

Text

Self test 17.1.5 from ABE Introduction to Financial Accounting December 2009; Self tests 17.1.6, 17.1.7 from ABE Introduction to Financial Accounting December 2007; Self tests 17.1.8, 25.5.1 from ABE Introduction to Accounting December 2009; Self test 30.1.16 from ABE Introduction to Accounting June 2007; Self test 30.1.17 from ABE Introduction to Accounting June 2009; Self test 37.1.17 from ABE Managerial Accounting Diploma December 2009; Self test 39.1.14 from AQA Financial Accounting ACC2 Question 1 January 2009, AQA examination questions are reproduced by permission of the Assessment and Qualifications Alliance; Self test 39.1.15 from AQA Financial Accounting Unit 3 Question 1 January 2009, AQA examination questions are reproduced by permission of the Assessment and Qualifications Alliance; Self test 39.1.16 from AQA Financial Accounting Unit 3 Question 4 January 2009, AQA examination questions are reproduced by permission of the Assessment and Qualifications Alliance; Self test 39.1.17 from AQA Introduction to Management Accounting Unit 4 Question 1 January 2009, AQA examination questions are reproduced by permission of the Assessment and Qualifications Alliance; Self test 39.1.18 from AQA Introduction to Management Accounting Unit 4 Question 3 January 2009, AQA examination questions are reproduced by permission of the Assessment and Qualifications Alliance; Self test 39.1.19 from AQA Financial Accounting Unit 5 Question 2 January 2009, AQA examination questions are reproduced by permission of the Assessment and Qualifications Alliance; Self tests 39.1.20, 39.1.21, 39.1.22 from Company Accounts F004 January 2009, Oxford, Cambridge and RSA Examinations (OCR), 2009; Self tests 39.1.20, 39.1.21, 39.1.22 from Company Accounts F004 January 2009, Oxford, Cambridge and RSA Examinations (OCR), 2009; Self tests 39.1.23, 39.1.24 from Accounting Applications F012RB, Oxford, Cambridge and RSA Examinations (OCR), 2009; Self tests 39.1.23, 39.1.24 from Accounting Applications F012RB, Oxford, Cambridge and RSA Examinations (OCR), 2009; Example on page 408 from www.powertoolssoftware.com/QBManual, PowerTools Software, Inc.; Extract on page 409 from www.powertoolssoftware.com, PowerTools Software, Inc.; Self tests 41.7.6, 41.7.7, 41.7.8 from ACCA Preparing Financial Statements June 2007.

In some instances we have been unable to trace the owners of copyright material, and we would appreciate any information that would enable us to do so.

Chapter 1

Introduction to accounting

Objectives After you have studied this chapter, you should be able to:

- understand and explain the purposes of accounting;
- explain the differences between financial and management accounting;
- explain the need for financial information;
- identify the main users of accounts and their information needs.

1.1 Introduction

During the course of your studies of this subject you will read about and work through the many varied aspects of accounting. You will understand that its main purposes are to measure, identify and record transactions. More importantly, accounting is a language for all businesses and it is the intention of this book to teach you how to understand this language and be able to communicate in it.

1.1.1 Terminology

At the very outset we need to clarify certain terms that we use throughout this book. When we speak about a 'business' we mean a commercial concern. This concern is involved either in manufacturing products, selling products or services, or both. The business invests its capital into resources so that it can make a profit for the owners. Because of this profit motive, organisations such as charities, or even local authorities, are excluded from the term.

Later in this work (see Chapter 28) we deal with 'companies', which in effect are merely a particular legal form. These companies, unlike the term 'business' above, can include a charity as well as the other forms described in the paragraph above.

The final term used is 'firm' and this is a rather vague term, which we will restrict to refer to any business that is unincorporated, i.e. not a company.

Before going into the detail of the language of accounting, let us examine the very basics. We do this by asking a most important question.

1.2 What is accounting?

In simple terms we can say that the collection, measurement, analysis and reporting of events in financial terms is what accounting is all about. If we expand this definition we can say that accounting is a process of identifying, recording, measuring and communicating information within a business so as to allow managers, lenders of finance, shareholders and the many other users of the information the opportunity and ability of making informed judgements and decisions.

Once we have identified the information, we need to examine the other key words incorporated into the above definition.

Recording

This is the starting point within the accounting system. Transactions, once identified, must be recorded in a systematic way, as the events take place. To do this, it must be possible to record events and these events must be of a financial nature.

Measurement

As we noted above, we need to be able to measure, no matter if it is our own wealth, the business profits or government spending. To do this there are rules that establish how events are measured.

You will all have had some experience of using the language of accounting, but many of you will probably not even have realised that you are, or have been, using it.

Individuals measure their wealth in terms of the financial value of their assets (house, motor car, stocks and shares, cash, etc.). To do this they use value as the means for measurement. This also applies to organisations which measure their success (i.e. the profit earned) in financial terms.

Governments also measure and report much of their success in financial terms as, for example, the amount spent on education, health, the police, etc.

Communication

This aspect of the definition implies that the message contained in the accounting system is delivered to the different classes of users. We discuss the classes of users in section 1.6, below.

1.3 Accounting groups

In accounting terms there are three groups of people that are usually recognised (see Figure 1.1):

1. Those who prepare accounts and are able to read and interpret accounting information.
2. Those who can read and interpret accounting information but would be unable to actually prepare accounts.
3. Those who can neither prepare nor read accounting information.

Figure 1.1 **Accounting groups**

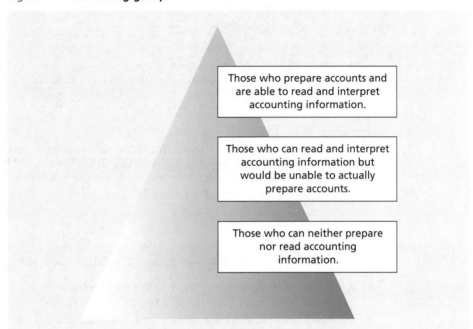

Those who prepare accounts and are able to read and interpret accounting information.

Those who can read and interpret accounting information but would be unable to actually prepare accounts.

Those who can neither prepare nor read accounting information.

Table 1.1 **The three accounting groups**

Group	Prepare	Read	Interpret
1	✓	✓	✓
2	✗	✓	✓
3	✗	✗	✗

It is anticipated that after studying the contents of this book you will not only be able to prepare accounts, but also read and interpret the information provided in accounts with relative ease.

1.4 Financial and management accounting

Accounting is divided into two parts (Figure 1.2). One is addressed to internal parties, while the other is intended for external use. The two areas have differences but are also closely related:

■ Financial accounting is concerned with the preparation of financial statements, covering the whole of the activities of the business, for use by people outside the business (users). This area of accounting is normally regulated by law.
■ Management accounting concerns itself with parts of the business, as well as the whole, and is used to help decision making by management. The main objective is planning and control.

Figure 1.2 **The areas of accounting**

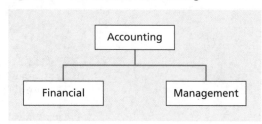

These distinctions do not mean that the basic information is different. The sources are one and the same and decisions are made by both management and users.

We will now examine the two areas in more detail.

1.4.1 Financial accounting

As financial accounts are required by law, the following applies:

■ Disclosure of information must conform to legal requirements and some businesses may show only the minimum requirements.
■ Reports contain financial information which is useful to users.
■ The information provided is geared to external users.
■ The results are based on past activities and, as such, the information provided may be out of date. The results, be they an annual report or an interim report (say, six-monthly), are always backward looking.
■ All information presented is based on accounting concepts and conventions, such as accruals and standards.
■ The results are shown in a set of accounts, which are published annually in a prescribed, summarised format. The information is aggregated and the detail is not shown.
■ For any event to be shown, it must be able to be quantified in monetary terms.

1.4.2 Management accounting

Management accounts provide specific information to managers for a very definite purpose. It may be for the introduction of a new product or the purchase of a new machine. The accounts, as prepared, will assist with planning, control, monitoring, decision making and investment.

All the above can only be possible because management accounting information has certain criteria. This can be summarised as:

■ The information is detailed and up to date. Reports could be weekly, monthly, etc.
■ The statements are usually forward looking (although some may look back).
■ Accounts are confidential and for internal use only.
■ There is no prescribed format and the accounts are not subject to external regulation.

- The information is both financial and non-financial (quantitative and qualitative).
- All information is based on cost accounting systems and not on bookkeeping principles or accounting conventions.

Because of these differences it is often asked if two systems are necessary within an organisation. As we see from the above, each gives different information so we can say that both are needed, but they can be undertaken through a good integrated system which feeds off one database. The larger the company, the greater is the need for good strategic management information, but the more information given, the greater the cost. Therefore, we must consider the costs and the benefits of preparing management accounts.

1.5 The need for financial accounting

Having reviewed the definition, let us continue our journey and examine the need for financial accounting.

Accounts are prepared for a variety of reasons:

- to assess the trading activities of a business;
- to enable external owners to see how managers are performing;
- to control the activities of the business;
- to plan future activities;
- to assist in raising finance; and
- to report on the activities of the business to interested parties.

1.6 Users of business accounts

The efficiency of a business is vitally important to many groups of people. These groups will have a different level of understanding of accounts. Nevertheless, attempts must be made to ensure effective communication to a diversified range of users. At this stage it is essential that we identify the main users of financial accounting.

1.6.1 Shareholders/owners

Owners of a business and existing and potential shareholders of a company will want to know how effectively the directors/managers are performing their stewardship function. This is important in all businesses and more so where the owners/shareholders are not involved in the day-to-day running of a business and rely on the financial statements to communicate the results. They will use the financial statements as a base for their decisions – to dispose of some, or all, of their shares or, in the alternative, to buy some additional shares. In addition, they will also use the financial statements to decide how profits are to be apportioned and allocated.

1.6.2 Trade creditors

These users are from the group of various businesses that supply goods and services to the reporting business. As such they are commonly called the suppliers. They would want to know if they are able to advance credit to a business and, if so, whether they will be paid on the due date. A supplier would also wish to consider whether to supply credit in the future to continue a business relationship.

1.6.3 Long-term creditors

The second division of creditors are those that provide finance to the business. These advances (loans) are usually repaid over an extended (long) period of time. The loan creditors will want to ensure that payments of interest will be made promptly and that capital repayments on loans will be made as agreed.

The loans can be in the form of a debenture (for a detailed explanation of a debenture see section 28.10) or other form of loan.

1.6.4 Employees

This group includes existing, potential and past employees as well as trade unions whose members are employees. Past employees will be mainly concerned with ensuring that any pensions paid by the business are maintained.

Present employees will be interested in ensuring that the business is able to keep on operating, so maintaining their jobs and paying them acceptable wages, and that any pension contributions are maintained.

In addition, they may want to ensure that the business is being fair to them, so that they get a reasonable share of the profits accruing to the business as a result of their efforts.

Trade unions will protect the interests of their members and will, possibly, use the financial statements in wage and pension negotiations.

Potential employees will be interested in assessing whether or not it would be worth seeking employment with that particular business.

1.6.5 Bankers

Where the bank has not given a loan or granted an overdraft, there will be no great need to see the financial statements. Where money is owed to the banks, they will want to ensure that payment of interest will be made when due, and that the business will be able to repay the loan or overdraft on the due date.

1.6.6 Customers

Customers will want to know whether or not the business is a secure source of supply.

1.6.7 Competitors

Business rivals will use the information to assess their own position, compared with that of the rival business. The information will serve as a benchmark for them to use.

Potential takeover bidders, or those interested in a merger, will want to assess the desirability of any such move.

1.6.8 The analyst/adviser group

Financial journalists need information for their readers, while stockbrokers need it to advise investors. Credit agencies want the information in order to advise present and possible suppliers of goods and services to the business as to its creditworthiness.

1.6.9 Inland Revenue

HM Revenue & Customs (HMRC) will need the financial statements to assess the tax payable by the business.

1.6.10 Other official agencies

Various organisations, concerned with the supervision of industry and commerce, may want the financial statements for their specific purposes, for example the Financial Services Authority (FSA), which is an independent body whose aim it is to promote efficient, orderly and fair financial markets (see www.fsa.gov.uk).

1.6.11 Management

In addition to the internally produced management accounts, management is also vitally concerned with any financial statements. This is because the financial statements give an overall view of the financial situation of the business. Management would then consider the effect of such financial statements on the local community and the world at large.

1.6.12 The public

This section of users consists of groups such as ratepayers, taxpayers, political parties, pressure groups and consumers. The needs of these parties will vary accordingly.

It should be noted that in a local community the business can be very important to the local economy.

1.7 Revising the basics

Before continuing with the next chapter it is important that you have a solid understanding of what accounting is about. To do this the following self-tests are set and you need to make sure that you are able to answer the questions posed in these tests.

1.7.1 Self-test

This book shows you how accounts are prepared. It also shows how the information provided is used.

List the six reasons for preparing accounts.

1.7.2 Self-test

There are many users of accounts and the information that they provide.

Identify six such users.

1.7.3 Self-test

Accounting is defined by many organisations, but it is agreed that there are three key words that are associated with accounting.

In your own words identify how you would describe accounting.

1.7.4 Self-test

Accounting is a vast subject and caters for many needs. Traditionally it is divided into two main areas or divisions.

List these two areas and briefly describe what each division provides to its users.

Chapter 2

Double entry

Objectives After you have studied this chapter, you should be able to:

- explain the meaning of double entry;
- describe the dual effect of a transaction;
- describe the layout and content of a ledger account;
- explain the meaning of debit and credit;
- enter transactions to the ledger using the double-entry system;
- understand the information contained in the books of account.

2.1 Double-entry system

Accounting is based on transactions. There are two effects for every transaction, as can be seen from the example below.

We have an existing business which has £1,000 in the bank and a stock of goods purchased for £200. We now buy an additional £300 of goods, for cash.

- Cash decreases ↓
- Stock (goods) increase ↑

From Figure 2.1 we can see that the original amount of cash and stock is reflected in the first section of the graph. You then see the increase in the purchases and the corresponding decrease in the cash balance.

It is this dual effect (duality) that lies behind the double-entry system.

We can say, therefore, that double entry is the system whereby the books of account reflect the fact that every transaction has two sides:

- receiving a benefit by one or more accounts; and
- giving a benefit.

That means that each transaction made in the books of account is made twice (hence the term 'duality'), a debit and a credit. The rule for determining which account is debited and which is credited is very simple and something that you must commit to memory:

The receiver is debited and the giver is credited.

Figure 2.1 **Movement of cash and stock**

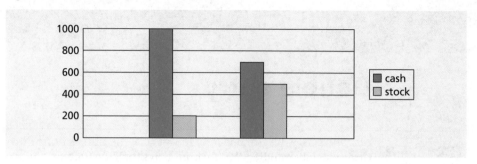

2.2 Source of transactions

A transaction is the act which involves a transfer of money or value, from one person or business to another. It is this act which is recorded in the books of account of the business. The accounts of a business are contained in a book, or a number of books, called ledger(s) (see section 2.3).

In order to record the transaction we need to have some record or proof of it having taken place as, without such, we cannot simply record a transaction.

This proof can be derived from one of two sources:

- *external* – from another person or business, e.g. invoice for purchases; or
- *internal* – from documents prepared by the business to record transactions, e.g. petty cash vouchers, cheque counterfoils, etc.

Make sure that you are fully conversant with double entry, its duality and debit and credit entries. In order to get you into the swing of things, let us set out below some basic transactions.

2.2.1 Worked example

You are given the following list of transactions:

(i)   The business buys a car for cash, paying £3,600.
(ii) The business sells goods on credit to Mr Brown, for £320.
(iii) The business pays £68 cash for an advertisement in the local newspaper.
(iv) The business pays, in cash, the weekly wages of £190.
(v)   The business buys £197 worth of goods on credit from Mr Green, for resale.

You are required to name each ledger account in which the above transactions will be recorded (at this stage ignore the debit or credit aspect of the entries).

Remember that every transaction must be posted to a ledger account and that all these accounts have a heading (or name). Given the above information, you will identify the accounts required for the above transactions as follows:

Transaction no.	Account name	Account name
(i)	Motor car	Cash
(ii)	Mr Brown	Sales
(iii)	Advertising	Cash
(iv)	Wages	Cash
(v)	Purchases	Mr Green

You will see from the above that each account has its own name, e.g. motor car, purchases, wages, etc. We do not mix the transactions into a single account. However, all transactions for one account are shown in that account, e.g. the Cash account will have three entries in the example above.

Now we move forward a step and you are asked to consider which account is increased and which account is decreased as a result of the above transactions.

Transaction no.	Increase	Decrease
(i)	Motor car	Cash
(ii)	Mr Brown	
	Sales	
(iii)	Advertising	Cash
(iv)	Wages	Cash
(v)	Purchases	
	Mr Green	

You will note from the above that in the case of transactions (ii) and (v) there has been no decrease in any account. This does not mean that we have not obeyed the rules of double entry. What it means is that increases can be brought about to both debit and credit entries. We will see this more clearly when we undertake the next part of the question.

Continuing with the example above, you are required to 'post' (that is, to enter) all the transactions to the ledger. Remember that this involves a debit entry and a credit entry. Remember also that the receiver is debited and the giver is credited. So before you start, make sure that you know who the giver is and who the receiver is in all the transactions.

Once you have made this determination, your answer should look like this:

Motor car

Date Cash	3,600	

Cash account

	Date Motor Car	3,600
	Advertising	68
	Wages	190

Sales

	Date	Mr Brown	320

Mr Brown (Debtor)

Date	Sales	320	

Advertising

Date	Cash	68	

Wages

Date	Cash	190	

Purchases

Date	Mr Green	197	

Mr Green (Creditor)

	Date	Purchases	197

2.3 The ledger

From the above examples you can see that all the transactions of a business are posted (entered) into a ledger or ledgers. The ledger can be described as a collection of accounts of a business (in simple terms it is a book with one page for each account), and it is the principal book of account where all financial transactions are recorded. We commonly talk about 'keeping the books' or 'writing up the books'. In this instance the word 'books' means the ledger (or ledgers).

An account is the place where all the information relating to one type of **asset**, **liability**, **income** or **expense** is to be found. It reflects a detailed record of all transactions insofar as they relate to a particular expense, receipt, asset or liability.

2.3.1 Definitions

- **Expenses** – when running a business all firms will have to make payments for expenses which include, for example, wages, rent of premises, telephone costs, electricity and motor expenses. All these costs are recorded in separate ledger accounts so that the business can see the total of each expense.
- **Drawings** – the owner of a business takes money from the business for his/her private needs which is called drawings. Also included as drawings could be the withdrawal, from the business, of goods as well as cash. As these withdrawals are of a private nature they are not classed as an expense of the business. The treatment of drawings is dealt with in detail in Chapter 26.

- **Income** is usually derived from the receipt of money for goods or services provided by the business. If, for example, the business is a dress shop, then the sale of dresses to its customers would generate income to the business. Other forms of income could be interest received from investment accounts, rent received from letting out premises, and even commission received for arranging a sale of a product for someone else.
- **Assets** are items of value that a business possesses. This could be the building it occupies, its delivery vehicles, the computers and other office equipment possessed (termed fixed assets). In addition, the business also has its stock, debtors (people that owe it money for goods or services) and cash in the bank or on hand (all termed current assets).
- **Liabilities** are amounts due by the business, in other words debts that must be paid. For example, amounts due to suppliers for goods or services sold, amounts due for rent and telephone. Any amount owing and to be paid within one year is a short-term liability (also called current liability). Any amounts to be paid for a time period of greater than one year is called a long-term liability.

2.4 A ledger account

Each ledger account, like an individual, has its own name, e.g. motor expenses, advertising, debtors, and all are similar in appearance.

A typical ledger account that we would expect to see in a business is illustrated in Figure 2.2.

The name of the account is placed at the top of the account. This describes the nature of the transaction contained in the account and from its title we can determine if it is an expense or income account, or an asset or liability.

The page is divided into two halves by a central vertical line. The left-hand side is the debit side (Dr) and the right-hand side is the credit side (Cr). Each side is ruled in exactly the same way, with a number of vertical columns.

The first column is for the date of the transaction. The next column gives the details of that transaction. The third column is the folio column. A folio number (page number) is used in cross-referencing between the subsidiary books (see section 2.5) and the ledger. As the folio is not used in exams this column is ignored throughout this text. It is hoped that in this way you will get to understand the principles of the accounting system without getting burdened with too much detail.

Figure 2.2 Ledger account

Dr.					(Name of Account)				Cr.
Date	Details	Folio	£	p	Date	Details	Folio	£	p

Throughout this book we will show a simplified ledger account – commonly known as a 'T' account (it takes the form of a capital 'T'). This shows the date of the transaction, description of the transaction and the amount.

Through the use of these two sides of the ledger, and depending on the type of account (e.g. asset, liability, etc.), we are able to show increases on the one side and decreases on the other. This does not mean that increases are always on the debit side or decreases are always on the credit side. This depends on the type of account that we are dealing with. To illustrate this, using the simplified T account, let us look at the examples below.

2.4.1 Worked example

The first account is for wages and shows the amounts that have been paid in January and February. We see that wages paid increased from £500 in January to a total of £970 by the end of February. To reflect this increase in wages we debited the wage account.

Wages		
31 Jan Bank	500	
28 Feb Bank	470	

The second account is one that relates to a fixed asset – a computer – and shows the purchase of a computer in April. In this account we see that we paid £1,200 by cheque on 30 April for a computer.

Computer (Office equipment)		
30 April Bank	1,200	

The third account is the capital account of the business. It shows how the business was started with a capital injection of £5,000 and another amount, some 3 months later, of £11,000.

In this account we see that capital increased from £5,000 at the end of January to £16,000 at the end of April. In this instance we credited the capital account to reflect the increase.

Capital		
	31 Jan Bank	5,000
	30 April Bank	11,000

From the above examples we learn that we can increase expenses, e.g. wages, by debiting the named account. This will also apply to assets, e.g. a computer, as they are on the debit side of the ledger.

We can increase a liability or capital by crediting the named account.

This will also apply to income, e.g. sales, which is a credit to the relevant ledger accounts.

We also see how the accounting system records the many transactions. Clearly we must record all transactions in at least two separate ledger accounts.

You must always ask yourself an important question when posting transactions and that is:

Have I recorded this transaction in two accounts?

If not, you have not entered the transaction according to the double-entry system. We will see the problem this causes when we discuss the trial balance in Chapter 15.

2.4.2 Self-test

You should now be able to answer the questions below:

Identify the following:	Asset	Liability
(a) Delivery vehicle		
(b) Bank loan		
(c) Stock		
(d) Cash on hand		
(e) Creditors		
(f) Debtors		
(g) Office equipment		
(h) Cash at bank		

Identify the following:	Expense	Income
(a) Rent received		
(b) Telephone charges		
(c) Sales		
(d) Wages and salaries		
(e) Commission paid		
(f) Advertising costs		
(g) Rent payable		
(h) Purchases		

2.4.3 Self-test

Answer the following questions on debits and credits.

Does a debit item:	Yes	No
(a) decrease capital		
(b) decrease income		
(c) decrease liabilities		
(d) decrease assets		
(e) decrease expenses		

Does a credit item:	Yes	No
(a) increase capital		
(b) increase income		
(c) increase liabilities		
(d) increase assets		
(e) increase expenses		

From now on do not think that a credit means an increase or that a debit means a decrease. In accounting, this is far from the truth!

As an additional guide we must remember that assets and expenses are debits while liabilities and income are credits. To illustrate this we look at the following examples of double entry.

2.4.4 Worked example

(i)   A motor vehicle is purchased for £1,145 cash on 2 June 2009.

Motor vehicle

2 June 2009 Cash	1,145	

Cash

	2 June 09 Motor vehicle	1,145

(ii) The owner of the business funded it with a cash deposit of £2,000 on 2 June 2009.

Capital

	2 June 09 Cash	2,000

Cash

2 June 09 Capital	2,000	

(iii) To start its trading activities the business purchased £1,600 of goods on 4 June 2009 from Wholesaler Ltd. An amount of £840 was paid in cash and the balance due for goods purchased was on credit.

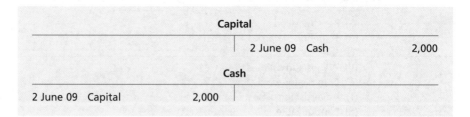

Purchases

4 June 09 Cash	840	
Wholesaler Ltd	760	

Wholesaler Ltd (Creditor)

	4 June 09 Purchases	760

Cash		
	4 June 09 Purchases	840

(iv) A business purchased office equipment from Supplier Ltd on 11 July 2009. The purchase was a credit purchase of £543.

Office equipment		
11 July 09 Supplier Ltd	543	

Supplier Ltd (Creditor)		
	11 July 09 Equipment	543

We can see that each of the items above are entered using a debit and a credit entry. We also note that in certain instances (items (i), (ii) and (iii)) the cash account has been credited with part of the double entry. Instead of having three separate accounts for cash we would have a single one. This account, showing all three transactions will appear as follows:

Cash				
2 June 09 Capital	2,000	2 June 09 Motor vehicle	1,145
		4 June 09 Purchases	840

It is important to note that posting of transactions to the ledger are done in a very formal way. The date of the transaction must be shown, as is the description of the transaction. This description is normally the title of the other account of the double entry and so allows anyone reading the ledger the opportunity of tracing the transaction to the opposite side.

All these accounts are collected together into a ledger and we will see later that it is from this ledger (or ledgers) that the financial statements are ultimately prepared.

2.5 Subsidiary books

The ledger can be divided into a number of smaller ledgers. These smaller ledgers are subsidiary to the main ledger and record transactions prior to entry (or posting) to the main ledger, hence they are called subsidiary books.

Examples of these subsidiary books are:

- the sales (or debtors') ledger (which records who owes us money);
- the purchase (or creditors') ledger (where we record what we buy and how much we owe); and
- the general ledger (where all our remaining transactions are recorded).

All of these subsidiary books will be discussed later (see Chapters 8 and 9).

2.5.1 Self-test

What you need to do at this stage is identify the ledger in which the following transactions would be shown.

Transactions	General ledger	Sales ledger	Purchase ledger
Cash sales			
Rent			
Bank			
Credit purchases			
Credit sales			
Wages paid			
Rent received			

2.6 Understanding ledger entries

You should also be able to interpret and understand what each ledger account tells you. It sets out a transaction and you need to interpret it. Take the following ledger accounts and by looking at each transaction, interpret what has happened.

Example 1

			Bank			
1 Mar 09	Capital	10,000	1 Mar 09	Rent		500
11 Mar 09	Sales	21,500	3 Mar 09	Gibson Wholesalers		1,000
			29 Mar 09	Drawings		1,000
			30 Mar 09	Motor expenses		1,900
				Sundry expenses		1,050
				Salaries		4,000

In the above account, we can 'read', for example, that rent of £500 was paid by the business on 1 March 2009. We also see that £10,000 was paid into the business as capital. We received £21,500 in cash sales and paid out various other items shown in the account above.

Example 2

		Creditor – J Smith			
31 May 09	Bank	15,300	31 May 09	Purchases	45,990

		Purchases		
31 May 09	J Smith	45,990		
	Cash	38,961		

In the accounts above we see that the credit purchase from J Smith amounted to £45,990. In addition we paid £38,961 for cash purchases. We also see that we paid J Smith £15,300 by cheque.

Example 3

	Sales	
	31 May 09 Cash	6,900
	J Jones	41,000

The above account shows us that we sold goods on credit to J Jones to the value of £41,000. A further amount of £6,900 was sold for cash.

	Debtor – J Jones	
31 May 09 Sales	41,000	

Once we are able to 'read' the various ledger accounts, we are closer to having a full understanding of double entry.

Before we continue let us work through some questions which will help illustrate the duality of transactions and highlight the accounts that we debit and those that we credit.

2.6.1 Worked example

Alex starts a new business on 1 January 2009 and the first thing he does is to invest £8,000 into the business bank account.

Bank account			
1 Jan 09 Capital	8,000	2 Jan 09 Purchases	1,200
4 Jan 09 Sales	2,100	8 Jan 09 Purchases	1,500
		Wages	110

We debit the bank account (money paid into the bank, which is the receiver) and credit the owner's (Alex) capital account (the giver).

Capital account		
	1 Jan 09 Bank	8,000

We are now in a position to start up the business, having received the necessary capital from the owner.

On 2 January Alex purchases, by cheque, stock for resale. Let us assume that he buys goods to the value of £1,200.

Purchases		
2 Jan 09	Bank	1,200
8 Jan 09	ABC	3,800
	Bank	1,500

We debit purchases with £1,200 and credit the bank account with a similar amount (*note we use one bank account for all transactions*).

The important thing to note in this last transaction is that we credit the bank account to reduce the amount remaining in that account. We do not show a minus figure on the debit side but a credit to the ledger account. After these transactions there is a positive bank balance of £6,800 and this will show as an asset of the business.

Having bought goods for resale Alex then sells the goods on 4 January for £3,500. Of this amount he receives a cheque for £2,100. The remainder of the transaction is a credit sale to G Bush.

Sales				
		4 Jan 09	Bank	2,100
			G Bush	1,400

Debtor – G Bush		
4 Jan 09	Sales	1,400

We credit the sales account with the £3,500 (total) and debit the bank account with £2,100 and the debtors' account of G Bush with £1,400.

On 8 January Alex buys additional goods for £5,300 of which £3,800 is bought on credit from I Supply & Co. He issues a cheque for £1,500 for the other purchases.

Creditor – I Supply & Co.				
		8 Jan 09	Purchases	3,800

He hires D Smith to work with him and agrees to pay him a wage of £110 per day.

Wages		
8 Jan 09	Bank	110

At the end of that day he would debit purchases with £5,000, credit the creditors' account of I Supply & Co. with £3,800 and credit the bank account with £1,200. He pays D Smith his wages for the day and so we debit the wages account and credit the bank account with £110.

Work through the above example very carefully and make sure that you understand why we debit and why we credit various accounts. Once you are confident that you understand this example, you are ready to work through a number of additional self-test questions on your own. You must at all times make sure that you are familiar with the debit and credit concept of the double-entry system.

2.6.2 Self-test

Mark has set up his business and is preparing to commence trading in his sports goods store as from 1 April 2009.

Before he starts to trade he introduced capital of £30,000. This was by way of a cheque paid into the business on 25 March 2009. On the same day he purchased a motor van and paid out £7,400 by cheque. In addition he paid for shop fittings (£2,900), purchases (£7,100) and half the rent for April for the shop (£2,000). All these payments were made by cheque. He purchased, on credit, goods for resale from Tennis Ltd to the value of £3,400.

Mark's business transactions for the first week in April 2009 are as follows:

1 April   Paid £150 by cheque to the local newspaper for an advertisement.
2 April   Paid £2,000 for the balance of rent due by cheque.
3 April   Sold goods for cash £150.
4 April   Sold goods for cash £210.
5 April   Sold goods for cash £80.
6 April   Sold goods for cash £153.
6 April   Purchased additional goods from Tennis Ltd on credit for £1,500.
7 April   Cash sales £197.
7 April   Paid £120 wages to shop assistant in cash.
7 April   Paid £600 cash into the bank.

You are required to open the necessary ledger accounts for all the above transactions and post the entries to those accounts. Make sure that both the debit and credit entries are made for each transaction.

At the end of this period you would balance the cash and bank accounts. (*If you have entered the accounts correctly you will see that an amount of £70 remains in the cash account and that the bank account shows a balance of £9,050.*)

Keep your ledger account balances as we will use these in a later chapter (section 15.1.2) when we prepare the trial balance. At this stage you have no proof that you have entered all the ledger accounts correctly. Only once we prepare the trial balance do we know that we have posted all the items.

2.6.3 Self-test

On 1 September 2009 Larry started an antiques business. The transactions of Larry for September 2009 were as follows:

1 September	Paid £40,000 into the business bank account.
2 September	Purchased antiques for £26,000. Cheque issued from the bank account.
4 September	Paid insurance premium of £980 for the year ending 31 September 2010. Payment was made by cheque.
10 September	Larry was charged £1,200 for packing material by Upack.
12 September	A bill was sent to Acquire for goods sold, £12,900.
19 September	A cheque for £8,000 was received from Acquire.
25 September	A bill for £5,300 was sent to Okay for antiques sold.
27 September	Larry paid D Brown, by cheque, wages for the month of £1,100. Larry withdrew £2,000 from the bank account for personal use.
28 September	Goods invoiced of £1,900 were damaged and sent back by Okay for credit.

You are required to prepare the ledger accounts for the month of September 2009 and balance each ledger account at the month end.

Note: in section 15.1.3 we will use these balances to prepare a trial balance.

2.6.4 Self-test

On 1 July 2009, J Cecil opened a gift store. He transferred £20,000 cash from a personal bank account to the business. During the remainder of the month he completed the following transactions, all of which were by cheque.

10 July	Paid rent, £900
11 July	Purchased a delivery truck from MotoTrade for £15,000. He paid £7,000 on date of purchase. The balance due is to be paid on 31 December 2009.
12 July	Purchased shelving and other fixtures, £3,700.
14 July	Purchased goods, £885.
14 July	Paid insurance premiums, £750.
15 July	Sold goods and received immediate payment of £1,200.
16 July	Purchased £1,240 worth of goods on credit from Hilcom Gifts.
17 July	Paid wages, £600.
24 July	Sold goods on credit, £3,100, to Monica.
27 July	Paid telephone expense, £1,205.
27 July	Paid gas expense, £173.
28 July	Received payment from Monica, £1,350.
31 July	Paid wages, £1,350.
31 July	Withdrew money for personal use, £1,500.

You are required to write up all the above transactions to the relevant ledger accounts and show the closing balances at 31 July 2009.

2.6.5 Self-test

On 1 June 2009, Jack started a clothing business. During the month, Jack completed the following transactions, all of which were by cheque unless stated otherwise:

5 June	Jack transferred £15,000 from a personal bank account to an account to be used for the business.
5 June	Paid rent for the month, £1,950.
7 June	Purchased office equipment on credit from File & Co. for £6,250.
8 June	Purchased a used car for £16,000 from NuVan Ltd and paid £9,500 on account. The balance was payable in 6 months.
10 June	Purchased goods, £725.
12 June	Cash sales of £1,600.
15 June	Paid wages of employees, £800.
20 June	Paid insurance premiums of £725.
22 June	Invoiced A Lu for clothes bought, £1,950.
24 June	Received an invoice from NuVan Ltd for motor expenses, £310.
26 June	Cash sales of £1,650.
28 June	Purchased goods, £590.
29 June	Paid gas and electricity expenses, £490.
29 June	Paid sundry expenses, £195.
30 June	Received from A Lu on account, £1,200.
30 June	Paid wages of employees, £200.
30 June	Paid File & Co. on account, £1,500.
30 June	Withdrew money for personal use, £500.

You are required to show the transactions in the ledger accounts.

After entering all the transactions you must balance the ledger accounts at 30 June 2009.

Note: this question will also be used in section 15.1.4 where we will be able to ensure that all the items above have been posted in accordance with the double-entry system.

2.6.6 Self-test

You are required to indicate whether the following ledger accounts are normally debits or credits.

	Debit	Credit
Creditors		
Capital		
Loan from bank		
Postages		
Drawings		
Liability		
Revenue		
Fixed asset		

2.7 What the books tell us

The various records contained in the books of account assist in providing an insight into the financial health and growth potential of the business.

In particular they set out:

- how much the business owes others, and how much others owe the business;
- the details of income, expenses, assets and liabilities;
- the source of profits or losses;
- the profit or loss for any given period; and
- the value of the business.

Accounting does not, and cannot, exist in a vacuum – it reflects the activities of the business which reacts and interacts with the external environment. This is shaped by many different forces which may be political, social, legal or economic.

Business decisions have social as well as economic consequences, and businesses must accept responsibility for the social implications of their activities, such as their impact on the environment, or the extent to which employment opportunities are provided.

Chapter 3

Ledger accounts

Objectives   After you have studied this chapter, you should be able to:

- explain the need for balancing the ledger;
- balance and close off ledger accounts;
- distinguish between debit and credit balances;
- explain the importance of dates, descriptions and balances.

3.1 | Balancing the ledger accounts

After all transactions are entered (posted), the ledger accounts are balanced –
i.e. the difference between the debit side and the credit side is calculated. This is
usually done at the end of a trading period.

The balance is transferred, as a single amount, to the following period, or to
the profit and loss account (see Chapter 20) or balance sheet (see Chapter 22).

Wages					
31 March	Cash	800	30 June	P&L account	2,700
30 April	Cash	600			
31 May	Cash	900			
30 June	Cash	400			
		2,700			2,700

In the above example, wages have been paid from March until June. At the end
of June a profit and loss account is to be prepared and therefore the total of the
ledger account is transferred to the profit and loss account at that date. As the full
amount (£2,700) is transferred to the profit and loss account there is no balance
on this account.

The balance is the amount by which one side of the account exceeds the other
side. This allows you to see at a glance a single amount for each ledger account –
what is in the bank, or the value of debtors, or what we owe.

In order to balance an account there are a number of steps that we have to take. These are:

■ Add the money columns on the debit and credit sides and find the difference (which is the balance).
■ Enter the balance on the side where the total is less than the other. This is the balance carried down (c/d).
■ The two sides are now equal and the totals are written on the same line on each side and ruled off.
■ The balance is brought down (b/d) to the side with the higher total. Write this balance immediately below the total. This completes the double entry which is inherent in the balancing process.
■ The balance b/d is the opening balance for the next period.

The following account illustrates the above process.

Cash account					
3 Apr	Sales	150	7 Apr	Bank	600
4 Apr	Sales	210	7 Apr	Wages	120
5 Apr	Sales	80	7 Apr	Balance c/d	70
6 Apr	Sales	153			
7 Apr	Sales	197			
		790			790
8 Apr	Balance b/d	70			

We have referred to the balancing of the accounts at the end of a period. We must understand that accounts can be balanced at any time, even when the ledger page is full and we need to carry the balance forward on to a new page. Usually we balance the accounts at the end of a month, or year, as it is then that we prepare the final accounts.

Once we have balanced off the ledger accounts the balances are then transferred to the trial balance. All debit balances are shown on the left side of the trial balance and all credit balances are on the right. After entering all the balances we total the trial balance to ensure that it balances. For more details on this see Chapter 15.

From this balanced trial balance we are then in a position to prepare the financial statements. We no longer have to page through the various ledger accounts to extract information – it is all in one place: the trial balance.

At this stage it is important that you practise balancing off various ledger accounts. In the following examples you are given ledger accounts with opening balances and details of transactions for the following month. Enter these transactions and then balance off the accounts as explained above.

3.1.1 Self-test

Olivier commenced business on 1 January 2009. An amount of £11,000 was paid in by J Olivier by cheque as capital and he also received a cheque for £7,000 as a loan from A Turner.

The transactions for the six months ended 30 June were as follows:

Account	Amount £
Drawings	9,000
Cash received from debtors	12,500
Cash paid to creditors	15,300
Expenses paid	7,900
Credit purchases	34,200
Cash purchases	21,900
Payment for motor vehicle	18,000
Cash sales	9,400
Credit sales	32,000
Returns inward	325
Returns outward	197

You are required to show the bank account (all cash is banked immediately) as well as ledger accounts of the sales and purchases for the six months. The debtors' and creditors' accounts at 30 June 2009 should also be shown.

Note: you can ignore dates in this answer. In most exam questions you must show the dates and carry down balances on the ledger accounts.

3.1.2 Self-test

You are presented with the following ledger account in the books of Ann. The account gives details of the bank transactions for the month of July 2009.

You are required to balance this account and show the opening balance at 1 August 2009.

	Bank				
1 Jul 09	Capital	40,000	10 Jul 09	Rent	1,900
15 Jul 09	Sales	3,587	11 Jul 09	Computer	2,100
28 Jul 09	Debtor	2,984	12 Jul 09	Phone	156
31 Jul 09	Interest	143	14 Jul 09	Purchases	1,123
	Sales	1,988		Drawings	1,200
			17 Jul 09	Wages	950
			27 Jul 09	Printer	287
				Electricity	342
			31 Jul 09	Wages	1,980
				Insurance	3,500

3.1.3 Self-test

	Cash account				
1 Sept 09	Loan	4,000	10 Sept 09	Wages	1,000
15 Sept 09	Sales	2,000	11 Sept 09	Rent	2,000
28 Oct 09	Commission	500	12 Oct 09	Postages	100
31 Oct 09	Interest	850	14 Nov 09	Purchases	2,300
11 Nov 09	Sales	2,300	19 Nov 09	Wages	500
			24 Nov 09	Purchases	900
			27 Nov 09	Rent	1,000

You are required to balance the cash account for September, October and November 2009.

In addition you are required to post the payments made for purchases and wages and show the balances on each of those accounts at 30 November 2009.

3.2 Carry forwards

Do not confuse the various terms used. We have read about the terms 'b/d' and 'c/d' in section 3.1. In addition, you will come across two other terms – carried forward (c/f) and brought forward (b/f). These terms are not used in carrying down a balance on an account. The only time they are used is when we carry an amount forward, from one page of the ledger to another. We add the two sides and carry forward the total of each side to the next page. At the top of the next page we show each total as having been brought forward. An example is shown below.

	Cash account				
3 Apr	Sales	150	7 Apr	Bank	600
4 Apr	Sales	210	7 Apr	Wages	120
5 Apr	Sales	80			
	Balance c/f	440		Balance c/f	720

As the ledger account continues on to the following page we need to transfer the balances at the end of page one to page two. We do this by 'carrying forward' the balances from the one page to the next.

	Cash account				
5 Apr	Balance b/f	440	7 Apr	Balance b/f	720
6 Apr	Sales	153	8 Apr	Balance c/d	70
7 Apr	Sales	197			
		790			790
8 Apr	Balance b/d	70			

3.2.1 Self-test

Marge started a gift shop on 1 March 2009. The following cheque payments are made during the month:

1 Mar 09   Marge transferred £10,000 to the business.
1 Mar 09   Paid rent for office, £500.
3 Mar 09   Purchased goods from Gift Wholesalers, £2,900.
8 Mar 09   Paid Gift Wholesalers on account, £1,000.
11 Mar 09   Cash sales, £21,500.
29 Mar 09   Withdrew cash for personal use, £1,000.
30 Mar 09   Paid motor expenses, £1,900, and sundry expenses, £1,050.
30 Mar 09   Paid office salaries, £4,000.

You are required to prepare all the ledger accounts for the above transactions and to balance them at month end.

You also are required to answer the following questions:

(a) What is the total revenue recorded in the ledger?
(b) State the amount of total expenses for the month
(c) What is the net income for March? (Assume that all goods purchased have been sold.)

Chapter 4

Cash book

Objectives After you have studied this chapter, you should be able to:

- explain the need for a cash book and how to write it up;
- write up a cash book and balance it off at the end of a period;
- post cash book entries to ledger accounts;
- explain the function of the discount columns.

4.1 Introduction

Two very important accounts are the cash account and the bank account. We need to know on a daily basis what funds the business has and keep a close watch on the flow of funds. These two accounts are kept in the cash book. The cash book is classed as a ledger.

Details of receipts and payments are kept in a separate book (or ledger) – the cash book[1] – which is a book of prime (original) entry (see section 8.1) and a division of the ledger.

Importantly, the cash book is part of the double entry system. All cash and bank transactions are first entered into this book and then afterwards posted to the ledger to complete the double entry.

All entries on the debit side of the cash book are posted to the credit side of their respective accounts and vice versa (see, however, section 4.4 and 7.3.1 where this does not apply).

To check the cash balance and make sure it is correct we can count the cash on hand and see that it agrees with the balance shown in our ledger account (cash book).

In the case of the bank account in the cash book there are other transactions such as bank charges that the bank may be taking from our bank account, but we do not yet know about them. Therefore we need to reconcile (agree) our bank balance in the cash book with that of the records kept by the bank. This topic is covered in detail in Chapter 5.

---

[1] Only the cash book can properly be described as a ledger account and the balances in the cash book are taken directly to the trial balance.

The 2-column cash book

The 2-column cash book refers to the two most important columns in the cash book – 'Cash' and 'Bank'. This is a very simple form of cash book. It is designed to record all transactions concerning money – cash, cheques, direct debits, etc. By maintaining this cash book it is possible to keep the cash account and the bank account in one ledger.

Without this 2-column cash book we would have to use two separate ledger accounts – one for 'Cash' and the other for 'Bank'. The 2 columns allow us to combine them in one book and to record transactions on a daily basis. At the end of a period, usually one month, we balance the bank and cash columns to determine what funds are available.

Cash book

Date	Details	Cash	Bank	Date	Details	Cash	Bank
1 Jun 09	Sales	255		3 Jun 09	Wages	45	
9 Jun 09	Cash		195	8 Jun 09	Rent		120
				9 Jun 09	Bank	195	

If we receive cash then we show it in the cash column on the debit side. Only when the money is banked do we remove the amount from the cash column (by a credit entry) and add it to the bank column (by a debit entry). This is illustrated in the transactions of 9 June 2009 above when £195 was paid into the bank.

Cash book

Date	Details	Cash	Bank	Date	Details	Cash	Bank
1 Jun 09	Sales	255		3 Jun 09	Wages	45	
9 Jun 09	Cash		195	8 Jun 09	Rent		120
10 Jun 09	Sales		100	9 Jun 09	Bank	195	
12 Jun 09	Bank	145		12 Jun 09	Cash		145

If cash is banked immediately (£100) then it is entered into the bank column at that stage.

If we need cash in the business, then we make out a cheque and enter this in the bank column (on the credit side) and also in the cash column (on the debit side). This is illustrated in the transactions of 12 June 2009 above, when £145 in cash was taken out of the bank.

Cash book

Date	Details	Cash	Bank	Date	Details	Cash	Bank
1 Jun 09	Sales	255		3 Jun 09	Wages	45	
9 Jun 09	Cash		195	8 Jun 09	Rent		120
10 Jun 09	Sales		100	9 Jun 09	Bank	195	
12 Jun 09	Bank	145		12 Jun 09	Cash		145
				15 Jun 09	Balance c/d	160	30
		400	295			400	295
15 Jun 09	Balance b/d	160	30				

When we balance the cash book the situation may arise where we have a debit balance in the cash column and a debit or credit balance in the bank column. If the latter is a credit balance then it means that the bank account is overdrawn. In other words we have paid out more than we have received and as a result the business is operating on an overdraft.

4.3 Source documents

To create all the entries there must be some form of documentation for writing up the cash book. The documents available as the source for the transactions are the till rolls (cash register slips) and paying-in books, which will establish the receipts by the business which become debit entries. Cheque books or the bank statement would be the source document for credit entries. Although these are not all the source documents, they are the most common.

4.4 The 3-column cash book

The difference between the 2-column cash book discussed in section 4.2 above and the 3-column cash book is that by adding the extra column, discounts can be recorded. By using the extra column for recording the discount we are able to post both discount received and discount allowed, in total, instead of individually.

Discount received occurs when a supplier allows us to pay a little less for the goods ordered because we have made a prompt payment. Discount allowed is when we accept a smaller amount than originally invoiced (billed) from a customer for prompt payment. Discount received and discount allowed are known as 'cash discounts' even though the invoice may be paid by cheque.

We must remember that the discount column is a 'memorandum' column[2] and as such is not part of the double-entry system. The total of the discount columns must be entered to the relevant ledger accounts, e.g. total discount received will be posted to the credit side of the discount received account. The total of the discount allowed column will be debited to the discount allowed account.

---

[2] This memorandum column is where a record can be made of the discount received or allowed. It serves as a record of the amounts and is used for convenience.

4.4.1 Worked example

The following example illustrates a 3-column cash book and shows the various ledger accounts to which items in the cash book are posted.

Note that the item for discount allowed (shown on the debit side of the cash book) is posted to the **DEBIT** side of discount allowed in the ledger. The credit entry for this discount is posted to the debtors' ledger account.

In a similar way the discount received entry from the credit side of the cash book is posted to the **CREDIT** side of the discount received account, with a corresponding debit entry to the creditors' account.

Cash book

Date	Details	Discount allowed	Cash	Bank	Date	Details	Discount received	Cash	Bank
4 Jul 09	Debtor A	20		103	3 Jul 09	Creditor	14		139
9 Jul 09	Sales		9	51	6 Jul 09	Wages			140
31 Jul 09	Sales		89	404	31 Jul 09	Purchase		35	200
						Balance c/d		63	79
		20	98	558			14	98	558
1 Aug 09	Balance b/d		63	79					

Debtor A

				4 Jul 09	Bank	103
					Disc allowed	20

Sales

				7 Jul 09	Cash	9
					Bank	51
				31 Jul 09	Cash	89
					Bank	404

Creditor

3 Jul 09	Bank	139		
	Discount received	14		

Wages

6 Jul 09	Bank	140		

Purchases

31 Jul 09	Cash	35		
	Bank	200		

Discount allowed

31 Jul 09	Cash book	20		

Discount received

			31 Jul 09	Cash book	14

4.5 Balancing the cash book

As is the case with any ledger account, the cash book must be balanced from time to time. This is usually done every month and is compared with the bank statement to ensure that all items are entered in the cash book (such as bank charges).

As was explained in the case of other ledger accounts (see section 3.1), the totals of the debit side and credit side are established and the difference is entered as the balance to be carried down (c/d). The columns are ruled off and the balance brought down (b/d) is shown directly below the total on the side which had the greater total.

The following example illustrates the procedure:

Cash book

Date	Details	Discount allowed	Cash	Bank	Date	Details	Discount received	Cash	Bank
4 Jul 09	Debtor	20		103	3 Jul 09	Creditor	14		139
9 Jul 09	Sales		49	51	6 Jul 09	Wages			140
15 Jul 09	Sales		39	104	9 Jul 09	Rent			170
19 Jul 09	Debtor	35		458	11 Jul 09	Creditor			230
24 Jul 09	Debtor			200		Purchase		35	200
					31 Jul 09	Balance c/d		53	37
		55	88	916			14	88	916
1 Aug 09	Balance b/d		53	37					

4.5.1 Self-test

Green is a sole trader who records all her cash and bank transactions in a 3-column cash book. During July 2009 the following transactions took place.

1   Cash balance £123 and bank balance £482 debit balance.
5   Received cheque of £98 from Lite in full settlement of her account of £106. The cheque was deposited into the bank account.
8   Received £87 cash from Noble in full settlement of her debt of £100.
11   Paid wages of £145 in cash.
16   Paid Walker £178 by cheque in full settlement of the £196 owing.
17   Received a cheque for £165 from King to settle the amount of £180 owing. The cheque was paid into the bank.
24   Paid Sharp £25 by cheque to settle the account due of £27.
27   Transferred £64 cash into the bank.
28   Bank debited Green with £41 as bank charges for the month.

You are required to:

(a) Write up a 3-column cash book for the month and balance it at the month end. Your three columns should be Discount, Cash and Bank (dates can be ignored).

(b) Show the totals of discount to be posted and indicate the respective ledger accounts.

4.5.2 Self-test

You are given the following information by Walker relating to his transactions for the month of July 2009.

Receipts during the month:

From Debtors:

  3 July 09   Jacks paid £320 by cheque.
11 July 09   Jacks paid £240 less £18 discount by cheque.
15 July 09   Martha paid £420 in settlement of her account of £450 by cheque.
21 July 09   Martha paid £149 by cheque (for which she was allowed a discount of £37).

From cash sales (all paid in cash):

  6 July 09   £220
19 July 09   £430
28 July 09   £172

Payments during the month:

Cash payments:

- Cash purchases of £60
- Petty Cash £195
- Wages £185

Cheque payments:

- Telephone £48
- Cash purchases £140
- Tom & Co. (creditor) £170 together with a £30 discount
- Green Bros (creditor) £165 in settlement of their account for £190
- Cash purchases £245

In addition £340 was transferred from the bank account to the cash account during the month.

    You are required to write up and balance the 3-column cash book for July 2009.

Chapter 5

Bank reconciliation

Objectives   After you have studied this chapter, you should be able to:

- explain the meanings of the various bank terms;
- understand the need for reconciling the cash book;
- reconcile the bank statement with the cash book balance;
- adjust the cash book balance as part of the reconciliation.

5.1   Introduction

We read in Chapter 4 how to write up a cash book. There are certain transactions with our bank that we may not be aware of until we receive the monthly bank statement. These transactions must obviously also be included in our cash book as they are either expenses of the business or income which must be accounted for in our accounts. We check the cash book with the bank statement on a regular basis. (In this chapter, as in others, we assume that by regular, we mean at least monthly.)

All entries in the bank statement must agree with those in the cash book. We must note, however, that all debits in the cash book are credits in the bank statements and vice versa. This is because the bank statement is a record of the customer's account in the bank's books. If there is a disagreement between the two balances this is because of some omission or error.

The figure in the cash book must reconcile with the balance in the bank statement – this ensures that both are accurate.

The bank reconciliation explains the difference between the cash book balance and that in the bank statement.

The reasons for the difference could be one or more of the following:

- errors that we or our bankers may have made;
- unpresented cheques – this could be an outstanding cheque which may only be presented for payment in the following period;
- outstanding deposits which would also be credited in the next period;
- deposits not yet shown on the bank statement where, for example, the deposit was not made at our own branch;
- a direct transfer (credit transfer) to our account by a debtor of which we are unaware;
- bank charges and interest;
- standing orders; and
- direct debits.

5.2 Definitions

There are a number of terms used in bank transactions such as:

- a dishonoured cheque is where a customer's cheque is not cleared (paid) by his/her bank;
- credit transfer is an amount paid directly into or out of your bank account;
- overdraft interest is the interest charged by your bank for allowing you to become overdrawn;
- bank charges are the charges levied by the bank for the services it provides you;
- a standing order is an instruction to the bank to pay out regular amounts at fixed dates, e.g. for rent;
- a direct debit is where the creditor obtains payment from your bank account but the amount is not a fixed amount, e.g. for insurance;
- interest may be added on to your balance if you do not become overdrawn.

5.3 Bank reconciliation statement

The reconciliation is done between the bank balance in the cash book and the bank balance shown in the bank statement. It checks the accuracy of the cash book through a comparison with the bank statement, which we normally receive on a monthly basis.

It is our balance in the cash book that is reflected in the balance sheet and not that in the bank statement.

In order to reconcile the two accounts we start by ticking off each item shown in the cash book on to the bank statement. Any unchecked item on the bank statement, if it is correct, must be entered into the cash book before it is balanced off. At the same time, any unchecked item in the cash book must be brought into the reconciliation statement unless, of course, it is an error on our part, in which case it must be cancelled in our cash book.

The frequent differences are the bank charges and bank interest where the bank shows it on their bank statement. Other differences could be for dishonoured cheques, direct debits and credit transfers.

As an example of the process, we take the case of a dishonoured cheque. This must be recorded in the cash book. We usually become aware that a cheque is dishonoured when the bank notifies us of this event, usually via the monthly bank statement. The entry (credit the bank and debit the debtor) is normally made when we reconcile the cash book with the bank statement, usually at the end of every month.

The reconciliation statement takes a particular form:

- We start with the balance in the cash book.
- To this we add cheques not yet presented or deduct errors of the bank.
- After this we deduct cash and cheques received by us but not yet shown on the bank statement.
- The final balance must agree with the bank statement.

5.3.1 Worked example

The following is the cash book of A Co. Ltd. To illustrate the reconciliation method this example shows that the cash book was balanced on 30 August. At that date the balance shown was £866. When we received the bank statement we note that the balance at 30 August as shown in the bank statement is £1,218. The reconciliation is now done in order to ensure that the cash book and the bank statement can be agreed with each other.

In the example below the additional entries in our cash book are done when we compare our balance of £866 with the one shown by the bank of £1,218.

Bank account

1 Aug 09	Balance b/d	688	5 Aug 09	Purchases	120✓
3 Aug 09	J Smith	378✓	29 Aug 09	Purchases	235
15 Aug 09	Cash sale	135✓	30 Aug 09	Wages	320
16 Aug 09	D Brown	165✓		Balance c/d	866
29 Aug 09	D Brown	175			
		1,541			1,541
31 Aug 09	Balance b/d	866	3 Aug 09	Unpaid Cheque	18✓
18 Aug 09	Cash sale	100✓	5 Aug 09	Standing order	50✓
			31 Aug 09	Bank interest	20✓
				Charges	40✓
				Balance c/d	838
		966			966
1 Sept 09	Balance b/d	838			

The monthly bank statement received by A Co. Ltd is as follows:

Bank statement

Date	Details	Withdrawal	Deposit	Balance
01 Aug 09				688
02 Aug 09	Deposit 29		✓ 378	1,066
03 Aug 09	Unpaid cheque	✓ 18		1,048
05 Aug 09	Standing order	✓ 50		998
07 Aug 09	Cheque 137	✓ 120		878
16 Aug 09	Deposit 31		✓ 300	1,178
21 Aug 09	Credit transfer		✓ 100	1,278
28 Aug 09	Interest	✓ 20		1,258
30 Aug 09	Bank charges	✓ 40		1,218

A Co. Ltd must ensure that the balance it shows in its cash book is correct. It does this by marking off [✓] all the items which are common to both the bank statement and cash book.

The first thing that must be done is to check the reconciliation of the previous month and agree the opening balance. We now move on to August. Any items on the bank statement for charges etc. are entered into the cash book. Finally the reconciliation can be done.

Reconciliation statement

Balance per cash book		838
Add unpresented cheques:	235	
	320	555
		1,393
Less outstanding deposit		175
Balance per bank statement		1,218

We could also show the reconciliation statement as follows:

Reconciliation statement

Balance per bank statement		1,218
Less unpresented cheques:	235	
	320	555
		663
Plus outstanding deposit		175
Balance per cash book		838

Note: If there is an overdraft then we would take the cash book overdraft and add outstanding deposits and deduct outstanding cheques to arrive at the bank statement figure.

5.3.2 Self-test

The following is the cash book of A Broad for the month of July 2009 together with a copy of the bank statement at the same date.

You are required to make any cash book adjustments necessary and then to balance the cash book and reconcile it with the bank balance.

Cash book

03 Jul 09	Sales	878	01 Jul 09	Balance b/d	3,100
15 Jul 09	Cash sale	224	05 Jul 09	Chq 121	700
31 Jul 09	Sales	1,435	29 Jul 09	Chq 122	432
			30 Jul 09	Chq 123	670

Bank statement

Date	Detail	Debit	Credit	Balance
01 Jul 09				3,100 OD
04 Jul 09	Deposit		878	2,222 OD
09 Jul 09	Cheque 121	700		2,922 OD
16 Jul 09	Deposit		224	2,698 OD
27 Jul 09	Unpaid cheque	150		2,848 OD
31 Jul 09	Bank charges	25		2,873 OD

5.3.3 Self-test

The bank columns of Enid's cash book for the month of February 2009 are shown below.

Cash book

2009		Bank	2009		Cheque No.	Bank
01 Feb	Balance b/d	480	04 Feb	Wages	335	180
22 Feb	Jones	250	05 Feb	Green	336	60
	White	136	11 Feb	Amir	337	110
	Dixon	208		Noble	338	244
26 Feb	Mann	85	23 Feb	Martha	339	401
			28 Feb	Balance c/d		164
		1,159				1,159
01 Mar	Balance b/d	164				

The following bank statement was received for the month of February:

Bank statement

		Debit	Credit	Balance
01-Feb-09	Balance			480
08-Feb-09	Cheque no. 335	180		300
16-Feb-09	Cheque no. 338	244		56
17-Feb-09	Cheque no. 336	60		4OD
23-Feb-09	Sundries		594	590
26-Feb-09	Mann – credit transfer		65	655
	Standing order – gas	26		629
	Bank charges	18		611

(a) Make the necessary entries in the cash book and ascertain the correct balance as at 28 February 2009.

(b) Reconcile your revised cash book balance with the balance shown in the bank statement.

5.3.4 Self-test

Michael received the following bank statement.

Bank statement

2009	Transaction	Debit	Credit	Balance
1 May	Balance			332
7 May	Cheque no. 119	102		230
11 May	Cash		518	748
18 May	Credit transfer – dividends		600	1,348
19 May	Cheque no. 121	340		1,008
26 May	Direct debit insurance	78		930

He checked the statement against his cheque counterfoils and found that cheques numbered 118 for £235 and 120 for £136 had not yet been presented. The names of the payees of the cheques are:

118   Steve
119   Wilcox
120   Adams
121   Nigel

You are required to write up, balance and reconcile the cash book for the month.

Chapter 6

Petty cash book

Objectives After you have studied this chapter, you should be able to:

- explain the need for a petty cash book;
- understand the imprest system of petty cash and its advantages;
- understand the control of cash and expenses;
- write up a columnar petty cash book;
- explain the function of the analysis columns in the petty cash book;
- balance the petty cash.

6.1 Introduction

The 'second' cash book is called the petty cash book. Its purpose is to keep a record of small cash payments. A business tries to restrict the use of cash payments because they are inconvenient and, because cash is involved, there is a risk of theft. One person is made responsible for maintaining the petty cash book and controlling the items of expenditure. This person receives cash and pays out any amounts due. These payments are recorded in the petty cash book using petty cash vouchers as the source documents.

The petty cash book is similar to a cash book and contains various columns. These columns are used to analyse the expense items in order to save time in recording the totals to the ledger accounts. The totals of the various columns are posted at the month end to the debit of the respective expense or asset account.

It is common for the imprest system to be used. Under this system the cashier responsible for making cash payments for the business receives a fixed amount of cash and uses that to pay expenses. This 'float' of cash is designed to cover the anticipated needs of (say) one month. At the end of the period, a cheque for the amount paid out for payments during the period is written out. This is a credit entry in the cash book with a corresponding debit to the petty cash account. The cheque is cashed and the cash is handed over to the cashier. This cash, together with whatever cash balance remained beforehand, will then represent the original cash amount at the beginning of the period.

This can be illustrated in the following way:

Cash given to cashier on 1 June (cash float)	300
Expenses for June month	198
Balance at end of June	102
Cash paid to cashier on 30 June	198
Balance on hand at 1 July (cash float)	300

Petty cash is normally only used for payments and should not have any cash added other than from the reimbursement (topping-up) of the float.

As is the case with the cash book, the petty cash book also has various columns for the more frequent payments. An example of a petty cash book using the imprest system is as follows.

Petty cash for June 2009

Date	Receipts	Details	Total	Postage	Travel	Printing	Wages
01 June	300	Cash					
01 June		Postage	28	28			
04 June		Printing	10			10	
11 June		Postage	62	62			
14 June		Wages	65				65
28 June		Travel	20		20		
30 June		Postage	13	13			
			198	103	20	10	65
30 June		Bal c/d	102				
	300	Total	300				
01 July	102	Bal b/d					
01 July	198	Cash*					

* This payment into petty cash is designed to bring the float back to its original amount of £300.

The petty cash book prevents the cash book and ledgers being cluttered up with a large number of small transactions. At the month end the totals, for example postage (£103), would be entered to the debit of the ledger account as would the totals of all the other accounts. In the case of postage you can see that without using totals we would have had to enter three separate amounts to the ledger.

At the month end, as we do with the cash book, we reconcile the petty cash. We do this by counting the cash to see that it is equal to the balance shown in the petty cash book (in this case we should have cash on hand of £102).

6.2 Petty cash vouchers

We saw in the previous section, that the petty cash is written up from petty cash vouchers. Before any payments are made the cashier will need proof of the expenditure. A special purpose form is used and any additional proof, such as a till slip, is attached to that form. The form is signed by the person receiving the cash and this then serves as proof of the expenditure (see Figure 6.1).

Figure 6.1 **Petty cash voucher**

Petty Cash Voucher						
Required for	TOTAL £	p	GOODS etc £	p	VAT £	p
Signature						
Passed by						
Date						

6.2.1 Self-test

You are required to prepare a petty cash book with four columns for cleaning, postage, travel and office expenses, and enter the items listed below.

The petty cash book of Josh is kept on the imprest system.

June 2009
1   Received £230 from the cashier as a float
    Bought postage stamps – £25.
2   Paid travel expenses – £48.
3   Bought office stationery – £37.
    Paid travel expenses – £26.
4   Bought postage stamps – £38.
    Bought office stationery – £24.
5   Paid for cleaning – £14.
6   Paid travel expenses – £12.
    Received cash from cashier to make up the imprest amount.

You are required to balance the petty cash book as at 6 June 2009.

6.2.2 Self-test

Jenny is a sole trader who keeps her petty cash on the imprest system. The float is a total of £400.

The following are the transactions for the month:

November 2009
1   Petty cash in hand £81.
2   Petty cash restored to the imprest amount.
6   Purchased envelopes £23.
    Paid wages £87.
11 Purchased postage stamps £41.
17 Paid cash purchases £87.
24 Paid wages £87.
30 Purchased stationery £25.

You are required to:

(a) Write up the petty cash book for November 2009 (show analysis columns for stationery, wages, postages and purchases).
(b) Balance the petty cash book as at 30 November 2009.
(c) Carry down the balance and show the amount received on 1 December.

6.2.3 Self-test

Jacques is a sole trader. He maintains the petty cash on the imprest system, with a float of £500.

During the month of July 2009 the following transactions took place:

July 2009
1   Petty cash in hand £31.
    Petty cash restored to imprest amount.
3   Paid wages £53.
5   Postage £36.
7   Cost of purchases £63.
11 Envelopes purchased £12.
17 Paid cash purchases £19.
22 Paid wages £61.
24 Postage £3.
26 Purchased stationery £13.
30 Cash purchases £29.
31 Cost of postage £8.

Prepare the petty cash book to record the above transactions, carry down the balance at 31 July 2009 and restore the petty cash balance at 1 August 2009.

As a suggestion the following analysis columns should be used: wages, postages, purchases and stationery.

Chapter 7

Value added tax

Objectives

After you have studied this chapter, you should be able to:

- explain the meaning of VAT;
- differentiate between input and output VAT;
- show how VAT is accounted for in the ledger;
- enter VAT in the subsidiary books;
- calculate VAT when trade and cash discounts are offered;
- prepare and comment on the VAT account.

7.1 Introduction

This is a tax on the supply of goods and services which is eventually borne by the final consumer but collected at each stage of the production and distribution chain. The seller, registered under VAT, acts as a collector and sends the amounts collected to the government. As such, the tax must not be included in any income or expense of the business, although it must show as a liability (output VAT) until paid. When buying in goods or services, the business must pay the full amount (including VAT) but the portion relating to VAT can be claimed back. Here again the VAT is not included in purchases but is shown as an asset (input VAT). A record must, however, be kept of all VAT paid and all VAT received, as the balancing figure is the amount owing by or owing to the authorities.

At present VAT in the UK is charged at a standard rate of 17.5 per cent on goods and services (although certain items are either VAT exempt or charged at a lower rate).[3] In the examples given here we will state a rate but you should remember that this is only done to make your calculations easier.

It is important that you note that VAT has no effect on profit, but where a business is not registered for VAT because of an exemption, then VAT is included as part of the cost and so will affect profits.

7.1.1 Worked example

We sell goods for £100 but we must add VAT of £17.50. Therefore the total selling price is £117.50.

---

[3] The standard rate of VAT will increase to 20% as from 4 January 2011.

If you are asked to calculate the VAT on an item then we use the following formula:

$$\frac{17.5}{100} \times \text{price} = \text{VAT}$$

Let us assume that we are given a total invoice amount (which includes VAT). We are asked to calculate the VAT component. To do this we must take the amount and multiply it by $\frac{17.5}{117.5}$ or $\frac{7}{47}$. The answer is the VAT portion of the selling price.

Using the first example above – we receive an invoice for £117.50. What amount has been charged on this invoice as VAT?

$$117.50 \times \frac{7}{47} = £17.50 \quad \text{or} \quad \frac{17.5}{117.5} \times 117.5 = £17.50$$

7.1.2 Worked example

Using the above formula we look at the following example:

Gross sales are £1,650. The VAT rate is 10 per cent.

Applying the formula:

$$\frac{10}{110} \times 1,650 = £150 \text{ which represents the amount of VAT.}$$

7.2 Adjustments to VAT

There are two occasions when we need make certain adjustments in our calculations:

- If goods are subject to trade discount then that discount is deducted prior to calculating the VAT (see section 7.4 below).
- Where a cash discount is allowed then VAT is calculated on the assumption that the cash discount will be taken (see section 7.5 below).

Both instances produce a lower amount of VAT than would otherwise be the case.

7.3 VAT ledger account

We must maintain a VAT account for all taxable supplies purchased and all VAT charged to customers. The VAT account is a summary of the totals of VAT. Remember VAT is neither income nor expenditure and does not appear in the profit and loss account. It is, however, a current asset (if owed to the business), or a current liability (if owed by the business), and therefore any balance on the account appears in the balance sheet.

Where a business is too small and not registered for VAT, then it would not charge out any VAT on sales but would still pay VAT on its purchases. In this instance the VAT paid would be included as an expense of the business.

VAT is also paid on the purchase of fixed assets and if this cannot be claimed (because the firm is not registered for VAT) then the VAT is capitalised in the same way as the fixed asset itself.

The ledger account is debited with VAT paid on purchases from suppliers (input VAT) and credited with all VAT charged on sales (output VAT). Once this is done we then need to pay over any shortfall, or claim back any overpayment from HMRC.[4]

We calculate the claim by reconciling our input VAT and our output VAT as follows:

VAT

Date		Amount	Date		Amount
	Purchases	850		Sales	1,000
	Balance due	150			

The above ledger account shows that we have VAT from sales (output) of £1,000. At the same time we paid VAT for purchases (input) of £850. This means that we have an amount to pay of £150.

In the case of the transactions below we find that we have paid VAT on purchases of £1,320 and have only received VAT from sales of £1,000. As such we are entitled to a refund of £320 for this period.

VAT

Date		Amount	Date		Amount
	Purchases	1,320		Sales	1,000
				Refund due	320

7.3.1 VAT in cash book

Where we include VAT in a payment, we enter the VAT in its own column in the cash book and only the net amount is shown in the purchases, or other expense column. This is only if the payment is a cash expense. If we pay a creditor then the VAT is dealt with when we enter the invoice in the purchase day book (see Section 8.2). A similar situation applies to sales where cash sales need to show the VAT element in the cash book but receipts from debtors only show the gross payment in the bank account.

Input VAT is the amount that we pay to a supplier based on the invoice price less any cash discount. Output VAT is that charged to customers on an invoice (less any cash discount).

[4] Her Majesty's Revenue and Customs, which is responsible for the collection of all taxes.

7.3.2 Analysis cash book

We have discussed the simple 2-column cash book and the need for additional analysis when dealing with multiple transactions. This is achieved by use of an analysis cash book which can contain three or more columns both on the debit side as well as the credit side. In the account below a basic 3-column cash book is illustrated.

Although we discussed a 3-column cash book showing both a cash and bank column, we have ignored the cash column in this example so that the additional VAT column can be illustrated.

We note that we have received cash from sales on 9 July and 15 July. Both receipts include amounts for VAT (£9 and £19). In a similar way we paid cash for certain purchases on 11 July. The payment included £35 for VAT.

					Cash book					
Date	Details	Discount	VAT	Bank	Date	Details	Discount	VAT	Bank
4 Jul 09	Debtor	20		103	3 Jul 09	Creditor	14		139
9 Jul 09	Sale		9	51	6 Jul 09	Wages			140
15 Jul 09	Sales		19	104	9 Jul 09	Rent			170
19 Jul 09	Debtor	35		458	11 Jul 09	Creditor			230
24 Jul 09	Debtor			200		Purchase		35	200

7.4 Trade discount

When we buy goods we are given a trade discount which is a reduction in the list price because we are buying large quantities or reselling to an end user. This discount is not shown in the books as it is deducted before the purchase is entered, as shown on the invoice below (Figure 7.1). It must not be confused with a cash discount which is when the supplier offers an inducement for a prompt payment.

Figure 7.1 **Invoice showing trade discount**

The Electrical Shop
323 Station Road
Anywhere

INVOICE No 148

Electrical Supply Company
22 High Road
Somewhere

To supply of Gas Cooker Model XYZ	£400.00
Less Trade Discount – 25%	£100.00
Net Invoice Value	£300.00
Add VAT @ 17.5%	52.50
	£352.50

Payment Terms:

Payment is to be made 45 days from date of invoice.

The trade discount may, for example, be 25 per cent. The list price of the goods we wish to purchase is £400 and the discount is £100. Remember that only after the trade discount is deducted do we calculate the VAT.

An example of a sale to Jenifer will illustrate the way in which VAT is calculated:

Sale to Jenifer of 300 units of product A @ £20 per unit = 6,000.00
Trade discount of 15%   =   900.00
                                                              5,100.00
Plus VAT at 17.5%   892.50
Total value of invoice   5,992.50

The amount of VAT charged in this example is termed the output VAT. This is calculated on £5,100 and not on the initial £6,000.

Purchases

Date		Amount	Date		Amount
Purchase day book		5,100.00			

VAT

Date		Amount	Date		Amount
Purchase day book		892.50			

Creditor

Date		Amount	Date		Amount
			Purchase day book		5,992.50

7.5 Cash discounts

A business tries to collect its outstanding debtors as quickly as possible. To do this it sometimes offers an incentive – a discount for cash. In effect the business tells the customer that if the amount owing is paid within a certain time (e.g. 30 days from invoice), the customer would be entitled to an additional discount (over and above any trade discount already given).

If this cash discount is offered on top of the trade discount, the VAT is calculated after deduction of the cash discount. This is in addition to the earlier deduction of the trade discount.

For example:

Sales of 300 units of product A @ £20 per unit = 6,000.00
Trade discount of 15%   =   900.00
                                                    5,100.00
Plus VAT* of 17.5%   847.87
Total value of invoice   5,947.87

* The VAT is calculated on £5,100 – 5% cash discount of £255 = £4,845

7.5.1 Self-test

You are given the following information relating to purchases and sales under-taken by Dani & Co. during the 3 months ended September 2009. Assume for this example that VAT is calculated at 10 per cent.

Purchases	Amount excluding VAT
July	£12,000
Aug	£16,000
Sept	£18,000

Sales	Amount excluding VAT
July	£18,000
Aug	£20,000
Sept	£30,000

You are required to prepare the VAT ledger account for the three months and indicate the amount either to be paid to or received from HMRC.

7.5.2 Self-test

Martha owns a retail clothing store.

Martha's trading during July showed that she had sold goods to Mrs Green for £820, plus VAT. She offered a 3 per cent cash discount for payment within 30 days. She also sold Miss Wydham goods to the value of £650 plus VAT. Here again a cash discount of 3 per cent was offered for payment by the end of August.

She purchased goods from Clothes & Co. The goods are priced at £4,800 but there is a trade discount of 20 per cent as well as a cash discount of 5 per cent for payment within 10 days. The goods are subject to VAT.

She also purchased goods from Jeans & Co. for £260 plus VAT. Here again a cash discount was offered of 5 per cent. Of the goods purchased from Jeans & Co., a dress for £94 plus VAT was returned as unsuitable.

VAT is calculated at 15 per cent unless the amount has been specified in the question.

You are required to prepare the VAT account at the end of July.

7.5.3 Self-test

Decker & Co. sells office desks to various retail stores. The stores are offered a trade discount of 25 per cent as well as a 10 per cent discount for all payments made within 10 days of the invoice date.

During July 2009 Decker & Co. issued the following invoices:

Date	Inv No.	Customer	Gross price (before trade discount)
11 July	407	Nudeal Supplies	£4,200
13 July	408	Executive Offices	£3,800
19 July	409	Fashion Desks	£8,400
27 July	410	Executive Offices	£7,600

On 20 July Executive Offices returned a desk because it was delivered damaged. The gross price of the desk was £1,400. Decker & Co. issued a credit note for the return.

Fashion Desks returned a small desk on 24 July, as it was the incorrect colour. The gross price of the unit was £620.

Only Nudeal Supplies pays all its invoices within 10 days of the date of invoice.

You are also required to prepare the VAT account at the end of July. VAT is calculated at 15 per cent.

You are also required to show the ledger account for Nudeal Supplies, which paid its invoice in full less the cash discount.

Chapter 8

Purchases and returns day books

Objectives

After you have studied this chapter you should be able to:

- explain the meaning of books of prime entry;
- understand how VAT is treated in all purchase transactions;
- write up and post the purchases day book;
- write up and post the purchases returns day book;
- post entries from the purchases and purchases returns day books to ledger accounts.

8.1 Books of original (prime) entry

In addition to the subsidiary books described in section 2.5, we also have books for recording original transactions. These books include the cash book and petty cash book, which we discussed in earlier chapters. In addition there are further books of original entry and these are the sales and purchases day books (which we discuss in this and the following chapter) and the journal (see Chapter 14).

With the exception of the cash book (see Chapter 4) all these books of prime entry are memorandum books and are used to collect transactions of a similar nature. By doing this we are able to reduce the number of entries in the ledger accounts.

These books are used to record the first details of business transactions. What are these details? They are invoices for goods purchased or sold by the business. When goods are returned, either by the business, or by a customer of the business, a credit note is issued. These credit notes are also transactions that have to be recorded. All these transactions are listed in the relevant subsidiary books as they occur.

At the month end the totals are posted to the relevant ledger accounts, e.g. sales, purchases, returns inwards and returns outwards.

The six books of original entry are:

- Purchase day book (or purchase journal), which lists all credit purchases from the creditors' invoices.
- Sales day book (or sales journal), which is written up from the invoices generated by the business.
- Sales returns (returns in) book, which is a record of all credit notes issued to customers for goods returned.

- Purchases returns (returns out) book records all credit notes received by the business from its suppliers for goods returned to the suppliers.
- Cash book, which we have already examined in Chapter 4.
- Journal, which we will discuss in Chapter 14 and which is only used when no other book of prime entry can be used.

8.2 Purchases day book

A large majority of transactions of a business consists of buying goods for resale. This results in a considerable number of purchase invoices which are recorded in the purchase day book. These purchases are entered in total to the debit of the purchases account and a credit to the individual creditor accounts.

We must remember that the source documents for the purchase day book are the invoices of the suppliers, but these invoices include VAT. It is important that VAT is not included as an expense and, therefore, we need show the VAT component separately. To do this an additional column for VAT is given in the purchase day book. (We discussed VAT in Chapter 7.) The ruling of the purchase day book is as follows:

Date	Supplier	Net amount	VAT	Total of invoice
1 July	ABC	1,000.00	175.50	1,175.50
4 July	XYZ	2,000.00	350.00	2,350.00

8.2.1 Worked example

You are required to write up the purchases day book for Julian for April 2009. The following are a list of purchases made by Julian in the month.

1   Bought goods on credit from Thomas. The price excluding VAT was £3,400.
5   Bought goods on credit from Geoffrey. The price excluding VAT was £1,600.
11   Bought goods on credit from Jay. The price excluding VAT was £900.
19   Bought goods on credit from Thomas. The price excluding VAT was £600.
28   Bought goods on credit from Geoffrey. The price excluding VAT was £900.

You are told that VAT on these goods is 10 per cent.

From the total columns of the day book we can then post in a single figure to the respective ledger accounts. The total net amount of £7,400 is posted to purchases and VAT of £740 to the VAT account. At the end of each line the total invoice amount will be posted to the individual creditors' accounts.

Purchases day book

Date	Supplier	Net amount	VAT	Total of invoice
01 Apr 09	Thomas	3,400	340	3,740
05 Apr 09	Geoffrey	1,600	160	1,760
11 Apr 09	Jay	900	90	990
19 Apr 09	Thomas	600	60	660
28 Apr 09	Geoffrey	900	90	990
	Total April 2009	£7,400	£740	£8,140

Purchases		Thomas	
Purchase journal 7,400		Purchases 3,740	
		Purchases 660	

VAT		Geoffrey	
Purchases 740		Purchases 1,760	
		Purchases 990	

Jay	
Purchases 990	

8.3 Purchases returns book

When goods are returned to a supplier, a credit note is received from them and this is recorded in a purchases returns book. The credit note, like the original invoice, includes VAT. So here again we have an additional column in which to record the amount of VAT.

The full amount of the credit note is debited to the supplier's account with the totals being entered to the purchase returns (returns out) account and the VAT account.

Date	Supplier	Net amount	VAT	Total of credit note
1 July	ABC	1,000.00	175.50	1,175.50

8.3.1 Worked example

Based on the above you are required to write up the purchases returns book for Julian for April 2009. The following returns of goods were made by Julian during the month.

6 April   Julian returned goods to Geoffrey and a credit note was issued for £110 including VAT of £10.

20 April   Julian returned goods to Thomas and a credit note was issued for £330 including VAT of £30.

Purchases returns day book

Date	Supplier	Net amount	VAT	Total
06 Apr 09	Geoffrey	100	10	110
20 Apr 09	Thomas	300	30	330
	Total April 2009	400	40	440

	Thomas			Purchases	
Returns	330			Returns	400
	Geoffrey			**VAT**	
Returns	110			Returns	40

From the total columns of the day book we are able to post them to the respective ledger accounts. The total net amount of £400 is posted to the credit of the purchases account and VAT of £40 is posted to the credit of the VAT account. At the end of each line the total of each credit note is posted to the individual creditors' account.

8.3.2 Self-test

The following is a list of transactions of Julian for the month of July 2009.

 5 July   Bought goods on credit from Jay & Co. for £260.
 8 July   Bought goods on credit from T Williams for £660.
21 July   Bought goods on credit from H Henry for £540.
26 July   Bought goods on credit from J Jones for £200.
29 July   Bought goods on credit from Green & Co. for £900.

All the above transactions are subject to VAT of 15 per cent which must be added to the cost price shown.

You are required to enter the above transactions into the purchases day book and indicate the accounts to be debited and credited.

In addition to the above transactions, Julian also returned certain goods to various suppliers. The following are the details:

 2 July   Returned goods to H Henry for £140.
23 July   Returned goods to J Jones for £80.

VAT of 15 per cent is payable on these transactions.

8.3.3 Self-test

You are required to write up the purchases and purchases returns day books of Leon to record the relevant transactions set out below. You also need to show the ledger account for purchases for March 2009. VAT can be ignored.

2009	Transaction	£
3 Mar	Bought goods on credit from Jay	914
6 Mar	Bought goods on credit from Emma	432
	Returned goods to Jay	106
8 Mar	Bought goods on credit from Jay	317
18 Mar	Bought goods on credit from Jay	204
	Paid cash for goods for resale	123
	Returned goods purchased for cash	119
22 Mar	Bought goods on credit from Emma	543
	Paid for carriage inwards* on goods	169
25 Mar	Bought goods on credit from Henry	802
26 Mar	Returned goods purchased for cash	105
	Discount received on purchase from Jay	182
31 Mar	Bought goods on credit from Jay	167
	Returned goods to Jay	198

* Carriage inwards must be charged to purchases.

Using the relevant day books, record all the above transactions and then enter the totals to the purchases account.

8.3.4 Self-test

You are required to write up the purchases and purchases returns day books of Norman to record all the transactions set out below. You also need to show the ledger account for purchases and the VAT account.

2009	Transaction	£
3 Aug	Bought goods on credit from Jay & Co.	1,200
6 Aug	Bought goods on credit from T Williams	1,400
	Returned goods to Jay & Co.	400
8 Aug	Bought goods on credit from Green & Co.	1,000
18 Aug	Bought goods on credit from Jay & Co.	400
22 Aug	Bought goods on credit from Jay & Co.	500
25 Aug	Bought goods on credit from H Henry	800
31 Aug	Bought goods on credit from T Williams	1,800
	Returned goods to Jay & Co.	120

VAT is to be calculated at 15 per cent on all the above transactions.

Chapter 9

Sales and returns day books

Objectives After you have studied this chapter you should be able to:

- write up and post the sales day book;
- write up and post the sales returns book;
- understand how VAT is treated in all sales transactions;
- post entries from the sales day book.

9.1 Sales day book

As sales is the cornerstone of a business, the bulk of transactions are from sales and therefore some form of summary needs to be kept so that there is not an abundance of entries and repetitive detail. This summary is kept in the sales day book which lists all sales and only posts the total amount to the sales ledger account.

All credit sales made by a business are invoiced and these invoices are posted to the credit of the sales account with the corresponding debit to the debtors account. (In the case of a cash sale the debit is shown in the cash book as the money is received immediately.)

As with purchases, a business is also obliged to charge VAT on its sales (this of course assumes that the business is liable to VAT). Here again the VAT must be recorded on the invoices sent to customers and is shown in a separate column in the day book.

The ruling of the sales day book would be as follows:

Date	Invoice No.	Customer	Net amount	VAT	Total of invoice
1 July	1234	XYZ	100.00	17.50	117.50
4 July	5678	ABC	200.00	35.00	235.00
			300.00	52.50	352.50

9.1.1 Worked example

You are given the transactions of Harold for the month of July 2009.

8 July	Inv 2	Sold goods on credit to Colin for £160.
11 July	Inv 3	Sold goods on credit to William for £360.
21 July	Inv 4	Sold goods on credit to Henry for £240.
24 July	Inv 5	Sold goods on credit to Jacques for £300.
31 July	Inv 6	Sold goods on credit to George for £180.

You are required to enter the above transactions into the sales day book and indicate the accounts to be debited and credited. All the transactions are subject to VAT (for this example we use 15 per cent) which must be added to the invoice price shown.

Sales day book

Date	Invoice No.	Customer	Net amount	VAT	Total
08 July	2	Colin	160	24	184
11 July	3	William	360	54	414
21 July	4	Henry	240	36	276
24 July	5	Jacques	300	45	345
31 July	6	George	180	27	207
	Totals		£1,240	£186	£1,426

The total of each invoice is posted to the debit of the individual customer. The totals are posted as follows:

(i) the net invoice amount of £1,240 is credited to sales; and
(ii) the VAT total of £186 is credited to the VAT account.

9.2 Sales returns book

When goods are returned by a customer the business issues a credit note. As this credit note is designed to cancel all or part of an earlier transaction (an invoice), the credit note must include VAT, if previously charged.

The credit note is entered into the sales returns book and posted to the credit of the debtors account. The totals, usually at month end, are posted to the debit of the sales and VAT accounts.

Date	Credit Note No.	Customer	Net amount	VAT	Total of credit note
1 July	987	XYZ	10.00	1.50	11.50
9 July	432	ABC	20.00	3.00	23.00
			30.00	4.50	34.50

9.2.1 Worked example

During July 2009 a number of customers returned goods to Harold. The following are the details:

10 July CN 6 Goods of £40 were returned by William.
22 July CN 7 Goods of £60 were returned by Henry.
29 July CN 8 Goods of £180 were returned by Jacques.

All the above credit notes must still have VAT, at the rate of 15 per cent, added to them.

Sales returns book

Date	CN No.	Customer	Net amount	VAT	Total of credit note
10 July	6	William	40	6	46
22 July	7	Henry	60	9	69
29 July	8	Jacques	180	27	207
		Totals	£280	£42	£322

Debits would be entered to the sales returns account for £280, and to the VAT account for £42. The debtors' accounts would be credited individually with the total amount of the credit notes.

Returns in

31 July Sales returns	280	

VAT

31 July Sales returns	42	

William

	10 July 09 Returns in	46

Henry

	22 July 09 Returns in	69

Jacques

	29 July 09 Returns in	207

9.2.2 Self-test

You are required to write up the sales and sales returns day books of Leon to record the relevant transactions set out below. You also need to show the ledger accounts for sales for March 2009. VAT can be ignored.

2009	Transaction	£
6 Mar	Sold goods on credit to Dee	375
	Cash sales banked	874
	Cash sale customer returned damaged goods	114
11 Mar	Sold goods on credit to Gert	192
12 Mar	Sold goods on credit to Henry	109
26 Mar	Sold goods on credit to Gert	147
29 Mar	Sold goods on credit to Gert	314
	Sold goods on credit to Henry	719

Using the relevant day books, record all the above transactions and then enter the totals to the sales ledger account.

9.2.3 Self-test

You are required to write up sales and sales returns day books of Norman to record all the transactions set out below. You also need to show the ledger account for sales and the VAT account.

2009	Transaction	£
5 Aug	Sold goods on credit to Jacques	2,400
11 Aug	Sold goods on credit to William	1,600
12 Aug	Sold goods on credit to George	440
18 Aug	George returned goods	240
26 Aug	Sold goods on credit to George	1,440
	William returned goods	480
29 Aug	Sold goods on credit to Henry	860
31 Aug	Sold goods on credit to William	640

VAT is to be calculated at 15 per cent on all the above transactions.

Chapter 10

Control accounts

Objectives   After you have studied this chapter, you should be able to:

- explain the meaning and use of a control account;
- understand how entries to individual accounts are 'copied' to a control account;
- write up individual debtors' and creditors' control accounts;
- transfer amounts from debtors' to creditors' accounts as contra payments;
- calculate ledger control balances.

10.1   Introduction

The accuracy of the double-entry system for recording transactions is checked through the trial balance (see Chapter 15). There are many entries made from the sales and purchase day books to the debtors' and creditors' accounts. Because of this we use control accounts to check the accuracy of the entries made in these ledgers. These control accounts record totals of transactions that pass through the accounts that they control. We have a control account for each ledger and so can identify the errors when they occur.

The control accounts consist of summaries of totals taken from other books. All individual entries are summarised, that is, an entry in any ledger account is duplicated in the control account.

The control account is a memorandum account only and not part of the double-entry system. We are able to use the balances of the control accounts in a trial balance instead of the individual balances. For example, if the opening balance on the debtors' control account is £10,000, this equates to the sum total of all the individual balances in the debtors' ledger.

Using the total we then add entries that increase the individual debtors' balances and deduct totals that decrease balances. The closing balance must equal the total of the individual debtors' balances and, if not, then it proves that there are errors in posting to the debtors' accounts. This, of course, also applies to the creditors' ledger and control.

10.2 Advantages of control accounts

There are several benefits for a business in using control accounts. By employing control accounts we are able to produce a trial balance without having to total each individual debtor's or creditor's account in order to incorporate those balances into our trial balance.

In addition, the control account acts as a check both on accuracy and control. It ensures that all payments made by debtors are accounted for and that no individual debtor's account is credited without a payment having been made or a credit note having been issued. Similarly, it ensures that all payments to creditors are accounted for and discounts given by creditors are recorded. This control also applies to all purchases and sales transactions.

We can say, therefore, that the main function of a control account is to facilitate finding errors by drawing attention to the ledger in which those errors are likely. This ensures that errors are kept to a minimum and that opportunities for fraud or theft of cash are minimal. This is achieved by a system of internal control that is set up within the business. Control accounts are of great value as they allow the splitting up of functions. Figures entered into the control account should be calculated by a number of different staff, which means the control accounts act as a check on their work.

10.3 Limitations of control accounts

We have said that the balances on the control accounts can be used in preparing a trial balance. This is because all the entries to debtors' and creditors' accounts have also been posted to the control accounts.

There are, however, times when the balances from the control accounts are wrong and do not allow the trial balance to balance. We would check and calculate the totals of the individual balances and see that they agreed with the control balances.

Figure 10.1 illustrates the use of the control account. You will note (in this illustration) the sales day book and returns day book have been posted to the various debtors' accounts. Entries from the cash book are also shown. At the same time, the totals from all subsidiary books are posted to the debtors' control account. From there a balance (in this case £74) is calculated. This balance can be used as the debtors' balance in the trial balance without reference to individual debtors' accounts. This speeds up the preparation of a trial balance and financial statements.

You will also see that the individual balances on each debtor's account will and must total the £74 shown as the control account balance. This is the check on the accuracy of our debtors' postings.

The balance of £74 is made up of the balances of:

- A £18
- B £32
- C £24

Figure 10.1 **The transfer of transactions to the control account**

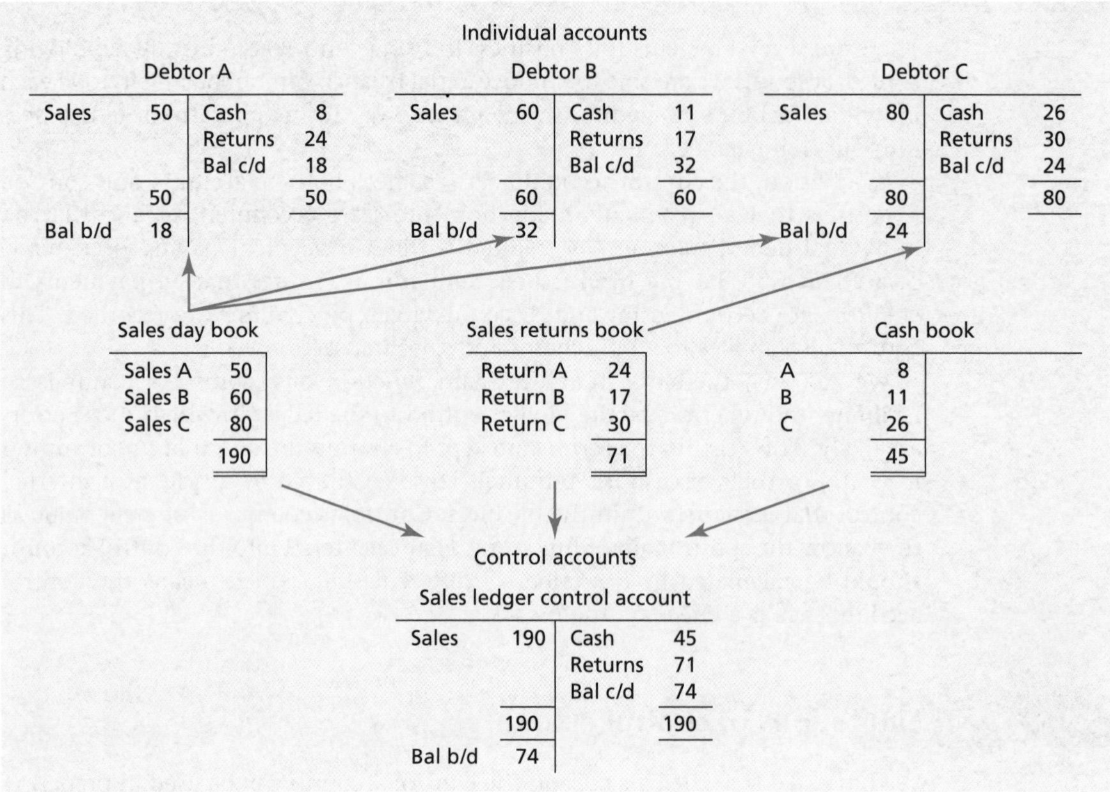

10.4 Sales ledger (debtors) control account

This control account copies all entries made in the individual ledger accounts. Remember that it is a memorandum account and the entries are on the same side as the individual ledger accounts. The entries made to the control account must *not* be reversed. All too often this is a common mistake made during examinations!

When we use the sales day book, each sale is entered into that subsidiary book and posted to the individual ledger account. The total would be credited to sales. Rather than enter each sales transaction again to the control account (remember – same side as ledger!) we enter the total thus saving time.

Sales ledger control account

1 Apr	Balance b/d	2,300	30 Apr	Bank	3,200
	Sales	5,650		Discount Allowed	120
				Returns inwards	350
				Bad debts	600
				Balance c/d	3,680
		7,950			7,950
1 May	Balance b/d	3,680			

The above example shows the items that are normally found in the debtors control account.

At the month end the business would extract a list of debtors' balances. The balance on the control account (£3,680) would equal the total of balances in the debtors' accounts in the sales ledger.

10.4.1 Self-test

The following is a list of transactions in the books of Gerta for May 2009.

01 May	Opening balance	6,035
31 May	Sales day book	29,549
31 May	Cheques from debtors	13,800
31 May	Discount allowed	1,003
31 May	Dishonoured cheque	622
31 May	Returns inwards	1,176
31 May	Bad debts written off	974

You are required to write up the sales ledger control account and show the closing balance at 31 May 2009.

10.5 Purchase ledger (creditors) control account

Here again we use totals, as shown in the purchase day book or in the cash book. There are limitations in the control accounts, as shown in section 10.3, but in the main they speed up the preparation of interim accounts. Although control accounts check the accuracy of the postings, they will not reveal all the errors (see section 15.2). If there is a discrepancy then all balances must be checked together with all totals.

10.6 Contra accounts (set-offs)

There is one additional item that could be recorded in a control account and that is a contra entry (or set-off). This comes about when a business deals with another business both as a supplier of goods (and therefore a creditor) and a purchaser of goods (and therefore a debtor). For example, suppose Ace Trading sells goods to Joe & Co. for £3,200 and also purchases goods from Joe & Co. for £4,500.

Ace Trading has a situation where Joe & Co. is owed £4,500 but it also owes £3,200 for the goods purchased from Ace Trading. Instead of paying the amount due to Joe & Co., Ace Trading sets off the amount owing of £3,200 and issues a cheque to Joe & Co. for £1,300.

The entries needed for such a transaction in the books of Ace Trading are shown below as individual ledger accounts:

Joe & Co. – debtor account			
Sales	3,200	Contra entry	3,200

Joe & Co. – creditor account			
Contra entry	3,200	Purchases	4,500
Bank	1,300		

To do the contra entry we would need to record it in the journal. Although we will only discuss journal entries in Chapter 14 it is useful at this stage to illustrate the entry required for a set-off of an account.

Joe & Co. (creditor)	Dr	3,200	
Joe & Co. (debtor)	Cr		3,200
The amount owing by Joe & Co. for goods is set off against an amount due to Joe & Co.			

The entry is also posted to the debtors' and creditors' control accounts. This means that the debit entry to the creditors account is also posted to the debit side of the creditors' control account.

Creditors' control account		
Contra entry	3,200	

Similarly, the credit entry is posted to the credit in the debtors' control account.

Debtors' control account		
	Contra entry	3,200

10.6.1 Worked example

Creditors at 1 January 2009	15,430
Credit purchases	21,000
Cash paid to creditors	16,570
Discounts received	6,020
Returns outward	1,000
Set-off of debtor balance	100

You are required to prepare the purchase ledger control account, showing the balance outstanding at the month end.

31 Jan	Bank	16,570	1 Jan	Balance b/d	15,430
	Returns outward	1,000	31 Jan	Purchases	21,000
	Set off – debtor	100			
	Discount received	6,020			
	Balance c/d	12,740			
		36,430			36,430
			1 Feb	Balance b/d	12,740

10.7 Balances on both sides

Finally we should note that there may be balances brought down on both sides of the ledger account. This means that in the debtors' control account there may be a credit balance brought down in addition to the normal debit balance. This means that certain debtors' accounts are in credit because they have either overpaid the account or they have returned goods after they paid their account.

In a similar way the creditors' control account may also show a debit balance in addition to the normal credit balance. The reason for this could be a return of goods after the account was paid or an overpayment of the account.

For example, we use the creditors' account of Joe & Co. as in section 10.6. After payment of £1,300 is made goods to the value of £430 are returned to Ace Trading. This will be shown as follows:

Joe & Co. – creditor account			
Contra entry	3,200	Purchases	4,500
Bank	1,300		
	4,500		4,500
Returns	430		

This will result in a debit balance in the creditors' account of £430. Similarly the purchase ledger control account will also show this debit balance.

It is important to note that all balances must be shown and not deducted from each other.

10.7.1 Self-test

The following information is available to allow you to prepare a creditors' control account for Nicholas at 30 June 2009.

1 June	Opening balance	8,512
30 June	Purchases	7,190
30 June	Payments to creditors	4,996
30 June	Discount received	711
30 June	Returns outward	657
30 June	Transfer to debtors	755

Show the ledger account and the closing balance at 30 June 2009.

10.7.2 Self-test

From the balances in the ledger account of Trudie, prepare the debtors' and creditors' control accounts at 30 June 2009.

1 June	Purchase ledger balance	9,843
1 June	Sales ledger balances	6,488
30 June	Purchases for month	12,992
30 June	Sales for month	19,745
30 June	Paid to suppliers	10,622
30 June	Discounts received	255
30 June	Returns inwards	790
30 June	Returns outwards	681
30 June	Discount allowed	1,003
30 June	Bad debts written off	780
30 June	Unpaid cheque of customer	147
30 June	Cheques received from customers	5,933

10.7.3 Self-test

The following is an extract from the books of Hellenco Trading for the year ended 31 March 2009.

Debtors' ledger control account balance on 1 April 2008 (debit)	22,060
Sales	153,900
Cheques received from debtors	92,282
Discounts allowed	4,160
Discounts received	3,021
Returns inwards	2,050
Returns outwards	1,604
Bad debts written off	1,901
Set-off to debtor of a credit balance	196
Amounts due from customers transferred to creditors' ledger	904
Interest charged on debtors' overdue account	68
Total of balances in debtors' ledger on 31 March 2009: (debit)	81,034
Total of balances in debtors' ledger on 31 March 2009: (credit)	6,107

You are required to prepare the debtors' ledger control account for the year ended 31 March 2009 using relevant figures selected from the data shown above.

10.7.4 Self-test

The books of Katie include three ledgers comprising the nominal (general) ledger, debtors' ledger and creditors' ledger.

The following information relates to the year ended 30 June 2010:

Debtors' ledger control account balance on 1 July 2009 (debit)	23,105
Creditors' ledger control account balance on 1 July 2009 (credit)	19,714
Cheques received from debtors	42,033
Cheques paid to creditors	41,206
Sales	104,500
Purchases	77,390
Returns outwards	12,120

Returns inwards	16,430
Discount received	5,619
Discount allowed	6,230
Bad debts	5,910
Cash received in respect of a debit balance from creditor	3,104
Amount due from debtors transferred to creditors' ledger	3,021
Total balances in creditors' ledger on 30 June 2010 (credit)	38,295

You are required to prepare the debtors' ledger and creditors' ledger control accounts as at 30 June 2010. The balances for debtors and any debit balances on creditors' accounts must be calculated as at 30 June 2010.

10.7.5 Self-test

The books of Hilmar & Co. include three ledgers comprising the general ledger, debtors' ledger and creditors' ledger. The general ledger contains debtors' ledger and creditors' ledger control accounts.

The following information relates to the month of March 2009:

Debtors' control account balance on 1 March 2009 (Dr)	5,900
Debtors' control account balance on 1 March 2009 (Cr)	425
Creditors' control account balance on 1 March 2009 (Dr)	370
Creditors' control account balance on 1 March 2009 (Cr)	7,290
Credit sales for the month	41,800
Credit purchases for the month	30,433
Debtors' balances set against accounts in the creditors' ledger	1,011
Returns inwards	884
Returns outwards	470
Cheques received from debtors	17,470
Interest charged on debtors' overdue accounts	185
Discount allowed	706
Discount received	471
Bad debts	902
Dishonoured (unpaid) cheques from debtors	1,940
Bad debts recovered	217
Cheques paid to creditors	20,084
Cash received from debtors	6,130
Cash paid to creditors	4,020
Creditors' control account balance on 31 March 2009 (Dr)	816
Debtors' control account balance on 31 March 2009 (Cr)	413

You are required to prepare the debtors' ledger and creditors' ledger control accounts for March 2009 and find the balances at the month end.

Chapter 11

Accruals and prepayments

Objectives   After you have studied this chapter you should be able to:

- explain the meaning of accruals and prepayments;
- adjust revenue and expense accounts;
- write up the ledger accounts of the revenue and expense items.

11.1 Accruals

An accrual can be defined as an expense that has been incurred but not yet paid for. As such the amount unpaid must be recorded in the books of account prior to preparing the financial statements.

There are also instances where accruals refer to accrued income. In this instance the income is due to the business but has not yet been paid. This would, for example, be in the case of interest on a deposit account or rent receivable by the business.

11.1.1 Worked example

Accruals refer mainly to items of expenditure. This is illustrated in the ledger accounts below.

At the year end the amount to be included for the expense in the profit and loss is transferred from the expense account to the profit and loss account. For example, the telephone and postages expense for the year is £2,414. However, the business has only paid £2,100 of this amount so the difference (£314) is shown as the balance in the telephone and postages account. This credit balance is called an accrual.

	Telephone and postages				
31 Dec 09	Bank	2,100	31 Dec 09	Profit & Loss	2,414
	Accrual c/d	314			
		2,414			2,414
			1 Jan 10	Balance b/d	314

Motor expenses

31 Dec 09	Bank	1,987	31 Dec 09	Profit & Loss	2,587
	Accrual c/d	600			
		2,587			2,587
			1 Jan 10	Balance b/d	600

Here again we accrue £600 for motor expenses unpaid at 31 December 2009.

Commission on sales

31 Dec 09	Bank	11,880	31 Dec 09	Profit & Loss	16,220
	Accrual c/d	4,320			
		16,220			16,220
			1 Jan 10	Balance b/d	4,320

The above account shows an accrual of £4,320 for commission payable.

All three accruals from above are transferred together with the amounts paid during the year to the profit and loss account as shown below.

Profit and loss account for the year ended 31 December 2009 (extract)

Telephone and postages	2,414
Motor Expenses	2,587
Commission on sales	16,220

The reason for this is that the accrual concept recognises the difference between the actual payment of cash and the accounting period.

In some cases accruals must be estimated as no invoice has been issued prior to the year end. For example, we receive our last phone bill on 10 December and our financial year end is 31 December. At the year end there are 21 days of calls made but not yet billed. In the event that the amount is material (this means that it is important to be shown in the financial statements), we must estimate the accrued amount.

There are also instances of accrued income, for example rent receivable, and this would be treated in the same way as an accrued expense except that the balance brought down would be on the debit side.

Rent receivable

31 Dec 09	Profit & Loss	24,000	31 Dec 09	Bank	22,100
				Accrual c/d	1,900
		24,000			24,000
1 Jan 10	Balance b/d	1,900			

11.1.2 The matching concept

The need for accruing items is dictated by the matching concept (see section 25.2.4). This states that expenses for the period must be matched against revenues of the same period.

Where expenditure is incurred but not yet paid for at the year end, expenditure must be accrued.

11.2 Prepayments

A prepayment is a payment in the current period for goods or services to be received in the subsequent accounting period. With a prepayment, for example insurance, the amount that is not related to the period of the profit and loss account must be 'taken out' (credited) of the insurance expense account with a corresponding debit to prepaid expenses or alternatively shown as a debit balance on the expense account, as illustrated below.

Prepaid expenses are items recorded in the books (whether paid or not). They relate wholly or partly to a later accounting period than when recorded. They are sometimes referred to as payments in advance, which is exactly what they are. The following example illustrates prepayments.

Our business year end is 31 December 2009. On 1 October we pay one year's insurance of £1,200. This payment is for the period 1 October 2009 to 30 September 2010. That means that only $^1/_4$ of £1,200 (£300) covering the months of 1 October 2009 to 31 December 2009 is relevant to the financial year. The remaining $^3/_4$ of £1,200 or £900 is prepaid and must be brought into account in the following year.

As is the case with accruals, adjustment for prepaid expenses can also be made in the one account. This is shown in the example below.

		Insurance			
1 Oct 09	Bank	1,200	31 Dec 09	Prepaid c/d	900
				P & L account	300
		1,200			1,200
1 Jan 10	Prepayment b/d	900			

In the balance sheet the prepayment is shown as a current asset. In the profit and loss account we show revenues for that accounting period exactly matched by the expenses incurred in earning those sales. As such we deduct the prepaid amount of insurance from the expenses in the profit and loss account, as it is a payment made against next year's trading.

11.2.1 Worked example

In this example we have paid an additional amount of £800 in December 2009 for rent which relates to the following year. We need take this amount and move it into the next year so that the profit and loss account reflects the correct figure for 2009.

Rent

11 Jan 09	Bank	600	31 Dec 09	P & L account	2,400
3 Apr	Bank	600		Balance c/d	800
1 July	Bank	600			
1 Oct	Bank	600			
29 Dec	Bank	800			
		3,200			3,200
1 Jan 10	Balance b/d	800			

11.2.2 Worked example

Although prepaid expenditure is the most common of prepayments, there are also instances of prepaid income, such as where we receive rent for premises rented out.

We may be paid in advance, so the treatment here would be to show the balance prepaid (in this example £600) as a credit in the balance sheet.

Rent receivable

31 Dec 09	P&L account	1,200	1 Jan 09	Bank	600
			1 July 09	Bank	600
			29 Dec 09	Bank	600
31 Dec 09	Prepaid c/d	600			
		1,800			1,800
			1 Jan 10	Balance b/d	600

11.2.3 Self-test

(a) Bill pays his rent quarterly, in arrears, at the end of March, June, September and December. The rent in 2009 is £84,000 p.a. His financial year-end is 31 May 2009.

Calculate the charge that is to be made to the profit and loss account, the accrual in the balance sheet and show the ledger account for rent.

(b) From 1 October 2009, Bill's rent increases to £96,000 p.a.

Calculate the charge in the profit and loss account for the year ended 31 May 2010, the liability as at that date and show the ledger account for rent.

(c) Bill pays insurance one year in advance. For the calendar year ended 31 December 2009 the payment was £18,000 and for the year ended 31 December 2010 it was £24,000.

Calculate the charge in the profit and loss account for the financial year ended 31 May 2010 and the prepayment as at that date. Show the insurance ledger account.

11.2.4 Self-test

Jay has taken out a 4-year loan of £20,000 at 7 per cent interest.
The following is the ledger account for the interest payable on the loan.

Interest payable		
15 Mar 10 Bank	350	
30 July 10 Bank	350	
5 Nov 10 Bank	350	

You are required to complete the interest payable ledger account to correctly reflect the amount to be charged to the profit and loss account for the year ending 31 December 2010. Show the balance at the start of the next financial year.

11.2.5 Self-test

The electricity account for the year ending 31 December 2010 is as follows:

Electricity			
15 Feb 10 Bank	550	1 Jan 10 Balance b/d	430
30 July 10 Bank	280		
31 Oct 10 Bank	310		

An amount of £425 due for charges to 31 December 2010 has not yet been paid.
You are required to prepare the electricity account to correctly reflect the amount to be charged to the profit and loss account for the year ending 31 December 2010 showing the balance at the start of the next financial year.

11.2.6 Self-test

Insurance is paid by BB & Co. in a single payment. This is due on 1 August each year. BB & Co. has its year end on 31 December.
The following is the ledger account for insurance:

Insurance		
1 Jan 10 Balance b/d	700	
1 Aug 10 Bank	1,800	

You are required to prepare adjustments to the insurance account to correctly reflect the amount for the year ending 31 December 2010.

Chapter 12

Depreciation

Objectives

After you have studied this chapter, you should be able to:

- explain how assets depreciate in value;
- calculate depreciation charges using various methods;
- prepare a depreciation account;
- show how depreciation is recouped;
- show how losses and profits on sale of fixed assets are treated.

12.1 Introduction

We have stated that a fixed asset is one that is purchased by a business to enable it to generate profits over a long period of time. An example would be the premises from which the business produces goods for resale, or a van for delivery of goods.

Now, although these fixed assets generate profits over more than one year, they do, nevertheless, cost the business some form of expense. This is depreciation which can be defined as the cost of an asset due to its fall in value over its useful economic life. Depreciation is due to the physical deterioration over a period of time or due to the asset wearing out because of usage. Depreciation may be caused by technical obsolescence; for example, a computer becomes obsolete with the development of newer and faster technology. At this point we must note, however, that the one fixed asset that does not normally depreciate is land, which often rises in value. Even so we may still apply depreciation to property, as depreciation can be viewed as the allocation of cost over the useful economic life of the asset.

We do not know that the life of the fixed asset is a definite 3 years or 5 years and therefore the depreciation charged is only an estimate, based on past experience. Only when the asset is finally sold, or scrapped, are we able to calculate the final cost. We apportion the estimated depreciation of the asset over its life expectancy and we do this using one of the methods described below.

When we examine the cash flow statement in Chapter 31 we will see that depreciation is excluded from the expenses in preparing this statement. This is because depreciation is not a cash expense. We may have a cash outflow when we buy the asset but we do not have any outflow when we depreciate it.

12.2 Straight line depreciation

This method allows for the same amount to be charged each year as an expense. The business estimates the fall in value of the fixed asset, taking into account any value that it may receive for that asset at the end of its life. This could be the resale value or the scrap value of the asset or even a trade-in value – collectively known as the residual value.

When the fixed asset is finally disposed of, the business is then able to determine if there is an underestimation or overestimation of depreciation.

12.2.1 Worked example

A business buys a machine at a cost of £55,000. The cost includes delivery and installation charges which are added to the capital amount of the machine. It is expected to use the machine for 5 years and at the end of the period it will be sold for £5,000 (the residual value). To calculate the depreciation the following formula is used:

$$\text{Depreciation per year} = \frac{\text{Cost less residual value}}{\text{Useful economic life}}$$

This formula divides the cost of the asset (original cost less residual value) into equal proportions according to its estimated useful life.

Depreciation charge for the year:

$$\frac{£55,000 - £5,000}{5} = £10,000 \text{ p.a.}$$

The depreciation charge remains fixed every year. This charge is shown in the profit and loss account as an expense although we must note that there is no payment for depreciation (hence no cash flows out of the business). The balance sheet shows the net book value of the asset, which is the original cost minus the accumulated (total to date) depreciation.

In the example above we see that after one year the value of the fixed asset is its cost less the accumulated depreciation which, in this case, is the depreciation for one year only. The balance is known as the net book value.

- Cost £55,000 less £10,000 = Net book value £45,000.

The position changes after two years and the calculation is as follows:

- Cost £55,000 less £20,000 = Net book value £35,000.

In this case the accumulated depreciation is the depreciation charged for two years.
At the end of year 5 the net book value is:

- Cost £55,000 less £50,000 (5 × £10,000) = Net book value £5,000.

This final balance equates to the anticipated scrap value of the fixed asset and when it is sold the cash received will be credited to the fixed asset account. If there is any difference on the account then this will be an over- or under-recovery of depreciation.

To illustrate fully how the fixed asset depreciates in value, the following table is given:

Detailed schedule of the machine over 5 years

	Year 1	Year 2	Year 3	Year 4	Year 5
Original cost	55,000	55,000	55,000	55,000	55,000
Accumulated depreciation at beginning of the year		10,000	20,000	30,000	40,000
Opening balance	55,000	45,000	35,000	25,000	15,000
Depreciation for year	10,000	10,000	10,000	10,000	10,000
Accumulated depreciation	10,000	20,000	30,000	40,000	50,000
Net book value	45,000	35,000	25,000	15,000	5,000

The highlighted figures show the build-up of depreciation each year and the reduction in the net book value year on year.

The entries in the Ledger accounts would be as follows:

Machine

Year 1	Cost	55,000		

Accumulated depreciation – machine

			Year 1	Depreciation	10,000
			Year 2	Depreciation	10,000
			Year 3	Depreciation	10,000
			Year 4	Depreciation	10,000
			Year 5	Depreciation	10,000

Depreciation

Year 1	Acc depreciation	10,000	Year 1	P&L account	10,000
Year 2	Acc depreciation	10,000	Year 2	P&L account	10,000
Year 3	Acc depreciation	10,000	Year 3	P&L account	10,000
Year 4	Acc depreciation	10,000	Year 4	P&L account	10,000
Year 5	Acc depreciation	10,000	Year 5	P&L account	10,000

We examine the under- and over-recoupment in sections 12.5.1 and 12.5.2 below.

12.3 Reducing balance method

Under this method a fixed percentage of depreciation is applied to the asset each year based on the net book value. It is considered that a fixed asset does not fall in value equally over its life but has its biggest fall in the early stages. As a result it is frequently found that this method is used in the case of motor vehicles as it reflects what actually occurs. When we buy a vehicle it loses a lot of value within the first year but less and less over the next few years. This we attempt to account for using the reducing balance method.

To use this method we need to have a fixed annual depreciation rate which is then applied to the net book value each year.

12.3.1 Worked example

For the purposes of this method, assume a percentage has been pre-calculated. Apply this percentage to the 'written down' or 'net book value' of the fixed asset to arrive at a charge for the year.

Using the same example as in section 12.2.1, we assume that the fixed percentage for this fixed asset is 20 per cent each year calculated on the reducing balance.

At the end of the first year the depreciation equals £11,000. This is arrived at by taking the fixed rate of 20 per cent and multiplying it by the cost of £55,000. This then gives us the net book value of £55,000 – £11,000 = £44,000.

At the end of the second year the depreciation for the year equals the fixed rate multiplied by the reduced balance. This is calculated as £44,000 × 20% = £8,800. We now have a net book value at the end of year 2 as the cost less the accumulated depreciation (year 1 and year 2). This is shown as £55,000 – £19,800 (i.e. £11,000 + £8,800) = £35,200.

The following is a detailed schedule of the machine over the five years using the reducing balance method.

	Year 1	Year 2	Year 3	Year 4	Year 5
Original cost	55,000	55,000	55,000	55,000	55,000
Accumulated depreciation at beginning of the year		11,000	19,800	26,840	32,472
Opening balance – net book value	55,000	44,000	35,200	28,160	22,528
Depreciation for year	11,000	8,800	7,040	5,632	4,506
Accumulated depreciation	11,000	19,800	26,840	32,472	36,978
Net book value	44,000	35,200	28,160	22,528	18,022

From the table above we can see that the net book value as calculated using this method is greater than that using the straight line method. We show this in the 'T' accounts below.

Machine			
Year 1 Cost	55,000		

Accumulated depreciation – machine			
	Year 1 Acc depreciation	11,000
	Year 2 Acc depreciation	8,800
	Year 3 Acc depreciation	7,040
	Year 4 Acc depreciation	5,632
	Year 5 Acc depreciation	4,506

Depreciation

Year 1	Acc depreciation	11,000	Year 1	P&L account	11,000
Year 2	Acc depreciation	8,800	Year 2	P&L account	8,800
Year 3	Acc depreciation	7,040	Year 3	P&L account	7,040
Year 4	Acc depreciation	5,632	Year 4	P&L account	5,632
Year 5	Acc depreciation	4,506	Year 5	P&L account	4,506

12.3.2 Illustration of depreciation methods

Reducing balance method

Figure 12.1 **Graph showing NBV using reducing balance method**

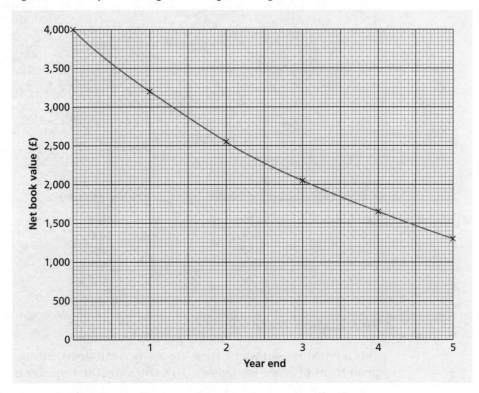

	Opening balance	20% depreciation p.a.	Year end NBV
Year 1	4,000	800	3,200
Year 2	3,200	640	2,560
Year 3	2,560	512	2,048
Year 4	2,048	409	1,639
Year 5	1,639	327	1,312

Straight line method

Figure 12.2 Graph showing NBV using straight line method

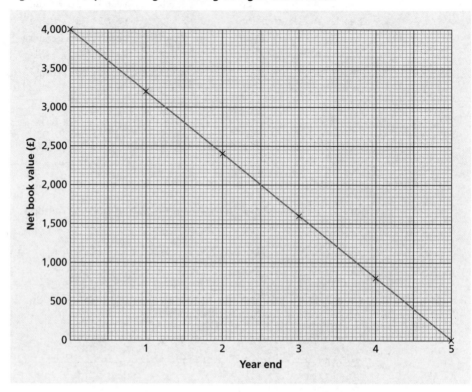

	Opening balance	20% depreciation p.a.	Year end NBV
Year 1	4,000	800	3,200
Year 2	3,200	800	2,400
Year 3	2,400	800	1,600
Year 4	1,600	800	800
Year 5	800	800	NIL

12.4 Revaluation method

This method is used where there are many small items, e.g. tools in a garage or small items of office equipment. To use this method the assets are valued each year and the fall in value is the depreciation for that year. No fixed percentage is used to reduce the value but the net book value is calculated by valuation. In this method only the reduction in value is taken into account in the profit and loss account and there is no write-up of appreciation in value.

12.4.1 Worked example

A business purchases office equipment on 1 January 2009 to a total value of £2,000. As this equipment consists of small items, it was decided that the best method of accounting for depreciation was the revaluation method. Accordingly at the end of each year a value was determined. The following are these values:

Year to 31 December 2009   £1,600
Year to 31 December 2010   £1,350
Year to 31 December 2011   £1,000

In calculating depreciation for each year, we deduct the new value from the old one, as follows

Year 2009   £2,000 – £1,600 = £400 depreciation for the year
Year 2010   £1,600 – £1,350 = £250 depreciation for the year
Year 2011   £1,350 – £1,000 = £350 depreciation for the year

12.5 Sale of fixed assets

When we sell a fixed asset we receive an amount which may be more or less than the net book value at the time. If it is more then we have made a profit, while if the amount received is less than the net book value, a loss is made. Both the profit and the loss must be recorded in the profit and loss account.

Using the examples in sections 12.2.1 and 12.3.1, let us assume that we sell the fixed asset at the end of year 3 for £20,000. The net book value (as shown in the table in section 12.3.1) using the reducing balance method is £28,160. Therefore, we have made an additional loss of £8,160 and this is the additional amount to be written off to the profit and loss account as a loss on the sale of the fixed asset.

In the case of the straight line method, as illustrated in section 12.2.1, the table shows a balance of £25,000 at the end of year 3. In this instance the additional amount to be written off is £5,000.

To record the profit or loss, we can open a disposal account to which we transfer the balances on the fixed asset account and the provision for depreciation account. We also credit that account with the amount received from the sale. The balance is then calculated and if it is a debit balance, it is a profit, while any credit balance reflects a loss on disposal. Whatever this balancing figure is, it is transferred to the profit and loss account.

12.5.1 Worked example

We have illustrated the accounting entries for straight line depreciation and the reducing balance method, under their respective paragraphs. In the example below we show how we would record the sale set out in section 12.5 above.

You will note that the initial entries are the same as those in the case of the reducing balance method but that at the end of year 3 we have disposed of the machine and received a payment of £20,000.

On doing this we transfer the cost of the machine sold and all the accumulated depreciation on that machine to the disposal account. After entering the payment received, we then determine if there is a profit or loss, which must then be written off. In this instance there is an additional loss of £8,160 and this is credited to the disposal account (to balance that account to nil), and the corresponding debit to the loss on sale account. This latter account is subsequently transferred to the profit and loss account.

Machine

Cost	55,000	Transfer to disposal account	55,000
	55,000		55,000

Accumulated depreciation – machine

Transfer – disposal account	26,840	Year 1	11,000
		Year 2	8,800
		Year 3	7,040
	26,840		26,840

Depreciation

Year 1	11,000	P&L ac	11,000
Year 2	8,800	P&L ac	8,800
Year 3	7,040	P&L ac	7,040

Disposal account – machine

Machine account	55,000	Acc depreciation	26,840
		Bank	20,000
		Loss on sale to P&L account	8,160
	55,000		55,000

Profit and loss account (extract)

Loss on sale of machinery	8,160		

12.5.2 Worked example

In this example we use the information shown in the above paragraph but are told that the sale in year 3 is for an amount of £32,000 instead of the £20,000 used in the above example.

As such we will show a profit on the sale, as illustrated in the disposal account shown below:

Disposal account

Machine account	55,000	Acc depreciation	26,840
Profit on sale to P&L	3,840	Bank	32,000
	58,840		58,840

12.6 Summary of depreciation

- Depreciation measures the reduction in the useful economic life of the asset and allocates the cost, less any estimated scrap or residual value, over the accounting periods expected to benefit from the asset.
- The depreciation charge for the year is shown as an expense in the profit and loss account.
- In the balance sheet we show the fixed assets at net book value (cost less accumulated depreciation).

The reasons for depreciation are:

- Attempts to match costs with revenues (matching/accruals concept).
- Ensuring that there is adequate capital maintenance.
- Attempts to maintain sufficient capital in the business to allow for the replacement of the asset when it wears out.

The problems of depreciation are:

- What is the cost?
- How do you quantify the 'useful economic life'?
- How is the residual value calculated?

These questions are a good illustration of the fact that accounting is not a precise science. Judgement is required and this may vary between different people with a corresponding difference in the calculation of depreciation and net profit.

12.7 Appreciation of fixed assets

Not all the fixed assets of a business depreciate. A common example is land, which generally shows an appreciation over a number of years.

Any gain can be shown in a revaluation of the asset but it is not shown in the profit and loss account as it is a capital gain and reflected as such in the balance sheet (see section 28.8.2).

12.7.1 Self-test

A machine is purchased by Kay & Co. for £450,000 on 1 January 2009. The machine has an expected life of 5 years and the scrap value is expected to be £100,000.

Using straight line depreciation, prepare calculations to show the charge to the profit and loss account each year as well as the balance sheet presentation during the life of the machine.

The business also purchased a building for £950,000 on 1 January 2009. The business depreciates all buildings at a rate of 2 per cent p.a. using the reducing balance method.

Prepare calculations to show the charge to the profit and loss account and the balance sheet entries for the first three years.

12.7.2 Self-test

At 31 December 2009 Maureen's ledger contained the following balances:

Plant and machinery   50,000
Provision for depreciation on plant and machinery   22,500

During the year ended 31 December 2010 the following transactions took place:

- On 31 March Maureen exchanged part of her machinery for more modern equipment.
- She received a trade-in allowance on the old plant of £7,000 and the balance of £2,000 was paid by cheque.
- The old plant cost £13,000 when it was originally purchased on 1 July 2007.
- Plant and machinery is depreciated on a strict time basis at 20 per cent p.a. using the reducing balance method.

You are required to show the ledger accounts for the above items. You need to show what charges are to be made to the profit and loss account for the year in respect of the plant sold.

12.7.3 Self-test

On 19 June 2009 Wilson purchased a new machine for his factory. The following are the payments made by him relating to this purchase:

Cost of machine   42,000
Less: Trade discount   4,000   38,000
Delivery costs incurred   3,100
Erection charge paid   5,200
Annual maintenance charge   1,300

You are required to show what amount is to be used as the total cost price of the machine.

(i) Prepare the ledger account for the new machine for the years ending 31 December 2009 and 2010, and allow depreciation of 15 per cent per annum on a reducing balance. *Note that depreciation is charged in full for the year in which the machine is purchased.*
(ii) Assuming that Wilson decides to use a straight line method of depreciation of 10 per cent per annum, what would the charges be for depreciation in the years ending 31 December 2009 and 2010?

12.7.4 Self-test

Sheryl started a business on 1 March 2008.

- She purchased both a printer for £1,300 and a photocopier for £870 on 1 March 2008.
- On 28 February 2009 she traded in the printer for a new one. The total price of the new printer was £1,900 and she received a credit for the trade-in of £985.

- On 1 March 2009 she also decided to purchase a second photocopier. The list price was £1,200 but she received a trade discount of 10 per cent and a cash discount of 5 per cent.
- Depreciation is charged at 15 per cent p.a. on the printer using the straight line method and at 10 per cent p.a. on the photocopiers using the reducing balance method.

You are required to show the ledger accounts for the fixed assets and the provision for depreciation accounts for the years ending 28 February 2009 and 2010.

Chapter 13

Bad debts

Objectives   After you have studied this chapter, you should be able to:
- explain the nature of bad debts;
- create provisions for bad debts;
- show the accounting entries for bad debts and provisions;
- account for bad debts recovered.

13.1 Introduction

We sell on credit and expect to be paid. But this does not always happen and businesses often have to write off amounts owing to them because of bad debts. To do this we debit the bad debt account and credit the debtors' account.

The balance on the bad debts account is then written off to the profit and loss account at the year end as an expense for the period. The debtors' balances, as shown in the balance sheet, are reduced by the amount of the bad debt written off.

13.1.1 Worked example

Alex Hardware sells goods to Smythe during the 2009 financial year. The total sales to 30 April 2009 were £872. On 12 May 2009 Smythe pays Alex Hardware £220 on account. In September 2009 Alex Hardware are informed that Smythe is insolvent and that no further payments can be expected.

You are required to show the ledger accounts for the above transactions.

			Smythe			
30 April	Sales	872		12 May	Bank	220
		___		30 Sept	Bad debt	652
		872				872

			Bad debts			
30 Sept	Smythe	652		31 Dec	P&L account	652

Provision for bad debts

We do not always know that a debtor is or will become bad – there is just a risk that we may not get paid. Based on this, we estimate the percentage of debtors that may not pay in the future because prudence (conservatism) demands that we do so. (The concept of prudence is discussed fully in section 25.2.3.)

This estimate is known as a provision for bad (or doubtful) debts. This, like other provisions, is an amount set aside for a known expense where the amount is not definite.

In a way this provision is similar to writing off a bad debt as it serves to reduce the total debtors as shown in the balance sheet and any increase in the provision is also shown in the profit and loss account as an expense.

The provision that we create is only an estimate of the possible amount of future bad debts. We could examine each and every debtor's account and see if the amount is likely to be paid. If not, then we could allow for that debtor to form part of the provision. This can be very time consuming and can also only be an estimate.

We could analyse the debtors' balances into an age category. The longer a debtor is outstanding, the more likely it is that it will ultimately become bad. By doing this we are able to allocate a fixed percentage to the different 'ages' of the debtors and so arrive at an amount for the provision. Here too the amount is an estimate but less time consuming than the first alternative.

In the table below, an age analysis of debtors and the calculation of the amount of the provision is shown.

Analysis of debtors by age

Months outstanding	Amount of debtors	Percentage doubtful	Provision amount
Under 1 month	8,800	0.5%	44
1 to 3 months	11,200	1.5%	168
4 to 6 months	2,000	3.0%	60
6 to 12 months	1,000	5.0%	50
Over 12 months	1,500	10.0%	150
Totals	24,500		472

Each year, after writing off all known bad debts, we calculate the amount of the provision. The difference is either an additional expense (when the provision increases), or is shown as a credit to the profit and loss account (when the provision is reduced).

In accounting terms we can say that if the provision is greater than it was in the previous year then we must debit the profit and loss account with the additional amount and credit the provision account. If, on the other hand, the provision is less, then the excess must be credited to the profit and loss account and deducted (debited) from the provision account.

13.2.1 Worked examples

(i) A business has debtors of £250,000 at 31 December 2009. It anticipates that 5 per cent of them will not pay their debts. You are required to calculate the amount to be charged in the profit and loss account and show the presentation of debtors as it would appear in the balance sheet.

Sundry debtors			
31 Dec 09 Bal b/d	250,000		

Provision for bad debts			
		31 Dec 09 P&L account	12,500

The profit and loss account is charged with £12,500 as a provision for bad debts. In the balance sheet we would show debtors of £250,000 − £12,500 = £237,500.

Any increase in the provision in later years is shown as an expense in the profit and loss account.

(ii) A business has a balance of £900,000 of outstanding trade debtors at 31 December 2010. Each year it calculates a provision of 5 per cent of year-end trade debtors. At 31 December 2009 the provision amounted to £30,000. You are required to calculate the amount to be shown in the profit and loss account and show the presentation of the debtors in the balance sheet as at 31 December 2010.

Sundry debtors			
31 Dec 10 Bal b/d	900,000		

Provision for bad debts			
		31 Dec 09 P&L ac	30,000
		31 Dec 10 P&L ac	15,000

In 2009 the provision was £30,000, while in 2010 we are told that the provision is 5 per cent of £900,000 = £45,000. Therefore, we only need increase the existing provision by an additional amount of £15,000.

In the 2010 balance sheet we would show debtors as follows:

Debtors	£900,000
Less provision for doubtful debts	(£45,000)
	£855,000

From this we see that it is the total provision of 5 per cent of the closing debtors' balances (£45,000) that is shown in the balance sheet in 2010. In the profit and loss account, however, only the additional amount of £15,000 is shown as a current year's expense.

Extract from profit and loss account 31/12/10	
Provision for bad debts	15,000

13.2.2 Worked example

A business has debtors at its year end of £40,000. One debtor of £2,500 is in liquidation and it is also thought that there could be other debtors, estimated as being 4 per cent of the outstanding balances, who may not pay. The business would write off the £2,500 as a bad debt and would then calculate a provision of 4 per cent on the remaining debtors of £37,500. The balance sheet would show debtors of £37,500 minus £1,500 = £36,000.

The bad debts (£2,500) and the provision (£1,500) are both treated as expenses in the profit and loss account.

Bad debts			
Year 1 Debtor A	2,500	Year 1 P&L account	2,500

The following year the provision is reversed and a new one is created. Only the increased amount (say £400) is charged to the profit and loss account in the new period. There may, of course, be a reduction in the provision and in this case the amount is credited to the profit and loss account.

Provision for bad debts		
	Year 1 P&L account	1,500
	Year 2 P&L account	400

We can define a provision as an amount deducted from profit to provide for expenses that are not known accurately at the time the accounts are prepared. If legal action is being brought against a business it might make a provision for legal costs and claims. This is acting prudently, recognising the possible costs as soon as possible.

13.2.3 Self-test

Ajax Electrical decides that 5 per cent of all debtors are assumed to be doubtful debts and makes a provision accordingly. You are told that the debtors' balances are as follows:

31 December 2009	£50,000
31 December 2010	£60,000
31 December 2011	£40,000

You are required to show the relevant ledger account for the provision for doubtful debts for each year. Also indicate what amounts will appear in the profit and loss account and balance sheet at the end of each year.

13.3 Recovery of bad debts

It may happen that a debtor, who we write off as bad, subsequently pays part, or all, of the amount due. We then show the amount in the cash book and post it to the credit of the bad debts recovered account. From there it is entered as a recovery of an expense in the profit and loss account.

13.3.1 Worked example

Let us assume that Smythe paid Alex Hardware £420 on 20 July 2010. Using the information in section 13.1.1 the ledger account would be as follows:

Smythe					
30 April 09	Sales	872	12 May 09	Bank	220
		___	31 Dec 09	Bad debt	652
		872			872

Note that the debtors account is not altered in any way. The recovery (in this case only a part recovery) is credited to the bad debts recovered account on the date it is received. At the end of the year the balance on this account is transferred to the profit and loss account, where it shows as an income item.

Bad debt recovered					
31 Dec 10	P&L account	420	20 Jul 10	Bad debt recovered	420

13.3.2 Self-test

At 31 December 2009 Mike's ledger contained the following balances:

Trade debtors	20,000
Provision for bad debts	3,340

The provision for bad debts consisted of a general provision of £800 and specific provisions for the following debtors:

D Swart	420
J Higgins	1,200
L Beck	920

During the year ended 31 December 2010 the following transactions took place:

(i) On 30 April D Swart was declared bankrupt and a payment of £95 was received on 18 July 2010.
(ii) On 15 June Mike was advised that the full debt due by J Higgins included in the debtors at 31 December 2009 was bad.
(iii) On 3 August L Beck paid the amount due by him in full.

Mike wishes to make provision for future bad debts by providing a general provision for bad debts of 5 per cent of the year-end debtors.

You are required to show the ledger accounts for the above items. You can assume that no other transactions took place on the debtors' ledger other than those given in the question.

Indicate clearly what charges are to be made to the profit and loss account for the year.

13.3.3 Self-test

Lyn commenced her business on 1 June 2008. She sells most of her goods on credit and therefore ensures that there is always an adequate provision for doubtful debts. She considers that the provision should be equal to 5 per cent of the outstanding debtors at the end of the financial year.

At 31 May 2009 the debtors outstanding were £14,800. Included in these debtors was an amount of £620 due by Martin, who had been declared bankrupt. Lyn decided she would write this amount off as a bad debt.

At 31 May 2010 the outstanding debtors amounted to £18,900. Lyn received a payment from the liquidators of Martin of 15 pence in the pound. This amount has not yet been recorded in her books. During the year Gary was unable to pay the £280 due and Lyn decided that the amount should be treated as a bad debt.

At 31 May 2011 the debtors outstanding were £21,000. Lyn considered that the provision for doubtful debts should be increased to 6 per cent of the debtors' balances.

You are required to show the entries to be made to the profit and loss account for the years ending 2009, 2010 and 2011.

You also are required to show the debtors' figure that is to be shown in the balance sheet for each year.

Chapter 14

The journal

Objectives

After you have studied this chapter, you should be able to:

- explain the purpose of the journal;
- identify and show how errors are rectified;
- enter journal transactions and narrations.

14.1 Introduction

Journals are often called day books and are not part of the double-entry system. They store details of transactions until they are entered into the accounts.

The journal is used for non-regular transactions, for example, the sale of a fixed asset. We deal with this form of journal in the paragraphs below.

14.2 Why use a journal?

No transaction can be entered directly into the ledger. They must first be recorded in a subsidiary book and then posted to the ledger. The journal is used for items which cannot be conveniently entered into any other subsidiary book. All journals are books of original entry because they record the first details of the transactions.

There are many instances when we would make use of the journal instead of another subsidiary book. For example:

- when we buy or sell a fixed asset on credit (if we paid cash then it would be entered via the cash book);
- to write off any bad debts;
- to correct errors (see section 15.2);
- when we undertake adjusting entries, such as adjustments for accruals and prepayments;
- for any year-end adjustments for depreciation; and
- to transfer amounts between accounts (inter ledger transfers).

The journal is ruled like this:

Figure 14.1 Example of a journal

Date	Details	Folio	DR		CR	

In the above example (Figure 14.1) the first money column is for the debit entry and the second money column is for the credit entries.

When we enter items into the journal we must decide which account is to be debited and which account is to be credited. An important part of the journal entry is the narration – that is, the 'story'. This describes the reason for making the journal entry. Without this we would often not know or understand why the journal entry was made.

It is extremely important that you familiarise yourselves with the journal as you have to plan, in advance, the account(s) to be debited and the one (or more) to receive the corresponding credit. To be a complete entry you must ensure that it is properly dated and described (the narration). All too often in answering examination questions, a near perfect journal entry loses marks because the student has failed to put in the date or narration.

14.2.1 Worked examples

On 1 August 2009 A Ltd purchased from X Motors a delivery van for the business. The purchase price was £8,000 and X Motors agreed that the total amount was payable over 8 months. You are required to record this transaction.

As payment is not made by cheque (and therefore there is no cash book entry) we must record it via the journal.

1 Aug 09	Delivery van	Dr	8,000	
	X Motors	Cr		8,000
	Purchase price of new van from X Motors payable over 8 months as from 1 August 2009.			

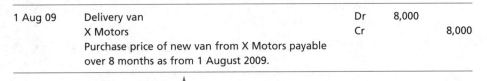

This statement is known as the narration

We have a debtor, J Smith, who owes us £300. He became insolvent on 30 June 2009 and therefore we need to write off the amount owing to us. To do this we can only use the journal.

30 Jun 09	Bad debts	Dr	300	
	J Smith	Cr		300
	Amount owing by J Smith on his account now written off due to his insolvency.			

On 31 August 2009 we buy a new machine from Planters Ltd for the factory. The purchase price is £1,500 and the payment for this machine will be made on 30 November 2009.

31 Aug 09	Plant and machinery	Dr	1,500	
	Planters Ltd	Cr		1,500
	Purchase of plant and machinery. Payment due on 30 Nov 2009.			

J Smith owes us £130 for goods that we sold to him. At the same time, we also purchase goods from him for the business. At 30 June 2009 we owe J Smith on his creditors' account a total of £90. On the same day, he sends us a cheque for £40 to settle his account. In the entry below we use the journal to offset the £90 credit balance with the £90 debit balance.

The journal entry would be:

30 Jun 09	J Smith (creditor)	Dr	90	
	J Smith (debtor)	Cr		90
	An off-set of the debtors' and creditors' accounts at 30 June 2009.			

14.2.2 Self-test

In preparing our year-end accounts for Fleck at 30 June 2009 we are told that the following adjustments are still to be made:

Electricity outstanding (no invoice yet received)	89
Telephone due	47
Motor car purchased (payment due 31 Dec 2009)	1,500

A debtor, J Smith, who owes us £69, has been declared insolvent.
We have also paid in advance the following:

Advertising	300
Rent	490

You are required to prepare the journal entries for the above transactions.

14.2.3 Self-test

Dee owes £162. She pays £102 on 31 July 2009 but makes no further payments. On 3 October 2009 she is declared bankrupt and we are informed that we will receive 20p in the pound on whatever is still owing. We receive this amount on 30 November 2009.

Calculate the amount of the bad debt for the year ended 31 December 2009.
Show the journal entry for the bad debt and also the debtors' ledger account.

14.2.4 Self-test

A Trader has the following bad debts for the year ended 30 June 2009:

Smith	£81
Jones	£94
Blake	£32
Currie	£14

The debtors at 30 June 2009, before the write-off of bad debts, were £8,981.

Show all the above journal entries and the ledger accounts for debtors and
bad debts.

14.2.5 Self-test

Raymond starts up a new business on 11 May 2009, having purchased certain
assets and liabilities from the previous owner.

The following is the list of assets and liabilities purchased:

Land and buildings	15,000
Electricity due	170
Stock	7,960
Creditors	960
Debtors	410
Overdraft	3,420
Equipment	11,640

Raymond paid for the net assets from his personal bank account. The net amount
paid is regarded as his capital in the business.

You are required to make the necessary journal entries to record the above
transactions.

Chapter 15

Trial balance

Objectives

After you have studied this chapter, you should be able to:

- describe the nature and purpose of a trial balance;
- prepare a trial balance from a set of ledger account balances;
- account for year-end adjustments such as accruals, prepayments, depreciation and bad debts.

15.1 Introduction

The trial balance is a list of balances taken from the ledger accounts at a set point in time. The trial balance is often prepared at month end using these balances and is done in order to test the accuracy of our recording of transactions.

The ledger accounts are balanced off and all the debit balances are shown in the debit column and all credit balances in the credit column. We saw in section 3.1 how we balance off the ledger accounts. We also noted how these balances are transferred to the trial balance. If the balance is at the month end then the balance brought down is dated as the 1st of the following month. It is also important to note that the trial balance is not part of the double-entry system but is simply a list of balances.

The following example shows a list of balances taken from the ledger at 31 December 2010. These balances are listed as below and then used (after any adjustment) in the relevant financial statement.

Trial balance for the year ended 31 December 2010

	DEBIT	CREDIT
Trade creditors		5,400
Cost of sales	11,500	
Wages	3,100	
Sales		27,500
Rent	1,900	
Office furniture	1,800	
Capital account		4,000
Bank overdraft		1,200
Debtors	19,800	
	38,100	38,100

If the trial balance balances this means that the postings have been made to the correct side of an account. It does not, however, indicate that a posting has been entered to the correct account. We discuss this in section 15.2 below.

Figure 15.1 shows the use of balances in the relevant financial statements.

Figure 15.1 **The division of the trial balance**

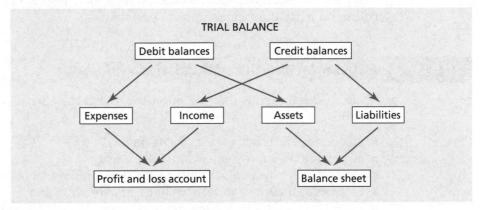

15.1.1 Self-test

The following balances were extracted from the books of A Jones at 31 December 2009:

Motor vehicles at cost	5,600
Fixtures and fittings at cost	4,200
Land and buildings at cost	5,600
Loan	1,680
Advertising	280
Administration expenses	1,316
Loan interest	56
Bank overdraft	840
Debtors	3,150
Creditors	2,086
Profit and loss account at 1 January 2009	5,250
Provision for doubtful debts at 1 January 2009	210
Jones – capital account	5,446
Sales	10,850
Purchases	5,180
Opening stock at 1 January 2009	3,500
Depreciation on motor vehicles at 1 January 2009	1,680
Depreciation on fixtures and fittings at 1 January 2009	840

You are required to prepare the trial balance of A Jones at 31 December 2009.

15.1.2 Self-test

Using the balances that you prepared in self-test 2.6.2 you are required to draw up the trial balance.

15.1.3 Self-test

Prepare a trial balance from the information you prepared in self-test 2.6.3.

15.1.4 Self-test

Using the balances from self test 2.6.5 you are now required to prepare a trial balance to prove the accuracy of your postings.

15.2 Errors affecting the trial balance

There are certain errors that will affect the trial balance from balancing. These can be:

- accounting errors due to items being omitted;
- an amount incorrectly entered into the ledger;
- balances of a ledger account incorrectly stated in the trial balance;
- balances in the ledger not shown in the trial balance; and
- credit balances shown as debit balances in the trial balance and debit balances shown as credit balances in the trial balance.

15.2.1 Self-test

Jillian is the owner of an electrical repair business. After the first year of operations she presented the following trial balance which was not balanced because a number of accounts were shown in the incorrect column. You are required to place the accounts in the correct column so as to check if the trial balance is in balance.

Cash	2,150	
Debtors	6,500	
Stock at 1 January 2009		1,900
Equipment	18,900	
Creditors		1,750
Accruals	3,000	
Jillian, capital account	13,000	
Jillian, drawings		1,800
Sales	37,250	
Wages		9,500
Rent	8,600	
Postage and telephone	3,750	
Travel and motor expenses		1,900

After working through the above example you will note that the trial balance does, in fact, balance.

There are, of course, many instances where this does not happen. This is usually because of errors in adding or posting but may be also brought about by some of the many other errors that we will discuss in Chapter 16. We will show how all these errors are corrected by journal entries (section 16.2.2).

15.3 Period-end adjustments

Having now ensured that the trial balance is correct, there may still be additional adjustments to be made. All the entries taken into the trial balance have originated from records of prime entry. Each transaction has originated from a source document such as an invoice, cheque payment, credit note, etc. There are, however, a number of additional entries that need be made at the end of a period to amend, alter or correct the accounts.

These additional adjustments are for accruals and prepayments as well as for the creation of a provision (such as for bad debts or for depreciation).

We examined accruals and prepayments in Chapter 11. Depreciation was covered in Chapter 12 and bad debts and the provision for bad debts was examined in Chapter 13.

15.3.1 Self-test

Nigel prepares a trial balance from his records. In doing so he places some debit and credit balances on the incorrect side of the trial balance. As a result the trial balance does not balance. The following trial balance was prepared for the year ended 31 December 2009.

Sales	21,860	
Purchases		11,180
Motor vehicles at cost		15,600
Fixtures and fittings at cost	4,200	
Advertising	980	
Bank interest	456	
Opening stock at 1 January 2009		6,500
Motor vehicles (accumulated depreciation at 1 Jan 09)	4,680	
Debtors		9,150
Creditors	9,086	
Provision for doubtful debts at 1 Jan 2009	1,910	
Nigel – capital account		27,446
Land and buildings at cost		19,600
Selling expenses	6,680	
Administration expenses		4,316
Bank overdraft	9,840	
Fixtures and fittings (accumulated depreciation at 1/1/09)		3,840

You are required to redraw the trial balance, placing the debit and credit balances in their correct columns. At the end of the exercise total the debits and credits to ensure that the trial balance now balances.

15.3.2 Self-test

You are given the following list of balances for W Thom at 30 September 2009. From this list of balances prepare the trial balance.

Advertising	9,600
Postage and telephone	3,280
Lighting and heating	5,104
Drawings	50,560
Bank overdraft	27,796
Insurance	15,584
Rent and rates	60,352
Salaries and wages	41,088
Motor expenses	37,172
Purchases	330,061
Returns inwards	1,440
Returns outwards	2,416
Stock at 1 October 2008	112,448
Debtors	65,005
Commission received	3,200
Creditors	51,028
Fixtures and fittings	49,280
Capital at 1 October 2008	150,432
Cash in hand	1,450
Bank interest and charges	4,928
Sales	604,960
Motor vehicles	52,480

15.3.3 Self-test

On 30 June 2009, Final Trading Co. extracted a list of balances from their ledger.

Office expenses	11,880
Postage and stationery	3,900
Rent and rates	7,500
Insurance	1,095
Lighting and heating	1,548
Motor expenses	5,880
Salaries and wages	14,550
Sales	109,800
Purchases	61,950
Bank charges	2,418
Vans	10,500
Creditors	9,750
Debtors	20,430
Land and buildings	84,000
Stock 1 July 2008	24,060
Cash at bank	3,402
Drawings	18,834
Capital	152,397

You need to place these balances in a trial balance to check the accuracy of the ledger postings.

Remember the rules to determine if the balances are debits or credits.

We read about them in section 2.1. To recap, they are:

- All assets are debits and liabilities are credits.
- Expenses are debits and incomes are credits.

With the above in mind, you only need identify what each account heading represents and from that you should be able to prepare the trial balance.

15.4 From trial balance to financial statements

In addition to being a check on the double-entry system the trial balance is also the springboard for the preparation of the final accounts. Once all these adjustments have been made, we can proceed to the next stage in the accounting process which is the preparation of the final accounts.

The first statement to be prepared is the trading and profit and loss account and this is fully discussed in Chapters 19 and 20. The resulting profit (or loss) is transferred to the balance sheet where all the assets and liabilities are shown. Here again, full details are given in Chapter 22.

15.4.1 Self-test

Using the information for A Jones, given in section 15.1.1, you are required to amend your trial balance at 31 December 2009 by incorporating the following additional items prior to preparing the final accounts. You only need prepare an adjusted trial balance in this question.

(i) Stock at 31 December 2009 was valued at £4,300.
(ii) Included in the figure for administration expenses is £144. This is an advance payment for 12 months rent from 1 October 2009.
(iii) Depreciation to be charged as follows:
    (a) Fixtures and fittings: 25 per cent using the straight line method;
    (b) Motor vehicles: 20 per cent using the reducing balance method.
(iv) Provision for doubtful debts should be made equal to 10 per cent of outstanding debtors.
(v) During the year the company engaged cleaners for their premises at a cost of £140. This amount must be provided for in administrative expenses.
(vi) The accountancy fees for 2009 will amount to £100, and should be included in administrative expenses.

It is important that you show all your workings for all the above adjustments.

15.4.2 Self-test

The following adjustments are to be made to the trial balance of W Thom that you prepared in self-test 15.3.2.

(i) At 30 September 2009 depreciation on fixtures and fittings of £4,928 had not been provided for in the books.
(ii) Rent and rates included a payment made on 30 September 2009 of £4,000 for October to December rent.
(iii) Salaries of £1,200 due on 30 September 2009 were only paid on 4 October 2009 and an allowance for this must still be made in the books of account.
(iv) Debtors of £430 were bad and had to be written off.

You are required to show the above adjustments by way of journal entries.

15.4.3 Self-test

Prepare a trial balance from the following list of ledger balances at 30 June 2010.

Office expenses	3,880
Lighting and heating	2,570
Motor expenses	5,820
Salaries and wages	4,650
Sales	79,850
Purchases	41,750
Bank charges	2,010
Delivery vehicles	23,580
Creditors	9,150
Debtors	29,930
Office equipment	24,530
Stock 1 July 2009	14,960
Cash at bank	9,450
Drawings	25,870
Capital	100,000

15.4.4 Self-test

Prepare a trial balance from the following list of ledger balances at 31 December 2010.

Purchases	103,400
Insurance	2,880
Office expenses	12,145
Salaries and wages	23,400
Drawings	34,600
Bank charges	3,150
Fittings and fixtures	12,670
Motor expenses	3,890
Debtors	45,320
Capital	94,000
Sales	214,700
Bad debts	55,875
Cash at bank	2,430
Creditors	28,920
Stock 1 January 2010	37,860

15.4.5 Self-test

When Mimi prepared her trial balance she incorrectly listed the balances in the wrong columns. As a result she was unable to balance her trial balance.

You are required to redo the trial balance to ensure that it is balanced.

Mimi & Co. Trial balance at 30 June 2009

Debtors		5,100
Purchases	24,000	
Insurance	350	
Electricity		700
Motor expenses	2,960	
Salaries and wages	5,830	
Sales	28,891	
Drawings	8,000	
Motor vehicle		7,500
Creditors		3,250
Fittings and fixtures	3,160	
Stock 1 July 2008	5,020	
Cash at bank		320
Capital	30,799	

15.4.6 Self-test

Max prepared a list of balances from his ledger accounts. You are required to prepare the trial balance from this list.

Max & Co. Balances at 30 June 2009

Postage and stationery	1,300
Rent and rates	2,500
Drawings	11,340
Capital	80,000
Motor expenses	1,960
Salaries and wages	4,850
Sales	63,400
Purchases	48,650
Motor vehicle	3,500
Creditors	7,100
Debtors	39,540
Bank overdraft	5,120
Fittings and fixtures	23,960
Opening stock	18,020

Chapter 16

Errors and suspense accounts

Objectives   After you have studied this chapter, you should be able to:

- describe the nature of the additional errors affecting a trial balance;
- prepare a suspense account and the adjustments to that account;
- journalise all trial balance adjustments;
- prepare a balanced trial balance.

16.1   Introduction

It is important that you are aware that even if the trial balance agrees (balances) there can still be errors. In order that you understand exactly what type of errors may exist, the following list, with a brief explanation of the meaning of the error type, is given.

(a) Errors of commission – this is where the correct amount is entered in the ledger but to the wrong account. For example, sales on credit to J Smith are debited to S Smith's account. The error does not affect the profit and loss account or the balance sheet, as the class of account (i.e. asset, liability, income or expenditure) is correct, but the asset, for example, is shown in the wrong asset account or, in the case of debtor's revenue items, is shown in the wrong revenue account (see (d) below).

(b) Complete reversal of entries – a debit is posted as a credit and vice versa. This could be where, for example, the sales account is debited and the debtors' account is credited with a sale. Both the profit and loss account and/or balance sheet may be affected.

(c) Errors of omission – here the transaction has not been entered into the ledger. This error does have an effect on the profit and loss account and/or the balance sheet.

(d) Errors of principle – the transaction is posted to an incorrect class of account, e.g. an asset is entered as an expense. This affects both the profit and loss account and the balance sheet.

(e) Errors of original entry – this is where the wrong amount is entered. For example, an amount of £93 is entered as £39 in both the debit and credit entry. This affects both the profit and loss account and the balance sheet.

(f) Compensating errors – where two mistakes, for the same amount, in two separate transactions, have the effect of cancelling each other. For example, the ledger account for interest paid is overcast (added) by £100. In addition the ledger account for discount receivable is also overcast by £100. As a result both accounts will be overstated in the trial balance. As interest is debited by £100 in excess and discount is credited by £100 excess, the trial balance will still balance. It must be noted that the one account could be an expense item while the other could be an asset or liability. As such, the profit and loss account and/or balance sheet may be affected.

16.2 Suspense account

If the trial balance does not balance, the difference is placed in a temporary account called a suspense account. If the debit column is smaller than the credit column then the suspense account is said to be in debit and vice versa.

The balance may be shown in the balance sheet until it is sorted out. Naturally this must be done before finalising the financial statements for the period. (In an exam you cannot leave a suspense account in the balance sheet as you would be penalised for that action.)

When the errors are found then the accounts are corrected. To do this we need a journal entry to effect the correction. The entry will be to the suspense account and also to another account to maintain the double-entry system.

The various errors that are shown in a suspense account are those listed in the section above.

Other errors will affect the balancing of the trial balance, such as where there is an incorrect posting. You need to enter the difference in the trial balance into a suspense account. This could either be a debit or a credit. All errors must be investigated and the corrections recorded in the journal with a proper narration (see Chapter 14).

16.2.1 Worked example

We have prepared a trial balance that does not balance. As such we create a suspense account to allow for the difference. The trial balance therefore appears as follows:

	Dr	Cr
Subtotal	59,875	61,960
Suspense account	2,085	
Totals	61,960	61,960

This suspense account is a temporary account and would be closed off after finding the errors.

We now need to find the difference and correct the trial balance. Once this is done we would use journal entries to make the adjustments.

On investigation we find the errors are as follows:

- The total of the purchases account is understated by £2,200 (that is, the total is £2,200 less than it should be).
- Cash received from debtors of £115 is not entered in the debtors account.

We show you these journal entries below so that you understand how they will eventually help us close off the suspense account and balance the trial balance.

Purchases Dr	2,200	
Suspense Cr		2,200

Because the purchases were undercast, the account must now be increased by that shortfall. As this is an expense account we need to debit it with the £2,200. The remainder of the entry (i.e. the credit entry) is not affected so we merely credit the suspense account.

Suspense Dr	115	
Debtor Cr		115

In a similar situation we find that we have not credited our debtor with the amount paid.

Remember: the debtor is the giver and so must be credited.

These journal entries are then posted to the suspense account, as shown below.

Suspense account

Date	Trial balance	2,085	Date	Purchases	2,200
	Debtors	115			
		2,200			2,200

16.2.2 Worked example

Martha Williams prepared a trial balance on 31 December 2009 but the totals did not agree. The difference was entered in a suspense account. After investigation the following errors were revealed:

(i) Martha had taken stock costing £900 from the business for her own use. No entries had been made for this. This error is one of omission (c) as the entry charging Martha for the goods has not been made.

(ii) Sales on credit to D Alexander for £800 were debited to the account of J Alexander. This is an example of an error of commission, as explained in (a) above. The debtors' account of J Alexander was incorrectly charged with goods purchased.

(iii) A sales invoice for M Wilson has been incorrectly totalled as £378 instead of £478. This error is one of original entry. The trial balance remains unaffected as both sales and debtors have been similarly posted with £378. As a result debits and credits are in balance but the profit is understated by £100 and the debtors in the balance sheet are undervalued by £100.

(iv) A cash refund of £110 was given to D Alexander. Martha entered the refund on the debit side of her cash book and credited the account of D Alexander. As there is a double entry there is no error shown in the trial balance. The refund should, however, have been shown on the credit side of the cash book and debited to D Alexander. This error is a complete reversal of entries, as explained in (b) above.

(v) A motor vehicle had been purchased during the year at a cost of £12,000. This amount had been debited to motor expenses in the accounts. This is fixed asset and should not show as an expense item. As such this error is one of principle (d) as the posting was to an incorrect class of account.

As a result of discovery of the above errors, Martha was able to balance the trial balance.

In a question such as this, you would be required to write up the suspense account, and show all the corrections as journal entries with full narrations.

Drawings	Dr	900	
Purchases	Cr		900
Correction of error of omission.			
D Alexander	Dr	800	
J Alexander	Cr		800
Correction of error of commission.			
M Wilson	Dr	100	
Sales	Cr		100
Correction of invoice no.111 – should be £478 instead of £378.			
D Alexander	Dr	220	
Cash book	Cr		220
Correction of entry reversal.*			
Motor vehicle	Dr	12,000	
Motor expenses	Cr		12,000
Correction of error of principle.			

* Note that the amount is double.

The above worked example shows the journal entries required to correct the various errors. If you have any problem with understanding the entries then you should read through Chapter 14 again.

As the above types of error lead to incorrect accounting information, it is important that you understand how they arise, what their effect is on the profit and loss account and the balance sheet and what steps you need take to rectify them.

Errors must be found and corrected before any accounts can be prepared. Additions of the trial balance should be checked and then the individual balances on every account must be checked to see that the accounts are correctly added up and balanced off.

Then the balances should be checked against the trial balance to make sure that the debits and credits are in the correct columns. Often this latter exercise can bring to light the errors without having to check all the additions.

16.2.3 Worked example

We extracted a trial balance at 30 June 2009 but as it does not balance it is vital that we investigate the causes of this imbalance. We find the following:

(i)   The rates are overcast by £20.
(ii) Sales are undercast by £100.
(iii) A credit to William (a debtor) of £35 has not been posted into his account.
(iv) The sale of goods to John for £45 has been entered as £54 in both accounts.

Journal entries to correct the above are:

Suspense	20	
Rates		20
Suspense	100	
Sales		100
Suspense	35	
William		35
Sales	54	
John		54
John	45	
Sales		45

Make sure that you understand why the above entries have been made. Remember who the receiver is and who the giver is. See which one has not been debited or credited. **Remember that one-half of the double entry has been made.** It is the other half that we have to make to balance the trial balance.

After writing up the entries in the journal, we must then post them to the ledger and close the suspense account.

Note that the error made by entering £45 as £54 does not affect the trial balance and therefore there is no correction to the suspense account. The error does, however, affect the sales as shown in the trial balance as well as the debtors' total.

Suspense account					
30 June 09	Rates	20	30 June 09	Trial balance	155
	Sales	100			
	William	35			
		155			155

16.2.4 Self-test

L Green cannot balance her trial balance at 31 December 2009 and opens a suspense account for the difference. This account shows a debit of £140. After checking the books she discovers the following errors:

(i)   A credit note for £18 was entered twice in a debtor's account.
(ii) An invoice for £96 entered correctly in the sales day book was incorrectly entered to a debtor's account as £69.
(iii) A payment of £110 to a creditor was entered in the cash book but not posted to the creditor's account.
(iv) The returns inwards day book total has been overcast by £90.
(v)   Two payments of £75 each were made to a creditor but only one was entered to the creditor's account.

Show the journal entries needed to adjust the suspense account and balance the trial balance.

16.2.5 Self-test

You are required to draw up the necessary journal entries in the books of Merle to correct the following:

2009

20 May	Machine repairs for £111 were posted to the plant and machinery account.
22 May	Discount allowed of £49 was posted to the debit of discount received.
24 May	A printer costing £820 was purchased for the office on credit from BB Stores, but the transaction has not yet been entered.
25 May	Goods valued at £90 were returned to A Brown, but the return had been posted to the account of D Brown.
27 May	A delivery van had been sold for £5,400 but the receipt was posted to sales.
30 May	Rent received of £100 was posted to commission received.

16.2.6 Self-test

During the year, the following events occurred:

(i) On 1 January 2008, Heinz buys fittings for £8,600 on credit from Joe.
(ii) On 31 March he sells the old fittings to Fritz for £600, the full amount payable in July.
(iii) Steve owes Joe £500. As the debt is outstanding for more than a year it is treated as bad.
(iv) Goods purchased on credit from A Bryan for £400 are incorrectly posted to L Bryan.
(v) On 30 June, Heinz sells the old delivery van for £200 to Martin.

You are required to show the journal entries, including the narrations and dates, for all the above transactions.

16.2.7 Self-test

At 31 December 2009, C Whyte prepared his trial balance for the year. It did not balance and he entered the difference into a suspense account. Thereafter he prepared his accounts and the net profit shown was £9,720.

It was subsequently discovered that the following errors had been made in the trial balance.

(i) Salaries of £4,200 had been debited to the office equipment account in error.
(ii) Purchases of £962 were correctly entered in the purchases day book, but were incorrectly credited to the creditors' account as £926.
(iii) The sales day book total of £6,280 was posted to the sales account as £6,820.
(iv) Total discount received of £192 was posted to the wrong side of the discount received account.

You are required to state how, and by how much, each of the errors above would affect the trial balance. Show the adjusted profit for the year.

16.2.8 Self-test

In preparing the trial balance for Jay & Co., a difference of £222 was entered as a credit to a suspense account in order to balance the trial balance.

Sometime later, after examining the books the following errors were discovered.

(i) The total of the returns inward book was overcast by £600.

(ii) When writing off a bad debt of £720, the bad debt account was incorrectly debited with £72.

(iii) A cheque for £110 received from a debtor was dishonoured but no entry reflecting this has been made in the books.

(iv) A receipt of £320 from Justin was credited to the account of Austin.

(v) A credit note from I Buy for £360 for goods returned was not entered in the books.

(vi) On 31 December 2009 the quarterly rent of £600, for the period 1 December 2009 to 28 February 2010 was paid. No adjustment has yet been made for the prepayment.

(vii) The total of the discount received column in the cash book of £135 was posted to the debit side of the discount allowed account.

Prepare journal entries for the above adjustments and show the adjustments to the suspense account.

You are required to show the effect of the above errors on the net profit of £12,380 for the year ended 31 December 2009.

16.2.9 Self-test

Alex prepares a trial balance on 30 June 2009. As it does not balance, he opens a suspense account with a credit balance of £101. He subsequently checks his books and discovers the following errors.

(i) Two payments of £90 each have been made to Thomas but only one has been entered in the creditor's account.

(ii) An invoice for £98 has been entered correctly in the sales day book but the entry to Smythe (debtor) is shown as £89.

(iii) A payment of £14 to Vashi has been entered in the cash book but no corresponding double entry has been made.

(iv) The returns inward day book has been overcast by £200.

(v) A credit note for £14 received from Hilife (creditor) has been entered twice in their account.

You are required to show the suspense account as it would appear after the correction of errors.

16.2.10 Self-test

Roger extracts a list of balances and presents the following trial balance at 31 July 2009.

Capital		22,350
Drawings	9,000	
Stock 1 August 2008	7,500	
Trade debtors	8,850	
Trade creditors		8,052
Shop fittings	4,590	
Purchases	15,420	
Sales		22,380
General expenses	2,580	
Discount received		120
Cash at bank	4,980	
Returns outwards		120
Suspense account	102	
	53,022	53,022

The following errors and omissions were subsequently discovered.

(i)   A credit balance of £48 in the purchases ledger had been omitted from the trial balance.

(ii)   A credit note for £39 issued by Roger to a customer had been omitted from the books.

(iii) Sales invoices for £450 entered in the sales day book had not been entered to a customer's personal account.

(iv) A purchase of shop fittings totalling £1,320 had been debited to purchases.

(v)   The sales day book was undercast by £300 in March 2009.

You are required to draw up an amended trial balance.

   You are required to show the journal entries for the above errors and also write up the suspense ledger account.

Chapter 17

Revision

Objectives After you have worked through all the questions in this chapter, you should be able to:

- prepare a trial balance incorporating adjustments;
- adjust a suspense account and correct errors;
- calculate any additional adjustments required.

17.1 Introduction

What is extremely important at this stage is to make sure that what you have studied can be accurately brought into your further learning.

From now on we will concentrate on the presentation of financial statements to the many users of these accounts.

For this reason we have introduced a chapter here which covers in some detail the revision of what has already been studied. Practise what you have studied as it is only in this way that you will reinforce your knowledge. Accuracy is vitally important and for this reason you should always show your workings. In an exam you will often receive marks for showing that you understand the method to be applied even though you may have an incorrect answer.

If there are any areas where you think that you need more revision, go back to the relevant chapter, read it again, do the self-tests within that chapter and only then come back to this revision chapter.

17.1.1 Self-test

Sylvia commenced business on 1 January 2009 with two delivery vehicles. The Ford pick-up had cost £4,000 and the Toyota had cost £6,000.

On 23 April 2009, the Ford was written off in an accident. No depreciation was charged for the period to the accident. The insurance company paid out £2,100 in settlement of the claim.

She purchases a replacement Honda on 28 April 2009 for a total cost of £8,000.

You are required to show the appropriate ledger accounts for the three years to 31 December 2009, 2010 and 2011 assuming that:

(i) the vehicles are depreciated at 20 per cent on the straight line method; and
(ii) the vehicles are depreciated at 25 per cent on the reducing balance method.

Note that a full year's depreciation is charged in the year of acquisition.

17.1.2 Self-test

You are presented with a trial balance at 31 October 2009.

Idea & Co. trial balance at 31 October 2009

Packing expenses	525	
General expenses	490	
Electricity expenses	2,416	
Insurance	205	
Rent	3,500	
Rates	906	
Salaries and wages	15,689	
Motor expenses	1,416	
Sales		88,300
Purchases	51,150	
Returns inwards	200	
Returns outwards		350
Stock 1 November 2008	15,690	
Debtors	16,314	
Creditors		10,170
Fixtures and fittings	6,300	
Drawings	10,950	
Capital		29,256
Cash in hand	150	
Cash at bank	2,175	
	128,076	128,076

After its preparation you are told that certain adjustments are to be made. The following is the list:

Expenses prepaid:

Insurance	25
Rates	256

Expenses owing:

Rent	700
General expenses	25
Motor expenses	310
Electricity expenses	104

Stock at 31 October 2009 amounts to £17,170.

You are required to produce the revised trial balance in preparation of the profit and loss account and balance sheet for the financial year. In so doing you will need to create an account for accruals and another for prepayments.

Note: as the preparation of the financial statements is only dealt with in Chapters 20 and 22, you are required to keep your adjusted trial balance until you have completed your studies of those two chapters.

17.1.3 Self-test

NuVenture prepares a trial balance for the year.

Trial balance at 31 March 2009

Purchases	89,185	
Stock 1 April 2008	18,160	
Sales		122,340
Carriage inwards	520	
Carriage outwards	1,470	
Returns outwards		640
Wages and salaries	20,240	
Rent and rates	3,015	
Telephone expenses	624	
Commissions payable	216	
Insurance	405	
General expenses	318	
Land and buildings	40,000	
Debtors	14,320	
Creditors		8,160
Fixtures	2,850	
Cash at bank	2,970	
Cash in hand	115	
Loan from K Blake		10,000
Drawings	7,620	
Capital		60,888
	202,028	202,028

The following adjustments are to be made:

Prepaid expenses:

Insurance	20
General expenses	29
Rates	200

Expenses owing:

Rent	250
Telephone expenses	98
Commission	240

Stock at 31 March 2009 is valued at £20,300.

You are required to prepare the revised trial balance.

Note: as the preparation of accounts is only dealt with in Chapters 20 and 22, you are required to keep your adjusted trial balance until you have completed your studies of those two chapters.

17.1.4 Self-test

The following is the list of balances extracted from the books of Wilmot Trading at 31 December 2009.

List of balances at 31 December 2009

Creditors	19,832
Returns inwards	390
Electricity and gas	4,711
Insurance	400
Capital – Wilmot	57,049
Rates	1,767
Salaries and wages	30,594
Motor expenses	2,761
Sales	172,185
Purchases	99,743
Cash in hand	293
Returns outwards	683
Stock 1 January 2009	30,596
Debtors	31,812
Rent	6,825
Fixtures and fittings	12,285
Drawings – Wilmot	21,353
Delivery expenses	1,979
Cash at bank	4,240

You are told that the following expenses are paid in advance:

Insurance	49
Rates	499

At year end the following expenses incurred were not yet recorded in the books:

Rent	1,365
Delivery expenses	49
Motor expenses	605
Electricity and gas	203
Stock at 31 December 2009	33,482

You are required to prepare an adjusted trial balance at 31 December 2009 which incorporates the above items.

17.1.5 Self-test

Howard Graham is the owner of HG Electricals. His business is VAT registered and all sales are standard rated at $17^1/_2$ per cent.

Sales are divided between fitting and servicing electrical equipment and supplying electrical goods.

Howard Graham maintains a double-entry bookkeeping system. He records work undertaken and goods supplied in a work log, along with the net sales value (excluding VAT). The work log is then used to prepare an analysed sales day book and to calculate VAT on sales.

An extract of the work log for the week ended 31 October 2009 is shown below:

Work log for the week ended 31 October 2009

Date	Customer	Fitting and servicing	Electrical goods	Invoice number allocated
27/10	Fred James	£120.00	–	INV 2044
28/10	Sally Baker	£80.00	£140.00	INV 2045
29/10	Klipper Ltd	£400.00	£1,600.00	INV 2046
30/10	K Benn	£200.00	–	INV 2047
31/10	Mouville & Sons	–	£300.00	INV 2048

Required:

(a) Write up the sales day book for the week ended 31 October 2009. You must calculate the VAT for each invoice and total the sales day book at the end of the week.

The sales day book should be prepared using the following format:

Date	Invoice number	Customer	Total £	VAT £	Fitting and servicing £	Electrical goods £

(b) The sales day book totals are transferred to the general ledger on a weekly basis. Using the information from (a), identify the figures that will be posted to the following accounts and state whether they will be a debit entry or a credit entry.
   (i) Fitting and servicing account.
   (ii) Electrical goods account.
   (iii) VAT account.
   (iv) Sales ledger control account.

(c) HG Electricals receives some purchase invoices from its suppliers which have VAT included at 5 per cent and some with VAT included at $17^1/_2$ per cent. During the week ended 31 October 2009, Howard Graham received the following five invoices:

Supplier	VAT inclusive invoice total £	VAT rate %
ABC Electricity	262.50	5
Smiths Wires	1,457.00	$17^1/_2$
Southern Gas	117.60	5
Clark Brothers	2,749.50	$17^1/_2$
Minnow Ltd	587.50	$17^1/_2$

Extract the VAT from each of the five invoices, using the appropriate VAT rate.

(ABE, Introduction to Financial Accounting, December 2009)

17.1.6 Self-test

Catena prepares a bank reconciliation at the end of each month.
The bank statement for May 2007 is as follows:

Bank statement

Mellor Bank plc
Park St   Sheet 1
Lower Gornal   1 May 2007–
West Midlands   31 May 2007

Account No. 89547325   **Account name**: Catena

Date	Payment type and details	Paid out	Paid in	Balance
01/05/07	Balance b/fwd			2,500.60 Cr
05/05/07	Counter credit		850.00	3,350.60 Cr
05/05/07	Bank charges	68.75		3,281.85 Cr
08/05/07	Counter credit		675.50	3,957.35 Cr
10/05/07	Cheque No. 100221	985.00		2,972.35 Cr
16/05/07	Cheque No. 100222	263.98		2,708.37 Cr
18/05/07	SO – Bank loan	457.00		2,251.37 Cr
22/05/07	Cheque No. 100223	335.50		1,915.87 Cr
24/05/07	Counter credit		1,200.63	3,116.50 Cr
29/05/07	Cheque No. 100224	85.62		3,030.88 Cr
31/05/07	DD – Council tax	135.00		2,895.88 Cr
31/05/07	BACS – Rent receivable		500.00	3,395.88 Cr

Cr: credit balance   SO: standing order
Dr: overdrawn balance   BACS: Banks Automated Clearing Service
DD: direct debit

You have been supplied with a partially complete cash book for Catena for May 2007.

Catena: Cash book May 2007

Date	Details	£	Date	Details	Chq No.	£
01/05/07	Balance b/d	2,500.60	06/05/07	Smith Ltd	100221	985.00
02/05/07	Sales	850.00	10/05/07	Brookmans	100222	236.98
05/05/07	Sales	675.50	18/05/07	Bank loan	SO	457.00
20/05/07	Sales	1,200.63	19/05/07	Hemming & Co.	100223	335.50
29/05/07	Sales	840.85	27/05/07	Leigh Ltd	100224	85.62
			30/05/07	Torrissi Bros	100225	695.00
			31/05/07	Council tax	DD	135.00
			31/05/07	Powerhen	100226	228.95
				Balance c/d		2,908.53
		6,067.58				6,067.58

Required:

(a) What are the outstanding paying in amounts and also unpresented cheques?
(b) Calculate the adjusted cash book balance for Catena as at 31 May 2007.

(c) Prepare a bank reconciliation statement for Catena as at 31 May 2007.

(d) Explain why it is important to perform regular bank reconciliations.

(ABE, Introduction to Financial Accounting, December 2007)

17.1.7 Self-test

Knowles started in business as a landscape gardener on 1 April 2006. Knowles has recorded all his transactions in a cashbook and the following extracts have been obtained from the accounting records covering the first year of trading to 31 March 2007.

Bank receipts (extract)

Date	Details	£
18/10/06	Insurance refund	60

Bank payments (extract)

Date	Details	£
15/04/06	Telephone installation charges	125
07/05/06	Insurance to 31/12/06	975
15/07/06	Telephone bill ¼ (three months) to 30/06/06	230
31/07/06	Road fund licence for the year to 31/07/07	165
15/08/06	Rates to 31/03/07	1,175
15/10/06	Telephone bill ¼ to 30/09/06	245
07/11/06	Motor repairs	430
25/12/06	Insurance to 31/12/07	1,500
15/01/07	Telephone bill ¼ to 31/12/06	262
31/03/07	Rates to 31/03/08	1,250

Knowles received a telephone bill on 15 April 2007 for the quarter ended 31 March 2007, totalling £295.

Required:

(a) Record the information from the bank receipts and bank payments extracts in the general ledger accounts for insurance, telephone, motor expenses and rates.

(b) Calculate the relevant accruals and prepayments at 31 March 2007 and record in the general ledger accounts for insurance, telephone, motor expenses and rates.

(c) Balance off the general ledger accounts for insurance, telephone, motor expenses and rates, clearly showing the total expense transferred to the trading, profit and loss account.

(d) Explain why a business would calculate and include accruals and prepayments in its financial statements and identify how accruals and prepayments are disclosed on the financial statements.

(ABE, Introduction to Financial Accounting, December 2007)

17.1.8 Self-test

You have been supplied with the following information from the accounts of Louise Phillips for the year ended 31 March 2009:

Balances b/d 1 April 2008:

– debtors control	7,400
– creditors control	3,180
Discounts received	100
Bad debts written off	840
Discounts allowed	220
Sales for the year to 31 March 2009	29,000
Purchases for the year to 31 March 2009	16,000
Receipts from debtors for the year ended 31 March 2009	12,400
Payments to creditors for the year ended 31 March 2009	6,900

Notes:

1. 10 per cent of the sales for the year were cash sales.
2. 85 per cent of the purchases were credit purchases.

Required:

(i) Prepare the debtors' control account for the year ended 31 March 2009.

(ii) Prepare the creditors' control account for the year ended 31 March 2009.

For both accounts clearly show the balance that will be brought down at the start of the next financial year.

(ABE, Introduction to Accounting, December 2009)

Chapter 18

The valuation of stock

Objectives

After you have studied this chapter, you should be able to:

- understand how opening and closing stock is valued;
- calculate the value of stock using LIFO, FIFO and AVCO methods;
- explain the use of net realisable value instead of cost.

18.1 Introduction

In Chapter 19 we will show how stock is treated in the trading account and later, in Chapter 21, in the manufacturing account. In many of the examples given in the self-tests, as well as in examinations, you will frequently be given a closing stock figure.

It is appropriate at this stage to examine how stock is valued. This applies to all forms of stock – raw materials, work in progress or finished goods.

18.2 Valuation methods

The cardinal rule is that stock is valued at the lower of cost or net realisable value. The latter method takes into account any additional costs that may be incurred in putting the goods for sale into a saleable condition.

We do not attribute cost to each item as and when it is brought into stock. Often we continue purchasing the same item during the year and we also sell that item at a fixed price during the year. We therefore make certain assumptions:

- The stock is sold in the order in which it was purchased – called the FIFO system (first in, first out).
- The more recently purchased stock is sold before the older stock – this is known as LIFO (last in, first out).
- We can make one further assumption and that is that every time stock is issued it is issued at the average cost up to the time of that sale. Here we use the weighted average cost – termed AVCO.

18.2.1 Worked example

The following are the purchase and sales transactions for can openers.

Date	Goods in		Goods sold
July	Quantity	Price per item	Quantity
5	300	85p	
6			250
8	400	82p	
9			350
11			100
16	500	88p	
19			200
24	800	91p	
28			300

You are required to calculate the value of the closing stock using the following valuation bases:

- FIFO
- LIFO
- AVCO

FIFO

Date	Goods in		Units issued	Stock in hand	
July	Quantity	Unit price	Quantity	Quantity	Value £
5	300	85p		300	255.00
6			250	50	42.50
8	400	82p		450	370.50
9			350	100	82.00
11			100	Nil	Nil
16	500	88p		500	440.00
19			200	300	264.00
24	800	91p		1,100	992.00
28			300	800	728.00

Using FIFO the closing balance is 800 units and the value must be equal to the purchase of 800 units at 91p each.

LIFO

Date	Goods in		Units issued	Stock in hand	
July	Quantity	Unit price	Quantity	Quantity	Value £
5	300	85p		300	255.50
6			250	50	42.50
8	400	82p		450	370.50
9			350	100	83.50*
11			100	Nil	Nil
16	500	88p		500	440.00
19			200	300	264.00
24	800	91p		1,100	992.00
28			300	800	719.00

* The amount is made up of 50 units @ 82p and 50 units @ 85p.

Using LIFO we see that our closing balance is 800 units. Of these 500 units are valued at 91p each and 300 units at 88p each.

AVCO

Date	Goods in		Units issued	Stock in hand	
July	Quantity	Unit price	Quantity	Quantity	Value £
5	300	85p		300	255.50
6			250	50	42.50
8	400	82p		450	370.50
9			350	100	82.33*
11			100	Nil	Nil
16	500	88p		500	440.00
19			200	300	264.00
24	800	91p		1,100	992.00
28			300	800	721.45

* The average price per unit is 82.3p and 350 units are issued. This amounts to £288.17 leaving the balance of £82.33.

Using AVCO we see that our closing balance is 800 units all of which are valued at an average price of 90.2p per unit.

18.2.2 Self-test

You are required to answer this question by the use of the different methods of stock valuation.

(i)   A buys 200 units of product ZZ at £1.20 each in April 2009.
(ii) A buys a further 400 units in September 2009 at £1.50 each.
(iii) During the manufacturing process 300 units of ZZ are issued in October 2009.

Using the different methods for the pricing of stock, you are required to show the cost of the 300 units using each method.

18.3 Using different methods

By using different methods of stock valuation, a variation of the final net profit is shown. As such, a business must elect to use one method and remain consistent with that chosen method. In some way the method selected should relate to the type of product sold by the business.

18.4 Net realisable value

In section 18.2 mention was made of the net realisable method. Whatever method is normally used by the business – LIFO, FIFO or AVCO – there is always the need to ensure that stock is not overvalued – this is an application of the prudence concept (see section 25.2.3).

The basis of determining that stock is not overvalued is to find out what the selling price is for the stock. From this we deduct any costs that must be incurred in order to make the sale. These can include repacking of the goods, new labels, delivery charges, etc. The final figure is the net realisable value.

If the value is below the cost price of the stock on hand then it is this value that must be used to value stock and not the cost price. Doing this ensures that the balance sheet does not overstate the value of the stock.

An example would be of a product of can openers purchased at a cost price of £1.30 each. Because of mass production it is now possible to purchase the identical openers for 84p each and they are currently being sold for 98p each. This in itself means that we cannot value our existing stock at any more than the realisable value, which is 98p each.

There is, however, one additional problem and that is that the boxes in which the openers were originally packed have been water damaged and new boxes, costing 11p each must be provided. The net realisable value therefore, would be 98p minus 11p = 87p each. As this is lower than the original cost, the stock of can openers must be valued at 87p each.

18.4.1 Self-test

Nat purchases 60 boxes of towels in February 2009 for £22 per box. He also buys an additional 30 boxes in April 2009 at £26 per box.

In July 2009 he sells 80 boxes for £68 per box.

You are told that closing stock at 31 December 2009 must be valued for use in the trading account of the business.

You are required to calculate the value of this stock using:

(a) FIFO;
(b) AVCO; and
(c) LIFO.

18.4.2 Self-test

Musicman & Co. purchase one model of DVD player. The cost of these players during the year ending 30 June 2010 varied but that company sold all the players at a fixed price of £800 each.

Stock was taken on 30 June 2009 and this amounted to 33 units at a total cost of £6,600.

The following details are for the players purchased during the year:

	No. of DVD players purchased	Price per player £
3.7.09	120	270
6.9.09	100	300
20.11.09	180	330
25.3.10	240	390
2.5.10	120	420

The following were the sales for the year:

	No. of DVD players sold
July–Aug	30
Sept–Oct	90
Nov–Dec	150
Jan–Mar	210
Apr–Jun	60

You are required to calculate the cost of the stock at 30 June 2010 using FIFO and LIFO methods.

18.4.3 Self-test

Sweet & Co. purchase sugar from a refinery for repacking and resale. At 1 January 2010 (the start of the financial year), Sweet & Co had a stock of 500 kilo valued at a cost of £1 per kilo. During January the following purchases were made:

	Kilo	£ per kilo
3 January	800	1.01
13 January	700	1.03
15 January	800	1.05
23 January	500	1.04

During the month the following sales took place:

	Kilo
5 January	900
11 January	100
18 January	400
25 January	600
31 January	900

You are required to calculate the value of the closing stock at 31 January using each of the following methods:

(i)   AVCO
(ii) LIFO
(iii) FIFO

Chapter 19

Trading account

Objectives   After you have studied this chapter, you should be able to:

- explain the meaning of the terms 'carriage' and 'returns';
- show the treatment of returns and carriage in the trading account;
- calculate the gross profit and cost of sales of a business;
- prepare a trading account.

19.1   Introduction

The trading and profit and loss account shows the profit, or loss, of the business. Both the trading account and the profit and loss account are part of the double-entry system and any entry in either account must have an opposite entry somewhere else.

All accounts that relate to the purchase and sale of goods and services are transferred from the respective ledger accounts and shown in the trading account. The difference between the cost of goods sold and the net sales turnover is called the gross profit.

The gross profit is an extremely important figure and we will learn more about its importance when we look at ratios (see Chapter 32). If the gross profit is too small then there is not enough profit to sustain business activity. Remember that other business expenses still have to be deducted from the gross profit and that the trading account only shows the gross profit from the buying and selling of goods.

The account is prepared for a period, which is usually one year. As such, the heading is 'Trading account for the year ended [date]' or 'Trading account for the month (or period) ended [date]'.

19.2   Returns and carriage

- Returns inwards or sales returns are when goods, previously sold by you, have been returned to you by the customer. There can be many reasons for the return. The goods may be defective; not suitable for what was required; wrong size or colour; or delivery may have been too late.
- Returns outwards or purchase returns, are goods that you return to your suppliers. Here again there are many reasons for the returns, including defective goods, late delivery, etc.

- Carriage inwards is the cost incurred by you in receiving goods from your suppliers. It includes amounts paid for freight, postage and packing of goods. This expense increases the cost of the purchases, as it is added to purchases.
- Carriage outwards is the cost paid by you to send goods to your customers. This is an expense of the business, although it may, in part, be recouped from the customers. Although this item is a charge to the business it is not an expense that adds to the cost of sales and as such is not recorded in the trading section of the account but rather in the profit and loss account.

19.3 Stock

There are three kinds of stock – raw materials, work in progress and finished goods. Only the latter is shown in the trading account in order to calculate the cost of sales.

Stock or inventory, as it is also called, can be defined as goods purchased or produced for resale that are not sold during the period. How do we calculate the cost of sales as shown in the table below?

Opening stock at 1 January 2009	42,000	
Purchases for the year	71,000	113,000
Closing stock at 31 December 2009		53,000
Cost of sales		£60,000

We take the opening stock, which is the closing stock figure of the previous period, and add purchases for the period. From this amount we deduct the closing stock.

The closing stock is usually found as a note to the trial balance. The stock figure in the trial balance is the opening stock.

19.3.1 Worked example

Jacques has £4,000 of goods in stock on 1 June 2009 and purchases £19,000 of stock during the month. This means that the total goods that he has for resale is £23,000.

His sales for the month amount to £31,000 but we cannot say that the gross profit is £8,000 (i.e. 31,000 – 23,000).

We must take into account any unsold stock at the month end. In this case the stock at 30 June is £2,800. Taking this into account we can now calculate the gross profit, which is £10,800.

The calculation is made as follows:

Sales		31,000
Cost of sales:		
Opening stock	4,000	
Purchases	19,000	
Closing stock	(2,800)	
Cost of goods sold		20,200
Gross profit		£10,800

We have, in effect, matched the goods sold with the sales. The goods unsold (i.e. the closing stock) are kept over for the following month.

19.4 Returns

What we saw above is the simple calculation involving purchases and sales. There are also additional items which must be included in the trading section. The first are those relating to returns.

Sales	55,000
Less returns inwards	4,000
Net sales (turnover)	£51,000
Purchases	49,000
Less returns outwards	3,800
Net purchases	£45,200

It is important to note that before we calculate the gross profit we must deduct the returns, both inwards and outwards. Make sure that you remember that the returns inwards are deducted from sales and returns outwards are deducted from purchases.

19.5 Treatment of carriage charges

Using the example in section 19.4 above we see that the cost of purchases is also changed to include carriage inwards.

Purchases	49,000
Less returns outwards	3,800
Net purchases	45,200
Add carriage inwards	2,100
Total purchases	£47,300

Carriage outwards on the other hand has no bearing on our trading account. It is our cost in sending out goods to the customers. It does not reduce the selling price of the goods sold and therefore would not be shown in the trading account but rather in the profit and loss account.

19.6 Sales

An important question that is often asked – when is sales revenue recognised? Is it when the sale is made, or when the cash comes in? Could it be when the goods are delivered or when the goods are invoiced?

The receipt of cash is irrelevant for its recognition, as the sale may be a cash sale or a credit sale. Therefore, recognition,[5] as revenue, is when the sale is agreed and this is usually when the invoice is raised. At this stage a contract of sale has been made and the goods are able to be delivered when required by the buyer.

We must not include revenue which has not yet been earned (accrued). This conforms to the prudence convention (see section 25.2.3) in accounting which states that we only bring into account income earned.

19.6.1 Self-test

Prepare a trading account for J Anthony from the following information:

Stock 1 January 2009	12,500
Stock 31 December 2009	16,400
Purchases	32,345
Sales	87,213
Returns inwards	1,106
Returns outwards	2,348
Carriage inwards	1,984

19.7 Transfer of balances

At the year end we balance our ledger accounts (see section 3.1) and transfer some balances to the trading account. Remember, although we prepare a trial balance (see Chapter 15) this is not part of the double-entry system but merely a check on accuracy.

	Sales				
August	Transfer to Trading a/c	139,327	March	Bank	5,100
				Debtors	23,400
			April	Bank	3,256
				Debtors	12,780
			May	Bank	3,897
				Debtors	18,234
			June	Bank	6,512
				Debtors	27,895
			July	Bank	5,478
				Debtors	16,542
			August	Bank	2,986
				Debtors	13,247
		139,327			139,327

[5] Recognition is based on the accounting realisation convention (see section 25.3.7).

Purchases					
March	Bank	1,659		Transfer to	
	Creditors	11,345	August	Trading a/c	89,513
April	Bank	1,278			
	Creditors	13,478			
May	Bank	1,349			
	Creditors	14,326			
June	Bank	1,265			
	Creditors	11,120			
July	Bank	1,137			
	Creditors	16,452			
August	Bank	1,784			
	Creditors	14,320			
		89,513			89,513

19.8 Cost of sales

The opening stock for the period, plus the goods purchased during the period, will represent the total goods available for resale. The closing stock will represent that portion of the total goods available for resale that remains unsold at the end of the period. Thus, the cost of goods sold during the period must be the cost associated with the total goods available for resale less the stock remaining at the end of the period.

Opening stock	20,000
Add goods purchased	165,000
This is what we are able to sell in the year	185,000

But certain goods are unsold at the end of the year so before we calculate the cost of sales we need to deduct that amount of unsold goods from the above.

Less closing stock	75,000
Cost of goods sold	£110,000

The trading revenue, which arises from selling goods, is the first item that appears in the account. Deducted from this item is the trading expense, which is the cost of acquiring the goods sold during the period. The difference between the trading revenue and trading expense is the gross profit. This represents the profit from simply buying and selling goods without taking into account any other expenses or revenues associated with the business.

The remainder of the account is referred to as the profit and loss account (see Chapter 20).

19.8.1 Worked example

In the following example, a trading account layout shows the sales less their cost, to determine the gross profit.

Henry Trading Co.
Trading account for the year ended 31 October 2009

Sales		232,000
Less cost of sales		
Opening stock	40,000	
Add goods purchased	189,000	
	229,000	
Less closing stock	75,000	154,000
Gross profit		78,000

19.9 Linking trading and profit and loss

Once we have determined the gross profit we move to the next stage which is the profit and loss account (see Chapter 20).

In effect there are two parts to the profit and loss account:

- The trading account section (shown above) is used to arrive at the gross profit.
- The profit and loss account, which contains all other revenue expenses. These are then deducted from the gross profit to calculate the net profit. This account also includes any revenue items from non-trading sources, for example interest received or discounts received.

19.9.1 Self-test

Larry presents you with a summary of certain transactions for the year ended 30 June 2009. He asks you to prepare the trading account for his first year of trading, so that he can determine the gross profit.

The following are the accounts given to you:

Sales	421,000
Purchases	214,000
Returns inwards	40,108
Carriage inwards	2,790

Larry also tells you that his closing stock amounts to £37,890. You are required to prepare the trading account so that the gross profit is shown.

19.9.2 Self-test

The following items are extracted from the books of Henry for the year ended 30 June 2009. You are required to prepare the trading account for the year.

Sales	43,988
Closing stock	8,967
Purchases	11,870
Opening stock	9,876
Returns to suppliers	1,245

19.9.3 Self-test

Gordon presents you with an extract from his ledger for the year ended 30 June 2009. The accounts he lists are not all needed for the trading account but he asks you to use those required to prepare a trading account.

Sales	211,980
Opening stock	43,650
Returns by customers	35,800
Closing stock	65,780
Purchases	98,650
Discount received	8,989
Carriage inwards	76,500
Delivery charges	51,900
Depreciation van	5,870
Discount allowed	6,997
Advertising	9,946

Chapter 20

Profit and loss account

Objectives After you have studied this chapter, you should be able to:

- understand the differences between expenditure and income;
- understand the differences between revenue and capital items;
- detail the expenses and income and show the net profit/loss;
- prepare a profit and loss account.

20.1 Introduction

We saw in Chapter 19 how the gross profit was determined. While that figure is extremely important we still need to establish if the business is making an overall profit. To do this we take the gross profit from the trading account and add any revenue receipts. From that we deduct all the remaining costs incurred in creating the revenue. There are no fixed names for the individual items of expenditure and different businesses may use different headings to describe the expenses. The important thing to note is that all these expenses must be of a revenue nature (see section 20.4). Once all the expenses are deducted we are left with the net profit (or loss) for the period.

20.2 Format of the profit and loss account

Although the format is similar for both sole trader and company, there are certain variations. In section 29.2.1 we will examine the format of the profit and loss account for a company as required under the Companies Act. At this stage we should note that a sole trader would want far more detail in the profit and loss account than that shown in the company's profit and loss account. In the accounts of a sole trader, or partnership, each expense account heading is shown in the profit and loss.

The classification of expenses is dependent on how useful it is to identify such an expense. For example, we could group telephone, postage and stationery as one item. However, if postage was a material item (that is, of considerable size and importance) then it may be prudent to show that item as a separate one from the others. This would not apply when we prepare the accounts for a company as the users, other than the internal users, are not too concerned with a detailed division of all costs.

The format of the account is either horizontal or vertical. Throughout this book we use vertical formats as it is by far the most commonly used form. It is easier to understand and is in common use in the UK.

In the format below we start our profit and loss account from the gross profit figure which, as shown in the previous chapter, is calculated in the trading section. The vertical format lists all the income (other than from sales, which is shown in the trading section) immediately after the gross profit. From this total all expenses including provisions (depreciation and bad debts) are deducted. The final figure is the net profit for the period – in this case for the year ended 31 December 2009.

Prima Trading Co.
Profit and loss account for the year ended 31 December 2009

Gross profit		104,000
Add Interest received		2,000
Commission received		5,000
		111,000
Less expenses		
Salaries and wages	31,500	
Rent and rates	10,000	
Heat and light	2,500	
Telephone and postage	1,400	
Insurance	1,200	
Motor expenses	2,400	
Interest paid	3,100	
Depreciation of fixed assets	4,000	
Provision for bad debts	900	57,000
Net profit for the year		54,000

20.3 What is profit?

Owners want to know how much profit they make in their business. This profit figure indicates the increase in wealth of the business over a period of time and is the excess of income over expenditure. The increase in wealth is shown by the increase in net assets (which, in effect, is the capital account).

20.4 Classification of expenditure

Before preparing the profit and loss account we need to examine and differentiate between the two types of expenditure that are incurred by a business. In doing so it is useful if you look back at Figure 15.1, which shows the division of expenditure as well as of income.

20.4.1 Capital expenditure

This form of expenditure relates mainly to amounts paid for fixed assets and includes the cost of buying, transporting and installing machinery, fixtures, etc. These items of capital expenditure are shown as assets on the balance sheet.

20.4.2 Revenue expenditure

This type of expenditure relates to everyday running costs such as wages, salaries, lighting, heating, office expenses, stationery etc. All these costs are shown in the profit and loss account. Revenue expenditure can be divided into different groups, such as:

- **administrative expenses**, which includes items such as wages and salaries, repairs and rent;
- **selling expenses**, such as advertising and commission; and
- **financial expenses**, which includes interest paid.

It should be noted that a similar division exists with income items and here again it is only revenue receipts that are shown in the profit and loss account, while those of a capital nature, such as the sale of a fixed asset, are brought into account in the balance sheet.

20.4.3 Self-test

Lionel

From the following list of account titles, you are required to identify revenue income and expenditure as well as capital income and expenditure. Remember that items of a capital nature do not feature in the trading and profit and loss account but rather in the balance sheet. On the other hand, revenue items are shown as part of the trading and profit and loss accounts.

The list is:

Item	Revenue		Capital	
	Income	Expenditure	Income	Expenditure
Wages				
Land and buildings				
Loans from bank				
Sale of computer				
Advertising				
Sale of goods				
Purchases of raw materials				
Carriage outwards				
Bad debts				
Motor vehicle				
Motor expenses				

20.4.4 Worked example

Using the example given in the previous chapter for Henry Trading Co. (see section 19.8.1) we can see how the other expenses of operating the business are deducted from the gross profit to arrive at the net profit for the period. The first part of the statement is concerned with calculating gross profit for the period. This first part is referred to as the trading account or trading section. We will now examine the second part of the statement – the profit and loss section.

Henry Trading Co.
Trading and profit and loss account for the year ended 31 October 2009

Sales		232,000
Less cost of sales		154,000
Gross profit		78,000
Interest received from investments		2,000
		80,000
Less		
Salaries and wages	24,500	
Rent and rates	14,200	
Heat and light	7,500	
Telephone and postage	1,200	
Insurance	1,000	
Motor vehicle running expenses	3,400	
Loan interest	1,100	
Depreciation of fixtures and fittings	1,000	
Depreciation of motor van	600	(54,500)
Net profit		25,500

In the above example we see that the gross profit calculated previously (£78,000) has had other income (interest) added to it before the various expenses are deducted. The net amount arrived at is the net profit for the period.

20.4.5 Self-test

Complete the following statements:

Capital expenditure is shown in the profit and loss account.	True/False
Revenue expenditure is shown in the profit and loss account.	True/False
Revenue receipts are shown in the profit and loss account.	True/False
Capital income is shown in the profit and loss account.	True/False

Income from the sale of an old motor van in excess of the net book value is shown in . . .
Expenditure on the purchase of a new computer for the office is shown in . . .
Expenditure on stationery is shown in . . .

20.5 Changes to net profit

We saw in Chapter 16 that errors may be found after we have prepared the profit and loss account. You will need to be able to determine the adjusted net profit caused by a number of errors or adjustments. All you need do is consider what account would be debited and what account is credited with these adjustments.

20.5.1 Self-test

How does each of the following errors affect the net profit of £29,000 as shown in the profit and loss account?

(i)   Opening stock was undervalued by £858.
(ii) Interest on a business investment of £289 was treated as interest charged.
(iii) A loan of £900 made to the business was credited to the profit and loss account.
(iv) Discounts received of £340 were debited to the profit and loss.
(v)   Credit purchases of £540 were omitted from the purchases day book.

20.5.2 Self-test

Martin prepared his final accounts and calculated that his net profit for the year was £9,862.

Subsequently the following errors were discovered:

(i)   Rent of £1,600 shown in the profit and loss account relates to the following year.
(ii)   Rent receivable of £1,020 was outstanding.
(iii)   A provision for bad debts of £240 had not been created.
(iv)   Sales of £1,905 had not been recorded.
(v)   Sales returns of £478 had not been entered in the books.
(vi)   Closing stock had been overvalued by £986.
(vii)   An invoice for telephone charges of £230 had not been paid.
(viii) Depreciation on motor vehicles of £450 had not been made.

You are required to prepare an adjustment of the net profit to reflect the above errors.

20.5.3 Self-test

Andrew has made a profit of £40,000 for the year. During that same period he has seen his bank balance decline by £23,000. You are asked to explain possible reasons for this decrease while making a profit of £40,000.

20.5.4 Self-test

You are required to complete the following table:

	Amount paid/received in year	Disclosure in P&L account
Salaries	6,000	
Rent payable	14,000	
Insurance		5,800
Property rates		7,000
Interest payable	4,000	
Interest receivable		9,400

You are told that the following accruals had to be allowed for in the above table:

- Salaries £5,000
- Rates £1,900
- Interest payable £1,100
- Interest receivable £2,100

In addition the following amounts were prepaid:

- Rent payable £2,000
- Insurance £1,200

20.5.5 Self-test

Ella has prepared a trading account showing a gross profit of £56,900. She asks you to prepare a profit and loss account for her as she is not sure what has to be shown in that account. The following is an extract of balances that she thinks are relevant.

Extract of balances at 30 June 2010		
Motor expenses	3,140	
Interest receivable		2,980
Bank charges	720	
Wages	1,360	
Rent payable	5,870	
Discount received		1,040
Insurance	3,800	
Postages	1,010	

20.5.6 Self-test

George opened a suspense account so that he could prepare the trading and profit and loss account. He showed a net profit of £6,920.

Subsequent to the above, the following errors were discovered:

(i) Wages were debited with £636. This was an amount paid for machine installation.

(ii) Sales of £910 had been entered in both the sales day book and debtors' account as £190.

(iii) The discount total of £313 on the debit side of the cash book was entered as discount received.

(iv) Closing stock was understated by £700.

Show the effect of each of the above errors on the net profit.

20.5.7 Self-test

The following is the trial balance of Jacques at 31 December 2009. You are required to prepare the profit and loss account, having been given the gross profit for the year.

Advertising	3,000	
Bank	700	
Creditors		6,900
Bank loan		7,000
Debtors	30,000	
Electricity	2,800	
Insurance	1,700	
Investments	2,800	
Investment income		400
Machinery:		
At cost	42,000	
Accumulated depreciation at 1 January 09		15,200
Office expenses	4,900	
Owner's capital		25,000
Interest paid	400	
Profit and loss account at 1 January 2009		13,200
Provision for doubtful debts		800
Rent and rates	7,500	
Stock at 31 December 2009	15,500	
Vehicles:		
At cost	8,000	
Accumulated depreciation at 1 January 09		4,000
Wages and Salaries	41,300	
Gross profit		88,100
	160,600	160,600

Depreciation for the year is £4,200 for machinery and £1,600 for vehicles.

Note that although you are given the complete trial balance, you must be aware that there are certain account balances that are not required for answering the above question as they are balance sheet items. We will deal with these in Chapter 22.

Chapter 21

Manufacturing account

Objectives After you have studied this chapter, you should be able to:

- understand the meaning of direct and indirect costs;
- apportion expenses between factory and office expenses;
- explain the purpose of a manufacturing account;
- calculate the prime cost and production cost;
- prepare a manufacturing account.

21.1 Introduction

In all manufacturing businesses the first account that needs to be prepared is the manufacturing account. This is done so that the costs of manufacturing can be transferred to the trading and profit and loss account. Unlike the latter, the manufacturing account is not published but is, instead, prepared as the first step in determining the cost of goods sold. The total cost of production, as calculated in this account, is transferred to the trading account and is shown with other items to make up the total cost of sales.

We can see, therefore, that the manufacturing account shows the cost of running and maintaining a factory. These costs are divided into:

- Direct costs, which are expenses that can be attributed to specific cost units; and
- Indirect costs, which are not directly attributed to specific unit costs.

Figure 21.1 **Manufacturing costs**

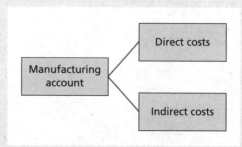

21.2 Direct costs

The total of the direct costs, namely raw material, direct wages and other direct costs are called prime costs because they are all costs incurred in the production process. These costs constitute the basic costs of manufacturing a product before the addition of factory overhead expenses.

Once we have established these costs we then add to it the indirect costs to arrive at the production cost.

21.3 Indirect costs

These are costs that are incurred in the factory (sometimes called 'factory overheads') and hence in the manufacturing process, but are not directly attributable to a specific product or cost centre.[6]

We know that they are costs of producing the items but do not know which particular item (or cost centre) to charge. It may be that the costs should be spread over all items being manufactured.

Examples of these costs are depreciation of fixed assets used in the factory and expenses, such as factory rent, power, insurance, repairs, etc.

21.4 Stock

When bringing stock into account, it is important that the three kinds of stock are separately identified:

- Raw materials
- Work in progress
- Finished goods

The first two are shown in the manufacturing account, while finished goods are shown in the trading account (see Chapter 19). We discussed the treatment of finished goods stock in section 19.3.

21.4.1 Work in progress

The cost of production is for all goods completed and ready for sale. As business is a continuing operation, this does not always happen and so, at the year end, there are goods that are still in the manufacturing process. They may have been partially manufactured but they are not yet ready for sale – they are termed work in progress.

---

[6] A 'cost centre' is a production activity or location to which costs can be allocated. With direct costs there is no problem in allocation, but where the costs are indirect, allocation is not possible.

For example, a clothing manufacturer may have spent the past week cutting material for a garment. The manufacturer has all these cut pieces of material but they still have to be sewed together to produce the garment.

Therefore, at the end of the year, we add the opening stock of work in progress and deduct the closing work in progress to arrive at the cost of production.

21.4.2 Worked example

Manufacturing account for the year ended 31 December 2010

Opening raw material stock		12,000
Direct material	13,000	
Less closing raw material	10,100	2,900
Cost of raw material consumed		14,900
Direct labour		10,200
Direct expenses		10,430
Prime cost*		35,530
Factory overhead expenses:		
Indirect costs	9,300	
Wages	8,710	
Depreciation	6,400	
Other factory costs, e.g. rent, rates, etc	3,100	27,510
		63,040
Add work in progress at beginning of year		10,100
		73,140
Less work in progress at end of year		23,060
Cost of production transferred to trading account		50,080

* Note: Prime cost is the total sum of all direct costs incurred in the manufacturing process. All indirect costs are then added to the prime cost to eventually obtain the total production cost.

21.5 Apportioning expenses

You will read later on that rent, for example, is shown in the profit and loss account. But we also show any factory rent in the manufacturing account as it is a cost of manufacturing. What if we only pay one cheque per month for rent? Where do we show the expense?

In actual fact we need to apportion this expense. One way of doing it is to determine the space (floor area) occupied by the manufacturing side of the business and the space occupied by the offices for administration, sales etc. The rent would then be apportioned on that basis.

There are many other expenses that are apportioned, some between selling expenses and administration expenses (both contained within the profit and loss account). All apportionments use some basic logical form.

The nature of the expense must be taken into account when deciding on how to apportion. Heating, for example, could be based on floor area while depreciation of equipment could be based on the book value of each item and where it is used.

21.5.1 Self-test

You are given the following extract of balances for Marmax Trading at 30 April 2010.

Sales		502,000
Sales returns	2,000	
Stocks at 1 May 2009:		
– Raw materials	16,000	
– Work in progress	800	
– Finished goods	4,800	
Purchases of raw material	117,000	
Carriage in on raw material	3,000	
Direct labour	145,000	
Carriage outwards	7,000	
Factory indirect labour	29,000	
Factory indirect material	1,700	
Factory expenses	20,100	
Plant and machinery	150,000	
Provision for depreciation on plant and machinery at 1 May 2009		90,000
Selling expenses	44,000	
Bank interest	6,000	
Administration expenses	35,000	

At the year end the closing stock is as follows:

Raw materials	14,000
Work in progress	1,000
Finished goods	3,900

Depreciation is calculated as follows:

Plant and machinery	10% on straight line
Land and buildings	2% on cost
Office equipment	5% on reducing balance

You are required to prepare the manufacturing account of Marmax Trading for the year.

Note: Included in the extract above are some accounts which are not required in the manufacturing account.

21.5.2 Self-test

The following balances are extracted from the books of Cast Manufacturers for the year ended 31 March 2010.

Stocks at 1 April 2009:	
Raw materials	76,688
Work in progress	107,269
Finished goods	144,263
Purchases: raw materials	615,000
Carriage on raw materials	17,269
Direct labour	996,788
Office salaries	175,950
Rent and rates	85,124
Office lighting and heat	59,100
Depreciation: plant and machinery	106,125
Depreciation: office equipment	18,563
Sales	2,402,250
Factory fuel and power	134,700

Rent and rates are to be apportioned:

Factory 75%   Office 25%

Stocks at 31 March 2010 were:

Raw materials	90,788
Work in progress	110,213
Finished goods	118,069

You are required to prepare a manufacturing account for the year ended 31 March 2010.

21.5.3 Self-test

The following balances are extracted from the books of Ezee Manufacturing for the year ended 31 March 2010.

Stocks at 1 April 2009:	
Raw materials	29,325
Work in progress	10,455
Finished goods	198,730
Purchases: raw materials	181,475
Carriage on raw materials	1,148
Direct labour	193,120
Direct expenses	1,105
Factory rent	12,070
Office lighting and heat	1,987
Depreciation: machinery	10,030
Depreciation: office equipment	21,300
Sales	198,761
Factory fuel and power	19,210
Indirect wages	76,755
Factory insurance	1,785
Repairs to factory	4,250
General factory expenses	3,783

The following additional information is available to you:

Stocks at 31 March 2010 were:

Raw materials	£30,813
Work in progress	£12,920
Finished goods	£192,410

You are required to prepare a manufacturing account using the relevant information in the above extract of balances.

21.5.4 Self-test

The following balances are extracted from the books of account of Reedy Manufacturing Co. for the year ended 31 December 2009.

Stocks at 1 January 2009:	
Raw materials	10,673
Work in progress	9,196
Finished goods	14,284
Purchases: raw materials	79,616
Carriage on raw materials	6,633
Manufacturing wages	112,101
Rent	11,028
Office expenses	5,983
Factory lighting and heat	4,144
Depreciation: machinery	8,208
Depreciation: office equipment	2,513
Purchases: finished goods	8,144
Sales	344,028
Factory fuel and power	5,913
Factory expenses	6,094
Salaries and wages	76,614
Advertising	14,127

You are required to prepare a manufacturing account using the relevant information in the above extract of balances.

The following additional information is available to you:

50% of salaries and wages and 75% of rent are to be treated as a cost of manufacturing.

Stocks at 31 December 2009 were:

Raw materials	15,005
Work in progress	12,130
Finished goods	32,331

21.5.5 Self-test

The following questions are designed to test your understanding of the contents of this chapter. Make sure that you are able to answer all the questions clearly.

Although full answers are not provided, you will find that the questions can be answered by reference to the contents of this chapter.

(a) Explain the difference between direct factory costs and factory overheads.
(b) Prepare a list of the direct costs that exist in a manufacturing business.
(c) What is the purpose of a manufacturing account?
(d) Why are factory costs adjusted for work in progress?

Chapter 22

Balance sheet

Objectives   After you have studied this chapter, you should be able to:

- explain the need for and purpose of a balance sheet;
- explain why and how a balance sheet is prepared;
- understand the differences between fixed and current assets, liabilities and capital;
- identify liabilities payable within 12 months;
- adjust for prepayments and accruals in the balance sheet;
- prepare a balance sheet allowing for adjustments.

22.1   Introduction

Having prepared the profit and loss account our next link is the balance sheet.

The communication of the affairs of a business is done via the profit and loss account and balance sheet. The balance sheet, consisting of assets and liabilities, shows the financial position of the firm at a specific time. For this reason it is important that we label the balance sheet correctly. We must always state the name of the firm, the fact that it is the balance sheet and end with the important words 'as at [date]'. The specific assets of the firm (resources) are shown on the asset side (section) of the balance sheet and how they are financed is shown on the liability/equity side (section).

The two sides (sections) must always balance.

Do you remember the accounting equation?

$$\text{Assets} \quad \text{minus} \quad \text{Liabilities} \quad = \quad \text{Capital}$$

Therefore:

$$\text{Assets} \quad \text{minus} \quad \text{Liabilities} \quad = \quad \text{Net assets} \quad = \quad \text{Capital}$$

You will note from this equation that there are really three sections:

- the assets (A);
- the liabilities (L); and
- the capital (C).

The balance sheet is affected by every transaction of the business, usually in two ways. Therefore, the equality of the balance sheet equation is maintained.

We have said that the balance sheet consists of assets and liabilities, so before we go on with our study of the balance sheet, we need to examine the definitions of these items.

22.2 Definitions – assets

Assets are resources of value owned by the business.

Once acquired, the asset remains in the business until its benefits are exhausted (e.g. motor car less annual depreciation) or it is sold. The two subsections are:

- fixed assets[7] and
- current assets.

22.2.1 Fixed assets

A fixed asset is one that is bought for ongoing use within business and likely to be held and used over a long term. This type of asset constitutes the 'tools of a business'. Examples are land and buildings, machinery, office equipment and motor vehicles. All these are tangible fixed assets – in other words, they are physical assets which have a real existence.

Figure 22.1 Division of fixed assets

In addition there are also fixed assets such as goodwill and brand names (e.g. Coca-Cola, Nike, Microsoft). These are intangible fixed assets, which are often more valuable than the tangible assets.

Typically, intangible assets have no physical substance – they cannot be touched – although they do provide future benefits. The most common and often the most valuable of all intangible assets is goodwill. As such, we will spend a little time discussing this important intangible asset.

One important point is that we never show goodwill that is internally generated in a balance sheet. Goodwill is only shown where it arises from a purchase of a business. At that stage goodwill (and other purchased intangible assets) are capitalised and disclosed as fixed intangible assets.

Once the asset is created (capitalised), it is depreciated (amortised) over its useful economic life. This becomes difficult in the case of most goodwill amounts as the question that will arise is what is its useful economic life? Consequently

---

[7] The term 'fixed assets' has been used rather than 'non-current assets'. See Chapter 41.

UK accounting standards (FRS 10) introduced a rule whereby intangible assets must be written off (amortised) over no more than 20 years.[8]

22.2.2 Current assets

A current asset is an asset that is held temporarily as a stage in the earning cycle. The usual intention is to turn the current asset into cash within one year. The most common current assets are stock, debtors, bank and cash.

We have discussed stock in earlier chapters and therefore only need focus a few words on the remaining current assets.

- Debtors arise where money is owed to the business as a result of sales made on credit.
- Prepayments are where goods and/or services are paid for at the end of the accounting period but will only be used in a future period.

In the case of current assets there is a listing order. This order is determined by answering the question, how quickly can the current asset be turned into cash? This allows us to prepare a list in descending order of liquidity – that is, the time it takes to convert an asset into cash. Using this order we would place stock first, then debtors, bank and lastly cash.

22.3 Definitions – liabilities

Liabilities are debts owed by the business and are either long term[9] or current. Here again these types of liabilities are separately defined.

22.3.1 Long-term liabilities

A long-term liability is a debt where the amount due is payable in more than one year. Examples are long-term loans and debentures. In all company accounts this heading is shown as 'creditors: amounts falling due after more than one year'. At present we will merely refer to these items as long-term liabilities, but you are advised to remember the correct description.

22.3.2 Current liabilities

A current liability is a debt where the amount is to be paid in the near future – usually within one year of the balance sheet date. In company accounts we use the term 'creditors: amounts falling due within one year'. Here we will be using the term current liabilities to identify this group, but when we deal with company accounts you will note that we change the term used.

---

[8] There is provision for an impairment test but this is outside the scope of this book.
[9] Throughout this book use is made of 'long-term liabilities' instead of the term 'non-current liabilities'. This is done even though balance sheets prepared under IAS use the 'non-current' term.

Remember that not all liabilities are shown as current liabilities and the date they are due for repayment plays a vital part in determining where they are shown in the balance sheet. This seems self-evident, but it is all too often forgotten or ignored in an examination.

The following list is of creditors that we would expect to see listed as current liabilities:

- Creditors (trade creditors) are amounts owed by the business to suppliers for goods or services, received in the accounting period, but paid for in the subsequent accounting period.
- Short-term loans and other creditors are also shown in this group and consist of all amounts due for repayment within 12 months. We would expect to find items such as bank overdraft, taxation due and dividends payable.
- Accruals are for expenses incurred during the accounting period, but still to be paid. This includes taxation, dividends and interest due but unpaid.

Although each business would have its unique types of assets and liabilities, they would fall into the main groupings as described above.

22.4 Definitions – capital

The third section of the accounting equation is the capital section. This is the amount put into the business by the owner(s). It is of fundamental importance as without capital no business can exist.

Capital is also a liability, but it is slightly different in that it represents a liability to the owner(s) of the business rather than to outsiders.

Capital varies depending on the nature of the entity.

- In a sole ownership the capital is the amount introduced by the owner. To this is added the accrual of profits earned during the past years less any drawings made by the owner(s).
- In a company it consists of the share capital plus retained profits and reserves. It is shown as shareholders' funds (see section 22.5).

22.5 Additional definitions

Although we will deal with the more advanced balance sheet layouts in section 22.6, we still need to familiarise ourselves with the terminology more commonly used in, but not limited to, company accounts.

- Working capital is the difference between current assets and current liabilities. It is also called 'net current assets'.
- Net assets consist of the total assets less total liabilities. It is the net asset figure which makes up one half of the balance sheet and is equal to the total capital (or net worth).

■ Shareholders' funds (or capital) constitutes the other half of the balance sheet. This term applies only to companies and comprises shareholders' funds (total amount invested by shareholders) plus reserves (e.g. retained profit). With a sole trader or a partnership we would show the capital account and accrued profits of the owner(s).

22.5.1 Self-test

Using the information in the preceding paragraphs, you are required to complete the table below:

Description	Fixed asset	Current asset	Current liability
Motor vehicle			
Cash			
Goods for resale			
Amount due to supplier			
Amount due by customers			
Rent outstanding			
Bank overdraft			
Office furniture			

22.5.2 Self-test

Identify the assets from the list below. State if the asset is a current or a fixed asset.

(a) Stock.
(b) Money owed to supplier.
(c) Computer equipment.
(d) Money outstanding for goods sold.

Identify the liabilities from the following list. Give the nature of the liability, i.e. current or long term.

(a) Loan due to be repaid to A Brown in 4 months' time.
(b) Money owed to a supplier.
(c) Fixtures and fittings.
(d) Money outstanding for goods sold by us.
(e) Loan due to be repaid to G Smythe in 3 years' time.
(f) VAT due to be paid to HMRC.
(g) Bank overdraft.

22.5.3 Self-test

Given the list below, you are required to identify the nature of each item and where each would appear in the financial statements.

Remember that all the items must appear in one of the first four columns and also in either column 5 or 6.

Details	Asset	Liability	Income	Expense	Bal sheet	P&L
Bank overdraft						
Rent paid quarterly in advance						
Motor vehicle						
Directors' salaries						
Factory premises						
Sale of goods						
Purchase of stationery						
Bank interest received						
Insurance premium						
Tax payable in three months' time						
Amount owed to stationery supplier						
Dividends received						
Stock held for resale						
Loan interest paid						
Computer equipment						
Shares held in another business						

22.5.4 Self-test

Wendy borrowed £30,000 for her business on 1 January 2010. The loan is repayable in full in 3 years' time but interest at the rate of 8 per cent is payable annually.

She has also financed the purchase of a delivery vehicle by a loan of £8,000, which is repayable in full over 4 years as from 1 January 2011. Interest of 7 per cent annually is payable on the loan.

The business has purchased goods for resale totalling £2,100. This amount is to be paid on 15 January 2011.

Show the total amount of current liabilities as at 31 December 2010 (show your workings). Assume that no payments have been made during 2010 either for interest or for capital.

22.6 Balance sheet layout

Having defined the various types of assets and liabilities, we now need to see where they are placed in the balance sheet.

The balance sheet has a fixed format – there are basically two formats: a horizontal one and a vertical one. The latter is called the narrative or columnar method.

The format is on the lines of the accounting equation that we first looked at in section 2.1.

Figure 22.2 **The accounting equation**

This rule always applies whether the business platform is a sole owner, a partnership, a small private company or a large international public company.

For purposes of illustration only we show you below an example of the balance sheet in a horizontal format.

Balance sheet of J Jones as at 31 December 2009

Fixed assets			Capital	
Land & buildings	120,000		J Jones capital	100,000
Plant & equipment	23,000	143,000	Plus profit	49,000
				149,000
Current assets			Current liabilities	
Stock	15,000		Creditors	18,500
Debtors	6,000			
Bank	3,500	24,500		
		£167,500		£167,500

For the remainder of this book we will only use a vertical format, as that is the one most commonly used, especially in the UK.

We will now compare the above balance sheet to one prepared in a vertical format, to highlight the differences. We use the same information and headings but place the items into the vertical format.

Balance sheet of J Jones as at 31 December 2009

Fixed assets		
Land & buildings	120,000	
Plant & equipment	23,000	143,000
Current assets		
Stock	15,000	
Debtors	6,000	
Cash at bank	3,500	
	24,500	
Less: **Current liabilities**		
Creditors	18,500	
Net current assets		6,000
		£149,000
Represented by:		
Capital		
J Jones – capital account	100,000	
Plus profit	49,000	149,000
		£149,000

From the above you can see that the balance sheet starts with the fixed assets and ends with capital. It is easier to read and it highlights the relationship between current assets and current liabilities (i.e. the net current assets or working capital).

22.7 Balance sheet presentation

In section 22.2.2 we showed that current assets are listed in the order of liquidity. In addition there is a very definite order of other assets and liabilities in balance sheet presentation. This is more so when we present company accounts, as the layout is more rigidly defined by the Companies Act. We will use this layout throughout as it makes sense to be familiar with the layout and it can be applied to sole traders and partnerships as well as limited liability companies.

Name of business: Balance sheet as at DATE

Assets	34,000
Less liabilities	18,000
= Net assets	16,000
Capital	16,000

To illustrate this in more detail we use a typical company layout which follows the prescribed format as required by the Companies Act 2006.[10]

Balance sheet as at DATE

Fixed assets			
Tangible			
Land and buildings	80,000		
Plant and machinery	65,000		
Fixtures and fittings	14,000		159,000
Intangible			
Goodwill			20,000
			179,000
Current assets			
Stock	26,000		
Debtors	17,000		
Prepaid expenses	1,000		
Cash on hand	3,000	47,000	
Current liabilities			
Overdraft	2,000		
Creditors	10,000		
Accruals	1,000	13,000	
Net current assets			34,000
Total assets less current liabilities			213,000
Long-term liability			
Loan			29,000
NET ASSETS			£184,000
Capital			
Share capital	3,000		
Retained profit	181,000		
SHAREHOLDERS' FUNDS			£184,000

[10] The accounts must comply with provision made by the Secretary of State by regulations as to the form and content of the balance sheet and profit and loss account (section 396 3(a) of CA 2006).

The order for the balance sheet groups are in the reverse order of liquidity. Fixed assets appear first and then current assets. Within the current asset heading the least liquid current asset (stock) appears first and the list descends to cash (the most liquid current asset).

22.7.1 Worked example

The above format is illustrated when we look at the following example.

At 31 December 2009 we are given the following information as it relates to balance sheet items:

Premises	80,000
Stock	5,000
Debtors	2,000
Cash at bank	2,500
Creditors	4,500

You are required to prepare the balance sheet using the above information.

The problem you have is that the balance sheet must balance – but there is an amount of £85,000 missing. We know this because we know that the accounting equation does not balance. We know that Assets – Liabilities = Capital. This can also be shown as Assets = Liabilities + Capital.

What we have in the details above are assets of £89,500 and liabilities of £4,500. This means that capital must be equal to the difference of £85,000. Once we have determined the missing number we are in a position to draw up the balance sheet.

Balance sheet as at 31 December 2009

Fixed assets		
Premises		80,000
Current assets		
Stock	5,000	
Debtors	2,000	
Cash at bank	2,500	
	9,500	
Less: **Current liabilities**		
Creditors	4,500	
Net current assets		5,000
		£85,000
Represented by:		
Capital		85,000
		£85,000

From the above example we now know that the value of the business is its net book value which is the total capital employed of £85,000. Another important thing that the balance sheet tells us is the liquidity of the business and we will discuss this in detail in Chapter 32 on ratios.

22.7.2 Worked example

The following list of balances was extracted from the books of Middlesex Ltd at 31 December 2009.

Trade creditors	75,000
Debtors	100,000
Overdraft	30,000
Debenture interest	2,000
Administrative expenses	47,000
Selling & distribution expenses	10,000
5% debentures	60,000
Freehold land & buildings at cost	200,000
Fixtures & fittings at cost	150,000
Motor vehicles at cost	200,000
Accumulated depreciation at 1 Jan 2009:	
– Fixtures & fittings	30,000
– Motor vehicles	60,000
Opening stock at 1 January 2009	125,000
Purchases	185,000
Sales	375,000
Share capital	160,000
Revaluation reserve	35,000
Provision for doubtful debts at 1 Jan 2009	7,000
Profit & loss account at 1 January 2009	187,000

You are also provided with additional information relating to the financial year end:

(i)   Closing stock at 31 December 2009 is valued at £175,000.

(ii) Included in the figure for administrative expenses is £18,000, being an advance payment for twelve months' rent from 31 August 2009.

(iii) Depreciation is to be charged as follows:
   (a) Fixtures and fittings: 20 per cent straight line.
   (b) Motor vehicles: 30 per cent reducing balance.

(iv) Provision for doubtful debts should be increased and made equal to 10 per cent of outstanding debtors.

(v)   During the year the company engaged computer consultants at a cost of £15,000. Their bill has not yet been paid but must be provided for.

(vi) It is expected that the accountancy fees for 2009 will amount to £12,000.

You are required to prepare the profit and loss account and balance sheet for 31 December 2009.

Note that in order to prepare the financial statements, we first need to ensure that the trial balance is in balance. To do this we must enter the balances into the debit or credit column.

Once completed, the trial balance will appear as follows:

Trade creditors		75,000
Debtors	100,000	
Overdraft		30,000
Debenture interest	2,000	
Administrative expenses	47,000	
Selling & distribution expenses	10,000	
5% debentures		60,000
Land & buildings at cost	200,000	
Fixtures & fittings at cost	150,000	
Motor vehicles at cost		200,000
Accumulated depreciation at 1 Jan 2009		
– Fixtures & fittings		30,000
– Motor vehicles		60,000
Opening stock at 1 Jan 2009	125,000	
Purchases	185,000	
Sales		375,000
Share capital		160,000
Revaluation reserve		35,000
Provision for doubtful debts at 1 Jan 09		7,000
Profit & loss account at 1 Jan 2009		187,000
	1,019,000	1,019,000

We have now established that the trial balance is balanced and we can proceed to do the adjustments listed above.

(i)   Administration expenses must be reduced for the £18,000 paid for rent. We need calculate how much of the rent is prepaid. This we do by matching the dates to the amounts paid. We note that the payment of £18,000 made on 31 August 2009 is for September to December (4 months) plus January to August (8 months). Therefore we can state that $1/3$ of the £18,000 is for the current period and the balance is for the year ending 31 December 2010. So we show a prepayment of £18,000 × $2/3$ = £12,000.

(ii) Depreciation is calculated for motor vehicles on the basis of the reduced balance which is £200,000 − £60,000 = £140,000. The rate given is 30% × £140,000 = £42,000.

(iii) For fixtures and fittings depreciation is calculated at 20% × £150,000 (cost) = £30,000.

(iv) For the next adjustment we are told that the provision for doubtful debts is 10% × £100,000 = £10,000. As the balance on the account is presently £7,000 we need to allow for an additional £3,000 in the profit and loss account.

(v)   Computer consultancy must be provided for in the year-end accounts. We are told that the amount to accrue is £15,000 and this must be taken into the profit and loss account as an additional expense.

(vi) In a similar vein the £12,000 for accountancy fees is also to be accrued.

Both the accruals ((v) and (vi)) are shown in the balance sheet as additional liabilities and, as they are most likely to be paid within 12 months, they will appear as current liabilities.

You will note that the only item of adjustment that has not yet been dealt with is that of the closing stock. We use the closing stock figure in the profit and loss account in order to calculate the cost of sales. That same figure is shown in the balance sheet as a current asset.

Having now prepared the workings for all the adjustments we can prepare the accounts. As we read in Chapter 20, we start off with the profit and loss account before moving to the balance sheet.

Profit and loss account of Middlesex Ltd for the year ended 31 December 2009

Sales		375,000
Opening stock	125,000	
Purchases	185,000	
	310,000	
Closing stock	175,000	
Cost of goods sold		135,000
Gross profit		240,000
Administration expenses	35,000	
Selling & distribution expenses	10,000	
Debenture interest*	3,000	
Increase in provision for doubtful debts	3,000	
Accrued expenses	27,000	
Depreciation	72,000	150,000
Net profit		90,000
Add balance at 1 January 2009		187,000
Balance at 31 December 2009		277,000

* The debentures are stated as being 5% debentures. This means that interest is payable at the rate of 5% per annum, or £3,000. As only £2,000 was shown in the trial balance it means that we must accrue for the additional £1,000.

Balance sheet of Middlesex Ltd as at 31 December 2009

Fixed assets		
Land & buildings		200,000
Fixtures & fittings	150,000	
Less acc depreciation	60,000	90,000
Motor vehicles	200,000	
Less acc depreciation	102,000	98,000
		388,000
Current assets		
Stock	175,000	
Debtors (net)	90,000	
Prepayments	12,000	
	277,000	
Current liabilities		
Creditors	75,000	
Overdraft	30,000	
Accruals**	28,000	
	133,000	
Net working capital		144,000
		532,000
Long-term liabilities		
Debentures		60,000
		472,000
Capital		
Share capital	160,000	
Reserves	35,000	
Profit & loss	277,000	
		472,000

** Accruals are made up of computer consultancy £15,000, accounting fees £12,000 and debentures interest £1,000.

22.7.3 Self-test

Complete the following table:

Fixed assets	Current assets	Long-term liabilities	Current liabilities	Capital
48,000	22,000	14,000	6,000	?
?	17,500	3,100	6,000	35,000
102,000	?	30,000	25,000	65,000
102,000	46,000	?	28,000	110,000
48,000	22,000	Nil	?	65,000

You will note from doing the table above that we can always find the missing part of the balance sheet if we remember the accounting equation of Assets minus Liabilities = Capital.

22.7.4 Self-test

The following is an extract of the trial balance of Brenda at 31 December 2009. You are required to prepare the balance sheet, having already determined that the net profit for the year amounted to £21,100.

Trial balance at 31 December 2009

Bank	700	
Creditors		6,900
Bank loan due 2010		7,000
Debtors	30,000	
Investments	2,800	
Machinery: at cost	42,000	
Accumulated depreciation – machinery, at 1 January 2009		19,400
Owner's capital		38,200
Provision for doubtful debts		800
Vehicles: at cost	8,000	
Accumulated depreciation – vehicles, at 1 January 2009		5,600
Closing stock	15,500	
Net profit for the year		21,100
	£99,000	£99,000

22.7.5 Self-test

Using the trial balance of W Thom that you prepared in self-test 15.3.2 together with the adjustments made in self-test 15.4.2, you now need to prepare the final accounts for W Thom for the year ended 30 September 2009.

There are no additional adjustments that need to be made for the final accounts except to allow for closing stock of £66,798.

22.7.6 Self-test

In self-test 15.3.3 you were required to prepare a trial balance of Final Trading Co. at 30 June 2009. Using the balances in that trial balance you are now required to prepare the profit and loss account and balance sheet at that date.

There are no additional adjustments that need be made for the final accounts except to allow for closing stock of £46,800.

22.7.7 Self-test

You are given the following trial balance and a list of additional adjustments to be made.

Michael Enterprise Trial balance at 31 October 2009

Creditors		71,190
Returns inwards	1,400	
Electricity and gas	16,912	
Insurance	1,435	
Capital		204,792
Rates	6,342	
Salaries and wages	109,823	
Motor expenses	9,912	
Sales		618,100
Purchases	358,050	
Cash in hand	1,050	
Returns outwards		2,450
Stock 31 October 2008	109,830	
Debtors	114,198	
Rent	24,500	
Fixtures and fittings	44,100	
Drawings	76,650	
Delivery expenses	7,105	
Cash at bank	15,225	
	896,532	896,532

The following amounts were prepaid:

Rates	2,304
Insurance	225

Amounts due but not yet paid are:

Rent	6,300
Delivery expenses	225
Motor expenses	2,790
Electricity and gas	936
Stock at year end	188,870

You are required to prepare the profit and loss account and balance sheet at 31 October 2009, incorporating the above adjustments.

22.8 Valuation in the balance sheet

Valuation of items appearing in the balance sheet is usually at historic cost. In current assets, however, if the net realisable value is less than the cost then the asset is shown at the former value (using the prudence convention).

In the case of a fixed asset it has a limited life and is, therefore, depreciated. But in some cases a fixed asset can appreciate in value, such as property. In this case it can be revalued to the current market value and this increase in value is shown in the balance sheet.

Chapter 23

Revision

Objectives	After working through this chapter, you should be able to:

- identify assets and liabilities;
- incorporate adjustments to the trial balance;
- prepare a trading, profit and loss account and balance sheet for sole traders.

23.1 Final accounts

These consist of the profit and loss account and the balance sheet. At this stage we need to recap on what you have read in earlier chapters and undertake some additional questions covering all the topics already studied. Before we do this, however, you need to remind yourselves of the two main accounting documents covered here.

23.1.1 Balance sheet

This is a 'snapshot' on a particular date of the assets, liabilities and capital (net worth) of a business. The balance sheet shows where the capital has come from and how it has been used in providing the assets required in the business.

Although the balance sheet is a measure of the net book value of a business at a point in time, it is not an indication of the current market value of a business. The main reason for this is that the balance sheet reflects assets and liabilities at cost (less depreciation) and not at current values. In addition, it does not bring into account any item that has not been purchased, such as goodwill.

By drawing up a balance sheet at two different points in time we can measure how much the wealth or the net worth has increased or decreased over the period. These changes in the net worth can largely be explained by the profit or loss of the past period but can also be as a result of additional capital being brought into the business or money withdrawn by the owner or shareholders.

23.1.2 Profit and loss account

This account shows the business's performance over a period of time, usually one year.

The structure of the profit and loss account is as follows:

> Revenue or income or sales or turnover (that is, earnings from selling products and/or services)
>
> *less* expenses (the costs incurred in earning that revenue)
> = profit earned

If expenses are greater than revenue then we have made a loss. When we make a profit, this profit may be paid out to owners as drawings (in the case of a sole trader or partnership), dividends (to shareholders of a company), or retained in the business as additional capital.

23.2 Net worth

The meaning of net worth can best be explained by the following illustrations:

Balance sheet as at 30 June

	2009	2010
Assets	30,000	37,000
Less liabilities	5,000	6,000
Net worth	£25,000	£31,000

In the above example net worth increased by £6,000. How was this achieved?

By preparing the profit and loss account for 2010, we see that the profit of £6,000 is responsible for the increase in the net worth.

Profit and loss account for the year ended 30 June

	2009	2010
Revenue	36,000	40,000
Less expenses	28,000	34,000
Profit	£8,000	£6,000

23.3 Revision questions

You should now practice what you have read in the preceding chapters and check that you are familiar with the way in which financial statements are prepared.

If you are in any doubt about an aspect of what you have read so far, go back to the relevant chapter/s and read them again before attempting this revision chapter.

23.3.1 Self-test

George opened a suspense account so that he could prepare the trading and profit and loss account. He showed a net profit of £6,920.

Subsequent to the above, the following errors were discovered:

(i) Wages were debited with £636. This was an amount paid for machine installation.

(ii) Sales of £910 had been entered in both the sales day book and debtors' account as £190.

(iii) The discount total of £313 on the debit side of the cash book was entered as discount received.

(iv) Closing stock was understated by £700.

Show the effect of each of the above errors on the net profit.

23.3.2 Self-test

Although the trial balance did not balance, we were asked by M Jones to prepare a balance sheet at 31 December 2009. After its preparation, we investigated the errors so as to eliminate the suspense account.

You are required to correct these errors (using journal entries) and show what the net profit should be after allowing for those corrections.

Fixed assets			
Land & buildings		300,000	
Plant & machinery at cost	8,000		
Less accumulated depreciation	1,500	6,500	
			306,500
Current assets			
Stock	5,190		
Debtors	6,200		
Bank	1,340		
		12,730	
Current liabilities			
Creditors	6,100		
Suspense	850	6,950	5,780
			312,280
Capital		286,000	
Add Net profit		62,800	
		348,800	
Less drawings		36,520	
			312,280

The errors revealed are:

(i) The ledger account for telephone expenses has been overcast by £200.

(ii) A payment of £350 to Joe & Co. (a creditor) was entered only in the cash book.

(iii) The sales account was undercast by £1,000.

(iv) A credit sale to Ace Traders for £450 was incorrectly entered in the sales journal as £540.

23.3.3 Self-test

Show how each of the following errors affect the net profit of J Black for the year ended 31 December 2009.

(i)   Opening stock is overvalued by £852.
(ii) A loan of £5,000 made to Black was credited to the profit and loss account.
(iii) Discounts received of £210 were debited to the profit and loss account.
(iv) Credit purchases of £760 were not entered into the purchases day book.
(v)   Interest on Black's bank deposit of £130 was treated as interest charged in the profit and loss account.

The net profit as calculated before the above errors were discovered was £6,700.

23.3.4 Self-test

Jay & Co. Trial balance at 30 June 2009

Postage and telephone	1,300	
Rent and rates	2,500	
Insurance	365	
Electricity	516	
Motor expenses	1,960	
Salaries and wages	4,850	
Sales		36,600
Purchases	20,650	
General expenses	806	
Motor vehicle	3,500	
Creditors		3,250
Debtors	6,810	
Land and buildings	28,000	
Fittings and fixtures	3,960	
Stock 1 July 2008	8,020	
Cash at bank	1,134	
Drawings	6,278	
Capital		50,799
	£90,649	£90,649

Stock at 30 June 2009 amounts to £11,700.

You are required to prepare a trading and profit and loss account and a balance sheet for the year ended 30 June 2009.

23.3.5 Self-test

Andrew List of balances at 31 December 2009

Motor vehicles at cost	5,600
Fixtures and fittings at cost	4,200
Land and buildings at cost	5,600
Loan	1,680
Advertising	280
Administration expenses	1,316
Loan interest	56
Bank overdraft	840
Debtors	3,150
Creditors	2,086
Profit and loss account at 1 Jan 2009	5,250
Provision for doubtful debts at 1 Jan 2009	210
Capital account – Andrew	5,446
Sales	10,850
Purchases	5,180
Opening stock at 1 Jan 09	3,500
Motor vehicles (acc depreciation at 1 Jan 2009)	1,680
Fixtures and fittings (acc depreciation at 1 Jan 2009)	840

You are required to prepare the trial balance at 31 December 2009. Thereafter, the following additional information must be brought into account. It is important that you show all your workings.

(i) Stock at 31 December 2009 is valued at £4,300.
(ii) Administration expenses include £144 which is an advance payment for rent for the 12 months from 1 September 2009.
(iii) Depreciation is to be calculated as follows:
    (a) Fixtures and fittings: 25 per cent using the straight line method.
    (b) Motor vehicles: 20 per cent using the reducing balance method.
(iv) Provision for doubtful debts should be made equal to 10 per cent of outstanding debtors.
(v) During the year the company engaged office cleaners at a cost of £140. No payment has been made and therefore the full amount has to be provided for in administrative expenses.
(vi) There is a charge of £100 for accounting fees for the year. This amount is unpaid and must be accrued as an additional administrative expense.

You are required to prepare a profit and loss account and balance sheet for Andrew for the year ended 31 December 2009.

23.3.6 Self-test

Miskien & Co. Trial balance at 31 December 2009

Cash	6,700	
Debtors	23,800	
Insurance	3,400	
Stock 1 January 2009	1,950	
Land	50,000	
Building at cost	141,500	
Accumulated depr – buildings		91,700
Equipment at cost	90,100	
Accumulated depr – equipment		65,300
Creditors		7,500
Interest receivable		6,000
Capital account – Miskien		81,500
Drawings – Miskien	10,000	
Sales		218,400
Purchases	80,200	
Electricity and gas	28,200	
Advertising	19,000	
Repairs	11,500	
Salaries	4,050	
	470,400	470,400

The following year-end adjustments need to be made:

(i)	Prepaid insurance at 31 December 2009	800
(ii)	Stock on hand at 31 December 2009	450
(iii)	Depreciation of buildings for the year	1,620
(iv)	Depreciation of equipment for the year	5,500
(v)	Interest due to Miskien at 31 December 2009	500
(vi)	Accrued salaries and wages 31 December 2009	2,000
(vii)	Sales delivered but not invoiced at 31 December 2009	2,750

You are required to show the above adjustments as journal entries and then to prepare an adjusted trial balance.

You are then required to prepare the profit and loss account and balance sheet for the year.

23.3.7 Self-test

Watno & Co. Trial balance at 30 June 2009

Cash	1,150	
Debtors	3,500	
Advertising	1,300	
Equipment	9,900	
Creditors		750
Prepaid fees		2,000
Capital account		10,500
Drawings	1,000	
Fees earned		36,750
Wages	19,500	
Rent	9,000	
Electricity and gas	3,750	
Sundry expenses	900	
	50,000	50,000

The following adjusting entries have still to be made to the above trial balance:

(i)   Fees earned but not invoiced at 30 June 2009   1,025
(ii) Depreciation of equipment for the year   750
(iii) Unpaid wages at 30 June 2009   510

You are required to show journal entries for the above adjustments. You are also required to prepare the profit and loss account and balance sheet for the year.

23.3.8 Self-test

Wasser & Co. Trial balance 31 December 2009

Cash	3,200	
Debtors	17,200	
Insurance	3,900	
Stock	2,450	
Delivery vehicles at cost	150,000	
Accumulated depreciation – delivery vehicles		95,700
Equipment at cost	90,100	
Accumulated depreciation – Equipment		65,300
Creditors		7,500
Rent receivable		4,000
Capital		165,900
Drawing	5,000	
Sales		218,400
Salaries and wages	78,700	
Gas and water	28,200	
Advertising	19,000	
Repairs	13,500	
Office expenses	4,050	
Purchases	141,500	
	456,800	456,800

The year-end adjustments are as follows:

(i) Prepaid gas and water at 31 December	825
(ii) Stock on hand at 31 December 2009	700
(iii) Depreciation of delivery vehicles for the year	1,500
(iv) Depreciation of equipment for the year	5,500
(v) Accrued salaries and wages at 31 December	1,250

You are required to prepare the profit and loss account and balance sheet for the year after taking into account the above adjustments.

23.3.9 Self-test

Show how each of the following errors has affected the net profit of £2,900 as shown in the profit and loss account and state what the adjusted profit is after correcting these errors.

(i)   Opening stock was undervalued by £942.
(ii) Interest on a business investment of £153 was treated as interest charged in the profit and loss account.
(iii) A loan of £300 made to the business was credited to the profit and loss account.
(iv) Discounts received of £40 were debited to the profit and loss account.
(v)   Credit purchases of £330 were omitted from the purchases day book.

23.3.10 Self-test

Martin prepared his final accounts and calculated that his net profit for the year was £7,875. This was before the following errors were discovered:

(i)   Rent receivable of £520 was outstanding.
(ii)   Sales of £928 had not been recorded.
(iii) A provision for bad debts of £700 should have been created.
(iv)   Depreciation of £800 had not been provided for.
(v)   An invoice for telephone charges of £120 had not been paid.
(vi)   Sales returns of £322 had not been entered.
(vii) Rent of £1,000 shown in the profit and loss account relates to the following year.
(viii) Closing stock had been overvalued by £648.

Show the corrected net profit for the year.

23.3.11 Self-test

Steve prepared a trial balance at 31 May 2009. The trial balance did not balance and Steve opened a suspense account so that he could prepare the trading and profit and loss accounts. He showed a net profit of £1,920.

Subsequent to the above, the following errors were discovered:

(i) Wages were debited with £376. This amount was for machine installation which should be added to the cost of the machine.

(ii) Sales of £191 had been entered in both the sales day book and debtors' account as £119.

(iii) The discount total of £132 on the debit side of the cash book was entered as discount received.

(iv) Stock at 31 May was understated by £340.

You are required to show the effect on the net profit of each of the above errors and to calculate the correct net profit.

23.3.12 Self-test

Nufashion Manufacturing

Trial balance at 30 April 2010	Debit	Credit
Factory machinery at cost	53,000	
Factory machinery depreciation 1 May 09		5,000
Office equipment	6,000	
Office equipment depreciation 1 May 09		1,200
Debtors and creditors	25,000	19,000
Cash at bank	3,800	
Loan due 30 April 2012		21,000
Stock of: raw materials 1 May 2009	5,000	
work in progress	12,200	
finished goods	17,000	
Carriage inwards	3,200	
Carriage outwards	1,500	
Purchases – raw materials	106,000	
Electricity and heat	5,000	
Rent and rates	8,000	
Direct factory wages	30,000	
Office wages	8,200	
Sales commission	3,400	
Sale of finished goods		215,000
Capital account		47,000
Drawings	20,900	
	308,200	308,200

Notes to the information above:

(i) At 30 April 2010, direct factory wages accrued amounted to £900 and office wages accrued were £400.

(ii) The rent and rates account includes £1,200 paid on 20 January 2010, for the period 1 January to 30 June 2010.

(iii) Records showed that, at the year end, stock values were as follows: raw materials £9,400; work in progress £22,000; finished goods £13,000.

(iv) Depreciation for factory machinery is on the straight line method over ten years, and office equipment on the reducing balance method at 25 per cent p.a.

(v) A provision of £3,000 should be made for doubtful debts.

(vi) Electricity and heat should be apportioned between the factory and office in the ratio 3:2 respectively and rent and rates in the ratio 3:1 respectively.

You are required to prepare manufacturing, trading, and profit and loss accounts for the year ended 30 April 2010 and a balance sheet at that date.

23.3.13 Self-test

From the following extract of information for Delta Manufacturing prepare manufacturing, trading and profit and loss accounts for the year ended 31 December 2009.

You are required to show clearly the prime cost, factory cost of completed production, cost of sales, gross profit, administrative overheads, selling and distribution overheads, and net profit.

Note: In your answer the purchase of finished goods is to be shown in the profit and loss account and sale of scrap material in the manufacturing account.

Stock of raw materials at 1 January 2009	3,920	
Work in progress at 1 January 2009	1,840	
Stock of finished goods at 1 January 2009	8,215	
Purchases of raw materials	64,600	
Purchases of finished goods	1,300	
Raw materials returned to suppliers		5,020
Carriage outwards	516	
Carriage inwards	809	
Direct factory wages	28,310	
Administrative salaries	11,530	
Supervisors' wages	6,320	
Electricity used in factory	3,508	
Electricity and heat for administrative offices	1,020	
Sales staff salaries	18,897	
Bad debts	830	
Discount received		3,020
Discount allowed	1,860	
Depreciation: plant and machinery	14,250	
delivery vehicles	4,160	
office fixtures and furniture	2,050	
Rent and rates (factory $^3/_4$, office $^1/_4$)	9,600	
Delivery expenses	725	
Postage and telephone	825	
Printing and stationery	460	
Income from the sale of scrap material		320
Interest payable on loan	4,600	
Bank charges	308	
Insurance on plant	2,812	
Advertising	735	
Repairs to plant	1,020	
Sales		187,300

Closing stock at 31 December 2009 is:

Raw materials	4,160
Work in progress	2,830
Finished goods	9,210

23.3.14 Self-test

Using relevant information from the balances of Nuage Manufacturing Co. below, you are required to prepare manufacturing, trading and profit and loss accounts for the year ended 31 December 2009.

In your presentation you should show clearly the prime cost, factory cost of completed production, cost of sales, gross profit and net profit.

Stock of raw materials at 1 January 2009	28,730
Work in progress at 1 January 2009	4,090
Stock of finished goods at 1 January 2009	11,310
Purchases of raw materials	146,900
Purchases of finished goods	38,620
Returns inwards	4,034
Returns outwards	6,150
Carriage outwards	1,423
Carriage inwards (raw material)	8,097
Factory wages	62,130
Factory power	27,900
Bad debts	6,830
Depreciation: plant and machinery	26,080
office equipment	11,320
Rent (factory $^2/_3$ office $^1/_3$)	60,000
Interest on overdraft	4,270
Repairs to machinery	4,340
Sales	384,980

Closing stock at 31 December 2009 is:

Raw materials	41,910
Work in progress	3,240
Finished goods	24,800

23.3.15 Self-test

From the following extract of information of Winter Manufacturing Co., prepare manufacturing, trading and profit and loss accounts for the year ended 31 May 2010.

You are required to show clearly the prime cost, factory cost of completed production, cost of sales, gross profit, administrative overheads, selling and distribution overheads, and net profit.

Stock of raw materials at 1 June 2009	11,080
Work in progress at 1 June 2009	3,920
Stock of finished goods at 1 June 2009	16,740
Purchases of raw materials	47,104
Purchases of finished goods	3,001
Raw materials returned to suppliers	1,002
Carriage outwards	961
Carriage inwards (raw material)	843
Direct factory wages	11,218
Administrative salaries	14,072
Supervisors' wages	4,794
Electricity used in factory	1,874
Electricity and heat for administrative offices	1,920
Sales staff salaries and commission	11,470
Bad debts	1,214
Discount received	806
Discount allowed	324
Depreciation: plant and machinery	962
delivery vehicles	109
office fixtures and furniture	803
Rent and rates (factory $^3/_4$ office $^1/_4$)	8,000
Delivery expenses	1,214
Postage and telephone	830
Printing and stationery	720
Interest payable on loan	1,009
Bank charges	131
Insurance on plant	906
Advertising	1,204
Repairs to plant	872
Sales	140,709

Closing stock at 31 May 2010 is:

Raw materials	14,720
Work in progress	4,870
Finished goods	18,310

23.3.16 Self-test

Richard Trial balance at 30 September 2009	Debit	Credit
Stock 1 October 2008	9,150	
Purchases	14,300	
Sales		22,580
Salaries and wages	2,720	
Rent and rates	900	
Insurance	110	
Motor expenses	640	
Printing and stationery	210	
Electricity and gas	140	
General expenses	300	
Motor vehicles	3,400	
Fixtures and fittings	1,050	
Debtors	4,900	
Creditors		2,200
Cash at bank	1,160	
Drawings	7,800	
Capital		22,000
	46,780	46,780

The stock at 30 September 2009 is valued at £7,300.

You are required to prepare a trading and profit and loss account for the year ended 30 September 2009 and a balance sheet at that date.

23.3.17 Self-test

Alan & Co. manufacture beach towels. The following balances appear in the books of the firm at 31 December 2008.

Stocks at 1 January 2008:

Raw materials	23,400
Work in progress	2,800
Finished goods	19,700

Wages:

Direct manufacturing	314,600
Factory supervisors	40,000
Administrative staff	17,350
Heating and electricity	24,000
Carriage outwards	1,001
Purchase of raw materials	187,400
Administration expenses	6,720
Sales	874,320

Stocks at 31 December 2008:

Raw materials	29,240
Work in progress	3,610
Finished goods	16,480

Note: Heating and electricity is to be apportioned: factory $^3/_4$ and office $^1/_4$.

You are required to prepare the following for the year ended 31 December 2008:

(i) the manufacturing account, showing clearly the prime cost and the cost of goods manufactured;

(ii) the trading account; and

(iii) the profit and loss account.

23.3.18 Self-test

Using the revised trial balance of Idea & Co. that you prepared in section 17.1.2 you are required to prepare the financial statements for the year ended 31 March 2009.

You are told that the closing stock is £17,170.

23.3.19 Self-test

Using the revised trial balance that you prepared for NuVenture in section 17.1.3 you are required to prepare the financial statements for the year ended 31 March 2009.

The value of the closing stock is £20,300.

23.4 Summary

Check through all your answers in this chapter and make sure that you are satisfied with the results.

If you are in any doubt about a section, or sections, of the revision then read the relevant chapters again and work through the various self-tests. Once you are satisfied, proceed to Chapter 24.

Chapter 24

Incomplete records

Objectives After you have studied this chapter, you should be able to:
- explain the nature of single entries;
- determine profit from limited information;
- construct ledger accounts from incomplete records;
- prepare accounts from incomplete records.

24.1 Introduction

Not all businesses maintain complete accounting records. This may be because the owner has neither the desire nor the skills to keep a complete set of accounting records. In some cases many of the figures used are estimates, resulting in the trading profit being found by approximation.

Some accounting records may be more complete than others. In some cases a firm may have little or no information, while others may have a cash book and even a debtors' and creditors' ledger. In the latter case, this becomes a good starting point. This is obviously not a complete set of books and the accountant may have to write up the rest of the books at year end. This will involve completing all double-entry work and preparing the final accounts.

In cases where the business has no books at all, the accountant may have to prepare the accounts from the original source documents.

24.2 Preparing accounting records

There are many ways to build accounting records from incomplete information. In doing this we will come across unidentified payments and drawings which must be dealt with in some logical manner. We also need to examine how to prepare accounting records and financial statements from the information and explanations.

One way is to start with the opening balance sheet and then prepare the cash book and petty cash book. To do this, use is made of cheque books and paying-in books as well as any cash vouchers that may exist.

Once these have been prepared the ledger entries are made and after all the postings have been completed, the accounts can be prepared, using the opening balances from the balance sheet of the previous year.

24.3 Calculating the trading results

Even with incomplete records, we may still need to calculate our purchases and sales so that we are able to assess the gross profit of the business. To do these calculations we need a list of receipts and payments. These can usually be obtained from the cash book or bank statement.

Once the lists are established we then need to identify receipts relating to sales and payments in connection with purchases. Naturally, any payments for other expenses and for capital expenditure must be excluded.

24.3.1 Worked example

In this example we want to calculate the sales for the year. Even with incomplete records we can establish the following:

Debtors' balances at 1 January 2009	6,580
Debtors' balances at 31 December 2009	7,345
Receipts from debtors during the year	47,200

To calculate sales we do the following:

Receipts	47,200
Less balances 1 January	6,580
	40,620
Plus balances 31 December	7,345
Sales for the year	£47,965

We looked at missing figures in the chapter on control accounts (see Chapter 10) and it would be useful if you re-read that chapter at this stage.

A similar method of calculation is used in determining purchases. The following example illustrates this:

Creditors' balances at 1 January 2009	9,300
Creditors' balances at 31 December 2009	6,135
Payments to creditors during the year	£51,320

To calculate purchases we do the following:

Payments	51,320
Less balances 1 January	9,300
	42,020
Plus balances 31 December	6,135
Purchases for the year	£48,155

24.4 Financial statements

In order to prepare the financial statements for a business we normally require a trial balance setting out all the balances at year end. When we have incomplete records we often have very limited data from which to build our financial statements.

By working through the many self-test questions in this chapter you will see the logical ways in which information for the financial statements can be obtained.

24.4.1 Worked example

In the following example we will examine such a case.

Statement of assets and liabilities at	1 January 09	31 December 09
Office fixtures at cost	3,500	3,500
Stock (as valued)	1,060	1,300
Debtors	6,580	7,345
Bank balance (from bank statement)	8,195	210
Total assets	19,335	12,355
Creditors	9,300	6,135
Net worth = Capital balance	£10,035	£6,220

We have been given details of the receipts from debtors and payments to creditors. From those details we have established the purchases and sales figures (see section 24.3.1 above).

We are also able to determine that payments for expenses during the year totalled £1,765 and drawings by the owner were £2,100.

We are told that the owner wants to depreciate his office fixtures by 10 per cent p.a.

From what seems very little information we are now able to construct the financial statements.

**Trading and profit and loss account for the year ended
31 December 2009**

Sales		47,965
Opening stock	1,060	
Purchases	48,155	
	49,215	
Less closing stock	1,300	
Cost of goods sold		47,915
Gross profit		50
Expenses	1,765	
Depreciation	350	2,115
Net loss for the year		£2,065

We can now prepare the balance sheet. We know from the opening statement that the capital account at 1 January is £10,035.

Balance sheet as at 31 December 2009

Fixed assets at cost	3,500	
Less depreciation	350	
		3,150
Stock	1,300	
Debtors	7,345	
Bank	210	8,855
		12,005
Less creditors		6,135
		£5,870
Capital at 1 January	10,035	
Drawings	2,100	7,935
Net loss		2,065
		£5,870

24.4.2 Self-test

Eve started a business with £18,000 of her own money. In addition she made use of a loan given by her uncle. This loan of £5,000 was deposited into the business bank account.

Using the money available she purchased office equipment for the business. The total cost of the equipment was £10,000.

What is the amount of her capital in the business?

24.4.3 Self-test

The following is a summary of the net assets of William.

(i) At 1 January 2009 he had assets of £65,000 and liabilities of £11,000.
(ii) On 31 December 2009 the assets amounted to £83,000 and the liabilities to £14,000.

During the year William withdrew £10,000. What is the profit for the year?

24.4.4 Self-test

On 1 January 2009 Todd had debtors owing him £17,400. During the year he received payments totalling £89,300. Todd gave discounts of £4,940 to the debtors.

At 31 December 2009 the balance on the debtors' ledger was £19,740.

Calculate the sales for the year.

24.4.5 Self-test

Sheila presented you with the following information:

(i) At 1 January 2009 she had assets of £70,000 and liabilities of £7,300.
(ii) At 31 December 2009 assets were £90,000 and creditors for goods purchased amounted to £8,700.

During the year Sheila was given a bank overdraft fixed for two years. At 31 December 2009 the balance was £17,000.

Sheila had drawings of £11,300 during the year.

You are required to determine the profit for the year.

24.4.6 Self-test

You are given the following information relating to assets and liabilities of J Jones for the 2009 year.

Assets and liabilities	1 January	31 December
Equipment at cost	3,000	3,000
Stock	2,550	3,600
Debtors	2,130	2,490
Creditors	1,620	1,680
Bank balance	480	420

During the year there were a number of transactions, all of which were entered into the bank account. A summary of these is as follows:

Receipts from debtors	20,670
Payments to creditors	9,600
Payments for trade expenses	5,430
Drawings	5,700

The equipment is depreciated annually at 10 per cent of its cost.

You are required to calculate the capital account of J Jones at 1 January 2009 and the profit and loss account and balance sheet for the year to 31 December 2009.

24.4.7 Self-test

Alice maintains limited records. At 31 December 2008 her balance sheet was as follows:

Balance sheet at 31 December 2008			
Delivery vehicles (cost £47,000)			29,470
Office equipment (cost £30,000)			26,740
			56,210
Stock	11,250		
Debtors	29,390		
Prepaid insurance	1,033		
Bank	7,840	49,513	
Creditors	7,320		
Wages accrued	1,403	8,723	40,790
			97,000
Capital – Alice			97,000

The following is a record of bank transactions for the year:

Cash sales	32,380
Debtors' payments	41,906
Additional capital paid in	5,800
Loan from Fry on 1 July 2009	10,000
Payment to creditors	49,320
Cash purchases	20,006
Wages	11,310
Motor expenses	8,670
Insurance	8,931
Bank charges	1,004

In addition Alice has taken cash from her sales before depositing it into the bank. She prepared a summary of those takings.

Drawings	21,010
Motor repairs	4,031
Cash purchases	1,610

The following additional information is also available at 31 December 2009:

(i)	Closing stock	13,210
(ii)	Debtors	31,047
(iii)	Creditors	8,240
(iv)	Insurance prepaid	924
(v)	Wages not yet paid	643
(vi)	The loan bears interest at 10% p.a.	
(vii)	Depreciation is calculated as follows:	
	(a) Vehicles 10% on reducing balance	
	(b) Office equipment 5% straight line	

You are required to prepare the profit and loss account and balance sheet for the year ending 31 December 2009.

24.4.8 Self-test

Balance sheet of Miro at 31 July 2009

Land and buildings (at cost)		45,000
Fixtures and fittings (cost £20,000)		14,800
		59,800
Stock	6,300	
Debtors	8,120	
Telephone prepaid	416	
Bank	6,000	
	20,836	
Creditors	6,140	
Electricity accrued	496	
	6,636	14,200
		74,000
Capital		74,000

The only record kept by Miro is a cash book in which all transactions that pass through the bank account are recorded.

A summary of the cash book for the year ended 31 July 2010 is as follows:

Cash book summary			
Balance b/d	6,000	Wages	7,301
Cash sales	14,310	Telephone	420
Payments from debtors	40,014	Electricity	680
Additional capital	4,000	Motor expenses	1,904
		Payments to creditors	32,061
		Printing	600
		Purchases	5,314
		Balance c/d	16,044
	64,324		64,324
Balance b/d	16,044		

From the supporting documents it has been ascertained that the following amounts were paid from the cash takings before they were banked:

Drawings	6,000
Purchases	1,803
Car repairs	1,002
Printing	210
Total	9,015

Additional information:

(i) Stock at 31 July 2010 was valued at £4,130.
(ii) At 31 July 2010 there are telephone charges prepaid of £240 and electricity accrued of £490.
(iii) The trade debtors and trade creditors outstanding at the end of the year are £6,840 and £5,930 respectively.
(iv) Miro has taken goods that cost £710 from the business for his own use.
(v) Fixtures and fittings are to be depreciated at 20 per cent per annum using the reducing balance method.

You are required to prepare a trading and profit and loss account for the year ended 31 July 2010 and a balance sheet at that date.

24.4.9 Self-test

Nadia owns a retail shop. The trading and profit and loss account and balance sheet are prepared annually by you from records consisting of a bank statement and a file of unpaid suppliers and outstanding debtors.

The following balances were shown on her balance sheet at 1 January 2009:

Creditors	937
Shop fittings (cost £1,800) at written down value	490
Stock in hand	535
Debtors	107
Cash at bank	192

The following is a summary of her bank statement for the year ended 31 December 2009:

Debtors' payments banked	7,430
Payments to suppliers	6,024
Rent of premises to 31 December 2009	800
Sundry expenses	44
Advertising	72
Repairs	94

You obtain the following additional information:

(i)   Stock in hand at 31 December 2009 was £1,021.
(ii) Debtors' payments are banked daily. Nadia withdraws £100 per week for herself, and pays her assistant £52 per week prior to banking any payments from debtors.
(iii) Amounts outstanding are: £630 due to suppliers, £24 due in respect of sundry expenses, and £103 outstanding debtors.
(iv) Nadia took £130 worth of goods for her own use without payment.
(v)   Depreciation on shop fittings is provided at 10 per cent of cost.

You are required to prepare Nadia's trading and profit and loss account for the year ended 31 December 2009, and her balance sheet as at that date.

Note: All weekly amounts are paid for 52 weeks.

24.4.10 Self-test

Monica keeps some basic records of her business activities, but requires you to prepare a balance sheet for her at the year end. She also wants to know what her profit was for the year.

The balance sheet information as at 1 April 2009 is as follows:

Creditors	2,901
Shop fittings (cost £6,200) at written down value	3,800
Stock in hand	4,090
Debtors	3,021
Cash at bank	1,064

The following is a summary of her bank statement transactions for the year ended 31 March 2010:

Bank charges	102
Repairs	194
Salaries to staff	3,040
Payments to suppliers	5,094
Rent for the year	1,021
Cash sales banked	4,920
Debtors payments	9,874
9% loan from George	4,000

All the receipts are banked although Monica takes £400 per month from the cash sales before banking.

At the year end the stock on hand was £5,260 and amounts due to Monica totalled £4,063. Monica also owed suppliers £2,830.

She depreciated the shop fittings at 10 per cent p.a. using the straight line method of depreciation.

The loan from George was given on 1 June 2009.

Chapter 25

Accounting concepts

Objectives   After you have studied this chapter, you should be able to:

- explain the nature of accounting principles and concepts;
- explain the underlying concepts of accounting;
- describe the objectives against which a business judges if accounting policies are appropriate;
- describe the assumptions made when recording accounting data;
- explain what accounting standards are and why they exist.

25.1   Introduction

We have shown that accounts are prepared for various users. In preparing these accounts we must abide by certain rules and guidelines, called accounting concepts or accounting principles or conventions. These rules are used by accountants and are intended to maintain objective accounting.

Some principles are found in law (such as in the Companies Act) and in accounting standards (such as IFRS or FRS).[11] Because we all use the same rules when we prepare accounts, we know that we can rely on the information and that the way in which items are shown in the accounts will be the same for all businesses.

25.1.1 Objectivity

No personal bias must exist when we prepare accounts. Whatever is done in the accounts must be based on facts and not on an opinion. For example, if we buy a fixed asset on the last day of the year, then this asset would be shown in the balance sheet at cost.

This we know is a fact and is not our own interpretation on how we think the particular asset should be reflected in the accounts. As a result, any user of the accounts is able to be sure that the original figure came from a cost value and not some mythical estimate.

This means that objectivity is paramount in accounting so that financial statements show no bias and all users can accept them with confidence.

---

[11] These are International Financial Reporting Standards and Financial Reporting Standards.

25.2 Fundamental concepts

There are rules which lay down the way in which we record all transactions. It is these rules that are known as accounting concepts. These are broken down further and we have a group of accounting concepts that are known as the fundamental accounting concepts (or accounting principles), and these are incorporated into accounting standards (such as FRS 18 in the UK) issued by the various accountancy bodies.

Let us now look at these accounting rules in some detail.

The fundamental accounting concepts are:

- Going concern
- Consistency
- Prudence
- Accruals concept
- Separate determination
- Substance over form

We will discuss each of these concepts in more detail in the paragraphs below.

25.2.1 Going concern

This means that we assume the business is to continue trading in the future and therefore the value of the business is shown at cost less depreciation and not at a price that we would receive on a liquidation or forced sale. It should be noted that if the business were to be forced to close down, and the assets sold, it is likely they would realise a great deal less than the figure shown in the balance sheet.

25.2.2 Consistency

This means that we must treat similar items in the same way; for example, we depreciate all motor vehicles at a rate of 25 per cent per annum, straight line method. This rate and method would be applied year after year. Although we are allowed to change a method – for example, we can move from straight line depreciation to the reducing balance method – we cannot change every year and we must remain consistent.

25.2.3 Prudence

In preparing any financial statement we adopt a cautious approach. Using this approach we must ensure that the assets are not overvalued and that the liabilities are not understated. This practice is known as prudence. As a result, all anticipated losses and expenses are shown even if they are uncertain. For example, a provision for bad debts may need to be shown. Similarly revenue is not taken into account by anticipating an event. This recognition of profits is covered in an additional concept known as the realisation concept, which we discuss in section 25.3.7.

25.2.4 Accruals or matching

The accounts should show the revenues earned in an accounting period, matched against the costs involved in earning those revenues.

We record sales in the profit and loss account when they are earned and not when we receive the money. This also applies to expenses, which we disclose when they are incurred and not when we pay for them.

25.2.5 Separate valuation principle

Under this concept we are told that the amount of each individual asset or liability is to be determined separately from all other assets and liabilities. This means that an office which has, say, five computers will show the value of those computers by calculating the value of each one individually and the asset figure, as it appears in the balance sheet, will be the sum of all five. As a result of this concept we are not able to hide any possible liabilities by netting off a liability against an asset. The only time this is done is where a provision for depreciation or a provision for bad debts is deducted from the relevant asset.

25.2.6 Substance over form

On occasion, the legal form of a transaction differs from the real substance, i.e. how the transaction affects the economic situation of the business. The rule here is that we treat transactions according to the real substance of the transaction and not the legal form.

A common example often used to illustrate this concept is when we buy a car under a hire purchase agreement. The legal view is that the car is not an asset of the business until all moneys owed under the agreement have been paid. When we prepare a set of accounts, we show the car as an asset, with a corresponding liability for outstanding amounts, as this is the economic view (the substance) of the transaction.

25.3 Other concepts

In addition to the fundamental concepts there are further accounting concepts which are not incorporated into accounting standards but which, nevertheless, are adopted and applied in financial statements through good accounting practice.

These concepts are listed and discussed below.

25.3.1 Historical cost

This concept deals with the way in which valuation is undertaken. If the value is based on the amount actually paid, it is objective and verifiable. As an example, it means that a fixed asset is normally shown at its cost less accumulated depreciation.

Shortcomings are that it is argued that by placing a historical cost value on assets no allowance is made for the changing value of money or for reflecting the current value of the resources available to the business. All this prevents a meaningful calculation of ratios (see Chapter 32).

For this reason the historical cost rule is not always applied and the Companies Act allows assets (especially property) to be accounted for at market value rather than at its historical cost.

25.3.2 Money measurement

Items are only shown in the accounts if they can be measured in money terms. As a result of this concept we cannot expect to be able to read in the financial statements about the quality of the management of a business, nor if the labour workforce is properly trained. We may be able to infer this from some indicators, but there can be no monetary value placed on any positive aspects, nor can there be a deduction in monetary terms for any negative situation.

25.3.3 Business entity

A business is separate from the owner and all transactions must be recorded this way.

Only business revenue and expenditure is recorded in the books of account and not private items. When, however, the owner introduces new capital or withdraws capital this is recorded within the business records.

25.3.4 Dual aspect (duality)

The concept is a simple one. It illustrates the two aspects of accounting and states that assets are always equal to liabilities (including capital). This concept can be shown by the fact that for every debit entry there is a credit entry.

25.3.5 Time interval

The time interval concept states that financial statements are prepared at regular intervals (usually annually). When management accounts are required these are usually prepared at more frequent intervals, such as monthly or quarterly.

25.3.6 Materiality

Any item appearing in the financial statements is governed by one major rule which is that the item should be material to that business. If the exclusion of an item would mislead users, then it is material. If the item is not material, then it is better to exclude it as otherwise the report is cluttered and makes for difficult reading. No useful purpose is served by adding non-material items into the financial statements. An example would be where we have a printer cartridge not yet used. No purpose is served in deducting the cost of that cartridge from the total stationery account for the year and treating the unused cartridge as a prepayment – it is not material.

In many businesses materiality is determined by a monetary amount. We may say that any item under £100 is not material to the financial statements of that firm. In a large multinational business, the amount may be set at £10,000 or even higher.

25.3.7 Realisation

This is often said not to be a separate concept but an addition to or part of the prudence concept. We only show items in any account if it has been realised. One important aspect of this is that we only recognise profits when the goods pass to the customer who accepts liability to pay for the goods. We do not inflate any value in the balance sheet, nor do we show profit if it is not yet realised. We saw in the prudence concept that in regard to assets, we err on the side of caution.

25.4 Qualitative characteristics – a summing up

It is a fixed rule that all accounts must have certain characteristics. These are:

- Relevance – the information must be relevant.
- Reliability – the information must be free from error or bias.
- Comparability – the same types of items are treated in the same way for measurement.
- Understandability – the accounts must be clear and be able to be understood by users.
- Materiality – only items that are significant are shown and therefore, if not material, they can be ignored.

Whenever you are required to prepare accounts, be sure that you take notice of the concepts detailed in the paragraphs above. These rules, or guidelines, must be used in the preparation of the final accounts. They have evolved over time and have been adopted for practical rather than theoretical purposes. The application of these concepts is often subjective and relies on a question of judgement. Remember that accounting is not a science!

25.4.1 Self-test

The table below lists various adjustments that need to be made to a trial balance prior to the preparation of financial statements.

You are required to state the relevant accounting concept that applies to each item listed below.

An amount of £4,000 due from debtor A was written off as a bad debt.

Stock of £9,000 was written down to its net realisable value of £8,000.

£1,000 paid for private travel was debited to drawings.

Motor vehicles were depreciated at 20% of cost.

£2,100 insurance was paid for the following financial year.

A computer mouse was written off as an expense even though it could last 3–5 years.

The DIY business has staff to show customers how to operate certain tools. This is considered to be worth £50,000 but is not recorded in the books.

Depreciation is charged at 20% but we want to increase it to 25% for this year only.

25.4.2 Self-test

What is meant by the term fundamental concepts? Give three examples.

25.4.3 Self-test

All accounts must contain certain characteristics. This allows users to compare one business with another.

Describe four such characteristics.

25.5 The requirements of accounting standards

In the UK, FRSs[12] and SSAPs[13] are classed as accounting standards for purposes of the Companies Act 2006. The Act requires that company accounts are prepared in accordance with these standards and even goes so far as to state that a company must give details of any departure from any standard and the reasons for this departure. The accounting standards, therefore, add to the statutory (legal) requirements by setting out specific ways in which to account for various transactions. They deal with the measurement, recognition and disclosure of the transactions and as such they deal with greater detail than the Companies Act.

We will see in later chapters that companies can be complex and that they are either a private company or a public company. In the case of the latter it could be a listed company or not. In addition, a number of companies can form themselves into a group. This group of companies may consist of a holding company and one or more subsidiary companies. Groups publish 'consolidated accounts' which add the results of the individual companies together.

---

[12] Financial Reporting Standards have been issued since 1990 by the Accounting Standards Board (ASB).

[13] Statements of Standard Accounting Practice. These were issued between 1970 and 1990. Many have been withdrawn or replaced by FRSs. For more details see www.frc.org.uk.

You can see that as accounts become more complex the understanding of them becomes ever increasingly difficult. We need ask ourselves a number of important questions:

■ Do users understand what is being communicated to them in the accounts?
■ Is the accounting information in the accounts relevant to the user's needs?

Accounting standards help in one major respect. They ensure that a user is able to rely on the information and is able to compare the information of company A with that of company B and know that both sets of accounts have been prepared in an identical manner.

Standards provide guidelines in many areas. Examples are cash flow statements, accounting policies and research and development expenses.

In an effort to promote international harmonisation, the adoption of international accounting standards has been gaining force. Today, all listed companies in the European Union, as well as companies in many other countries, have adopted international standards. As this topic is a new one being introduced into the syllabus, an additional chapter is included to cover it (see Chapter 41).

25.5.1 Self-test

Define, and illustrate with an example, the use of each of the following accounting concepts:

(i)   Going concern
(ii)   Consistency
(iii) Prudence
(iv)   Accrual
(v)   Historical cost
(vi)   Materiality
(vii) Dual aspect

(ABE, Introduction to Accounting, December 2009)

Chapter 26

Partnerships

Objectives   After you have studied this chapter, you should be able to:

- explain the differences between a sole trader and a partnership;
- prepare final accounts for a partnership;
- understand the need for a goodwill adjustment;
- make the necessary entries for partnership goodwill.

26.1 Introduction

Businesses are classified according to their form of ownership. We have discussed in earlier chapters the sole trader. In the following chapters we will focus on businesses owned by a partnership as well as those owned by limited companies. In so doing we will see what, if any, differences arise in the preparation of financial statements.

Before we move to that area it is useful to remind ourselves of the ownership of a business by a sole trader.

26.2 Sole trader

In all the earlier chapters we have dealt with a single (sole) trader. Here a business is owned by one person. Under this form of ownership the following points apply:

- a single owner provides capital and has total control;
- the owner is entitled to all profits earned;
- the owner is personally liable for income tax;
- the owner is personally responsible for all debts of the business and is said to have unlimited liability; and
- the owner can sue or can be sued.

From the above we can see that legally the owner and the business are one and the same, i.e. the owner is the legal entity. The business can be set up with very few legal restrictions and there are no legal requirements to publish financial statements although the business must produce annual accounts for the Inland Revenue authorities.

The big problem of a sole trader is that it is difficult for a business to grow beyond a certain size. This is because of the difficulties of control, finance and supervision. Ownership needs to be divided and from this we can conclude that a team of owners can expand a business.

We move, then, to the simplest form of 'combined' ownership, which is the partnership.

26.3 Partnership

This is when two or more people own a business jointly. This is quite common, especially in professional practices. It is important to note that not all partnerships are small in size and it must not be thought that a partnership indicates a small business.

It is quite a simple process to set up a partnership and, unlike a company, where there are fixed regulations, little formality exists.

Under this form of ownership certain points apply. These can be described as:

- No formal agreement is required although it is usual to have a written partnership agreement as set out in section 26.5 below. It should be noted that in the absence of such an agreement, the Partnership Act of 1890 applies.[14]
- Partners are entitled to a share of the profits, in proportion to an agreed ratio.
- Each partner is an agent for the partnership, which means that each partner can enter contracts and otherwise commit the partnership.
- Risk is shared – each partner is 'jointly and severally liable' for all the debts of the partnership – i.e. if one partner is unable to pay his or her share of the debt, the other partner will have to pay this, as well as their own share.
- There is no legal requirements to disclose financial information to the public, but specific accounting records must be maintained.
- The death of a partner effectively means the dissolution (end) of the partnership.

26.4 Accounting for partnerships

Partnership accounts are similar to those of a sole trader but with one important exception – the profits have to be shared between partners. It is also important that the capital accounts of each partner are shown and recorded separately. The capital account of each partner is similar to that of a sole proprietor. Fixed amounts are introduced into the business and these amounts are credited to the partners' capital accounts.

	A	B			A	B
			Capital accounts			
			Bank		23,000	18,000

[14] This Act states that in the absence of a partnership agreement, the profits and losses will be shared equally.

Profits (and losses) of a partnership are divided between partners. The way in which the division is made depends on the partnership agreement. It may be that each partner shares equally in profits and losses, or there may be some other percentage allocation. The addition of profits, interest on capital and salaries are credited to a current account of the partner concerned. Unlike the sole proprietor, the partners each have a current account and not a drawings account. This current account also records drawings made by a partner.

		Current accounts				
	A	B		A	B
Drawings	2,100	1,900	Interest	300	200
Balance c/d	10,200	13,300	Salary	5,000	8,000
			Profit share	7,000	7,000
	12,300	15,200		12,300	15,200
			Balance b/d	10,200	13,300

Often interest is credited to capital accounts – this is especially the case where the capital accounts are not equal. In some cases interest is charged on drawings. This is the amount taken by the partners in anticipation of profits and is debited to the partners' current accounts.

At the year, or period, end, the capital account and current account of each partner must be shown. While the capital account reflects the amount each partner has invested in the partnership, the current account records the share of profit (or loss) and drawings made by each partner.

26.5	**Partnership agreement**

All partnerships enter into an agreement which is designed to regulate the way in which the business affairs are conducted. The agreement usually states the amount of capital that each partner will contribute. In addition, it states whether interest is given on the capital amount and at what rate.

During the year, partners are allowed to draw out money in anticipation of their share of profits. The agreement would state the limits on drawings, and if interest is charged on these drawings and the rate. Certain partners are entitled to salaries and this is also covered in the agreement.

Finally the agreement states the way in which profits (or losses) are shared amongst the partners.

26.5.1 Worked example

Green and White are in partnership. Their agreement states that interest is given on capital accounts at the rate of 10 per cent p.a. As White works for the business, a salary of £6,000 is paid to him before the profits are shared on the basis of 80 per cent to Green and 20 per cent to White.

The business shows a net profit of £30,000 for the year prior to any payments to the partners. You are required to make all the necessary apportionments to give effect to the partnership agreement.

You are told that the capital accounts are Green £80,000 and White £20,000.

Net profit				30,000
Interest:	Green	8,000		
	White	2,000	10,000	
Salary	White		6,000	16,000
Apportionment of profit				14,000
	Green	11,200		
	White	2,800		14,000

Current accounts

	Green	White		Green	White
Balance c/d	19,200	10,800	Interest	8,000	2,000
			Salary		6,000
			Profit share	11,200	2,800
	19,200	10,800		19,200	10,800
			Balance b/d	19,200	10,800

26.6 Profit and loss appropriation account

You will see in the worked example above that there were adjustments made after the net profit had been calculated. These adjustments were appropriations of the net profit.

There are a few rules relating to partnerships which must be observed:

- Each partner has his/her own capital account as well as a current account and drawings account.
- The capital account is usually a fixed amount and no additional entries are made to this account in any year.
- All adjustments for interest, salary and share of profit or loss are shown in the current account to which the drawings account is also transferred at the year end.
- If any loans are made by the partners to the partnership, then they are shown separately.
- Interest on these loans is shown in the profit and loss account before arriving at the net profit.
- From the net profit all debits and credits are appropriations of it. The appropriations shown are interest on drawings, current accounts and capital accounts, salaries to partners and allocation of net profit, or loss.

26.6.1 Self-test

Smith and Jones decided to go into partnership and that they would contribute £30,000 and £20,000 respectively. It was agreed that Jones would work in the business and receive a salary of £5,000 p.a. Interest of 10 per cent p.a. was to be allowed on the capital accounts and the partners were to share the remaining profit in the ratio of 60 per cent for Smith and 40 per cent for Jones.

The business makes a profit of £140,000 in the first year. Show the amount to be credited to each partner.

26.6.2 Self-test

Dun and Swail are equal partners. The partnership agreement provides for annual salaries of Dun, £24,000 and Swail, £23,000. It also provides for interest on capital of 7 per cent per annum and interest on drawings of 3 per cent per annum.

The following information relates to the accounting year ending 30 June 2010:

	Dun	Swail
Capital at 1 July 2009	120,000	80,000
Current account at 1 July 2009	23,850	11,490
Drawings – 1 October 2009	6,000	4,000
– 1 March 2010	7,000	3,000
Capital introduced – 1 November 2009	24,000	
– 1 February 2010		36,000

The net profit shown in the profit and loss account for the year ended 30 June 2010 was £97,400.

You are required to prepare the profit and loss appropriation account, capital and current accounts at 30 June 2010.

26.6.3 Self-test

X and Y prepare their annual accounts to 31 December. Interest on drawings is charged at 10 per cent p.a. while interest of 8 per cent p.a. is allowed on capital account balances. X receives a salary of £18,000 p.a. The profit or loss is shared in the ratio of 2:3.

At 1 January 2009 the balances are:

	X	Y
Capital account	£85,000 credit.	£60,000 credit.
Current account	£11,000 credit.	£8,000 credit.

The net profit to 31 December 2009 is £80,000.

The partners' drawings during the year were:

X	Y
£12,000	£10,000

You are required to prepare the appropriation account as well as the ledger accounts of both partners' current accounts.

26.6.4 Self-test

Lane and Hill have decided to form a partnership. Lane is to contribute £150,000 as capital and Hill £20,000.

Hill is to work full-time in the business and Lane, one day a week. Because Hill has no other income, she anticipates making drawings of £1,000 per month from the partnership.

Lane expects to make drawings of about £1,000 per quarter (every three months).

Using the information above, explain the difference between each of the following ledger accounts in the books of a partnership:

(a) capital account;
(b) current account;
(c) drawings.

26.6.5 Self-test

Black and Whyte share profits in the ratio of 7:3. The balances on the capital accounts at 1 June 2009 were:

Black	300,000
Whyte	180,000

The partners' current account balances (credits) as at 1 June 2009 were:

Black	20,000
Whyte	14,000

During the year ended 31 May 2010 the partners made the following drawings from the partnership bank account:

Black

Amount	Date of drawing
£12,000	31 July 2009
£10,000	30 November 2009
£12,000	31 March 2010
£13,000	31 May 2010

Whyte

Amount	Date of drawing
£6,000	31 July 2009
£2,000	30 November 2009
£6,000	31 March 2010
£3,000	31 May 2010

Interest is charged on drawings at the rate of 10 per cent per annum, while interest of 6 per cent per annum is allowed on capital accounts and credit balances on current accounts. Whyte is allowed a salary of £25,000 per annum.

The net profit of the partnership for the year ended 31 May 2010 is £126,700.

You are required to prepare the partnership appropriation account for the year ended 31 May 2010.

You are also required to show the current account of each partner as at 31 May 2010.

26.6.6 Self-test

The partnership agreement of North, East and West stipulates that profits should be apportioned in the ratio of 3:2:1 after allowing interest on capital at 6 per cent per annum and crediting North with a salary of £28,000.

The following information relates to their first financial year which ended on 31 July 2010.

The partners introduced the following amounts as capital on 1 August 2009:

North	60,000
East	50,000
West	40,000

Cash drawings during the year were:

North	7,000
East	6,300
West	5,100

The profit and loss account for the year shows a net profit before any partner adjustments of £72,400.

No entries had been made in the accounts to record the following:

(i) During the year North had taken goods for his own use. The cost of those goods was £2,100.
(ii) Included in the travelling expenses account for the year was a payment of £650, which related to East's private travelling expenses.

You are required to prepare a revised profit and loss account for the year ended 31 July 2010, to include all partnership adjustments.

The partners have agreed to fix their capital accounts at the amounts originally contributed. All other transactions are recorded in their current accounts.

You also are asked to show the current ledger accounts for each partner at 31 July 2010.

26.6.7 Self-test

The following is the trial balance of Jack and Jill as at 31 December 2009.

Capital: Jack		20,000
Capital: Jill		15,000
Current account: Jack	1,900	
Current account: Jill	4,100	
Purchases/sales	44,823	71,460
Debtors/creditors	6,507	6,561
Building at cost	22,000	
Fixtures at book value	7,150	
Salaries	6,004	
Electricity	2,103	
Stationery	460	
Bank interest and charges	64	
Stock	6,890	
Bank	4,020	
Drawings – Jack 1 July 2009	4,000	
– Jill 1 September 2009	3,000	
	113,021	113,021

Additional information:

(i)   Stock at 31 December 2009 was valued at £13,813.

(ii) Electricity accrued at the end of the year – £95.

(iii) Depreciation on fixtures for the year is £1,600.

The partnership agreement provides that each partner is to be credited with interest on capital at 9 per cent per annum and charged interest on any current account debit balances at 5 per cent p.a. No interest is charged on drawings during the year.

Salaries are to be provided of £8,000 per annum for Jack and £6,800 per annum for Jill. The remainder of the profit is to be divided equally between the partners. All adjustments are made to the current account as the capital account is fixed.

You are required to prepare the profit and loss account and appropriation account for the year and a balance sheet at 31 December 2009. Your workings must include the current accounts of the partners.

26.6.8 Self-test

Mike and Jean are partners in a gift business. The agreement they have is that profits are shared equally, but interest is paid on their capital accounts.

The trial balance of Mike and Jean for the year ended 31 December 2009 is as follows:

Fittings and fixtures	22,000	
Accumulated depreciation		6,600
Debtors	38,700	
Creditors		21,400
Bank	6,512	
Stock	93,460	
Purchases	195,220	
Sales		298,715
General expenses	6,448	
Salaries and wages	43,309	
Bad debts	1,912	
Provision for doubtful debts		900
Capital account – Mike		67,000
Capital account – Jean		41,000
Current account – Mike		3,144
Current account – Jean		1,102
Drawings – Mike	15,800	
Drawings – Jean	16,500	
	439,861	439,861

The following adjustments have still to be made:

(i) Closing stock of £132,880.
(ii) Partnership salary to Mike £2,600.
(iii) Interest on drawings, Mike £460 and Jean £340.
(iv) Interest on capital at 10 per cent p.a.

You are required to prepare the profit and loss account and balance sheet for the year.

26.7 Changes in the partnership

Any changes, be it a withdrawal of a partner, the change in profit and loss sharing ratios, or the admission of a new partner, results in the termination of the existing partnership and the creation of a new partnership. This is because a partnership, unlike a company, does not have perpetual succession.[15]

As a result two separate sets of accounts are prepared – the one when the partner leaves or ratios are changed or before a new partner is admitted – and the other at the end of the trading year.

An important aspect is the revaluation of assets at the date of change. At that date the capital accounts of the partners are equal to the net worth of the partnership.

---

[15] In a winding-up the firm is dissolved and the partners do not carry on in the same way as before. In this case assets are realised, creditors paid and any surplus is divided among the partners.

This net worth is determined by placing a current value on assets and liabilities. Any increase (or decrease) is transferred to the capital accounts of the partners in the proportion in which they share profits and losses (before any change).

	Kay	Dan			Kay	Dan
			Capital accounts			
			1/1/2010	Bal b/d	20,000	18,000
			2/1/2010	Revalue	4,500	4,500

Prior to revaluation net worth of partnership = £38,000.

After revaluation on 2/1/2010 the net worth increases to £47,000.

Kay and Dan share profits (and losses) equally. Therefore the increase in value of the partnership must have £4,500 credited to each account.

If a new partner is to be admitted, then there is the need to determine the goodwill of the old partnership. This is not usually shown in the books and so each of the old partners have their capital account credited with their share of goodwill.

The new partner can either pay for his/her share of goodwill, or a new goodwill account is opened and the original partners are credited with their share of that goodwill with a corresponding debit to the goodwill account.

Other changes can be the sale of a partnership to a company or an amalgamation of partnerships. From an accounting point of view the balance sheets of the two (or more) partnerships are added together after the adjustment to partner capital accounts for goodwill or the revaluation of assets. Sometimes certain assets are not taken over and these are then adjusted accordingly.

26.7.1 Worked example

At 31 December 2008 a partnership between Ell and Emm existed. They shared profits and losses in the ratio of 3:2. They agreed that because Ell was going to take some time off from the partnership, the ratio would be amended as from the beginning of January 2009 to 2:2.

The annual balance sheet was prepared at 31 December 2008 and the following information was contained in this balance sheet:

Office equipment		9,600
Motor vehicles		3,500
		13,100
Current assets		
Stock	4,860	
Debtors	2,520	
Cash at bank	1,040	
	8,420	
Creditors	1,920	6,500
		19,600
Capital account Ell	11,760	
Emm	7,840	19,600

The partners agree that they will revalue the office equipment at £8,000 and the motor vehicles at £2,000. All the other assets and liabilities are as per the balance sheet.

The first step is to credit the office equipment account with £1,600 and to credit motor vehicles with £1,500. These amounts represent the decrease in value of the assets. The corresponding debit of £3,100 is to be posted to the capital accounts of the partners in their old profit and loss sharing ratio, i.e. £1,860 to Ell and £1,240 to Emm.

Office equipment

31 Dec 08	Balance b/d	9,600	1 Jan 09	Revaluation	1,600
				Balance c/d	8,000
		9,600			9,600
1 Jan 09	Balance c/d	8,000			

Motor vehicles

31 Dec 08	Balance b/d	3,500	1 Jan 09	Revaluation	1,500
				Balance c/d	2,000
		3,500			3,500
1 Jan 09	Balance c/d	2,000			

Revaluation account

1 Jan 09	Office equipment	1,600	1 Jan 09	Capital Ell	1,860
	Motor vehicles	1,500		Capital Emm	1,240
		3,100			3,100

26.7.2 Self-test

A and B share profits 3:2. A receives a salary of £20,000 p.a.

On 1 January 2009 the capital account balances were:

A	B
£17,000	£11,000.

On 1 July 2009, C was admitted as a partner and the profit sharing ratio was changed to 5:3:2.

(i)   C was to receive a salary of £16,000 p.a.
(ii) At that date, A transferred £5,000 from her capital account to a loan account and she was to receive interest on the loan of 8 per cent p.a. The interest was to be credited to her current account.
(iii) C brought in machinery to the partnership which was valued at £7,000.

On 31 December the balances (not taking into account any of the above) were:

Sales £14,000 p.m. × 12	168,000
Cost of sales	42,000
Rent	12,000
Wages	17,000
Office expenses	5,000

Machines are depreciated at 15 per cent p.a. using the reducing balance method. Assume that the gross profit percentage is fixed and that wages paid were £13,000 for the first 6 months and the balance for the remainder of the year.

You are required to prepare the trading, profit and loss account and appropriation account for the year.

Also prepare the current accounts for the partners at year end.

26.8 Limited liability partnership

A limited liability partnership (LLP), governed by the Limited Liability Partnership Act of 2000, includes many of the features of a normal partnership, but it also offers reduced personal responsibility for business debts. Unlike members of ordinary partnerships, the LLP itself is responsible for any debts that it incurs and not the individual partners. (In this way LLPs are similar to limited liability companies, in that it is a corporate body which has a continuing legal existence independent of its members.)

The LLP has increased administrative duties when compared to those of a partnership, but these extras are compensated for by creating the limited liability.

The requirements needed to establish an LLP is that it must have at least two members. The responsibilities and rights of all members would usually be laid out in a 'Deed of Partnership'. This document is a legally binding agreement between members and is similar to a partnership agreement, although it would nominate a 'Designated Member' who would be responsible for preparing the accounts and acting for the LLP if it is ultimately dissolved. In addition, the amount of capital each partner will inject into the business, their individual duties in the running of the business and the effects if a partner leaves the business are fully set out in this deed.

All profits in an LLP are divided between the members and, as is the case with partnerships, the tax liability falls on the individual members and not the partnership.

Chapter 27

Non-profit making organisations

Objectives

After you have studied this chapter, you should be able to:

- explain the differences between financial statements of sole traders and non-profit organisations;
- prepare receipts and payments accounts;
- prepare income and expenditure accounts for non-profit organisations;
- understand the need for special treatment of subscriptions and life membership;
- prepare balance sheets for non-profit organisations.

27.1 Introduction

The not-for-profit organisations in this group are charities, associations or clubs. Their main purpose is not to trade or make a profit but to operate for the benefit of the members. These organisations receive subscriptions to cover their annual overheads. Although there may be a small profit (surplus) at the year end, this is ploughed back into the organisations' funds for the following year.

As such they do not prepare a trading or profit and loss account but, as they still need to report to their members, they prepare either an income and expenditure account or a receipts and payments account.

The latter account is merely a summary of the cash book for the period and only tells members what transactions took place during the year. It is a simple account to prepare and as such does not cater for the disclosure of any assets or liabilities that the organisation may have at the year end.

Income and expenditure account for the year ended 31 December 2010			
Rent	1,500	Subscriptions	6,580
Salaries	1,200	Entrance fees	900
Meeting expenses	1,100		
Telephone and postage	600		
Surplus for the year	3,080		
	7,480		7,480

Many clubs and other associations have certain assets and liabilities – it may be office equipment, stock of badges, stock to be sold by the bar, club ties or even outstanding debtors, or there may be a liability to the printers for the cost of the report or for telephone rental or even rent.

As such, a balance sheet for the members disclosing these assets and liabilities is required. In addition, the members must also be shown what income and expenditure has been made during the year.

Thus an income and expenditure account is prepared together with a balance sheet at year end. The income and expenditure account is similar to the trading and profit and loss account although there is a slight variation in terminology – where we use 'net profit' in the profit and loss account we now use the term 'surplus of income over expenditure'. Conversely, where 'net loss' is shown, we use the words 'excess of expenditure over income'. The surplus, or deficit, in this account is transferred to the balance sheet where it is shown as part of the 'accumulated fund' which is the term used instead of capital account.

Although we have described these organisations as non-profit organisations, there are times when these organisations prepare a profit and loss account. This is when they run a club bar or undertake some project to make a profit. This may be a club dance or barbeque, where a trading and profit and loss account would be prepared. If it is a non-trading activity, such as a raffle, then the income is shown in the income and expenditure account with the costs of prize money or goods being deducted from that income.

In the following worked example you will see that the preparation of an income and expenditure account is very similar to that of a profit and loss account. Subscriptions due to a club would be shown as debtors for subscriptions and all forms of accruals and prepayments are taken into account.

	Subscriptions receivable				
1.1.10	Balance b/d	810	31.12.10	Cash received	6,340
31.12.10	Inc & exp account	5,730		Balance c/d	200
		6,540			6,540
1.1.11	Balance b/d	200			

In a club there is often the opportunity of paying for a life membership. The correct treatment would be to show the income over the approximate period of benefit to the member with the balance being recorded as a prepayment. In practice the amount is often shown in the year in which it is received. This practice of immediate recognition also applies to the payment for entrance fees to a club.

27.1.1 Worked example

The London Football Club has the following transactions during the year ending 31 December 2008:

Subscriptions for the year	3,547	
Arrear subscriptions	435	
Subscriptions for 2009	124	4,106
Donations received		1,680
Raffle ticket sales		3,500
Dance income		7,340
Total income for the year		16,626
Ground rental	4,800	
Wages for staff	3,750	
Repairs	520	9,070
Band costs for dance	1,800	
Food for dance	1,940	3,740
Telephone charges	310	
Postages	124	434
Raffle prizes		2,000
Total expenditure for year		15,244
Opening bank balance	1,950	
Income	16,626	18,576
Expenditure		15,244
Closing bank balance		3,232

While the table above would constitute an acceptable receipts and payment account it would not show the club assets and liabilities.

The following additional information is available:

(i)   The club training equipment is valued at £11,900 at 1 January 2008. It is depreciated at 15 per cent per annum.
(ii) The office equipment is valued at £5,430 at 1 January 2008 and it is depreciated at 10 per cent per annum.
(iii) Members still owe £1,980 for 2008 subscriptions. The arrears received in 2008 were all amounts due at 31 December 2007.
(iv) The club still has to pay £145 for repairs and £48 for telephone charges. Both these amounts were due at 31 December 2008.

The first step is to prepare a profit and loss account for the dance. This account would show income of £7,340 and expenditure of £3,740 which results in a net profit of £3,600 which is transferred to the income and expenditure account.

Dance			
Band	1,800	Receipts	7,340
Food	1,940		
Profit c/d	3,600		
	7,340		7,340
Inc & exp account	3,600	Profit b/d	3,600

Income and expenditure account for the year ended 31 December 2008

Income

Subscriptions (3,547 + 1,980)	5,527	
Profit from dance	3,600	
Raffle ticket income (3,500 – 2,000)	1,500	
Donations received	1,680	12,307
Expenditure		
Ground costs (9,070 + 145)	9,215	
Telephone charges (310 + 48)	358	
Postages	124	
Depreciation – training equipment	1,785	
Depreciation – office equipment	543	12,025
Surplus of income over expenditure		182

Having determined the surplus for the year the next process is to prepare the balance sheet for the members.

Balance sheet as at 31 December 2008

Fixed assets			
Training equipment	11,900	1,785	10,115
Office equipment	5,430	543	4,887
	17,330	2,328	15,002
Current assets			
Debtors	1,980		
Bank	3,232	5,212	
Current liabilities			
Creditors (145 + 48)	193		
Subscriptions in advance	124	317	4,895
			19,897
Accumulated fund			
Balance at 1 January 2008*	19,715		
Surplus for the year	182		19,897

* The opening balance in the accumulated fund is calculated by taking all opening balances at 1 January 2008. Assets are added together and all liabilities are deducted. This calculation uses the formula that we have discussed of assets – liabilities = capital. In this case capital is the accumulated fund at 1 January 2008. The calculation is as follows:

£11,900 (training equipment) + 5,430 (office equipment) + 435 (arrear subscriptions) + 1,950 (bank balance) = £19,715

You can see from this example that the preparation of these accounts is similar in some aspects to those you have done for a sole trader. As with a sole trader, accruals and prepayments are taken into account.

27.1.2 Self-test

The Valley Sports Club closes its financial year on 31 December. The following are the assets and liabilities of the club at year end:

	at 31.12.08	at 31.12.09
Exercise equipment	4,700	6,200
Cash at bank	1,900	11,080
Outstanding amounts: Telephone	48	65
Electricity	120	140
Rent	200	300
Purchases for restaurant unpaid	690	950
Restaurant stock	1,200	1,400

The following are the receipts and payments made for the year ended 31 December 2009:

Receipts	
Subscriptions	14,600
Raffle tickets sold	3,800
Restaurant sales	21,700
Payments	
Exercise equipment	3,100
Wages in restaurant	5,000
Raffle prizes	1,800
Printing	500
Rent	2,400
Electricity	700
Telephone	400
Repairs to equipment	620
Purchases for restaurant	16,400

You are required to prepare the income and expenditure account for the year and the balance sheet as at 31 December 2009.

As there is a trading section you are also required to prepare a trading account for that section.

27.1.3 Self-test

The Trainer Club prepares its accounts at 31 December each year. At 31 December 2008 the following was the balance sheet at that date:

Gym equipment	8,900
Bar stocks	1,200
Cash at bank	700
	10,800
Accumulated funds	10,800

The receipts for the year to 31 December 2009 were:

Subscriptions for the year	4,730
Subscriptions in advance	260
Bar sales	3,980
Raffle ticket sales	1,200
Competition fees	905

The payments for the year were:

Rent	2,000
Bar purchases	1,250
Wages for barman	800
Repairs to equipment	200
Postage and telephones	140

The bar stock at 31 December 2009 is £1,040 and the gym equipment is to be depreciated at 10 per cent p.a.

You are required to prepare the accounts at 31 December 2009 for submission to the members.

Chapter 28

Limited liability companies

Objectives

After you have studied this chapter, you should be able to:

- explain the meaning of limited liability;
- differentiate between private and public companies;
- differentiate between ordinary and preference shares;
- show how dividends are calculated and paid;
- understand the various terms – bonus shares, rights issue, reserves and debentures;
- discuss the process of issuing shares;
- prepare accounts to record a share issue.

28.1 Introduction

In the UK, the Companies Act 2006 requires that companies prepare annual accounts.[16] So far we have dealt with businesses in general and their ownership by sole proprietors or partnerships. We now move to businesses where ownership is held through limited companies.

28.2 The nature of limited companies

It is apparent from the discussion in the previous chapter that the partnership suffers from some severe drawbacks. This can be overcome by the creation of a limited company, which has a number of advantages:

- The company is a separate legal entity, distinct from its owners. The company, not the owners, can make contracts and incur debts, and can sue or be sued.
- Owners are shareholders in the company but are not necessarily involved in the day-to-day running of the business.
- The company is managed by directors, appointed by the owners or shareholders. These directors become caretakers of the shareholders' investment.
- The liability of shareholders for the debts of the company is limited to the amount of money invested.

[16] There are a number of exemptions for certain companies so it is no longer the case that all companies prepare annual accounts (www.companieshouse.gov.uk).

- It is the company that is liable for corporation tax on the profits.
- Profits are distributed to shareholders by way of dividends.
- The company is unaffected by any change of ownership.

To become incorporated there are a number of documents and regulations that need to be prepared. There are requirements that one or more shareholders must:

- own at least one share each;
- file a Memorandum and Articles of Association and register the company with the Registrar of Companies at Companies House; and
- appoint a director and a company secretary (a secretary is no longer required under CA 2006).

Once incorporated, the company must:

- hold an annual general meeting of all shareholders;
- submit annual returns to the Registrar of Companies; and
- comply with the rules and regulations of the Companies Act.

The statutory requirement is to prepare accounts annually in compliance with the Companies Act. The accounts must follow a strict format as set out in the Act. Once filed, these accounts are available for inspection by any member of the public. One special requirement is that the accounts are audited by an independent, registered auditor. It must be noted that this latter requirement does not apply to small companies.

Why do limited companies exist? We have seen the small sole trader with a modest capital. This trader has unlimited liability for all debts of the business and has little or no access to additional capital. As the business grows there is the need for additional capital and outside investors are needed to bring in their money, by buying equity in the business.

Limited companies are better able to raise capital and give investors some form of security. The capital of the company is divided into shares. The person investing becomes a shareholder and is a part-owner of the company. Limited liability means that shareholders have their liability for the debts of a company limited to the amount subscribed for shares.

The limitation of liability is a big plus as it means these outside investors, who in point of fact have no control on the day-to-day management of the business, have little risk and cannot lose more than the capital they have invested.

28.3 Private limited companies (Ltd)

This is by far the largest section of companies, outnumbering public companies in the UK by about 20 to 1. They are allowed to have up to 50 shareholders (this excludes employees and former employees). The public cannot be invited to subscribe for shares in these companies and they are not traded on the stock exchange. Shares cannot, therefore, be freely sold and the company is able to restrict a shareholder from transferring shares.

28.4 Public limited companies (Plc)

Public companies, on the other hand, can offer their shares to members of the public. These shares are usually traded on the stock exchange and are, therefore, more marketable than shares in a private company.

When an issue of ordinary shares is offered for sale (floated) on the market it is first advertised in what is called a prospectus. The investor will apply for shares, which are to be issued, and sends in his/her application money. The terms of the issue of a £1 share may be 25p on application and 25p on allotment, with additional calls thereafter. This means that when a potential shareholder applies for shares in the issue, the application money of 25p per share must be paid for all the shares applied for, even if, ultimately, the number is cut down because of oversubscription.

The board of the company will review the applications for their issue, and if it is oversubscribed (more applications for the shares than there are shares available) they will scale down applications by lottery or selection.

If a share issue is likely to be popular with the investing public it is possible to issue it at a premium (i.e. a £1 share can be issued for (say) £1.50). If 10,000 of such shares are issued, the ordinary share capital of the company is increased by £10,000 and a share premium of £5,000 is created. This is a capital reserve (see section 28.8) and is credited to an account called the 'share premium account'.

There are certain differences between the public company and the private company. Unlike the private company, a public company requires a minimum number of seven shareholders, with no maximum limit. Their shares and debentures (if any) are traded on the stock exchange with no restriction on transfer of ownership.

In all companies, directors are responsible for the day-to-day running of the business and are appointed by the shareholders at a general meeting. Each year they report on their stewardship to the annual general meeting of shareholders and submit audited accounts together with their annual reports.

28.5 Share capital

In a partnership the partners introduce capital in order to finance the business. In a similar way a company is financed by capital. The difference here is that it is termed share capital and not simply capital. In examinations there is often confusion as to what is meant by the various terms relating to capital and, therefore, the following summary is inserted as an aid to understanding the terminology used.

Called-up capital	In some instances only part of the amount of the issued share capital has been asked for – called up. For example, if a £1 share has been issued and the investor has been asked to pay in 80p at this stage then that is the called-up amount.
Uncalled capital	The remaining amount of 20p, from the above example, would be the uncalled amount. This indicates that the total due is £1, but part of it has not yet been called.

Calls in arrear	Payment is required for shares issued as and when called for. If payment is not made when due then it becomes a call in arrears. For example, if the 80p had not been paid in full (say only 55p had been paid), then the called-up capital would show 80p and calls in arrear would show 25p.
Paid-up capital	The total share capital paid for by investors (shareholders) is shown and called the paid-up share capital.

28.5.1 Authorised share capital

When a company is formed it must state in its Memorandum and Articles of Association how many shares of each class it may wish to issue. This becomes that company's authorised capital and is the maximum amount that it is legally allowed to raise by a share issue. Naturally this sum varies from company to company.

There is no need for the company to issue all of its shares at once, hence the need in the balance sheet to state how many shares have been authorised and how many have actually been issued. All too often this important division within the balance sheet is omitted in examinations.

28.5.2 Issued share capital

The issued share capital is the amount of each class of share issued to shareholders. As this amount can never exceed the authorised capital it means that if a company wishes to raise extra share capital it would need to increase its authorised capital. This can be done with the agreement of shareholders at a general meeting.

28.5.3 Worked example

Alter plc has an authorised capital of 500,000 ordinary shares of £1 each.

It issues a prospectus offering shares to the public. As a result 350,000 shares are issued.

The company requires shareholders to pay in a total amount of 75p per share. All payments due have been made, except for a shareholder holding 20,000 shares. In this instance only the amount of 55p per share, due on application, was paid.

You are asked to complete the following table (answers and computation are shown in this example):

Authorised capital	£500,000
Issued capital	£350,000
Called-up capital	£262,500 (350,000 × 75p)
Calls in arrears	£4,000 (20,000 × 20p)
Uncalled capital	£87,500 (350,000 × 25p)
Paid up capital	£258,500 (350,000 − 87,500 = 262,500 − 4,000)

28.5.4 Types of shares

Ordinary shares

These are issued to the owners of the company and give the shareholders voting rights. Therefore, the shareholders can appoint and dismiss the directors and vote on all resolutions of the company.

Although ordinary shareholders (as opposed to preference shareholders) take the greater risk, they do have a right to a share of the profit or loss, and the return of capital should there be any money left in the event of a winding-up. When a business ceases, the assets are sold and the funds are used to repay the business liabilities. Only when all other claims have been paid will the shareholders be paid out. The ordinary shareholders, however, have a right to divide equally among themselves the entire value of the business on a winding-up after the preference shareholders have received the face value of their shares. There is, therefore, a risk that no money will be left for them to receive. This is why ordinary shares are often referred to as risk or venture capital or equity shares.

Anyone who possesses over 50 per cent of the voting shares is said to have a controlling interest in a company, while the other shareholders are known as the minority interest.

The disadvantage of ordinary shares is that the shareholders can lose their investment should the company fail. In addition, the company has no obligation to pay any dividend at all. If profits are low then no dividend, or low dividends, may be paid.

There are, however, advantages in holding ordinary shares, such as the possession of the right to all profits remaining after the preference share dividend has been paid and the potential capital growth (i.e. a rise in the share price) from profits retained in the business.

Owning shares gives its owner voting rights at the company's general meetings. At the annual general meeting (AGM), the directors must be appointed or reappointed by the shareholders. The directors must also present their report and audited accounts to the shareholders and the dividend to shareholders must be approved. The dividend is the shareholders' share of the company's profits as recommended by the directors and approved by those shareholders at the AGM. The shareholders can vote to reduce the dividend but cannot increase it.

Preference shares

These shares give their shareholders the right to a fixed amount of dividend which is only paid if the company earns sufficient profit.[17] The dividend on such a share is, however, limited to a fixed percentage of the face value (nominal or par value), which is stated on the share certificate. They receive their dividend before the ordinary shareholders and, in a liquidation, are also able to get repaid before the ordinary shareholders.

For example, 10 per cent preference shares are shares whose owner has a right to a dividend of 10 per cent each year, but no more. If a company has issued

---

[17] In addition, there are cumulative preference shares where the dividends are allowed to accumulate year on year until the company has profit which enables it to pay out a dividend.

10,000 10 per cent £1 preference shares, and has made a profit of only £1,000, then the preference shareholders will have a right to receive a dividend before any payment is made to the ordinary shareholders.

Preference shares carry no right to vote at a general meeting of the company, but if an extraordinary meeting is called to discuss matters which prejudice their preferential rights, for example capital reorganisation schemes, then preference shareholders are usually allowed to vote.

All shares have a nominal value (i.e. the face value), and this is shown together with the amount paid per share. This total is known as the paid-up capital (see section 28.5).

28.5.5 Worked example

We can illustrate the above share capital structure in the following example:

Authorised share capital

500,000 ordinary shares of 50p each	£250,000
100,000 6% preference shares of £1 each	£100,000
	£350,000

Issued share capital

200,000 ordinary shares of 50p each, fully paid	£100,000
80,000 6% preference shares of £1 each, fully paid	£80,000
	£180,000

Note: Both the authorised and the issued capital must be shown when you prepare a company balance sheet. The authorised capital is not added into any totals but it is shown for information purposes. All too often the student loses marks by not showing the authorised capital.

Another important point to observe in preparing a company balance sheet is that the number of shares and the nominal value of each type of share must be shown. Here again, marks are lost by simply omitting this detail.

28.5.6 Nominal and market value

It is important to know that the nominal value is not the market value of the share. In the case of a public company, listed on the stock exchange, it is fairly simple to obtain the market value from the closing prices each day.[18] In a private company a value can be calculated, but this requires considerable expertise.

Table 28.1 **Market price of listed shares showing movements on the day**

Name	Price	+/–	%+/–
Home Retail	263.10	+1.60 ▲	+0.61
Kingfisher	215.10	−1.50 ▼	−0.69
Marks & Spencer	352.40	+0.40 ▲	+0.11
Next	2,017.00	+33.00 ▲	+1.66

[18] The market value can be obtained from newspapers, teletext or the internet.

The term nominal value is the same as the term face value. On the other hand, market value is the price that someone will pay for the shares. It does not depend on the nominal or face value but rather on the investor's valuation of the company.

Shares can be of any denomination. Most shares in UK companies are of a nominal value of 25 pence, 50 pence or £1. Dividends, as we will see later in this chapter, are expressed as a percentage of the nominal value or as an amount per share.

The market price of a share is usually different to the nominal value. If the company is doing well the market price will be high and if it is thought to be in difficulties then the market price will fall. The market price of a company's shares is the concern of the company's directors. If the share price falls then shareholders get upset and the directors could be voted out at the next meeting, or the business could be taken over by another company. It is in the directors' interest, therefore, to ensure the shareholders' confidence in their management.

28.5.7 Net worth

At year end the company earns profit. From that it pays corporation tax and then a dividend. Any amount left over is held by the company as a general reserve (see Figure 28.1).

Figure 28.1 Chart showing available profit after dividends and taxation

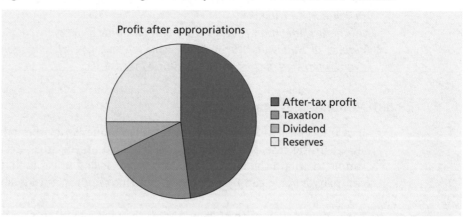

Although reserves belong to the shareholders, they are not credited to each shareholder. The share capital and reserves show how much the company is worth in the books. They show how the assets are financed using the accounting equation, which we can modify slightly to read as follows:

Fixed and current assets – liabilities
= share capital and reserves (shareholders' funds)

28.5.8 Self-test

To ensure that you are aware of the differences in the terms market value and nominal value, the following exercise is given. You are asked to fill in the amounts in the missing spaces.

Number of shares	Nominal value	Total value
300,000	?	£300,000
?	50p	£250,000
?	40p	£320,000
1,500,000	10p	?

28.6 Dividends

By holding ordinary shares, the shareholder expects to receive a return via a dividend. If there is a large profit then it could be expected that a higher dividend would be paid out, while if there is a loss, then little or nothing would be paid. Thus it is said that shareholders receive rewards from a company in the form of dividends which are an appropriation of after-tax profits (see Figure 28.1).

A company would not pay out all its profits but transfer some to reserves. These reserves would be used at a later time to pay a dividend when there is no profit or very little profit, providing, of course, that cash is available.

Often a company will pay out two dividends a year. The first is paid during the year and is known as an interim dividend. The second is a final dividend. Before a final dividend can be paid it must be proposed by the directors and agreed to by members of the company at the annual general meeting. This does not apply to the interim dividend, where directors can make a payment during the year to shareholders. Although dividends are paid with an eye on the profits achieved, the interim payment will not be based on profits alone. The directors must ensure that the profits will be maintained for the full year and also that there are sufficient liquid funds to make the payment. Of course, liquidity is vital to all dividend payments to shareholders.

In recommending a dividend to shareholders, the directors must be sure that there are distributable profits and that the necessary liquid resources are available for a dividend without depleting funds needed for growth or to cover liabilities.

The company can express the amount of dividend as x pence per share or as x per cent (this means the percentage of the nominal value of the share).

Figure 28.2 features a notice sent by Tate & Lyle plc to its shareholders. In the notice (which is one relating to the annual general meeting), shareholders are asked to approve a resolution (no. 3) to declare the final dividend.

Unlike the ordinary shareholder, the preference shareholder receives a fixed rate of dividend each year, subject of course to the availability of profit. There are two types of preference share – the cumulative and the non-cumulative share. In the former case any dividend not paid in one year is accumulated to the

Figure 28.2 **Extract from the annual report of Tate & Lyle plc**

> Notice is hereby given that the one hundred and seventh Annual General Meeting (AGM) of Tate & Lyle plc will be held at the Queen Elizabeth II Conference Centre, Broad Sanctuary, Westminster, London SW1P 3EE on Thursday 22 July 2010 at 11.00 am for the following purposes:
>
> **Ordinary business**
>   1. To receive the reports and accounts of the directors and of the auditors for the year ended 31 March 2010.
>   2. To approve the directors' remuneration report set out in the report and accounts for the year ended 31 March 2010.
>   3. To declare a final dividend on the ordinary shares of the Company.
>   4. To re-elect Liz Airey as a director of the Company.
>   5. To re-elect Evert Henkes as a director of the Company.
>   6. To re-elect Sir Peter Gershon as a director of the Company.
>   7. To re-elect Javed Ahmed as a director of the Company.
>   8. To re-elect William Camp as a director of the Company.
>   9. To re-elect Douglas Hurt as a director of the Company.
>   10. To re-appoint PricewaterhouseCoopers LLP as auditors.
>   11. To authorise the directors to set the remuneration of the auditors.
> **Resolution 3**
> **Declaration of a final dividend**
> You will be asked to declare a final dividend of 16.1 pence per ordinary share for the year ended 31 March 2010. If approved, the dividend will be paid on 30 July 2010 to shareholders on the Register of Members at the close of business on 25 June 2010.

following year and can then be paid. This means that the shareholder always receives a dividend, although it may not be paid out annually. All preference shares are cumulative unless otherwise stated.

28.6.1 Worked example

A company has issued 100,000 ordinary shares of 50p each at 31 December 2008. For the 2009 year the company pays a dividend on 15 May 2009 of 5p per share as an interim dividend and an 8 per cent final dividend at the year end.

You are asked to calculate the total dividend that shareholders will receive during 2009 (the answer is shown in the table below).

Number of shares	Nominal value	Total value	Interim dividend	Final dividend
100,000	50p each	£50,000	£5,000	£4,000

On 1 January 2010 the company issues an additional 100,000 shares of 50p each, at a premium of 20p. In the ledger there are two separate accounts for this issue of additional capital. The one ledger account would be for the additional issued share capital of 100,000 shares × 50p = £50,000 and the other account would show the share premium account of £20,000 (100,000 × 20p).

Share capital account

1 Jan 10		31 Dec 08	Ordinary shares	50,000
		1 Jan 10	Ordinary shares	50,000

Share premium account

1 Jan 10		1 Jan 10	Ordinary shares	20,000

The capital of the company has now increased to 200,000 shares with a share premium of £20,000.

If dividends on the share capital are paid at the same rate as in 2009 then the interim dividend would be 5p × 200,000 = £10,000 and a final dividend of 8 per cent of £100,000 = £8,000. The additional amount of £20,000 (the share premium) does not come into the calculation as the dividend is only paid on the nominal value of the shares.

If we take the total dividend paid out during 2010, we can say that the company has declared a total dividend of 18 per cent, or 9p per share for the year, that is, £18,000 on a capital amount of £100,000.

28.7 Bonus shares

It can happen that a company wishes to reward its shareholders, but finds that it does not have sufficient liquidity to make the necessary payment. As a result of good trading results over the past periods it is able to make use of the reserves created from past profits. The company utilises these reserves to issue additional shares to existing shareholders in proportion to the number of shares already held by them.

This issue is called a bonus share issue or capitalisation issue. The shareholders do not pay for the shares – they are a bonus. In effect the company is giving shareholders part of the reserves which they already own.

For example, assume there are 50,000 ordinary shares of £1 each in issue. The company decides to take part of the reserves and use them to give bonus shares to shareholders. It decides that 1 bonus share will be given for every five ordinary shares held. This means that a total of 10,000 bonus shares are to be issued and the amount due of £10,000 is transferred from the reserves to the share capital account. The transaction does not affect the shareholders' funds which still total £80,000.

Share capital account

		1 Jan 10	Balance b/d	50,000
		1 Mar 10	Bonus shares	10,000

General reserve

1 Mar 10	Bonus shares	10,000	1 Jan 10	Balance b/d	30,000

28.8 | Reserves

In the previous section we spoke of the utilisation of reserves. So what are they?

A reserve, by definition, is not created to meet any known liability, but is simply an appropriation of retained profits. For example, some of the profit after tax could be placed in the general reserve.

It is different to a provision, which is an amount set aside from profit to meet a specific, although estimated, liability. A provision (such as for depreciation) would be entered into the profit and loss account as an expense, before arriving at the net profit.

The ordinary share capital, known as the equity capital, includes reserves. The shareholders' fund is the total of all share capital (both ordinary and preference) and all the reserves.

The reserves are divided into revenue reserves and capital reserves.

28.8.1 Revenue reserves

Revenue reserves are an appropriation of distributable profits (which belong to the ordinary shareholders). Some examples are the profit and loss reserve, general reserve and the fixed asset replacement reserves.

28.8.2 Capital reserves

Capital reserves are not appropriations of profit but arise from the following:

(i) issuing of shares at a premium would result in a share premium reserve;
(ii) a revaluation of assets would lead to the creation of a revaluation reserve;
(iii) when a company buys back its own shares without issuing new shares to fund the redemption, a capital redemption reserve is created.

Capital reserves cannot be used to pay out dividends. Their usage is regulated by the Companies Act.

Capital reserves could be used for a bonus share issue. In the case of the share premium account, it could be used to write off preliminary expenses or share issue expenses or to pay a premium on share or debenture redemption.

All reserves are not a source of cash but are amounts that are represented by assets. It is often thought that if there are reserves then the company is able to pay out increased dividends. This is far from the truth as all too often these reserves have been invested in fixed assets for future growth of the company and are, therefore, not liquid enough to be used for payment of dividends.

28.9 | Rights issue

During the life of a company there could be the need for additional capital. While outside loans are often available, the company may decide that a further issue of shares is more appropriate.

In issuing shares to the public there are many formalities and costs of an issue are high. Using the existing shareholders, a company can raise additional finance by offering those shareholders the right to buy additional shares. These rights are less costly to the company as there are not as many formalities.

The rights allow existing shareholders to apply for new shares in proportion to their existing holding. The rights are stated in the offer document where the price is also given. If the shareholder does not take up the rights they can be sold to another person as the rights are often quoted on the stock exchange.

An advantage of the issue, besides the lower costs, is that control remains with the existing shareholders, although there can be a slight change if rights are sold to outsiders.

Often the rights issue is underwritten by a financial house, for example a merchant bank. This ensures that any shares not subscribed for by existing shareholders will be taken up (and purchased) by the finance house.

28.10 Debentures

A company is able to raise extra money either by the issue of new shares or through a long-term loan, known as a debenture issue. Generally debentures are secured against the assets of the company and can either be a specific security (against a particular asset, such as property – here the debenture is called a 'fixed charge debenture') or a floating security where no specific assets are identified. In this latter case the debenture holders are allowed to take control of the assets of a company in the event of default (such as when the company fails to repay debenture holders on a due date). The holders are then allowed to sell the assets in order to recoup the amount due.

Debentures are usually for a fixed period[19] and are entitled to a fixed rate of interest. (The period is often shown as '8 per cent debenture 2010/2015'. This means that the debenture, with interest of 8 per cent p.a., is repayable by the company in any of the years 2010 to 2015.) The interest is a charge against profits and is paid whether the company makes a profit or not.

An important aspect of a debenture is that it is not part of the share capital and does not form part of the shareholders' funds. In a company balance sheet (see Chapter 22) the debentures are shown as long-term liabilities (assuming that they are repayable in more than 12 months).

Many companies prefer to issue debentures rather than additional shares. The main disadvantage of companies issuing more ordinary shares is that the creation of extra votes may change control in the company. It will also give more investors the chance to join in the distribution of the same amount of profit and therefore each share could get a smaller dividend.

---

[19] Holders may also be able to convert their loan at some future date into shares at a predetermined price. This allows debenture holders the right to continue having an interest in the company and to get future dividends. These loans are known as convertible debentures.

28.10.1 Self-test

Green Ltd has issued 500,000 ordinary £1 shares, 60,000 6 per cent £1 preference shares and £200,000 9 per cent debentures. You are told that the effective tax rate is 30 per cent.

You are required to calculate the return to ordinary shareholders if the operating profits (before debenture interest) were:

(i)   £25,000
(ii) £100,000

If the preference shares were cumulative, what would be the significance to ordinary shareholders?

28.11 Application and allotment of shares

This comprises an offer, acceptance and payment. The application for shares is the offer to the company and when they advise of the allotment, that constitutes the acceptance. The invitation is issued as a prospectus (the offer). Investors (applicants) apply and send in money due on application (the acceptance).

When shareholders apply for shares as a result of the offer, the money received is credited to the application and allotment account. Once the allotment is made then the additional money that may be due on allotment is also placed in this account which is then closed by a transfer to share capital and share premium accounts.

	Application and allotment account				
Date	Share capital	130,000	Date	Bank	120,000
	Share premium	180,000		Bank	190,000
		310,000			310,000

The company allots the shares and returns all or any surplus money to the unsuccessful applicants. On allotment of the shares the company notifies the applicants that further funds are due and the successful applicants send in the additional amounts required. There may be further calls later if any shares are not fully paid.

28.11.1 Worked example

A Co. plc decides to raise capital through an issue of 200,000 ordinary shares of £1 each. The terms of the offer are as follows:

(i)   The shares are to be issued at a premium of £1.10.
(ii) Payment for the shares is to be 60p on application of which 35p is premium and a further 95p on allotment of which 55p per share is the amount of the premium.

(iii) A final call of 55p per share will be made 3 months after allotment. Of this amount 20p is allocated to the share premium account.

Assume that all payments are made as and when required. You are required to show the journal entries to reflect the above.

Bank	Dr	120,000	
Application and allotment	Cr		120,000
Application money sent			
Bank	Dr	190,000	
Application and allotment	Cr		190,000
Money paid for allotment			
Application and allotment	Dr	310,000	
Share capital	Cr		130,000
Share premium	Cr		180,000
Shares allotted and paid			
Bank	Dr	110,000	
Call account	Cr		110,000
Call made for money			
Call account	Dr	110,000	
Share capital	Cr		70,000
Share premium	Cr		40,000
Call money allocated			

28.11.2 Self-test

Bee Co. plc has an authorised share capital of 500,000 £1 ordinary shares. At present the issued capital is 200,000 ordinary shares issued at a premium of 40p each.

The company decides to issue a further 200,000 ordinary shares at a premium of 60p each. Payment is to be 90p on application and the balance on allotment. Applications were received by the company for 500,000 shares. The directors agreed to allot 2 shares for every 5 applied for and refund all excess money to the applicants.

You are required to prepare the ledger accounts for the above transactions.

28.11.3 Self-test

Explor Limited is incorporated on 3 January 2010 with an authorised capital of £1,800,000 divided into 1,800,000 ordinary shares of £1 each.

On 3 January it issues 500,000 shares at a premium of 30p per share. The full amount is due and paid on 3 January 2010.

On 11 January 2010 the company offers for sale 450,000 ordinary shares at a price of £1.60. The offer is made subject to the following conditions:

(i)   30p is payable on application;
(ii) 60p is to be paid when the allotment of the shares are confirmed (this includes 20p share premium);
(iii) 70p must be paid as a first and final call.

At 15 January 2010 the company closes its share issue and at that stage had received applications for a total of 700,000 shares. The company agreed that all the applicants would receive shares. These would be allocated pro rata to their original application. All monies in excess of that due for the shares issued were to be applied to the amounts due on allotment. All balances still due were to be paid to the company by 31 January 2010.

On 15 June 2010 the first and final call was made for the balance due and was received by the company on 30 June 2010.

Explor Limited made a 2 for 5 rights issue at £1.40 per share during the following financial year. The full amount was due by 18 January 2011 and all monies were received by that date.

On 15 March 2011 the company made a 1 for 4 bonus issue of shares, using the share premium account.

You are required to show the relevant ledger accounts for the 2011 financial year to reflect all the above transactions.

28.12 Shares or debentures?

It is important to consider what form of capital a company should look for when raising money. From an investor's point of view an investment in a company can be in ordinary shares, preference shares, debentures or convertible loan stock.

The investor will note that debentures are safe as they are usually secured. Interest is paid whether the company makes a profit or not. A disadvantage is that interest is fixed and, if interest rates in the economy increase, the reward is less attractive. A better return could be obtained elsewhere. The repayment is often worth less as, when the debenture is repaid, it is worth less than at the time of the original investment due to inflation. For this reason holders of convertible loans have the advantage of being able to convert their loan into shares in the future.

Dividends for preference shares are fixed and if they are cumulative preference shares then any arrear dividends are made good at a later date, when there are profits. The important thing to note is that the rate of dividend does not increase with increased profits. The investor in preference shares is aware that in the event of a company going into liquidation, the preference shares are repaid (if there is sufficient money) in priority to the ordinary shareholders.

Ordinary share dividends are paid from profits and with increased profits the dividend can also increase. All the reserves in the company belong to the ordinary shareholders so the investor is not only rewarded by increasing dividends but may also enjoy capital growth. One disadvantage is that dividends are only from profits and even then the company must have sufficient liquidity to pay out the dividends.

The following table is a quick guide to the advantages and disadvantages of raising funds by debentures or shares from a company point of view.

	Advantage	Disadvantage
Shares	■ Dividends are only paid if there are profits. ■ There is no requirement to repay the shares. ■ If the shares are popular then they could be issued at a premium and the company would be able to receive extra cash. ■ Popular shares make it easier to sell additional shares.	■ High cost of making a share issue. ■ Dividends will be reduced if the profit remains the same. ■ Voting rights can be affected if new shares are issued.
Debentures	■ Can be redeemed in the future. ■ They have no voting rights. ■ They will not affect equity dividends where there are increasing profits.	■ Debenture interest must be paid. ■ They must be redeemed at the agreed date and this could affect liquidity. ■ Debentures create adverse gearing (see s. 28.10). ■ They are repaid in priority to the shareholders.

28.13 Amalgamations

Many companies expand through external growth. They can either buy the net assets of another company or buy the shares of the other company or form a new company which buys the shares of both companies.

When the transaction is the purchase of assets, the acquired company balances are not always the figure taken over. Often there are different amounts. A purchase price is agreed and any excess of the purchase price over the value of the net assets is classed as goodwill. This is illustrated in the worked example below.

As a result of the takeover, the acquiring company's balance sheet is adjusted.

28.13.1 Worked example

		Company A		Company B
Plant and machinery		42,000		
Motor vehicles		16,000		11,000
Office equipment		1,500		4,000
Computer equipment				12,000
		59,500		27,000
Current assets				
Stock	6,000		3,200	
Debtors	8,400		2,900	
Bank	11,700		4,000	
	26,100		10,100	
Creditors	2,600	23,500	1,300	8,800
		83,000		35,800
Share capital		45,000		30,000
Profit and loss account		38,000		5,800
		83,000		35,800

Company A acquires the net assets of Company B (except the bank account) at book value. Company A also accepts responsibility for the creditors. The purchase price is 30,000 ordinary shares of £1 each, issued at par, with the balance in cash.

You are required to show the balance sheet of Company A after the acquisition.

Acquisition account			
Motor vehicles	11,000	Creditors	1,300
Office equipment	4,000	Purchase price	
Computer equipment	12,000	Ordinary shares	30,000
Stock	3,200	Cash	1,800
Debtors	2,900		
	33,100		33,100

The first thing to do is to calculate the total value of the assets acquired: £35,800 − £4,000 = £31,800. Company A pays £30,000 in shares and £1,800 in cash.

We now add the assets taken over (from Company B) to those already shown in the balance sheet of Company A.

		Company A
Plant and machinery		42,000
Motor vehicles		27,000
Office equipment		5,500
Computer equipment		12,000
		86,500
Current assets		
Stock	9,200	
Debtors	11,300	
Bank (11,700 − 1,800)	9,900	
	30,400	
Creditors	3,900	26,500
		113,000
Share capital (45,000 + 30,000)		75,000
Profit and loss account		38,000
		113,000

Note: After the purchase by Company A, Company B shows assets of £5,800 in cash and £30,000 in shares held by it in Company A. The capital remains at £30,000 issued shares and £5,800 of profit and loss account.

28.13.2 Worked example

Use the same balance sheets as above for Company A and Company B.

In this example the facts are: Company A acquires the net assets of Company B including the bank account. The agreed purchase price is £90,000 which Company A pays by the issue of ordinary shares of £1 each at a premium of 80p.

Prepare the balance sheet of Company A, reflecting the additional assets acquired.

The first thing you are required to do is to calculate the goodwill paid by Company A. To do this we take the total purchase price of £90,000 and deduct the net value of the assets and liabilities of Company B that we purchased (£35,800). This results in goodwill of £54,200.

You also need to determine the number of additional shares issued in satisfaction of the purchase price. This is shown in the notes below.

Once these calculations are prepared it is then a matter of combining the assets of Company B with those of Company A to produce the new balance sheet.

		Company A
Goodwill*		54,200
Plant and machinery		42,000
Motor vehicles		27,000
Office equipment		5,500
Computer equipment		12,000
		140,700
Current assets		
Stock	9,200	
Debtors	11,300	
Bank	15,700	
	36,200	
Creditors	3,900	32,300
		173,000
Share capital (45,000 + 50,000)**		95,000
Share premium account**		40,000
Profit and loss account		38,000
		173,000

Note: * Goodwill is equal to the purchase price (£90,000) minus the net assets as shown in worked example above (£35,800).
** The purchase price consists of 50,000 ordinary shares of £1 each (£50,000) plus a share premium of 50,000 × 80p per share (£40,000).

28.13.3 Self-test

This question uses the same information as contained in sections 28.13.1 and 28.13.2 above. Prior to the acquisition it is agreed that the following values will be placed on the assets of Company B:

Motor vehicles	6,000
Office equipment	4,000
Computer equipment	8,000
Stock	2,000
Debtors	2,100

Company A agrees to acquire the assets (excluding bank account) of Company B for a purchase price of £46,000. The consideration is to be satisfied by the issue of 20,000 £1 ordinary shares at a premium of 50p each and a payment in cash of the balance.

You are required to prepare the balance sheet of Company A after the acquisition.

28.13.4 Self-test

Highway Connections Ltd, which builds roads, and Wessex Quarries Ltd, which mines stone used in the construction industry, have merged. The new company is called Roadworks Ltd and has an authorised share capital of 2,500,000 ordinary shares of £1 each. The new company was formed on 1 April 2009.

The balance sheets of the two companies on 31 March 2009 were as follows:

| | Highway Connections Ltd | | Wessex Quarries Ltd | |
	£000	£000	£000	£000
Fixed assets				
Buildings	200		120	
Machinery	950		480	
Furniture	70		37	
Vehicles	550		186	
		1,770		823
Current assets				
Stock	58		43	
Debtors	22		39	
Bank	36		12	
Cash	21		2	
	137		96	
Current liabilities				
Creditors	(46)		(72)	
Working capital		91		24
Net assets		1,861		847
Ordinary shares of £1 each	800		800	
Share premium	200		50	
Profit & loss reserve	861		(3)	
Capital employed		1,861		847

Roadworks Ltd settled the purchase consideration by issuing to shareholders of Highway Connections Ltd and Wessex Quarries Ltd, £1 ordinary shares in Roadworks Ltd. These shares were valued at £1.50 each, which included a premium of £0.50 per share.

Roadworks Ltd took over the assets and liabilities of Highway Connections Ltd and Wessex Quarries Ltd at book value, with the following exceptions:

(i)   Buildings were revalued:
    (a) Highway Connections Ltd to £280,000.
    (b) Wessex Quarries Ltd to £160,000.
(ii) Machinery of Wessex Quarries Ltd was valued at £380,000.
(iii) Furniture of Highway Connections Ltd was valued at £60,000.
(iv) Vehicles of Wessex Quarries Ltd were valued at £145,000.
(v)   Net realisable value of the stock was:
    (a) Highway Connections Ltd £55,000.
    (b) Wessex Quarries Ltd £25,000.
(vi) Debtors (£17,000) of Wessex Quarries Ltd were written off as bad debts.

In addition:

(i) Goodwill was valued at:
    (a) £274,000 for Highway Connections Ltd; and
    (b) £30,000 for Wessex Quarries Ltd.
(ii) The purchase price of Highway Connections Ltd was £2,202,000.

Required:

(a) Calculate:
    (i) the purchase price of Wessex Quarries Ltd;
    (ii) how many shares the members of Wessex Quarries Ltd received in Roadworks Ltd.
(b) In the books of Highway Connections Ld, prepare the:
    (i) realisation account; and
    (ii) sundry shareholders' account.
(c) Prepare the balance sheet of Roadworks Limited as at 1 April 2009.
    Angelina was a shareholder in Highway Connections Limited.
(d) Evaluate the merger from the point of view of Angelina.

(Edexcel Accounting 6002 June 2009)

28.13.5 Self-test

The directors of Sun Limited and Land Limited decided to combine the companies with effect from 1 January 2006.

The current summarised balance sheets of the two companies are given below.

Balance sheets at 31 December 2005

	Sun Limited	Land Limited
Buildings	70,000	–
Machinery	20,000	80,000
Vehicles	–	40,000
Stock	2,300	21,000
Debtors	1,500	14,050
Bank	18,800	12,000
	112,600	167,050

	Sun Limited	Land Limited
Issued capital	100,000	150,000
Profit and loss balance	8,000	9,600
General reserve	–	4,000
Creditors	4,600	3,450
	112,600	167,050

The new company was registered with a capital of 800,000 ordinary shares of 50p each, under the name SunLand Limited. It was agreed that shareholders of Sun Limited and Land Limited should receive shares in SunLand Limited in satisfaction of the purchase price.

All the assets and liabilities were taken over by SunLand Limited at the above values with the following exceptions:

(i)   Goodwill of the two companies was agreed at £20,000 for Sun Ltd and £14,000 for Land Ltd.
(ii) Buildings were valued at £90,000.
(iii) One vehicle was sold to a director of Land Ltd for £3,000 cash, which was £800 less than book value.

Required:

(a) In the books of Sun Limited, prepare the:
    (i) realisation account;
    (ii) sundry shareholders' account.
(b) Show your calculations of the purchase price of Land Limited and indicate how many shares its members will receive in SunLand Limited.

(Edexcel Accounting 6002 May 2006)

Chapter 29

Company financial reports

Objectives   After you have studied this chapter, you should be able to:

- prepare a company profit and loss account and balance sheet;
- understand and comply with the requirements of the Companies Act 2006;
- detail and discuss the contents and use of a directors' report;
- discuss the need for an auditors' report.

29.1 Introduction

The first thing we should note is that the accounting basics for companies are the same as those for other businesses. The system of double entry is the same, the keeping of subsidiary books is the same and even the conventions are much the same. There are, however, some differences and this is covered in the extensive legislation that exists. The Companies Act sets out the minimum information that companies must disclose in their accounts and requires companies to file a copy of their annual accounts with the Registrar of Companies. It is important to note that the companies must prepare annual audited financial statements comprising a balance sheet and profit and loss account together with the notes to the accounts and a directors' report.

The accounts are prepared so that they show a true and fair view, both of the profit (or loss) for the period and of the state of affairs at balance sheet date. It is an additional requirement of accounting standards that a cash flow statement is prepared.

29.2 The content of financial statements

We will read in the following paragraphs about the items that appear in the profit and loss account and balance sheet. We should pause for a minute and think why these items appear where they do, and what determines the form that they take.

There are three factors which contribute to this determination.

They are:

- The **theoretical framework**, under which accounting concepts have developed over a period of time. We discussed accounting concepts in Chapter 25.

- The **legal framework** such as the company law as set out in the Companies'
  Act. The law is also supplemented by the various judicial decisions made and
  embodied in case law.
- The **regulatory framework**, which incorporates the many rules and standards
  set by the professional accountancy bodies and the users of accounts.

In addition, public companies are also regulated by the stock exchange 'yellow
book' regulations, which apply to all listed companies and which cover items
such as the need for interim accounts and timely notices of any events relating
to the particular company which may affect its value.

29.2.1 Company profit and loss account

We have said that there is very little difference in the layout used by a sole proprietor and a company. One major difference is that, in the case of a company, a
great deal of the detail is relegated to the notes to the accounts. This allows for
an uncluttered appearance of the typical company profit and loss account.

As such, the profit and loss account will group expenses and it is important
that you familiarise yourself with these groupings.

- Administration expenses consist of, for example, office salaries, printing,
  postage and telephones, property rates, electricity and bank charges.
- Selling and distribution expenses consist of, for example, salaries and commission of sales staff, advertising, carriage and packing, and motor expenses.
- Financial expenses would include interest payments.

The other item of note is that there is a deduction from profits of corporation
tax – something we did not see with the sole trader or partnership. The tax
deduction illustrates the fact that a company is a separate legal persona and is
liable for taxation on profits it makes.

The following is a company layout for the profit and loss account.

**Profit and loss account for Any Company plc for the year ended
31 December 2009**

Turnover		100,000
Cost of sales		38,000
Gross profit		62,000
Income from investments		28,000
		90,000
Distribution costs	24,000	
Administration expenses	19,000	
Financial expenses	11,000	54,000
Profit before tax		36,000
Tax		14,000
Profit after tax		22,000
Dividends: Preference	4,000	
Ordinary	5,000	9,000
Retained profit for the year		13,000
P&L account as at beginning of the year		142,000
P&L account as at end of the year		155,000

29.2.2 Company balance sheet

The following example shows the layout of the balance sheet of a typical company. Here again we must note that the balance sheet is also very much like that of a sole trader or partnership but again there is an exception. This time it is the very detailed capital section, in addition to the extensive use of notes to the accounts.

We discussed in Chapter 12 the aspects of depreciation. We saw that fixed assets (except land) are depreciated over a period of time. The company balance sheet is prepared with various headings that show the cost, accumulated depreciation and the net book value of the fixed assets. In addition, there is a split of fixed assets as follows:

- Intangible fixed assets, which are non-physical assets, e.g. brands, patents, goodwill.
- Tangible fixed assets, which are those that can be seen and touched, e.g. delivery van, computer.
- Investments, which are also classed as a fixed asset when they are kept for a number of years and not purchased for resale.

As we go down the face of the balance sheet (it is presented in a vertical format) we come to the current assets, which are set out in a fixed order. This order is a descending one, from the least liquid to the most liquid asset and is identical to the order used in the sole traders' accounts.

Balance sheet of Any Company plc as at 31 December 2009

Fixed assets		
Tangible assets		
Buildings	40,000	
Motor lorries	20,000	60,000
Intangible assets		
Goodwill		25,000
Current assets		85,000
Stocks		
Stocks of finished goods	40,000	
Debtors	10,000	
Cash at bank and in hand		
Bank	7,000	
Cash	8,000	
Prepayments and accrued income	3,000	
	68,000	
Creditors: amounts falling due within one year		
Trade creditors	14,000	
Bank interest	1,000	
Net current assets (liabilities)	15,000	53,000
Total assets less current liabilities		138,000
Creditors: amounts falling due after more than one year		
Bank loan	15,000	
Provisions for liabilities and charges		
Taxation provision	2,500	
Pension and similar obligations	6,500	24,000
		114,000

Balance sheet of Any Company plc as at 31 December 2009 (*continued*)

Capital and reserves	
Ordinary share capital called up	12,000
Share premium account	4,000
Revaluation reserves	18,000
General reserves	60,000
Profit and loss account	20,000
	114,000

From the current assets we deduct the short-term liabilities. We no longer use the term current liabilities but instead use the term 'Amounts falling due within one year'. These liabilities are our trade and other creditors and also include dividends and other accruals.

After deducting these current liabilities from the current assets, we arrive at the net current assets or working capital. To that figure we add the total of the fixed assets and that gives us a figure for the total assets, less current liabilities.

We still have additional creditors which are the long-term creditors and described as 'amounts falling due after more than one year'. These creditors consist of loans and debentures. We also have a section for provisions and other charges. Deducting both these items from the subtotal above we arrive at the net worth of the company. If you recall our accounting equation, the total here is the assets minus liabilities. We know, then, that the answer to the equation $(A - L = ?)$ is the capital and this is the final part of the balance sheet.

This final part shows the total of the capital and reserves. We show in the notes to the accounts the amount of the authorised capital as well as the issued capital. As the authorised capital is for information only we do not add the amount into our balance sheet.

The next part consists of the issued capital. Under this heading we show the class of share (ordinary shares or preference shares) and the number of shares issued in each class. We also show the nominal value of the shares and if they are fully paid. If the shares are only partly paid then it means that the difference can still be collected by the company and constitutes a liability due by the shareholders.

For example, if we show 10,000 ordinary shares of £1 each, 75p paid, with the amount of £7,500, this still means that the company can call up the remaining £2,500 due (25p per share).

The capital section also discloses the reserves and these are the capital reserves and the revenue reserves (see section 28.8). In the case of the former, these reserves consist of the share premium account, revaluation reserves[20] and capital redemption reserves.

The revenue reserves are those apportioned from profits. Importantly, the profit and loss account (the retained profit) is one of those reserves.

Adding the capital and all the reserves gives us the final figure on the balance sheet, which equates to the shareholders' funds. This figure is the last part of the accounting equation and represents the total assets less the liabilities.

---

[20] Revaluation reserves are capital reserves and retained in the company accounts until the gain is realised.

29.2.3 Self-test

Larnaca Limited has an authorised capital of £350,000 in ordinary shares of £1 each. The financial year ends on 31 March. At 31 March 2006 the following figures were extracted from the books, subject to final adjustment.

	Debit	Credit
Ordinary shares issued, fully paid		200,000
Profit and loss account at 1 April 2005		19,000
Bank balance	25,789	
8 per cent debentures		25,000
8 per cent loan		10,000
Remuneration of auditors	800	
Remuneration of directors	32,000	
Interest on loan	800	
Interest on debentures	2,000	
Office expenses	74,800	
Delivery expenses	68,000	
Leasehold workshop at cost	180,000	
Provision for depreciation on leasehold workshop		60,000
Machinery at cost	160,000	
Provision for depreciation on machinery		27,000
Additions to machinery at cost during the year	10,000	
Stock at 31 March 2006	86,000	
Debtors	95,200	
Prepaid expenses	700	
Trade creditors		50,500
Accrued expenses		5,340
Sales		900,000
Materials consumed	560,751	
	1,296,840	1,296,840

The following matters are to be taken into consideration:

(i) The lease on the workshop expires on 31 March 2015. Provide for the annual depreciation at the appropriate rate.

(ii) Depreciation on machinery is 15 per cent on cost. A full year's depreciation is charged on all machinery owned at 31 March 2006.

(iii) A dividend of 5 per cent is proposed on the share capital.

(iv) The only distribution cost during the year was delivery expenses.

(v) A provision for corporation tax of £11,000 is to be made.

You are required to prepare the profit and loss account for the year ended 31 March 2006 and a balance sheet as at that date in a form satisfying the minimum requirements of the Companies Act.

Note 1 You must show relevant working outside the profit and loss account and balance sheet but there is no need to show any of the notes required by the Companies Act.

Note 2 Ignore all exemptions permitted for small and medium-sized companies.

(Edexcel Accounting 6002 May 2006)

29.2.4 Self-test

Trial balance of Lister Limited at 30 June 2009

Carriage outwards	3,000	
Bank	700	
Trade creditors		13,900
Trade debtors	32,800	
Directors' remuneration	5,500	
Electricity and gas	2,800	
Insurance	1,700	
Plant and machinery – at cost:	42,000	
Accumulated depreciation at 1 July 2008		15,200
Office expenses	4,900	
Ordinary issued share capital		25,000
Dividend	625	
Profit and loss account at 1 July 2008		13,200
Provision for doubtful debts		800
Purchases	124,000	
Rent and rates	7,500	
Sales		210,625
Stock at 1 July 2008	13,400	
Motor vehicles: at cost	8,000	
Accumulated depreciation at 1 July 2008		4,000
Wages and salaries	35,800	
	282,725	282,725

You are given the following additional information:

(i)   Stock at 30 June 2009, valued at cost, amounts to £15,500.

(ii)   Depreciation, using the reducing balance method, is to be provided as follows:
  (a) Plant and machinery at 20 per cent.
  (b) Motor vehicles at 25 per cent.

(iii) The provision for bad debts is to be equal to 5 per cent of outstanding debtors as at 30 June 2009.

(iv)   The insurance account includes £300 which covers the business from 1 July 2009 until 31 December 2009.

(v)   Rent due but unpaid at 30 June 2009 amounts to £250.

(vi)   The directors agreed to pay a dividend of 5 per cent for the year. This includes the interim dividend already paid.

(vii) Lister Limited has an authorised capital of 200,000 50p ordinary shares.

Prepare a trading and profit and loss account for the year ended 30 June 2009, and a balance sheet as at that date.

29.2.5 Self-test

Allied Holdings Ltd was registered with an authorised capital of £3,000,000. This is divided into 800,000 6 per cent preference shares of £1 each and 4,400,000 ordinary shares of 50p each. All the preference shares and 2,000,000 ordinary shares were issued and fully paid.

You are required to prepare the profit and loss account, for Allied Holdings Ltd for the year ended 31 December 2009 and the balance sheet at that date.

Trial balance as at 31 December 2009

Ordinary share capital		1,000,000
Preference share capital		800,000
Share premium account		100,000
Profit and loss account		62,000
Stock 1 January 2009	43,000	
Land and buildings	1,950,000	
Plant and equipment (at cost)	143,000	
Motor vehicles (at cost)	25,000	
Fixtures and fittings (at cost)	12,000	
Debtors	38,300	
Creditors		19,600
Purchases	191,000	
Sales		503,000
Salaries	93,600	
Directors' remuneration	48,000	
Motor expenses	6,300	
Audit fees	3,500	
Bad debts	12,100	
Provision for bad debts		1,100
Acc depreciation – plant and equipment		14,000
Motor vehicles		9,300
Fixtures and fittings		1,100
Cash at bank	11,100	
Ordinary share dividend		12,000
Debentures		78,800
	2,588,900	2,588,900

(i) Stock at 31 December 2009 was £18,900.

(ii) Depreciation of 10 per cent per annum is to be provided on cost for:
   (a) plant and equipment; and
   (b) fixtures and fittings.

(iii) Depreciation of 20 per cent per annum on reducing balance for motor vehicles.

(iv) The provision for bad debts is to be made equal to 10 per cent of sundry debtors.

The directors recommend that:

(a) The final preference dividend should be paid.

(b) A final dividend of 1p per share should be paid to ordinary shareholders.

29.2.6 Self-test

Delta Furnishing Ltd Trial balance – 31 December 2009

Bad debts	700	
Provision for bad debts 1st January 2009		250
Profit and loss account 1 January 2009		43,000
Stock – 1 January 2009	18,800	
Freehold property – at cost	180,850	
Creditors		24,640
Ordinary share capital – fully paid		90,000
Furniture and fittings – at cost	24,000	
Debtors	5,000	
Sales		199,000
Purchases	80,200	
Carriage outwards	9,240	
Office expenses	12,400	
Advertising	12,940	
10 per cent debentures		18,000
Debenture interest paid	1,800	
Rates and insurance	1,760	
Cash in hand	300	
Cash in bank	400	
Provision for depreciation – furniture and fittings		19,000
Salaries and wages	45,500	
	393,890	393,890

You are required to prepare the trading and profit and loss account for Delta Furnishing Ltd for the year ended 31 December 2009 and the balance sheet on that date after taking into account the following adjustments:

(i)	Stock – 31 December 2009	34,000
(ii)	Salaries accrued	1,000
(iii)	Rates prepaid	460
(iv)	Provision for bad debts is to be reduced to	200
(v)	Depreciation of 10 per cent p.a. on the cost furniture and fittings	
(vi)	A dividend of 3 per cent on ordinary share capital	
(vii)	Directors' remuneration unpaid during the year is now due	2,000

The company has an authorised capital of 10,000 6 per cent preference shares of £1 each and 100,000 ordinary shares of £1 each.

29.2.7 Self-test

Hilmor Ltd has an authorised capital of £200,000 divided into 20,000 6 per cent preference shares of £1 each and 180,000 ordinary shares of £1 each. All the preference shares and 100,000 ordinary shares were issued and fully paid.

Trial balance as at 31 December 2009

Ordinary share capital		100,000
Preference share capital		20,000
Share premium account		10,000
Profit and loss account		12,400
General reserve		15,000
Stock 1st January 2009	17,460	
Freehold land and buildings	100,000	
Plant and equipment (at cost)	22,000	
Motor vehicles (at cost)	15,000	
Furniture and fittings (at cost)	6,000	
Debtors and creditors	14,200	17,700
Purchases and sales	280,020	451,000
Wages	80,000	
Salaries	42,000	
Directors' remuneration	29,000	
Motor expenses	4,700	
Auditors' fees	1,300	
Rates and insurance	1,700	
Advertising	17,400	
Bad debts written off	2,600	
Bad debt provision		600
Depreciation provisions – Plant		6,000
Motor vehicles		6,700
Furniture		1,000
Preference dividend	600	
Cash at bank	6,420	
	640,400	640,400

Prepare the trading and profit and loss account for the year ended 31 December 2009 and the balance sheet at that date taking the following additional information into account.

(i)   Stock at 31 December 2009 is £46,500.
(ii) Depreciation:
   (a) 10 per cent per annum on cost of plant and equipment and furniture and fittings.
   (b) 20 per cent per annum on cost of motor vehicles.
(iii) The provision for bad debts is to be made equal to 10 per cent of sundry debtors.
(iv) The directors recommend that a dividend of 10 per cent should be paid on the paid-up value of the ordinary shares.
(v)   The final dividend was also paid to preference shareholders.

29.2.8 Self-test

Washer Trading Ltd was formed with an authorised share capital of 500,000 £1 ordinary shares.

The following is the list of balances of Washer Trading Ltd at 31 December 2010.

Trade creditors	195,000
Trade debtors	260,000
Bank overdraft	78,000
Bank interest	5,200
Office expenses	122,200
Selling expenses	26,000
Share premium account	156,000
Land and buildings at cost	520,000
Office fittings at cost	390,000
Accumulated depreciation at 1 January 2010	78,000
Motor vehicles at cost	520,000
Accumulated depreciation at 1 January 2010	156,000
Opening stock at 1 January 2010	325,000
Purchases	481,000
Sales	975,000
Issued share capital	416,000
Revaluation reserve	91,000
Provision for doubtful debts at 1 January 2010	18,200
Profit and loss account at 1 January 2010	486,200

The following additional information must be taken into account in preparing the financial accounts:

(i) Stock at 31 December 2010 was valued at £216,000.
(ii) Rent is payable annually in advance. Payment of £36,000 was made on 1 September 2010 for the year to 31 August 2011.
(iii) Depreciation is to be charged as follows:
    (a) Office fittings: 20 per cent straight line.
    (b) Motor vehicles: 30 per cent reducing balance.
(iv) Provision for doubtful debts should be increased and made equal to 10 per cent of outstanding debtors.
(v) During the year computer consultants were engaged. Their bill has not yet been paid, nor provided for in the accounts. The amount due is £28,000.
(vi) It is expected that the audit fees for 2010 will be £14,000.

Prepare the trading and profit and loss account for the year ended 31 December and the balance sheet at that date.

29.2.9 Self-test

Nuwaste Trading Ltd was formed with an authorised share capital consisting of 1,500,000 £1 ordinary shares.

The following is the list of balances extracted from the company books at 31 December 2010.

Debtors	480,000
Overdraft	144,000
Debenture interest	9,600
Selling commissions and rent	225,600
Office expenses	48,000
5 per cent debentures	288,000
Creditors	360,000
Freehold land and buildings at cost	960,000
Fixtures and fittings at cost	720,000
Motor vehicles at cost	960,000
Accumulated depreciation at 1 January 2010:	
Fixtures and fittings	144,000
Motor vehicles	288,000
Opening stock at 1 Jan 2010	600,000
Purchases	888,000
Sales	1,800,000
Share capital	768,000
Revaluation reserve	168,000
Provision for doubtful debts at 1 January 2010	33,600
Profit and loss account at 1 January 2010	897,600

The following additional information must be taken into account in preparing the financial accounts.

(i) Stock at 31 December 2010 was valued at £398,000.
(ii) Rent paid in advance amounts to £44,000.
(iii) Depreciation is to be charged as follows:
   (a) Fixtures and fittings: 20 per cent straight line.
   (b) Motor vehicles: 30 per cent reducing balance.
(iv) Provision for doubtful debts should be increased and made equal to 10 per cent of outstanding debtors.
(v) During the year computer consultants were engaged at a cost of £38,000. The amount has not yet been paid, nor provided for in the accounts.
(vi) It is expected that the audit fees for 2010 will be £20,000.

Prepare the trading and profit and loss account for the year ended 31 December and the balance sheet at that date.

29.2.10 Self-test

The following is the list of balances of Camden Trading Ltd at 31 December 2010.

Trade creditors	75,000
Trade debtors	100,000
Bank overdraft	30,000
Debenture interest	2,000
Administrative expenses	47,000
Selling and distribution expenses	10,000
5 per cent debentures	60,000
Land and buildings at cost	200,000
Fixtures and fittings at cost	150,000
Accumulated depreciation at 1 January 2010	30,000
Motor vehicles at cost	200,000
Accumulated depreciation at 1 January 2010	
Motor vehicles	60,000
Stock at 1 January 2010	125,000
Purchases	185,000
Sales	375,000
Issued share capital	160,000
Revaluation reserve	35,000
Provision for doubtful debts at 1 January 2010	7,000
Profit and loss account at 1 January 2010	187,000

Additional information:

(i) Stock at 31 December 2010 is valued at £175,000.

(ii) £12,000 paid for administrative expenses belongs to the year to 31 December 2011.

(iii) Depreciation is to be charged as follows:
   (a) Fixtures and fittings: 20 per cent straight line.
   (b) Motor vehicles: 30 per cent reducing balance.

(iv) Provision for doubtful debts should be increased and made equal to 10 per cent of outstanding debtors.

(v) Provide £15,000 for consultants' fees.

(vi) Audit fees of £12,000 are to be allowed for in the accounts.

Camden Trading Ltd was formed with an authorised share capital of 200,000 £1 ordinary shares.

Prepare the financial statements for the year to 31 December 2010.

29.3 Annual report

Before we review some of the details contained in an annual report of a public company we should be aware of exactly what we expect to find.

The following list is a summary of the contents:

■ Chairman's statement – review of progress, changes in management and future prospects.

■ Business review (see section 29.3.2).

- List of directors.
- Directors' report – dividend declaration, principal activities, political and charitable donations, directors' shareholding, employment policy, creditors' payment policy, appointment of auditors (see section 29.3.1).
- Report of remuneration committee.
- Corporate governance – statement of compliance.
- Audit report (see section 29.3.3).
- Financial statements – profit and loss, balance sheet, cash flow, statement of recognised gains and losses and the parent company balance sheet.
- Historical record of financial performance – 10-year summary.
- Notice of the annual general meeting.

As the full contents are outside the scope of this book we suggest that you have a look at the website of a public company such as Tate & Lyle plc (www.tateandlyle.com) and Arriva plc (www.arriva.co.uk).

Now that we have this list of contents we can see that the annual report is much more than the balance sheet and profit and loss account. Among other things it contains a cash flow statement (see Chapter 31), together with a report from the company directors as well as the auditors' report.[21]

In the following paragraphs we will set out an extract of a directors' report as well as an extract of an auditors' report to the shareholders.

29.3.1 Directors' report

This report is required by the Companies Act 2006. The Act lists what is required in the report and it is useful to examine the details required. The legal requirements as set out in CA 2006 are detailed in paragraphs 416–418 of Chapter 5 of the Act.

The report is a summary of the main activities undertaken during the year and details changes in those activities. An important part of the report is the statement of directors' responsibilities as regards the annual report. This statement is illustrated in Figure 29.1.

The directors' report outlines the progress of the company over the past year and examines the future performance potential. It also discloses future plans for the business.

The report must contain a review of the past year; the position at the year end; the company activities; changes to non-current assets; donations to charities and many other items which are non-financial in nature. These include:

- information about environmental matters (including the impact of the company's business on the environment);
- the company's employees; and
- social and community issues.

---

[21] It should be noted that all company accounts, apart from small company accounts, with reporting periods beginning on or after 1 October 2007, are expected to include a business review.

Figure 29.1 **Directors' responsibilities**

Statement of directors' responsibilities
The directors are responsible for preparing the Annual Report, the directors' remuneration report and the group and parent company financial statements in accordance with applicable law and regulations.
Company law requires the directors to prepare financial statements for each financial year. Under that law the directors have elected to prepare the group financial statements in accordance with International Financial Reporting Standards (IFRS) as adopted by the European Union (EU), and the parent company financial statements in accordance with United Kingdom Generally Accepted Accounting Practice (United Kingdom Accounting Standards and applicable law). In preparing the group financial statements, the directors have also elected to comply with IFRS, issued by the International Accounting Standards Board (IASB). Under company law the directors must not approve the financial statements unless they are satisfied that they give a true and fair view of the state of affairs of the group and the company and of the profit or loss of the company and group for that period.

Figure 29.2 shows an extract from the directors' report of Arriva plc for the year ended 31 December 2009. It should be noted that the list below is only of the main headings and that the report sent to shareholders is in far greater detail.[22]

Figure 29.2 **Contents of the directors' report of Arriva plc**

Directors' Report
The directors submit their report and the audited accounts of Arriva plc for the year ended 31 December 2009.

- Principal activities of the group
- Business review
- Key performance indicators
- Results and dividends
- Share capital
- Directors
- Indemnification of directors
- Statement of directors' responsibilities
- Directors' interests
- Purchase of own shares
- Charitable and political donations
- Annual general meeting
- Employees
- Policy regarding payment of suppliers
- Substantial shareholdings
- Corporate governance
- Health, safety and environment
- Auditors

29.3.2 The business review

This is a new requirement and applies to all companies with reporting periods beginning on or after 1 October 2007. This review forms part of the directors' report and all companies, except companies that file small-company accounts, are required to prepare such a review.

The purpose of the business review is to inform members of the company and help them assess how the directors have performed their duties.

---

[22] The full report can be viewed at www.arriva.co.uk.

It differs slightly from the traditional directors' report in that it is a fair review of the company's business within the reporting period. It must be a balanced and comprehensive analysis of the development and performance of the company, with a description of the principal risks.[23]

29.3.3 Auditors' Report

The Companies Act (section 475) requires that all companies, excluding dormant companies and small companies, are audited every year. A small company is defined as one with a turnover of not more than £5.6 million and a balance sheet total of not more than £2.8 million.

The report is attached to the financial statements of a company and is a statutory requirement of the Companies Act. This report is made to shareholders (not the directors) of the company at the same time as the financial statements – in other words, at the annual general meeting.

Figure 29.3 gives an extract from the auditors' report of Tate & Lyle plc for the year ended 31 March 2010.

Figure 29.3 **Extract of an auditors' report to shareholders**

Independent Auditors' Report to the Members of Tate & Lyle plc

We have audited the Group financial statements of Tate & Lyle plc for the year ended 31 March 2010 which comprise the Consolidated income statement, the Consolidated statement of comprehensive income, the Consolidated statement of financial position, Consolidated statement of cash flows, the Consolidated statement of changes in shareholders' equity and the related Notes to the consolidated financial statements. The financial reporting framework that has been applied in their preparation is applicable law and International Financial Reporting Standards (IFRSs) as adopted by the European Union.

We have reported separately on the Parent company financial statements of Tate & Lyle plc for the year ended 31 March 2010 and on the information in the Directors' remuneration report that is described as having been audited.

29.3.4 What does an auditor do?

There is often confusion as to what an auditor is required to do. One important point is that auditors do not guarantee to discover fraud within the company. This is not what the audit sets out to do.

The auditors ensure that the company has kept proper accounting records and that the accounts prepared agree with the books of account. There is the added requirement that the report must state that the accounts give a true and fair view, both of profit or loss and of the assets and liabilities, at the end of the period.

There is the added requirement that the report confirms that the directors' report is consistent with the accounts of the company.

The auditor will check the accounts and accounting records of the company and prepare a report for the members.

[23] See Section 417 of the Companies Act 2006 (www.companieshouse.gov.uk).

For financial years beginning on or after 1 January 2008, the auditors' report must include:

■ An introduction identifying the accounts that were the subject of the audit and the financial framework that has been applied in their preparation (i.e. whether UK Generally Accepted Accounting Practice (GAAP) or International Financial Reporting Standards (IFRS) has been adopted).

■ A description of the scope of the audit identifying the accounting standards used in the audit.

■ A statement as to whether, in the auditors' opinion, the accounts have been properly prepared in accordance with the Companies Act.

■ A statement as to whether the accounts, in accordance with the relevant financial reporting framework, give a true and fair view of the company's (or group's) financial affairs.

■ The auditors' report may be either unqualified or qualified and must include a reference to any matters to which the auditors wish to draw attention by way of emphasis without qualifying the report. In the case of a qualified report the auditors indicate that they are not satisfied that the financial statements show a true and fair view. In effect, it is a warning to the users that there may be something wrong.

Section 29.3.5 contains an extract from the full audit report to shareholders of Arriva plc for the year ended 31 December 2008. The subheadings are those of the author, in order to draw your attention to specific items dealt with in the report.

29.3.5 Extract from an auditors' report

Respective responsibilities of directors and auditors

As explained more fully in the Directors' statement of responsibilities, the directors are responsible for the preparation of the Group financial statements and for being satisfied that they give a true and fair view. Our responsibility is to audit the Group financial statements in accordance with applicable law and International Standards on Auditing (UK and Ireland). Those standards require us to comply with the Auditing Practices Board's Ethical Standards for Auditors.

This report, including the opinions, has been prepared for and only for the Company's members as a body in accordance with Chapter 3 of Part 16 of the Companies Act 2006 and for no other purpose. We do not, in giving these opinions, accept or assume responsibility for any other purpose or to any other person to whom this report is shown or into whose hands it may come save where expressly agreed by our prior consent in writing.

Opinion on financial statements

In our opinion the Group financial statements:

■ give a true and fair view of the state of the Group's affairs as at 31 March 2010 and of its profit and cash flows for the year then ended;

■ have been properly prepared in accordance with IFRSs as adopted by the European Union; and

- have been prepared in accordance with the requirements of the Companies Act 2006 and Article 4 of the IAS Regulation.

In our opinion the information given in the Directors' report for the financial year for which the Group financial statements are prepared is consistent with the Group financial statements.

Paul Cragg (Senior Statutory Auditor)
for and on behalf of PricewaterhouseCoopers LLP
Chartered Accountants and Statutory Auditors
London
26 May 2010

29.4 Reporting on the internet

With the introduction of the Companies Act 2006, new provisions (section 430) have been made for reporting by companies on the internet.

Previously companies incurred large sums of money in printing and distributing annual reports to their shareholders and other interested users. Now the Act requires a company to make its reports available on the company's website on the internet.[24] It also stipulates that the annual accounts and reports remain posted until the following year when the new annual report is posted.

The Companies Act also stipulates that the annual report be made available as soon as reasonably practicable and without any charge. This ensures the timeliness of the report which is so important to users of the financial statements.

You are encouraged to use the internet to view a number of annual reports. To help you, the following sites are suggested:

- www.ft.com
- www.precisionir.com
- www.londonstockexchange.com
- www.carol.co.uk

You may well find that in reading these reports there is a change of terminology. This is brought about by the companies in question adopting International Accounting Standards.

Throughout this book we have emphasised accounting methods and illustrated the current practice in the UK. In Chapter 41 we introduce you to International Accounting Standards.

Many of the examination bodies have not yet brought into their syllabus the changeover to international accounting.

At this stage you are advised to focus on learning and understanding the basic accounting procedures, layout of financial statements and the terminology used by accountants.

[24] Annual reports on the internet are the responsibility of the directors. The work carried out by the auditors does not involve consideration of these matters and, accordingly, the auditors accept no responsibility for any changes that may have occurred to the financial statements since they were initially presented on the website.

Chapter 30

Revision

After you have worked diligently through this chapter, you should be able to:

- apply any adjustments required to the trial balance;
- understand the format of annual accounts;
- prepare partnership accounts;
- prepare a company profit and loss account and balance sheet.

30.1 Introduction

It is important at this stage to check your understanding of company accounts. You have read that there are similarities between company accounts and those of a sole trader. But having said this, you should be aware that **there are differences** and that the differences are important in the drafting of any accounts.

This chapter is devoted exclusively to self-test questions. Work through each one in turn and make sure that you are comfortable with the suggested answers. Once you have completed this task and you are satisfied that you have been able to answer all the tests, proceed to the next chapter.

A word of caution, however: do not proceed if you have any doubts about the previous chapters. Make sure that you have mastered all the points discussed previously, or worked through additional questions, before going on to Chapter 31.

30.1.1 Self-test

Kitt Ltd Trial balance at 31 December 2009

Ordinary share capital		100,000
7% preference shares		100,000
Share premium account		110,000
Profit and loss account at 1 January 2009		190,000
7% debentures		200,000
Stock at 1 January 2009	400,000	
Purchases	700,000	
Sales		1,500,000
Sales returns	6,000	
Delivery vehicles at cost	200,000	
Delivery vehicles: accumulated depr at 1 Jan 09		120,000
Machinery at cost	240,000	
Machinery: accumulated depreciation at 1 Jan 09		100,000
Buildings at cost	460,000	
Administrative expenses	406,000	
Selling and distribution costs	20,000	
Creditors		400,000
Debtors	388,000	
Interest payable on overdraft	10,000	
Bank overdraft		10,000
	2,830,000	2,830,000

The following adjustments are to be made to the above trial balance:

(i) Closing stock at 31 December 2009 was £360,000.

(ii) On 19 June 2009 the company paid the insurance account for the year to 30 June 2010. This amount of £8,000 is included in administrative expenses.

(iii) Accountancy fees for the year of £2,000 have not yet been paid.

(iv) A sum of £40,000 included in debtors relates to a customer who has gone bankrupt.

(v) The full amount of interest is to be paid to debenture holders.

(vi) Depreciation for the year is to be charged on the straight line basis. Rates to be used are 20 per cent on delivery vehicles and 15 per cent on machinery.

(vii) Sales agents were owed December commission. The amount of £12,000 had not yet been entered in the books of the company.

You are required to prepare a profit and loss account and a balance sheet for the year ended 31 December 2009.

30.1.2 Self-test

Muddle Ltd Trial balance at 31 December 2008

Ordinary share capital		220,000
Profit and loss account		380,000
9% debentures		320,000
Opening stock at 1 January 2008	640,000	
Purchases	1,150,000	
Sales		2,200,000
Sales returns	49,600	
Goods returned to suppliers		70,000
Motor vehicles at cost	320,000	
Motor vehicles: acc depreciation at 1 January 2008		192,000
Office equipment at cost	384,000	
Office equipment: acc depreciation at 1 January 2008		160,000
Fixtures and fittings at cost	436,000	
Fixtures and fittings: acc depreciation at 1 January 2008		384,000
Administration expenses	649,600	
Selling and distribution costs	102,000	
Creditors		540,000
Debtors	620,800	
Interest on bank overdraft	46,000	
Cash at bank	68,000	
	4,466,000	4,466,000

Adjustments to the above trial balance:

(i)   Closing stock at 31 December 2008 = £493,000.

(ii) Insurance of £5,000 is due for November and December. This is to be included in administration expenses.

(iii) Commission on sales of £8,600 for December is outstanding.

(iv) A provision for doubtful debts of 3 per cent is to be made.

(v)   No interest has yet been paid to debenture holders.

(vi) Depreciation is calculated:

   (a) on the straight line basis for motor vehicles at 15 per cent.

   (b) on the reducing balance for office equipment at 5 per cent and fixtures and fittings at 10 per cent.

You are required to prepare the profit and loss account and a balance sheet for the year ended 31 December 2008.

30.1.3 Self-test

Allie Ltd Trial balance at 30 June 2009

Advertising	30,130	
Bank	19,900	
Creditors		69,214
Debentures 10%		70,000
Debtors	301,440	
Directors' remuneration	55,000	
Electricity	22,134	
Insurance	17,890	
Investments – fixed asset	28,500	
Investment income		4,240
Machinery:		
At cost	410,320	
Accumulated depreciation at 1 July 2008		168,900
Office expenses	43,210	
Ordinary share capital		220,000
Dividend	4,400	
Profit and loss account at 1 July 2008		121,300
Provision for bad debts		8,500
Purchases	1,203,980	
Rent and rates	67,210	
Commission received		5,700
Sales		2,104,090
Stock at 1 July 2008	126,900	
Vehicles:		
At cost	83,240	
Accumulated depreciation at 1 July 2008		51,100
Wages and salaries	321,900	
Discount received		12,340
Discount allowed	51,430	
Goods returned by customers	47,800	
	2,835,384	2,835,384

Additional information:

(i) Stock at 30 June 2009, valued at cost, amounted to £195,000.
(ii) Depreciation is to be provided on machinery and vehicles at a rate of 20 per cent and 25 per cent respectively, using the reducing balance method.
(iii) The provision for bad debts is to be made equal to 5 per cent of outstanding debtors as at 30 June 2009.
(iv) Provision is to be made for machine repairs of £8,000.
(v) Provision is to be made for interest to debenture holders.

You are required to prepare a profit and loss account for the year ended 30 June 2009, and a balance sheet as at that date.

30.1.4 Self-test

Trial balance of Sunnie Ltd as at 30 June 2009

Telephone and postages	12,032	
Cash at bank	19,870	
Creditors		236,788
12% debentures		200,000
Debtors	452,310	
Directors' salaries	165,000	
Electricity and gas	26,780	
Insurance and rates	12,114	
Loose tools	29,760	
Interest received		8,135
Plant and machinery:		
At cost	246,880	
Accumulated depreciation at 1 July 2008		134,400
Office salaries and commissions	12,322	
Ordinary share capital		240,000
Interim dividend	6,000	
Profit and loss account at 1 July 2008		187,600
Provision for doubtful debts		11,220
Purchases	1,672,230	
Rent	86,200	
Commission received		11,330
Sales		2,133,245
Stock at 1 July 2008	341,570	
Delivery vehicles:		
At cost	113,087	
Accumulated depreciation at 1 July 2008		67,807
Bank charges	2,314	
Discount received		2,483
Discount allowed	10,874	
Goods returned by customers	23,665	
	3,233,008	3,233,008

Additional information:

(i) Stock at 30 June 2009, valued at cost, amounted to £443,100.

(ii) Depreciation is to be provided on plant and machinery at a rate of 20 per cent, using the reducing balance method.

(iii) Interest is to be paid to the debenture holders for the year.

(iv) Depreciation on delivery vehicles is at 25 per cent on a straight line basis.

(v) Loose tools are revalued annually. At 30 June 2009 the value was £26,000.

(vi) The provision for bad debts is to be made equal to £22,615 as at 30 June 2009.

(vii) Provision is to be made for machine repairs of £11,300.

You are required to prepare a profit and loss account for the year ended 30 June 2009, and a balance sheet as at that date.

30.1.5 Self-test

Terry Ltd prepared their profit and loss account and balance sheet for the year but were not able to use the correct formats. You are presented with the accounts as prepared and required to redraft them and present them in the correct format.

Profit and loss account as at 30 June 2008

Sales	316,800	
Less cost of sales	214,200	102,600
Add interest received		1,011
Discount received		3,879
Gross profit		107,490
Less depreciation	4,512	
Interest on loans	3,008	
Bank charges	1,014	
Office expenses	2,873	
Bad debts	1,984	
Taxation	2,430	15,821
Net profit		91,669
Less dividends	5,700	
Debenture dividend	6,000	11,700
Retained profit		79,969

Balance sheet for the year ending 30 June 2008

Fixed assets		
Machinery	123,420	
Office equipment	11,800	
Goodwill	40,000	
Stock	5,900	181,120
Current assets		
Cash at bank	1,003	
Prepayments	2,970	
Debtors	5,890	9,863
		190,983
Current liabilities		
Taxation	4,142	
Debentures	6,000	
Accruals	1,772	
Creditors	5,662	
Loan due 2012	12,900	30,476
		160,507
Financed by		
Ordinary shares	30,000	
Share premium	5,830	
Preference shares	19,000	
Profit for the year	79,969	
Retained earnings	20,008	
Dividends due	5,700	160,507

30.1.6 Self-test

Sarah and Mary commenced business on 1 January 2008. They are equal partners and each contributed £50,000 capital. Interest of 7 per cent was to be paid on this capital and, in addition, each partner would receive a salary of £28,000 and an equal share of profits.

The following are extracts of the balances shown in the partnership at 31 December 2008:

Plant and machinery	82,000
Stock	3,859
Office equipment	7,448
Cash on hand	106
Cash at bank	1,942
Creditors	2,314
Debtors	8,177
Net profit for the year	64,718
Capital – Sarah	50,000
Capital – Mary	50,000
Drawings – Sarah	28,900
Drawings – Mary	34,600

During the year each partner withdrew her salary from the business.

You are required to prepare:

(a) The profit and loss appropriation account for the year ended 31 December 2008 reflecting all adjustments for interest, drawings and salary.

(b) A statement showing the balance of each partner's current account at 31 December 2008.

30.1.7 Self-test

NuDeal Ltd was formed with an authorised share capital of 2,000,000 ordinary shares of 50p each.

NuDeal Ltd Trial balance at 31 December 2010

Bad debts	2,800	
Provision for bad debts		1,000
Profit and loss account 1 January 2010		172,000
Stock at I January 2010	75,200	
Land and buildings at cost	723,400	
Creditors		98,560
Issued share capital – fully paid		360,000
Equipment at cost	96,000	
Debtors	20,000	
Sales		796,000
Purchases	320,800	
Carriage inwards	2,960	
Carriage outwards	34,000	
Office expenses	49,600	
Advertising	51,760	
10 percent debentures		72,000
Debenture interest paid	7,200	
Rates	7,040	
Cash in hand	1,200	
Cash in bank	1,600	
Provision for depreciation of equipment		76,000
Salaries and wages	182,000	
	1,575,560	1,575,560

The following additional information is provided:

(i)   Stock at 31 December 2010 is £123,500.

(ii)   Salaries accrued: £12,600.

(iii) Rates prepaid: £1,250.

(iv) Provision for bad debts is to be reduced to £740.

(v)   Depreciation of 10 per cent p.a. on the cost of equipment must be provided.

(vi) A dividend of 4p per ordinary share is declared.

(vii) Taxation is provided at 20 per cent.

You are required to prepare the final accounts for Nudeal Ltd for the year ended 31 December 2010.

30.1.8 Self-test

James Ltd was registered with an authorised capital of £200,000 divided into 20,000 6 per cent preference shares of £1 each and 360,000 ordinary shares of 50p each.

Trial balance as at 31 December 2010

Ordinary share capital		100,000
Preference share capital		20,000
Share premium account		10,000
Profit and loss account		12,400
General reserve		15,000
Stock at 1 January 2010	17,460	
Land and buildings	100,000	
Plant and equipment (at cost)	22,000	
Motor vehicles (at cost)	15,000	
Furniture and fittings (at cost)	6,000	
Debtors and creditors	14,200	17,700
Purchases and sales	280,020	451,000
Wages and salaries	122,000	
Directors' remuneration	29,000	
Motor expenses	4,700	
Audit fees	1,300	
Rates and office expenses	1,700	
Commission	17,400	
Bad debts written off	2,600	
Bad debt provision		600
Accumulated depreciation – Plant and equipment		6,000
– Motor vehicles		6,700
– Furniture and fittings		1,000
Preference dividend	600	
Cash at bank	6,420	
	640,400	640,400

The following adjustments are to be made to the above trial balance:

(i) Stock on 31st December 2010 amounts to £86,500.

(ii) Depreciation at 10 per cent per annum on cost of plant and equipment.

(iii) Depreciation at 10 per cent per annum on the reducing balance of furniture and fittings.

(iv) Depreciation at 20 per cent per annum on cost of motor vehicles.

(v) The provision for bad debts is to be made equal to 10 per cent of sundry debtors.

(vi) Tax should be provided at 30 per cent of taxable income.

(vii) The directors recommend that:

(a) The final preference dividend should be paid.

(b) A dividend of 5 per cent should be paid on the ordinary shares.

You are required to prepare the financial statements of James Ltd for the year ended 31 December 2010.

30.1.9 Self-test

Aye Ltd has an authorised capital of 400,000 ordinary shares of £1 each. The company has issued 120,000 ordinary shares. At the year end it declares a dividend of 8 per cent. What is the total dividend to be paid?

30.1.10 Self-test

Which of the following statements is correct?

A company is able to improve its cash balance by:

(a) An issue of bonus shares.
(b) A rights issue.
(c) A transfer of money from the share premium account.
(d) A redemption of debentures.

30.1.11 Self-test

In the following question, Top Ltd acquires Bottom Ltd.

It acquires all the assets, except the bank account. In addition it assumes responsibility for the creditors. The purchase price is £30,000 of which 27,000 £1 ordinary shares are issued at par and the balance paid in cash.

You are required to prepare the balance sheet of Top Ltd after the acquisition.

	Top Ltd		Bottom Ltd	
Equipment	30,000		17,000	
Motor vehicles	15,000		8,000	
Office fixtures	3,0000	48,000	_____	25,000
Current assets				
Stock	6,000		3,000	
Debtors	7,200		1,100	
Cash at bank	9,800		1,700	
	23,000		5,800	
Less creditors	7,000	16,000	1,800	4,000
		64,000		29,000
Ordinary shares		50,000		25,000
Revenue reserves		14,000		4,000
		64,000		29,000

30.1.12 Self-test

Using the details in section 30.1.11 assume that Top Ltd purchases Bottom Ltd for £120,000. Neither the bank account nor the liabilities to creditors are taken over by Top Ltd.

Prior to the acquisition it is agreed that the assets of Bottom Ltd will be revalued as follows:

Equipment	£14,000
Vehicles	£7,000
Stock	£2,400
Debtors	£900

Payment of the purchase price is as follows:

- 80,000 £1 ordinary shares issued at a premium of 40p each.
- The balance in cash.

You are required to prepare the balance sheet of Top Ltd after the acquisition.

30.1.13 Self-test

Robin and Ann trade as partners. Their year end is 30 June and after allowing for the adjustments, as contained in their partnership agreement, the remainder of the profits or losses are to be shared equally between them.

The following are the additional adjustments to be made:

(i)   Salaries: Robin £36,000 per annum and Ann £24,000 per annum.
(ii) Interest on capital of 10 per cent is allowed.
(iii) Interest on drawings amounted to £160 to Robin and £475 to Ann.

The trial balance as at 30 June 2009 is as follows:

Capital – Robin		180,000
– Ann		110,000
Current accounts – Robin	1,021	
– Ann	14,060	
Salaries and wages	24,620	
Plant and machinery at cost	127,000	
Motor vehicles at cost	42,100	
Electricity accrued at 1 July 2008		158
Land and buildings at cost	316,734	
Provision for depreciation on plant and machinery		24,800
Stock	7,320	
Debtors	4,580	
Creditors		8,960
Bank	8,103	
Electricity	3,672	
Selling expenses	2,086	
Postage and telephone	4,930	
Printing and stationery	2,460	
Sales		197,000
Provision for bad debts		316
Provision for depreciation on motor vehicles		22,480
Mike – loan account		42,000
Purchases	21,008	
Rates and taxes	6,020	
	585,714	585,714

The following additional information is given:

(i)   Stock at 30 June 2009 is £9,820.
(ii)   The debtors shown in the trial balance include bad debts of £425.
(iii) Depreciation, using the straight line method, is calculated at 10 per cent per annum on plant and machinery and 20 per cent per annum on motor vehicles.
(iv)   Electricity accrued at 30 June 2009 is £135, while rates of £98 are prepaid.
(v)   A provision for bad debts of £630 is to be made at 30 June 2009.
(vi)   A loan from Mike was received on 1 July 2008. Interest of 7 per cent p.a. is payable and the loan itself is to be repaid on 1 July 2009.
(vii) Included in salaries and wages are drawings made by Robin of £8,000 and by Ann of £9,500.

You are required to prepare a profit and loss account and appropriation account for the year ended 30 June 2009 and a balance sheet at that date.

30.1.14 Self-test

Monica, Cyril and Gene are in partnership. The trial balance at 31 December 2010 is as follows:

Capital accounts – Monica		55,000
– Cyril		35,000
– Gene		15,000
Current accounts – Monica	8,600	
– Cyril	3,800	
– Gene	4,800	
11 per cent loan due 1 December 2012		49,000
Land and buildings	211,590	
Delivery vehicles at cost	40,000	
Provision for depreciation on vehicles		30,210
Office expenses	2,210	
Debtors' control account	26,900	
Creditors' control account		22,850
Sales		287,300
Stock	44,970	
Investment income		1,100
Goodwill at cost	19,800	
Purchases	84,070	
Rates	13,150	
Salaries to staff	17,080	
Motor expenses	3,100	
Provision for bad debts		2,100
Bank	13,050	
Loan interest	1,900	
Bank charges	370	
Returns	1,900	1,600
Printing and stationery	1,870	
	499,160	499,160

The following additional information must be taken into account:

(i) The stock at 31 December 2010 is valued at £31,000.

(ii) Motor expenses of £240 are to be accrued and rates of £160 have been paid in advance.

(iii) Debtors of £2,000 are to be written off as bad.

(iv) The bad debt provision at year end is £498.

(v) Depreciation on delivery vehicles is calculated at 10 per cent per annum using the straight line method.

(vi) Investment income of £320 is still to be received.

(vii) Loan interest must be provided for at the end of the year.

Monica and Gene are entitled to salaries of £19,000 and £23,000 per annum, respectively.

    All the partners receive interest on capital of 9 per cent per annum.

The remaining profit or loss is divided between Monica, Cyril and Gene in the ratio of 2:2:1.

You are required to prepare a profit and loss account and appropriation account for the year ended 31 December 2010 and a balance sheet at that date.

30.1.15 Self-test

K, L and M are in partnership, sharing profits and losses 2:1:1. They prepare accounts to 31 December each year.

The following is the balance sheet as at 31 December 2008:

			Cost	Depr	NBV
Fixed assets					
Delivery vehicles			46,000	11,000	35,000
Office computers			11,000	4,000	7,000
			57,000	15,000	42,000
Current assets					
Stock			16,000		
Debtors			11,000		
Cash at bank			3,000	30,000	
Current liabilities					
Creditors			4,000	4,000	26,000
					68,000
	K	L	M		
Capital accounts	26,000	18,000	14,000	58,000	
Current accounts	4,000	3,000	3,000	10,000	
				68,000	

You are given the following information:

(i) Depreciation is charged as follows:
   (a) Delivery vehicle 20 per cent straight line.
   (b) Computers 15 per cent reducing balance.
(ii) Annual salary K £16,000.
(iii) Interest on capital balances at beginning of the year – 5 per cent p.a.

On 30 June 2009 L retired from the partnership. The agreement set out the following:

(a) The goodwill at the date of retirement was valued at £48,000 but it was agreed that this would not be shown in the books of the partnership.
(b) L would leave a loan account of £15,000 with the new partnership. This loan would carry interest of 10 per cent p.a.
(c) The balance of L's capital and current accounts would be paid out in cash on 30 June 2009.

K and M continue in partnership but with the following changes as from 1 July 2009:

(i) K continues to receive an annual salary of £16,000 and M is to be paid £12,000 p.a.
(ii) All remaining profits and losses are shared equally.

For the year ended 31 December 2009 the following details are available:

Sales	401,800
Purchases	198,300
Wages to staff	82,100
Office expenses	14,900
Drawings to 30 June 2009 – K	11,000
– L	8,000
– M	6,000
Drawings to 31 December 2009 – K	13,000
– M	9,000
Debtors at 31 December 2009	14,000
Cash at bank at 31 December 2009	41,356
Creditors at 31 December 2009	4,600
Stock at 31 December 2009	5,000

You are required to prepare a trading, profit and loss account and appropriation account for the 6 months to 30 June 2009 and for 6 months to 31 December 2009.

You are also required to prepare a balance sheet at 31 December 2009 and the partners' accounts at that date.

Assume the profit is earned on a uniform basis throughout the year.

30.1.16 Self-test

Rush and Aldridge are in partnership sharing profits and losses in the ratio 3:2 respectively. The following list of balances has been extracted from the books of the business for the year ended 30 November 2006.

	£
Land at cost	120,000
Fixtures and fittings (cost)	70,000
Fixtures and fittings (depreciation)	20,000
Creditors	17,000
Debtors	21,000
Balance at bank (Cr)	7,500
Bank loan	20,000
Provision for bad debts	1,000
Sales	98,000
Purchases	39,000
Stock (1-12-05)	11,000
Rent and rates	3,000
Insurance	1,500
Salaries and wages	13,700
Office expenses	2,800
Heating and lighting	1,750
Advertising	900
Capital account – Rush	80,000
– Aldridge	50,000
Current account – Rush (cr)	3,850
– Aldridge (dr)	2,000
Drawings – Rush	3,700
– Aldridge	7,000

The following information is also available:

(i) At 30.11.06:
- Closing stock £13,800.
- Rent outstanding £500.
- Salaries outstanding £1,120.
- £80 insurance prepaid for the following year.

(ii) Provision for bad debts needs increasing to £1,150.

(iii) Interest of £2,000 on the bank loan needs to be included in the accounts.

(iv) Fixtures and fittings are depreciated at 10 per cent on a reducing balance basis.

(v) Partnership salaries are as follows:
- Rush £8,000.
- Aldridge £2,000.

(vi) Interest on capital is allowed at 10 per cent.

Required:

(a) From the list of balances (at 30.11.06) prepare the trial balance for Rush and Aldridge.

(b) Prepare a trading and profit and loss account and a balance sheet as at 30 November 2006.

(ABE, Introduction to Accounting, June 2007)

30.1.17 Self-test

Dixon and Phillips are in partnership sharing profits and losses in the ratio 2:1 respectively. The following trial balance has been drawn up at 31 March 2009.

	DR £	CR £
Land – at cost	100,000	
Buildings – at cost	126,000	
Fixtures – at cost	8,000	
Cumulative depreciation (at 1 April 2008)		
– Buildings		9,450
– Fixtures		1,600
Stock (at 1 April 2008)	2,100	
Debtors	4,900	
Creditors		1,300
Bank overdraft		840
Sales		78,600
Purchases	31,700	
Rent	1,120	
Rates	2,360	
Insurance	3,540	
Heating	8,020	
Salaries and wages	14,290	
Capital – Dixon		150,000
– Phillips		75,000
Current – Dixon	1,750	
– Phillips	2,650	
Drawings – Dixon	4,180	
– Phillips	6,180	
	316,790	316,790

The following information is also available:

(i) Closing stock at 31 March 2009 was £4,240.
(ii) Rent accrued at 31 March 2009 was £400.
(iii) Insurance prepaid at 31 March 2009 was £720.
(iv) Depreciation was to be provided as follows:
- Buildings at 2.5 per cent per year on a straight line basis assuming nil residual value.
- Fixtures at 20 per cent per year on a reducing balance basis.
(v) Partnership salaries are as follows:
- Dixon £2,000.
- Phillips £500.
(vi) Interest on capital is allowed at 5 per cent per year.

Required:

(a) Prepare the trading, profit and loss account and appropriation account for Dixon and Phillips for the year ended 31 March 2009.
(b) Prepare a balance sheet for Dixon and Phillips at 31 March 2009.

(ABE, Introduction to Accounting, June 2009)

30.1.18 Self-test

Filling and Kap are partners in a dentistry business. The following trial balance was extracted from their books on 31 March 2006.

	Debit £	Credit £
Capital accounts 1 April 2005 – Filling		100,000
– Kap		50,000
Current accounts 1 April 2005 – Filling		5,000
– Kap	15,000	
Drawings – Filling	100,000	
– Kap	95,000	
Bank	7,500	
Wages to assistants	40,000	
Creditors		3,415
Administration expenses	8,500	
Fittings and equipment at cost	60,000	
Provision for depreciation on fittings and equipment 1 April 2005		18,000
Advertising	840	
Materials bought and fees received	22,000	420,000
Stock of materials 1 April 2005	2,000	
Cash in hand	275	
Loan from Filling		10,000
Premises	255,300	
	606,415	606,415

Their partnership agreement provides that

- Profits and losses are to be shared in the ratio 3:2 to Filling and Kap respectively.
- Interest on fixed capital is allowed at 5 per cent per year.
- Each partner is paid an annual salary of £80,000.

Additional information:

1. Stock of materials at 31 March 2006 was £640.
2. The fittings and equipment are to be depreciated by 10 per cent of cost per annum.
3. Interest at 5 per cent per annum on the loan is to be paid to Filling, through her current account.
4. Filling's family has used the business for dental care. This has not been recorded in the accounts. The estimated cost is £500.
5. An insurance bill amounting to £1,800 and covering the year from 1 October 2005 had not been paid.
6. Interest on drawings: Filling £1,000 and Kap £950.

From the information given, prepare for the partnership for the year ended 31 March 2006:

(a) a profit and loss account;
(b) a profit and loss appropriation account;
(c) partners' current accounts;
(d) a balance sheet at 31 March 2006.

Note: You are not required to show details of the current accounts in the balance sheet. You need only show the balances of the current accounts at 31 March 2006.

(Edexcel Accounting 7011, May 2006)

30.1.19 Self-test

Sylett Cricket Club has been in existence for a number of years.

On 1 April 2005 the club's assets and liabilities were as follows.

	£
Sports equipment	40,000
Subscriptions due	250
Subscriptions received in advance	100
Cash at bank	10,000

Members pay an annual subscription of £50, which entitles them to use the club's facilities. During the year ended 31 March 2006 the club had 1,000 members.

The club's treasurer has produced the following summary of receipts and payments for the year ended 31 March 2006.

Receipts	£	Payments	£
Subscriptions	50,250	Clubhouse rent	1,600
Interest free loan from a member	4,000	Groundsman's wages	8,500
Competition receipts	800	Repairs to equipment	320
Sale of surplus sports equipment	240	Competition fees	350
		Sports equipment	4,000

Notes:

(i) On 31 March 2006 the groundsman was owed £140 wages, and £120 clubhouse rent was prepaid.

(ii) Depreciation on sports equipment was estimated at £2,500 for the year.

(iii) The surplus sports equipment sold during the year had a net book value of £600.

(iv) Members' subscriptions at 31 March 2006:
  - all subscriptions outstanding at 1 April 2005 had been received;
  - £50 subscriptions had been received in advance;
  - some subscriptions had not been paid.

For the Sylett Cricket Club for the year ended 31 March 2006, prepare:

(a) the subscriptions account;

(b) the income and expenditure account.

(Edexcel Accounting 7011, May 2006)

30.1.20 Self-test

The Charford Social Club presents you with the following receipts and payments for the year ended 31 December 2002.

Receipts	£	Payments	£
Subscriptions	4,200	Rent	500
Sales of draw tickets	900	New furniture	200
Sales of annual dance ticket	1,000	Caretaker's wages	5,200
Sales of refreshments	4,000	Light and heat	1,870
		Draw prizes	400
		Dance expenses	340
		Purchase of refreshments	1,500

Additional information:

- £80 subscriptions received were owing from last year (2001) and £120 was received for the next year (2003). On 31 December 2002, £90 subscriptions are in arrears.
- Furniture is to be depreciated by 10 per cent on the year-end value (value of furniture at 1 January 2002 was £6,000).
- Creditors for refreshments amounted to £500 at 1 January 2002, and to £600 at 31 December 2002.
- An electricity account for £100 is unpaid at 31 December 2002.

Prepare an income and expenditure account for the year ended 31 December 2002.

(Edexcel Accounting 7011, January 2003)

30.1.21 Self-test

Staff at Bromsgrove High School take students camping each year during the summer holiday. The School Camp accounts showed the following balances on 1 August 2001, immediately after the 2001 camp:

- tents £20,000;
- cash at bank £6,200;
- pots and pans £460;
- debtors £320.

Three hundred students attended the 2002 Camp, paying fees of £100 each. The students operated in groups of five and paid £5 per group for ownership of a map of their walking area.

Payments relating to the 2002 Camp were as follows:

- hire of coaches £7,500;
- site fees £6,000;
- purchase of additional tents £5,000;
- purchase of food and drink £4,000;
- mountain rescue fees £280;
- ambulance fees £150;
- staff travelling expenses £2,300;
- maps £420.

On 31 July 2002, site fees of £225 were still outstanding, a stock of tinned food was valued at £400 and there was £10,970 at the bank. Debtors remaining after the 2001 camp were written off as irrecoverable. Total fixed assets were to be depreciated by £1,800.

(a) Prepare the income and expenditure account for the Bromsgrove High School Camp for the year ended 31 July 2002.
(b) Explain how the accumulated fund was made up at 1 August 2001.
(c) Using the available information, explain whether you would increase or decrease the fees to be charged to students for the next camp in 2003. Give two reasons for whatever course of action you think appropriate.

(Edexcel Accounting 7011, May 2003)

Chapter 31

Cash flow statements

Objectives After you have studied this chapter, you should be able to:

- explain the reasons for the difference between profit and changes in cash balances;
- prepare a reconciliation statement between operating profit and the cash flow from operating activities;
- understand the importance of cash to a business;
- prepare a cash flow statement in the format consistent with FRS1;
- describe how information can help the assessment of the current financial position and future prospects.

31.1 Introduction

Cash is the lifeblood of a business. Although a business can operate at a loss and survive in the short term, without a positive cash flow it will not succeed. We have seen that the balance sheet is a 'snapshot' at a point in time and, as such, portrays a static picture of cash balances. It does not show how a business finances its various activities.

The profit and loss account, on the other hand, explains the reasons for the changes in the net worth of a business through its showing of the profit (or loss) for the period. It does not, however, give any information on the liquidity of the business.

Many simple organisations, such as small clubs and other not-for-profit associations, limit their accounting activities to a record of cash receipts and cash payments (see Chapter 27). Periodically (normally annually) a summary of all cash transactions is produced for the members. This summary would show one single figure for each category of payment or receipt, for example, membership subscriptions. Using this summary, decisions are made by the club. This cash summary is the main means of the committee fulfilling its moral duty to its members.

Clearly, businesses, which are more complex than simple clubs, need to produce a profit and loss account which reflects movements in wealth and the net increase (profit) or decrease (loss) for the period concerned. Although in the past it was felt that there was no need for businesses to produce more than a profit and loss account and balance sheet, it has now been shown that in the short to medium term, this is not sufficient. In the past there existed the implicit belief that if a business were profitable, then automatically it would have plenty of cash.

We can see that in preparing accounts, the cash flow does not feature when determining, for example, the amount of sales or an expense in the profit and loss account. The accruals-based nature of the profit and loss account obscures the question of how and where a business generates its cash. For this reason we now produce a statement which reflects movements in cash.

31.2 Why is cash so important?

We have seen that cash and profit do not go hand in hand, so why the current preoccupation with cash? After all, cash is only one of the assets which a business needs to help it to function. For a business, the term cash implies cash (notes and coins) and also the funds in the bank. The reason for its importance is that claims against a business need to be settled in cash. Employees must be paid in cash. If a business buys stock then it must be paid for in cash. When businesses fail, it is their inability to find the cash to pay creditors (including taxation due) that forces them into liquidation. Therefore, it is cash that analysts and other users watch most carefully in trying to assess the ability of the business to survive and/or to take advantage of commercial opportunities as they arise. (You will also see the importance of cash when we discuss ratios in Chapter 32.)

The cash flow statement is now accepted, along with the profit and loss account and balance sheet, as one of the standard accounting statements. In the UK, FRS1 (Cash flow statements) requires most companies to publish a cash flow statement as part of their annual accounts.

31.3 What is a cash flow statement?

The cash flow statement is a summary of the cash receipts and payments over the period concerned. All payments of a particular type, for example cash payments to acquire additional fixed assets, are added together to give just one figure which appears in the statement. The net total of the statement is the net increase or decrease of the cash of the business over the period. The statement is, therefore, an analysis and summary of the business' cash movements for the period. It serves as an indicator of the ability of the business to generate cash.

The balance sheet reflects the combination of assets and claims of the business at a particular point in time. Over the period there are changes to some items in the balance sheet caused by the trading of the past period. These items include the net worth of the business and cash.

It is the cash flow statement that tells us how the business has generated cash during the period and where that cash has gone. By tracking the sources and the ways in which cash is used over several years we are able to show the financing trends of a business. This assists a user of the statements to make predictions on likely future behaviour of the business and its ability to meet future commitments.

We have said before that it is important that a business generates cash in order to survive. We must emphasise that profit is not equal to cash and therefore the profit disclosed in the profit and loss account does not give any indication as to the extent of cash generated by the business.

It must also be borne in mind that the amount of profit shown in the profit and loss account may be that which the business considers appropriate and this could be determined by what is commonly called creative accounting. Cash, however, cannot be manipulated and the cash flow statement, by focusing on the sources of the cash and its uses, discloses the full amount of cash generated.

31.3.1 Self-test

To illustrate the difference between cash and profit you need to complete the following table. In each case state if the transaction affects profit or cash flow or both. Indicate if the transaction increases, decreases or has no effect on the profit and/or cash flow.

Transaction	Effect on profit	Effect on cash flow
Issue of new shares		
Bad debt written off		
Goods bought for cash		
Bonus share issue		
Dividend paid to shareholders		
Goods purchased for credit		
Delivery van purchased for cash		

31.4 The contents of the cash flow statement

We set out in section 31.3 a description of a cash flow statement and how it links in with the profit and loss account and balance sheet. We now need to examine the contents.

There is a standard format for a cash flow statement. In the UK, it is set out in FRS 1 (an accounting standard issued by the Accounting Standards Board).[25]

The starting point for a cash flow statement is the reported net profit or loss for the period. The end point is the total increase, or decrease, in cash and bank balances. Although both figures are available in the balance sheet, the cash flow statement reconciles the one with the other. It does this by showing the sources of the cash and then how that cash is used. For this purpose we must note that cash is cash in hand and deposits repayable on demand less any bank overdrafts.

The cash flow statement consists of a number of standard headings:[26]

- Net cash flow from operating activities.
- Returns on investments and servicing of finance.
- Taxation.

[25] This and other standards can be viewed at www.frc.org.uk.
[26] FRS1 requires that each section be separately identified and shown on the cash flow statement. Internationally IFS 7 'Statement of cash flows' is issued – see www.iasb.org and also Chapter 41, section 41.6.3.

- Capital expenditure and financial investments.
- Acquisitions and disposals.
- Equity dividends paid.
- Management of liquid resources.
- Financing.

The end result after adding or deducting the various headings shows us the increase, or decrease, in cash over the period.

In preparing the cash flow statement we must remember that there are various activities over and above the items reflected in the profit and loss account that are a source of (or application of) cash. These are:

- dividends paid;
- purchase and sale of fixed assets;
- financing activities such as loans; and
- investing activities such as the purchase of shares.

31.4.1 Operating activities

This section shows the net cash flows that have been generated from trading operations during the period. Operating activities include such items as changes in stock, debtors and creditors.

It must be noted that certain adjustments must be made to the net profit figure, such as that for depreciation, which must be added back in the cash flow statement as it does not involve a flow of cash. Another item not involving a flow of cash is the loss or profit made on the sale of a fixed asset as it is, in effect, a depreciation adjustment. The profit and loss account also shows other provisions such as a bad debt provision. These, too, must be eliminated from the cash flow statement.

An example of the method of reconciling profit with the cash flow from operating activity is given below:

Operating profit	21,000
Add: Non-cash expenses	
Depreciation of fixed assets	1,500
Loss on sale of fixed asset	2,500
	25,000
Deduct: Stock decrease (increase)	2,000
Debtors decrease (increase)	5,000
Creditors increase (decrease)	1,000
Cash flow from operating activity	17,000

Once this figure (£17,000) has been calculated we can start our cash flow statement with the first section, namely 'Net cash flow from operating activities'. There is no need to show the reconciliation in the cash flow statement.

31.4.2 Returns on investments and servicing of finance

Returns on investments and the servicing of finance include the payment of preference dividends on shares and interest paid on loans. Investment income such as interest and dividends received are also included in this section.

One point often forgotten in exams is that certain items are added in the cash flow statement while others are deducted. In this section, for example, we would add to our opening figure of cash inflow all interest received and deduct interest and preference dividends paid. The final figure in this section would either be a net cash inflow or outflow. In the latter instance it is deducted from the opening amount in the cash flow statement.

31.4.3 Taxation

Taxation shows only the payments and receipts made during the period. Any provisions created in the accounts are ignored as they do not involve any movement of cash. Here again you must remember to deduct all payments made.

31.4.4 Capital expenditure and financial investment

Capital expenditure includes the sale and/or the purchase of fixed assets as well as investments in or from other businesses. When fixed assets are sold the amount received in cash from the sale is shown under this section.

This section can have both expenditure (on fixed assets) as well as receipts (from the sale of fixed assets).

31.4.5 Equity dividends paid

This section reflects the dividends paid in cash to the ordinary shareholders during the period – preference dividends are shown as 'Returns on investments and servicing of finance' as explained in section 31.4.2. Here again, any provision for dividend is ignored in the cash flow statement.

31.4.6 Management of liquid resources

This section shows the cash receipts and payments from the purchase or sale of disposable investments (current asset investments). These include short-term deposits or investments (short-term) in a company.

31.4.7 Financing

Financing shows all the long-term borrowings. This includes receipts from share issues, loans and debentures less any expenses paid in connection with such receipts. It also shows as a deduction any repayments made when the source of the finance, such as the debentures, is redeemed or repaid.

31.4.8 Reconciliation of net cash flow

Having completed the cash flow statement, we would show a final figure which equates to either an increase in cash or a decrease (outflow) of cash. It is important that this final figure is reconciled to the cash movement that has taken place during the period.

One way to prepare this reconciliation is to take the opening balances of cash and bank and adjust them to the closing balances at the end of the period. The difference (either positive or negative) is then shown as the inflow or outflow of funds during the period and must agree with the cash flow statement prepared earlier.

The following layout is suggested for this reconciliation:

Changes in cash and bank balances for the year ended 31 December 2009

	1 January 2009	31 December 2009	Change in year
Cash	7,000	4,000	(3,000)
Bank	11,000	(5,000)	(16,000)
Total	18,000	(1,000)	(19,000)

In the above layout we are given the opening cash and bank balances – a total of £18,000. During the year there is a cash outflow of £19,000 and this results in our cash on hand reducing to £4,000 and the cash at bank moving into an overdraft of £5,000.

This change (outflow) of cash must agree with the cash flow statement.

31.5 The working capital cycle

Before we examine in greater detail the prescribed format of the cash flow statement we need to understand what is meant by the working capital cycle. In a business the assets are used to acquire goods for resale. Acquisition is either in cash or through the use of credit. Ultimately the creditors are paid in cash. If we buy raw material this goes through the manufacturing process with all the expenses being paid in cash. The work in progress is, at some point, converted to finished goods. These finished goods are sold for cash, or on credit, but if the latter then the debtors eventually pay in cash.

This, then, is the cycle of cash in a business and it is illustrated by Figure 31.1.

31.5.1 Worked example

The following is a simple form of cash flow:

Amounts received from debtors	1,950
Less: Amounts paid to creditors	1,800
Net cash inflow	£150

There are a number of situations where we can determine the effects on the cash flow of a business without having to prepare a full statement. For example, if the debtors increase then the cash received from debtors is less than the credit sales.

We can take another example where we are given the profit for the period.

Operating profit	350	
Decrease in debtors	150	This represents an increase in cash as debtors are paying monies owed
	500	
Less decrease in creditors	250	This shows an outflow of cash as we are paying out monies owed
Less increase in stock	200	Extra stock is a cash outflow
Cash inflow	£50	

Figure 31.1 **The cash flow cycle**

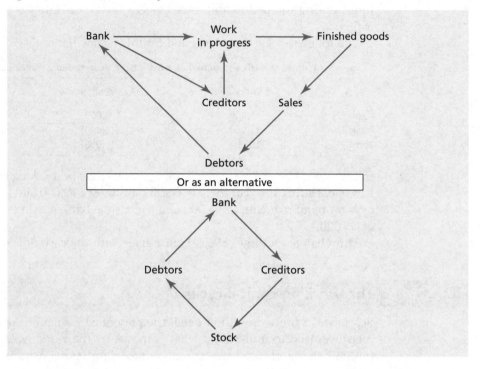

31.5.2 Worked example

A company shows a net profit of £18,300 for the year. This is after allowing for depreciation of £180 on furniture and £750 on motor vehicles.

An extract of the balance sheet of the company for the year is shown below:

	2009	*2010*
Furniture – net book value	980	800
Motor vehicles	3,750	3,000
Stock	670	510
Debtors	900	1,100
Creditors	780	920
Accrued expenses	180	140

We are required to reconcile the operating profit of £18,300 with the cash flow from operating activities.

Operating profit	18,300
Add: Non-cash expenses (depreciation)	930
	19,230
Add: Stock decrease	160
Creditors increase	140
Less: Debtors (increase)	200
Accrued expenses (decrease)	40
Cash flow from operating activity	19,290

31.5.3 Self-test

The following table has certain areas where the amount is missing. Using the information that you have read, you are required to complete the table.

	A	B	C
Change in stock	+2	−50	+70
Change in debtors	+30	−15	−10
Change in creditors	+5	?	−18
Depreciation	15	20	25
Operating profit (after depreciation)	+100	−80	+40
Cash – opening balance	+200	−160	?
Cash – closing balance	?	−100	−10

Remember that the cash flow statement only shows cash flows. We must remove the effects of accruals and other balances.

31.5.4 Self-test

Complete the following table:

Increase in debtors	4,250
Sales	?
Bad debts written off	170
Cash received	19,331
Increase in creditors	3,320
Purchases	17,192
Cash paid	?

31.6 The cash flow statement

The cash flow statement has as its first item the net cash inflow from operating activities. To find this figure we need to prepare a statement as illustrated below:

Net operating profit (before interest and taxation)
Add back:
Depreciation charges
Loss on sale of fixed assets
Decrease in stocks
Decrease in debtors
Increase in creditors
Deduct:
Profit on sale of fixed assets
Increase in stocks
Increase in debtors
Decrease in creditors
Net cash flow from operating activities*

* Note: It is this figure that is shown in the cash flow statement.

Having calculated the net cash flow (it is not always an inflow – if more cash has gone out then you show it as an outflow of cash), we can proceed to the cash flow statement.

The following is the format of a cash flow statement as used by companies.[27]

Sample plc Cash flow statement for the year ended 31 December 2009

Net cash inflow from operating activities
Returns on investments and servicing of finance
Interest received
Interest paid
Preference share dividend paid
Taxation
Corporation tax paid
Capital expenditure and financial investment
Payment to acquire intangible fixed assets
Payment to acquire tangible fixed assets
Receipts from sale of tangible fixed assets
Receipts from repayment of loan
Equity dividends paid
Ordinary share dividend paid
Management of liquid resources
Disposal of securities
Cash withdrawn from deposit account
Financing
Issue of ordinary share capital
Repurchase of debentures
Repayment of long-term loan
Increase/decrease in cash

The final increase or decrease should agree with the increase or decrease in the bank account and other liquid resources.

31.7 Advantages of a cash flow statement

The statement helps the user understand where the business has generated its cash and how it is applied. It is important if this user is an investor and this will be looked at and discussed in detail in Chapter 32. Users have many questions, such as:

- What amount of cash is generated internally?
- Why is the bank balance less when the business made a profit?
- How are the fixed assets financed?
- How did (or how will) the business pay dividends if it made a loss?

We cannot stress the importance of the fact that without cash, a business will fail. All businesses must plan their cash flow, both for the long term and short term. Often a cash flow statement is prepared too late and it becomes a difficult

---

[27] As required by FRS1 (Revised 1996). Note also that the headings in **bold** must be shown.

rescue mission. Sometimes a cash flow statement is prepared with figures that are simply too optimistic. We need to estimate what cash is needed and, at the same time, estimate the time taken to pay and receive cash from sales and purchases. When preparing the cash flow statement it is important to be realistic and use minimum sales figures and maximum expenses.

Once the cash flow statement is prepared the business is in a position to:

- ensure adequate cash is available;
- see that there is enough cash for future capital expenditure;
- manage the cash and invest any surplus; and
- identify short-term shortages and help raise funds.

31.7.1 Worked example

You are given the balance sheet of Raymond Ltd and are required to prepare a cash flow statement at 31 December 2009. You are told that one delivery van was sold during the year for £1,600. The book value at the date of sale was £3,400.

Balance sheet of Raymond Ltd as at 31 December

	31.12.2008		31.12.2009	
Fixed assets				
Delivery vans – cost	45,000		39,000	
Accumulated depreciation	16,000	29,000	18,000	21,000
Current assets				
Stock	49,000		27,500	
Debtors	8,400		12,700	
less Provision for bad debts	(600)		(900)	
Cash on hand and bank	5,350		3,980	
	62,150		43,280	
Creditors	(5,320)		(7,140)	
Net current assets		56,830		36,140
		85,830		57,140
Long-term loan		15,000		7,000
		70,830		50,140
Share capital	56,200		31,330	
Profit and loss account	14,630		18,810	
		70,830		50,140

Reconciliation of operating profit to operating cash flow

Cash flow from operating activities		
Net profit for the year*		4,180
Depreciation (added back)	4,600	
Loss on sale of fixed asset	1,800	
Increase in provision for bad debts	300	
Decrease in stock	21,500	
Increase in debtors	(4,300)	
Increase in creditors	1,820	25,720
Net cash flow from operating activities		29,900

* The net profit for the year is the difference between the opening and closing balances of the profit and loss account.

Cash flow statement for the year ended 31 December 2009

Net cash flow from operating activities		29,900
Capital expenditure and financial investment		
Proceeds from sale of van		1,600
Financing		
Decrease in share capital	(24,870)	
Loan repaid	(8,000)	
		(32,870)
Decrease in cash		(1,370)

An analysis of the changes in the cash on hand and bank is shown as follows:

Balance at 1 January 2009	**5,350**
Decrease in cash	(1,370)
Balance at 31 December 2009	**£3,980**

Note: The depreciation added back is calculated as follows:

We know that the original cost of the van sold was £6,000 (the difference between the cost in 2008 and the cost in 2009 as per balance sheet). As the book value at the time of sale was £3,400 this means that the depreciation on the van sold was £2,600 (£6,000 – 3,400).

The additional accumulated depreciation shown in the 2009 balance sheet is £2,000 (18,000 – 16,000). Add to this the depreciation of the van sold of £2,600 and we arrive at a total depreciation for the year of £4,600 (2,000 + 2,600).

The loss on sale of the van is calculated as follows:
Net book value (given in question) = £3,400. Sale price = £1,600. Therefore, loss on sale is £3,400 – 1,600 = £1,800.

31.7.2 Self-test

You are presented with the following balance sheet for J J Motors Ltd. The company has made a profit in 2009 of £30,600. The director advises you that he is short of funds and, in fact, has an overdraft at the year end of £3,240. He does not understand where all the money has gone and asks you to prepare a cash flow statement to answer this problem.

Balance sheet as at 31 December

	2008			2009	
Fixed assets		55,800			66,600
Provision for depreciation		5,400			6,120
		50,400			60,480
Current assets					
Stock	11,160			21,240	
Debtors	14,040			12,240	
Bank	5,400				
	30,600			33,480	
Current liabilities					
Creditors	7,200			7,920	
Overdraft				3,240	
	7,2000	23,400		11,160	22,320
		73,800			82,800
Share capital		48,600			27,000
Profit and loss account		25,200			55,800
		73,800			82,800

31.7.3 Self-test

You are presented with the following balance sheet for Maxwell & Co. Ltd. You are required to prepare the cash flow statement for the year.

Balance sheet as at 31 December 2009

	2008			2009	
Fixed assets		115,475			137,825
Provision for depreciation		11,175			12,665
		104,300			125,160
Current assets					
Stock	23,095			43,955	
Debtors	29,055			25,330	
Bank	11,175				
	63,325			69,285	
Current liabilities					
Creditors	14,900			16,390	
Overdraft				6,705	
	14,900	48,425		23,095	46,190
		152,725			171,350
Share capital		100,575			55,875
Profit and loss account		52,150			115,475
		152,725			171,350

31.7.4 Self-test

You are required to prepare the cash flow statement for the year ended 31 December 2009 for Hilmar Trading Ltd from the information provided below:

Profit and loss account for the year ended 31 December 2009

Net profit before charging the following:		1,182
Depreciation	251	
Loss on sale of fixed asset	38	289
Operating profit		893
Less interest payable		60
Profit before tax		833
Taxation		264
Profit after tax		569
Ordinary share dividend		153
Profit retained for the year		416
Add balance brought forward		1,042
		1,458

Balance sheet as at 31 December

	2008		2009	
		2008		*2009*
Fixed assets				
at cost		3,315		3,200
Plus additions		–		191
		3,315		3,391
Depreciation		476		676
		2,839		2,715
Current assets				
Stock	43		52	
Debtors	106		140	
Bank	119		102	
	268		294	
Current liabilities				
Creditors	13		26	
Taxation	183		217	
Proposed dividend	34		43	
	230		286	
Working capital		38		8
		2,877		2,723
Long-term loan		1,063		425
		1,814		2,298
Share capital		723		765
Share premium		49		75
Profit and loss		1,042		1,458
		1,814		2,298

31.7.5 Self-test

The balance sheet of Peter Paul plc as at 30 June 2009 is given below, together with a summary profit and loss account for the year. You are required to prepare the cash flow statement for inclusion with the annual report.

Balance sheet as at 30 June

	2008		*2009*	
Fixed assets				
Land and buildings at cost	260		260	
less Accumulated depreciation	60	200	64	196
Plant and machinery at cost	140		160	
less Accumulated depreciation	34	106	46	114
		306		310
Current assets				
Stock	50		48	
Debtors	32		58	
Short-term investments	10		40	
Cash at bank	6		14	
	98		160	
Creditors: Amounts due in less than one year				
Trade creditors	38		54	
Taxation	30		24	
Dividends	24		28	
	92		106	
Net current assets		6		54
		312		364
Creditors: Amounts due in more than one year				
10% debentures		40		80
		272		284
Financed by:				
Share capital		200		200
Revenue reserves		72		84
		272		284

Profit and loss account for the year ended 30 June 2009

Sales	346	
less Cost of sales	192	
Gross profit		154
less Expenses	48	
Depreciation – buildings	4	
– Plant and machinery	32	
Loss on sale of fixed asset	2	86
Net operating profit		68
Interest receivable		4
		72
Interest payable		8
Profit before tax		64
Corporation tax		24
Net profit after tax		40
Proposed dividend		28
Net profit unappropriated		12

Note: During the year plant and machinery costing £30m, with accumulated depreciation of £20m, was sold for £8m.

31.7.6 Self-test

You are given the following extract of balance sheet items:

	31.12.08	31.12.09
Creditors		
Taxation	40,000	51,000
Proposed dividends	78,000	68,000
Debenture interest	40,000	40,000
Ordinary shares	75,000	32,000
Share premium	24,000	24,000
General reserve (ex P&L account)	34,000	48,000
Profit and loss reserve	141,000	115,700

You are required to calculate the net profit before interest and taxation for the year ended 31 December 2009.

31.7.7 Self-test

A company had an opening balance of £70,000 for interest receivable and a closing balance of £84,000. The profit and loss account for the year shows an amount of £180,000 as interest received.

What amount is shown in the cash flow statement?

31.7.8 Self-test

You are given the following information at the year ends:

Balance sheet extract

	31.12.08		31.12.09	
Land and buildings		700,000		930,000
Plant at cost	274,000		324,000	
Accumulated depreciation	48,800		52,300	
		225,200		271,700
Motor vehicles at cost	31,200		53,200	
Accumulated depreciation	9,100	22,100	14,300	38,900
		947,300		1,240,600
Asset revaluation reserve				230,000

On 1 January 2009 plant costing £46,000 (NBV £18,000) was sold for £11,000. A motor vehicle costing £12,000 was sold on 1 January 2009 for £7,000. This resulted in a profit of £2,500.

You are required to calculate the figures that would be shown in the cash flow statement at 31 December 2009.

31.7.9 Self-test

The following information is given as it relates to corporation taxation.

Tax liability 2008	£764,000
Liability 2009	£932,000
P&L for 2009 shows a taxation provision of	£816,000

Calculate the amount of tax paid in 2009.

31.7.10 Self-test

A cash flow statement includes dividends paid.

The following is an extract from the balance sheet of Que Ltd as at 31 December:

	2008	2009
Creditors for dividends	186,000	257,000

The profit and loss account for the year ending 31 December 2009 shows that the dividend paid and proposed amounts to £349,000.

You are required to calculate the amount of dividends paid in 2009 for inclusion in the cash flow statement.

Chapter 32

Analysis of financial statements – an introduction

Objectives   After you have studied this chapter, you should be able to:

- explain how financial information can be interpreted;
- explain the usefulness and importance of ratio analysis and its limitations;
- understand the uses of and be able to calculate ratios;
- apply ratios in interpreting a set of accounts;
- use ratios to determine how a business is performing.

32.1   Introduction

Ratio analysis is the calculation and comparison of ratios which are derived from the information in a business' financial statements. The ratios are used to examine the performance of a business over a period of time. They can also be used to compare the current year's performance of the business with a previous year or with the performance of a similar business.

32.2   Key factors in using ratios

There are certain key factors that apply when using ratios. These are:

- they provide a comparison between two or more variables in the accounts;
- they compare the results from two or more sets of accounts to disclose the trends and relationships that are not evident from the figures alone (in isolation, ratios provide very little information about the performance of a business); and
- they allow us to compare the results with other businesses in the same industry, sector or even in other sectors.

32.3   How are ratios used?

Many ratios are available, and the question that arises is which ratio or ratios should be used? Different users have different needs, but even then the ratios cannot be considered in isolation. Ratios are used by companies, investors, analysts and competitors to provide additional information to that provided in the financial statements.

One aspect of the accountant's work is to interpret statements to provide information to management. An important aspect of interpretation is that ratios must always be considered in relation to other information.

Because different groups need to look at different aspects of behaviour in the business, we categorise the many types of ratios into groups.

Companies usually calculate as many ratios as they find useful to monitor their own performance. When outsiders look at the performance of a business, they normally use a few of the major ratios and then, if a particular area seems to require further explanation, they will use as many other ratios as are necessary to draw adequate conclusions.

When we compare ratios there must be a relationship between the figures. They need to be relevant to each other to ensure that the ratio will have meaning. For example, if we compare the profit to cash at bank, there is no relevance in this comparison and in such a case the ratio is meaningless.

32.4 Limitations of ratios

Ratio analysis is an extremely useful tool but it has its limitations.

- Accounts are historical and, therefore, concerned with the past. The results are old and things could have improved, or deteriorated, since the date of the accounts. Great care must be exercised to determine if historical cost or inflation adjusted data is used.
- Comparing the results of different businesses can be problematic as there are different methods of measuring charges against profit.
- There are different ways of valuing stock and tangible and intangible fixed assets. These differences affect the comparative ratios between companies.
- Ratios calculated from information in the published accounts may not be comparable. Notes to the accounts may give us information, allowing us to adjust the accounts so that the figures are calculated on the same basis as those of another business, but in practice this is not easy.
- When use is made of accounts produced in different countries the problem is increased. Valuation methods may be different, and there may be insufficient information.
- An acceptable ratio in some countries would be considered dangerous in others. This applies particularly to liquidity and gearing ratios. Comparison therefore must take account of these differences.

32.4.1 Profitability ratios

These ratios measure performance and examine the extent of the profit in relation to the size of the business and the amount of capital invested. They allow an outsider to evaluate the effectiveness of management in the utilisation of the many resources at its disposal.

In your study of this aspect of the course you need to ensure that you are familiar with the way in which each ratio is determined. This requires a comprehensive knowledge of the particular formula and an ability to undertake the calculations.

Gross profit margin

$$\frac{\text{Gross profit}}{\text{Sales turnover}} \times 100$$

Using the above formula, we relate the gross profit to the turnover generated. A decrease in the gross profit could mean increased competition, increasing costs of purchases, or a bad pricing strategy. With high profit margins it is easier to cover the expenses of a business, including interest charges, when there is a decline in income.

A simple example of the gross profit margin is given below:

Alex buys a clock for £25 and sells it for £35. What is the gross profit margin?

We calculate the gross profit by deducting the cost price from the selling price:

Selling price £35 less cost of £25 = Gross profit of £10

From this we can calculate that the gross profit margin is:

$$\frac{10}{35} \times 100 = 28.6\%$$

Often you are asked to determine the mark-up. In this case we would use the following formula:

$$\frac{\text{Gross profit}}{\text{Cost of sales}} \times 100$$

Using the example above we calculate this as:

$$\frac{10}{25} \times 100 = 40\%.$$

In other words Alex makes a 40 per cent mark-up on the cost price of his goods. When you look at the percentage of gross profit, make sure that you know the difference between the **mark-up** and the **gross profit margin**.

Net profit margin

$$\frac{\text{Operating profit*}}{\text{Turnover}} \times 100$$

* Operating profit = Net profit before interest and tax (PBIT)

This ratio compares the profit to turnover and does vary from one type of business to another. The net profit can be influenced by competition, economic climate and type of customer, so no definitive percentage can be set for this ratio.

Note: You need be aware that any individual expense (or income) can be expressed as a percentage of turnover. This serves as a check against increases in year-on-year expenditure.

Return on investment (ROI)

$$\frac{\text{Operating profit*}}{\text{Total assets}} \times 100$$

* Operating profit = PBIT

This ratio can also be described as the return on total assets. The ratio shows what a business earns from all the money invested in it, without distinguishing between borrowed capital and equity.

Return on equity (ROE)

$$\frac{\text{Net profit after preference dividend and tax}}{\text{Equity}} \times 100$$

This ratio shows the return due to the owners (shareholders).

The shareholders want to know what percentage return they receive on their investment. This is not shown by the return on investment ratio (ROI) as that ratio shows the total return on all money invested. This ratio (ROE) only relates the net income to equity (that is, ordinary shares plus reserves), and therefore the return is only on the equity investment.

Return on capital employed (ROCE)

$$\frac{\text{Profit (before interest and tax)}}{\text{Capital employed**}}$$

** Capital employed consists of the shareholders' interest plus long-term liabilities.
It can also be expressed as total assets less current liabilities.

This ratio measures the percentage return achieved on the firm's assets, before paying interest or dividends. In effect it shows the relationship between the net profit and the long-term capital invested in the business.

32.4.2 Worked examples

Why do we bother to measure both gross profit to turnover and operating profit to turnover? Surely it is only the remaining net profit that matters?

We can explain this by examining the results for Perform Ltd.

2008	2008	Profit and loss account for the year ended 31 December	2009	2009
£000	£000		£000	£000
	2,000	Turnover		3,200
88		Stock at 1 January	90	
960		Purchases	1,040	
1,048			1,130	
90		Stock at 31 December	110	
	958	Cost of sales		1,020
	1,042	Gross profit		2,180
380		Distribution expenses	630	
410	790	Administrative expenses	440	1,070
	252	Net profit before interest and tax		1,110
	42	Interest charges		67
	210	Net profit before tax		1,043
	46	Corporation tax		125
	165	Net profit after tax		918
40		Preference share dividend	80	
80		Ordinary share dividend	260	
	(120)			(340)
	45	Retained earnings for the year		578

For 2009, the gross profit margin is $\dfrac{2,180}{3,200} \times 100 = 68.1\%$ and the net profit margin

is $\dfrac{1,110}{3,200} \times 100 = 34.7\%$.

In addition to calculating every ratio for 2009 to determine the trend of the business, we also need to know whether the two ratios shown above are moving in the same direction – are they both increasing or decreasing?

Only by doing this are we able to link various ratios and so attempt to make sound and well-considered judgements.

For 2008, the gross profit margin is $\dfrac{1,042}{2,000} \times 100 = 52.1\%$ and the net profit

margin is $\dfrac{252}{2,000} \times 100 = 12.6\%$.

From the ratios calculated above we see that both the gross profit margin and the net profit margin ratios have improved from 2008 to 2009.

Another form of analysis is to determine how profitable the business is from the point of view of the money invested.

We are required to calculate the ROCE, ROI and ROE for Perform Ltd. To do this, however, we need additional information to that provided in the profit and loss account.

Extracts from balance sheet as at 31 December 2009

	£000	£000
Share capital		
Ordinary shares of £1 each	2,000	
5% preference shares of £1 each	1,600	
		3,600
Reserves		
Share premium	600	
Retained earnings	800	1,400
		5,000
Fixed assets		5,500
Current assets		
Stocks	110	
Trade debtors	320	
Prepayments	90	
Bank	95	
	615	
Current liabilities		
Trade creditors	130	
Accrued expenses	5	
Corporation tax	60	
Proposed·dividend	70	
	265	350
		5,900
Long-term liability		
6% Debentures 2012		900
		5,000

In 2009 the operating profit is £1,110; therefore, the return on capital employed is:

$$\text{ROCE} = \frac{1,110}{5,900} \times 100 = 18.8\%$$

$$\text{ROI} = \frac{1,110}{6,165} \times 100 = 18.0\%$$

$$\text{ROE} = \frac{838^*}{3,400^{**}} \times 100 = 24.6\%$$

* The ordinary shareholders are obviously not entitled to the interest paid to the debenture holders, nor to the preference share dividends. Therefore, their entitlement is to the profit after tax of £918,000 less the preference share dividend of £80,000.

** Equity refers to issued ordinary shares and reserves. Therefore, we take the share capital for ordinary shares (£2,000,000) and add the reserves of £1,400,000.

32.4.3 Self-test

You are presented with the following information for Calculator Ltd for the year ended 31 December 2009.

Balance sheet data	2008	2009
Fixed assets	9,650	9,530
Current assets including debtors	11,470	12,424
Debtors included above	4,800	4,200
Creditors: amounts due within one year	4,720	4,954
Trade creditors included above	4,420	4,562
Creditors: amounts due in more than one year	6,000	1,200
Ordinary share capital of 50p each	5,700	6,028
Reserves	4,700	9,772

Profit and loss data	2008	2009
Turnover	44,800	52,620
Opening stock	4,820	6,000
Purchases	37,080	42,840
Closing stock	6,000	7,400
Cost of goods sold	35,900	41,440
Gross profit	8,900	11,180
Interest payable	480	130
Net profit after interest but before tax	4,345	5,464
Net profit after tax	4,224	5,312
Dividends proposed	180	240

The following notes apply to the information above and must be taken into account in your calculations:

(i) All purchases and sales are made on credit.
(ii) The market value of the 50p ordinary shares of Calculator Ltd at the end of each year was £2.50 and £3.50 respectively.
(iii) The issue of equity shares during the year ended 31 December 2009 occurred at the beginning of that year.

You are required to calculate (to the nearest one decimal place) the following ratios for the years 2008 and 2009:

(a) Gross profit margin.
(b) Net profit margin.
(c) Return on capital employed.

32.4.4 Liquidity ratios

This selection of ratios deals with the relationship between assets and liabilities. It measures a business' immediate ability to pay its short-term debts. In calculating the various ratios in this section we must note that there are certain current assets, such as stock, which may not be readily convertible into cash. It is for this reason that the quick ratio is used.

The key ratios within this group are:

- current or working capital ratio; and
- acid test or quick ratio.

Listed below are the formulae for calculating the liquidity ratios. Again, you are reminded of the need to be familiar with the way in which each ratio is determined. This requires a comprehensive knowledge of the formula and an ability to undertake the calculations.

Current or working capital ratio

$$\frac{\text{Current assets}}{\text{Current liabilities}}$$

Acid test or quick ratio

$$\frac{\text{Current assets} - \text{stock}}{\text{Current liabilities}}$$

While profitability ratios are extremely important, no matter how much profit a business makes, if its cash flow is inadequate, it will not be able to continue in business. Liquidity ratios are, therefore, key in determining the viability of any business.

32.4.5 Worked examples

This example shows the information that liquidity ratios can provide. We will use the extract from the balance sheet of Perform Ltd for the year ended 31 December 2009 in section 32.4.2.

Our first step is to examine the working capital ratio.

$$\frac{\text{Current assets}}{\text{Current liabilities}} = \frac{615,000}{265,000} = 2.3{:}1 \text{ or } 2.3 \text{ times}$$

From the above calculation we see that current liabilities are covered 2.3 times. Having determined this ratio, we must consider if this is adequate. An acceptable ratio in one industry is not necessarily acceptable in another, so we look at similar businesses in the same industry to give us a guide. To establish a trend we also look at the ratio for several past years. If we assume that 2.0:1 is reasonable, then we can make some comment on this ratio.

For the purposes of this example, let us assume that we are given ratios for the past three years as per the table below:

	2006	2007	2008
Perform Ltd	1.3:1	1.4:1	1.9:1
Industry average	1.9:1	1.7:1	2.1:1

We are asked to assess how Perform Ltd is doing. It would appear that in 2009, the company is too liquid and needs to invest some of its surplus funds in more profitable areas. This is borne out by the fact that the current ratio is increasing all the time.

A high liquidity ratio indicates poor management of resources. Adequate working capital is essential, but too much is unnecessary and does not generate extra profits.

The next step is to examine the liquidity situation. If all creditors demanded payment at once, would Perform Ltd be able to meet its obligations? We can answer this by using the acid test ratio.

$$\frac{\text{Current assets} - \text{stock}}{\text{Current liabilities}} = \frac{615,000 - 110,000}{265,000} = 1.9{:}1 \text{ or } 1.9 \text{ times}$$

The result is good, as 1:1 is normally the minimum figure required for this ratio. Again, we need to look at the trend to make sure that it was not consistently downwards, as this could eventually prove dangerous.

If the current ratio, as calculated above, had been rising because stock was increasing, the results for the acid test ratio over the same period would decrease. This could be dangerous for the company, as it would show a build-up of stock, or a slowing down of turnover.

32.4.6 Self-test

Using the information in self-test 32.4.3, you are now required to prepare the following ratios for 2008 and 2009 for Calculator Ltd.

(a) Current or working capital ratio.
(b) Acid test or quick ratio.

Your answer should be given to the nearest one decimal place.

32.4.7 Gearing ratios

The term 'gearing' often creates confusion with students. All it refers to is the extent to which a business is dependent on fixed-return capital such as loans (with a fixed rate of interest) or preference shares (with a fixed dividend rate), as opposed to equity capital (ordinary shares). By calculating the gearing ratio it is possible to determine the degree of risk attached to a business and also its sensitivity to changes in profitability.

The amount of gearing is important if we want to raise extra capital and, as such, gearing ratios become extremely meaningful because they express the relationship between long-term liabilities and shareholders' funds. If the gearing is too high then it may be difficult to get a loan. One reason for this is that the bank may feel the interest payments may not be met. Another reason could be that the lender believes that it is the ordinary shareholders who should provide the capital.

There are a number of advantages to gearing:

■ First, and most importantly, debt capital is cheaper. The reason for this is that the interest is fixed, and therefore may diminish (in real terms) if there is inflation. While an ordinary shareholder expects a dividend growth year on year, this is not the case where there is a fixed interest charge.

- The reward (interest payments) on secured debt may be lower than that paid to equity (dividend payments) because the debt bears a lower risk to an investor.
- It should also be noted that interest is tax deductible, while dividends are only a distribution (appropriation) of profit after tax.
- Shareholders are entitled to a vote at company meetings but debt capital does not have a vote and therefore cannot affect control over a company.

A company is said to be highly geared when it has a large proportion of its capital as fixed-return capital. In this case there is a greater risk of insolvency, but the return to shareholders will grow when the profits grow. A low-geared company has scope to increase its borrowings when a potentially profitable project becomes available. Usually companies with a low gearing are able to borrow far easier than companies with a high gearing.

The situation may be complicated by the existence of preference shares, as is the case in Perform Ltd. Holders of long-term debt are creditors of the company, whereas preference shareholders are owners and they receive their dividend before any dividends are paid to ordinary shareholders. Businesses with preference shareholders include them with the long-term debt in the main gearing ratio. This is because these shareholders have the right to a fixed rate of dividend.

The following is the formulae for the various ratios in this category:

Gearing

$$\frac{\text{Long-term loans} + \text{preference share capital}}{\text{Capital employed}} \times 100$$

Or

$$\frac{\text{Prior charge capital}}{\text{Equity}} \times 100$$

Or

$$\frac{\text{Debt}}{\text{Equity}} \times 100$$

Once we have determined the percentage of gearing, it is then fundamentally important that we interpret it correctly. All too often the calculations are correct but the interpretation is weak. We can say that a company's gearing is low if the resultant percentage is less than 100 per cent. At the same time, we can conclude that it is high if the ratio exceeds 100 per cent.

Interest cover

$$\frac{\text{Profit before interest payable and tax}}{\text{Interest payable}}$$

There is always a risk in gearing and that is that the company may not earn enough to pay the interest due. Interest cover indicates if a company is able to pay interest from profits. If the cover is low, then ordinary shareholders should be aware that their dividends may be at risk because the profits will be absorbed by interest payments. As a rule of thumb, cover of less than 2 is considered unsatisfactory.

32.4.8 Worked example

Using the information for Perform Ltd (in section 32.4.2), we calculate the percentage of gearing.

To do this we add the debentures and preference shares together and divide that total by the total capital employed (ordinary share capital + reserves + preference shares + long-term liabilities).

$$\frac{2,500}{5,900} \times 100 = 42.4\%$$

The alternate method of calculation is to use the additional formula of

$$\frac{\text{Prior charge capital}}{\text{Equity}}$$

Stated numerically this is:

$$\frac{900 + 1,600}{2,000 + 1,400} \times 100 = 73.5\%$$

We saw in Chapter 28 that the shareholders are the owners of the company and they should therefore benefit from growth. As debt capital interest is fixed, any rising profits benefit the ordinary shareholder.

Having determined the gearing of a company, it is possible to reduce gearing by the simple exercise of issuing additional ordinary shares and also by retaining profits within the company – thereby increasing the reserves. In the case of a low-geared company, it may be decided to increase the gearing, which can be done by issuing debentures or preference shares. Naturally, any decision made is determined, in part, by the trading results of the past and the attractiveness or otherwise of the company to new investors.

32.4.9 Worked example

A ratio that lenders and potential lenders look at is the ability of a business to pay their interest charges.

Using the information from Perform Ltd (see section 32.4.2), you are asked to determine if the company would be able to meet its interest obligations.

$$\frac{\text{Operating profit}}{\text{Interest payable}} = \frac{1,110}{54^*} = 20.5 \text{ times}$$

* Interest is 6% on 900

This means that the business should have no difficulty in meeting its obligations to pay interest.

32.4.10 Self-test

Using the financial statements of Calculator Ltd in self-test 32.4.3, you are required to calculate (to one decimal place) the following ratios for the years 2008 and 2009:

(a) Gearing.
(b) Interest cover.

32.4.11 Investment or shareholder ratios

Usually the value of an investment depends on future returns and not those of the past. However, this does not mean that these ratios cannot be used where only past information is available. If nothing else, then at least the trend of a business can be established and an investment decision can be made on that trend.

Earnings per (ordinary) share (EPS)

$$\frac{\text{Profit (on ordinary activities) after tax less preference dividends}}{\text{Number of issued ordinary shares}}$$

This ratio shows the amount of earnings generated by a business and available to ordinary shareholders. This ratio is important when looking for capital growth.

Earnings yield per share

$$\frac{\text{Earnings per share}}{\text{Current market price per share}} \times 100$$

This ratio, as a percentage, is used to calculate the amount of earnings of each ordinary share to the market price of the share at the time.

Price/earnings ratio (PE ratio)

$$\frac{\text{Current market price per share}}{\text{Earnings per share}}$$

Using the above ratio we are able to show if the particular shares are overpriced or inexpensive. It shows how many years of current earnings an investor is willing to pay. A high PE ratio indicates that future growth is expected, for which investors would pay a higher multiple. If it is low then growth prospects are considered poor by investors.

Dividend payout

$$\frac{\text{Total dividends for the year}}{\text{Average distributable earnings for the year}} \times 100$$

The available earnings are normally the net profit after tax and after preference dividends. This ratio shows the percentage of earnings which a company pays out to shareholders as a dividend.

Dividend yield

$$\frac{\text{Dividend per share}}{\text{Current market price per share}} \times 100$$

This ratio is important if you are seeking income rather than capital growth. Generally, this ratio is an indicator of dividend policy and not performance. All too often a company will pay out only a proportion of its profits. Dividend yield reflects this approach. The yield on ordinary shares gives the shareholders a method of comparing what their dividend really represents based on the market value of the shares.

Dividend cover

$$\frac{\text{Earnings per share}}{\text{Net dividend per ordinary share}}$$

This ratio indicates how secure dividends are by showing how many times a business could have paid its current dividend from available earnings. If the cover is less than 2, it is inadequate. While a high dividend yield may attract investors, the dividend cover may be low. The low cover shows a greater possibility of future dividends being cut.

Net assets per share

$$\frac{\text{Net assets (shareholders' funds)}}{\text{Number of shares}}$$

Where this has a value greater than the total market price of the shares, it may be considered that the business could be broken up to realise these higher values. It should also be noted that net assets are based on tangible assets. One problem that must be recognised is that the values in the balance sheet may not reflect current market values.

Where employees are the key to the success of a business, it is not possible to account for this factor in a ratio. As a result, net assets do not reflect the true value of a business even if there has recently been a revaluation of fixed assets.

32.4.12 Worked example

Using the information provided for Perform Ltd in section 32.4.2, we are able to calculate the following ratios.

The earnings per share (EPS) shows what the available profit is actually worth, per ordinary share. In this ratio it is important that you state the answer as x pence per share.

For this calculation we use the after-tax profit less the preference share dividend and divide this amount by the number of ordinary shares issued.

$$\frac{838}{2{,}000} = 41.9 \text{ pence per share}$$

Note: It is important that you divide by the number of shares and not by their value. In this case it is easy, as the shares are £1 each. Where we have, for example, 50p shares, then we must remember to multiply the value in £ by 2 to arrive at the number of shares.

$$\text{Dividend cover} = \frac{41.9}{13} = 3.22 \text{ times, or the dividend is 32.2\% of the sum available}$$

The calculation above is based on the total EPS (41.9p) divided by the dividend paid to each ordinary shareholder, which in this example is £260,000 divided by the shares in issue (2,000,000).

In 2008, £125,000 was available and £80,000 was distributed as a dividend. In 2009, the amount available was £838,000 and £260,000 was distributed. The dividend cover ratio measures the ability of the company to maintain equity dividends.

The price/earnings ratio uses the share's market price and its earnings per share. It is a measure of the stock market's valuation of a company.

Let us assume that the market value of a share in Perform Ltd is £1.50. The PE ratio is therefore calculated as follows:

$$\frac{150}{41.9} = 3.6 \text{ times}$$

The result is the price as a multiple of earnings.

32.4.13 Worked example

You are given the following information relating to two companies:

	First Ltd	Second Ltd
Ordinary share capital of £1 each	10,000	4,000
10% loan		6,000
Total long-term capital	£10,000	£10,000

What would the earnings per share be if profits before interest and tax are:

(a) £500?
(b) £2,000?
(c) £3,000?

For purposes of the answer, let us assume that the rate of tax is 50 per cent.
Solution to (a) above.

PBIT*	500	500
Interest		600
Profit (loss) before tax	500	(100)
Tax	250	
Earnings	£250	(100)
No. of shares	10,000	4,000
EPS	2.5p	Nil

Solution to (b) above.

PBIT*	2,000	2,000
Interest		600
Profit before tax	2,000	1,400
Tax	1,000	700
Earnings	1,000	700
No. of shares	10,000	4,000
EPS	10.0p	17.5p

Solution to (c) above.

PBIT*	3,000	3,000
Interest		600
Profit before tax	3,000	2,400
Tax	1,500	1,200
Earnings	1,500	1,200
No. of shares	10,000	4,000
EPS	15.0p	30.0p

* PBIT is the profit before interest and tax.

You will note from the above examples that once profits increase, the EPS grows faster in high-geared companies.

To determine if there is sufficient profit to pay the fixed interest charges we use the interest cover ratio. In the case of Second Ltd we can calculate the interest cover for (c) above as follows:

$$\frac{\text{PBIT}}{\text{Interest paid}} = \frac{3,000}{600} = 5 \text{ times}$$

If the resultant answer is less than 1 it means that the company has not earned enough to cover interest charges.

We need to understand why interest cover is so important. Loan creditors are paid interest whether the company makes a profit or not. These loans, or debentures, are frequently secured on company property and, if any problems arise with the payment of interest and/or capital, the company could find that its fixed assets are being sold off by the debenture holders.

Creditors cannot vote, nor determine company policy. A new project that is likely to pay for itself within a few years is often funded by a long-term liability rather than the issue of shares. This liability can be repaid once the project contributes to the company cash flow.

Naturally, if a company has many loans outstanding, it may not have the security to obtain additional loans and may be forced to issue shares.

32.4.14 Worked example

In addition to the above, there are tax advantages in issuing debentures rather than shares.

The following worked example illustrates this.

A company, John Ltd, is wholly financed by 500,000 £1 ordinary shares, and pays a dividend of 10 per cent on the shares. Assume that corporation tax is 20 per cent.

Net profit before tax	650,000
Corporation tax	(130,000)
	520,000
Ordinary share dividend	(50,000)
Retained earnings	470,000

In our second company, James Ltd, there are 100,000 £1 ordinary shares and £400,000 8 per cent debentures. A 10 per cent dividend is paid to its ordinary shareholders.

Operating profit	650,000
less debenture interest	(32,000)
Net profit before tax	618,000
Corporation tax	(123,600)
Net profit after tax	494,400
Ordinary share dividend	(10,000)
Retained earnings	484,400

The retained earnings are growing faster in the latter case, because interest is deductible for tax purposes. This means that James Ltd will expand more quickly. For this reason there is a great deal of support for high gearing. From the point of view of ordinary shareholders they stand to lose out when profits are low, but gain when profits rise, because the debentures still attract a fixed rate of interest.

32.4.15 Self-test

Using our last example for John Ltd and James Ltd, what would have been available to the ordinary shareholders (EPS) if the profit figure had been:

(i) £60,000?
(ii) £800,000?

32.4.16 Self-test

You are required to calculate (to one decimal place) the following ratios of Calculator Ltd for 2008 and 2009 using the financial information in self-test 32.4.3:

(a) Earnings per share.
(b) Price/earnings ratio.
(c) Dividend payout.
(d) Dividend cover.

32.4.17 Efficiency or activity ratios

These ratios deal with the use of funds, and measure the performance of management in relation to the use of working capital and assets.

We detail the formulae for each of these ratios below.

Stock turnover period

$$\frac{\text{Cost of sales}}{\text{Average stock}} = \text{number of times a year}$$

Or

$$\frac{\text{Stock}}{\text{Cost of sales}} \times 365 = \text{number of days' sales that stock is held}$$

The rate of turnover measures how quickly stock passes through the business. The faster we turn our stock over, the smaller the amount of stock we need hold. This reduces storage costs and releases capital for other avenues of investment.

The formula measures the cost of sales against the average stock of finished goods. Stock values are always at cost (or occasionally at net realisable value, if lower), therefore we need to measure average stock against cost of sales.

Debtors' turnover

$$\frac{\text{Trade debtors}}{\text{Credit sales}} \times 365^*$$

If the number of days increase, then it could be because of a lack of invoicing, slow payments, bad debts or market competition forcing increased terms.

Creditors' turnover

$$\frac{\text{Trade creditors}}{\text{Credit purchases}} \times 365^*$$

If this increases it may signify cash flow problems.

* In the above calculations, if we multiply by 12 instead of 365 then the collection period is expressed in terms of months. If we multiply by 52 then it is expressed in weeks. Always ensure that you state exactly what the result is; that is, is it a percentage, a number of days or the number of weeks? Do not just leave a number without stating what it is.

Ideally, the figures used for debtors and creditors should be an average figure for the year, as the balance sheet figures may not be representative.

In the following ratios we need to see whether the assets are being used to good effect and if they are producing enough turnover. The ratios are designed to monitor any asset or group of assets against turnover.

All three ratios use turnover as the one part of the calculation. Each of the three ratios describes the other part of the calculation. The answer is then expressed either as a percentage or as a number of times.

Fixed asset turnover

$$\frac{\text{Turnover}}{\text{Fixed assets}}$$

In this formula, fixed assets means the 'net book value of all fixed assets, including investments and intangibles', but it is usual to only use tangible fixed assets.

Working capital turnover

$$\frac{\text{Turnover}}{\text{Net current assets}}$$

Asset turnover

$$\frac{\text{Turnover}}{\text{Capital employed}}$$

Or

$$\frac{\text{Turnover}}{\text{Net assets}}$$

Net assets means 'all assets less external liabilities', but this ratio is usually calculated using 'all assets less current liabilities'.

32.4.18 Worked example

We now use the information for Perform Ltd from section 32.4.2 to calculate the efficiency ratios discussed above.

Taking the measures normally used for net assets and net fixed assets, we are able to determine the net asset turnover and the fixed asset turnover for 2009.

$$\frac{\text{Turnover}}{\text{Net assets}} \quad \frac{3,200}{5,900} = 54.2\%$$

$$\frac{\text{Turnover}}{\text{Fixed assets}} \quad \frac{3,200}{5,550} = 57.7\%$$

The answers need to be compared to previous years' figures and/or an industry average.

Note: Net assets are equal to the share capital + reserves + long-term liabilities (3,600 + 1,400 + 900). Remember the accounting equation A = C + L.

The next aspect to examine is debtors and creditors, and how cash flows in and out of the company. We need to know what percentage of turnover is on credit and if all purchases are paid using credit terms.

For purposes of this example we will assume that Perform Ltd deals entirely on a credit basis and allows its customers 40 days' credit. We can also assume that it receives similar terms from its creditors.

To undertake these calculations we need the sales and purchases figures. If we had access to the published accounts, only the turnover figure would be available. Ideally, we would use an average figure for debtors and creditors, just in case the figures taken from current assets and current liabilities are not really representative.

Using the information from the profit and loss account (see section 32.4.2), we see that the turnover for 2009 was £3,200,000 and that purchases for the year were £1,040,000. We would then have a debtors' collection period of

$$\text{Debtors/Turnover} \quad \frac{320}{3,200} \times 365 = 37 \text{ days}$$

and a creditors' payment period of

$$\text{Creditors/Purchases} \quad \frac{130}{1,040} \times 365 = 46 \text{ days}$$

The results are good, as the company wants to receive cash from its debtors before it has to pay its creditors. Here again, the trend of previous years is important. However, the firm may wish to reduce the creditors' payment period to below 46 days so as to avail itself of cash discounts when offered.

The final ratio in this section is the rate of stock turnover. This, too, is an important ratio as a great deal of the liquidity of the company depends on the amount of stock carried in a business.

$$\frac{\text{Cost of sales}}{\text{Average stock}} \quad \frac{1,020}{(90 + 110) \div 2^*} = 10.2 \text{ times.}$$

* The denominator is the average of the opening stock and the closing stock.

We need to compare this figure with those of previous years to see if there has been an improvement or not. A decreasing rate of stock turnover not only means that holding costs have risen; it may also mean that there is increased competition, or that the demand for products is no longer as great.

32.4.19 Self-test

Using the information for Calculator Ltd in self-test 32.4.3, you are now required to prepare the following ratios for 2008 and 2009. Your answer should be given to the nearest one decimal place.

(a) Stock turnover.
(b) Debtors' turnover.
(c) Creditors' payment period.
(d) Asset turnover ratio.

32.4.20 Self-test

The financial statements of Valued Ltd are given below:

Trading and profit and loss account for Valued Ltd for the year ended 31 December

	2008		2009	
Turnover		1,350,000		1,800,000
Cost of sales				
Opening stocks	90,000		72,000	
Net purchases	750,000		1,080,000	
Closing stock	(60,000)	780,000	(36,000)	1,116,000
Gross profit		570,000		684,000
Investment income		135,000		72,000
		705,000		756,000
Distribution expenses	265,500		342,540	
Administrative expenses	178,050		200,160	
Debenture interest	24,000	467,550	36,000	578,700
Net profit before tax		237,450		177,300
Corporation tax		72,000		45,000
Net profit after tax		165,450		132,300
Ordinary share dividend		112,500		108,000
		52,950		24,300
Balance 1 January		101,100		184,860
Balance 31 December		154,050		209,160

Balance sheets of Valued Ltd at 31 December 2008 and 2009

	2008		2009	
Fixed assets		2,034,000		2,335,320
Current assets				
Stock	60,000		36,000	
Debtors	165,000		189,000	
Bank	45,000		253,800	
	270,000		478,800	
Current liabilities				
Creditors	72,000		108,000	
Accruals	3,450		3,960	
Corporation tax	72,000		45,000	
Ordinary share dividend	112,500		108,000	
	259,950		264,960	
Net current assets		10,050		213,840
		2,044,050		2,549,160
Long-term liability				
10% debentures 2009		240,000		360,000
		1,804,050		2,189,160
£1 ordinary shares		1,350,000		1,620,000
Reserves				
Share premium	300,000		360,000	
Profit and loss	154,050		209,160	
		454,050		569,160
		1,804,050		2,189,160

Using the information provided, you are required to calculate the following ratios:

(a) Working capital ratio.
(b) Acid test.
(c) Debtors' collection period.
(d) Creditors' payment period.
(e) Gross profit percentage.
(f) Operating profit percentage.
(g) Earnings per share.
(h) Dividend cover.

Give your answers correct to two decimal places.

32.4.21 Self-test

You are given the following financial information for Rekon Ltd and are required to calculate the gross profit margin, mark-up, net profit margin and return on capital.

Profit and loss account for the year ended 31 December 2009

Turnover	312,524
Cost of sales	269,332
Gross profit	43,192
Administrative expenses	33,633
Profit before interest	9,559
Interest receivable	4,606
Interest payable	(3,058)
Net profit before tax	11,107
Taxation	3,902
Profit after taxation	7,205

Balance sheet as at 31 December 2009

Fixed assets		32,000
Current assets	48,403	
Current liabilities	(16,290)	
Net current assets		32,113
		64,113
Creditors falling due after more than one year		(19,082)
		45,031
Share capital – 1,788 ordinary shares of £1 each	1,788	
Share premium account	6,020	
Other reserves	2,827	
Profit and loss account	34,396	
		45,031

32.4.22 Self-test

The following financial statements relate to November plc for the financial years ending 31 March.

Balance sheets as at 31 March

	2009		2010	
	£000	£000	£000	£000
Fixed assets				
Land and buildings at cost		651		651
Fixtures and fittings at cost	189		195	
Less accumulated depreciation	61	128	103	92
		779		743
Current assets				
Stock at cost	520		670	
Trade debtors	280		219	
Bank	39		47	
	839		936	
Creditors: amounts due within one year				
Trade creditors	229		247	
Dividends proposed	48		72	
Corporation tax due	103		109	
	380	459	428	508
		1,238		1,251
Creditors: amounts due in more than one year 10% debentures		300		100
		938		1,151
Capital and reserves				
£1 ordinary shares		680		680
General reserve		37		44
Retained profit		221		427
		938		1,151

Profit and loss accounts for the years ended 31 March

	2009		2010	
	£000	£000	£000	£000
Sales		2,340		2,984
Less cost of sales				
Opening stock	441		520	
Purchases	1,986		2,563	
	2,427		3,083	
Less Closing stock	520	1,907	670	2,413
Gross profit		433		571
Expenses excluding interest	76		167	
Interest payable	30	106	10	177
Net profit before tax		327		394
Less corporation tax		103		109
Net profit after tax		224		285
Retained profit brought forward		45		221
		269		506
Less:				
Transfer to general reserve				7
Dividends proposed		48		72
Retained profit carried forward		221		427

Notes:

- All sales and purchases are made on credit.
- The market value of the shares of the company at the end of each year was £2.50 and £3.50 respectively.

You are required to calculate the following ratios:

(a) Working capital ratio
(b) Acid test
(c) Debtors' collection
(d) Creditors' payment
(e) Gross profit %
(f) Net profit %
(g) ROCE
(h) Earnings per share
(i) Gearing
(j) Interest cover
(k) Stock turnover

32.4.23 Self-test

Traveller Ltd was awarded a contract to construct a new bridge.

The funds provided by the shareholders were not sufficient to complete the contract and the company decided to issue 9 per cent debentures as a way of obtaining the necessary additional finance.

The following is an extract from the balance sheet as at 31 December 2008.

Fixed assets		2,600,000
Current assets	320,000	
Current liabilities	(260,000)	
Net current assets		60,000
		2,660,000
Long-term liabilities 9% debentures		(980,000)
		1,680,000
Capital and reserves		
Ordinary shares of £1	1,000,000	
Share premium account	220,000	
Profit and loss account	460,000	
		1,680,000

During the trading period ended 31 December 2008, only a small profit was made by the company after paying debenture interest.

You are required to record the following:

(i) On 1 January 2009, the directors decided to use all the distributable reserves to pay the ordinary shareholders a dividend. Calculate the dividend per share, expressing your answer in pence per share.

(ii) At 1 January 2009 the market price was quoted at £1.80 per share. Calculate the dividend yield based upon this price.

(iii) As a result of discussions with the debenture holders, the company converted £500,000 of the debentures to 500,000 of £1 ordinary share at par, on 1 March 2009. Calculate the gearing ratio for the company after the conversion of the debentures into shares.

Chapter 33

Introduction to cost accounting

Objectives

After studying this chapter, you should be able to:

- understand the terminology applied in costing;
- calculate the cost of a product using both absorption and marginal costing;
- understand how costing helps in decision making;
- understand the meaning of contribution;
- calculate the contribution towards fixed costs;
- use contribution in a decision-making process.

33.1 Introduction

In section 1.4 we explained the difference between financial and management accounting. In the next four chapters we discuss and explain some of the aspects of management accounting.

Remember that management accounting, unlike financial accounting, is a forward-looking method dealing with future events. It is presented as an aid to management and assists management in decision making. It does this by presenting various reports to management in the form of budgets and cost statements.

While cost accounting is adopted for control purposes, such as the control of expenditure, budgets are used to provide information for planning (and control), based on the objectives of the business and designed to allow the attainment of its goals. We will examine budgeting in Chapter 35.

In this chapter we examine how costs are collected and used. We need to know where the costs are incurred – the cost centres. We also need to know the different jobs that are being undertaken at each cost centre so that we can determine the unit costs. Two methods are commonly used to collate costs and we discuss these in section 33.3.

33.2 Terminology

Before we start to examine the various costing methods we need to understand the terms being used.

A distinction is drawn between direct and indirect costs.

Direct costs are costs that are easily identified with, or traceable to, a product or service. These costs consist of direct material, direct labour and direct overheads.

Indirect costs are not linked directly to a product or service, but are shared costs, which need to be apportioned on some logical basis (see section 33.3.1). For example:

- Indirect labour which includes wages of cleaning staff, supervisors etc.
- Indirect materials, such as maintenance materials etc.
- Indirect expenses including heating, lighting, rent etc.

When output increases all costs increase, although often at different rates. These increases must be known so that informed decisions can be made by the manager.

There are four divisions that can be made when we look at costs:

1. **Variable costs.** This is where the increase is in direct proportion to activity. An example of this is in the case of material used in production. Each unit produced consumes £1 of material. Therefore, 10 units consume £10 worth of material and 50 units have costs of £50. Almost all variable costs are direct costs.
2. **Fixed costs.** These costs remain the same, irrespective of activity levels. An example is factory rent. If there is an increase this is because of a commercial decision by the landlord and not because there is an increase in production. As rent is not attributable to a single product, but to the whole factory, it is classed as an indirect cost.
3. **Semi-variable costs** combine 1 and 2 above. With increased activity, costs do increase. An example would be where we pay a fixed rental, such as for the use of a telephone line (this is a fixed cost) and, in addition, we pay for each telephone call (which is a variable cost).
4. **Semi-fixed costs** increase as activity increases. Although an existing factory is large enough for a certain output, more space is needed if the output increases, resulting in an increase in rent.

33.3 Costing methods

In costing we measure the cost of all inputs and compare them with the value of the output of the business.

There are two methods that are commonly used:

- full costing or absorption costing; and
- marginal costing.

The difference between the two is the way in which overheads are treated.

In absorption costing the overheads (both fixed and variable) are included in the cost of production and the value of stock.

In marginal costing, only the variable overheads are included in stock. The fixed overheads are all written off against production, in the year of production, and not incorporated into closing stock. The overheads are considered to relate more to time than to the volume of production and, therefore, are written off in the year incurred.

33.3.1 Full costing (absorption costing)

In determining the unit cost, all direct and indirect production costs, whether variable or fixed, are included. If a business wants to set prices for its output in order to make a profit, the prices charged must cover all costs. Under this method the full cost of production is absorbed into the unit cost.

Overheads are apportioned to the product cost. In the case of variable overheads, they are directly traceable to the product, while with fixed overheads, they need to be apportioned to the product. This can be expressed as:

$$\text{Total product cost} = \text{Direct cost} + \text{share of overheads}$$

If only one product is produced then the total fixed overheads are divided to get a fixed overhead per unit. For example, if 5,000 units are produced, and the total fixed overhead cost is £20,000 then the fixed overhead per unit is equal to:

$$\frac{20,000}{5,000} = \text{£4 per unit}$$

If several products are produced, the common costs, such as electricity costs, need to be shared out. These costs are said to be apportioned, and this must be done using an appropriate basis. This basis could be by dividing the total electricity bill by the number of machine hours needed.

For example, we are given the following facts:

Estimated overhead: £20,000
Estimated number of machine hours: 8,000 hours

We now need to apportion the overheads of £20,000 so that a proportion of this fixed overhead is absorbed by every machine hour.

$$\frac{20,000}{8,000} = \text{£2.50 per machine hour}$$

The £2.50, as calculated above, is known as the 'overhead recovery rate'.

33.3.2 Worked example

This example is of a manufacturing firm, which produces and sells party bags. Each unit (party bag) requires the following:

- £7 of raw materials;
- £4 of direct labour;
- £3 of variable factory overhead; and
- £2 of variable selling expense.

Additional costs incurred during the year are as follows:

- total fixed factory overheads of £90,000;
- fixed selling and distribution overheads of £20,000; and
- fixed administration overheads of £50,000.

The firm makes and sells 20,000 units in the year, and management expects to make a profit of 50 per cent on cost.

In this example we examine two scenarios [A] and [B].

[A] In the first case the firm is able to set its own selling price. This is because the firm is in a monopoly (sole supplier) position, and the demand for its product is inelastic (i.e. the demand does not fall if the price rises).

	Unit cost
Raw materials	7.00
Direct labour	4.00
Variable factory overhead	3.00
Variable selling expense	2.00
Fixed factory overhead*	4.50
Fixed selling/distribution expense*	1.00
Fixed administration expense*	2.50
Total cost per unit	24.00
Required profit (50%)	12.00
Selling price per unit	36.00

* In the above calculation the firm has simply taken its fixed overheads and divided them by the number of units produced.

[B] In the second case, the firm has several competitors, and must take note of the market price for its product. This is set at £30 per unit.

Using the figures above, we can see that the profit obtained can only be £30 (market price) – £24 (unit price) = £6, which is 25 per cent of cost.

In this case, therefore, the firm will have to accept a lower profit than it would have liked. Production would still be worthwhile, provided there are no alternative products the firm could make that would yield a higher return.

33.3.3 Advantages and disadvantages of full costing

There are a number of advantages and disadvantages of full costing.
The advantages:

- it aims to ensure that all overheads are covered by revenues received;
- it is a good base for 'cost plus' pricing (see above example); and
- it is the normal method used for stock valuation for financial accounts.

The disadvantages:

- overheads could be estimated, or apportioned, in an inaccurate fashion; and
- there is an under- or over-absorption of overheads. This is brought about by incorrectly apportioning the total overheads or by them not being totally absorbed.

33.3.4 Worked example

Major placed an order for 65,000 units of product X. The producer needed to give a price to Major for the order and so it had to do cost calculations.

(i) Material consisted of 12,400 metres of material at £6 per metre.
(ii) Labour required to manufacture the units would be 500 hours at £20 per hour.
(iii) Additional material for packing would cost £12,800.
(iv) Factory indirect costs would have to be allowed for 500 hours at £30 per hour.

Once all this is known a costing sheet can be prepared so that Major can be given a price for the order.

Material	74,400
Labour	10,000
Additional material	12,800
Indirect costs	15,000
Total cost	112,200

Using absorption (full) costing we know that we adhere to the formula of:

Direct cost + Overheads + Profit = Selling price

Using the above example, we would have a total cost of £112,200 to which selling and distribution costs of £6,800 are to be added. This gives a total of £119,000.

To this, a mark up of (say) 10 per cent is added (Figure 33.1), which gives a selling price of £130,900.

Figure 33.1 **The constituents of the selling price**

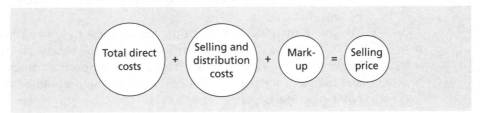

33.3.5 Marginal costing

In marginal costing only variable or marginal costs are considered in determining the cost of a product. Marginal costs are the costs involved in the production of an extra unit of output. Fixed costs, although they exist, are irrelevant for decision-making in any marginal cost calculation as all decisions are based on the contribution calculation. Marginal costing asks how much it costs to produce one more unit. Only the additional costs are variable costs.

Before examining marginal costing in detail we need to understand what is meant by the term 'contribution'.

Contribution is an important concept in management accounting. It is defined as the difference between the selling price and the total variable cost.

Contribution = sales revenue − variable costs

The contribution is the amount contributed towards the fixed costs of a business and to its ultimate profit. The profit will be brought about when the variable costs are covered and there is a surplus.

Once we have calculated the amount of the contribution, we then deduct the fixed costs from the total contribution to arrive at a profit or loss. The full equation therefore is:

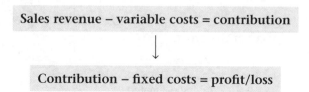

$$\textbf{Sales revenue} - \textbf{variable costs} = \textbf{contribution}$$

$$\downarrow$$

$$\textbf{Contribution} - \textbf{fixed costs} = \textbf{profit/loss}$$

33.3.6 Advantages of marginal costing

- There is no attempt to relate the fixed costs to production.
- The profits are not overstated because the fixed costs are not being absorbed in the closing stock. The fixed costs are all written off in the time period to which they apply. They are not taken forward to the next time period in the closing stock.

33.3.7 Disadvantages of marginal costing

- Current year's losses cannot arise if the products are manufactured for later periods.
- The use of marginal costing in processing leads to low prices when demands are slack and, as a result, customers may demand this all the time.
- Firms with few variable costs, but a large proportion of fixed costs, would find marginal costing less significant. An example would be where automated production exists.
- Absorption costing shows a more consistent profit (see section 33.3.17).

33.3.8 Decision making

In order to best utilise costing information, a business must compare the various proposals made to it by its customers. We will see that the determination of a profit or loss is irrelevant in marginal costing. What is relevant, however, is if there is a positive contribution. If there is a negative contribution, then the proposal must be rejected.

In this section we examine a number of different possibilities which we, as managers, need to ask ourselves. In all cases, we require some form of costing to assist in making a decision.

[A] The selling price for our product or service is capped, i.e. it cannot rise above a certain price. Is the market price sufficient to make it worth continuing?
[B] Should we cease production of an item, or close down a section of our business?
[C] Should we add a new product or service to what we offer?
[D] If we are limited by shortages of space, machine hours, materials, labour or anything else related to our business, what action should we take?

33.3.9 Worked examples

[A] Limited price for product

Using the cost information set out in section 33.3.2, we need to see what would happen if the market price fell to £22 per unit, as new competitors introduce cheaper units.

The way in which we present our figures is important. We see that the layout in the first case, where the fixed costs are allocated to each unit, is not particularly helpful.

The contribution approach will give us a far clearer view of the situation.

	Full costing		Contribution	
Selling price per unit		22.00		22.00
Unit cost:				
Raw materials	7.00		7.00	
Direct labour	4.00		4.00	
Variable factory overhead	3.00		3.00	
Variable selling expense	2.00		2.00	
Fixed factory overhead	4.50		–	
Fixed selling expenses	1.00		–	
Fixed administrative expenses	2.50		–	
Total unit cost		(24.00)		(16.00)
Loss per unit		(2.00)		
Total unit variable cost				
Contribution per unit				6.00
Total contribution (20,000 units)				120,000
less Total fixed costs				160,000
Loss				(40,000)

A loss of £40,000 on the 20,000 units appears to be the same as a loss of £2 per unit. However, if we say we are losing £2 for each unit, we might make the mistake of thinking that we will continue to lose money if we increased production to, say, 30,000 units.

Using the contribution approach, the result based on a production of 30,000 units, would be:

Contribution: £6 × 30,000	180,000
less fixed costs	(160,000)
Profit	£20,000

It seems logical for a firm to divide its fixed costs between the units that it produces if the number of these units remains constant. When the number varies, however, the profit position can be seen far more clearly if we know what contribution each unit makes.

In this example we note that although we would lose £40,000 on an output of 20,000 units, we would show a £20,000 profit if we could push our output to 30,000 units.

We can conclude, therefore, that if the selling price per unit (£22) is greater than the variable cost per unit (£16), then production should continue in the short run.

[B] Close down a department

We now need to make a decision based on the facts as set out in [B]. This requires us to decide if a department should be closed. In this example a department store is considering the closure of one of its departments, as it is making a loss. The profit statement of the department in question reads as follows:

Sales	800,000
Cost of sales*	(500,000)
Gross profit	300,000
Variable overheads	(160,000)
Fixed overheads	(180,000)
Net loss	(£40,000)

* All costs are variable.

What should the store do?

To answer this question, we make use of marginal costing to calculate the contribution.

Sales	800,000
Cost of sales	(500,000)
Gross profit	300,000
Variable overheads	(160,000)
Contribution	£140,000

There is a positive contribution of £140,000. If the department closes, the store will be worse off by £140,000. This is because the fixed overheads are unavoidable and, therefore, irrelevant in the decision. If we base a decision only on numbers, then the decision may be to keep the department open.

[C] Buy in/subcontract or not

Using the facts set out in [C] above as our next area for decision making, we ask ourselves, how do we decide if we should make or buy in a component?

In this example, Arthur & Co. is considering the alternatives of either purchasing a component from an outside supplier or producing the component itself.

The estimated costs to the company of producing the component are as follows:

Variable costs	£450
Fixed overheads	£100
	£550

The outside supplier has quoted a figure of £500 for supplying the component.

We know that the variable costs are £450 and that the buy-in price is £500. If we buy in the product our costs would be £500 plus our fixed overheads[28] of £100 – a total of £600. Clearly, therefore, the decision must be to manufacture the product as there is a positive contribution of £50 (manufactured cost being £50 less than the buy-in cost) towards fixed costs.

---

[28] We have assumed that the fixed costs will remain at £100 and that these costs will have to be absorbed either by this product or another.

There are, however, other considerations, such as the qualitative factors (i.e. factors not expressed as numbers) and opportunity cost. These considerations include:

- effect on competition;
- effect on staffing;
- quality may be affected;
- how suppliers are affected;
- customer may be dependent on the product; and
- future orders from customers.

[D] Scarce resources (limiting factor)

More decisions can be made using marginal costing and in this example we use the problems of [D], above, to see what the case is if resources are scarce.

It is not only the demand in the marketplace that limits the amount produced but also the availability, or lack, of resources such as skilled labour, raw materials, time available on certain machinery and working or storage space.

What happens when there is such a shortage of resources? Under these circumstances we cannot consider the answer on the basis of a positive contribution.

A ranking system is required, which is based on the usage of the scarce factor, so that the contribution is maximised.

The method used is to isolate the scarce resource and recalculate the contribution per unit of the scarce factor. The most profitable combination of products will be when the contribution per unit of the scarce factor is maximised. This is best illustrated by the following worked example.

33.3.10 Worked example

A manufacturer wishes to produce three products (figures given are for one unit of production):

	Product 1	Product 2	Product 3
Selling price	10	18	23
Raw material costs	3	2	8
Variable labour costs	4	8	10
Labour hours	1	2	2.5

The limiting factor is the number of labour hours. The cost of labour is £4 per hour.

The company wishes to maximise profits, and therefore it requires to determine the order in which it should rank the three products.

To establish this, we first must calculate the contributions made by each product.

	Product 1	Product 2	Product 3
Selling price	10	18	23
Variable costs	7	10	18
Contribution	3	8	5
Ranking	3rd	1st	2nd

All products show positive contributions and therefore all products are equally possible. In the above table we have ranked them by contribution.

But we have been told that labour hours are the scarce factor and, therefore, we must establish what the contribution of each product, per labour hour, is.

$$\text{Contribution per scarce factor} = \frac{\text{Contribution per unit}}{\text{Number of labour hours per unit}}$$

	Product 1	Product 2	Product 3
Contribution	3	8	5
Labour hours	1	2	2.5
Contribution per labour hour	3	4	2
Ranking	2nd	1st	3rd

This gives us the information required for our decision. We need to manufacture in the order of product 2, then product 1 and finally (if any labour hours are still available) product 3.

33.3.11 Self-test

Multi Ltd produces two products – a hair curler and a hairdryer. They each sell at a different price. The following information is given:

	Hair curler		Hairdryer	
Selling price per unit		25.0		35.0
Unit cost:				
materials	10.0		14.0	
labour	7.0		9.0	
other variable costs	3.5		2.0	
fixed costs	5.0		5.0	
Total costs		25.5		30.0
(Loss)/Profit per unit		(0.5)		5.0
Units produced		2,500		1,000
(Loss)/Profit per product		(1,250)		5,000

Overall profit for both products   £3,750
Total fixed costs are £17,500

We can see from the above calculations that the firm makes a loss of £0.5 per unit for every hair curler it produces, while the hairdryer produces a profit of £5 per unit.

Like most firms, this one has a policy of not producing loss-making items. So, it could decide to dispense with the hair curler production and concentrate on producing hairdryers.

You are told that the demand for hairdryers will remain constant and that all the fixed costs relate to the firm as a whole, rather than to a particular product.

Advise management whether to continue to produce hair curlers or not. Show all your calculations to support the advice given.

33.3.12 Self-test

Jason Ltd is a company with only one product, and spare capacity – that is, it could make and sell more if only there was a greater demand for the product. We are given the following information:

	Normal production
Selling price per unit	40
Total variable costs per unit	30
Units demanded	5,000

The fixed costs of Jason Ltd are £40,000.

Jason Ltd has now received an order for an additional 1,000 units but the purchaser is only willing to pay £36 per unit for these extra 1,000 units. What should the company do with this extra order at the lower price? Show all the calculations necessary to arrive at your conclusion.

33.3.13 Self-test

In the following case you are required to advise Cindy & Co. the order of ranking based on the scarce resource, namely machine hours.

Product	A	B	C
Selling price	25	20	23
Variable cost	10	8	12
Demand	25	20	30
Machine hours	4	3	4

Ignore fixed costs because the products all use the same machine. There is a time limit of 148 hours for the use of this machine.

33.3.14 Self-test

You are required to determine the ranking for the following products, based on the fact that there is a limit on available labour. You are required to advise Bertha & Co. which product is the most profitable to produce.

	A	B	C
Selling price per unit	50	40	65
Variable costs per unit	25	19	29
Contribution	25	21	36
Hours of labour per unit	5	3	6

33.3.15 Self-test

Erin & Co. is not able to recruit sufficient skilled employees (the scarce factor) to fulfil the demand for the three different catering services it provides. The firm has only 144,200 hours of skilled time available and must decide how it is going to utilise that resource.

Our first step is to examine the income and expenses associated with those services.

Service	Gold	Silver	Bronze
Revenue per service	2,000	1,340	1,600
Variable salaries per service	800	600	700
Variable selling expenses per service	400	200	300
Contribution per service	800	540	600

Total fixed costs £400,000

Erin & Co. would like to provide as much of the Gold service as possible, followed by the Bronze service and finally the Silver service because the higher the contribution, the more speedily it would be able to cover its fixed costs.

The following information is available:

Service	Gold	Silver	Bronze
Staff hours per service	40	30	35
Demand for catering service	2,000	2,000	1,200
Total hours to meet demand	80,000	60,000	42,000

This results in a total demand requiring 182,000 hours. Erin & Co. only has 144,200 hours available. Therefore, it is apparent that it will not be able to satisfy the total demand.

You are to determine how the company should use the available hours so that it makes as much profit as possible.

33.3.16 Self-test

Pat Fabrics designs, makes and sells silk ties. The selling price is £28 each.
The variable costs per silk tie are as follows:

Material	£7
Trimmings	£2
Wages	£3
Packaging	£2

Fixed overheads are £3,000 per month.

You are required to calculate the contribution made by each tie sold.

Pat Fabrics has had an offer from a retail outlet to purchase 400 ties at £18 per tie. Acceptance of this offer would entail renting additional premises at £300 per month. The order would be completed in two months.

Calculate whether Pat Fabrics should accept this order.

The following season, Pat Fabrics plans to make three new designs. The costs for the new styles are as follows:

	Style 1	Style 2	Style 3
Material	£4	£3	£5
Trimmings	£2	£1	£2
Wages	£3	£3	£3
Packaging	£1	£1	£1
Selling price	£25	£20	£31
Machine hours per tie	5	3	4
Demand in units per month	20	15	25

Although the fixed overheads are expected to remain at £3,000 per month, Pat Fabrics has a limiting factor. The firm has only one machine and, as a result, machine hours are limited to 200 hours per month.

What is the most profitable combination of styles for Pat Fabrics to make?

33.3.17 Comparing marginal and absorption costing

We have discussed the two methods of costing. We have noted that each has its own advantages and disadvantages. In this section we examine the differences between the two methods in the pricing of a product. The costs have all been based on a production of 12,000 units in year 1 and 13,000 units in year 2.

	Absorption costing		Marginal costing	
Year 1				
Sales 10,000 units @ £10 each		100,000		100,000
Cost of sales				
Opening stock	Nil		Nil	
Variable costs £6 per unit	72,000		72,000	
Fixed costs	18,000		18,000	
Total cost (12,000 units)	90,000		90,000	
Closing stock (2,000 units)	15,000	75,000	12,000	78,000
Net profit		25,000		22,000
Year 2				
Sales 12,000 units @ £10 each		120,000		120,000
Cost of sales				
Stock (2,000 units)	15,000		12,000	
Variable costs £6 per unit	78,000		78,000	
Fixed costs	18,000		18,000	
Total cost (13,000 units)	111,000		108,000	
Closing stock (3,000 units)	22,200*	88,800	18,000	90,000
Net profit		31,200		30,000

* Note: Closing stock of £22,200 is the cost of production (£78,000) and fixed costs for the year (£18,000) divided by the units produced (13,000) and multiplied by the units of stock held at year end (3,000). The answer, correct to one decimal place is £7.4 per unit which is equal to £22,200 for the closing stock of 3,000 units. In marginal costing only variable costs are taken into account in closing stock.

Using absorption costing, the profit is greater than with marginal costing, as seen in the above example for year 2.

33.3.18 Self-test

Able & Co. produce 5,000 units of toothbrushes per month.
You are provided with the following information relating to costs:

Material	60 pence per unit
Labour	40 pence per unit
Factory rent	£1,000 per month
Production manager	£24,000 per annum
Sales of 2,000 units are made at	£3 per unit

You are required to compare marginal and absorption costing by showing your calculations, side by side.

33.3.19 Self-test

Myco Ltd is able to use the same machines to produce different grades of its product, for which the unit costs and revenues are shown below

	Small	Medium	Large
Selling price	100	140	200
Materials	40	48	60
Labour	20	32	52
Other variable costs	8	12	16
Machine hours	4	8	6
Demand (units)	40,000	32,000	20,000

The total fixed costs for the period are £330,000.
There is a limit to the number of machine hours available and this is currently 296,000 hours.
You are required to calculate the output, per product, during this period in order to maximise the profit of Myco Ltd.

33.3.20 Self-test

Paula Ltd, currently producing 20,000 units, makes a single product, which it sells for £150 per unit. Until recently the company has only sold to the UK market. It is now interested in securing markets in the rest of Europe.
The company has received an order, at its normal selling price, for 5,000 modified units from a Spanish firm. The modifications would mean that the Spanish order would be subject to the following adjustments:

(i) an increase in material costs of 10 per cent;
(ii) an increase in labour costs of 5 per cent;
(iii) a reduction in variable selling expenses of 20 per cent.

A new machine would have to be purchased in order to produce the modified units, and this would result in additional fixed costs of £16,000 per year.

The present costs are as follows.

	£ per unit
Materials	60
Labour	30
Variable factory costs	10
Variable selling costs	15
Total fixed factory costs	£195,000
Total fixed selling and administrative costs	£135,000
Additional fixed cost	£16,000

You are required to determine if the order should be accepted.

33.3.21 Self-test

Norman Ltd is worried about the production of its saxophones, which appear to be loss-making. The directors question whether they should cease production of them, and concentrate on the production of the trumpets. The products are made in different factories and the company has a separate administrative/distribution centre. You are provided with the following details:

	Trumpets	Saxophone
Sales revenue	750,000	540,000
Material cost	312,000	279,000
Labour cost	180,000	120,000
Other variable costs	60,000	48,000
Fixed costs	105,000	99,000

£33,000 of the fixed costs of the saxophone production would cease if the factory were to be closed, but the remaining costs would still have to be paid unless the site was to be sold.

The market for saxophones remains constant, and no further cost increases are predicted for the next year.

Would you advise the directors to close the saxophone factory? Show all your calculations.

33.3.22 Self-test

Nathan Ltd manufactures Kiddie Kites (their sole product). Several new competitors have entered the market for kites, and the market price for Kiddie Kites has fallen by £5.50 to £23.50 per unit.

You are required to advise the directors as to whether it is worthwhile for them to continue production of Kiddie Kites, bearing in mind that they require a minimum return on capital employed of 16 per cent. The capital employed by Nathan Ltd is, at present, £130,000. The company considers that there is an expected demand of 30,000 units.

In order to provide this advice, you are given the following information relating to the unit costs of Kiddie Kites:

Materials	4.80
Direct labour	3.15
Other factory variable costs	0.60
Variable selling costs	0.75
Total fixed costs	£63,750

33.3.23 Self-test

In this example, Clothes & Co. makes several products. Each of these products – shirts, ties, pants and jackets – is made in a separate department. Apart from the shirts and ties, the other items are usually bought separately, rather than in combination.

Revenues and variable costs per unit are given in the table below. The total fixed costs amount to £180,000 per annum.

£ per unit	Shirts	Ties	Pants	Jackets
Selling price	12.0	6.0	15.0	42.0
Materials	3.0	2.7	6.0	31.5
Labour	2.1	2.7	3.3	9.0
Other variable costs	1.5	0.9	1.8	3.0
Contribution	5.4	(0.3)	3.9	(1.5)
Sales volume (units)	40,000	40,000	80,000	20,000
Contribution per product (£)	216,000	(12,000)	312,000	(30,000)
Total contribution	486,000			
Fixed costs	180,000			
Profit	306,000			

Based on the information you have been given above, you are required to recommend to Clothes & Co. what you consider to be the best option for them. You are told that there are no scarce factors.

33.3.24 Self-test

Using the information for Clothes & Co. in section 33.3.23, above, and the results of your calculations, you are now required to consider another option open to the company.

The company has now decided to specialise in shirts and ties. It has approached Dress Ltd for a quotation for the manufacture of pants. It has now received a price for this and has been assured of delivery times and quality.

Dress Ltd has quoted £11.20 for each pair of pants. This seems to give Clothes & Co. a profit of £3.80 per pair.

You are required to examine this proposition and recommend to the management of Clothes & Co. whether they should specialise and buy in pants for resale. Give all the necessary calculations to support your recommendations.

Chapter 34

Break-even analysis

Objectives   After you have studied this chapter, you should be able to:

■ distinguish between semi-variable, fixed and variable costs;

■ understand the term margin of safety and the need for its calculation;

■ explain the meaning of the break-even point;

■ calculate the break-even point of a product;

■ recognise the limitations of break-even analysis.

34.1   Introduction

Break-even analysis calculates the break-even point and analyses the consequences of any changes in costs. A business reaches the break-even point when the level of activity produces no profit or loss. Stated another way, the break-even point (BEP) is that point where the total sales revenue (TR) equals the total costs (TC) (both fixed and variable).

In formula terms, this means that the breakeven point is $TR - TC = 0$ (see section 34.3.5). At that point, the firm makes no profit or loss. It goes some way to answer the age-old question asked by new businesses – 'When are we going to start to make a profit?'

From your study of Chapter 33 you know the importance of fixed and variable costs per unit. It is these costs, shown as the contribution per unit, that are used in calculating the break-even point. This calculation would then tell us how many units have to be sold in order to cover the total fixed costs.

The formula used is:

$$\text{Break-even point} = \frac{\text{Total fixed costs}}{\text{Contribution per unit}} = \text{No. of units}$$

If we wish to look at this in terms of total revenue, we can multiply the break-even point in units by the selling price per unit.

34.2   Types of cost

We have read in previous chapters that there are a variety of costs that can be incurred in production and selling. In this chapter we shall assume for purposes of our calculations that all the costs can be classified either as fixed or variable. This, of course, is not always the case in practice.

34.2.1 Worked example

We are given the following information:

Fixed costs   £6,000
Selling price   £5 per unit
Variable cost   £2 per unit

The first thing to do is to determine the value of the contribution. This is the selling price per unit, less the variable cost per unit, in other words, £5 – £2 = £3 contribution per unit.

Selling price per unit – Variable costs per unit = Contribution per unit

We next calculate the break-even point. This is the fixed costs divided by the contribution per unit.

$$\text{BEP} = \frac{\text{Fixed costs}}{\text{Contribution per unit}} = \frac{6{,}000}{3} = 2{,}000 \text{ units}$$

If we want to achieve a certain profit then we need to add the required profit figure to the total fixed cost and divide that total by the contribution.

Let us assume that we wish to make a profit of £36,000. To calculate the number of units required to be sold in order to make a profit of £36,000 we need to take the fixed cost of £6,000 and add the profit required of £36,000 and divide the total by the £3 (contribution).

$$\frac{\text{Fixed costs} + \text{Profit}}{\text{Contribution per unit}} = \frac{6{,}000 + 36{,}000}{3} = 14{,}000 \text{ units}$$

This tells us that we need to sell 14,000 units to achieve the £36,000 profit.

34.3   Margin of safety

The margin of safety is the gap between the current production or sales level and the break-even point. This is the extent to which the planned volume of sales lies above the break-even point and shows how much leeway exists before the firm ceases to be profitable. In other words, it gives us an indication of the risk factor. The greater the margin of safety, the lower the risk. The margin of safety is shown in units or in pounds of sales revenue. It could also be shown as a percentage of the present sales level (see section 34.3.5).

34.3.1 Worked example

In this example, we use the same facts as in section 34.2.1, above. We are told that the budgeted sales are 3,000 units. We had also previously calculated that the breakeven point is 2,000 units.

Using this information, we deduct the number of units required to break even from the (budgeted) sales to determine the margin of safety.

$$3,000 - 2,000 = \text{Margin of safety} = 1,000 \text{ units}$$

This tells us that the gap between the break-even point and the sales level is 1,000 units (our margin of safety).

34.3.2 Worked example

Kirk & Co. are manufacturers of garden benches. They sell these at an average selling price of £50 per bench. The following variable costs are incurred in the manufacture of each bench:

Material	20
Labour	18
Other variable costs	2
Total	£40

Other information:

(i)   monthly output is 500 benches;
(ii) fixed costs are £4,000 per month; and
(iii) break-even point is 400 benches.

Note: The break-even point is calculated by taking the contribution of £10 per unit and dividing it into the fixed costs of £4,000.

You are required to calculate the monthly sales that are required to achieve a profit of £1,000 if advertising costs of £3,000 p.m. are incurred in addition to all the above items.

Remember! Contribution – Fixed costs = Profits

Sales	500 × £50	£25,000
Contribution	£10 × 500	£5,000
Net profit before advertising	£5,000 – £4,000	£1,000

To cover the additional costs of advertising we would need to produce an additional 300 units, (i.e. £3,000 ÷ 10). This would then give a break-even of 800 units.

Note: We can prove this answer by multiplying 800 by £10 (contribution) = £8,000. From this we deduct the fixed costs of £4,000 and the advertising costs of £3,000. The remainder is profit, which equals £1,000.

What output would be required if the selling price is decreased to £48? Keep in mind that we still wish to achieve a monthly profit of £1,000.
    We calculate that the contribution is 48 – 40 = £8 per unit.
    The total costs are fixed costs of £4,000 plus advertising of £3,000 = £7,000.
    This amount together with a £1,000 profit is divided by the contribution of £8 per unit. This means that we need to produce 1,000 units to cover costs and show a £1,000 profit.

$$\frac{7,000 + 1,000}{£8} = 1,000 \text{ units}$$

34.3.3 Self-test

Bob Ltd has one product, which has the same selling price for each unit sold. Variable costs and fixed costs do not vary at any level of activity during the period. The company sells its entire production.

Once we know where the current break-even point is, we can experiment with what will happen if various items in the formulae change.

You are given the following information:

(i)   Bob Ltd has fixed costs of £160,000 for the period;
(ii) the selling price of its product is £38 per unit; and
(iii) total variable cost per unit amounts to £30.

You are required to calculate the number of units required to break even.

You are now required to examine the effects of the following changes on the break-even point.

(i)   the selling price is increased to £40 per unit;
(ii) the fixed costs have increased to £180,000 and the selling price remains at £38 per unit; and
(iii) the variable costs increase to £36 per unit; the selling price remains at £38 per unit and the fixed costs are £160,000.

As a result of this examination can you arrive at some general conclusion relating to the movement of the break-even point?

34.3.4 Movements in break-even

It is not always ideal to have low variable costs and therefore a high contribution. We must also consider the level of fixed costs.

Using your answer to the self-test above, we can see the effects on the break-even point by having a higher level of fixed costs. It is going to take far longer for the firm to achieve its break-even point. This can be particularly crucial for a new firm, especially when funding is needed to repay short-term loans, or where investors require a return on capital.

The relationship between fixed and variable costs is of vital importance to any firm. Where a firm has a high level of fixed costs in proportion to its variable costs, it will take a long time before it is able to reach break-even point. However, once that point is reached, profits should increase fairly quickly as the high contribution is now being channelled mainly to profit.

If the firm runs into difficulties, it will slide back towards its break-even point, and risks the possibility of a loss, far quicker than a firm with comparatively low fixed costs in relation to its variable costs. This aspect is a crucial factor for many highly automated manufacturing firms, having high borrowings and fixed overheads.

34.3.5 Graphic illustration of terminology

Figure 34.1 illustrates various terms used.

Figure 34.1 Relationship between terms

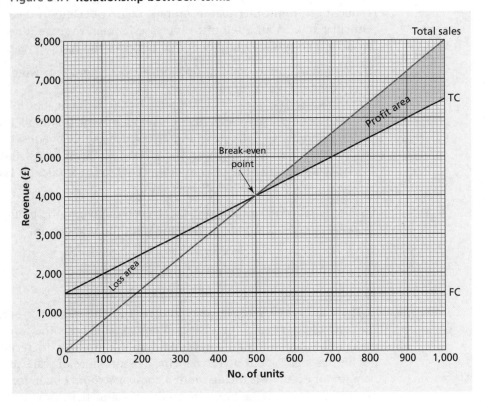

Cost sheet

Fixed costs	£1,500 p.m.
Variable costs	£500 per 100 units
Sales	£8 per unit

34.3.6 Self-test

The following information relates to the costs of toy manufacturing by Excel Toys:

Selling price per unit	£90
Materials per unit	£18
Labour per unit	1 hour @ £6 per hour (skilled)
	3 hours @ £3 per hour (unskilled)
Variable overhead	£14 per unit
Fixed overhead	£430,000

The estimated turnover is £945,000 per annum.

Taking the current position, you are required to calculate the following:

(a) the break-even point (in units);
(b) the margin of safety (in units);
(c) the profit that is currently expected; and
(d) how many toy units need to be sold to achieve a target profit of £215,000.

Excel Toys notices a decline in its sales over the years. This may be due to strong competition from other manufacturers, or to a decline in the demand for that particular toy. In an attempt to increase its market share, the management of Excel Toys proposes a number of new ideas for the coming year. These are:

(i) To reduce the current selling price by 30 per cent, which is expected to generate 50 per cent more sales.

(ii) To reduce the current selling price by 30 per cent, but to accompany this with an aggressive advertising campaign which should increase sales by 60 per cent. Advertising will increase the variable overheads by 50 per cent.

(iii) To offer a second toy free. The second toy would cost the company £15 but, as a result of the offer, it is expected to boost sales by 120 per cent. The selling price remains at £90 per unit.

You are required to calculate the break-even point and the profit or loss for each proposal in order to advise management on the best option.

34.3.7 Limitations to break-even analysis

There are a number of limitations to break-even analysis.

There are many variable costs that remain the same, per unit, regardless of the level of activity. In the case of other variable costs they are not necessarily going to be the same at all levels of activity. For example, there are reducing costs per unit brought about by the benefits of economies of scale and specialisation. A common example is the discount a company could obtain for buying in larger quantities. At the same time, we could also find that some unit costs increase. This could, for example, be where a manufacturer has to work overtime in order to complete a job.

In the case of semi-variable costs, part of the cost changes according to the level of activity. This means that part of the cost is fixed, while the remaining part is variable. An example would be the fixed cost of rental for a telephone and the variable part for usage.

We assume that every single unit will be sold for the same price during the period. This is not true. Discounts are given to customers that buy in bulk, or that buy for resale. Discount is also given to encourage speedy payments. All these discounts influence the amount received (total revenue).

After providing a certain number of units, fixed costs will increase as, for example, where more factory space (and therefore rent costs) is required.

34.3.8 Self-test

Howard Ltd is a new company, anxious to become profitable as soon as possible. It has fixed costs of £96,000 per period. Present demand for its product is 30,000 units, but this is expected to rise shortly to 36,000 units. This increase will be accompanied by a £0.20 drop from the present selling price of £8 per unit. Material costs £2 per unit but, if the production level rises, the company will be able to get a quantity discount of 20 per cent. Labour costs are £2.50 per unit. Other variable costs amount to £0.60 per unit.

Calculate:

(i) the present break-even point for Howard Ltd, in units and pounds of sales revenue;
(ii) the break-even point, together with the margin of safety, if the above changes take place.

34.3.9 Self-test

Pat Fabrics (see section 33.3.16) designs, makes and sells silk ties. The selling price is £28 each.
   The variable costs per silk tie are as follows:

(i)   Material   £7
(ii) Trimmings   £2
(iii) Wages   £3
(iv) Packaging   £2

Fixed overheads are £3,000 per month.
   You are required to calculate how many ties Pat Fabrics must sell every month to break even.
   If the fixed costs increase to £3,700 per month and the selling price falls by 25 per cent, how many ties will have to be sold to make a monthly profit of £4,000?

34.3.10 Self-test

The following information, based on a budgeted sales and production volume of 9,000 units, relates to EZee, the only product made by Design Ltd.

Sales (9,000 units)		585,000
Less:		
Direct materials	156,600	
Direct labour	256,500	
Variable production overhead	21,600	
Fixed production overhead	54,000	(488,700)
		96,300
Less:		
Administration, selling and distribution costs		
Variable	10,800	
Fixed	27,000	(37,800)
Net profit		58,500

In addition, you are advised that there is no opening or closing stock.
   You are required to:

(a) Calculate the break-even point in units sold and in sales revenue.
(b) Calculate the margin of safety in units and in sales revenue.

Design Ltd anticipates that profits will increase if the following proposals are adopted:

(i) that the selling price be reduced by £8 per unit; and

(ii) that an additional investment of £45,000 be made in fixed production overheads.

The company expects that these proposals will help increase sales volume by 4,000 units and reduce labour costs by £5 per unit.

You are required to determine the new expected profit and the new break-even point (in units) if the proposals are adopted.

34.3.11 Self-test

Rocky Ltd has produced the following results for the month of July 2008:

Sales (15,000 units @ £10 each}		150,000
Costs:		
Variable	90,000	
Fixed	30,000	120,000
Profit		30,000

You are required to

(a) Calculate the break-even point using the above data

(b) Calculate the breakeven point on the assumption that the sale price increases by 20 per cent and the variable costs increase by 50 per cent.

Assume the number of units sold remained the same.

34.3.12 Self-test

First Aid Ltd manufactures bandages and dressings which are supplied to doctors' surgeries, nursing homes and hospitals.

The company advises you of the following:

Sales (in units) per month

Product	Doctors	Nursing homes	Hospitals	Total units per month	Total units per year
Bandages	1,200	1,800	3,900	6,900	82,800
Dressings	1,700	1,300	2,400	5,400	64,800

There is no trend and the company uses the above information for its annual sales budget.

The selling price of bandages is £1.00 each and dressings are £1.40 each.

To produce the above, the company has invested in a number of machines for which they paid a total price of £28,000. These machines have an expected life of 10 years with a residual value of £2,000. The company writes off the machines using the straight line method. Costs are apportioned between bandages and dressings in the ratio of 7:3.

Other costs in the factory are:

	Bandages	Dressings
Direct material	30p per bandage	45p per unit
Direct labour	28p per bandage	52p per unit
Variable overheads	£1.80 per hour	£2.40 per hour
Production time per unit	3 minutes	6 minutes

Rental for the premises is £36,000 p.a.

You are required to calculate the break-even point in units for both products.

Prepare a budget showing the profit or loss account for the year ending 31 December 2011.

34.3.13 Self-test

X Ltd manufactures biscuits. These are sold at £20 per box. The monthly turnover is 200 boxes and the company wishes to increase sales.

If they reduce the selling price to £18 then it is anticipated that sales will increase to 450 boxes per month. The sales director believes that if the selling price is further reduced to £17 per box then sales could be 600 boxes per month.

The following budget is prepared for 200 boxes:

Direct material	1,000
Direct labour	1,500
Selling and distribution costs	600
Fixed overheads	700
Total costs	3,800

You are required to prepare for each of the above scenarios:

(i) the profit or loss;
(ii) the break-even point.

Recommend which policy should be adopted.

Chapter 35

Budgeting

Objectives After you have studied this chapter, you should be able to:

- understand what key factors are required for a budget;
- prepare an annual budget for individual items;
- prepare a master budget;
- create a flexible budget for different levels of activity;
- understand the use of budgets to measure performance.

35.1 Introduction

Businesses must plan for the future and, in doing so, must see that managers have a clear direction and know where the business is going. To do this, they must have long-term goals, which are broken down into short-term budgets.

It is the discipline of management accounting that provides the information for planning and control. Through this, business is able to achieve its goals.

Before undertaking any form of budgeting we must identify the objectives of the business. These objectives (or strategic plans) deal with a varied mixture of items.

Before developing these plans we need be aware of the present situation of the business. We do this by undertaking a number of things:

- We need to analyse the environment in which the business operates. We examine the current position to see if the business faces opportunities or competition.
- We examine the resources that the business possesses in order to understand its ability to compete.

Once this is completed we can then prepare our strategic plans. To do this, we detail our requirements in the form of questions, which are both asked and answered by management.

- What is the economic mission of the company?
- What line of business should the company be in?
- What goods and services should be sold?
- What markets should be served?
- What share of the market is desired?
- What rate of growth is required in sales, assets, investment, etc.?

Once the plan has been established, it is the function of management to identify a range of possible courses of action that will enable the company's objectives to be achieved.

35.2 Budget

A budget is a plan prepared in advance for a fixed period. It could show the anticipated value and in some cases quantities of revenue, expenditure, assets, liabilities and cash flow. It forecasts the result that a business would like to achieve, if the plan is adopted. Usually the budget is based on past experience and takes into account future anticipated trends in the products manufactured.

The budget itself translates this long-term plan into an annual operating plan. Although this is the typical budget period, predictions are likely to be more accurate at the beginning of, rather than later in, the budget period.

We can define a budget as a plan expressed in financial terms. The budget period is often one year, broken down into quarters, months, weeks, days, etc.

Budgets are prepared for each area of the business such as sales, materials, labour etc. and are known as functional budgets. Each functional budget is allocated to a budget centre under the responsibility of a budget manager or budget holder.

While the cash budget is the most well known budget, there are many other budgets. These feed into both the cash budget and the budgeted profit and loss account and balance sheet – known as the master budget.

35.3 The objectives of budgeting

Budgeting is a method designed to maximise the use of the economic resources of the business. It records:

- market expectations and product changes;
- alterations to the business structure; and
- capital investments and inflation forecasts.

Managers constantly need to make decisions. For example, they must decide if they should make a product or bring in a new product or subcontract the work.

This decision-making process is not only a financial one, but also takes into account qualitative factors. For example:

- Should employees be kept on or should staff be reduced?
- What are the future prospects for the company?
- Is it possible and profitable to introduce new business and products to the company?

35.4 Budget preparation

A great deal of work is involved in the process of preparing budgets. The figures used are estimates derived from previous experience, or from market research. Those responsible for implementing the budget need to be involved in its preparation and the data from all sections of the business must be coordinated.

A successful budget that will achieve its objectives needs the involvement and cooperation of departmental managers. These managers are unlikely to be motivated to achieve targets unless they have played a part in preparing the overall budget.

It is also important that key factors (see section 35.4.1) are taken into account in the budget preparation. For example, it would be pointless for the budget to be based on sales data if the production side of the business is unable to meet these targets.

The individual budgets feed through to a budgeted profit and loss account as well as, in most cases, to the cash budget. It is important to understand that the individual budgets affect the cash budget and the budgeted operating statement. At the end of the budget period, a budgeted statement of affairs can be drawn up. These two statements (budgeted profit and loss account and budgeted balance sheet) are referred to as the master budget.

35.4.1 The key factors

There are several key factors in budget preparation. Before starting preparation the firm must:

- determine its financial objectives;
- identify its sales potential or its limitations in production or labour;
- prepare calculations for its requirements which are limited to a level of activity; and
- prepare a system of budgetary control which identifies those responsible for each cost centre and ensures that any departures from budget are recognised and acted upon quickly.

Financial data, involving a great deal of work, is needed to prepare any budget. In addition, a number of key areas must be calculated:

- fixed and variable costs;
- semi-variable costs; and
- can any fixed costs be avoided?

The cash flow identifies the actual cash expended and collected as a result of the decision. It is vital that the exact timing of cash flows is identified.

We know that the profit and loss account shows groups of costs. These are shown as administration costs, or selling and distribution costs. Although this form of classification is used by accountants in the profit and loss account, it is not of much use to the managers of a business. The managers need to know, in far greater detail, the individual costs and if they are variable or fixed, or something in between.

If a business manufactures products for resale, then the manager would want a clear distinction between manufacturing costs and non-manufacturing costs.

35.5 Benefits of a budget

We now look at the many benefits that can be achieved by producing budgets. These are listed in the paragraphs below.

35.5.1 Planning

This forces management to:

- plan ahead;
- set targets; and
- anticipate problems.

35.5.2 Control

Events must conform to plans. It is important that we compare the actual results with the planned figures and that any, and all, variances (that is, the difference between the planned amount and the actual amount) are identified and corrective action is taken. This is known as management by exception.

35.5.3 Communication

No budget can exist without proper and full communication to those who must implement it. This is done in two ways:

- vertically, through line management; and
- horizontally, by co-ordination with other budget centres.

35.5.4 Coordination

In all businesses, and especially in manufacturing, it is vital that the efforts of all involved in the process work together as a team. With this in mind, we must understand that functional budgets are interrelated and that, in the construction of the budgets, the managers are forced to negotiate with each other. This highlights the fact that the activities of departments are interlinked and that one department complements another; for example, the production and sales departments.

35.5.5 Motivation

In motivating staff it is important to ensure that the targets are attainable. If the targets are too high or too low, then the staff is insufficiently motivated. The best way in which to maximise motivation would be by following the steps below:

- managers and staff participate in the budget preparation;
- budget managers are accountable only for controllable costs; and
- management information systems are perceived to be efficient.

35.5.6 Performance evaluation

Managers are only held accountable for matters that are within their control. When the budgeted figures for one month are compared with the actual results of that month, some of the adverse variances may involve items that could have been predicted or avoided. On the other hand, some items might have been impossible to predict or avoid. For example, if time has been lost because a manager failed to authorise maintenance on a machine, which subsequently broke down, that manager would be held responsible for the problem and, consequently, for the budget variance. But if time was lost because of a trade union strike, this would be outside the control of the manager. Any variance would therefore be classed as a non-controllable variance for which the manager could not be held responsible.

35.6 Stages in the budget process

To undertake the preparation of budgets we need to consult all departments involved using a 'bottom-up' approach. Budgets cannot be prepared without considerable discussion and negotiation and, therefore, we must always recognise that a good budget is one where we have negotiated, coordinated and reviewed the process. Budgeting is a continuous process of feedback, control and review.

There are a number of stages that are implemented in setting a budget. These are listed in the paragraphs below.

35.6.1 Critical factors

We first need to identify any possible critical factors. By examining these we can take them into account in determining the budgets. These factors could be the level of sales that can be achieved by a business, or the amount of capital available for growth and expansion, or there could be a scarcity element, such as shortages of skilled labour or machinery.

In Chapter 33 we examined the effects of limited factors on decision making.

35.6.2 Order of budgeting

Invariably there is an order commonly used in budget preparation. We begin with the **sales budget**. This requires an estimate of the number of units that can be sold. In so doing, we must also consider the external environment and seasonal factors. Although prior knowledge and experience may help, it is also desirable to conduct market research. The sales budget would show the number of units of each product, the selling price per unit and the total sales value.

Sales budget	Article A	Article B	Total £
Sales in units	600	300	
Unit selling price	£400	£1,000	
Total annual sales	£240,000	£300,000	£540,000

Our next task is the preparation of the **production budget**. This would use the number of units expected to be sold, adjusted for the net difference between the opening and closing stock. This final figure would then determine the production required.

Production budget	Article A	Article B
Production units	550	320

The third budget is that set to determine the **material requirements**. Having previously calculated the number of units of each product to be produced, we simply multiply this figure by the amount of material required for each unit. If this is multiplied by the price per unit, we would be able to establish the direct material cost.

Material budget	Article A	Article B	Total £
Production units	550	320	
Raw material per unit	10 kilo	6 kilo	
Cost per kilo	£10	£10	
Total cost	£55,000	£19,200	£74,200

We then move on to the **labour budget**, where we calculate the direct labour hours required and multiply it by the rate paid to workers.

Labour budget	Article A	Article B	Total £
Production units	550	320	
Hours per unit	6	15	
Labour cost per unit	£200	£500	
Total cost	£110,000	£160,000	£270,000

No budgeting process can be complete without preparing a **cash budget**. We have, in the earlier budgets, set out our expectations, all involving capital requirements. These expectations can only be feasible if we have sufficient cash flow to meet the needs of the business. It is the cash budget that will show us if this is so.

The final budget (the **master budget**) is a summary of all the other budgets. This budget is, in essence, the budgeted profit and loss account.

Master budget	Article A	Article B	Total £
Sales	£240,000	£300,000	£540,000
Less:			
Material	£55,000	£19,200	£74,200
Labour	£110,000	£160,000	£270,000
Total variable costs	£165,000	£179,200	£344,200
Contribution	£75,000	£120,800	£195,800
Fixed costs			£42,450
Net profit			£153,350

35.6.3 Delegation

Once budgets are agreed, responsibility for them is delegated to the line managers by means of subsidiary budgets. This allows these managers to have some control over their smaller areas, thus achieving the targets as set.

35.7 Different types of budget

There are two different types of budget. They are:

- the fixed budget; and
- the flexible budget.

In the case of the fixed budget, it only shows one level of activity or production, while the flexible budget shows the situation covering several levels of activity.

It should be noted that budgets are not only presented in money terms but may also show quantities, e.g. 200 units produced each week.

35.7.1 Rolling (continuous) budgets

No matter how much experience the budgeting team has, it is difficult to predict future events. To overcome this problem some firms use a rolling budget.

In this type of budget, the period is constantly extended and the estimates updated so that we are always working with a full budget period. We prepare a one-year budget but after each month the remaining figures (for the next 12 months) are revised and an extra month is added. This method is particularly useful when there are high levels of inflation or where firms are faced with fluctuating interest rates and/or exchange rates.

35.7.2 Zero-based budget

In contrast, the zero-based budget is built up from scratch. The budget starts with expenditure for each department or category at zero. Department heads must present a case to justify expenditure, which senior management may grant. All existing requirements must be justified, and any new proposals must be properly adopted.

Zero-based budgeting considers:

- the objectives of each activity;
- whether the activity is really necessary;
- if there are alternative ways of achieving the stated objectives; and
- the cost consequences should the activity not take place.

35.7.3 Flexible budgets

We need to decide if we should maintain a fixed or flexible budget bearing in mind that actual circumstances and levels of activity may change during the budget period.

With a fixed budget the original budget is maintained, while with a flexible budget it is adjusted to reflect fluctuations in units produced, increases or decreases in costs or changes in production capacity.

With a flexible budget the variable cost element is revised or 'flexed'. This means that different cost behaviour patterns are allowed for and therefore changes are made as the volume of activity changes.

When preparing a budget we estimate the output that can be achieved. If the firm operates at a different percentage (e.g. 70 per cent) of its maximum capacity, it will not achieve the results budgeted for at 100 per cent. To measure performance against this wrong target is unrealistic. Any difference is called a volume variance. By creating a flexible budget this volume variance is eliminated.

A flexed budget is based on different levels of activity. Costs must be analysed into fixed and variable costs so that the expenditure at different levels of activity can be determined. We must remember that the fixed overheads budget would not change. It is also possible that the sales budget would not change with changes in production activity, as the business may have sufficient stock to meet the demand that was originally projected.

35.7.4 Worked example

The budget below was produced for the output of 100,000 units of product Y. During April 2009 the actual units produced were 120,000. You are required to present a budget based on the April production, so that it can be compared to the actual costs during the month.

	Budget	Flexed budget	Actual
No. of units	100,000	120,000	120,000
Sales	£150,000	180,000	175,000
Variable costs	£80,000	96,000	94,000
Fixed costs	£30,000	30,000	32,000
Profit	£40,000	£54,000	£49,000

By flexing the budget it is possible to compare the actual achievement with a revised budget (the flexed budget) and so get a better comparison.

35.7.5 Self-test

Rainbow Limited produces saris. It uses a flexible budgeting system and prepares monthly budgeted production figures. The budget and actual figures for production for April are given below.

	Budget	Actual
Production (in units)	5,500	6,600
	£	£
Direct materials	17,600	20,592
Direct labour	45,650	55,968
Fixed overheads	2,300	2,300
Total cost of production	65,550	78,860

Management was satisfied that some budget figures were met exactly:

- each sari was budgeted to use 4 metres of material in production, and this was achieved;
- each sari should have taken 2 hours' labour to produce and this was achieved.

Required:

Prepare the flexible budget for a production of 6,600 saris.

(Edexcel Accounting 6002, June 2007)

35.8 Cash budget

The purpose of this budget is to ensure that the business has sufficient cash to meet its obligations. It is crucial that a business should predict its future cash flow. This will prevent any overcommitment to expansion or development. The budget identifies cash deficits and cash surpluses well in advance, so that prompt action can be planned.

As it is used internally (unlike the cash flow statement), there are no fixed formats. Like all budgets, it is broken down into periods. It shows receipts under one heading and payments under another. The final figure shows the surplus, or deficit, for each period and the balance at the end of each period.

The receipts shown in the budget are cash from sales, rental income, investments, bank interest, etc. The outflows are cash payments for product costs, overheads and other expenses, capital expenditure, bank interest, etc. (It is important to remember that all non-cash items, such as depreciation, are ignored.)

Because of the importance of liquidity, there are occasions when it will be necessary to prepare a separate cash budget. For example, a business might wish to show its bankers that it will be generating sufficient funds to repay any loan by a certain time. The cash budget can be prepared by using only receipts and payments.

35.8.1 Self-test

Daniel is a manufacturer of dining tables and chairs. You are required to prepare a number of budgets for April 2009 based on the following information.

	Tables	Chairs
Forecast sales	40 units	100 units
Selling price	£500	£140
Stock at 1 April 09	20 units	40 units
Material – kg per unit	12 kg	5 kg
Labour hours per unit	11 hours	6 hours
Material cost per kg	£14	£14
Labour cost per hour	£9	£9

In addition to the above, you are advised that there is administration, selling and distribution overheads budgeted at £900 for the month of April. These expenses are apportioned on the basis of total budgeted labour hours in the month.

Daniel aims to produce sufficient tables and chairs so that the closing stock is equivalent to 15 per cent of the sales for April.

You are required to prepare the following budgets:

(a) Sales budget in units and £.
(b) Production budget in units.
(c) Materials usage budget in £.
(d) Labour usage budget in £.
(e) Budgeted profit and loss in £.

35.8.2 Self-test

The following is a projection of income and expenditure from February to July 2009.

You are required to prepare a cash budget for Jetset Ltd for the 3 months ending 30 June 2009.

	Cash sales	Credit sales	Purchases
Feb	100,000	50,000	76,000
March	110,000	60,000	86,000
April	124,000	64,000	90,000
May	120,000	58,000	64,000
June	96,000	48,000	50,000
July	84,000	36,000	40,000

You are given the following additional information:

(i)   Bank balance at 31 March 2009 is expected to be £15,000.
(ii)   Payment for purchases is made in cash, two months later.
(iii) Payment for credit sales is received in cash, one month later.
(iv)   Wages per month are estimated at £24,000.
(v)   Overheads per month are estimated at £36,000.
(vi)   Last instalment on a loan amounting to £70,000 must be paid in April.
(vii) VAT payment due in May. This amounts to £23,000.
(viii) Depreciation per month amounts to £13,000.
(ix)   A tax rebate of £50,000 is due, to be paid in June.

You are required to list the action you would take if the resultant cash budget shows that there is a shortage of cash for the period under review. What action can be taken to prevent a deficit?

35.8.3 Self-test

The following estimates are made for Outdoor Shopping:

	Sales	Purchases	Wages and salaries
Jan	80,000	30,000	12,000
Feb	100,000	40,000	12,000
Mar	50,000	10,000	10,000
Apr	40,000	60,000	14,000
May	40,000	10,000	18,000
June	60,000	30,000	18,000
Jul	50,000	20,000	14,000
Aug	40,000	15,000	10,000
Sept	60,000	40,000	12,000

The following information is available:

(i)   20 per cent of all sales are cash sales and the remainder are credit sales.
(ii)   The payments from debtors are:
        (a) 60 per cent of the amount due is made within one month after the sale, and
        (b) the balance due in the second month.
(iii)   Purchases are paid for in the following month.
(iv)   Interest on a loan of £480,000 is paid quarterly. The interest rate is 10 per cent and the first quarter's payment is made in April 2010.
(v)   Rent is £2,800 per month.
(vi)   Monthly depreciation is calculated at £8,500.
(vii)   Outdoor Shopping purchased new office equipment for a total price of £28,000. Payment is to be made in two equal instalments, in May and September 2010.
(viii) The opening cash balance is £5,900.

You are required to prepare a cash budget for Outdoor Shopping for the period March to August 2010.

35.8.4 Self-test

Rose Fashions Ltd prepares monthly budgets for the 3 months ending 30 September 2010. Forecasts have been drawn up as follows:

Month (2010)	Sales	Purchases	Overheads
May	130,000	75,000	12,000
June	150,000	65,000	12,000
July	140,000	50,000	10,000
August	90,000	90,000	7,000
September	160,000	100,000	11,000
October	170,000	120,000	14,000

The following additional information is given:

(i)   Bank balance on 1 July 2010 is estimated at £5,000.
(ii)   50 per cent of the sales are credit sales. Payments from debtors are received two months after the transaction takes place.
(iii) All purchases are on credit. Payments to suppliers are made one month after the transaction takes place.
(iv)   The forecasts for the overheads, in the table above, refers to cash payments, which are paid when due.
(v)   Wages are £35,000 per month and are paid by cheque.
(vi)   Rent is £72,000 p.a. and is paid quarterly, in advance, on 1 January, 1 April, 1 July and 1 October.
(vii) Depreciation is estimated at £2,500 per month.
(viii) Corporation tax of £10,000 is due in August.
(ix)   A new computer system was purchased in July for £50,000. Payment is due in August 2010.

You are required to prepare a cash budget for Rose Fashions Ltd for the 3 months ending 30 September 2010.

35.8.5 Self-test

Jack Ltd manufactures a hand-held recorder which sells for £64. The company has prepared a projection of units that could be demanded for the first 5 months of 2009.

This projection of demand is:

Month	January	February	March	April	May
No. of units	194	210	280	320	400

At 1 January 2009 the company has stock of 46 recorders. It is the agreed company policy that the stock at the month end will equal 40 per cent of the following month's planned sales.

Each recorder requires 1.5 kg of raw material, costing £8.20 per kg, for its manufacture. At 1 January the raw material stock is 140 kg and company policy is that the month-end stock balance must equal 60 per cent of the following month's planned production needs.

You are required to prepare stock and raw material budgets for January to March 2009.

35.8.6 Self-test

One-one Ltd produces a single product. The budget is as follows:

Selling price		98
Less direct material	28	
Direct labour	18	
Direct overheads	8	
Direct selling costs	4	58
Contribution		40

Unit sales are expected to be:

July	Aug	Sept	Oct	Nov	Dec	Jan
800	600	500	300	400	550	700

You are given the following information:

(i) Credit sales account for 55 per cent of the total sales. Debtors are expected to pay in the month following the sale. All cash sales receive a 2 per cent discount.

(ii) Purchases budget for August–November 2010:

Aug	Sept	Oct	Nov
£8,400	£11,200	£15,400	£18,300

Material suppliers are paid in the month following purchase.

(iii) Labour budget for August–November 2010:

Aug	Sept	Oct	Nov
£7,400	£9,000	£5,400	£7,200

Payments are paid in the month in which they are incurred.

(iv) Variable expenses budget for August–November 2010:

Aug	Sept	Oct	Nov
£6,000	£3,600	£4,800	£4,200

Expenses are paid in the month following that in which they are incurred.

(v) Monthly fixed expenses (including £1,150 depreciation) are £7,000.

(vi) At 1 September 2010, the bank balance is £11,800.

You are required to prepare a cash budget for the three months ending 30 November 2010.

35.9 Budgets for control

Budgets are prepared as a means of controlling anticipated revenue and expenditure. This does not mean that things will go exactly as planned. It often happens that a budget, having been carefully prepared, is found to be unattainable for one reason or another. When this happens it is important that the budget be amended as soon as possible. We describe this as flexing the budget (see section 35.7.3).

Flexing relates to a revision of the variable cost element. It recognises that there are different cost behaviour patterns and, therefore, changes need to be made in volume of activity or unit costs.

35.9.1 Self-test

Wood Products Ltd manufactures a standard design dining room table. It prepares annual budgets based on previous financial information and current market indications of demand for the product. It is now preparing the budget for 2010 and has collected the following external information:

(i) Sales in the UK are expected to remain at 700 tables per month.
(ii) Due to an extensive marketing operation, the company anticipates sales in the USA during the year. The directors consider that table sales will be 300 tables per month from July, with a further increase to 500 for October and November. After that date, sales are expected to increase by 15 per cent per month.

Required:

(a) You are required to prepare a sales budget showing the expected number of tables to be sold for the six months ending December 2010.
(b) Wood Products Ltd prepares cash, production, sales and stock budgets. These budgets need to be prepared in a certain order. Indicate this order with reasons for your answer.

Chapter 36

Standard costing

Objectives After you have studied this chapter, you should be able to:

- understand the benefits of standard costing;
- set standards for manufacturing;
- calculate the different variances and explain the reasons for such variances;
- identify and analyse the causes of the different types of variances;
- reconcile the variances with the actual performance.

36.1 Introduction

We saw in the previous chapter that a budget is a financial plan for a future period. The budgets are prepared from past information as to price, quantity, etc. This information is from existing standards which set the data for quantities and costs of units.

The standards are targets, or yardsticks, by which actual performance is measured. They are arrived at by extremely thorough calculations of both the quantities and prices involved. In controlling the budgets, it is important that we monitor them to see that the standards set are achieved and, if not, the reasons why there has been an over- or underachievement of the standard.

36.2 Benefits of standard costing

There are a number of ways in which a firm will benefit from setting standard costs. Of course, the benefit will only be attained if there is a continuous monitoring of the budget and the achievements.

The following is a list of what is considered to be the benefits:

- Employees may be motivated to work more efficiently to achieve the standards set.
- Managers are given responsibility for seeing that standards are met. This in itself will help to motivate the managers.
- Only those items that have departed from the norm will need to be investigated (this is management by exception). By doing this, reporting is speeded up and the costs of monitoring and control are reduced.

36.3 Setting the standards

In preparing the budget, it is important that the standards set are those that can be achieved. Reference is made to recent past periods, and to future expectations. With fluctuating prices and changing technology, both prices and quantities change fairly frequently, so standards must be reset whenever there is a marked departure from the old criteria.

Standards must be monitored regularly and the variances investigated. These variances may be classified as 'controllable' or 'uncontrollable' and it is important that managers are not held responsible for variances outside their control.

Because standard setting is of vital importance, it is useful, at this stage, to work through the three main cost groups and see how each standard is determined.

36.3.1 Materials

A careful examination of the material specifications is required in order to produce a unit or a predetermined output. This will tell us the quality of material required, as well as the quantities that will be needed. Quantities will vary, according to who is going to be handling the materials and what machinery is going to be used in the production process. If unskilled labour (or outdated machinery) is to be used, wastage will normally be higher than if skilled labour or new machines are available.

Prices, allowing for any trade discounts, must be calculated and any possible price increases must be brought into the calculation.

36.3.2 Labour

Several different operations may be involved in the production of an item, and these may involve different labour skills which will be paid at different rates.

To calculate the standard time needed to carry out a particular operation, it is necessary to know what equipment the employees will have to work with and the quality of the material they are processing. Usually the production manager provides this information so that these standard times can be determined.

36.3.3 Overheads

The prices that are expected to be paid for all overheads are usually based on recent costs. Any known future increases must be taken into account.

It is important to distinguish between fixed and variable overheads. The standards are set for one level of activity, and include a charge per product for fixed overheads. This can result in significant differences should production be completely different. The level of production chosen is one that is likely to be achieved, and must be realistic.

36.4 Variance analysis

Having set the standards and the way in which the budget is constructed, we must now consider the question of monitoring the results.

To do this we must decide on how many standards can be set and how many variances must be calculated.

The answer is as many as will be useful for guiding the business.

Some firms will need several types of material and will employ different categories of direct labour to make their products. They will, therefore, have separate variances for each category of material or labour. Some firms may vary the combination of material, or labour, and are interested in determining the 'mix' variances.

We must also take into account sales variances. We must investigate the differences between standard and actual sales. This will allow us to reconcile the profit originally predicted with what has been achieved.

36.4.1 Adverse variance

As a general rule, an adverse variance means that we have spent more than the budget allowed – actual costs are greater than budgeted costs. Another cause of an adverse variance is that we have not sold what was anticipated – actual sales are less than budgeted sales.

Let us look at a few specific instances and try to determine the reasons for the adverse variances:

- an adverse material usage variance can be brought about by the use of inferior raw material, or poor training of staff;
- an adverse price variance may be because of a sudden price increase, or the withdrawal of a supplier from the market;
- adverse labour hour variances are because of an unskilled person doing a job that requires more skill or a delay in getting materials, which delays labour; and
- an adverse rate variance may be because trade unions have increased rates after the budget was prepared, or the wrong kind of labour was used for the job.

It is not possible to list every single reason for adverse variances but by working through the many self-tests later you will quickly come to identify extra causes.

36.4.2 Favourable variance

Favourable variances show that we have spent less than planned – actual costs are lower than budgeted costs. It can also show that we have sold more than planned – actual sales are greater than budgeted sales.

Under favourable variances there can also be a price variance where we purchase material at a better price, or where we can use less skilled labour (at a lower hourly rate) than originally thought.

| 36.5 | **Types of variance** |

If we are shown a budget for a particular month then, given the actual results for that month, we are easily able to determine whether the profit is more or less than anticipated. But it is important to determine the reasons for the difference – this is where the calculation of variances becomes important.

In the above paragraphs we dealt, in very general terms, with the types of variance that can be determined. The importance of ascertaining the many variances cannot be understated, as part of the budget process is just for that purpose – control. By calculating the many variances it is possible to isolate the area or areas that need special attention. It may be a labour rate variance, or a material usage variance, or even a sales price variance. All these can lead to a difference between what was actually achieved and what was anticipated in the budget.

The following example is given to show you how a variance is determined.

In our budget we are told that a product Y requires 8 kg of material costing £2 per kg. We know that if we manufacture 10 items of product Y we should use 80 kg of material at a total cost of £160.

$$\text{Total cost} = \text{Units} \times \text{kg per unit} \times \text{cost per kg} = 10 \times 8 \times 2 = £160$$

At the end of the period we are told that the material costs were £180. We cannot say that this is an adverse £20 on the cost unless we analyse the results in more detail.

In this example let us assume that we have manufactured 10 items as per the budget. We have used 120 kg of product costing £1.50 per kg. We can see, therefore, that the price is favourable – it is 50p per kg less than budgeted. On the other hand, usage is 40 kg more – an adverse variance.

In the following paragraphs we will show the way in which variances are calculated.

36.5.1 Raw material variances

These variances consist of usage and price variances, either or both of which can be favourable or adverse.

The usage variance is the result of the difference between the quantity budgeted (the standard usage) and the actual quantity used. To determine the value of this variance, the difference between the two quantities is multiplied by the standard cost. The formula is:

$$\text{Material usage variance} = (\text{Standard quantity} - \text{Actual quantity}) \times \text{Standard price}$$

If, for example, we budget using 260 kg of material but in actual fact we use 280 kg, then the difference of 20 kg is the additional amount used. The variance is that amount multiplied by the standard cost (say £11 per kg), resulting in an adverse raw material usage variance of £220 (20 kg × £11).

In addition, we need to calculate the variance brought about by a change in price. That variance, like all others, can be favourable or adverse. Here we use the following formula:

Material price variance = (Standard price – Actual price) × Actual quantity

Using the example above, let us assume that the price we paid for the material was £9 per kg instead of the £11 that we had set out in the budget. This would result in a favourable price variance of £560 (£2 (11 – 9) × 280 kg).

In total, therefore, we would show a budget for material at £2,860 (260 kilo × £11), and an actual amount spent of £2,520 (280 kilo × £9). At first glance we may say that we have a favourable variance of £340 and, therefore, this need not be investigated further, as the amount shows how efficiently we are manufacturing.

But this is not the case. We have a favourable variance of £560 and an adverse variance of £220, which results in the overall favourable variance of £340. This is important, as it highlights the fact that there is an adverse variance resulting from a greater usage of material than budgeted. It is this adverse variance that requires immediate attention. Does it mean that the labour force are not trained properly and are therefore using more material than necessary? Or, is it that the quality of the material is inferior than that purchased previously, and therefore more material has to be used?

36.5.2 Labour variances

As was the case with material, labour can also show a number of variances. The rate at which labour is paid can vary from that budgeted to the amount actually paid. We also plan and budget for a set number of labour hours per item but this too can vary.

As a result we have a labour rate variance, which is the difference between the rate in the budget and the rate paid. The formula is:

Labour rate variance = (Standard rate – Actual rate) × Actual hours

Suppose we budget for a labour rate of £6 per hour. We also establish that we need 60 hours to complete the budgeted output. The budget would show an amount of £360 for labour (£6 × 60 hours). The actual number of hours decreased to 56 hours, but the rate was increased to £7 per hour, The actual amount paid for labour shows as £392, an increase over the budget of £32.

We must now consider if this adverse variance needs investigating, but we cannot do so without splitting the variance into two sections. The first is that dealing with the labour rate. We know it was set at £6 per hour and is now £7 per hour. This means that there is an adverse rate variance of £60 (£1 × 60 hours).

To calculate the efficiency variance we use the following formula:

Labour efficiency variance = (Standard hours – Actual hours) × Standard rate

On the other hand, the number of hours spent on production was reduced by 4 hours (60 – 56) and this would produce a favourable efficiency variance of £28 (4 hours × £7). The overall result would be an adverse variance of £32 (£60 – £28).

This immediately highlights the area for concern. It is the rate being paid for labour rather than the number of hours spent on production. Is it better to employ more expensive labour, with better training, who can produce more efficiently? Or less skilled labour as originally budgeted for, who may require additional training or who are slower in production?

36.5.3 Self-test

Using the information for Rainbow Ltd in section 35.7.5 you are required to complete the following:

Calculate, clearly stating the formula used, the:

(i) materials price variance;
(ii) labour rate variance.

Explain three possible causes of the materials price variance calculated above.

Evaluate how accurately the management accountant has set the budget for April for Rainbow Limited.

(Edexcel Accounting 6002, June 2007)

36.5.4 Overhead variances

The fixed overheads can also vary as between the budget and the actual amount spent. In this case there is only one variance that can be calculated and this is the overhead variance.

The formula used is:

$$\text{Overhead variance} = \text{Budgeted overhead expenditure} - \text{Actual overhead expenditure}$$

Assume that a budget shows overheads at £2,400 and that the actual expenditure is £2,310. We can then say that the overhead variance is a favourable one of £90. It is, of course, possible to investigate each component of the overheads to determine where changes have taken place.

36.5.5 Sales variances

As is the case with the expenditure variances, the sales are also capable of having different variances. In one case the volume of sales can be different to that budgeted, while in another instance the selling price can be higher or lower than that budgeted.

Assume that we budget for sales of 2,000 units at £8 each and that, in fact, we sell 2,300 units at a price of £7 each. Our budget sales are £16,000 and our actual sales are £16,100. We can say that we have increased sales revenue above what we budgeted and, therefore, not look any further, or we can investigate the different variances.

In the first instance we have a sales volume variance. For this we use the following formula:

$$\text{Sales volume variance} = (\text{Budgeted sales volume} - \text{Actual sales volume}) \times \text{Selling price}$$

The volume difference is 300 units resulting in a favourable volume variance of £2,400.

We next investigate the price at which we sell the product. Here we use the following formula:

$$\text{Sales price variance} = (\text{Budgeted selling price} - \text{Actual selling price}) \times \text{Actual sales volume}$$

Using the example above we find that there is a difference of £1 on every unit sold. This equates to an adverse sales price variance of £2,300. It could be that this area of the budgeted selling price needs further investigation and it would have been missed if we had not extracted the different variances of sales.

36.5.6 Self-test

Ralph & Co. manufacture computer stands. The company prepares annual budgets and controls the results on a monthly basis. The following is the monthly budget for December 2010 based on the production and sale of 1,600 units.

Sales	1,600 units		32,000
Direct materials:	Plastic £25 per kg	6,000	
	Colourants £10 per litre	8,000	
Direct labour	Skilled £2.5 per hour	2,000	
	Unskilled £2 per hour	5,000	
Fixed overheads		6,000	27,000
Budgeted profit			5,000

You are given the following information regarding the events that took place in December 2010.

(i) During the month a total of 1,900 units were produced and sold for £36,500.
(ii) Material usage was:
   (a) 155 kg plastic costing a total of £7,595 was used for production.
   (b) 460 litres of colourants costing £9,200 was used during the month.
(iii) Skilled labour worked for 845 hours and cost a total of £2,197 while the unskilled labour worked 2,375 hours at a cost of £5,225.
(iv) The total cost of the fixed overheads amounted to £5,980.

You are required to prepare the actual profit and loss account and compare the achievement of the month against the budget. Indicate all variances.

36.5.7 Self-test

Mervyn & Co. has produced an annual budget for the manufacture of product Z. This budget has now been broken down into months so that the production team can ensure targets are met.

The following is the budget for June 2010:

Number of units	2,200 units
Direct material	£88,000
Direct labour	£44,000
Fixed overheads	£40,000
Profit	£48,000
Sales	£220,000
Material used	88,000 kg
Labour	5,500 hours

During June, Mervyn & Co. achieved an increased output of 2,300 units all of which were sold. The following are the results for the month.

Number of units	2,300 units
Direct material	£92,600
Direct labour	£46,400
Fixed overheads	£38,600
Profit	£49,400
Sales	£227,000
Material used	92,600 kg
Labour	5,920 hours

As a result of the increased production, the monthly profit increased by £1,400. Nevertheless, the firm still needs to find out where the areas are for improvement and where the production was favourable.

Accordingly you are required to prepare a revised budget for the increased output level (2,300 units) and then calculate all the variances. Reconcile these variances with the budget.

36.5.8 Self-test

Francis & Co. prepared a monthly budget for its production and found that there was a 10 per cent reduction in the amount produced.

A flexed budget was prepared and, based on that, the actual profit achieved was £1,800 greater than the flexed budget amount of profit.

Francis & Co. nevertheless decided to investigate all the variances to determine the reasons for the profit increase and to ascertain if there were areas that required further control.

	Budget	Flexed budget	Actual
Number of units	2,000 units	1,800 units	1,800 units
Direct material	£80,000	£72,000	£73,800
Direct labour	£40,000	£36,000	£35,000
Fixed overheads	£40,000	£40,000	£41,400
Profit	£40,000	£32,000	£33,800
Sales	£200,000	£180,000	£184,000
Material used	80,000 metres	72,000 metres	74,000 metres
Labour	5,000 hours	4,500 hours	4,300 hours

You are required to calculate the following variances:

(i)   Material usage and price variances.
(ii) Labour rate and efficiency variances.
(iii) Fixed overhead variance.
(iv) Sales price variance.

To check your answer, reconcile the variances calculated to the original budgeted profit.

36.5.9 Self-test

Marcel Ltd manufactures a product which has the following standard costs:

Selling price		262
Direct materials (2 kg)	104	
Direct labour (3 hours)	61	
Fixed overheads	9	174
Standard profit		88

In July the company budgets production of 1,400 units. The actual production is 1,700 units and the total sales for the month amounts to £579,020. The company sells its entire production and therefore incurs no costs in holding stock.
   The actual costs for July were as follows:

Direct materials	Usage is 2.16 kg per unit	£264,384
Direct labour	Total hours were 5,440	£136,000
Fixed overheads		£18,000

You are required to calculate the following variances and reconcile them with the difference between the actual and budgeted results.

(i)   Material usage and price variances.
(ii) Labour rate and efficiency variances.
(iii) Fixed overhead variance.
(iv) Sales price and volume variances.

36.5.10 Self-test

Vera Ltd manufactures table cloths. The company introduced a system of costing in January 2008 using the information of the previous year.

The following is the budget for 2008:

(i)   Vera Ltd has a factory staff of 15 people. They all work 8 hours a day and a 5-day week.
(ii) Wages are paid at the rate of £6.40 per hour. All overtime is paid at the rate of basic wage plus £3.60 per hour.
(iii) All workers are required to produce one table cloth every 15 minutes. They are allowed to work overtime in order to achieve the target output for any period.
(iv) For purposes of control the company divides its costing periods into 4-week portions.
(v)   As a result of material supplies being delayed in week 2 of the first 4-week period, workers were required to work an extra 2 hours per day in weeks 2 to 4 in order to achieve the target.

You are required to calculate the following information for the first 4-week period:

(a) standard hours worked;
(b) actual hours worked;
(c) labour efficiency variance;
(d) total standard wages;
(e) total actual wages;
(f) total wages variance;
(g) actual wage rate;
(h) wage rate variance.

Chapter 37

Revision

Objectives After you have worked carefully through the self tests in this chapter, you should be able to:

- interpret financial statements;
- prepare and interpret budgets;
- apply marginal costing for decision making;
- calculate and interpret the reasons for variances.

37.1 Introduction

Although you have only studied a few chapters since the last set of revision questions, it is important that you revise what you have learnt in those chapters before continuing on to the final stages of this book.

The interpretation of accounts, as well as the costing aspects of accounting, are both vital for a business to function smoothly and effectively.

Budgets need to be prepared and constantly revised in the light of ever changing circumstances. These changing circumstances can be detected by a well-informed interpretation of the financial statements.

So here are the revision questions for you. Once again, if you feel that you have difficulty in answering any question, go back to the relevant chapter and study it again.

Not all the revision in this chapter is focused on calculations. In many ways there is also the need for an understanding of words, so that you are able to identify accurately and speedily with the problems in an examination.

In this next section you are required to test this knowledge by answering the multiple-choice questions set out therein. Make sure that you know the answer – do not try to guess it!

In the next four self-tests, you are required to circle the correct answer. If you are unsure, go back to the relevant chapter and read through the section to which the question relates. In that way you will achieve maximum benefit.

37.1.1 Self-test

1. Fixed costs:
   (a) Tend to remain fixed irrespective of the level of activity.
   (b) Tend to remain fixed over the short and medium term.
   (c) Both of the above.

2. Martin has a budgeted profit of £350,000. The actual results show an adverse sales variance of £70,000. This is in spite of a favourable production variance of £90,000. What profit has been actually achieved?
   (a) £440,000
   (b) £420,000
   (c) £370,000
   (d) £280,000

3. What system of costing values output only in terms of the variable costs of production?
   (a) Marginal costing
   (b) Activity-based costing
   (c) Full (absorption) costing
   (d) Costing by management discretion

4. When a company faces a shortage of skilled labour, it needs to decide which products it should continue to manufacture. To do this it ranks the products. What criteria does it use?
   (a) the contribution earned per unit;
   (b) the profit margin earned per unit;
   (c) the gross profit margin earned per skilled labour hour;
   (d) the contribution earned per skilled labour hour.

37.1.2 Self-test

Musical Ltd produces gift boxes of three CDs with a birthday greeting card. These boxes sell at £20 per box. This product is in high demand and the company sales during 2010 totalled £1,200,000.

In 2010 the costs were as follows:

CDs and royalties cost (each)	9.00
Birthday card	0.30
Packaging (per box)	1.25
Direct labour (per box)	0.80
Variable overheads (per box)	0.65
Fixed overheads	£96,000

Using the above information, answer the following questions:

1. Musical Ltd's contribution per unit is:
   (a) £8.00
   (b) £12.00
   (c) £14.00
   (d) £20.00

2. Musical Ltd's break-even point (in boxes) is:
   (a) 4,800
   (b) 8,000
   (c) 12,000
   (d) 32,000

3. Musical Ltd's break-even point (in sales revenue) is:
   (a) £48,000
   (b) £160,000
   (c) £240,000
   (d) £640,000

4. How many boxes need to be sold to achieve a target profit of £1,000,000?
   (a) 98,000
   (b) 137,000
   (c) 120,000
   (d) 180,000

5. How many boxes need to be sold to achieve a target profit of £3,200,000?
   (a) 1,600,000
   (b) 209,800
   (c) 160,000
   (d) 412,000

37.1.3 Self-test

Esef Ltd wishes to produce three products. The following costs relate to these three products:

Product	1	2	3
Selling price (£)	15	27	39
Raw materials (£)	5	3	12
Labour (£)	6	12	18
Production	180	90	80

The labour rate is £6 per hour and the maximum hours available is 450 hours. The fixed costs of the company are £56,000.

1. Which one of the following statements is correct?
   (a) Labour hours is the limiting factor.
   (b) Raw materials is the limiting factor.
   (c) Both labour hours and raw materials are limiting factors.
   (d) There is no limiting factor.

2. What is the contribution per unit for Products 1, 2 and 3?
   (a) £4, £12 and £9
   (b) £10, £24 and £27
   (c) £9, £15 and £21
   (d) £15, £27 and £39

3. What is the contribution per scarce factor for each of Products 1, 2 and 3?
   (a) £4, £6 and £3
   (b) £4, £12 and £9
   (c) £10, £24 and £27
   (d) £9, £15 and £21

4. How should Esef Ltd rank the three products so that the most profitable product is produced first?

	Rank 1	Rank 2	Rank 3
(a)	Product 2	Product 1	Product 3
(b)	Product 1	Product 2	Product 3
(c)	Product 2	Product 3	Product 1
(d)	Product 3	Product 2	Product 1
(e)	Product 3	Product 1	Product 2

5. How many units of each product should be produced in order to maximise profit?

Product	1	2	3
(a)	30	90	80
(b)	180	45	60
(c)	180	90	30
(d)	180	90	60

37.1.4 Self-test

Master Ltd decides to reduce its gearing. Which of the following methods can be used?

	Increases gearing	Reduces gearing
Issuing new debentures		
Issuing new ordinary shares		
Issuing new preference shares		
Redeeming ordinary shares		
Redeeming debentures		

37.1.5 Self-test

Mushtaq and Hasan have decided to start their own business, Chatanooga Timber Limited. They plan to buy timber and sell to builders and other customers.

Mushtaq and Hasan will each invest £10,000 as share capital. There is £20,000 additional capital in the form of a bank loan.

At the start of month 1, Mushtaq and Hasan will pay:

- £12,500 for premises.
- £13,000 for fixtures and fittings with an expected life of 10 years.
- £22,000 for stock.

During the next three months purchases of stock are expected to be:

Month 2   £7,000
Month 3   £8,400
Month 4   £10,080

During this period, credit is not available from suppliers.

Sales are expected to be £14,000 for the first month, increasing by 20 per cent every month as the business builds up customers. From month 1, Chatanooga Timber Limited will offer credit terms to customers, to be paid in the month following the sale. Each month 25 per cent of sales are expected to be on credit.

General expenses are expected to be £4,000 per month, payable during the month incurred.

Mushtaq and Hasan plan to make directors' drawings of £400 each a week. Assume 4 weeks in every month.

Required:

(a) Prepare a cash budget for the first four months of trading.
(b) Prepare a debtors' budget to show the value of debtors at the end of each month.

(Edexcel Accounting 6002, January 2008)

37.1.6 Self-test

Milly & Co. are preparing their sales budget for the year ending 31 December 2011. The following information is available for the year ended 31 December 2010.

Units sold	80,000
Selling price	£50 per unit
Variable costs	£27 per unit
Fixed costs	£430,000

The company wishes to increase its profitability and is considering one of the following plans:

■ Plan 1 is to reduce the selling price by 10 per cent. In this case they anticipate a 30 per cent increase in demand.
■ Plan 2 is to increase the selling price by 12 per cent. Although this will result in a loss in sales, the company forecasts higher revenue.
■ Plan 3 is where the selling price remains fixed at £50. Sales would be generated by commission agents, thereby eliminating the fixed staff costs of £85,000. The commission agents would be paid 10 per cent on all sales.
  (a) You are required to calculate the break-even point in units, and the profit earned in the year ended 31 December 2010.
  (b) What volume of sales is required under the various plans if Milly & Co. wishes to maintain its profit level in 2011?
  (c) Assuming plan 3 was adopted, what would be the break-even point?
  (d) Which plan should be adopted if the company wishes to maintain the current profit level?

37.1.7 Self-test

Seehow Ltd would like to repay a loan in advance and so save interest. The total amount of the loan is £25,000. As interest is calculated on 31 December 2010 it would, if possible, elect that date for the repayment.

The accountant prepares an extract of sales and expenses for the 3 months ending 31 December 2010.

	October	November	December
Sales	75,000	42,000	46,000
Purchases	55,000	30,000	35,000
Wages	7,600	4,800	5,200
Expenses	5,200	5,000	4,800

Forty per cent of the above monthly sales are cash sales, while the remainder are paid in the following month. The purchases are paid in the following month, except for 25 per cent of them which are paid for in cash. Both the wages and expenses are paid for at the end of each week.

The company has a short-term investment on which it receives a monthly interest payment of £600. At 1 November 2010 the accountant calculates that the cash on hand is £3,200.

You are required to prepare a cash budget for the two months ending 31 December 2010. By using this budget indicate whether Seehow Ltd will be in a position to pay back all (or part) of the loan.

37.1.8 Self-test

Kayla Ltd has prepared a budget for the year to 31 December 2008. The company manufactures three products and separate budgets are prepared for each product.

Product	1	2	3
Sales in units	10,000	30,000	50,000
Selling price per unit	£25	£20	£15
Variable material costs	£9	£7	£6
Other variable costs	£3	£2	£1
Variable labour costs	£40,000	£120,000	£200,000

Other budgeted fixed costs are £400,000.
Total assets employed are £1,000,000.

You are required to:

(a) Calculate the unit contribution for each product.
(b) Calculate the total contribution.
(c) Calculate the total profit for the year.
(d) Calculate the return on assets for the year.

37.1.9 Self-test

Ices Ltd manufactures an ice cream party cake. Its monthly production for July 2010 is 1,200 units. During the month it sells 1,000 units, with the remainder being kept in the freezers for August 2010.

The production costs are:

Direct labour	£7 per cake
Direct material	£4 per cake
Variable overheads	£3,000 plus 50p per cake
Selling price	£21 per cake

The factory has annual fixed costs of £36,000.

You are required to prepare the profit and loss account for July 2010. In doing this, you are required to show management what the profit would be using marginal costing and absorption costing.

During October–December 2010 a decline in orders is usual. At that time it is anticipated that the selling price will reduce to £16 per cake. Ices Ltd intends to maintain normal production of 1,200 units per month and needs to know if the price of £16 could be accepted.

You are required to assist management in making a decision based on an anticipated decline in orders.

37.1.10 Self-test

Kings Ltd manufactures a range of four products for which it has had a steady demand during 2010. The company has now experienced a month (March 2011) when it was unable to meet the increased demand and feels that it is possible that this higher demand level will continue throughout the year and beyond.

An initial report was presented to management which showed that unless additional machinery was purchased, the demand could not be satisfied.

Kings Ltd has decided that it does not want to commit to additional machinery at this stage because of the high capital cost. It therefore requires you to advise the company of the optimum production that can be achieved in order to maximise profits.

The following data relates to the four products:

Product	1	2	3	4
Selling price per unit	60	40	70	80
Variable costs per unit	33	20	40	42
Machine hours per unit	3	5	6	7
Maximum sales in units	1,800	1,900	1,400	1,100

The company has at present three machines which all make the four allied products. The total capacity of these machines is 21,900 hours.

The directors of Kings Ltd also require you to forecast monthly profit using the optimum production levels where fixed costs for the month total £62,000.

37.1.11 Self-test

Many decisions for internal expenditure also make use of costing methods. In this example a company provides a canteen for teas and snacks for its employees.

Management have to make a decision based on the following:

The company can contract with an outside firm by paying them an annual fee of £18,000 or it can use its own staff which will cost £11,000 plus the cost of various food purchases of £700.

In addition, the company would have to hire certain equipment at a cost of £120 per month. This would apply irrespective of whether the company uses its own staff or a contractor.

You are required to determine which option is best for the company.

37.1.12 Self-test

A clothing manufacturer of ladies' skirts requires pleating as one of the processes. At present the manufacturer does not have the required equipment or staff to complete this process and investigates the alternative of buying in this process.

The company is told that the contract for an outside pleater would be £35,500 p.a. while to employ its own staff the cost would be £16,400 p.a. In addition, the company would have to hire pleating machines at £3,700 p.m. This latter charge would apply even if outside pleaters were contracted. One additional charge for the company if it used its own staff would be the purchase of trimmings required in the process. This would amount to £2,600 p.a.

You are required to advise the company of the best choice.

37.1.13 Self-test

A manufacturing company requests you to suggest whether they establish their own machine repair shop or contract with outside companies.

They are told that an outside firm will contract with them for £74,000 p.a.

If they establish their own department they will have to hire staff at £52,500 p.a., purchase tools for the department which will cost £13,200 and also hire lathes for the department at £12,000 p.a.

You are asked to make a recommendation to the directors.

37.1.14 Self-test

Company X manufactures ladies' shoes in three styles. The following table shows the costs for each style, the anticipated sales per style and the budgeted profit. The company has no problem selling all the products manufactured but it does have a limit on the machine hour capacity of its factory.

The object of the manufacturer is to make the best possible profit, taking into account any capacity restraints. In this case it is not possible to manufacture all the styles that could be sold because of a scarce resource (the machine hours). Therefore, Company X must manufacture the styles that produce the highest contribution per unit of the scarce resource.

The following is the budget for 31 December 2009:

	A	B	C	TOTAL
Machine hours	98	90	82	270

	A	B	C	TOTAL
Direct material costs	309,000	104,400	362,500	775,900
Direct labour	129,000	88,200	183,000	400,200
Variable overheads	46,900	42,000	96,120	185,020
Direct costs	484,900	234,600	641,620	1,361,120
Fixed overheads	40,000	34,000	42,000	116,000
Total costs	524,900	268,600	683,620	1,477,120
Profit	240,100	325,400	218,780	784,280
Sales	765,000	594,000	902,400	2,261,400

The directors ask you to investigate the problem and recommend to them which styles should be manufactured assuming the machine hours available amount to 250 per annum.

37.1.15 Self-test

A hat manufacturing company produces 3 different styles of hat. Each requires a proportion of skilled labour to attend to the finishing process. The skilled labour is in short supply and therefore the company will have to reduce the amount of hats manufactured to the limit of skilled labour hours available. At present style A requires 25 hours of skilled labour; style B 31 hours and style C 47 hours. Total available hours are 80 for the production of all three styles.

Given the following information you are required to make your recommendation to the board of directors.

	A	B	C	TOTAL
Direct material costs	103,000	87,000	145,000	335,000
Direct labour	43,000	49,000	61,000	153,000
Variable overheads	67,000	21,000	80,100	168,100
Direct costs	213,000	157,000	286,100	656,100
Fixed overheads	20,000	14,000	22,000	56,000
Total costs	233,000	171,000	308,100	712,100
Profit	32,000	27,000	67,900	126,900
Sales	265,000	198,000	376,000	839,000

37.1.16 Self-test

Eezysnooze Limited is to go into business producing beds. The following information is available.

- Materials for production will be delivered from Week 1 in Month 1. Each week, £2,400 of materials will be delivered. These materials are the quantity required to produce 60 beds.

- Production will start in Week 2 in Month 1. In each week, 60 beds will be produced, which is the maximum production capacity of the factory.
- Sales are budgeted to be 55 beds a week, starting from Week 3 in Month 1. Any beds produced but not sold will be placed into stock in the warehouse.
- Materials are budgeted to be paid for 3 weeks after delivery, e.g. materials delivered in Week 1 will be paid for in Week 4.
- Customers are budgeted to pay 4 weeks after a sale, e.g. a bed sold in Week 3 Month 1 will be paid for in Week 3 Month 2.
- The budgeted selling price of beds is £300 per bed.
- Assume 4 weeks in each month.

Required:

(a) Prepare, for the first three months of trading for Eezysnooze Limited (for each of the three months, the budgets should show total figures for each month, *not* weekly figures):
  (i)   A purchases' budget in pounds (£s).
  (ii) A purchases' budget in units (beds).
  (iii) A production budget in units (beds).
  (iv) A sales budget in units (beds).
  (v)   A stock budget in units (beds). The budget should show the number of units going into stock each month and the total number of units in stock at the end of each month.
  (vi) A creditors' budget in pounds (£s) showing the creditors' figure at the end of each month.
  (vii) A debtors' budget in pounds (£s) showing the debtors' figure at the end of each month.
  Production is determined by the maximum production capacity of the factory, *not* by the number of beds ordered by customers.
(b) Evaluate the decision to produce a quantity determined by the maximum capacity of the factory instead of producing a quantity determined by customers' orders.

(Edexcel Accounting 6002, June 2009)

37.1.17 Self-test

DEF Ltd manufactures and sells a single product. The following budget details are available:

	£ per unit	£ per unit
Selling price		150
Less:		
Materials	60	
Labour	30	90
Contribution		60

Additional information:

(i) Budgeted sales units are as follows:

	January	February	March	April
Sales units	5,000	2,000	2,500	6,000

(ii) Opening stock of finished goods at the start of January will be 1,000 units. Closing stock of finished goods at the end of each month is budgeted at 10 per cent of the sales volume for that month.

(iii) DEF Ltd operates a just-in-time ordering system. The stock of raw materials is therefore always zero.

(iv) Raw material purchases are paid for in the month of purchase and labour costs are paid for in the month of production.

(v) All goods are sold on credit. Sales revenue is received 60 per cent in the month of sale and 35 per cent during the following month. The remaining 5 per cent is treated as being irrecoverable.

(vi) Fixed overheads are £80,000 per month. This figure includes depreciation of £20,000.

(vii) Fixed overheads are paid for in the month in which they are incurred.

(viii) Machinery costing £200,000 is due to be installed in February and paid for in March.

(ix) Taxation of £150,000 and proposed dividends of £75,000 are due for payment in April.

(x) At the beginning of January, trade debtors will total £130,000 and the usual collectible amount will be received during January.

(xi) Overdraft interest of 1 per cent per month will be paid in respect of the closing bank balance at the previous month end.

(xii) The opening bank balance of DEF Ltd in January will be £200,000 overdrawn.

Required:

(a) Prepare a production budget, in units, for each of the four months, January to April.

(b) Prepare, in columnar form, a cash budget for each month. The cash balance at the end of each month must be clearly shown.

(c) Comment on the cash budget prepared in (b) and the implications for the company.

(ABE Managerial Accounting Diploma, December 2009)

37.1.18 Self-test

Solar Chocolates plc is a major producer selling three chocolate bar products – Jupiter, Neptune and Saturn.

Normal monthly sales for these bars are:

Jupiter 3 million   Neptune 2 million   Saturn 4 million

The following information relates to sales in exceptional months:

(i)   In November, sales for Jupiter and Neptune will double.
(ii) In November, sales for Saturn will increase by 50 per cent.
(iii) In December, sales for Jupiter and Neptune will be four times greater than a normal month.
(iv) In December, sales for Saturn will increase by another 50 per cent on the November figure.

Required:

(a) Construct a sales budget for each of the 6 months July to December. Within the total sales budget, show the forecast sales for the Jupiter, Neptune and Saturn bars.

Keeping all stocks to a minimum is a policy of Solar Chocolates plc. Production is normally carried out one month before sales take place in the shops. This is not always possible in relation to the exceptional months because the monthly capacity for production is:

Jupiter 6 million   Neptune 5 million   Saturn 6 million

Production facilities for one bar cannot be used to produce another bar. In order to meet exceptional sales in November and December, production schedules may have to be adjusted, but a minimum of one month's lead time must apply.

In January, sales for all three bars will return to normal.

(b) Construct a production budget for each of the 6 months July to December. Within the total production budget, show the forecast production for the Jupiter, Neptune and Saturn bars.

An essential ingredient in all three bars is 'chocolate crumb'. Each of the three bars contains 2 grams of chocolate crumb. In order to keep stocks to a minimum, the chocolate crumb required is delivered in the same month as production.

(c) Construct a total stock budget for each of the 6 months July to December for chocolate crumb.
(d) Evaluate the policy of Solar Chocolates plc of keeping stock to a minimum.

(Edexcel Accounting 6002, June 2007)

37.1.19 Self-test

Consider the following figures for Gleaston plc:

Profit and loss account for the year ended 30 September 2009

	£000
Sales	28,980
Less: cost of sales	(15,295)
Gross profit	13,685
Less: expenses	(3,785)
Net profit	9,900

Balance sheet at 30 September 2009

	£000	£000
Fixed assets		49,910
Current assets:		
– stock	13,860	
– debtors	8,030	
– bank	1,080	
	22,970	
Current liabilities:		
– creditors	(4,650)	
– accruals	(6,960)	
Net current assets		11,360
		61,270
Financed by:		
Ordinary share capital		46,400
Profit and loss		14,870
		61,270

Notes:

1. All purchases and sales are on credit.
2. Credit purchases for the year were £12,608,000.

Required:

Calculate the following ratios for Gleaston plc:

(i)   Gross profit
(ii) Net profit
(iii) Current ratio
(iv) Acid test (liquidity)
(v) Debtors' collection period (in days)
(vi) Creditors' payment period (in days)

(ABE Introduction to Accounting, December 2009)

37.1.20 Self-test

Sharma has obtained the figures of a rival restaurant owned by Mustapha. The following information is available.

	Mustapha	Sharma
Rate of stock turnover	52 times	40 times
Net profit to sales percentage	10%	10%
Gross margin	30%	40%
Acid test ratio	1.1:1	0.5:1

It is known that the ideal liquid capital ratio for these businesses is 1:1.

(a) Give the formula for each of the following:
   (i)   acid test ratio;
   (ii) gross margin;
   (iii) rate of stock turnover.

(b) State one strategy that Sharma could use to improve the profitability of her business.

(c) State one strategy that Sharma could use to improve the liquidity of her business.

(Edexcel Accounting 7011, May 2006)

37.1.21 Self-test

Andreas Sugaro is considering investing £100,000 in the shares of either Thessaloniki plc (current market price 64p per share) or Athena plc (current market price 98p per share).

Information on each company, relating to the year ended 30 April 2006, is given below.

Thessaloniki plc

Figures from the profit and loss account	£000
Profit after taxation	1,136
Preference dividend	360
Interim dividend	300
Final proposed dividend	500
Retained profit (loss)	(24)

Balance sheet extracts at 30 April 2006	Athena plc	Thessaloniki plc
	£000	£000
Ordinary shares of 50p each	6,000	8,000
12% preference shares of £1 each	–	3,000
Share premium account	900	1,200
Reserves	1,840	860
	8,740	13,060
8% debentures	–	6,000
	8,740	19,060

	Athena plc	Thessaloniki plc
Earnings per share	6.37p	
Price earnings ratio	15.4	
Dividend yield	4.6%	
Gearing	Not geared	
Dividend cover	1.41	0.97
Dividend per share	4.5p	5p

Required:

(a) For Thessaloniki plc, calculate (stating the formula in each case) the following investment ratios:

   (i)   earnings per share;

   (ii) price earnings ratio;

   (iii) dividend yield;

   (iv) gearing.

(b) Commenting on the price earnings ratio, dividend policies and gearing, advise Andreas in which company he should make his investment.

(Edexcel Accounting 6002, May 2006)

Chapter 38

Investment appraisal

Objectives   After you have studied this chapter, you should be able to:

- explain the various methods used for investment decisions;
- understand the differences between the various cash flow methods;
- calculate and formulate answers for management;
- understand the drawbacks of some of the appraisal methods.

38.1 Introduction

In this chapter we consider whether it is worth financing the capital cost of a new project. The alternative is to remain as we are, showing profits that may be smaller than we could achieve with an additional investment.

38.2 Financial management

The return on capital is affected by the way in which a company raises finance. In today's climate it can be seen that although gearing up a company may enhance the return, it does carry risks.

For this reason it is important that we examine the various techniques of investment appraisal. It is these techniques that help directors, owners and managers decide on the methods of raising finance or even if expansion should be undertaken. Whatever form of capital is introduced, there is a cost. To meet this cost the company needs to generate income equal to or greater than that cost. Many companies set a minimum return required before they consider raising fresh capital.

We will see that there are two areas from which fresh capital can be raised. A company can issue new shares, or it can decide to take an outside loan, be it a secured debenture or a bank overdraft. Most companies do not rely on share capital alone. They usually combine the raising of fresh capital with external loans. The link between the two determines the gearing of the company.

The following shows the different gearing levels of a company based on its method of financing the business.

	High gearing	Low gearing
Equity capital	100,000	180,000
Debentures	60,000	10,000
Preference shares	40,000	10,000
Total capital	200,000	200,000

In the case of the first company, non-equity capital (the debentures and preference shares) amounts to 50 per cent of the total capital, while in the second case it is only 10 per cent of the total capital.

Some companies operate at a high gearing of 50 per cent while others may not even use borrowed capital. Although the latter reduces risk considerably it does not mean that the company in question operates in a more efficient way.

38.2.1 Worked examples

We illustrate the paragraph above with the following worked example.

	High gearing	No gearing
Ordinary shares	100,000	180,000
Revenue reserves	60,000	60,000
8% debentures	80,000	–
	240,000	240,000
Scenario 1		
Profit before interest and taxation	300,000	300,000
Debenture interest	6,400	–
	293,600	300,000
Taxation – at 20%	58,720	60,000
Profit after tax	234,880	240,000
Return on shareholders' funds	146.8%	100%
Scenario 2		
Profit before interest and taxation	600,000	600,000
Debenture interest	6,400	–
	593,600	600,000
Taxation – at 20%	118,720	120,000
Profit after tax	474,880	480,000
Return on shareholders' funds	296.8%	200%

Where there is no gearing then the return increases in proportion to the profit increase. When the profit doubled, the return increased by the same amount. Where there is gearing then the increase in profit of 100 per cent results in a more than a twofold increase in the return to shareholders.

38.3 Initial assessment

Businesses need to grow to satisfy increasing demand for their products. This means that they need new machinery and other fixed assets. One of the most important aspects of the initial assessment is to decide what, and when, to buy.

For any new idea, we need to:

- fund the original capital costs;
- ensure a positive contribution towards any additional fixed costs;
- be certain that any interest due on borrowed money can be met; and
- determine the profit remaining.

Although there are many methods that can be used in assessing a new investment, managers are not in agreement as to which method is best. This is mainly because of the many unknown factors that can arise when we try to look several years ahead.

Some managers prefer to use a simple method, or a combination of methods, to predict results, while others are drawn to more complicated, but more logical, procedures.

The most important distinction between the various methods is whether or not they take account of the fact that money now is worth more than money in the future.

Discounted methods take this fact into account, whereas non-discounted methods do not. Although non-discounted cash flow methods are easier to calculate manually, even the most complicated discounted cash flow calculations can be performed relatively easily on a computer spreadsheet.

Whatever method is used, we must start with a calculation of the expected cash flow of the project. (A common mistake is the inclusion of depreciation. This must be excluded from costs when we prepare the cash flow.)

To prepare the cash flow we need to predict revenues and relevant costs. In so doing we must make sure that we identify when revenue will be received and costs paid, ignoring the accruals concept.

The only exception to this rule is when we use the accounting rate of return method. This method, as we will see later in the chapter, is based on net profit divided by the investment.

38.3.1 Investment appraisal

The chapter heading describes the way decisions on when and how to spend money on capital projects are arrived at. More importantly, it even asks if the project should be undertaken. The benefits are compared with the costs. If the return is not reasonable then investors will stay away from that company in the future.

Whatever appraisal method is used, the yearly cash flows have to be estimated for the project being considered. There is usually an initial cash outflow which could be for the purchase of a capital asset such as a new machine or vehicle. Further cash outflows may occur such as extra parts for the new machine or modification to the vehicle.

Cash flows into the business from sales while the outflows consist of the expenses incurred in generating those sales. The income is not reduced by depreciation as we charge the total cost as a cash outflow and depreciation is not a cash item.

There are two methods that may be considered crude and therefore rather weak. Nevertheless they are easy to calculate and understand.

38.4 Methods of calculation

There are two main groups of method. They are:

- non-discounted methods; and
- discounted methods.

38.4.1 Non-discounted methods

Payback method

This is a simple calculation and easy to understand. As such it is highly favoured by managers. In this method the positive cash flows are deducted from the initial cost of the project. We are then able to calculate, from the net cash inflow, how long it takes to pay back the full cost of the project.

It does not measure total profitability over the life of the investment but merely tells how long it will take to recover the initial investment.

By using this method, which emphasises liquidity, calculations are both quick and easy.

The best way to explain this method is by way of an example.

We are told that the initial cost of two possible projects are £730,000 and £985,000 respectively. The net cash flows for these projects are as follows.

	Project I	Project II
Year 1	200,000	225,000
Year 2	210,000	225,000
Year 3	220,000	290,000
Year 4	240,000	360,000

We must now establish the payback period for each project.

	Project I	Project II
Initial cost	(730,000)	(985,000)
Cash-flow year 1	200,000	225,000
	(530,000)	(760,000)
Cash-flow year 2	210,000	225,000
	(320,000)	(535,000)
Cash-flow year 3	220,000	290,000
	(100,000)	(245,000)
Cash-flow year 4	240,000	360,000
	140,000	115,000
Payback time	3 years 5 months	3 years 8.2 months

Note: In year 4 our cash flow for project I is £240,000, or £20,000 per month. This means that after 5 months (5 × £20,000) we receive the additional amount (£100,000) required. Project II is calculated in the same way (£30,000 × 8.2 = £245,000).

Payback occurs quicker in Project I. If payback time is important then Project I must be selected.

There are many questions not covered by the payback method, including:

■ do the cash flows continue after the payback period? and
■ are the cash flows static or do they increase year on year?

These questions must always be considered before an investment can take place.

In the above example the cash flows of Project I increase each year. The cash flows of Project II, on the other hand, are static for the first two years and then increase.

Where projects have identical payback periods, the one giving the greatest cash flows in the early years would be preferred. This returns the cash invested sooner and allows us to reinvest the cash into new projects at an earlier date.

This example illustrates that while the payback method is a useful and simple tool for the initial consideration of a project's acceptability, managers must also examine the continuation of cash flows after payback, and the pattern of these cash flows.

Irrespective of this, however, this method would still not address the time value of money.

Accounting rate of return (ARR) method

The ARR method takes the average profit that the investment will generate and expresses it as a percentage of the average investment in the project. For a positive decision to invest, a firm must achieve a pre-determined minimum ARR.

This method gives us the profitability of the investment by dividing the average annual profit by the average investment. To find these figures we take the total profits earned over the life of the investment and divide it by the life expectancy of the project. The problem with this method is that timing differences are ignored as it assumes that the return stays constant throughout the period of the project.

For example, we have the following profit figures:

Year 1	Year 2	Year 3
1,000	1,500	5,000

The total profit for the 3 years = £7,500 and therefore the average profit over the 3 years = £2,500. If the cost of the investment is £15,000 over 3 years then the average cost = £5,000.

$$\text{The ARR} = \frac{\text{Average annual profit}}{\text{Average investment}} \times 100\% = \frac{2,500}{5,000} = 50\%$$

Although this method is very similar to the ROCE ratio (see Chapter 32), it only relates to a single investment and, in addition, only looks at the performance before the event and not at the end.

Note: In investment appraisal it is cash flows that are important and not profits. It is cash that acquires resources and pays dividends or interest. The profit of any firm is only a measure of success – not an indication of liquidity.

We must not overlook the fact that ARR does not take into account the fact that the value of money changes over time. To receive £100 in 2 years' time has less value than receiving £100 today.

38.4.2 Worked example

Using the figures given for Projects I and II in section 38.4.1 above, we now use the accounting rate of return method. For this method we need to know the annual profit figures rather than the cash flow figures.

Let us assume that there are no relevant accruals or prepayments; that there is no estimated scrap value for either project; and that depreciation is calculated using the straight line method for both projects.

We also need to know what percentage rate of return would be considered acceptable by the firm.

We must calculate the annual depreciation charge. For Project I it is £182,500 (730,000 ÷ 4), and for Project II £246,250 (985,000 ÷ 4). By deducting the depreciation from the cash flows calculated in section 38.4.1 we arrive at the following annual profits:

	Project I	*Project II*
Year 1	17,500	−21,250
Year 2	27,500	−21,250
Year 3	37,500	43,750
Year 4	57,500	113,750
Total profit	140,000	135,000

To find the average profit, we divide the total profits by 4. We also need to calculate the average sum invested. To do this we take the investment at the start and the investment at the end (0) and divide by 2.

	Project I	*Project II*
Average profit	35,000	33,750
Average investment	730,000 ÷ 2	985,000 ÷ 2
	= £365,000	= £492,500
ARR	9.58%	6.85%

Project I has a higher average rate of return. This should be compared with the company's required return on investment or its cost of capital. If more than one project could be carried out then the ARR of Project II could also be considered.

This does not mean that this method is without fault. Here too, no attention is paid to the time value of money. We also see that the pattern of the cash flows is not important, as an average is being calculated.

One important thing to note is that profit, rather than cash flow, is used in these calculations. We should be aware that this could be a disadvantage for firms interested in their liquidity positions.

38.4.3 Self-test

Why Ltd contemplates the purchase of a new machine to produce additional units of its product. It has a choice of three different machines, each of which have similar technical specifications, but have different costs.

The company prepares a forecast of its cash flows covering each of the three machines.

	Machine A	Machine B	Machine C
Purchase price	150,000	180,000	165,000
Net cash flows			
Year 1	45,000	36,000	30,000
Year 2	45,000	42,000	39,000
Year 3	45,000	90,000	39,000
Year 4	30,000	60,000	75,000
Year 5	24,000	45,000	75,000

The management of Why Ltd use the payback method to assist them in deciding which machine it should choose.

You are required to show your workings and state clearly the recommendation you would make to the company.

38.4.4 Discounted methods

Net present value (NPV)

This method applies the time value of money to cash flows. In so doing it gives greater importance to the early receipt of cash. Present value tables show the value of the discount factor for a range of values. For example, a table shows how £1 diminishes in the future, assuming an opportunity cost of 8 per cent p.a. For this reason, it is agreed that the NPV is a better method than either the ARR or payback methods. (A present value table is given in Appendix 2.)

The NPV allows us to assess the profitability of the project. If the present value is positive then the project is viable. To do this we need know the initial cost, the cost of capital, the annual cash flows, and the expected life of the project and if there is any residual value. From this information we can then calculate the net present value (NPV) which, if it shows a surplus, means that the project is viable.

In using this method, we must use the appropriate discount factors for the particular business and for this we must know the business' cost of capital.

38.4.5 Worked example

In this example, let us assume that the cost of capital is 8 per cent.

We know that we would rather have £500 now, instead of waiting until next year. We could invest the £500 at the current rate of interest and obtain an additional £40 interest after one year. This shows that the later we receive the £500, the more interest we lose.

By not receiving the £500 until the end of the year, we have lost interest. We use the discount factor of 0.926 (8 per cent for one year). The net present value therefore is simply the sum of the discounted values of the cash flows, minus the initial sum invested.

We illustrate this method by using the earlier information (see section 38.4.1). We use the figures for the first four years and apply it to the cash flows for Projects I and II. The assumption is that the cash outflow for financing the projects occurs at the beginning of year 1 – or we could say year 0 – but that the net cash inflows do not occur until the end of each year.

	Discount factor	Project I		Project II	
		Cash flow	Discounted cash flow	Cash flow	Discounted cash flow
Year 0	1.000	(730,000)	(730,000)	(985,000)	(985,000)
Year 1	0.926	200,000	185,200	225,000	208,350
Year 2	0.857	210,000	179,970	225,000	192,825
Year 3	0.794	220,000	174,680	290,000	230,260
Year 4	0.735	240,000	176,400	360,000	264,600
Net present value			140,000		(88,965)

The results tell us that we should consider accepting Project I as it shows a positive net present value using the given rate of 8 per cent.

Internal rate of return (IRR)

The IRR is closely related to the NPV method because it also discounts cash flow.

In this method, we need to determine the rate of interest which will give us a net present value (NPV) of zero for a particular project. If this rate is higher than our current cost of capital then the project will be worthwhile.

The biggest problem with the IRR method is that without using a computer, trial and error is the only approach in arriving at the answer.

We do know that, as the discount rate increases, there is a decrease in the NPV. Ultimately we arrive at a stage where the NPV = 0 and this is the IRR.

We have seen that Project I has a positive NPV. We now need to establish the interest rate for Project II to become feasible. To do this we need to find one NPV which is a low positive and another NPV which is a low negative in order to determine this rate.

38.4.6 Worked example

Using the information in section 38.4.1 we can apply different interest rates to Project II.

		Project II at 5%	
	Discount factor	Cash flow	Discounted cash flow
Year 0	1.000	(985,000)	(985,000)
Year 1	0.952	225,000	214,200
Year 2	0.907	225,000	204,075
Year 3	0.864	290,000	250,560
Year 4	0.823	360,000	296,280
Net present value			(19,885)

		Project II at 4%	
	Discount factor	Cash flow	Discounted cash flow
	1.000	(985,000)	(985,000)
	0.962	225,000	216,450
	0.925	225,000	208,125
	0.889	290,000	257,810
	0.855	360,000	307,800
			5,185

Using the information of these two tables we find that the IRR is approximately 4 per cent as it is that rate that gives us a net present value of almost zero (in the above example the amount is £5,185).

38.4.7 Worked example

Y Ltd wishes to buy a new printing press for £150,000. Profit before depreciation is estimated at £60,000 for the first 4 years and then reducing to £20,000 for years 5 and 6.

At the end of year 6 the printing press will be scrapped as it would have reached a non-economical period. The company requires a minimum return on all projects of 20 per cent p.a. You are required to advise the directors of the viability of the project.

Year	Annual cash flow	PV factors at 20%	Present value
0	(150,000)	1.000	(150,000)
1	60,000	0.833	49,980
2	60,000	0.694	41,640
3	60,000	0.579	34,740
4	60,000	0.482	28,920
5	20,000	0.402	16,080
6	20,000	0.335	6,700
			128,060

Using the 20 per cent return expected we see that there is a positive NPV at the end of the sixth year. This gives us the go-ahead for the project. It does not tell us what the expected rate of return is on this project and to do this we use a further method to determine the internal rate of return (IRR).

Using a higher rate of interest we redo our calculations. Let us assume that we guess at a rate of 30 per cent for the project. The NPV would then be as follows:

Year	Annual cash flow	PV factors at 30%	Present value
0	(150,000)	1.000	(150,000)
1	60,000	0.769	46,140
2	60,000	0.592	35,520
3	60,000	0.455	27,300
4	60,000	0.350	21,000
5	20,000	0.269	10,760
6	20,000	0.207	4,140
			(5,140)

We find that in this case there is a deficit which tells us that the IRR is less than 30 per cent but more than the minimum required by the directors of 20 per cent. We may eventually find that the rate is 28 per cent, which is the true rate of return and called the internal rate of return (IRR). This means that the IRR is the rate which, when used, will give an NPV of zero. This method is also known as the discounted cash flow yield.

38.5 Analysis of discounted methods

In the preceding paragraphs we have discussed four methods and to best illustrate them we look at three different projects and apply each method to each project.

Year	Project A	Project B	Project C
0	(200,000)	(200,000)	(200,000)
1	20,000	80,000	60,000
2	40,000	60,000	60,000
3	60,000	60,000	60,000
4	60,000	40,000	60,000
5	60,000		40,000
6	68,000		20,000
Total profit	108,000	40,000	100,000
Payback period	4$\frac{1}{3}$ years	3 years	3$\frac{1}{3}$ years
ARR	18%	10%	16.7%
NPV at 12%	(£884)	(£12,580)	£15,100
IRR	12%	8.5%	15%

The payback method selects B but does not take into account the short life remaining after payback. Using IRR it highlights the short life of B and shows it as the least profitable of all three projects.

ARR selects A but when timing of profits are taken into account by using IRR, then A only shows a return of approximately 12%. The extra profit of £8,000 achieved by A when compared to C does not compensate for the slow build-up of the project. Even though C earns less profit than A, it is more profitable, as shown by IRR.

This shows that payback should not be used by itself. Using a discounting method is far more accurate.

38.5.1 Self-test

Using the data given for Why Ltd in section 38.4.3, calculate the net present values of each of the possible machine investments, assuming a cost of capital of 12 per cent.

Compare the results to the previous self-test for Why Ltd (section 38.4.3). Using these results, which machine, if any, would you recommend that Why Ltd purchase?

38.6 Choosing a method

Of the four methods discussed in section 38.4, only NPV and IRR give the same result. Both these methods showed that Projects A and B would not give a 15 per cent return.

Often, when firms undertake investment appraisal, only one project can be accepted. We may find that the NPV and IRR give different solutions. To overcome this we use IRR to rank any project. We must also take into account the availability of capital.

38.6.1 Limited capital

In expanding a firm, additional capital is often required. There are, however, times when capital is limited and choices have to be made. Not all projects showing the highest NPVs will be accepted. The firm may want to do so, but would have to choose projects which the firm could undertake with the limited capital resources.

Any project falling within the available funds would be adopted. Many projects are divisible and part of a project could be adopted but limited, in that case, to the level of available funds. Where, on the other hand, a project was indivisible, then it may well have to be rejected.

38.6.2 Worked example

In this example a firm has five different projects. The table below shows the cost and NPV of each. There is no problem with funding all projects. Therefore, we can rank the projects. Those giving the highest NPVs would be the first ones accepted.

Project	Cost £s	NPV £s
A	250,000	50,000
B	230,000	40,000
C	150,000	28,000
D	120,000	20,000
E	40,000	10,000

We are now told that funds are limited to £600,000. The total initial cost of, say, A, B and C, is £630,000, which is unacceptable.

If we replace C with D, we need £600,000, while if we adopt E instead of D, we would not be using the full £600,000.

The firm now has a number of alternatives. These are:

(i) go ahead only with A and B (costing £480,000), giving a total NPV of £90,000;
(ii) also undertake D (total costing £600,000), achieving a total NPV of £110,000; or
(iii) invest in A, B and E (costing £520,000), when NPV would total £100,000.

Earlier we assumed that a project could be divisible. As such, it may be possible to invest in only part of a project. We can perform a further calculation (that is, NPV per £ of initial investment) and see if it is possible to obtain a better result. This is applying the limiting factor technique.

Using these facts the following are the results:

Project		NPV per £	Ranking
A	50,000 ÷ 250,000	0.200	2
B	40,000 ÷ 230,000	0.174	4
C	28,000 ÷ 150,000	0.187	3
D	20,000 ÷ 120,000	0.167	5
E	10,000 ÷ 40,000	0.250	1

On this basis the firm should accept:

Project	Ranking	Capital needed	NPV per £	NPV
E	1	40,000	0.250	10,000
A	2	250,000	0.200	50,000
C	3	150,000	0.187	28,000
B (part only $^{16}/_{23}$)	4	160,000	0.174	27,840
		600,000		£115,840

By doing this the firm would invest its total available funds of £600,000. These investments would then give a total NPV of £115,840.

However, if we use this ranking above where projects cannot be split, we will only achieve an NPV of £88,000 (10,000 + 50,000 + 28,000). For this reason, ranking by NPV per £ of investment should be used with caution.

38.6.3 Self-test

Martin & Co. are printers. They were forced to reject a printing order because of insufficient machine capacity. As a result they investigated the purchase of a new press. This would cost £400,000, but its capacity allows for additional work of £500,000. The annual cost of running this press would be:

- 2 operators at £25,000 each; and
- materials at £100,000.

You are required to calculate the payback period.
   You are also required to:

(a) calculate the net present value, assuming that the company discounts 4 years of cash flow at 20 per cent p.a.; and
(b) calculate the accounting rate of return, assuming the press is depreciated over 4 years.

In addition to the facts above, Martin & Co. currently have their heavy-duty card cut out of sheets. This is done by an outside contractor. On investigation, they found that they could purchase a machine for £300,000, which would then allow them to do this themselves. The annual cost of the new machine would be £100,000, but there would be a saving of £325,000, which is the amount that they currently pay the outside firm.
   For the machine you are required to:

(a) calculate the payback period;
(b) calculate the net book value based on a 20 per cent discount rate;
(c) calculate the ARR.

As the company does not have sufficient funds for both the new press and the card cutter, you are required to advise them on which machine to purchase.

38.6.4 Self-test

Art Ltd wants to introduce a new product. To do this the company needs to buy a new machine costing £100,000. The life of the new product is anticipated as 4 years. At that time Art Ltd will sell the machine as scrap and should receive £10,000. To finance the cost of the machine the company will borrow money at 10 per cent p.a.
   You are given the following net cash flows:

Year 1	(10,000)
Year 2	60,000
Year 3	95,000
Year 4	75,000

You are also told that the discount factor, using 10 per cent p.a., is as follows:

Year	Discount factor
1	0.909
2	0.826
3	0.751
4	0.683

You are required to calculate the NPV to determine if the investment is worthwhile.

You are also given the following discount factors for interest rates of 20 per cent, 25 per cent and 30 per cent. Using this information calculate the IRR.

Year	20% Discount factor	25% Discount factor	30% Discount factor
1	0.833	0.800	0.769
2	0.694	0.640	0.592
3	0.579	0.512	0.455
4	0.482	0.410	0.350

38.6.5 Self-test

Fred Ltd manufacturers sports blazers. The company has over the past 2 years shown declining profits and the directors have decided that major capital investment is needed in the business if it is to succeed in the future.

A modern finishing machine which will improve the cut and finish of the blazers can be bought at a total cost, including installation charges, of £400,000. As this is a highly specialised machine, the full amount would be due and payable on 1 January 2011.

At present the company produces and sells 20,000 blazers p.a. Research into the new machine convinces the directors that a higher production than their present one is possible. The production manager produces the following data showing the additional output of blazers resulting from the new machine:

Year	Blazer units
2011	2,500
2012	3,400
2013	3,900

The cash flow is to be based on the information given by the production manager and also to take into account the fact that all production can be sold without any difficulty.

You are given the following additional information:

	2011	2012	2013
Cost of sale	£80	£87	£96
Selling price	£146	£164	£180

Finance is available to the company at 10 per cent p.a.

The following table gives the present values for £1 at 10 per cent.

Year 1   0.909
Year 2   0.826
Year 3   0.751

Required:

(a) You are required to calculate the net cash flows for the years 2011, 2012 and 2013.

(b) You are also required to calculate the net present value for the purchase of the machine.

(c) Describe each of the following investment appraisal methods:
  (i) payback period;
  (ii) accounting rate of return.

(d) Evaluate whether Fred Limited should purchase the machine.

(e) State how the net present value could be used to find the internal rate of return of purchasing the cutting machine.

(f) Why would the internal rate of return be more valuable to Fred Limited than the net present value?

38.6.6 Self-test

Helico Ltd received a contract for providing helicopter emergency services for the next 6 years in London.

Before deciding on accepting the contract they undertook an evaluation of the project. The following information is available:

The initial cost of purchasing a helicopter will be £950,000. Depreciation, using the straight line method, is calculated over the contract period on the basis that at the end of the period the scrap value of the helicopter will be £50,000.

Monthly expenses, including depreciation, for the first two years are anticipated to be £315,000. This will increase in year 3 by £40,000 per year and in year 6 by an additional £26,000 per year.

The emergency services are expected to operate for 300 days per year. Each emergency will be paid £690. As the service becomes better known, more people will be making use of the service, and it is expected that by year 3 the service will be operating for 320 days a year and also be used twice per day.

In year 4 the amount payable for the service will be increased by 20 per cent and this price will remain fixed until the end of the contract.

Helico Ltd considers that the project would only be worthwhile if it could have a payback period of four years on the project.

Funding for the project would be by way of a loan bearing interest at 15 per cent p.a.

You are required to calculate, in years and days, the payback period, the net present value and the average rate of return.

Give your recommendations to the company using the information you have calculated (assume that it is company policy only to invest in projects achieving an average return of 10 per cent per year).

The following is an extract of the present value table for £ at 15 per cent:

Year 1	0.870
Year 2	0.756
Year 3	0.658
Year 4	0.572
Year 5	0.497
Year 6	0.432

Chapter 39

Revision

Objectives After you have carefully worked through the self tests in this chapter, you should be able to:

- undertake calculations of the various methods used for investment decisions;
- undertake calculations using the various cash flow methods;
- calculate and formulate answers for management;
- interpret the results of your calculations.

39.1 Introduction

This revision chapter is designed to test you on your ability to calculate the many methods used in investment appraisal and, more importantly, being able to interpret the results for management.

In addition, this final revision chapter also allows you to try your hand at a few examination questions that have been set by various bodies over the past few years. Although answers are not provided to all these questions you can often find answers on the website of the relevant body. Each question is clearly marked indicating its origin.

39.1.1 Self-test

Walter & Co. has developed a new product, X2X, at a total cost of £1,000,000. The product is expected to have a four-year life.

The following are estimated revenues and costs for the product for the next four years:

	Sales	Costs
2010	£1,500,000	£1,000,000
2011	£2,000,000	£1,000,000
2012	£2,500,000	£1,120,000
2013	£3,000,000	£1,500,000

X2X will require an additional £2,000,000 investment in additional production machinery. The cost of capital to the company is 10 per cent.

Sales revenues are expected to increase by 5 per cent above the estimates, while costs will increase by 3 per cent. All these increases will become effective from 2011.

385

You are required to:

(a) calculate the revised budgets for sales and costs for each year; and
(b) calculate the NPV of the project.

39.1.2 Self-test

Gems Ltd manufactures a ladies fashion brooch which it sells to an exclusive group of fashion shops. During the past year the company has been operating at 75 per cent of its capacity and its results were as follows:

Sales	600,000 brooches at £12 each
Variable costs	£7.20 per brooch
Fixed costs	£1,300,000

A fashion shop, not presently being supplied by Gems Ltd, has offered to purchase the total output from the excess capacity for the forthcoming year at a fixed price of £9 per brooch.

You are required to evaluate this offer.

Explain whether the decision would be different if, on further investigation, it is determined that:

(i) the company would need to spend an additional sum of £280,000 on additional premises and other overheads; and
(ii) the offer is likely to depress the existing sales by 5 per cent.

39.1.3 Self-test

Healthy Products uses a unique chemical (WX234) in the production of its range of pharmaceuticals. The only supplier of WX234 has just had a fire at its plant and for the next year supply will be restricted to 34,500 kilo per month.

Before the fire Healthy Products' budgeted usage each month was:

Product	A	B	C
Sales (units)	24,000	15,000	30,000
Unit selling price £	6	8	12
Unit variable cost £	4	5	7
WX234 kilo	0.5	1	2

Fixed costs are £45,000 per month.

You are required to:

(i) rank the products in contribution per unit of WX234 used;
(ii) determine if there are any limiting factors; and
(iii) determine the current maximum possible monthly profit.

39.1.4 Self-test

Motorman Ltd supplies car parts to garages. Estimated figures for August to November are as follows:

	Sales	Wages	Expenses
August	190,000	15,000	16,800
September	225,000	16,000	18,750
October	250,000	18,000	11,400
November	220,000	18,000	20,150

Seventy per cent of sales are on credit and all debtors pay in the following month. The remaining sales are for cash. Goods are sold at cost, plus a mark-up of 25 per cent. Goods for resale are purchased one month before the month of sale, at the forecast level but all the manufacturers allow the firm two months' credit. All other costs are paid in the month in which they are incurred. Expenses include a monthly charge for depreciation of £5,000.

The firm plans to buy a new delivery van at the end of November for £25,000 cash and expects to pay tax amounting to £38,500 in September. The forecast cash balance at the end of August is £25,000.

You are required to prepare a cash budget for September, October and November.

39.1.5 Self-test

Alex Ltd anticipates the following costs will be incurred in the manufacture of Product X:

Variable costs:	
Raw materials	£12 per unit
Direct labour	£4 per unit
Variable cost	£2 per unit
Semi-variable costs:	
Repairs and maintenance	£150 per 1,000 units + £10,000 per month
Indirect wages	£750 per 1,000 units + £2,000 per month
Fixed costs:	
Depreciation	£2,400 per month
Insurance	£800 per month
General factory costs	£4,800 per month

The company has a normal production capacity of 40,000 units per month. All the costs above, other than the fixed costs, are based on this output.

You are required to prepare the monthly budget based on an output of 40,000 units.

Alex Ltd expects to achieve a higher production level during the next three months and estimates it at 45,000 units. The company also estimates that later in the year demand will decrease and output will be reduced to 30,000 units.

You are required to prepare flexible budgets to cover the 30,000 unit and 45,000 unit capacities.

39.1.6 Self-test

Doris and Eric have been trading in partnership for many years, preparing accounts to 31 March each year and sharing profits or losses in the ratio 2:1. As from 1 October 2008, they agree to amend the partnership agreement as follows:

(i) Each partner will be entitled to a monthly salary. This will be £800 per month for Doris and £1,000 per month for Eric;

(ii) Any remaining profits or losses will be shared between the partners equally.

The partnership's trial balance at 31 March 2009 is as follows:

	£	£
Capital accounts – Doris		20,000
– Eric		15,000
Current accounts at 1/4/08 – Doris		14,110
– Eric	1,060	
Drawings – Doris	11,500	
– Eric	13,600	
Purchases and sales	132,760	203,170
Carriage inwards	2,050	
Returns inwards and outwards	5,550	3,330
Inventory at 1/4/08	31,440	
Operating expenses	68,200	
Discounts allowed and received	4,230	3,740
Bad debts written off	2,900	
Allowance for doubtful receivables at 1/4/08		750
Equipment, at cost	56,000	
Allowance for depreciation at 1/4/08		32,570
Disposal of equipment		4,000
Trade receivables and payables	22,400	33,760
Bank balance		21,260
	351,690	351,690

The following information is also available:

1. The partnership's equipment is depreciated on the reducing balance basis at a rate of 30% per annum. A full year's depreciation charge is made in the year of acquisition but no depreciation is charged in the year of disposal. Equipment which had cost £10,000 in June 2005 was sold for £4,000 in February 2009. The proceeds of £4,000 were debited to the bank account and credited to a disposal account but no other entries were made in relation to this disposal.

2. Closing inventory (at cost) on 31 March 2009 was £28,560. This included an item with a cost of £1,400 and an estimated selling price of £1,500. Further costs of £250 would have to be incurred so as to make this item saleable.

3. Prepaid operating expenses of £3,150 and accrued operating expenses of £1,430 at 31 March 2009 have not yet been accounted for.

4. The allowance for doubtful receivables is to be 2.5% of trade receivables.

5. It may be assumed that net profits or losses are spread evenly over the year.

Requirement for question

(a) Prepare the partnership's income statement for the year to 31 March 2009.

(b) Prepare an appropriation account for the year to 31 March 2009.

(c) Write up the partners' current accounts for the year to 31 March 2009.

(d) Prepare a statement of financial position (balance sheet) as at 31 March 2009.

(e) Explain the significance of the Partnership Act 1890 in the absence of a partnership agreement.

         (Financial Accounting CIPFA Certificate Stage June 2009)

Note: this question contains terms used internationally. They are discussed in Chapter 41.

39.1.7 Self-test

Delamare Ltd is a small company which prepares accounts to 30 April each year. The company operates a manual double-entry book-keeping system but does not maintain any control accounts.

A trial balance extracted at 30 April 2009 revealed that debit balances exceeded credit balances by £5,020. This difference was placed into a suspense account and the company then proceeded to prepare a draft income statement for the year to 30 April 2009. The draft income statement showed a profit of £27,780. The balances remaining in the company's books *after* this income statement had been prepared were as follows:

	£	£
Property, plant and equipment, at cost	242,500	
Allowance for depreciation of PPE		113,400
Inventory at 30 April 2009	43,610	
Trade receivables and payables	49,120	54,570
Prepayments and accruals	1,880	3,030
Bank balance	13,450	
Dividend paid in January 2009	10,000	
Retained earnings at 1 May 2008		76,760
Ordinary shares of £1		50,000
Loan repayable in 2012		30,000
Suspense account		5,020
Profit for year to 30 April 2009		27,780
	360,560	360,560

The company's books of original entry and ledgers were then searched and the following four errors were located:

E1. The sales daybook had been overcast by £100.
E2. Discounts received in April 2009 totalling £690 had been recorded correctly in suppliers' personal accounts but had been omitted from the discounts received account in the nominal ledger.
E3. A purchase invoice of £6,100 had been recorded correctly in the purchases daybook but had been credited to the supplier's personal account as £1,600.
E4. Bank charges of £70 had been recorded in the cashbook but nowhere else.

When these errors have been corrected, it will also be necessary to adjust for the following items that have not yet been recorded in the company's books:

A1. Non-depreciable land which is included in property, plant and equipment at its cost of £30,000 is to be revalued to £75,000;
A2. A 1 for 5 bonus issue of ordinary shares was made on 30 April 2009, financed out of retained earnings.

Requirement for question
(a) Identify the books of original entry (or prime entry) in which each of the following types of transaction should be recorded:
   (i) a cash sale;
   (ii) a purchase return;
   (iii) the payment of a minor expense in cash;
   (iv) an increase in an allowance for doubtful receivables.

(b) Write journal entries to correct errors E1 to E4 and to make adjustments A1 and A2. (Narratives are not required).

(c) Prepare a statement of financial position (balance sheet) for Delamare Ltd as at 30 April 2009. Ignore taxation.

(Financial Accounting CIPFA Certificate Stage June 2009)

39.1.8 Self-test

Damon plc prepares accounts to 31 December each year. The company's issued share capital consists of 2,500,000 ordinary shares of 20p each and 250,000 6% preference shares of £1 each. The following information relates to the year ended 31 December 2008:

1. On 1 January 2008, the company issued £1,000,000 of loan stock, repayable in 2013. This was the only loan outstanding during 2008;
2. Retained earnings brought forward on 1 January 2008 were £22,500. The only other reserve on that date was a share premium account of £100,000;
3. The company's profit after tax for the year was £280,000;
4. Dividends paid in the year (including the full preference dividend) were £152,500;
5. The market value of the company's ordinary shares at 31 December 2008 was 79.5p per share.

Requirement for question

(a) Calculate the maximum amount of dividends that the company could have paid for the year to 31 December 2008 and explain why this maximum cannot be exceeded.

(b) Calculate the following accounting ratios for the year to 31 December 2008:
    (i)   ordinary dividend cover;
    (ii) ordinary dividend yield;
    (iii) earnings per ordinary share;
    (iv) price earnings ratio;
    (v) capital gearing ratio.
Explain how each ratio is calculated and explain the significance of each ratio.

(Financial Accounting CIPFA Certificate Stage June 2009)

39.1.9 Self-test

The following extract has been taken from the statement of cash flows of Grutyer plc:

	£
Net profit before taxation	433,444
Adjustments for:	
Depreciation	214,530
Surplus on sale of non-current assets	(14,400)
Interest expense	32,120
Operating profit before working capital changes	665,694
Increase in inventories	(18,500)
Decrease in trade receivables	22,600
Increase in trade payables	27,400
Cash generated from operations	697,194
Interest paid	(32,120)
Corporation tax paid	(39,820)
Net cash from operating activities	625,254

The following additional information is available:

	£
Sales	12,133,014
Purchases	9,564,500
Corporation tax payable at end of year	158,600
Corporation tax payable at the start of the year	98,420
Wages and salaries	1,010,500
Other expenses excluding interest and depreciation	893,800
Discounts allowed	33,560
Discounts received	16,540

Requirement for question

Prepare a clear calculation of the cash from operating activities using the direct method.

(Financial Reporting CIPFA Certificate Stage Examination 9 June 2009)

39.1.10 Self-test

Hazel is a sole trader. She runs a small shop (operating from rented premises) and prepares accounts to 31 October each year. Her business records consist solely of a cashbook in which she records amounts paid into and out of her business bank account. The following information relates to the year ended 31 October 2003:

1. Nearly all of Hazel's sales are to customers who pay her immediately, but some customers have an account with Hazel and pay her once a month.
2. Each week, Hazel uses part of her takings to pay certain business expenses and then banks most of the remainder. However, she retains a small amount of cash in her till. The expenses paid out of takings in the year to 31 October 2003 were as follows:

	£
Wages to part-time sales assistant	5,840
Hazel's own wages as shop manager	13,000
Sundry expenses	1,170

3. A summary of the cashbook for the year to 31 October 2003 is as follows:

		£	£
Bank balance at 1 November 2002			1,470
Add:	Takings paid into bank	80,710	
	Premium Bond prize paid in	1,000	81,710
			83,180
Less:	Cheques to suppliers	61,890	
	Shop rent	8,400	
	Business rates	1,250	
	Insurance	1,570	
	Electricity	1,090	
	Sundry expenses	880	
	Bank charges and interest	340	
	New shop display cabinet	3,600	79,020
Bank balance at 31 October 2003			4,160

4. The October bank statement shows a closing balance at 31 October 2003 of £5,380. Hazel has compared her cashbook with the statement and has prepared the following reconciliation:

	£	£
Bank balance per cashbook		4,160
Add: Cheque payments shown in cashbook		
but not yet shown on bank statement		1,420
		5,580
Less: Items not recorded in cashbook:		
Bank charges 25 October 2003	30	
Dishonoured cheque 2 October 2003	170	200
Bank balance per bank statement		5,380

5. Shop equipment is depreciated at 25% per annum on the straight line basis, with a full year's charge in the year of acquisition and no charge in the year of disposal. All of the shop equipment owned by Hazel at the start of the year to 31 October 2003 had been acquired in 1998 or earlier. One item of equipment was sold for scrap during the year. Hazel gave the proceeds of £50 to her son as a present.

6. Apart from the bank balance and the shop equipment, Hazel's only business assets and liabilities at the start and end of the year to 31 October 2003 were as follows:

	31 October 2002	31 October 2003
	£	£
Stock of goods at cost	9,430	10,160
Amounts owed by customers	610	550
Amounts owed to suppliers	4,920	5,280
Cash float	250	270
Accrued electricity charges	210	180
Prepaid business rates	400	490

The figure of £550 shown for amounts owed by customers at 31 October 2003 is *before* accounting for the dishonoured cheque of £170 (see Note 4 above). The customer concerned seems to be in financial difficulties and Hazel has decided to provide in full for this doubtful debt.

The stock figure of £10,160 at 31 October 2003 includes £120 for the cost of certain items of damaged stock. In their undamaged state, these items could have been sold for £175 but their expected sale value is now only £80.

7. During the year to 31 October 2003, Hazel took stock items costing £490 from the shop for her own use. She did not reimburse the shop for these goods.

Requirement for question
(a) Prepare Hazel's trading, profit and loss account for the year to 31 October 2003.
(b) Prepare Hazel's balance sheet as at 31 October 2003.

(CIPFA Financial Accounting Certificate Stage Examination 8 June 2004)

39.1.11 Self-test

Emma is a sole trader operating from rented premises. She prepares accounts to 31 August each year. Her balance sheet at 31 August 2001 was as follows:

Balance Sheet as at 31 August 2001

	£	£	£
Fixed assets			
Shop equipment at cost		7,400	
Less: Depreciation to date		2,880	4,520
Current assets			
Stock		21,730	
Prepaid rent, rates and insurance		3,170	
Cash in hand		420	
		25,320	
Current liabilities			
Bank overdraft	2,450		
Trade creditor	10,590		
Accrued heat and light	170	13,210	
Net current assets			12,110
			16,630
Capital			
As at 31 August 2001			16,630

The following information is available in relation to the year ended 31 August 2002.

1. All of Emma's sales are to customers who pay immediately either in cash or by cheque. She sells goods at a constant markup of 40% on cost.
2. At the end of each week, Emma uses £200 of the week's takings to pay her assistant's wages and a further £300 to pay her own salary. She then pays most of the remainder into her business bank account, retaining only a small cash float. Cash in hand at 31 August 2002 was £400.
3. All of Emma's purchases of stock for resale are from a single supplier who offers a 2.5% discount for prompt payment. Emma always takes advantage of this discount. She owed £11,980 to her supplier at 31 August 2002.
4. The business bank statements for the year to 31 August 2002 show the following receipts and payments:

	£	£
Receipts:		
Takings paid into bank	169,470	
Business loan from Emma's sister	5,000	
Sale of shop equipment	200	174,670
Payments:		
Cheques paid to supplier	139,230	
Purchase of shop equipment	3,200	
Rent, rates and insurance	16,850	
Heat and light	6,110	
Sundry expenses	2,920	
Bank interest and charges	740	169,050

Takings of £3,350 paid into the bank on 31 August 2002 did not appear on the bank statement until 2 September 2002.

5. Rent of £12,000 per annum is paid quarterly in advance on 1 January, 1 April, 1 July and 1 October. Insurances and business rates are payable annually in advance on 1 January and 1 April respectively. The insurance premium paid on 1 January 2002 was £1,260 and the rates payment made on 1 April 2002 was £3,600.

6. During the year to 31 August 2002, Emma began paying for heat and light by monthly direct debit. The monthly payments are based on an estimate of her electricity consumption for the year ahead. A statement received from the electricity company at 31 August 2002 showed that she was in credit by £140.

7. Shop equipment bought in January 1998 for £1,000 was sold in February 2002 for £200. Depreciation on shop equipment is provided at 12.5% per annum on the straight line basis, with a full charge in the year of acquisition and no charge in the year of disposal. None of Emma's shop equipment had been fully depreciated by 31 August 2001.

8. The business loan from Emma's sister is interest-free. Emma repaid £300 of this loan out of her own private bank account during the year to 31 August 2002.

9. Unfortunately, Emma forgot to take stock on 31 August 2002. In consequence, she now has no idea of the value of her stock on that date.

Requirement for question

(a) Prepare Emma's trading and profit and loss account for the year to 31 August 2002.

(b) Prepare Emma's balance sheet as at 31 August 2002.

(CIPFA Financial Accounting Foundation Stage December 2002)

39.1.12 Self-test

Eastwood plc is a manufacturing company which prepares annual accounts to 31 July. On 1 July 2002, the company had a stock of 13,000 units of raw material X. These units had cost £6 each. During July 2002, purchases and sales of material X were as follows:

	Bought	*Sold*
7 July	8,000 units at £7 each	
10 July		12,000 units
18 July	15,000 units at £8 each	
25 July		20,000 units
30 July	3,000 units at £10 each	

The stock of Eastwood plc at 31 July 2002 also included 1,000 units of product Y. These units had been manufactured by the company in late July but were not complete at the year-end. Manufacturing costs of £11,500 had been incurred in relation to these units so far and it was anticipated that further costs of £3,400 would be necessary in order to complete production. The units had an estimated selling price of £18,000. When the units were sold, the company would incur delivery costs of £500 and selling expenses amounting to 5% of selling price.

Requirement for question

(a) Calculate the cost of the closing stock of raw material X at 31 July 2002, using each of the following stock valuation methods:
  (i) FIFO
  (ii) LIFO
  (iii) AVCO.
(b) Explain how the cost and net realisable value of a manufactured item are calculated.
(c) Calculate the value at which the 1,000 units of product Y should be shown in the financial statements of Eastwood plc at 31 July 2002.

(CIPFA Financial Accounting Foundation Stage December 2002)

39.1.13 Self-test

The balance sheets of Essex Ltd at 30 September 2001 and 2002 are as follows:

Balance sheets as at				
	30/9/01		30/9/02	
	£000	£000	£000	£000
Tangible fixed assets:				
At cost or valuation	3,770		4,890	
Depreciation to date	1,420	2,350	1,660	3,230
Current assets:				
Stocks	1,760		1,860	
Trade debtors	1,300		1,550	
Cash at bank	990		–	
	4,050		3,410	
Current liabilities:				
Trade creditors	900		1,190	
Corporation tax	720		–	
Proposed dividends	1,400		–	
Bank overdraft	–		510	
	3,020		1,700	
Net current assets		1,030		1,710
		3,380		4,940
7% debentures		–		1,000
		3,380		3,940
Capital and reserves:				
Ordinary shares of 50p		1,000		1,200
Share premium account		750		1,070
Revaluation reserve		–		500
Profit and loss account		1,630		1,170
		3,380		3,940

The following information is also available:

1. During the year to 30 September 2002, freehold land included in tangible fixed assets was revalued from its cost of £400,000 to its estimated market value of £900,000.

2. In January 2002, tangible fixed assets which had cost £600,000 in 1998 were sold for £250,000. The accumulated depreciation provided in relation to these assets at the date of disposal was £320,000.
3. The 7% debentures were issued on 1 October 2001. Interest is payable annually on 30 September and has been paid on the due date.
4. Bank overdraft interest paid during the year to 30 September 2002 was £27,000.
5. No interim dividend was paid during the year to 30 September 2002 and no final dividend is proposed. The previous year's proposed dividend was paid in December 2001.
6. The corporation tax creditor at 30 September 2001 was underestimated by £26,000.
7. In March 2002, 400,000 ordinary shares were issued at £1.30 per share.

Requirement for question
(a) Prepare a cash flow statement for Essex Ltd for the year to 30 September 2002 in accordance with the requirements of accounting standard FRS1 (Revised) using the indirect method. The reconciliation to movement in net debt is not required.
(b) Briefly explain why the cash position of Essex Ltd has deteriorated during the year to 30 September 2002.

(CIPFA Financial Accounting Foundation Stage December 2002)

39.1.14 Self-test

Karen Lamb Limited sells books. The draft final accounts for the year ended 30 November 2008 have been prepared and show a retained profit for the year of £84,000.
The following adjustments have not yet been made.

1. The directors propose a total final dividend of £5,000 on the ordinary shares.
2. A cheque for £2,000 received from a debtor on 29 November 2008 has not yet been entered in the accounts.
3. A cheque payment of £14,000 for the purchase of a new motor vehicle has not yet been entered in the accounts.
4. Stock at 30 November 2008 has been entered as £44,000. The correct figure is £46,000.
5. The directors propose a transfer of £10,000 to a general reserve.

Required:
(a) Calculate the corrected retained profit of Karen Lamb Limited for the year ended 30 November 2008.
(b) Detail any changes to the balance sheet as a result of each of these adjustments. Identify each sub-heading and item(s) involved and the effect, if any, on the net current assets.

(AQA Financial Accounting ACC 2 January 2009)

39.1.15 Self-test

The following trial balance has been extracted from the books of account of Spartre plc after the trading and profit and loss and appropriation accounts have been prepared.

Trial Balance at 31 December 2008

Accrued expenses		11,700
Bank balance		6,590
Fixed assets at cost	1,900,000	
General reserve		60,000
Ordinary shares of £1 each fully paid		500,000
Prepaid expenses	1,250	
Profit and loss account balance 1 January 2008		252,320
Proposed ordinary share dividends		60,000
Provision for corporation tax		45,000
Provision for depreciation of fixed assets		760,000
Retained profit for the year		78,140
Share premium account		200,000
Stock at 31 December 2008	43,000	
Trade creditors		26,500
Trade debtors	56,000	
	2,000,250	2,000,250

Required:

Prepare a balance sheet extract showing the ordinary share capital and reserves at 31 December 2008.

(AQA Financial Accounting Unit 3 January 2009)

39.1.16 Self-test

Tilly Teasdale owns a general store. She provides the following information at 31 December 2008.

Bad debts written off	88
Equipment at cost	12,000
General expenses	50,841
Motor expenses	7,217
Motor vehicles at cost	65,000
Provisions for depreciation – equipment	3,600
– motor vehicles	55,040
Purchases	107,087
Rent and rates	2,140
Sales	264,255
Stock at 1 January 2008	8,132
Stock at 31 December 2008	7,611
Wages	71,637

Additional information at 31 December 2008

The following items have not yet been taken into account.

1. Tilly took goods to the value of £1,700 from the business for her own personal use.
2. Wages remaining unpaid amounted to £830.
3. Rates prepaid for the year ended 31 December 2009 amounted to £400.
4. A motor vehicle purchased during the year for £23,000 had been included in the general expenses account.
5. A repair costing £2,000 to one of the vehicles had been included in the motor vehicles account.
6. Depreciation is to be charged at the following rates:
   - equipment at 10% per annum using the straight-line method;
   - motor vehicles at 40% per annum using the reducing balance method.

It is Tilly's policy to charge a full year's depreciation on the value of assets held at the end of the financial year.

Required:
Prepare a trading and profit and loss account for the year ended 31 December 2008.

(AQA Financial Accounting Unit 3 Jan 2009)

39.1.17 Self-test

Simon Paul sells CDs to music shops.
He provides the following information at 31 March 2008.

Trade debtors	28,000
Trade creditors	18,000
Sales for the year	260,000
Purchases for the year	180,000

All sales and purchases are on a credit basis.

Required:
(a) Calculate the debtors' collection period. State the formula used.
(b) Calculate the creditors' collection period. State the formula used.
(c) Briefly comment on the results obtained in (a) and (b) above.

(AQA Introduction to management Accounting Unit 4 Jan 2009)

39.1.18 Self-test

Niklas Ltd is a small company which sells clocks.

The following budgeted information is available for the five months ending 31 October.

	June	July	August	September	October
Expected purchases (clocks) Each clock costs £12.50	60	80	120	100	80

Each month, 25% of the purchases are expected to be on a cash basis.
Sixty per cent of the amount owed to the creditors is expected to be paid after one month. The remainder is expected to be paid after two months.

Required:
(a) Prepare a creditors' budget for Niklas Ltd for each of the three months ending 31 October.

(AQA Introduction to management Accounting Unit 4 Jan 2009)

39.1.19 Self-test

Drumfet plc is a manufacturing company. The directors feel that the time is right to expand the business. To fund this expansion, they must raise a substantial amount of finance. They are considering the following options:

either

1. by issuing 8% debentures repayable in the year 2049; the debentures will be secured on the company's land and buildings;

Or

2. selling the land and buildings and leasing them back from the new owners.

Required:
Advise the directors, giving reasons, which of the two methods of raising finance they should use.

(AQA Financial Accounting Unit 5 Jan 2009)

39.1.20 Self-test

The following balances were extracted from the books of Kumble plc on 31 October 2008.

	Dr £	Cr £
Purchases	820,000	
Sales		1,800,000
Stock 1 November 2007	58,000	
Discounts	8,300	4,200
Sales returns	4,600	
£1 Ordinary shares		700,000
£1 6% Preference shares		300,000
Rent received		50,000
General distribution costs	195,000	
General administrative expenses	145,000	
Profit and Loss	56,000	
Debtors	82,000	
Creditors		47,000
Equipment	220,000	
Vehicles	440,000	
Land and buildings	994,600	
Provision for depreciation of equipment		38,000
Provision for depreciation of vehicles		180,000
General reserve		75,000
Share premium		140,000
Bank	64,000	
Provision for doubtful debts		3,300
Salaries	250,000	
	3,337,500	3,337,500

Additional information.

(i) Stock at 31 October 2008 was valued at £53,000.
(ii) General distribution costs owing £4,300.
   General administrative expenses prepaid £3,000.
(iii) Salaries are split in the ratio of 3:2 between distribution costs and administrative expenses.
(iv) Rent receivable of £1,200 has been paid in advance.
(v) A cheque for £1,500 from a debtor has not been recorded in the accounts.
(vi) The provision for doubtful debts is to be made up of a specific provision of £800, plus a general provision of 3% on the remainder of debtors.
(vii) Depreciation is to be provided as follows:
   ● equipment 20% per annum on cost;
   ● vehicles 25% per annum reducing balance method.
   Equipment is split in the ratio of 3:1 between distribution costs and administrative expenses. Vehicles are treated as a distribution cost.
(viii) The directors recommend:
   ● a transfer to the general reserve of £70,000;
   ● an ordinary share dividend of 10 pence per share;
   ● the payment of the preference share dividend.
(ix) Corporation Tax for the year is estimated at £90,000.

Required:
(a) The Profit and Loss Account for the year ended 31 October 2008, together with the Balance Sheet as at that date (in accordance with the minimum requirements for publication).

(OCR Accounting (F004) Jan 2009)

39.1.21 Self-test

The following balances were taken from the accounts of Khan plc on 30 November 2008.

£1 ordinary shares	280,000
£1 6% preference shares	180,000
General reserve	90,000
Share premium	140,000
Land and buildings (land £350,000)	800,000

During the month of December 2008 the following took place.

(i) On 1 December 2008 a one for four rights issue was made at a premium £0.50 per share. Shareholders took up the full rights issue. On the same date, a further 50,000 £1 6% preference shares were issued.

(ii) A proposed dividend of 20% on the ordinary share balance as at 31 December 2008 utilising the general reserve was declared.

(iii) An independent surveyor revalued land to £450,000.

Required:

(a) Journal entries to record each of (i) to (iii) above (narratives are not required).

(b) The Capital and Reserves section of the Balance Sheet as at 31 December 2008.

(c) Explain the differences between a bonus issue and a rights issue.

(d) Discuss why a company might decide to make a bonus issue of shares.

(OCR Accounting (F004) Jan 2009)

39.1.22 Self-test

The following information is available for two companies engaged in a similar type of business for the year ended 31 October 2008.

	Gray plc £	Brew plc £
Turnover	900,000	1,200,000
Gross profit	360,000	540,000
Expenses	260,000	275,000
Profit before interest and taxation	100,000	265,000
Interest payable	10,000	25,000
Net profit before tax	90,000	240,000
Net profit after tax	72,000	192,000
Total capital employed	640,000	700,000
£1 ordinary shares	400,000	100,000
£1 5% debentures	200,000	500,000
£1 8% preference shares	40,000	100,000
Market price per ordinary share	1.50	2.00
Ordinary dividend	20,000	50,000

The preference share dividend is paid on time by both companies.

	%	%
Gross profit as a % of sales	40	45
Net profit as a % of sales	10	20
Return on capital employed	14	34

Required:

(a) Assess the relative profitability of Gray plc and Brew plc.

(b) Calculate for Brew plc: (where appropriate calculations should be made to two decimal places)
   (i)   earnings per share;
   (ii) dividend yield;
   (iii) interest cover.

(c) Assess the significance of the earnings per share for the shareholders of Brew plc.

(d) Assess two limitations of ratio analysis.

(OCR Accounting (F004) Jan 2009)

39.1.23 Self-test

Eastview Ltd is preparing its cash budget for the three months ending 30 June 2009. The following forecasts are available.

	Feb	Mar	Apr	May	June	July
Sales	120,000	120,000	130,000	140,000	150,000	150,000
Purchases	76,000	72,000	74,000	78,000	50,000	60,000
Wages	21,000	20,000	22,000	24,000	18,000	18,000
Rent	3,800	3,800	4,000	4,000	4,000	4,000
General expenses	38,000	40,000	40,000	44,000	36,000	36,000

The following information is also available.

(i)   40% of sales are on a cash basis. The remainder is received one month after the sale is made.

(ii)   20% of purchases are on a cash basis. The remainder is paid two months after the purchases are made.

(iii)   90% of wages are paid in the month they are earned, and 10% are paid during the following month.

(iv)   Rent is paid one month in advance.

(v)   General expenses include depreciation of £3,000 per month. General expenses are paid 75% in the month incurred and 25% in the following month.

(vi)   Eastview Ltd has negotiated a loan of £10,000 which will be paid into its bank account on 20 April 2009. Interest on the loan is included in the general expenses.

(vii)   The company intends to purchase a new motor van on 1 May 2009 for £12,000, paying half in the month of purchase and half in the following month. It also plans to sell a motor van on 15 June 2009 for £4,500 cash.

(viii) The budgeted bank balance on 1 April 2009 is £12,000.

Required:

(a) The Cash Budget of Eastview Ltd for each of the three months April, May and June 2009.

(b) Evaluate two benefits to a business of budgeting.

(OCR Accounting (F012) Jan 2009)

39.1.24 Self-test

Jacques is a sole trader. A trial balance was extracted for the year ended 31 December 2008. The trial balance did not agree. The Profit and Loss Account had, however, been prepared and a net profit of £22,600 had been calculated.

The following errors have now been discovered.

(i)   A new machine purchased for £2,500 had been entered as a debit in the machinery repairs account. Depreciation had been correctly entered in the accounts.

(ii) The purchases account had been undercast by £6,400.

(iii) Rent received of £7,900 had been entered on the debit side of the electricity account.

(iv) A credit sale to Heath Ltd of £900 had been omitted from the books.

(v)   A cheque for £1,600 from Sumner Ltd, a debtor, had been correctly entered in the bank account, but no other entry had been made.

(vi) A cheque paid for insurance of £140 had been correctly entered in the insurance account, but had been entered in the bank account as £400.

(vii) Purchase returns of £500 had been entered on the credit side of the sales account.

(viii) A purchase on credit from Wayne Ltd of £2,100 had been entered in the Purchases Journal as £2,000 and had also been posted to the Purchases Ledger and the General Ledger as £2,000.

Required:

(a) Journal entries to correct the errors (narratives are not required).

(b) A statement to show the revised net profit.

(c) Jacques is considering forming a partnership with Jill who operates a similar business. Evaluate the disadvantages to Jacques of forming a partnership.

(OCR Accounting (F012) Jan 2009)

Chapter 40

Computerised accounting

Objectives

After you have studied this chapter, you should be able to:

- explain the meaning of a microprocessor;
- understand and explain the advantages of computer-based accounts;
- identify the differences in systems.

40.1 Introduction

Traditionally accounts have been maintained by means of handwritten records. With the decrease in costs of computers and the simplification in their use, increasing numbers of firms have decided to computerise their own accounting records. This is aided by the reduction in size (and not only cost) of computers with some being not much more than advanced desktop calculators.

As a result many businesses today maintain all, or part, of their accounting records on computer. In some cases only a spreadsheet such as Excel is used and all the data is taken from a manual system. The spreadsheet would, in effect, be the trial balance and from that the final accounts would be produced.

You may think, then, that there is no need to know all about double entry, trading and profit and loss accounts and balance sheets, accruals, prepayments and all the many other aspects dealt with in the previous chapters. But you are wrong! There is a growing need to understand the processes of the computer system. You need to know what functions the computer system is doing. You also need to ensure that the system is operating correctly and that there are no 'bugs' in the system.

There are a great number of computerised accounting systems. These range from the very simple to the highly complex. The basic system is an extended cash book. As the cash book is written up (entered) on the computer, the ledger accounts are updated and from there a trial balance is automatically prepared.

The transactions are processed very quickly, but that is not to say that they are correct! All transactions must be entered by a person and if that person enters an incorrect item or amount, or even wrongly identifies a debit or a credit entry, then the ensuing result is incorrect.

40.2 Buying a system

When buying a computerised accounting system you need to consider a number of points:

- Is it best to buy a package off the shelf or have a system designed for the particular business? The latter, known as a 'bespoke' system, is expensive and can take a long time to install.
- Will the new system run alongside the manual system for a while? This is the best option – it makes sure there are no problems.
- Are you implementing the system yourself or will you get outside assistance?

40.2.1 Accounting software packages

There are many accounting software packages that can be purchased. These packages will perform many, if not all, of the tasks that would normally be manually entered. Transactions may be entered into the computer package and many will produce the double-entry records based on this one entry. Although the exact capabilities of each package will vary, it is possible that most, if not all, of these packages will be able to produce invoices for purchases and sales. They calculate VAT returns, discounts and all the other areas of the accounting information system. Logically, these packages will also produce the final accounts for the business when required.

It is important that each system is reviewed before making a decision. The cost of a mistake can be extremely high and often will result in many lost hours in trying to correct past errors. For larger firms this software can actually be tailor-made to the firm's own specific requirements. This sort of package is known as a 'bespoke' system. They are normally produced by a specialist computer software firm who have experience in producing accounting packages.

It is not intended to recommend any system in this book. To give you some idea of what is available you can look at the following websites:

- TAS software (www.tassoftware.co.uk);
- Pegasus (www.pegasus.co.uk);
- Sage software (www.sage.co.uk); and
- QuickBooks (www.quickbooks.intuit.co.uk).

Software must be able to grow with the business. No business wants to change from one system to another because the original system cannot be expanded to meet current needs.

The accounting system is only one component of the entire management information system. Reports do help control business but it must be noted that the reports and the information from them are only as good as the data going in – GIGO (garbage in, garbage out). It is important to check that the input is accurate and timely. Improved reporting can result in an information overload where too much detail is supplied to management, who are then unable to apply it, or even understand the reports.

40.2.2 Advantages of computerised systems

When we use a paper-based system, considerable time is required to input the data and to post it to the relevant ledgers.

Advantages of a computer system are:

- it is quicker to write up the books;
- it can be more accurate than the manual system;
- the information is up to date;
- it is faster to provide annual accounts; and
- it has advantages of cost savings.

In credit control, which is so vital to the well-being of a business, the computerisation allows for reports such as debtors' statements and cash flows to be prepared with little delay. This allows the business to determine if a debtor exceeds the credit limit allowed and monitors that expenses are within the budget. In addition, the system can produce payroll, cash flows and VAT returns faster than a manual system.

All entries are processed on a double-entry basis, but the difference is that with a computer system we only need to enter the transaction once and the software automatically completes the double entry. Each account has a unique number (code). We divide the accounts into balance sheet and profit and loss accounts, and also subdivide them into fixed assets, current assets, income and expenditure, etc.

From this we can see that whatever system is brought into a business it still uses the processes that we have read about in this textbook. Although we no longer worry about the accounts balancing, because the entries are made automatically, we still need to ensure that the entries are accurate.

40.2.3 Advantages of computers

Although the previous section listed the many advantages of a computerised accounting system, it is still possible to utilise a computer without any accounting package and still achieve many benefits.

These can be listed as:

- time saving;
- handle vast amounts of input and use reduced staff;
- increased accuracy;
- speedy production of reports;
- reports are produced at lower cost;
- increased job satisfaction for operators; and
- more effective use of the operator's time.

All this allows for management to receive information quickly. Using a simple spreadsheet a business will still be able to obtain debtor and creditor information as often as needed, although it may still take more time than if there were an accounting package in place.

The spreadsheet is ideal for invoicing and the preparation of payroll and VAT returns. Other uses would be in the preparation of cash flows and operating budgets.

40.2.4 Disadvantages

Having listed all the many advantages gained by using computers for some or all of the accounting functions, there are still a number of disadvantages.

- costs of installation are high;
- staff has to be trained;
- some staff may feel threatened if they are not computer literate;
- modification of a package/system requires expertise and is costly; and
- possible computer crash or malfunction with a loss of information when there is no back-up.

40.3 Accounting by computer

Ledger accounts are identified by a unique number – the whole list consists of a chart of accounts. The firm can make up its own list to suit its own uses.

They could break down the list into groups, for example:

- stock control;
- debtors and creditors including invoicing and record keeping;
- investments and cash;
- fixed asset records;
- equity, provisions and long-term liabilities;
- purchases and expenses;
- income;
- wages and salary payroll system.

40.3.1 Spreadsheets

Spreadsheets are very commonly used in a computer system. The screen is divided into vertical columns and horizontal rows and each cell thus formed has a unique grid reference. Using this template, it is possible to build financial and statistical models. These will be used for budgets and cash flow charts, as well as aids in preparing job estimates or profit projections.

Spreadsheets are ideal for producing and maintaining stock records and statistical projections which a business may need.

The following illustration of a spreadsheet shows the grid references used.

40.4 Limitations of computers

It must not be thought that a computer, with or without an accounting system, is the solution for accurate, detailed records. The input of inaccurate information, the incorrect coding or the incorrect allocation will also produce inaccurate information.

Many accounting systems try to include every feature which the designer thinks will be used. All too often this is far in excess of what is needed by the business. So many options are offered that the accountant would have to spend considerable time in deciding which features to activate and which are surplus to the needs of that particular business.

Alternatively some features may be missing and then it becomes a case of having to buy a bespoke system at far higher costs. The modification of an existing system is often far more costly than the bespoke system.

Another major problem is the inflexibility of a system. When businesses merge they may find that their two systems are not compatible. This can lead to lengthy and cumbersome amendments to the system finally adopted.

One important limitation that may or may not arise is that of vulnerability. Every system should have good anti-virus protection. It must be designed to prevent hackers gaining access, especially when the system is open to public ordering on the web.

40.4.1 Security on information

- Back-ups are important as they ensure that if anything goes wrong there is a copy available to access.
- When we use a computer system passwords must be created to restrict the use of access. This gives management some form of control and prevents an operator from gaining unlimited access to the entire system.
- Operators can only access the areas for which they are responsible.

Cost accounting makes great use of computers. Each cost centre gets a number so that expenses relative to that cost centre are correctly applied. The number – a code – also determines the nature of the expense and the job to which it is to be allocated.

The following is an example of a chart of accounts, showing how it is structured. This chart of accounts was prepared for the construction industry and issued by Power Tools Software Inc. (see www.powertoolssoftware.com/QBManual).

Chart of accounts

1. The Chart of Accounts contains the two basic types of accounts.
   A Balance Sheet accounts and
   B Profit and Loss Accounts.

2. The Chart follows Generally Accepted Accounting Principals (GAAP) and groups items as below:

    A 1000 Assets

    B 2000 Liabilities & Equity

    C 3000 Income

    D 4000 Direct Costs (Cost of Goods Sold)

    E 5000 Overheads (Expenses)

The above chart shows how the codes are split in the first instance, into balance sheet items and profit and loss items. The next division is between assets and liabilities, and income and expenditure.

The table below (prepared by Power Tools) is an extract from a more comprehensive list of special purpose codes.

Special purpose accounts

Number	Name	Description
1080	Costs Paid by Third Parties	Used to enter income and costs actually paid through bank accounts maintained by others (companies, banks, property owners, etc.).
1090	Petty Cash	Used to track petty cash. Using a petty cash account is the least recommended of the three available methods.
1100	Accounts Receivable	Used to track amounts due from customers.
1120	Rental Property Leases	Used to track rental property. Allows automatic billing at the 1st of each month, tracking of who's not paid.
1350	Loans Made to Principals	Used to track money you may have borrowed from the company.

40.4.2 Self-test

You have been asked to justify the installation of a computerised accounting system. In your answer indicate the advantages of the system.

40.4.3 Self-test

Describe the functions of a spreadsheet and give examples of their use.

40.4.4 Self-test

Hitesh is a sole trader who prepares accounts to 30 September each year. He uses a manual double-entry book-keeping system and maintains sales ledger and purchase ledger control accounts. The balance on the purchase ledger control account at 30 September 2003 was £24,791 (credit). However, the list of balances which was extracted from the purchase ledger on that date showed totals of £24,312 (credit balances) and £185 (debit balances).

On investigation, the following errors were found:

1. A batch of purchase invoices totalling £2,755 and received in early September 2003 had not been recorded in the books at all.
2. The credit side of a supplier's account in the purchase ledger had been overcast by £100.
3. The debit side of the purchase ledger control account had been undercast by £1,000.
4. A debit balance of £57 had been listed as a credit balance in the list of balances extracted from the purchase ledger.
5. A cheque to a supplier of £1,570 had been entered in the cashbook and supplier's account as £1,750.
6. A discount of £231 received from a supplier had been entered on the wrong side of the supplier's account in the purchase ledger.
7. Contras amounting to £340 had been recorded correctly in the individual supplier accounts in the purchase ledger but had not been recorded at all in the purchase ledger control account.

Hitesh is now thinking of switching to a computer-based accounting system and he hopes that this will eliminate errors such as those listed above.

Requirement for question

(a) State and briefly explain the principle of duality on which double-entry book-keeping systems are based.
(b) Prepare an amended purchase ledger control account and reconcile the balance on this account to the corrected total of the purchase ledger balances at 30 September 2003.
(c) If Hitesh transfers to a computer-based accounting system, will the types of errors that have occurred during the year to 30 September 2003 be eliminated? If not, why not?
(d) Briefly explain the advantages and disadvantages of computer-based accounting systems.

(CIPFA Financial Accounting Certificate Stage Examination 8 June 2004)

Chapter 41

International accounting – the future

Objectives   After you have studied this chapter, you should be able to:

■ explain the international standard-setting process;

■ understand the extent to which financial reporting is regulated by national and international authorities;

■ understand the role and structure of the International Accounting Standards Board;

■ understand the ways in which international standards can interact with local regulatory frameworks.

41.1   Introduction

Financial reporting is entering a period of change. The use of International Financial Reporting Standards (IFRS) is fast becoming widespread throughout the world. In the UK we find that, while the large listed companies are adopting international standards, very few of the smaller companies, which make up 90 per cent or more of all companies in the EU, are following that route – using national standards instead.

National standards are moving closer to the international standards. This seems to indicate that at some point, national standards, such as here in the UK, will conform (harmonise) with international standards.

In Chapter 1 we listed the many users of financial statements. Today, as a result of the globalisation of world capital markets, these users have a need to read and understand financial statements from anywhere in the world. Because there are national financial reporting differences which makes reading and understanding of financial statements more difficult, this is not always possible. Differences are brought about because of differences in the national legal systems and the way in which business is financed. Language, tax usage and even accounting theory have all contributed to these differences.

It is therefore argued that all these differences and problems can be overcome by having a single worldwide accounting standard.

It is beyond the scope of this book to examine in any detail the reasons for these differences but it is nevertheless important to examine briefly what steps are being taken to reduce these differences. We can accept that there have been many significant changes, not least of which is the acceptance by the EU countries that a single reporting system is good.

41.2 Accounting practices

There are a great variety of practices throughout the world. Where no national accounting standards exist there could even be a variety of practices within the same country. Here in the UK, accounting is well regulated with uniform rules both from the Companies Act and from accounting standards of the Accounting Standards Board (ASB).

The Financial Reporting Council (FRC) in its report 'The State of Financial Reporting – a review' (November 1991, p. 36) stated:

> The variety of accounting practices around the world remains a major source of concern both for standard setters and for preparers and users of accounts. Multi-national companies increasingly look for consistency throughout all the countries in which they operate. Consistency reduces the internal costs of a multinational in collecting, processing and disseminating financial information. More significantly it makes for clear reporting of performance and financial position to an international audience of shareholders, creditors and potential investors. As the technical and political barriers to global capital markets are progressively eroded, the need for high quality universally understood financial reporting becomes even more insistent.

It is accepted that there should really be only one way of accounting for similar transactions throughout the world. Here in the UK, the ASB tries to align its standards with the International Accounting Standards Board (IASB). By doing this we find that adherence to UK standards results mainly in compliance with international standards.

41.3 Financial statements

We have seen that the annual accounts are prepared for many different user groups. Each of these groups places reliance on the reports to achieve their specific objective. Where reports are prepared for individual shareholders, who have no other source of information, much more detail is required than, for example, where board members are the users. In this latter instance directors are able to obtain information additional to that provided in the financial statements as they have access to internal financial information.

So why do we need a single set of accounting standards? Let us remind ourselves that data is reflected in the balance sheet, profit and loss account (income statement) and other financial statements. The way in which transactions and events are disclosed is by the use of a **measurement** policy. The extent of detail of disclosure is determined in the **disclosure** policy. These two policies are coupled together to form the **accounting** policy.

It is this accounting policy which can and does vary from company to company and group to group. This is the reason why there is the need to establish both measurement and disclosure harmonisation.

41.4 Accounting standard setters

As this is not intended to be a detailed section on standard setters we will only look at those in the UK and the international body.

41.4.1 Accounting Standards Board

Since 1960 the accounting profession in the UK has regulated ways of dealing with measurement, disclosure and presentation of financial information. Many methods were used, resulting in profit fluctuation between companies. This was caused by the method of presentation used by the companies and led to confusion and uncertainty for the users.

In December 1969 the Accounting Standards Steering Committee was formed by the Institute of Chartered Accountants in England and Wales (ICAEW). Other accountancy bodies joined over the next five years. This committee resulted in the creation, in 1976, of the Accounting Standards Committee (ASC).

In 1990 an independent Accounting Standards Board (ASB) took over. This is the body responsible for issuing accounting standards. These standards apply to all companies, and are intended to provide a true and fair view.

The ASB endorsed the existing Statements of Standard Accounting Practice (SSAPs) but started replacing them with Financial Reporting Standards (FRSs). It should be noted that most of these SSAPs (25 had been issued) have been replaced by FRSs.

Another important function of the ASB is its collaboration with the IASB and other national standard setters in developing international accounting standards.

As the main body, the professional staff of the Financial Reporting Council (FRC) supports all the operating bodies. The main aim of the FRC is to ensure a high quality of reporting which it does by setting standards and monitoring and enforcing accounting and auditing standards. All these functions are undertaken by the various operating bodies shown in Figure 41.1. Further details on the FRC and the operating bodies can be seen at www.frc.org.uk.

41.4.2 International Accounting Standards Board

In 1973, an organisation – the International Accounting Standards Committee (IASC) – was established with the object of harmonising standards on a worldwide basis.

From 1 April 2001 a new body, the IASB, was established and took over standard-setting responsibilities.

Figure 41.1 Current structure of the FRC

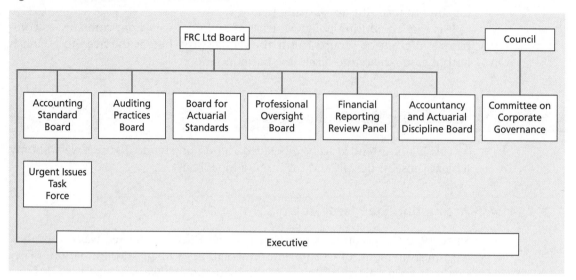

The IASB is an independent standard-setting body established with the purpose of introducing international standards so that convergence between countries could be made easier. This would reduce accounting costs and make the training of accountants easier.

This body adopted all previously issued International Accounting Standards (IASs) and is responsible for the development of new or revised International Financial Reporting Standards (IFRSs).[29]

The Board, like its UK counterpart, is in constant communication with standard setters and the accountancy profession throughout the world. In this way it hopes to achieve its objective – 'a single set of high quality, understandable and enforceable global accounting standards'.

41.5 Changes in terminology

As a result of the adoption of IASs certain changes have occurred in the terminology used. In the latest version of IAS 1 the titles 'balance sheet' and 'cash flow statement' have been changed to 'statement of financial position' and 'statement of cash flows' to describe two of the statements within a complete set of financial statements.

In the list below we have attempted to highlight the main changes brought about by the adoption of IASs.

---

[29] Until 2000 international standards were shown as IASs. After that date all new standards are IFRSs. The first IFRS was published in June 2003 (IFRS 1, First-time Adoption of International Financial Reporting Standards).

Current UK usage	International usage
Final accounts	Financial statements
Balance sheet	Statement of financial position
Fixed assets	Non-current assets
Land and buildings	Property
Goodwill, trademarks etc.	Intangible assets
Stock	Inventory
Debtors	Trade receivables
Prepayments	Other receivables
Current liabilities – Creditors: amounts due within 12 months	Current liabilities
Accruals	Other payables
Creditors	Trade payables
Long-term liabilities – Creditors: amounts falling due after more than one year	Non-current liabilities
Capital	Capital or shareholders' equity

Trading and profit and loss account	Income statement
Sales	Revenue
Cost of goods sold	Cost of sales
Sundry income	Other operating income
Sundry expenses (administration and distribution)	Other operating expenses
Interest payable	Finance costs
Interest receivable	Investment revenues or finance income
Net profit	Profit (before tax) for the year

41.6 Changes in financial statement presentation

IAS 1 lists the various statements required in a complete set of financial statements. These are:

(a) a statement of the financial position as at the end of the period;
(b) a statement of comprehensive income for the period;
(c) a statement of changes in equity for the period;
(d) a statement of cash flows for the period;
(e) notes to the accounts, comprising a summary of significant accounting policies and other explanatory information.

There is also an obligation on the entity to present 'with equal prominence' all of the above statements.

The UK wording of a 'true and fair view' is replaced by the requirement that financial statements shall 'present fairly' the financial position, financial performance and cash flows of an entity.

> Fair presentation requires the faithful representation of the effects of transactions, other events and conditions in accordance with the definitions and recognition criteria for assets, liabilities, income and expenses set out in the Framework. The application of IFRSs, with additional disclosure when necessary, is presumed to result in financial statements that achieve a fair presentation.

IAS 1 states that only an entity that complies with all the requirements of IFRSs is able to use the term 'present fairly'.

41.6.1 The statement of financial position

As can be expected, there are a number of changes in the way in which the final accounts (financial statements) are presented. To illustrate this we have taken a balance sheet from section 29.2.2 and used the international terms and layout.

Statement of financial position of Any Company plc as at 31 December 2009

Assets		
Non-current assets		
Intangible assets	25,000	
Tangible assets	60,000	85,000
Current assets		85,000
Inventory	40,000	
Trade receivables	10,000	
Other receivables	3,000	
Bank	7,000	
Cash	8,000	68,000
Total assets		153,000
Equity and liabilities		
Equity		
Ordinary shares	12,000	
Share premium account	4,000	
Revaluation reserves	18,000	
General reserves	60,000	
Retained earnings	20,000	114,000
Liabilities		
Non-current liabilities		
Bank loan		15,000
Current liabilities		
Trade payables	14,000	
Other payables	10,000	24,000
Total equity and liabilities		153,000

Besides the changes in terminology you will note that the balance sheet (statement of financial position) is presented in two parts. We still have our accounting equation but now it is more visible.

We have a total of all our assets (£153,000). We then have a total of our liabilities (current and non-current) amounting to £39,000. Our third part of the equation is the capital and here we have a total of £114,000.

41.6.2 Income statement

We now examine a profit and loss account (income statement). Here we have taken the one prepared in section 29.2.1 and amended it to conform to international standards.

Income statement for Any Company plc for the year ended 31 December 2009

Turnover		100,000
Cost of sales		38,000
Gross profit		62,000
Investment revenues		28,000
		90,000
Distribution costs	24,000	
Administration expenses	19,000	
Financial expenses	11,000	54,000
Profit before tax		36,000
Tax		14,000
Profit for the year attributable to equity holders		22,000

Cost of sales is made up of:	
Inventories 1 January 2009	34,000
Purchases	44,000
	78,000
Inventories 31 December 2009	40,000
Cost of sales	38,000

The earlier version of IAS 1 permitted disclosure in the **statement of changes in equity**, or in the notes, of the amount of dividends paid to equity holders (now referred to as 'owners') and the related amount per share. The amended IAS 1 requires dividends recognised as distributions to owners and related amounts per share to be presented in the **statement of changes in equity** or in the notes. This is illustrated below:

Statement of changes in equity

Balance 1 January 2009	142,000
Profit for the year	22,000
	164,000
Dividends paid*	9,000
Balance at 31 December 2009	155,000

* It should be noted that only dividends paid in the financial year will be shown in the accounts. This means that we show the previous year's proposed final dividend and the current year's interim dividend. The proposed final dividend for the current year is subject to approval by shareholders at the AGM and therefore has not been included as a liability in the year-end statements.

Also included under this heading would be any new issues of shares and any unrealised profits, for example an upward revaluation of property.

41.6.3 Statement of cash flows

The statement of cash flows reports on cash flows during the period. In doing so it groups flows into three categories – operating, investing and financing activities.

- **Operating activities** are the main revenue-producing activities of the entity. The cash flows shown here are derived from the principal revenue-producing activities of the entity.
- **Investing activities** are the acquisition and disposal of long-term assets and other investments not included in cash equivalents (see later).
- **Financing activities** are activities that result in changes in the size and composition of the equity and borrowings of the entity.

At the end of the statement of cash flows, disclosure is made of cash and cash equivalents at the year end, which must agree with the balance sheet (statement of financial position) amounts.

The following is an example of a statement of cash flows as required by IAS 7:

Cash flows from operating activities

Profit for the year	8,798
Income tax expense recognised in profit or loss	1,312
Investment revenue recognised in profit or loss	(1,004)
Gain on disposal of property, plant and equipment	(82)
Depreciation and amortisation of non-current assets	11,579
Movements in working capital	
Increase in trade and other receivables	(4,877)
(Increase)/decrease in inventories	(6,882)
Increase in other assets	(98)
Decrease in trade and other payables	(1,022)
Increase/(decrease) in provisions	548
(Decrease)/increase in other liabilities	(154)
Cash generated from operations	8,118
Interest paid	(1,760)
Income taxes paid	(2,570)
Net cash generated by operating activities	3,788

Cash flows from investing activities

Payments to acquire financial assets	(3,000)
Proceeds on sale of financial assets	1,102
Interest received	2,115
Dividends received	90
Payments for property, plant and equipment	(12,680)
Proceeds from disposal of property, plant and equipment	7,400
Payments for intangible assets	(984)
Net cash (used in)/generated by investing activities	(5,957)

Cash flows from financing activities

Proceeds from issue of equity shares	2,344
Payment for share issue costs	(87)
Proceeds from issue of redeemable preference shares	10,000
Proceeds from borrowings	12,400
Repayment of borrowings	(21,742)
Dividends paid on redeemable cumulative preference shares	(980)
Dividends paid to owners of the Company	(8,774)
Net cash used in financing activities	(6,839)
Net decrease in cash and cash equivalents	(9,008)
Cash and cash equivalents at the beginning of the year	12,480
Cash and cash equivalents at the end of the year	3,472

Note: The above example illustrates the indirect method of reporting cash flows from operating activities.

41.7 International Accounting Standards

A number of examination boards have introduced International Accounting Standards into their syllabus. At this stage a basic knowledge of IAS 7, dealing with the important report on cash flow is required. In addition the presentation of financial statements as set out in IAS 1 is important and should be studied where international accounting forms part of the syllabus. Both these standards can be found on the web site of the IASB (www.iasb.org). In addition there is a site (www.iasplus.com) created by Deloitte, where summaries of IASs can be found.

It is useful to list some of the topics dealt with by the IASB and link them to the UK equivalent.

IAS	Topic	UK equivalent
IAS 1	Presentation of financial statements	FRS 3
IAS 2	Inventories (stocks)	SSAP 9
IAS 7	Statements of cash flows	FRS 1
IAS 8	Accounting policies	FRS 18
IAS 10	Events after balance sheet date	SSAP 17
IAS 16	Property, plant and equipment	FRS 15

While no detailed knowledge (except for IAS 7) is currently required, any examination candidate should be able to explain and comment on the purpose and importance of the international standards.

These standards do not alter the way in which accounting is recorded. The accounting concepts of going concern, accruals, consistency and materiality still apply, as do those of prudence, business entity, measurement, historical cost and duality.

41.7.1 Self-test

Explain the need to have an international accounting standard setter.

41.7.2 Self-test

A company reporting under IASB rules pays dividends to its owners. Where are these dividends shown?

(a) Income statement
(b) Statement of financial position
(c) Statement of cash flows
(d) Statement of changes in equity

41.7.3 Self-test

Which of the following items are shown in the statement of cash flows?

(a) Dividends paid
(b) Revaluation of non-current assets
(c) A rights issue of shares
(d) A bonus issue of shares

41.7.4 Self-test

Camden Trading Ltd. Using the answers from section 29.2.10 you are required to prepare the income statement and the statement of financial position for the company in compliance with international standards.

41.7.5 Self-test

Hilmor Ltd. You have prepared the final accounts for the company based on the information given in section 29.2.7. You are now told that the company wishes to report using IASB standards.

Using the information available you are required to:

(a) prepare the income statement;
(b) the statement of financial position, and
(c) the statement of changes in equity for the company.

41.7.6 Self-test

Hasta is an antique dealer operating from rented premises. He keeps few accounting records. All his sales and purchases are for cash, except for some sales to other dealers which are made on credit.

The following information is available to prepare his income statement for the year ended 31 December 2006.

Assets and liabilities $	As at 31 December	
	2005	2006
Equipment	1,200	2,000
Inventory	85,000	88,500
Trade receivables	4,800	6,400
Payable for expenses	1,100	1,400

Cash summary

2006			2006		
1 Jan	Balance – float	100	31 Dec	Wages for assistant	15,600
31 Dec	Cash from sales	191,400		Sundry expenses	8,300
	Proceeds of sale of			Purchases of new	
	equipment	700		equipment	2,000
				Purchases	?
				Drawings	?
				Balance – float	150
		192,200			192,200

Hasta keeps cash that is in hand at the end of each week as drawings, subject to the retention of the float. No record has been made of payments for purchases of goods for sale. He fixes his selling price for all items by doubling their cost. He allowed a trade discount of $9,000, representing 30% on selling price, for sales to dealers with a normal price of $30,000. ($30,000 less $9,000 discount = $21,000).

All the equipment held at the beginning of the year was sold for $700, and new equipment purchased for $2,000.

A full year's depreciation is to be charged on the new equipment at 20%, with no depreciation on the items sold.

Required:

(a) Prepare Hasta's income statement for the year ended 31 December 2006.
 Your answer should include a detailed calculation of cost of sales.
(b) Calculate Hasta's drawings for the year ended 31 December 2006.

(ACCA Preparing Financial Statements (International Stream) June 2007)

41.7.7 Self-test

The receivables ledger control account of Atanga at 31 December 2006 shows a debit balance of $487,600. The list of receivables ledger balances at the same date totalled $455,800 debit. There were no credit balances.

On investigation the following errors and revisions were found:

1. The sales day book had been overcast by $2,000.
2. A debt of $8,400 is to be written off.
3. A credit note for $1,200 was entered on the debit side of the customer's account.
4. Contras against amounts owing to Atanga in the payables ledger totalling $16,100 were entered on the debit side of the receivables ledger control account.
5. A credit note for $5,600 sent to a customer and recorded at that figure should have been for $4,500.
6. Cash discount allowed and agreed at $150 has not been recorded in the accounting system.

Required:

(a) Prepare a statement showing the necessary adjustments to the receivables ledger control account balance.
(b) Prepare a statement showing the necessary adjustments to the total of the list of receivables ledger balances.

(ACCA Preparing Financial Statements (International Stream) June 2007)

41.7.8 Self test

Hathan has just concluded a ratio analysis comparing its performance and position at 31 December 2006 with those at 31 December 2005. The directors are concerned to see that the current ratio and quick ratio show a considerable decline.

Required:

(a) State and explain TWO possible causes for the decline in one or both of these ratios.
(b) State and explain TWO ways in which the company could improve these ratios.

(ACCA Preparing Financial Statements (International Stream) June 2007)

Appendix 1

Self-test answers

Preface to Appendix 1

This appendix contains suggested answers to the self-test questions in the various chapters of the textbook. Where answers are not provided you can often find answers on the website of the relevant body. Each question is clearly marked indicating its origin.

If there are questions where your answers are different to the solution given, you are advised to check the answers thoroughly and to reattempt the question at a later stage. It is only through practice that students can learn the methods of accounting and apply what you have read in the text.

Students need to be well prepared for their exams and this is only achieved by reading the chapters *and* working through all the self-test questions.

Make sure you understand what is asked for in the exam questions. There are certain terms commonly used by examiners and to gain good marks you need to answer the question in response to what was asked and not what you think the examiner would like to hear. Also, you are reminded that workings are vital to all answers and should be shown. You can often gain additional marks by showing the workings even when the numeric answer is incorrect.

Read through the list of terms below and make sure that you understand what the examiner is asking. If you do not answer what is asked for, you cannot expect to gain any marks!

Advise means you need to consider the information given in the question and use this to arrive at a decision. If calculation is required then that must be used to advise.

Analyse requires a descriptive answer. You would need to argue both for and against a situation. Using this analysis you may be asked to **assess** the information which then requires a conclusion.

Calculate asks you to mathematically find an answer. Show your workings. All too often this is not done and many marks are lost. If you make an error in your calculations and the examiner can see it in the workings you will still get a part score. You may be asked to comment on the calculations in which case analyse what you have calculated and then arrive at a conclusion.

Discuss requires both sides of a problem to be considered and a conclusion to be reached.

Evaluate is where you consider all the information of a question and make a decision using your own opinion.

Explain is often used in a question. This requires you to use your own words to define whatever is asked. It is always a good idea to try to give an example in addition to your definition or description.

If you are asked to **recommend** then you need to consider the facts given to you and advise on a course of action to be taken.

Chapter 1

1.7.1 Self-test

Reasons for preparing accounts are set out in detail in section 1.5.

1.7.2 Self-test

Users of accounts are listed in detail in the subparagraphs of section 1.6.

1.7.3 Self-test

Three key words are:

- the **recording** function;
- the ability to **measure**; and
- the **communication** of results.

1.7.4 Self-test

The divisions of accounting are:

- financial accounting and
- management accounting.

Section 1.4 describes each area.

Chapter 2

2.4.2 Self-test

Identify the following:	Asset	Liability
(a) Delivery vehicle	✓	
(b) Bank loan		✓
(c) Stock	✓	
(d) Cash on hand	✓	
(e) Creditors		✓
(f) Debtors	✓	
(g) Office equipment	✓	
(h) Cash at bank	✓	

Identify the following:	Expense	Income
(a) Rent received		✓
(b) Telephone charges	✓	
(c) Sales		✓
(d) Wages & salaries	✓	
(e) Commission paid	✓	
(f) Advertising costs	✓	
(g) Rent payable	✓	
(h) Purchases	✓	

2.4.3 Self-test

Does a debit item:	Yes	No
(a) decrease capital	✓	
(b) decrease income	✓	
(c) decrease liabilities	✓	
(d) decrease assets		✓
(f) decrease expenses		✓

Does a credit item:	Yes	No
(a) increase capital	✓	
(b) increase income	✓	
(c) increase liabilities	✓	
(d) increase assets		✓
(e) increase expenses		✓

2.5.1 Self-test

Transactions	General ledger	Sales ledger	Purchase ledger
Cash sales	✓		
Rent	✓		
Bank	✓		
Credit purchases			✓
Credit sales		✓	
Wages paid	✓		
Rent received	✓		

2.6.2 Self-test

Mark's ledger

Bank account

25 Mar	Capital	30,000	25 Mar	Rent	2,000
7 Apr	Cash	600	25 Mar	Purchases	7,100
			25 Mar	Fittings	2,900
			25 Mar	Motor Van	7,400
			1 Apr	Advertisement	150
			2 Apr	Rent	2,000
			7 Apr	Balance c/d	9,050
		30,600			30,600
8 Apr	Balance b/d	9,050			

Rent account

25 Mar	Bank	2,000	
2 Apr	Bank	2,000	

Shop fittings account

25 Mar	Bank	2,900		

Purchases account

25 Mar	Bank	7,100		
25 Mar	Tennis Ltd	3,400		
6 Apr	Tennis Ltd	1,500		

Motor van

25 Mar	Bank	7,400		

Advertising

1 Apr	Bank	150		

Sales

			3 Apr	Cash	150
			4 Apr	Cash	210
			5 Apr	Cash	80
			6 Apr	Cash	153
			7 Apr	Cash	197

Cash account

3 Apr	Sales	150	7 Apr	Bank	600
4 Apr	Sales	210	7 Apr	Wages	120
5 Apr	Sales	80	7 Apr	Balance c/d	70
6 Apr	Sales	153			
7 Apr	Sales	197			
		790			790
8 Apr	Balance b/d	70			

Wages

7 Apr	Cash	120		

Tennis Ltd

			25 Mar	Purchases	3,400
			6 Apr	Purchases	1,500

Capital

			25 Mar	Bank	30,000

To prove the duality of the transactions we would extract a trial balance. This would show that our total debits are equal to our total credits. We continue this part of the question in section 15.1.2 self-test.

2.6.3 Self-test

Larry's ledger

Bank

1/9/09	Capital	40,000	2/9/09	Purchases	26,000
19/9/09	Acquire	8,000	4/9/09	Insurance	980
			27/9/09	Wages	1,100
				Drawings	2,000
			30/9/09	Balance c/d	17,920
		48,000			48,000
1/10/09	Balance b/d	17,920			

Capital

			1/9/09	Bank	40,000

Drawings

27/9/09	Bank	2,000			

Purchases

2/9/09	Bank	26,000			

Insurance

4/9/09	Bank	980			

Packing material

10/9/09	Upack	1,200			

Upack

			10/9/09	Packing	1,200

Wages

27/9/09	Bank	1,100			

Sales

28/9/09	Okay	1,900	12/9/09	Acquire	12,900
30/9/09	Balance c/d	16,300	25/9/09	Okay	5,300
		18,200			18,200
			1/10/09	Balance b/d	16,300

Acquire

12/9/09	Sales	12,900	19/9/09	Bank	8,000
			30/9/09	Balance c/d	4,900
		12,900			12,900
1/10/09	Balance b/d	4,900			

Okay

25/9/09	Sales	5,300	25/9/09	Returns	1,900
			30/9/09	Balance c/d	3,400
		5,300			5,300
1/10/09	Balance b/d	3,400			

To prove the duality of the transactions we would extract a trial balance. This would show that our total debits are equal to our total credits. We continue this part of the question in section 15.1.3 self-test

2.6.4 Self-test

J Cecil's ledger

Capital – J Cecil

			1/7/09	Bank	20,000

Drawings

31/7/09	Bank	1,500

Sales

			15/7/09	Bank	1,200
			24/7/09	Debtors – Monica	3,100

Wages

17/7/09	Bank	600
31/7/09	Bank	1,350

Debtor – Monica

24/7/09	Sales	3,100	28/7/09	Bank	1,350

Fixtures and fittings

12/7/09	Bank	3,700

Delivery truck

11/7/09	Bank	7,000
	MotoTrade	8,000

Creditor – Hilcom Gifts

			16/7/09	Purchases	1,240

Insurance

14/7/09	Bank	750

Purchases

| 14/7/09 | Bank | 885 | |
| 16/7/09 | Creditor | 1,240 | |

MotoTrade

| | | | 11/7/09 | Van | 8,000 |

Telephone

| 27/7/09 | Bank | 1,205 | |

Gas

| 27/7/09 | Bank | 173 | |

Bank

1/7/09	Capital	20,000	10/7/09	Rent	900
15/7/09	Sales	1,200	11/7/09	Truck – MotoTrade	7,000
28/7/09	Debtor – Monica	1,350	12/7/09	F&F	3,700
			14/7/09	Purchases	885
				Insurance	750
			17/7/09	Wages	600
			27/7/09	Phone	1,205
				Gas	173
			31/7/09	Wages	1,350
				Drawings	1,500
				Balance c/d	4,487
		22,550			22,550
1/8/09	Balance b/d	4,487			

Rent

| 10/7/09 | Bank | 900 | |

2.6.5 Self-test

Jack's ledger

Capital – Jack

| | | | 5/6/09 | Bank | 15,000 |

Drawings

| 30/6/09 | Bank | 500 | |

Rent

5/6/09	Bank	1,950			

NuVan Ltd

30/6/09	Balance c/d	6,810	8/6/09	Motor car	6,500
			24/6/09	Motor exp	310
		6,810			6,810
			1/7/09	Balance b/d	6,810

Purchases

10/6/09	Bank	725	30/6/09	Balance c/d	1,315
28/6/09	Bank	590			
		1,315			1,315
1/7/09	Balance b/d	1,315			

Insurance

20/6/09	Bank	725			

A Lu (Debtor)

22/6/09	Sales	1,950	30/6/09	Bank	1,200
				Balance c/d	750
		1,950			1,950
1/7/09	Balance b/d	750			

Motor expenses

24/6/09	NuVan Ltd	310			

Sundry expenses

29/6/09	Bank	195			

Gas and electricity

29/6/09	Bank	490			

Motor car

8/6/09	Bank	9,500	30/6/09	Balance c/d	16,000
	NuVan	6,500			
		16,000			16,000
1/7/09	Balance b/d	16,000			

Bank

5/6/09	Capital	15,000	5/6/09	Rent		1,950
12/6/09	Sales	1,600	8/6/09	Motor car		9,500
26/6/09	Sales	1,650	10/6/09	Purchases		725
30/6/09	A Lu	1,200	15/6/09	Wages		800
			20/6/09	Insurance		725
			28/6/09	Purchases		590
			29/6/09	Gas & elect		490
				Sundry exp		195
			30/6/09	Wages		200
				File & Co		1,500
				Drawings		500
			30/6/09	Balance c/d		2,275
		19,450				19,450
1/7/09	Balance b/d	2,275				

Sales

30/6/09	Balance c/d	5,200	12/6/09	Bank	1,600
			22/6/09	A Lu	1,950
			26/6/09	Bank	1,650
		5,200			5,200
			1/7/09	Balance b/d	5,200

Office equipment

7/6/09	File & Co	6,250	

Wages

15/6/09	Bank	800	30/6/09	Balance c/d	1,000
30/6/09	Bank	200			
		1,000			1,000
1/7/09	Balance b/d	1,000			

File & Co (Creditor)

30/6/09	Bank	1,500	7/6/09	Off equip	6,250
	Balance c/d	4,750			
		6,250			6,250
			1/7/09	Balance b/d	4,750

To prove the duality of the transactions we would extract a trial balance. This would show that our total debits are equal to our total credits. We continue this part of the question in section 15.1.2 self-test.

2.6.6 Self-test

Ledger account title	Debit	Credit
Creditors		✓
Capital		✓
Loan from bank		✓
Postages	✓	
Drawings	✓	
Liability		✓
Revenue		✓
Fixed asset	✓	

Chapter 3

3.1.1 Self-test

Oliver's ledger

Bank

Capital	11,000	Drawings	9,000
A Turner – loan	7,000	Creditors	15,300
Debtors	12,500	Expenses	7,900
Sales	9,400	Purchases	21,900
Balance c/d	32,200	Motor Car	18,000
	72,100		72,100
		Balance b/d	32,200

Debtors

Sales	32,000	Bank	12,500
		Sales returns	325
		Balance c/d	19,175
	32,000		32,000
Balance b/d	19,175		

Creditors

Bank	15,300	Purchases	34,200
Return	197		
Balance c/d	18,703		
	34,200		34,200
		Balance b/d	18,703

Purchases

Bank	21,900	Puchases return	197
Creditors	34,200	Balance c/d	55,903
	56,100		56,100
Balance b/d	55,903		

Sales				
Returns	325	Bank		9,400
Balance c/d	41,075	Debtors		32,000
	41,400			41,400
		Balance b/d		41,075

3.1.2 Self-test

Ann's ledger

Bank					.
1/7/09	Capital	40,000	10/7/09	Rent	1,900
15/7/09	Sales	3,587	11/7/09	Computer	2,100
28/7/09	Debtor	2,984	12/7/09	Phone	156
31/7/09	Interest	143	14/7/09	Purchases	1,123
	Sales	1,988		Drawings	1,200
			17/7/09	Wages	950
			27/7/09	Printer	287
				Electricity	342
			31/7/09	Wages	1,980
				Insurance	3,500
				Balance c/d	35,164
		48,702			48,702
1/8/09	Balance b/d	35,164			

3.1.3 Self-test

Cash account					
1 Sept 09	Loan	4,000	10 Sept 09	Wages	1,000
15 Sept 09	Sales	2,000	11 Sept 09	Rent	2,000
			30 Sept 09	Balance c/d	3,000
		6,000			6,000
1 Oct 09	Balance bd	3,000	12 Oct 09	Postages	100
28 Oct 09	Commission	500	31 Oct 09	Balance c/d	4,250
31 Oct 09	Interest	850			
		4,350			4,350
1 Nov 09	Balance b/d	4,250	14 Nov 09	Purchases	2,300
11 Nov 09	Sales	2,300	19 Nov 09	Wages	500
			24 Nov 09	Purchases	900
			27 Nov 09	Rent	1,000
				Balance c/d	1,850
		6,550			6,550
1 Dec 09	Balance b/d	1,850			

Purchases

14 Nov 09	Cash book	100	30 Nov 09	Balance c/d	1,000
24 Nov 09	Cash book	900			
		1,000			1,000
1 Dec 09	Balance c/d	1,000			

Wages

10 Sept 09	Cash book	1,000	30 Nov 09	Balance c/d	1,500
19 Nov 09	Cash book	500			
		1,500			1,500
1 Dec 09	Balance c/d	1,500			

3.2.1 Self-test

Marge's ledger

Bank

1/3/09	Capital	10,000	1/3/09	Rent	500
11/3/09	Sales	21,500	8/3/09	Gift W/saler	1,000
			29/3/09	Drawings	1,000
			30/3/09	Motor exp	1,900
				Sundry exp	1,050
				Salaries	4,000
			31/3/09	Balance c/d	22,050
		31,500			31,500
1/4/09	Balance b/d	22,050			

Drawings

29/3/09	Bank	1,000			

Capital

			1/3/09	Bank	10,000

Rent

1/3/09	Bank	500			

Purchases

3/3/09	Gift W/saler	2,900			

Gift Wholesalers

8/3/09	Bank	1,000	3/3/09	Purchases		2,900
31/3/09	Balance c/d	1,900				
		2,900				2,900
			1/4/09	Balance b/d		1,900

Sales

		11/3/09	Bank	21,500

Motor expenses

30/3/09	Bank	1,900

Salaries

30/3/09	Bank	4,000

Sundry expenses

30/3/09	Bank	1,050

The total revenue recorded = £21,500.
Total expenses = 500 + 2,900 + 1,900 + 4,000 + 1,050 = £10,350.
Net Income = 21,500 − 10,350 = £11,150.

Chapter 4

4.5.1 Self-test

Green's ledger

Cash book

	Discount allowed	Cash	Bank		Discount received	Cash	Bank
Balance b/d		123	482	Wages		145	
Lite	8		98	Walker	18		178
Noble	13	87		Sharp	2		25
King	15		165	Transfer Bank		64	
Transfer Cash			64	Bank charges			41
				Balance c/d		1	565
	36	210	809		20	210	809
Balance b/d		1	565				

The discount allowed of £36 is posted to the debit of discount allowed and the credit of debtors. The discount received is debited to creditors and credited to discount received. Remember that the discount columns are only memorandum columns and therefore must be entered twice – once as a debit and once as a credit.

Note that dates have not been shown in this suggested answer due to space limitations. In all your work dates must be shown.

4.5.2 Self-test

Walker's cash book

		Discount allowed	Cash	Bank		Discount received	Cash	Bank
3/7/9	Jacks			320	Purchases		60	
6/7/9	Sales		220		Petty cash		195	
11/7/9	Jacks	18		222	Wages		185	
15/7/9	Martha	30		420	Telephone			48
19/7/9	Sales		430		Purchases			140
21/7/9	Martha	37		149	Tom & Co.	30		170
28/7/9	Sales		172		Green Bros	25		165
	Transfer		340		Purchases			245
					Transfer			340
					Balance c/d		722	3
		85	1,162	1,111		55	1,162	1,111
1/8/9	Balance b/d		722	3				

Chapter 5

5.3.2 Self-test

A Broad's cash book

		Cash book				
3/7/09	Sales	878	1/7/09	Balance b/d	3,100
15/7/09	Cash sale	224	5/7/09	Chq 121	700
31/7/09	Sales	1,435	29/7/09	Chq 122	432
	Balance c/d	2,540	30/7/09	Chq 123	670
			31/7/09	Unpaid cheque	150
				Bank charges	25
		5,077			5,077
			1/8/09	Balance b/d	2,540

Reconciliation statement

Overdraft per cash book		2,540
Less unpresented cheques – 122	432	
123	670	1,102
		1,438
Plus outstanding banking		1,435
Overdraft per bank statement		2,873

Note: the reconciliation can be started using the bank overdraft and working down to the cash book overdraft.

5.3.3 Self-test

Enid

(a) Additional cash book entries:

Cash book balance	164	
Add credit transfer	65	229
Less standing order	26	
Bank charges	18	44
Revised cash book balance at 1/3/09		185

(b) **Reconciliation statement**

Balance per cash book		185
Plus outstanding cheques:		
No. 337	110	
No. 339	401	511
		696
Less outstanding deposit		85
Balance per bank statement		611

5.3.4 Self-test

Michael

Cash book

1/5/09	Balance b/d	332	1/5/06	118	Steve	235
11/5/09	Sales	518		119	Wilcox	102
18/5/09	Dividends	600		120	Adams	136
				121	Nigel	340
				D. Debit	Insurance	78
			31/5/09		Balance c/d	559
		1,450				1,450
1/6/09	Balance b/d	559				

Reconciliation statement

Balance per cash book		559
Plus outstanding cheques:		
No. 118	235	
No. 120	136	371
Balance per bank statement		930

Chapter 6

6.2.1 Self-test

Josh

Petty cash for June 2009

Date	Receipts	Details	Total	Cleaning	Postage	Travel	Office
1 June	230	Cash					
		Stamps	25		25		
2 June		Travel	48			48	
3 June		Stationery	37				37
		Travel	26		26		
4 June		Stamps	38		38		
		Stationery	24				24
5 June		Cleaning	14	14			
6 June		Travel	12			12	
	224	Cash					
		Bal c/d	230				
	454	Total	454	14	63	86	61
7 June	230	Bal b/d					

6.2.2 Self-test

Jenny

Petty cash for November 2009

Date	Receipts	Details	Total	Stationery	Wages	Postage	Purchases
1 Nov	81	Bal b/d					
2 Nov	319	Cash					
6 Nov		Envelopes	23	23			
		Wages	87		87		
11 Nov		Stamps	41			41	
17 Nov		Purchases	87				87
24 Nov		Wages	87		87		
30 Nov		Stationery	25	25			
		Bal c/d	50				
	400	Total	400	48	174	41	87
1 Dec	50	Bal b/d					
	350	Cash					

6.2.3 Self-test

Jacques

Petty cash for July 2009

	Receipts	Details	Total	Wages	Postage	Purchases	Stationery
1 July	31	Bal b/d					
	469	Cash					
3 July		Wages	53	53			
5 July		Postage	36		36		
7 July		Purchases	63			63	
11 July		Envelopes	12				12
17 July		Purchases	19			19	
22 July		Wages	61	61			
24 July		Postage	3		3		
26 July		Stationery	13				13
30 July		Purchases	29			29	
31 July		Postage	8		8		
		Bal c/d	203				
	500	Total	500	114	47	111	25
1 Aug	203	Bal b/d					
	297	Cash					

Chapter 7

7.5.1 Self-test

Dani & Co.

VAT

31 July	Purchases	1,200	31 July	Sales	1,800
31 Aug	Purchases	1,600	31 Aug	Sales	2,000
30 Sept	Purchases	1,800	30 Sept	Sales	3,000
	Balance c/d	2,200			
		6,800			6,800
				Balance b/d	2,200

The firm has collected in £6,800 in VAT through sales and paid out £4,600 when purchasing goods. Therefore it owes £2,200 to HMRC. This is shown as a credit balance in the VAT account.

7.5.2 Self-test

Martha

Note: although the question does not require you to prepare day books, these have been shown here to assist you in understanding the entries in the VAT account.

Purchase day book

Date	Supplier	Net amount	VAT	Total of invoice
July 2009	Clothes & Co.	3,840.00	547.20	4,387.20
	Jeans & Co.	260.00	37.05	297.05
	Totals	4,100.00	584.25	4,684.25

Returns outwards day book

Date	Supplier	Net amount	VAT	Total of return
July 2009	Jeans & Co.	94.00	14.10	108.10
	Totals	94.00	14.10	108.10

Sales day book

Date	Customer	Net amount	VAT	Total of invoice
July 2009	Mrs Green	820.00	*119.31	939.31
	Miss Wydham	650.00	*94.57	744.57
	Totals	1,470.00	213.88	1,683.88

* VAT is calculated on the basis of the invoice value less the cash discount.

VAT

31 July 09	Purchases	584.25	31 July 09	Credit sales	213.88
				Purchase returns	14.10
				Balance c/d	256.27
		584.25			584.25
1 Aug 09	Balance b/d*	256.27			

* This amount is due to Martha by HMRC. As VAT is not accounted for on a monthly basis the balance is carried down to the following month.

7.5.3 Self-test

Decker & Co.

Note: although the question does not require you to prepare day books, these have been shown here to assist you in understanding the entries in the VAT account.

Sales day book

Date	Inv No.	Customer	Net	VAT	Inv total
11 July	407	Nudeal Supplies	3,150.00	425.25	3,575.25
13 July	408	Executive Offices	2,850.00	427.50	3,277.50
19 July	409	Fashion Desks	6,300.00	945.00	7,245.00
27 July	410	Executive Offices	5,700.00	855.00	6,555.00
		Total for month	18,000.00	2,652.75	20,652.75

Sales returns day book

Date	C/N No.	Customer	Net	VAT	C/N total
20 Jul		Executive Offices	1,050.00	157.50	1,207.50
24 Jul		Fashion Desks	465.00	69.75	534.75
		Total for month	1,515.00	227.25	1,742.25

VAT

31 July 09	Sales returns	227.25	31 July 09	Sales day book	2,652.75

Nudeal Supplies

31 Jul 09	Sales	3,575.25	31 Jul 09	Cash	3,260.25
				Discount	315.00
		3,575.25			3,575.25

Chapter 8

8.3.2 Self-test

Julian

Purchase day book

Date	Supplier	Net amount	VAT	Total of invoice
5/7/09	Jay & Co.	£260	£39	£299
8/7/09	T Williams	£660	£99	£759
21/7/09	H Henry	£540	£81	£621
26/7/09	J Jones	£200	£30	£230
29/7/09	Green & Co.	£900	£135	£1,035
		£2,560	£384	£2,944

Each supplier will be credited with the total invoiced amount. Purchases will be debited with £2,560 and VAT debited with £384.

Purchase returns book

Date	Supplier	Net amount	VAT	Total of credit note
2/7/09	H Henry	£140	£21	£161
23/7/09	J Jones	£80	£12	£92
		£220	£33	£253

Each supplier will be debited with the total of the credit note. Purchases will be credited with £220 and VAT with £33.

8.3.3 Self-test

Leon

Purchases day book

Date	Supplier	Net amount
3.3.09	Jay	914
6.3.09	Emma	432
8.3.09	Jay	317
18.3.09	Jay	204
22.3.09	Emma	543
25.3.09	Henry	802
31.3.09	Jay	167
	Total March 2009	3,379

Purchases returns journal

Date	Supplier	Net amount
6.3.09	Jay	106
31.3.09	Jay	198
	Total March 2009	304

Purchases

18.3.09	Cash	123	18.3.09	Returns	119
22.3.09	Carriage in	169	26.3.09	Returns	105
31.3.09	Purchase journal	3,379		Discount received	182
			31.3.09	Purchase returns	304
				Balance c/d	2,961
		3,671			3,671
1.4.09	Balance b/d	2,961			

8.3.4 Self-test

Norman

Purchase day book

Date	Supplier	Net amount	VAT	Total of invoice
3/8/09	Jay & Co.	1,200	180	1,380
6/8/09	T Williams	1,400	210	1,610
8/8/09	Green & Co.	1,000	150	1,150
18/8/09	Jay & Co.	400	60	460
22/8/09	Jay & Co.	500	75	575
25/8/09	H Henry	800	120	920
31/8/09	T Williams	1,800	270	2,070
	TOTALS	£7,100	£1,065	£8,165

Purchase returns book

Date	Supplier	Net amount	VAT	Total of credit note
6/8/09	Jay & Co.	400	60	460
31/8/09	Jay & Co.	120	18	138
	TOTALS	£520	£78	£598

VAT

31/08/09	Purchases	1,065	31/08/09	Purchases returns	78

Purchases

31/8/09	Creditors	7,100	31/8/09	Creditors	520
				Balance c/d	6,580
		7,100			7,100
1/9/09	Balance b/d	6,580			

Chapter 9

9.2.2 Self-test

Leon

Sales day book

Date	Customer	Net amount
6.3.09	Dee	375
11.3.09	Gert	192
12.3.09	Henry	109
26.3.09	Gert	147
29.3.09	Gert	314
31.3.09	Henry	719
	Total March 2009	1,856

Sales

6.3.09	Returns	114	6.3.09	Cash sales	874
31.3.09	Balance c/d	2,616	31.3.09	Sales journal	1,856
		2,730			2,730
			1.4.09	Balance b/d	2,616

9.2.3 Self-test

Norman

Sales day book

Date	Invoice No.	Customer	Net amount	VAT	Total of invoice
5/8/09		Jacques	2,400	360	2,760
11/8/09		William	1,600	240	1,840
12/8/09		George	440	66	506
26/8/09		George	1,440	216	1,656
29/8/09		Henry	860	129	989
31/8/09		William	640	96	736
		TOTALS	**£7,380**	**£1,107**	**£8,487**

Sales returns book

Date	Credit Note No.	Customer	Net amount	VAT	Total of credit note
18/8/09		George	240	36	276
26/8/09		William	480	72	552
		TOTALS	**£720**	**£108**	**£828**

Sales

31/8/09	Sales returns	720	31/8/09	Sales journal	7,380
	Balance c/d	6,660			
		7,380			7,380
			1/9/09	Balance b/d	6,660

VAT

31/8/09	Sales returns	108	31/8/09	Sales	1,107
	Balance c/d	999			
		1,107			1,107
			1/9/09	Balance b/d	999

Chapter 10

10.4.1 Self-test

Gerta

Sales ledger (debtors) control account

1 May	Balance b/d	6,035	31 May	Returns	1,176
31 May	Sales journal	29,549		Bank	13,800
	Bank – unpaid	622		Discount allowed	1,003
				Bad debts	974
				Balance c/d	19,253
		36,206			36,206
1 June	Balance b/d	19,253			

10.7.1 Self-test

Nicholas

Creditors' control account

30 June	Bank	4,996	1 June	Balance b/d	8,512
	Discount received	711	30 June	Purchases	7,190
	Returns	657			
	Debtors – contra	755			
	Balance c/d	8,583			
		15,702			15,702
			1 July	Balance b/d	8,583

10.7.2 Self-test

Trudie

Purchase ledger control account

30 June	Bank	10,622	1 June	Balance b/d		9,843
	Discount received	255	30 June	Purchases		12,992
	Returns out	681				
	Balance c/d	11,277				
		22,835				22,835
			1 July	Balance b/d		11,277

Sales ledger control account

1 June	Balance b/d	6,488	30 June	Returns in	790
30 June	Sales	19,745		Discount allowed	1,003
	Unpaid cheque	147		Bad debts	780
				Bank	5,933
				Balance c/d	17,874
		26,380			26,380
1 July	Balance b/d	17,874			

10.7.3 Self-test

Hellenco Trading

Debtors' control account

1/4/08	Balance b/d	22,060	31/3/09	Contra – creditors	904
31/3/09	Sales	153,900		Returns inwards	2,050
	Contra account	196		Cheques	92,282
	Interest	68		Discount allowed	4,160
	Balance c/d	6,107		Bad debts	1,901
				Balance c/d	81,034
		182,331			182,331
1/4/09	Balance b/d	81,034	1/4/09	Balance b/d	6,107

10.7.4 Self-test

Katie

Debtors' control account

1/7/09	Balance b/d	23,105	30/6/10	Bank	42,033
30/6/10	Sales	104,500		Returns inwards	16,430
				Bad debts	5,910
				Discount allowed	6,230
				Contra – creditors	3,021
				Balance c/d	53,981
		127,605			127,605
1/7/10	Balance b/d	53,981			

The balance on the debtors' control account is calculated after all items have been posted to this ledger account.

Creditors' control account

30/6/10	Bank	41,206	1/7/09	Balance b/d	19,714
	Returns outwards	12,120	30/6/10	Purchases	77,390
	Contra – debtors	3,021		Cash refund	3,104
	Discount received	5,619		Balance c/d*	53
	Balance c/d	38,295			
		100,261			100,261
1/7/10	Balance c/d	53	1/7/10	Balance c/d	38,295

* The £53 is calculated after allowing for the given credit balance at month end.

10.7.5 Self-test

Hilmar & Co.

Debtors' control account

1/3/09	Balance b/d	5,900	1/3/09	Balance b/d	425
31/3/09	Sales journal	41,800	31/3/09	Returns journal	884
	Unpaid cheques	1,940		Bank	17,470
	Interest	185		Discount allowed	706
	Balance c/d	413		Bad debts	902
				Cash	6,130
				Contra – creditors	1,011
				Balance c/d	22,710
		50,238			50,238
1/4/09	Balance b/d	22,710	1/4/09	Balance b/d	413

You are told that there is a credit balance on the debtors' control account. After all the postings have been made the remainder is the debit balance on this account.

Note: the bad debts recovered of £217 is not posted to the debtors' control as the amount is not credited to any debtor account. The amount is a recovery of an expense (bad debt) previously written off.

Creditors' control account

1/3/09	Balance b/d	370	1/3/09	Balance b/d	7,290
31/3/09	Returns journal	470	31/3/09	Purchases journal	30,433
	Bank	20,084		Balance c/d	816
	Contra – debtors	1,011			
	Discount received	471			
	Cash	4,020			
	Balance c/d	12,113			
		38,539			38,539
1/4/09	Balance c/d	816	1/4/09	Balance c/d	12,113

You are told that there is a debit balance on the creditors' control account. After all the postings have been made the remainder is the credit balance on the account.

Chapter 11

11.2.3 Self-test

Bill

(a) Charge to P&L is £84,000. Accrue £14,000 in the balance sheet (April and May only paid at the end of June).

Rent

30/06/08	Bank – 1 month	7,000	31/5/09	P&L account	84,000
30/09/08	Bank – 3	21,000			
31/12/08	Bank – 3	21,000			
31/03/09	Bank – 3	21,000			
31/05/09	Accrual c/d	14,000			
		84,000			84,000
			1/6/09	Accrual b/d	14,000

(b) Charge to P&L £92,000. Accrue £16,000.

		Rent			
30/06/09	Bank	21,000	1/6/09	Accrual b/d	14,000
30/09/09	Bank	21,000	31/5/10	P&L	92,000
31/12/09	Bank	24,000			
31/03/10	Bank	24,000			
31/05/10	Accrual c/d	16,000			
		106,000			106,000
			1/6/10	Accrual b/d	16,000

(c) Charge to P&L £20,500. Prepaid £14,000. (The charge is £1,500 × 7 = £10,500 + £2,000 × 5 = £10,000.)

		Insurance			
1/1/09	Bank	18,000	31/5/09	Prepaid c/d	10,500
				P&L account	7,500
		18,000			18,000
1/6/09	Prepayment b/d	10,500	31/5/10	Prepaid c/d	14,000
1/1/10	Bank	24,000		P&L account	20,500
		34,500			34,500
1/6/10	Prepaid c/d	14,000			

11.2.4 Self-test

Jay

		Interest payable			
15 Mar 10	Bank	350	31 Dec 10	P&L acc	1,400
30 July 10	Bank	350			
5 Nov 10	Bank	350			
31 Dec 10	Balance c/d	350			
		1,400			1,400
			1 Jan 11	Balance b/d	350

Total interest for the year is 7 per cent on a loan of £20,000 = £1,400. This amount is an expense and is written off in the profit and loss account. The £350 balance is an accrual.

11.2.5 Self-test

Electricity					
15 Feb 10	Bank	550	1 Jan 10	Balance b/d	430
30 July 10	Bank	280	31 Dec 10	P&L acc	1,135
31 Oct 10	Bank	310			
31 Dec 10	Balance c/d	425			
		1,565			1,565
			1 Jan 11	Balance b/d	425

Of the £550 paid in February 2010, £430 is for the previous year.

11.2.6 Self-test

BB & Co.

Insurance					
1 Jan 10	Balance b/d	700	31 Dec 10	Balance c/d	1,050
1 Aug 10	Bank	1,800		P&L acc	1,450
		2,500			2,500
1 Jan 11	Balance b/d	1,050			

Payment in August 2010 is for 12 months. Of this, 7 months are advance payments (amounts prepaid).

Chapter 12

12.7.1 Self-test

Kay & Co.

Straight line depreciation: £450,000 − £100,000 ÷ 5 years = £70,000 p.a. Each year depreciation of £70,000 is shown as an expense in the profit and loss account.

In the balance sheet the following details are shown:

Balance sheet	Cost	Accumulated depreciation	Net book value
31/12/09	450,000	70,000	380,000
31/12/10	450,000	140,000	310,000
31/12/11	450,000	210,000	240,000
31/12/12	450,000	280,000	170,000
31/12/13	450,000	350,000	100,000

Reducing balance method: the profit and loss account would be debited with the annual depreciation. In 2009 the amount is £19,000 (2% × £950,000). In 2010 depreciation is £18,620 (2% of £931,000) and in 2011 it is £18,247 (2% of £912,380).

In the balance sheet the following would be shown:

Year end	At cost	Accumulated depreciation	Net book value
31/12/09	950,000	19,000	931,000
31/12/10	950,000	37,620	912,380
31/12/11	950,000	55,867	894,133

12.7.2 Self-test

Maureen

Plant and machinery

1/1/10	Balance b/d	50,000	31/03/10	Transfer old plant	13,000
31/3/10	New plant – cash	2,000	31/12/10	Balance c/d	46,000
	Trade-in	7,000			
		59,000			59,000
1/1/11	Balance b/d	46,000			

Provision for depreciation

31/03/10	Transfer depr	5,512	1/1/10	Balance b/d	22,500
31/12/10	Balance c/d	16,988			
		22,500			
					22,500
			1/1/11	Balance b/d	16,988

Plant disposal account

31/3/10	Ex P&M	13,000	Dec 2007	Depreciation	1,300
			31/12/07	Balance c/d	11,700
		13,000			13,000
1/1/08	Balance b/d	11,700	Dec 2008	Depreciation	2,340
			31/12/08	Balance c/d	9,360
		11,700			11,700
1/1/09	Balance b/d	9,360	Dec 2009	Depreciation	1,872
			31/12/09	Balance c/d	7,488
		9,360			9,360
1/1/10	Balance c/d	7,488	31/3/10	Loss on sale P&L acc	488
				P&M – Trade-in	7,000
		7,488			7,488

Note: the depreciation calculation is shown as above to illustrate the calculation. Normally a transfer would be made from the provision for depreciation account of a single figure – in this case £5,512.

12.7.3 Self-test

Wilson

Plant and machinery

19 June 09	Bank	38,000	31 Dec 09	Depreciation	6,945
	Delivery	3,100		Balance c/d	39,355
	Erection	5,200			
		46,300			46,300
1 Jan 2010	Balance b/d	39,355.00	31 Dec 10	Depreciation	5,903.25
				Balance c/d	33,451.75
		39,355.00			39,355.00
1 Jan 2011	Balance b/d	33,451.75			

Machine cost = £46,300. Depreciation in 2009 = 15% × £46,300 = £6,945. In year 2010 machine value is £46,300 − £6,945 = £39,355; 15% depreciation = £5,903.25.

If Wilson uses the straight line method then depreciation for each year would be 10% of £46,300 = £4,630.

12.7.4 Self-test

Sheryl

Printer

1/3/08	Bank	1,300	28/2/09	Accumulated depr	195
			28/2/09	Trade in	985
			28/2/09	Loss on sale	120
		1,300			1,300
1/3/09	Bank	1,900			

Accumulated depreciation – printer

28/2/09	Printer – transfer	195	28/2/09	Depreciation	195
			28/2/10	Depreciation	285

Photocopier

1/3/08	Bank	870	
1/3/09	Bank	1,026	

Accumulated depreciation photocopiers

	28/2/09	Depreciation	87
	28/2/10	Depreciation*	78
		Depr – new*	102

* For 2010 the following are the calculations:
10% on reduced balance of £783(870 − 87) = £78
10% on new photocopier of £1,026 = £102

Chapter 13

13.2.3 Self-test

Ajax Electrical

At 31 December 2009 the debtors amounted to £50,000. Based on this the provision for doubtful debts is equal to 5% × £50,000 = £2,500.

In the balance sheet at year end, the debtors of £50,000 would be reduced by the provision for doubtful debts of £2,500. This means that a net amount is shown of £47,500.

The profit and loss account for 2009 would show the provision for doubtful debts of £2,500.

In 2010 the provision would be 5% × £60,000 = £3,000. As we already have a provision (created in 2009), we only need to increase it by £500, being the difference between the 2009 provision and the new one. This additional amount of £500 is also shown in the profit and loss account for the year.

In the balance sheet of 2010 we would show debtors at £60,000 less the provision for doubtful debts of £3,000 = £57,000.

In 2011 the debtors' balances are £40,000 and using the 5 per cent provision, we would only need a total provision of £2,000. The current balance on the provision account is £3,000. This means that we must reduce the provision by £1,000.

The 2011 profit and loss account would be credited with this reduction of £1,000, while in the balance sheet the debtors would be shown at £40,000 − 2,000 = £38,000.

Provision for doubtful debts

31 Dec 2011	P&L account	1,000	31 Dec 09	P&L account	2,500
	Balance c/d	2,000	31 Dec 10	P&L account	500
		3,000			3,000
			1 Jan 2011	Balance b/d	2,000

13.3.2 Self-test

Mike

Debtors control account

1/01/10	Balance b/d	20,000	30/04/10	Bad debt – Swart	420
			15/06/10	Bad debt – Higgins	1,200
			31/12/10	Balance c/d	18,380
		20,000			20,000
1/01/11	Balance b/d	18,380			

Provision for doubtful debts

31/12/10	P&L account	2,421	1/1/10	Balance b/d	3,340
	Balance c/d*	919			
		3,340			3,340
			1/1/11	Balance b/d	919

* 5% × 18,380 = 919

Bad debts

30/4/10	Swart	420	18/07/10	Bad debt recovered	95
15/6/10	Higgins	1,200	31/12/10	P&L account	1,525
		1,620			1,620

13.3.3 Self-test

Lyn

Debtors

31/5/09	Balance b/d	14,800	31/5/09	Bad debt – Martin	620
				Balance c/d	14,180
		14,800			14,800
1/6/09	Balance b/d	14,180			

Debtors

31/5/10	Balance b/d	18,900	31/5/10	Bad debt – Gary	280
				Balance c/d	18,620
		18,900			18,900
1/6/10	Balance b/d	18,620			

Debtors

31/5/11	Balance b/d	21,000	31/5/11	Balance c/d	21,000
		21,000			21,000
1/6/11	Balance b/d	21,000			

Provision for bad debts

			31/5/09	P&L account	709
			31/5/10	P&L account	222
			31/5/11	P&L account	329

Bad debts

31/5/09	Debtors – Martin	620	31/5/09	P&L account	620
31/5/10	Debtors – Gary	280	31/5/10	Bad debt recovered*	93
				P&L account	187
		280			280

* The amount recovered from Martin is based on the total written off as a bad debt – £620 × 15p = £93.

Debtors' amounts in balance sheet:

Debtors before bad debts	Bad debts written off	Provision for bad debts	Debtors' balance at year end
14,800	620	709	13,471
18,900	280	931	17,689
21,000	Nil	1,260	19,740

Chapter 14

14.2.2 Self-test

Fleck's journal

Electricity	Dr	89	
Accrued expenses	Cr		89
Telephone	Dr	47	
Accrued expenses	Cr		47
Motor vehicle	Dr	1,500	
Creditors	Cr		1,500
Bad debts	Dr	69	
J Smith	Cr		69
Prepaid expenses	Dr	790	
Advertising	Cr		300
Rent			490

14.2.3 Self-test

Dee's journal

Bad debt	Dr	48	
Debtor Dee	Cr		48
Shortfall after distribution, now written off as bad debt			

Debtors' account – Dee					
1/1/09	Balance b/d	162	31/07/09	Cash	102
			30/11/09	Cash	12
			31/12/09	Bad debt	48
		162			162

14.2.4 Self-test

A Trader's journal

30/6/09	Bad debts	Dr	221	
	Debtors – Smith	Cr		81
	– Jones			94
	– Blake			32
	– Currie			14

Amounts written off as bad debts.

Debtors' control

30/6/09	Balance b/d	8,981	30/6/09	Bad debts	221
				Balance c/d	8,760
		8,981			8,981
1/7/09	Balance b/d	8,760			

Bad debts

30/6/09	Debtors	221	30/6/09	Profit & Loss	221

14.2.5 Self-test

Raymond

11/5/09	Land and buildings	Dr	15,000	
	Equipment		11,640	
	Stock		7,960	
	Debtors		410	
	Overdraft	Cr		3,420
	Creditors			960
	Electricity due			170
	Capital account – Raymond			30,460

Opening journal entries at 11 May 2009 showing the assets and liabilities purchased by Raymond at that date.

Chapter 15

15.1.1 Self-test

Trial balance of A Jones at 31 December 2009

Motor vehicles at cost	5,600	
Fixtures and fittings at cost	4,200	
Land and buildings at cost	5,600	
Loan		1,680
Advertising	280	
Administration expenses	1,316	
Loan interest	56	
Bank overdraft		840
Debtors	3,150	
Creditors		2,086
Profit and loss account at 1/1/09		5,250
Provision for doubtful debts at 1/1/09		210
Jones – capital account		5,446
Sales		10,850
Purchases	5,180	
Opening stock at 1/1/09	3,500	
Motor vehicles depreciation at 1/1/09		1,680
Fixtures and fittings depreciation at 1/1/09		840
	28,882	28,882

15.1.2 Self-test

Mark

Trial balance as at 7 April 2009

Bank	9,050	
Rent	4,000	
Shop fittings	2,900	
Purchases	12,000	
Motor van	7,400	
Advertising	150	
Sales		790
Wages	120	
Cash	70	
Tennis Ltd		4,900
Capital		30,000
	35,690	35,690

The trial balance above has proved that our accounting entries to the ledger are correct.

15.1.3 Self-test

Larry

Trial balance as at 30 September 2009

Bank	17,920	
Capital		40,000
Drawings	2,000	
Purchases	26,000	
Insurance	980	
Packing	1,200	
UPack (creditor)		1,200
Wages	1,100	
Acquire (debtor)	4,900	
Sales		16,300
Okay (debtor)	3,400	
	57,500	57,500

15.1.4 Self-test

Jack

Trial balance as at 30 June 2009

Capital		15,000
Drawings	500	
Rent	1,950	
Bank	2,275	
NuVan Ltd (creditor)		6,810
Office equipment	6,250	
Wages	1,000	
Motor car	16,000	
File & Co. (creditor)		4,750
Sales		5,200
Insurance	725	
Motor expenses	310	
Sundry expenses	195	
A Lu (debtor)	750	
Gas and electricity	490	
Purchases	1,315	
	31,760	31,760

15.2.1 Self-test

Jillian

Trial balance at 31 December 2009

Cash	2,150	
Debtors	6,500	
Stock at 1 Jan 2009	1,900	
Equipment	18,900	
Creditors		1,750
Accruals		3,000
Jillian, Capital account		13,000
Jillian, Drawings	1,800	
Sales		37,250
Wages	9,500	
Rent	8,600	
Postage and telephone	3,750	
Travel and Motor expenses	1,900	
	55,000	55,000

15.3.1 Self-test

Nigel

Trial balance at 31 December 2009

Sales		21,860
Purchases	11,180	
Motor vehicles at cost	15,600	
Fixtures and fittings at cost	4,200	
Advertising	980	
Bank interest	456	
Opening stock at 1/1/09	6,500	
Motor vehicles (accumulated depreciation at 1/1/09)		4,680
Debtors	9,150	
Creditors		9,086
Provision for doubtful debts at 1/1/09		1,910
Nigel – capital account		27,446
Land and buildings at cost	19,600	
Selling expenses	6,680	
Administration expenses	4,316	
Bank overdraft		9,840
Fixtures and fittings (accumulated depreciation at 1/1/09)		3, 840
	78,662	78,662

15.3.2 Self-test

W Thom

Trial balance as at 30 September 2009

Advertising	9,600	
Postage and telephone	3,280	
Lighting and heating	5,104	
Drawings	50,560	
Bank overdraft		27,796
Insurance	15,584	
Rent and rates	60,352	
Salaries and wages	41,088	
Motor expenses	37,172	
Purchases	330,061	
Returns inwards	1,440	
Returns outwards		2,416
Stock at 1.10.08	112,448	
Debtors	65,005	
Commission received		3,200
Creditors		51,028
Fixtures and fittings	49,280	
Capital at 1.10.08		150,432
Cash in hand	1,450	
Bank interest and charges	4,928	
Sales		604,960
Motor vehicles	52,480	
	839,832	839,832

15.3.3 Self-test

Final Trading Co.

Trial balance at 30 June 2009

Office expenses	11,880	
Postage and stationery	3,900	
Rent and rates	7,500	
Insurance	1,095	
Lighting and heating	1,548	
Motor expenses	5,880	
Salaries and wages	14,550	
Sales		109,800
Purchases	61,950	
Bank charges	2,418	
Vans	10,500	
Creditors		9,750
Debtors	20,430	
Land and buildings	84,000	
Stock 1 July 2008	24,060	
Cash at bank	3,402	
Drawings	18,834	
Capital		152,397
	271,947	271,947

15.4.1 Self-test

A Jones

Trial balance as at 31 December 2009

Motor vehicles at cost	5,600	
Fixtures and fittings at cost	4,200	
Land and buildings at cost	5,600	
Loan		1,680
Advertising	280	
Administration expenses	1,448	
Loan interest	56	
Bank overdraft		840
Debtors	3,150	
Creditors		2,086
Profit and loss account at 1/1/09		5,250
Increase in doubtful debts provision	105	
Provision for doubtful debts at 1/1/09		315
Jones – capital account		5,446
Sales		10,850
Purchases	5,180	
Opening stock at 1/1/09	3,500	
Depreciation fixtures and fittings	1,050	
Depreciation motor vehicles	784	
Motor vehicles (acc depr at 1/1/09)		2,464
Fixtures and fittings (acc depr 1/1/09)		1,890
Prepayments	108	
Accruals		240
	31,061	31,061

Workings

Administration expenses £1,316 − 108 = £1,208 + £140 + £100 = £1,448
Depreciation – Fixtures and fittings 25% × £4,200 = £1,050
             Motor vehicles 20% × (5,600 − 1,680) = £784
Provision for doubtful debts: 10% × £3,150 = £315 − £210 = £105 increase
Prepayments are £108 rent
Accruals are £140 + £100.

Note that depreciation is shown as an expense (debit side) and has also been added to accumulated depreciation (credit side).

    The increase in the provision for doubtful debts has also been shown as a debit (the extra expense) and has been added (on the credit side) to the provision account.

    The closing stock has not been brought into the trial balance, although it could be shown as a debit to closing stock (balance sheet item) with a corresponding credit as closing stock (profit and loss account item).

15.4.2 Self-test

W Thom

Depreciation of fixtures and fittings	Dr	4,928	
Fixtures and fittings	Cr		4,928
Annual depreciation.			

Prepaid rent	Dr	4,000	
Rent and rates	Cr		4,000
Rent Oct–Dec paid in advance.			

Salaries and wages	Dr	1,200	
Accruals	Cr		1,200
Accrual of salaries due on 30/9/09.			

Bad debts	Dr	430	
Debtors	Cr		430
Bad debt written off.			

15.4.3 Self-test

Office expenses	3,880	
Lighting and heating	2,570	
Motor expenses	5,820	
Salaries and wages	4,650	
Sales		79,850
Purchases	41,750	
Bank charges	2,010	
Delivery vehicles	23,580	
Creditors		9,150
Debtors	29,930	
Office equipment	24,530	
Stock 1 July 2009	14,960	
Cash at bank	9,450	
Drawings	25,870	
Capital		100,000
	189,000	189,000

15.4.4 Self-test

Purchases	103,400	
Insurance	2,880	
Office expenses	12,145	
Salaries and wages	23,400	
Drawings	34,600	
Bank charges	3,150	
Fittings and fixtures	12,670	
Motor expenses	3,890	
Debtors	45,320	
Capital		94,000
Sales		214,700
Bad debts	55,875	
Cash at bank	2,430	
Creditors		28,920
Stock 1 January 2010	37,860	
	337,620	337,620

15.4.5 Self-test

Mimi & Co.

Mimi & Co. Trial balance at 30 June 2009

Debtors	5,100	
Purchases	24,000	
Insurance	350	
Electricity	700	
Motor expenses	2,960	
Salaries and wages	5,830	
Sales		28,891
Drawings	8,000	
Motor vehicle	7,500	
Creditors		3,250
Fittings and fixtures	3,160	
Stock 1 July 2008	5,020	
Cash at bank	320	
Capital		30,799
	£62,940	£62,940

15.4.6 Self-test

Max & Co.

Max & Co. Balance at 30 June 2009

Postage and stationery	1,300	
Rent and rates	2,500	
Drawings	11,340	
Capital		80,000
Motor expenses	1,960	
Salaries and wages	4,850	
Sales		63,400
Purchases	48,650	
Motor vehicle	3,500	
Creditors		7,100
Debtors	39,540	
Bank overdraft		5,120
Fittings and fixtures	23,960	
Opening stock	18,020	
	155,620	155,620

Chapter 16

16.2.4 Self-test

L Green's journal

31 Dec 09	Debtor	Dr	18	
	Debtor	Dr	27	
	Creditor	Dr	110	
	Returns inwards	Cr		90
	Creditor	Dr	75	
	Suspense account	Cr		140

16.2.5 Self-test

Merle's journal

20 May	Machine repairs	Dr	111	
	Plant and machinery	Cr		111
	Correction of posting.			
22 May	Discount allowed	Dr	49	
	Discount received	Cr		49
	Correction of incorrect posting.			
24 May	Office equipment	Dr	820	
	BB Stores	Cr		820
	Purchase of printer on credit.			
25 May	A Brown	Dr	90	
	D Brown	Cr		90
	Goods returned wrongly posted.			
27 May	Sales	Dr	5,400	
	Delivery van	Cr		5,400
	Van sold incorrectly posted to sales.			
30 May	Commission received	Dr	100	
	Rent received	Cr		100
	Rent incorrectly posted to commission.			

16.2.6 Self-test

Heinz

1 Jan 08	Fittings	Dr	8,600	
	Creditor Joe	Cr		8,600
	Fittings purchased on 1/1/08.			
31 Mar 08	Debtor Fritz	Dr	600	
	Fittings	Cr		600
	Fittings sold to Fritz on 31 March.			
	Bad debts	Dr	500	
	Debtor Steve	Cr		500
	Amount written off as bad debt.			
	Creditor L Bryan	Dr	400	
	Creditor A Bryan	Cr		400
	Reversal of incorrect entry.			
30 June 08	Debtor Martin	Dr	200	
	Motor van	Cr		200
	Van sold to Martin on 30 June.			

16.2.7 Self-test

C Whyte

(i)   No effect on balancing the trial balance as the amount has been posted.

(ii) The trial balance requires an additional credit of £36.

(iii) The credit to the trial balance is overstated by £540.

(iv) The trial balance has been incorrectly debited with £192. To correct this we must credit the trial balance by £384 (i.e. £192 × 2).

Net profit before adjustments		9,720
Plus credit – discount received		384
		10,104
Less salaries to be debited	4,200	
Sales adjustment – overstated	540	4,740
Adjusted net profit		£5,364

Note that item (ii) does not affect the net profit as the purchases are correctly stated.

16.2.8 Self-test

Jay & Co.

Adjustment to net profit:

Net profit as initially shown		12,380
add: Return inwards error	600	
Credit note now entered	360	
Rent prepaid	400	
Discount received now credited	270	1,630
		14,010
less: Bad debt – entry corrected		648
Adjusted net profit		£13,362

Journal entries:

Supense	Dr	600	
Returns in	Cr		600
Bad debts	Dr	648	
Supense	Cr		648
Debtor	Dr	110	
Bank	Cr		110
Austin	Dr	320	
Justin	Cr		320
I Buy (creditor)	Dr	360	
Purchases returns	Cr		360
Prepayment	Dr	400	
Rent	Cr		400
Suspense	Dr	270	
Discount received	Cr		135
Discount allowed			135

Suspense account

Returns in	600	Balance b/d	222
Discount received	135	Bad debts	648
Discount allowed	135		
	870		870

16.2.9 Self-test

Alex

Suspense account

Returns in	200	Balance b/d	101
Credit note (Hilife)	14	Thomas (creditor)	90
		Smythe (debtor)	9
		Vashi	14
	214		214

16.2.10 Self-test

Roger

Suspense	Dr	48	
Creditor	Cr		48
Sales	Dr	39	
Debtor	Cr		39
Debtor	Dr	450	
Suspense	Cr		450
Shop fittings	Dr	1,320	
Purchases	Cr		1,320
Suspense	Dr	300	
Sales	Cr		300

Suspense account

Balance b/d	102	Debtor	450
Creditor	48		
Sales	300		
	450		450

Amended trial balance at 31 July 2009

Capital		22,350
Drawings	9,000	
Stock 1 August 2005	7,500	
Trade debtors	9,261	
Trade creditors		8,100
Shop fittings	5,910	
Purchases	14,100	
Sales		22,641
General expenses	2,580	
Discount received		120
Cash at bank	4,980	
Returns outwards		120
	53,331	53,331

Chapter 17

17.1.1 Self-test

Sylvia

Using straight line method:

Motor vehicle – Ford

1 Jan 2009	Balance b/d	4,000	23 April 09	Bank		2,100
				Loss on disposal		1,900
		4,000				4,000

Motor vehicle – Toyota

1 Jan 2090	Balance b/d	6,000	31 Dec 2009	Depreciation	1,200
			31 Dec 2010	Depreciation	1,200
			31 Dec 2011	Depreciation	1,200
				Balance c/d	2,400
		6,000			6,000
1 Jan 2012	Balance c/d	2,400			

Motor vehicle – Honda

28 April 2009	Bank	8,000	31 Dec 2009	Depreciation	1,600
			31 Dec 2010	Depreciation	1,600
			31 Dec 2011	Depreciation	1,600
				Balance c/d	3,200
		8,000			8,000
1 Jan 2012	Balance c/d	3,200			

Using reducing balance method:

Motor vehicle – Toyota

1 Jan 2090	Balance b/d	6,000	31 Dec 2009	Depreciation	1,500
			31 Dec 2010	Depreciation	1,125
			31 Dec 2011	Depreciation	844
				Balance c/d	2,531
		6,000			6,000
1 Jan 2012	Balance c/d	2,531			

Motor vehicle – Honda

28 April 2009	Bank	8,000	31 Dec 2009	Depreciation	2,000
			31 Dec 2010	Depreciation	1,500
			31 Dec 2011	Depreciation	1,125
				Balance c/d	3,375
		8,000			8,000
1 Jan 2012	Balance c/d	3,375			

17.1.2 Self-test

Idea & Co.

Revised trial balance at 31 October 2009

Packing expenses	525	
General expenses	515	
Electricity expenses	2,520	
Insurance	180	
Rent	4,200	
Rates	650	
Salaries and wages	15,689	
Motor expenses	1,726	
Sales		88,300
Purchases	51,150	
Returns inwards	200	
Returns outwards		350
Stock 1 November 2008	15,690	
Debtors	16,314	
Creditors		10,170
Fixtures and fittings	6,300	
Drawings	10,950	
Capital		29,256
Prepayments	281	
Accruals		1,139
Cash in hand	150	
Cash at bank	2,175	
	129,215	129,215

17.1.3 Self-test

NuVenture

Revised trial balance at 31 March 2009

Purchases	89,185	
Stock 1 April 2008	18,160	
Sales		122,340
Carriage inwards	520	
Carriage outwards	1,470	
Returns outwards		640
Wages and salaries	20,240	
Rent and rates	3,065	
Telephone expenses	722	
Commissions payable	456	
Insurance	385	
General expenses	289	
Land and buildings	40,000	
Debtors	14,320	
Creditors		8,160
Fixtures	2,850	
Cash at bank	2,970	
Cash in hand	115	
Loan from K Blake		10,000
Drawings	7,620	
Accruals		588
Prepayments	249	
Capital		60,888
	202,616	202,616

17.1.4 Self-test

Wilmot Trading

Adjusted trial balance as at 31 December 2009

Creditors		19,832
Returns inwards	390	
Electricity and gas	4,914	
Insurance	351	
Capital – Wilmot		57,049
Rates	1,268	
Salaries and wages	30,594	
Motor expenses	3,366	
Sales		172,185
Purchases	99,743	
Cash in hand	293	
Returns outwards		683
Stock 1 January 2009	30,596	
Debtors	31,812	
Rent	8,190	
Fixtures and fittings	12,285	
Drawings – Wilmot	21,353	
Delivery expenses	2,028	
Cash at bank	4,240	
Prepayments	548	
Accruals		2,222
	251,971	251,971

17.1.5 Self-test

HG Electricals

(a) Sales day book

Date	Inv. No.	Customer	Total	VAT	Fitting and servicing	Electrical goods
			£	£	£	£
27/10/09	INV 2044	Fred James	141.00	21.00	120.00	
28/10/09	INV 2045	Sally Baker	258.50	38.50	80.00	140.00
29/10/09	INV 2046	Klipper Ltd	2,350.00	350.00	400.00	1,600.00
30/10/09	INV 2047	K. Benn	235.00	35.00	200.00	
31/10/09	INV 2048	Mouville & Sons	352.50	52.50		300.00
			3,337.00	497.00	800.00	2,040.00

(b) (i)   Fitting and servicing account   £800.00 Cr
    (ii) Electrical good account   £2,040.00 Cr
    (iii) VAT account   £497.00 Cr
    (iv) Sales ledger control account   £3,337.00 Dr

(c)

Supplier	VAT inclusive invoice total £	VAT rate	VAT £
ABC Electricity	262.50	5%	12.50
Smiths Wires	1,457.00	17½%	217.00
Southern Gas	117.60	5%	5.60
Clark Brothers	2,749.50	17½%	409.50
Minnow Ltd	587.50	17½%	87.50

17.1.6 Self-test

Catena

(a) Outstanding lodgements (paying in amounts) are amounts that have been paid into the bank but are not yet shown on the bank statement.

Unpresented cheques are cheques that have been written but are not yet shown on the bank statement.

(b) Adjusted cash book balance for Catena at 31 May 2007

Balance per cash book	2,908.53
Add: Rent receipt not entered	500.00
	3,408.53
Less: Bank charges	(68.75)
Less: Cheque 100222 understated	(27.00)
Adjusted cash book balance 31/05/07	3,312.78

(c) Bank reconciliation for Catena at 31 May 2007

Balance per bank 31/05/07	3,395.88
Add: Outstanding lodgement	840.85
	4,236.73
Less: Unpresented cheque 100225	(695.00)
100226	(228.95)
Balance per adjusted cash book 31/05/07	3,312.78

(d) There are a number of reasons why it is important for a business to prepare regular bank reconciliations:

i. The bank statement is an independent accounting record and when used to confirm the accuracy of accounting records maintained by the business, will assist in deterring fraud because irregularities should be detected.

ii. By comparing entries on the bank statement with those in the cash book, accounting errors can be detected.

iii. The business will have an up to date cash book figure to enter into its trial balance.

iv. The bank reconciliation will identify any old and unpresented cheques.

17.1.7 Self-test

Knowles

(a), (b), (c)

Calculation of accruals at 31 March 2007

Telephone — invoice received 15 April 2007   £295

Calculation of prepayments at 31 March 2007	
Insurance 9/12 × £1,500	1,125
Road Fund Licence 4/12 × £165	55
Rates to 31 March 2008	1,250

Insurance

Date	Details	£	Date	Details	£
07/05/06	Bank payment	975	18/10/06	Bank receipt	60
25/12/06	Bank payment	1,500	31/03/07	Profit & Loss	1,290
			31/03/07	Balance c/d	1,125
		2,475			2,475

Telephone

Date	Details	£	Date	Details	£
15/04/06	Bank payment	125			
15/07/06	Bank payment	230			
15/10/06	Bank payment	245			
15/01/07	Bank payment	262			
31/03/07	Balance c/d	295	31/03/07	Profit & Loss	1,157
		1,157			1,157

Motor Expenses

Date	Details		Date	Details	
31/07/06	Bank payment	165	31/03/07	Profit & Loss	540
07/11/06	Bank payment	430	31/03/07	Balance c/d	55
		595			595

Rates

Date	Details		Date	Details	
15/08/06	Bank payment	1,175	31/03/07	Profit & Loss	1,175
31/03/07	Bank payment	1,250		Balance c/d	1,250
		2,425			2,425

(d) In an accounting period, income and expenses must be matched so that they concern the same goods and services in the same accounting period. This is the accruals concept.

Accruals and prepayments are accounting adjustments which help to ensure that income and expenses are correctly matched.

Accruals increase the cost of an expense in the Trading, Profit and Loss Account and are shown under Current Liabilities on the Balance Sheet.

Prepayments decrease the cost of an expense in the Trading, Profit and Loss Account and are shown under Current Assets on the Balance Sheet.

17.1.8 Self-test

Louise Philips

Debtors Control Account

Balance b/d	7,400	Bad debts	840
Credit sales: (90% × 29,000)	26,100	Discounts allowed	220
		Bank	12,400
		Balance c/d	20,040
	33,500		33,500
Balance b/d	20,040		

Creditors Control Account

Discounts received	100	Balance b/d	3,180
Bank	6,900	Credit purchases: (85% × 16,000)	13,600
Balance c/d	9,780		
	16,780		16,780
		Balance b/d	9,780

Chapter 18

18.2.2 Self-test

Method	Calculation	Cost used
FIFO	200 units at £1.20 plus 100 units at £1.50	£390
LIFO	300 units at £1.50	£450
Average	300 units at £1.40	£420

It is noticeable that FIFO shows a higher profit when prices rise.

18.4.1 Self-test

Nat

	Goods in	
Date	Quantity	Unit Price
February	60	£22
April	30	£26

	Goods out
Date	Quantity
July	80

Balance at 31 December 2009 = 10 units.

(a) FIFO value is £10 × 26 = £260
(b) AVCO = 60 × 22 = 1,320 + 30 × 26 = 780 = 2,100. Average cost per unit is £23.33. Therefore balance is valued at 10 × 23.33 = £233.30
(c) LIFO value = 10 × 22 = £220

18.4.2 Self-test

Musicman & Co.

	Stock in	Unit price	Stock out	Balance
1.7.09	33	200		
3.7.09	120	270	30	123
6.9.09	100	300	90	133
20.11.09	180	330	150	163
25.3.10	240	390	210	193
2.5.10	120	420	60	253

Using the above information we can calculate the value of the stock.

FIFO

	Balance
31 Aug	123
31 Oct	133
31 Dec	163
31 Mar	193
30 June	253

The balance is made up of 120 units × £420 + 133 units × £390 = £50,400 + £51,870 = £102,270.

LIFO

	Balance	Value of stock balance
		$33 \times 200 = 6,600$
31 Aug	123	$90 \times 270 = 24,300$
31 Oct	133	$10 \times 300 = 3,000$
31 Dec	163	$30 \times 330 = 9,900$
31 Mar	193	$30 \times 390 = 11,700$
30 June	253	$60 \times 420 = 2,520$

Here the balance is valued at £58,020.

18.4.3 Self-test

Sweet & Co.

	Kilo in	£ per kilo	Kilo out	Balance
1 January	500	1.00		500
3 January	800	1.01		1,300
5 January			900	400
11 January			100	300
13 January	700	1.03		1,000
15 January	800	1.05		1,800
18 January			400	1,400
23 January	500	1.04		1,900
25 January			600	1,300
31 January			900	400

Using the above information we can calculate FIFO. Only part of the last purchase on 23 January remains in stock. Therefore value at 31 January is $400 \times £1.04 = £416$.

LIFO assumes that the last purchase is the first used. Therefore, the balance consists of 100 kilo at £1.03 + 300 kilo at £1.00 = £103 + £300 = £403.

AVCO uses average cost and the remaining balance is 400 kilo at an average price of £1.032 per kilo = £412.

Chapter 19

19.6.1 Self-test

J Anthony

Trading account for the year ending 31 December 2009

Sales		87,213
Less returns inwards		1,106
		86,107
Stock at 1/1/09	12,500	
Purchases	32,345	
Carriage in	1,984	
	46,829	
Less returns out	2,348	
	44,481	
Less stock 31/12/09	16,400	
Cost of sales		28,081
Gross profit		58,026

19.9.1 Self-test

Larry

Trading account for the year ended 30 June 2009

Sales		421,000
Less returns inwards		40,108
		380,892
Purchases	214,000	
Carriage inwards	2,790	
	216,790	
Less closing stock	37,890	178,900
Gross profit		201,992

19.9.2 Self-test

Henry

Trading account for the year ended 30 June 2009

Sales		43,988
Opening stock	9,876	
Purchases	11,870	
	21,746	
Returns to suppliers	1,245	
	20,501	
Less closing stock	8,967	11,534
Gross profit		32,454

19.9.3 Self-test

Gordon

Trading account for the year ended 30 June 2009

Sales		211,980
Less returns		35,800
		176,180
Opening stock	43,650	
Purchases	98,650	
Carriage inwards	76,500	
	218,800	
Less closing stock	65,780	153,020
Gross profit		23,160

Chapter 20

20.4.3 Self-test

Lionel

Item	Revenue		Capital	
	Income	Expenditure	Income	Expenditure
Wages		✓		
Premises				✓
Loans from bank			✓	
Sale of computer			✓	
Advertising		✓		
Sale of goods	✓			
Purchases of raw materials		✓		
Carriage outwards		✓		
Bad debts		✓		
Motor vehicle				✓
Motor expenses		✓		

20.4.5 Self-test

Capital expenditure is shown in the profit and loss | False |

Revenue expenditure is shown in the profit and loss | True |

Revenue receipt is shown in the profit and loss | True |

Capital income is shown in the profit and loss | False |

Income from the sale of an old motor van is shown in **the profit and loss account** as a recoupment of depreciation.

Expenditure on the purchase of a new computer for the office is shown in **the balance sheet**.

Expenditure on stationery is shown in **the profit and loss account**.

20.5.1 Self-test

Net Profit before adjustments		29,000
Add Interest received* (289 × 2)	578	
Discount received ** (340 × 2)	680	1,258
		30,258
Less stock adjustment	858	
Loan***	900	
Additional purchases	540	2,298
Adjusted net profit for the year		£27,960

* We need reverse the deduction and add the amount twice.
** Cancel the charge and show as an income item.
*** This is a capital item and show in balance sheet.

20.5.2 Self-test

Martin

Net Profit before adjustments		9,862
Add Rent prepaid	1,600	
Rent receivable outstanding	1,020	
Sales	1,905	4,525
		14,387
Less: sales returns	478	
Provision for bad debts	240	
Closing stock overvalued	986	
Outstanding telephone charges	230	
Depreciation on motor vehicles	450	2,384
Adjusted net profit for the year		£12,003

20.5.3 Self-test

Andrew

The profit can be as a result of increased sales which are mainly on credit. As such there is an increase in debtors but not in cash.

Andrew may have decided to withdraw cash from his business during the year. This is not an expense and would not affect profits.

Andrew may have purchased assets during the year. Payment from cash resources would have depleted the balance.

He may have decided to repay an outstanding liability (such as a loan). This would also deplete cash resources.

20.5.4 Self-test

	Amount paid/received in year	Disclosure in P&L account
Salaries	6,000	11,000
Rent payable	14,000	12,000
Insurance	7,000	5,800
Property rates	5,100	7,000
Interest payable	4,000	5,100
Interest receivable	7,300	9,400

20.5.5 Self-test

Ella

Gross profit		56,900
Add		
Interest received	2,980	
Discount received	1,040	4,020
		60,920
Less		
Motor expenses	3,140	
Bank charges	720	
Wages	1,360	
Rent payable	5,870	
Insurance	3,800	
Postages	1,010	15,900
Net profit for the year		£45,020

20.5.6 Self-test

George

Net Profit before adjustments		6,920
Add capital wages	636	
Sales	720	
Closing stock undervalued	700	2,056
		8,976
Less discount allowed		626
Adjusted net profit for the year		£8,350

20.5.7 Self-test

Jacques

Profit and Loss account for the year ended 31 December 2009

Gross profit		88,100
Investment Income		400
		88,500
Advertising	3,000	
Electricity	2,800	
Insurance	1,700	
Office expenses	4,900	
Interest paid	400	
Rent and rates	7,500	
Wages and Salaries	41,300	
Depreciation	5,800	67,400
Net profit for the year		21,100

Chapter 21

21.5.1 Self-test

Marmax Trading

Manufacturing account for the year ended 30 April 2010

Opening raw material stock		16,000
Direct material	117,000	
Carriage inwards	3,000	120,000
		136,000
Less closing raw material		14,000
Cost of raw material consumed		122,000
Direct labour		145,000
Prime cost		267,000
Factory overhead expenses		
Indirect costs (materials)	1,700	
Wages	29,000	
Depreciation	15,000	
Other factory repairs, heating, etc.	20,100	65,800
		332,800
Add work in progress at beginning of year		800
		333,600
Less work in progress at end of year		1,000
Cost of production transferred to trading account		332,600

21.5.2 Self-test

Cast Manufacturers

Manufacturing account for the year ended 31 March 2010

Stock of raw materials 1.4.09		76,688
Add purchases	615,000	
Add carriage inwards	17,269	632,269
		708,957
Less stock raw materials 31.03.10		90,788
Cost of raw materials consumed		618,169
Direct wages		996,788
Prime cost		1,614,957
Factory overhead expenses:		
Power and fuel	134,700	
Rent and rates	63,843	
Depreciation of machinery	106,125	304,668
		1,919,625
Add work in progress 1/4/09		107,269
		2,026,894
Less work in progress 31/3/10		110,213
Total production cost		1,916,681

21.5.3 Self-test

Ezee Manufacturing

Manufacturing account for the year ended 31 March 2010

Stock of raw materials 1.4.09		29,325
Add purchases	181,475	
Add carriage inwards	1,148	182,623
		211,948
Less stock raw materials 31.03.10		30,813
Cost of raw materials consumed		181,135
Direct wages	193,120	
Direct expenses	1,105	194,225
Prime cost		375,360
Factory overhead expenses:		
Power and fuel	19,210	
Indirect wages	76,755	
Factory rent	12,070	
Depreciation of machinery	10,030	
Factory insurance	1,785	
Repairs to factory	4,250	
General factory expenses	3,783	127,883
		503,243
Add work in progress 1/4/09		10,455
		513,698
Less work in progress 31.03.10		12,920
Total production cost		500,778

21.5.4 Self-test

Reedy Manufacturing Co.

Manufacturing account for the year ended 31 December 2009

Stock of raw materials 1.1.09		10,673
Add purchases	79,616	
Add carriage inwards	6,633	86,249
		96,922
Less stock raw materials 31/12/09		15,005
Cost of raw materials consumed		81,917
Direct wages		112,101
Prime cost		194,018
Factory overhead expenses:		
Fuel and power	5,913	
Indirect wages	38,307	
Factory rent	8,271	
Depreciation of machinery	8,208	
Factory expenses	6,094	
Factory lighting and heat	4,144	70,937
		264,955
Add work in progress 1/1/09		9,196
		274,151
Less work in progress 31/12/09		12,130
Total production cost		262,021

21.5.5 Self-test

(a) Direct costs are expenses that can be attributed to specific cost units. Overheads are costs that are incurred in the factory during the manufacturing process but are not directly attributable to a specific product or cost centre.

(b) Direct wages, repairs to specific factory machinery and any other expense that can be identified with a specific cost unit.

(c) This is prepared so that the costs of manufacturing can be transferred to the trading and profit and loss account.

(d) The cost of production is for all goods completed and ready for sale. As business is a continuing operation, this does not always happen and so, at the year end, there are goods that are still in the manufacturing process. They may have been partially manufactured but they are not yet ready for sale – they are called work in progress.

Chapter 22

22.5.1 Self-test

Description	Fixed asset	Current asset	Current liability
Motor vehicle	✓		
Cash		✓	
Goods for resale		✓	
Amount due to supplier			✓
Amount due by customers		✓	
Rent outstanding			✓
Bank overdraft			✓
Office Furniture	✓		

22.5.2 Self-test

Stock	current asset
Computer equipment	fixed asset
Money outstanding for goods sold	current asset
Loan due to A Brown in 4 months' time	current liability
Money owed to a supplier	current liability
Loan due to G Smythe in 3 years' time	long-term liability
VAT due to HMRC	current liability
Bank overdraft	current liability

22.5.3 Self-test

Details	Asset	Liability	Income	Expense	Balance Sheet	P&L
Bank overdraft		✓			✓	
Rent paid quarterly in advance	✓				✓	
Motor vehicle	✓				✓	
Directors' salaries				✓		✓
Factory premises	✓				✓	
Sale of goods			✓			✓
Purchase of stationery				✓		✓
Bank interest received			✓			✓
Insurance premium				✓		✓
Tax payable in three months' time		✓			✓	
Amount owed to stationery supplier		✓			✓	
Dividends from another business			✓			✓
Stock held for resale	✓				✓	
Loan interest paid				✓		✓
Computer equipment	✓				✓	
Shares held in another business	✓				✓	

22.5.4 Self-test

Wendy

As no payments were made during the year, all interest due for the year must be shown as a current liability.

Interest on £30,000 at 8% = £2,400.

Interest on £8,000 at 7% = £560.

Repayment for one year on the loan is also due to be paid within 12 months and is therefore a current liability = £2,000.

Creditors are also payable for goods = £2,100.

Total current liabilities = £7,060.

22.7.3 Self-test

Fixed assets	Current assets	Long-term liabilities	Current liabilities	Capital
48,000	22,000	14,000	6,000	50,000
26,600	17,500	3,100	6,000	35,000
102,000	18,000	30,000	25,000	65,000
102,000	46,000	10,000	28,000	110,000
48,000	22,000	NIL	5,000	65,000

22.7.4 Self-test

Brenda

Balance sheet as at 31 December 2009

Fixed assets			
Machinery	42,000	19,400	22,600
Vehicles	8,000	5,600	2,400
Investments	2,800		2,800
	52,800	25,000	27,800
Current assets			
Stock	15,500		
Debtors 30,000 – 800	29,200		
Cash	700	45,400	
Less **Current liabilities**			
Creditors	6,900	6,900	
Working capital			38,500
			66,300
Long-term creditor – Bank loan			7,000
			59,300
Financed by			
Capital			38,200
Add Net profit			21,100
			59,300

22.7.5 Self-test

W Thom

Trading and profit and loss account for the year ended 30 September 2009

Sales		604,960	
Less returns inwards		1,440	603,520
Less cost of sales			
Stock		112,448	
Add purchases	330,061		
Less returns outwards	2,416	327,645	
		440,093	
Less stock		66,798	373,295
Gross profit			230,225
Add income			
Commission received			3,200
			233,425
Less expenses:			
Advertising		9,600	
Bad debts		430	
Depreciation – fixtures & fittings		4,928	
Postage and telephone		3,280	
Lighting and Heating		5,104	
Insurance		15,584	
Rent and rates		56,352	
Salaries and wages		42,288	
Motor expenses		37,172	
Bank interest and charges		4,928	179,666
Net profit			53,759

Balance sheet as at 30 September 2009

Fixed assets			
Fixtures and fittings	49,280	4,928	44,352
Motor vehicles	52,480		52,480
	101,760	4,928	96,832
Current assets			
Stock	66,798		
Debtors	64,575		
Prepaid rent	4,000		
Cash	1,450	136,823	
Less **current liabilities**			
Bank overdraft	27,796		
Accruals	1,200		
Creditors	51,028	80,024	56,799
			153,631
Financed by			
Capital			150,432
Add Net profit		53,759	
Less drawings		50,560	3,199
			153,631

22.7.6 Self-test

Final Trading Co.

Trading and profit and loss account for the year ended 30 June 2009

Sales			109,800
Less cost of sales			
Stock		24,060	
Add purchases		61,950	
		86,010	
Less stock		46,800	39,210
Gross profit			70,590
Less expenses:			
Office expenses		11,880	
Postage and stationery		3,900	
Lighting and heating		1,548	
Insurance		1,095	
Rent and rates		7,500	
Salaries and wages		14,550	
Motor expenses		5,880	
Bank charges		2,418	48,771
Net profit			21,819

Balance sheet as at 30 June 2009

Fixed assets			
Land & buildings			84,000
Motor vans			10,500
			94,500
Current assets			
Stock	46,800		
Debtors	20,430		
Cash	3,402	70,632	
Less **Current liabilities**			
Creditors	9,750	9,750	
Working capital			60,882
			155,382
Financed by			
Capital		152,397	
Add Net profit	21,819		
Less drawings	18,834	2,985	
			155,382

22.7.7 Self-test

Michel Enterprise

Adjusted trial balance as at 31 December 2009

Creditors		71,190
Returns inwards	1,400	
Electricity and gas	17,848	
Insurance	1,210	
Capital		204,792
Rates	4,038	
Salaries and wages	109,823	
Motor expenses	12,702	
Sales		618,100
Purchases	358,050	
Cash in hand	1,050	
Returns outwards		2,450
Stock 31 October 2008	109,830	
Debtors	114,198	
Rent	30,800	
Fixtures and fittings	44,100	
Drawings	76,650	
Delivery expenses	7,330	
Accruals		10,251
Prepayments	2,529	
Cash at bank	15,225	
	906,783	906,783

Note: The adjusted trial balance is shown for information only. It is not necessary to prepare an adjusted trial balance before preparing the financial statements.

Trading and profit and loss account for year ended 31 October 2009

Sales			618,100	
Less returns inwards			1,400	616,700
Less cost of sales:				
Stock opening			109,830	
Add purchases	358,050			
Less returns outwards	2,450		355,600	
			465,430	
Less stock closing			188,870	276,560
Gross profit				340,140
Less expenses				
Delivery expenses	7,105	225	7,330	
Electricity and gas	16,912	936	17,848	
Insurance	1,435	225	1,210	
Rent	24,500	6,300	30,800	
Rates	6,342	2,304	4,038	
Salaries and wages			109,823	
Motor expenses	9,912	2,790	12,702	183,751
Net profit				156,389

Balance sheet as at 31 October 2009

Fixed assets				
Fixtures and fittings				44,100
Current assets				
Stock		188,870		
Debtors		114,198		
Prepayments	2,304　225	2,529		
Cash at bank		15,225		
Cash in hand		1,050	321,872	
Less **Current liabilities**				
Creditors		71,190		
Accruals		10,251	81,441	
Working capital				240,431
				284,531
Financed by				
Capital				204,792
Add Net profit		156,389		
Less drawings		76,650		79,739
				284,531

Chapter 23

23.3.1 Self-test

George

Net profit (before adjustments)		6,920
Plus:		
Wages (capital expenditure)	636	
Additional sales (910 – 190)	720	
Additional closing stock	700	2,056
		8,976
Less:		
Discount allowed (313 × 2)		616
Adjusted net profit		£8,360

23.3.2 Self-test

M Jones

The journal entries are:

Suspense	Dr	200	
Telephone	Cr		200
Correcting the amount overcast.			
Joe & Co.	Dr	350	
Suspense	Cr		350
Completion of double entry.			
Suspense	Dr	1,000	
Sales	Cr		1,000
Sales have been understated – now adjusted.			
Sales	Dr	540	
Ace Traders	Cr		540
Ace Traders	Dr	450	
Sales	Cr		450
Correcting incorrect entry and entering correct amount.			

Following the correction of the above errors, the net profit will now be recalculated as follows:

Net profit as per balance sheet		62,800
Add telephone expenses overstated in P&L	200	
Sales understated in P&L	1,000	1,200
		64,000
Less sales overstated – Ace Traders		90
Amended net profit		£63,910

In the balance sheet, debtors are reduced by £90 and creditors are reduced by £350. The capital balance at 31 December 2009 is increased by the additional profit earned, namely £1,110.

23.3.3 Self-test

J Black

As a result of the errors, the net profit was adjusted as follows:

Net profit (before adjustments)		6,700
Less: Stock	852	
Loan	5,000	
Purchases	760	6,612
		88
Plus: Discount received (210 × 2)	420	
Interest received (130 × 2)	260	£680
Adjusted net profit		£768

23.3.4 Self-test

Jay & Co.

Trading and profit and loss account for the year ended 30 June 2009

Sales			36,600
Less cost of sales			
Stock	8,020		
Add purchases	20,650	28,670	
Less stock		11,700	16,970
Gross profit			19,630
Less expenses:			
Postage and telephone		1,300	
Electricity		516	
Insurance		365	
General expenses		806	
Rent and rates		2,500	
Salaries and wages		4,850	
Motor expenses		1,960	12,297
Net profit			7,333

Balance sheet as at 30 June 2009

Fixed assets			
Land and buildings		28,000	
Fittings and fixtures		3,960	
Motor vehicle		3,500	35,460
Current assets			
Stock	11,700		
Debtors	6,810		
Cash	1,134	19,644	
Less **Current liabilities**			
Creditors	3,250	3,250	
Working capital			16,394
			51,854
Financed by			
Capital			50,799
Add net profit	7,333		
Less drawings	6,278		1,055
			51,854

23.3.5 Self-test

Andrew

Trial balance at 31 December 2009

Motor vehicles at cost	5,600	
Fixtures and fittings at cost	4,200	
Land and buildings at cost	5,600	
Loan		1,680
Advertising	280	
Administration expenses	1,316	
Loan interest	56	
Bank overdraft		840
Debtors	3,150	
Creditors		2,086
Profit and loss account at 1/1/09		5,250
Provision for doubtful debts at 1/1/09		210
Andrew – capital account		5,446
Sales		10,850
Purchases	5,180	
Opening stock at 1/1/09	3,500	
Motor vehicles (acc depr at 1/1/09)		1,680
Fixtures and fittings (acc depr at 1/1/09)		840
	28,882	28,882

Profit and loss account for the year ended 31 December 2009

Sales		10,850
Opening stock	3,500	
Purchases	5,180	
	8,680	
Closing stock	4,300	
Cost of sales		4,380
Gross profit		6,470
Advertising	280	
Administration	1,460	
Depreciation: Fixtures and fittings	1,050	
Motor vehicle	784	
Interest	56	
Provision for doubtful debts	105	3,735
Net profit		2,735

Balance sheet as at 31 December 2009

Fixed assets – tangible	Cost	Acc depr	NBV
Motor vehicle	5,600	2,464	3,136
Fixtures and fittings	4,200	1,890	2,310
Land and buildings	5,600		5,600
	15,400	4,354	11,046
Current assets			
Stock	4,300		
Debtors			
Less provision doubtful debts	2,835		
Prepaid rent	96	7,231	
Current liabilities			
Overdraft	840		
Creditors	2,086		
Accruals	240	3,166	
Net current assets			4,065
			15,111
Less loan			1,680
			13,431
Capital		5,446	
Profit and loss 1/1/09	5,250		
Net profit for the year	2,735	7,985	13,431

Workings

Depreciation of fixtures and fittings. This is 25% of the cost of £4,200 = £1,050.

Depreciation of motor vehicle is 20% of the reduced balance. We take cost £5,600 less accumulated depreciation to 1/1/09 of £1,680.

The reduced balance at 1/1/09 is therefore £3,920 and 20% of that = £784.

Prepayment of rent. We have prepaid 8 months' rent. That is 2/3 of £144 = £96. This is deducted from administration expenses.

We also owe the cleaners £140 and accounting £100. Both these amounts are added to administration expenses. So we have £1,316 – 96 + 100 + 140 = £1,460.

Provision for doubtful debts. We are told that the provision must equal 10% of £3,150 = £315. We already have a provision of £210 so all we must do is increase the amount by the difference which is 315 – 210 = £105.

23.3.6 Self-test

Miskien & Co.

Prepayment	Dr	800	
Insurance	Cr		800
Depreciation – buildings	Dr	1,620	
Accumulated depreciation – bldg	Cr		1,620
Depreciation – equipment	Dr	5,500	
Accumulated depreciation – equip.	Cr		5,500
Accrued income	Dr	500	
Interest receivable	Cr		500
Salaries and wages	Dr	2,000	
Accruals	Cr		2,000
Debtors	Dr	2,750	
Sales	Cr		2,750

Adjusted trial balance at 31 December 2009

Cash	6,700	
Debtors	26,550	
Insurance	2,600	
Stock 1 January 2009	1,950	
Land	50,000	
Building	141,500	
Accumulated depreciation – buildings		93,320
Equipment	90,100	
Accumulated depreciation – equipment		70,800
Creditors		7,500
Interest receivable		6,500
Capital account – Miskien		81,500
Drawings – Miskien	10,000	
Sales		221,150
Purchases	80,200	
Depreciation – equipment	5,500	
Depreciation – buildings	1,620	
Electricity and gas	28,200	
Advertising	19,000	
Repairs	11,500	
Salaries	6,050	
Prepayments	800	
Accrued income	500	
Accruals		2,000
	482,770	482,770

Profit and loss account for the year ended 31 December 2009

Sales		221,150
Opening stock	1,950	
Purchases	80,200	
Closing stock	450	
Cost of sales		81,700
Gross profit		139,450
Interest receivable		6,500
		145,950
Advertising	19,000	
Insurance	2,600	
Depreciation: Equipment	5,500	
Buildings	1,620	
Repairs	11,500	
Electricity and Gas	28,200	
Salaries	6,050	74,470
Net profit		71,480

Balance Sheet as at 31 December 2009

	Cost	Acc Depr	NBV
Fixed assets – tangible			
Equipment	90,100	70,800	19,300
Land	50,000		50,000
Buildings	141,500	93,320	48,180
	281,600	164,120	117,480
Current assets			
Stock	450		
Debtors	26,550		
Prepayments – insurance	800		
Accrued income – interest	500		
Cash	6,700	35,000	
Current liabilities			
Creditors	7,500		
Accruals – salaries	2,000	9,500	
Net current assets			25,500
			142,980
Capital		81,500	
Net profit for the year		71,480	
		152,980	
Less drawings		10,000	142,980

23.3.7 Self-test

Watno & Co.

Journal entries:

Accrued income	Dr	1,025	
Fees	Cr		1,025
Wages	Dr	510	
Accruals	Cr		510
Depreciation	Dr	750	
Equipment	Cr		750

Profit and loss account for the year ended 30 June 2009

Fees		37,775
Advertising	1,300	
Depreciation of equipment	750	
Rent	9,000	
Sundry expenses	900	
Electricity and gas	3,750	
Wages	20,010	35,710
Net profit		2,065

Balance sheet as at 31 December 2009

	Balance at 1/7/08	Depreciation	Net Book Value
Fixed Assets – tangible			
Equipment	9,900	750	9,150
Current assets			
Debtors	3,500		
Accrued income	1,025		
Cash	1,150	5,675	
Current liabilities			
Creditors	750		
Prepaid income	2,000		
Accruals	510	3,260	
Net current assets			2,415
			11,565
Capital	10,500		
Net profit for the year	2,065	12,565	
Less drawings		1,000	
			11,565

23.3.8 Self-test

Wasser & Co.

Profit and loss account for the year ended 31 December 2009

Sales			218,400
Opening stock	2,450		
Purchases	141,500	143,950	
Closing stock		700	
Cost of sales			143,250
Gross profit			75,150
Rent receivable			4,000
			79,150
Advertising		19,000	
Insurance		3,900	
Depreciation: Equipment		5,500	
Delivery vehicles		1,500	
Office expenses		4,050	
Repairs		13,500	
Gas and water		27,375	
Salaries and wages		79,950	154,775
Net loss			75,625

Balance sheet as at 31 December 2009

	Cost	Acc Depr	NBV
Fixed assets			
Equipment	90,100	70,800	19,300
Delivery vehicles	150,000	97,200	52,800
	240,100	168,000	72,100
Current assets			
Stock	700		
Debtors	17,200		
Prepayments	825		
Cash	3,200	21,925	
Current liabilities			
Creditors	7,500		
Accruals	1,250	8,750	
Net current assets			13,175
			85,275
Capital	165,900		
Net loss for the year	75,625		
	90,275		
Less drawings	5,000		85,275

23.3.9 Self-test

(i)   Increased profit by £942.
(ii) Decreased profit by £306.
(iii) Increased profit by £300.
(iv) Decreased profit by £80.
(v) Increased profit by £330.

Net profit before allowing for errors		2,900
Interest	306	
Discount	80	386
		3,286
Stock	942	
Loan	300	
Purchases	330	1,572
Adjusted net profit		1,714

23.3.10 Self-test

Martin

Net profit – initial		7,875
Add:		
Rent receivable	520	
Sales	928	
Rent	1,000	2,448
		10,323
Less:		
Provision for bad debts	700	
Depreciation	800	
Telephone	120	
Sales returns	322	
Closing stock	648	2,590
Adjusted net profit		£7,733

23.3.11 Self-test

Steve

Net profit – initial		1,920
Add:		
Wages	376	
Sales	72	
Stock	340	788
		2,708
Less discount		264
Adjusted net profit		£2,444

23.3.12 Self-test

Nufashion Manufacturing

Manufacturing account for the year ended 30 April 2010

Raw materials		
Opening stock	5,000	
Purchases	106,000	
Carriage inwards	3,200	
	114,200	
Less closing stock	9,400	104,800
Direct wages (30,000 + 900)		30,900
Prime cost		135,700
Factory overheads		
Electricity and heat	3,000	
Rent and rates	5,700	
Depreciation – machinery	5,300	14,000
Manufacturing costs		149,700
Add work in progress		12,200
		161,900
Less closing work in progress		22,000
Factory cost of production		139,900

Trading and profit and loss account for the year ended 30 April 2010

Sales		215,000
Less:		
Opening stock	17,000	
Factory cost of production	139,900	
	156,900	
Less closing stock	13,000	
Cost of sales		143,900
Gross profit		71,100
Administrative overheads		
Office wages (8,200 + 400)	8,600	
Electricity and heat	2,000	
Depreciation – equipment	1,200	
Rent and rates	1,900	
	13,700	
Selling and distribution overheads		
Carriage outwards	1,500	
Sales commission	3,400	
Provision for bad debts	3,000	
	7,900	21,600
Net profit		49,500

Balance sheet as at 30 April 2010

Fixed assets	Cost	Acc Depreciation	Net Book Value
Factory machinery	53,000	10,300	42,700
Office equipment	6,000	2,400	3,600
	59,000	12,700	46,300
Current assets			
Stock	44,400		
Debtors	25,000		
Less provision for bad debts	−3,000		
Prepaid rent	400		
Cash at bank	3,800	70,600	
Current liabilities			
Trade creditors	19,000		
Accrued expenses	1,300	20,300	
Net current assets			50,300
Total assets less current liabilities			96,600
Less **long-term liabilities**			
Loan			21,000
			75,600
Capital			
Opening balance		47,000	
Net profit for the year		49,500	
		96,500	
Less drawings		20,900	75,600

23.3.13 Self-test

Delta Manufacturing

Manufacturing account for the year ended 31 December 2009

Raw materials:		
Opening stock	3,920	
Purchases & carriage inwards	65,409	
Less returns	−5,020	
	64,309	
Less closing stock	4,160	60,149
Direct wages		28,310
Prime cost		88,459
Factory overheads:		
Supervisors' wages	6,320	
Electricity	3,508	
Depreciation on plant	14,250	
Rent and rates	7,200	
Insurance on plant	2,812	
Repairs to plant	1,020	35,110
Factory costs		123,569
Add work in progress		1,840
		125,409
Less closing work in progress		2,830
		122,579
Less sale of factory scrap		320
Factory cost of production		122,259

Trading and profit and loss account for the year ended 31 December 2009

Sales		187,300
Less:		
Opening stock	8,215	
Factory cost of production	122,259	
Purchases finished goods	1,300	
	131,774	
Less closing stock	9,210	
Cost of sales		122,564
Gross profit		64,736
Add discount received		3,020
		67,756
Administrative overheads		
Salaries	11,530	
Electricity and heat	1,020	
Depreciation – office fixtures and furniture	2,050	
Rent and rates	2,400	
Postage and telephones	825	
Printing and stationery	460	
	18,285	
Selling and distribution overheads		
Carriage outwards	516	
Salaries – sales staff	18,897	
Bad debts	830	
Discount allowed	1,860	
Depreciation – vehicles	4,160	
Delivery expenses	725	
Advertising	735	
	27,723	
Financial charges		
Loan interest	4,600	
Bank charges	308	
	4,908	50,916
Net profit		16,840

23.3.14 Self-test

Nuage Manufacturing Co.

Manufacturing account for the year ended 31 December 2009

Raw materials		
Opening stock	28,730	
Purchases	146,900	
Carriage inwards	8,097	
	183,727	
Less returns	6,150	
	177,577	
Less closing stock	41,910	135,667
Direct wages		62,130
Prime cost		197,797
Factory overheads		
Power	27,900	
Depreciation on machinery	26,080	
Rent	40,000	
Repairs to machinery	4,340	98,320
Factory costs		296,117
Add work in progress		4,090
		300,207
Less closing work in progress		3,240
Factory cost of production		296,967

Trading and profit and loss account for the year ended 31 December 2009

Sales less returns		380,946
Less cost of sales		
Opening stock	11,310	
Factory cost of production	296,967	
Purchases finished goods	38,620	
	346,897	
Less closing stock	24,800	
Cost of sales		322,097
Gross profit		58,849
Depreciation – office equipment	11,320	
Rent	20,000	
Carriage outwards	1,423	
Bad debts	6,830	
Overdraft interest	4,270	43,843
Net profit		15,006

23.3.15 Self-test

Winter Manufacturing Co.

Manufacturing account for the year ended 31 May 2010

Raw materials		
Opening stock	11,080	
Purchases and carriage inwards	47,947	
Less returns	−1,002	
	58,025	
Less closing stock	14,720	43,305
Direct wages		11,218
Prime cost		54,523
Factory overheads		
Supervisors' wages	4,794	
Electricity	1,874	
Depreciation on plant	962	
Rent and rates	6,000	
Insurance on plant	906	
Repairs to plant	872	15,408
Factory costs		69,931
Add work in progress		3,920
		73,851
Less closing work in progress		4,870
Factory cost of production		68,981

Trading and profit and loss account for the year ended 31 May 2010

Sales		140,709
Less cost of sales		
Opening stock	16,740	
Factory cost of production	68,981	
Purchases finished goods	3,001	
	88,722	
Less closing stock	18,310	
Cost of sales		70,412
Gross profit		70,297
Add discount received		806
		71,103
Administrative overheads		
Salaries	14,072	
Electricity and heat	1,920	
Depreciation – fixtures and furniture	803	
Rent and rates	2,000	
Postage and telephones	830	
Printing and stationery	720	
	20,345	
Selling and distribution overheads		
Carriage outwards	961	
Salaries and commission	11,470	
Bad debts	1,214	
Discount allowed	324	
Depreciation – vehicles	109	
Delivery expenses	1,214	
Advertising	1,204	
	16,496	
Financial charges		
Loan interest	1,009	
Bank charges	131	
	1,140	37,981
Net profit		33,122

23.3.16 Self-test

Richard

Trading and profit and loss account for the year ended 30 September 2009

Sales		22,580
Cost of sales		
Stock – opening	9,150	
Purchases	14,300	
	23,450	
Closing stock	7,300	16,150
Gross profit		6,430
Salaries and wages	2,720	
Rent and rates	900	
Insurance	110	
Motor expenses	640	
Printing and stationery	210	
Electricity and gas	140	
General expenses	300	5,020
Net profit for the year		1,410

Balance sheet as at 30 September 2009

Fixed assets		
Motor vehicles	3,400	
Fixtures and fittings	1,050	4,450
Current assets		
Stock	7,300	
Debtors	4,900	
Bank	1,160	
	13,360	
Current liabilities		
Creditors	2,200	
Net current assets		11,160
Net assets		15,610
Capital		
Balance at 1 October 2005	22,000	
Add profit for the year	1,410	
	23,410	
Less drawings	7,800	15,610

23.3.17 Self-test

Alan & Co.

Manufacturing account of Alan & Co. for year ended 31 December 2008

Opening stock raw material	23,400		
Purchases	187,400	210,800	
Less closing stock		29,240	181,560
Direct wages			314,600
Prime cost			496,160
Supervisors' wages		40,000	
Heating and electricity		18,000	58,000
			554,160
Add work in progress			2,800
			556,960
Less closing work in progress			3,610
Cost of goods manufactured			553,350

Trading and profit and loss account for year ended 31 December 2008

Sales			874,320
Opening stock	19,700		
Cost of goods manufactured	553,350	573,050	
Less closing stock		16,480	556,570
Gross profit			317,750
Salaries		17,350	
Administration expenses		6,720	
Heating and electricity		6,000	
Carriage outwards		1,001	31,071
Net profit			286,679

23.3.18 Self-test

Idea & Co.

Trading and profit and loss account for the year ended 31.10.09

Sales		88,300	
Less returns inwards		200	88,100
Less cost of sales:			
Stock 1/11/08		15,690	
Add purchases	51,150		
Less returns outwards	350	50,800	
		66,490	
Less stock 31/10/09		17,170	49,320
Gross profit			38,780
Less expenses			
Packing expenses		525	
General expenses (490 + 25)		515	
Electricity expenses (2,416 + 104)		2,520	
Insurance (205 − 25)		180	
Rent (3,500 + 700)		4,200	
Rates (906 − 256)		650	
Salaries and wages		15,689	
Motor expenses (1,416 + 310)		1,726	26,005
Net profit			12,775

Balance sheet as at 31 October 2009

Fixed assets			
Fixtures and fittings			6,300
Current assets			
Stock	17,170		
Debtors	16,314		
Prepayments	281		
Cash at bank	2,175		
Cash in hand	150	36,090	
Less current liabilities			
Creditors	10,170		
Accruals	1,139	11,309	
Working capital			24,781
			31,081
Financed by			
Capital			29,256
Add net profit		12,775	
Less drawings		10,950	1,825
			31,081

23.3.19 Self-test

NuVenture

Trading and profit and loss Account for the year ended 31 March 2009

Sales			122,340
Less Cost of Sales:			
Stock 1/04/08		18,160	
Add Purchases	89,185		
Carriage Inwards	520		
Less Returns Outwards	640	89,065	
		107,225	
Less Stock 31/03/09		20,300	86,925
Gross Profit			35,415
Less Expenses			
Carriage Outwards		1,470	
Sundry Expenses (318 − 29)		289	
Telephone expenses (624 + 98)		722	
Commission (216 + 240)		456	
Insurance (405 − 20)		385	
Rent and Rates (3,015 − 200 + 250)		3,065	
Salaries and Wages		20,240	26,627
Net Profit			8,788

Balance sheet as at 31 March 2009

Fixed assets			
Fixtures and fittings			2,850
Land and buildings			40,000
			42,850
Current assets			
Stock	20,300		
Debtors	14,320		
Prepayments	249		
Cash at bank	2,970		
Cash in hand	115	37,954	
Less current liabilities			
Creditors	8,160		
Accruals	588	8,748	
Working capital			29,206
			72,056
Less Loan – K Blake			10,000
			62,056
Financed by			
Capital			60,888
Add net profit		8,788	
Less drawings		7,620	1,168
			62,056

Chapter 24

24.4.2 Self-test

Eve's capital is £18,000. She has not withdrawn any capital but merely used it to purchase fixed assets.

24.4.3 Self-test

Net assets at 1/1/09 = £54,000. At 31/12/09 = £69,000. Net difference = £15,000. William's profit for the year is £15,000 + £10,000 (drawings) = £25,000.

24.4.4 Self-test

	Debtors control					
01.1.09	Balance b/d	17,400	31.12.09	Payments	89,300
	Sales	96,580		Discounts	4,940
				Balance c/d	19,740
		113,980			113,980
	Balance b/d	19,740			

Todd's sales for the year is £96,580.

24.4.5 Self-test

Sheila's profit for the year is calculated as follows:

$$£62,700 - £64,300 = £1,600 + £11,300 = £12,900$$

24.4.6 Self-test

J Jones

First we need calculate the statement of assets and liabilities at 1 January 2009.

Assets	
Equipment	3,000
Stock	2,550
Debtors	2,130
Bank balance	480
	8,160
Less liabilities	
Creditors	1,620
Capital	6,540

Next we need calculate the purchases and sales for the year. This we can do using a ledger account for each, as follows:

Creditors control

31.12.09	Paid	9,600	01.01.09	Balance b/d	1,620
	Balance c/d	1,680	31.12.09	Purchases	9,660
		11,280			11,280
			1/1/10	Balance b/d	1,680

Debtors control

01.01.09	Balance b/d	2,130	31.12.09	Receipts	20,670
31.12.09	Sales	21,030		Balance c/d	2,490
		23,160			23,160
1/1/10	Balance b/d	2,490			

Profit and loss account for the year ending 31 December 2009

Sales		21,030
Opening stock	2,550	
Purchases	9,660	
	12,210	
Less closing stock	3,600	8,610
Gross profit		12,420
Expenses	5,430	
Depreciation	300	5,730
Net profit		6,690

Balance sheet as at 31 December 2009

Fixed assets		
Equipment	3,000	
Less depreciation	300	2,700
Current assets		
Stock	3,600	
Debtors	2,490	
Bank	420	
	6,510	
Less creditors	1,680	4,830
		7,530
Capital at 1.1.09	6,540	
Net profit for the year	6,690	13,230
Less drawings		5,700
		7,530

24.4.7 Self-test

Alice

Cash book

Balance b/d	7,840	Creditors	49,320
Cash sales	32,380	Purchases	20,006
Debtors	41,906	Wages	11,310
Capital	5,800	Motor expenses	8,670
Loan – Fry	10,000	Insurance	8,931
Balance c/d	1,315	Bank charges	1,004
	99,241		99,241
		Balance b/d	1,315

Debtors control

Balance b/d	29,390	Receipts	41,906
Sales	43,563	Balance c/d	31,047
	72,953		72,953
Balance b/d	31,047		

Creditors control

Payments	49,320	Balance b/d	7,320
Balance c/d	8,240	Purchases	50,240
	57,560		57,560
		Balance b/d	8,240

Sales = 43,563 + 26,651 (ex drawings of Alice) + 32,380 = £102,594
Purchases = 20,006 + 50,240 + 1,610 = £71,856

Profit and loss account for the year ending 31 December 2009

Sales		102,594
Opening stock	11,250	
Purchases	71,856	
	83,106	
Closing stock	13,210	69,896
Gross profit		32,698
Wages (11,310 – 1,403 + 643)	10,550	
Motor expenses (8,670 + 4,031)	12,701	
Insurance (1,033 + 8,931 – 924)	9,040	
Bank charges	1,004	
Depreciation – vehicle	2,947	
Depreciation – equipment	1,500	
Interest on loan	500	38,242
Net loss for the year		5,544

Balance sheet as at 31 December 2009

Vehicles	26,523		
Equipment	25,240		51,763
Stock	13,210		
Debtors	31,047		
Prepayment	924		
		45,181	
Creditors	8,240		
Accruals (500 + 643)	1,143		
Overdraft	1,315	10,698	34,483
			86,246
Loan – Fry			10,000
			76,246
Capital Alice	97,000		
Additional capital	5,800	102,800	
Drawings		21,010	
		81,790	
Net loss		5,544	
			76,246

24.4.8 Self-test

Miro

Creditors

31/7/10	Bank	32,061	1/8/09	Balance b/d		6,140
	Balance c/d	5,930	31/7/10	Purchases		31,851
		37,991				37,991
			1/8/10	Balance b/d		5,930

Debtors

1/8/09	Balance b/d	8,120	31/7/10	Bank	40,014
31/7/10	Sales	38,734		Balance c/d	6,840
		46,854			46,854
1/8/10	Balance b/d	6,840			

Profit and loss account for the year ended 31 July 2010

Sales ex debtors	38,734	
Ex cash sales (14,310 + 9,015)	23,325	62,059
Opening stock	6,300	
Purchases*	38,258	
	44,558	
Closing stock	4,130	40,428
Gross profit		21,631
Wages	7,301	
Telephones (416 + 420 – 240)	596	
Electricity (680 – 496 + 490)	674	
Printing (600 + 210)	810	
Motor expenses (1,904 + 1,002)	2,906	
Depreciation	2,960	15,247
Net profit		6,384

* Purchases are: ex creditors £31,851, bank £5,314, cash £1,803 less goods taken £710 = £38,258

Balance sheet as at 31 July 2010

Fixed assets			
Land and building – at cost		45,000	
Fixtures and fittings (cost 20,000)		11,840	56,840
Current assets			
Stock	4,130		
Debtors	6,840		
Prepayments	240		
Cash at bank	16,044	27,254	
Current liabilities			
Creditors	5,930		
Accruals	490	6,420	20,834
			77,674
Capital at 1/8/09		74,000	
Additional capital		4,000	
Net profit for the year		6,384	
		84,384	
Less drawings		6,710	77,674

24.4.9 Self-test

Nadia

Creditors

31/12/09	Cash	6,024	1/01/09	Balance b/d	937
	Balance c/d	630	31/12/09	Purchases	5,717
		6,654			6,654
			1/1/10	Balance b/d	630

Debtors

1/01/09	Balance b/d	107	31/12/09	Cash	7,430
31/12/09	Sales P&L	15,330		Cash withdrawn	7,904
				Balance c/d	103
		15,437			15,437
1/1/10	Balance b/d	103			

Cash withdrawn $= 100 \times 52$ (drawings) $+ 52 \times 52$ (wages) $= 5,200 + 2,704 = 7,904$

Purchases

31/12/09	Creditors	5,717	31/12/09	Drawings	130
				P&L	5,587
		5,717			5,717

Bank

1/1/09	Balance b/d	192	31/12/09	Creditors	6,024
31/12/09	Debtors	7,430		Rent	800
				Repairs	94
				Advertising	72
				Sundry exp	44
				Balance c/d	588
		7,622			7,622
1/1/09	Balance c/d	588			

Profit and loss account for the year ended 31 December 2009

Sales		15,330
Opening stock	535	
Purchases (5,717 − 130)	5,587	
	6,122	
Closing stock	1,021	5,101
Gross profit		10,229
Rent	800	
Repairs	94	
Advertising	72	
Sundry	68	
Depreciation	180	
Wages	2,704	3,918
Net profit		6,311

Balance sheet as at 31 December 2009

Fixed assets			
Fixtures and fittings (cost 1,800)			310
Current assets			
Stock	1,021		
Debtors	103		
Cash at bank	588	1,712	
Current liabilities			
Creditors	630		
Accruals	24	654	1,058
			1,368
Capital at 1/1/09*		387	
Net profit for the year		6,311	
		6,698	
Less drawings		5,330	1,368

* A – L = C i.e. 1,324 – 937 = £387

24.4.10 Self-test

Monica

Cash book summary

Balance b/d	1,064	Salaries	3,040
Cash sales	4,920	Repairs	194
Payments from debtors	9,874	Rent	1,021
Loan – George	4,000	Bank charges	102
		Payments to creditors	5,094
		Balance c/d	10,407
	19,858		19,858
Balance b/d	10,407		

Creditors

31/3/10	Bank	5,094	1/4/09	Balance b/d	2,901
	Balance c/d	2,830	31/3/10	Purchases	5,023
		7,924			7,924
			1/4/10	Balance b/d	2,830

Debtors

1/4/09	Balance b/d	3,021	31/3/10	Bank	9,874
31/3/10	Sales	10,916		Balance c/d	4,063
		13,937			13,937
1/4/10	Balance b/d	4,063			

Capital account

31/3/10	Drawings	4,800	1/4/09	Balance b/d		9,074
	Balance c/d	15,780	31/3/10	Net profit		11,506
		20,580				20,580
			1/4/10	Balance b/d		15,780

Profit and loss account for the year ended 31 March 2010

Sales			20,636
Opening stock		4,090	
Purchases		5,023	
		9,113	
Closing stock		5,260	3,853
Gross profit			16,783
Rent		1,021	
Repairs		194	
Salary		3,040	
Bank charges		102	
Depreciation		620	
Loan interest		300	5,277
Net profit			11,506

Balance sheet as at 31 March 2010

Fixed assets			
Fixtures and fittings	3,800	620	3,180
Current assets			
Stock	5,260		
Debtors	4,063		
Cash at bank	10,407	19,730	
Current liabilities			
Creditors	2,830		
Accruals	300	3,130	16,600
			19,780
Loan – George			4,000
Capital	9,074		
Net profit for the year	11,506	20,580	
Less drawings		4,800	15,780
			19,780

Chapter 25

25.4.1 Self-test

An amount of £4,000 due from debtor A was written off as a bad debt.	**Prudence**
Stock of £9,000 was written down to its net realisable value of £8,000.	**Prudence**
£1,000 paid for private travel was debited to drawings.	**Business entity**
Motor vehicles were depreciated at 20% of cost.	**Matching and prudence**
£2,100 insurance was paid for the following financial year.	**Matching**
A computer mouse was written off as an expense even though it could last 3–5 years.	**Materiality**
The DIY business has staff to show customers how to operate certain tools. This is considered to be worth £50,000 but is not recorded in the books.	**Money measurement**
Depreciation is charged at 20% but we want to increase it to 25% for this year only.	**Consistency**

25.4.2 Self-test

Fundamental concepts are rules which lay down the way in which we record all transactions.

- Going concern
- Consistency
- Prudence
- Accruals concept
- Separate valuation principle
- Substance over form

25.4.3 Self-test

- Relevance – the information must be relevant.
- Reliability – the information must be free from error or bias.
- Comparability – the same types of items are treated in the same way for measurement.
- Understandability – the accounts must be clear and be able to be understood by users.
- Materiality – only items that are significant are shown and therefore, if not material, they can be ignored.

25.5.1 Self-test

The chapter gives you details of each concept. This answer gives you examples only.

(i) Going concern – we value stock on the basis that the business is going to continue.

(ii) Consistency – we use one depreciation method for each asset and do not change the method from year to year.

(iii) Prudence – we only include profit when we are sure that we will receive it.

(iv) Accrual – we charge each year with an appropriate amount for that year.

(v) Historical cost – transactions are recorded at their original price.

(vi) Materiality – we ignore items of small value as insignificant and not material.

(vii) Dual aspect – this is our double-entry system.

Chapter 26

26.6.1 Self-test

Smith and Jones

Net profit before adjustments		140,000
Interest Smith	3,000	
Interest Jones	2,000	
Salary Jones	5,000	10,000
		130,000
Share of balance Smith	78,000	
Jones	52,000	130,000

26.6.2 Self-test

Dun and Swail

Profit and loss appropriation account for the year ended 30 June 2010			
Net profit			97,400
Add interest on drawings:			
Dun	205		
Swail	120		325
Adjusted profit			97,725
Salaries:			
Dun	24,000		
Swail	23,000	47,000	
Interest on capital:			
Dun	8,400		
Swail	5,600	14,000	
Interest on new capital:			
Dun	1,120		
Swail	1,050	2,170	63,170
Net profit available for partners			34,555
Dun		17,277.50	
Swail		17,277.50	34,555

Workings: Interest on drawings
3% × 6,000 for 9 months =135 plus 3% × 7,000 for 4 months = 70 = £205
3% × 4,000 for 9 months = 90 plus 3% × 3,000 for 4 months = 30 = £120

	Dun	*Swail*
Current accounts		
Balance b/d	23,850	11,490
Cash introduced*	24,000	36,000
Salary	24,000	23,000
Interest	8,400	5,600
Interest	1,120	1,050
Net profit	17,277	17,277
	98,647	94,417
Drawings and Interest on drawings	13,205	7,120
Balance at year end	85,442	87,297

* It is assumed that the additional amounts are not part of the fixed capital.

26.6.3 Self-test

Profit and loss appropriation account for the year ended 31 December 2009

Net profit			80,000
Interest on drawings – X		1,200	
Y		1,000	2,200
			82,200
Interest on capital – X	6,800		
Y	4,800	11,600	
Salary – X		18,000	29,600
Net profit for the year			52,600
Share of profit – X		21,040	
Y		31,560	52,600

Current accounts

	X	Y		X	Y
Interest drawings	1,200	1,000	Balance b/d	11,000	8,000
Drawings	12,000	10,000	Interest	6,800	4,800
Balance c/d	43,640	33,360	Salary	18,000	
			Profit	21,040	31,560
	56,840	44,360		56,840	44,360
			Balance c/d	43,640	33,360

In the balance sheet the capital is shown as $85,000 + 60,000 = £145,000$

26.6.4 Self-test

Lane and Hill

(a) The capital account is used to denote the amount of fixed capital introduced by each partner. In this partnership the total capital is £170,000.

(b) Any changes during a year through drawings or the introduction of additional capital, or the award of a salary or interest on capital is shown in the current account.

(c) Drawings are that amount withdrawn by a partner in cash or through the use of goods or services of the partnership. Hill has drawings of £12,000 p.a. and Lane has drawings of £4,000 p.a. These amounts will be shown in the current account.

26.6.5 Self-test

Black and Whyte

Interest at 6%

	Black	300,000	18,000
	Whyte	180,000	10,800

Interest at 6%

	Black	20,000	1,200
	Whyte	14,000	840

Black – interest charged at 10% p.a.

Amount	Date of drawing	Number of months	Interest
£12,000	31 July 2009	10	1,000
£10,000	30 November 2009	6	500
£12,000	31 March 2010	2	200
£13,000	31 May 2010	0	0

Whyte – interest charged at 10% p.a.

Amount	Date of drawing	Number of months	Interest
£6,000	31 July 2009	10	500
£2,000	30 November 2009	6	100
£6,000	31 January 2010	4	200
£3,000	31 May 2010	0	0

Profit and loss appropriation account for the year ended 31 May 2010

Net profit			126,700
Interest on drawings			
Black	1,700		
Whyte	800		2,500
			129,200
Interest on capital			
Black	18,000		
Whyte	10,800	28,800	
Interest on current account			
Black	1,200		
Whyte	840	2,040	
Salary			
Whyte		25,000	55,840
Net profit for partners			73,360
Black		51,352	
Whyte		22,008	73,360

Current accounts

	Black	Whyte		Black	Whyte
Interest drawings	1,700	800	Balance b/d	20,000	14,000
Drawings	47,000	17,000	Interest	19,200	11,640
Balance c/d	41,852	54,848	Salary		25,000
			Profit	51,352	22,008
	90,552	72,648		90,552	72,648
			Balance c/d	41,852	54,848

26.6.6 Self-test

North, East and West

Profit and loss account for the year ended 31 July 2010

Net profit			72,400
Add travelling expenses – East	650		
Goods at cost – North	2,100		2,750
			75,150
Interest on capital accounts:			
North	3,600		
East	3,000		
West	2,400	9,000	
Salary – North		28,000	37,000
Net profit available for partners			38,150
Apportionment of profits			
North		19,075	
East		12,717	
West		6,358	38,150

North – current account

31/7/10	Drawings	7,000	31/7/10	Interest	3,600
	Goods	2,100		Salary	28,000
	Balance c/d	41,575		Profit share	19,075
		50,675			50,675
			1/8/10	Balance b/d	41,575

East – current account

31/7/10	Drawings	6,300	31/7/10	Interest	3,000
	Travel exp	650		Profit share	12,717
	Balance c/d	8,767			
		15,717			15,717
			1/8/10	Balance b/d	8,767

West – current account

31/7/10	Drawings	5,100	31/7/10	Interest	2,400
	Balance c/d	3,658		Profit share	6,358
		8,758			8,758
			1/8/10	Balance b/d	3,658

26.6.7 Self-test

Jack and Jill

Profit and loss account for the year ended 31 December 2009

Sales		71,460
Stock	6,890	
Purchases	44,823	
	51,713	
Closing stock	13,813	37,900
Gross profit		33,560
Depreciation fixtures	1,600	
Salary	6,004	
Electricity	2,198	
Stationery	460	
Bank interest and charges	64	10,326
		23,234
Interest on current accounts (95 + 205)		300
		23,534
Interest on capital (1,800 + 1,350)	3,150	
Salaries (8,000 + 6,800)	14,800	17,950
Profit for partners		5,584
Jack	2,792	
Jill	2,792	5,584
		5,584

Balance sheet as at 30 June 2009

Fixed assets			
Building			22,000
Fixtures			5,550
			27,550
Current assets			
Stock	13,813		
Debtors	6,507		
Cash at bank	4,020	24,340	
Current liabilities			
Creditors	6,561		
Accruals	95	6,656	17,684
			45,234
Capital – Jack		20,000	
Capital – Jill		15,000	35,000
Current accounts:			
Jack		6,597	
Jill		3,637	10,234
			45,234

Current accounts

	Jack	Jill		Jack	Jill
Balance b/d	1,900	4,100	Interest	1,800	1,350
Interest	95	205	Salary	8,000	6,800
Drawings	4,000	3,000	Profit	2,792	2,792
Balance c/d	6,597	3,637			
	12,592	10,942		12,592	10,942
			Balance c/d	6,597	3,637

26.6.8 Self-test

Mike and Jean

Profit and loss account for the year ending 31 December 2009

Sales		298,715
Opening stock	93,460	
Purchases	195,220	
	288,680	
Closing stock	132,880	155,800
Gross profit		142,915
Less general expenses	6,448	
Salaries and wages	43,309	
Bad debts	1,912	51,669
Net profit for the year		91,246

Appropriation of net profit	Mike	Jean	Total
Interest on capital	6,700	4,100	10,800
Interest on drawings	(460)	(340)	(800)
Salary	2,600		2,600
Share of balance	39,323	39,323	78,646
	48,163	43,083	91,246

Balance sheet as at 31 December 2009

	Cost	Acc depr	NBV
Fixed assets			
Fittings and fixtures	22,000	6,600	15,400
Current assets			
Stock	132,880		
Debtors	37,800		
Cash at bank	6,512	177,192	
Current liabilities			
Creditors		21,400	155,792
			171,192
Capital – Mike		67,000	
Capital – Jean		41,000	108,000
Current accounts: *(see workings below)*			
Mike		35,507	
Jean		27,685	63,192
			171,192

Workings

Current accounts	Mike	Jean
Balance b/d	3,144	1,102
Salary	2,600	
Interest on capital	6,700	4,100
Net profit	39,323	39,323
	51,767	44,525
Drawings	15,800	16,500
Interest on drawings	460	340
Balance at year end	35,507	27,685

26.7.2 Self-test

A, B and C

Trading account for the year ended 31 December 2009

Sales	168,000
Cost of sales	42,000
Gross profit	126,000

Profit and loss account for the period

	1.1.09–30.6.09		1.7.09–31.12.09	
Gross profit		63,000		63,000
Rent	6,000		6,000	
Wages	13,000		4,000	
Office expenses	2,500		2,500	
Depreciation			525	
Interest on loan A		21,500	200	13,225
Net profit	41,500	41,500		49,775
Salary A	10,000		10,000	
Salary C		10,000	8,000	18,000
		31,500		31,775
Profit A	18,900		15,887	
Profit B	12,600		9,532	
Profit C		31,500	6,356	31,775

Note: Interest paid on a loan from a partner is not shown in the appropriation account but in the main body of the profit and loss account. The current account is still credited with the interest.
In all questions the capital accounts of the partners should be treated as fixed and any debit or credit entries should be made to the current account. In the same way the drawings should be transferred to the current account at year end.

Current accounts	*A*	*B*	*C*
1 Jan 09 Balance b/d	17,000	11,000	
Add salary	10,000		
Interest on capital			
Net profit	18,900	12,600	
Credit balance at 1.7.09	45,900	23,600	
Add machinery introduced			7,000
Salary	10,000		8,000
Interest on loan	200		
Net profit at 31 Dec	15,887	9,532	6,356
Total credit	71,987	33,132	21,356
Less transfer to loan account	5,000		
Credit balance at year end	66,987	33,132	21,356

Chapter 27

27.1.2 Self-test

The Valley Sports Club

Restaurant trading account for the year ending 31.12.09

Takings		21,700
Stock at 1.1.09	1,200	
Purchases (16,400 + 950 − 690)	16,660	
	17,860	
Closing stock	1,400	16,460
Gross profit		5,240
Less wages		5,000
Profit transferred to income & expenditure account		240

Income and expenditure account for the year ending 31.12.09

Subscriptions		14,600
Profit from restaurant		240
Raffle ticket sales	3,800	
Less expenses on raffle	1,800	2,000
Total income		16,840
Rent (2,400 + 300 − 200)	2,500	
Printing	500	
Electricity (700 + 140 − 120)	720	
Telephones (400 + 65 − 48)	417	
Repairs to equipment	620	
Depreciation of equipment (4,700 + 3,100 − 6,200)	1,600	6,357
Excess income over expenditure		10,483

Balance sheet as at 31.12.09

Fixed assets		
Exercise equipment at 1.1.09	4,700	
Additions	3,100	
	7,800	
Depreciation for the year	1,600	6,200
Current assets		
Stock	1,400	
Cash at bank	11,080	12,480
		18,680
Current liabilities		
Creditors for purchases	950	
Accrued charges	505	1,455
		17,225
Accumulated funds at 1.1.09	6,742	
Excess income over expenditure for the year	10,483	17,225

27.1.3 Self-test

The Trainer Club

Bar trading account for the year ending 31.12.09

Takings		3,980
Stock at 1.1.09	1,200	
Purchases	1,250	
	2,450	
Closing stock	1,040	1,410
Gross profit		2,570
Less wages		800
Profit transferred to income & expenditure account		1,770

Income and expenditure account for the year ending 31.12.09

Subscriptions		4,730
Profit from bar		1,770
Raffle ticket sales		1,200
Competition fees		905
Total income		8,605
Rent	2,000	
Postages and telephones	140	
Repairs to equipment	200	
Depreciation of equipment	890	3,230
Excess income over expenditure		5,375

Balance sheet as at 31.12.09

Fixed assets		
Exercise equipment at 1.1.09	8,900	
Depreciation for the year	890	8,010
Current assets		
Stock	1,040	
Cash at bank*	7,385	8,425
		16,435
Current liabilities		
Subscriptions in advance		260
		16,175
Accumulated funds at 1.1.09	10,800	
Excess income over expenditure for the year	5,375	
		16,175

* You need to calculate this figure. Add all receipts plus opening balance and deduct all payments.

Chapter 28

28.5.8 Self-test

- Nominal value £1
- Number of shares 500,000
- Number of shares 800,000
- Total value £150,000

28.10.1 Self-test

Green Ltd

Profit for the year	25,000	100,000
Less debenture interest	18,000	18,000
Profit before tax	7,000	82,000
Less tax	2,100	24,600
Profit after tax	4,900	57,400
Less preference dividends	3,600	3,600
Profit available to ordinary shareholders	1,300	53,800

$$\text{Return to equity} \quad \frac{1,300}{500,000} = 0.26\% \qquad \frac{53,800}{500,000} = 10.76\%$$

Preference shareholders receive their dividends before ordinary shareholders. In the case of cumulative preference shares, then, if the dividend cannot be paid because of a lack of funds, or a loss made by the company, it must still be paid in later years before the ordinary shares receive their dividend.

28.11.2 Self-test

Bee Co. plc

Issued share capital

Dr				Cr
Balance c/d	400,000		Balance b/d	200,000
			App & allotment	200,000
	400,000			400,000
			Balance b/d	400,000

Share premium account

Dr				Cr
Balance c/d	200,000		Balance b/d	80,000
			App & allotment	120,000
	200,000			200,000
			Balance b/d	200,000

Application and allotment account

Dr					Cr
Refunds	270,000		Bank		450,000
Share capital	200,000		Bank		140,000
Share premium	120,000				
	590,000				590,000

28.11.3 Self-test

Explor Ltd

Ordinary share capital

Dr					Cr
31 Dec 2010	Bal c/d	950,000	3 Jan 2010	Bank	500,000
			31 Jan 2010	App & allotment	315,000
			30 Jun 2010	Call account	135,000
		950,000			950,000
31 Dec 2011	Balance c/d	1,662,000	1 Jan 2011	Balance b/d*	950,000
			18 Jan 2011	App & allotment	380,000
			15 Mar 2011	Bonus – ex premium	332,000
		1,662,000			1,662,000
				Balance b/d	1,662,000

* Opening balance at 1/1/11 is made up of original offer of 500,000 shares plus offer on 11 January of 450,000 = Total of 950,000.

Share premium

Dr					Cr
31 Dec 2010	Bal c/d	420,000	3 Jan 2010	Bank	150,000
			31 Jan 2010	App & allotment	90,000
			30 Jun 2010	Call account	180,000
		420,000			420,000
15 Mar 2011	Bonus shares**	332,000	1 Jan 2011	Balance b/d*	420,000
31 Dec 2011	Balance c/d	240,000	18 Jan 2011	App & allotment	152,000
		572,000			572,000
			31 Dec 2011	Balance b/d	240,000

* Opening balance at 1/1/11 is made up of premium of 30p on original offer of 500,000 shares plus 60p premium on offer on 11 January of 450,000.

Application and allotment

Dr					Cr
31 Jan 2010	Share capital	315,000	15 Jan 2010	Bank	210,000
31 Jan 2010	Share premium	90,000	31 Jan 2010	Bank	195,000
		405,000			405,000
18 Jan 2011	Share capital	380,000	18 Jan 2011	Bank*	532,000
	Share premium	152,000			
		532,000			532,000

* The rights offer is based on issued capital of 950,000 shares. 2 shares are issued for every 5 held
= 380,000 shares.
** Bonus shares are calculated on basis of 1,330,000 shares in issue.

28.13.3 Self-test

In this question Company A acquires the assets (not net assets). Therefore we must ignore the creditors in the calculation.

Total assets acquired are £22,100 and the purchase price is £46,000. Goodwill therefore amounts to £23,900.

Payment is made by the issue of 20,000 shares for a consideration of £30,000. The balance of £16,000 is paid in cash.

The combined balance sheet will be as follows:

Balance sheet of A and B after merger

Plant and machinery		42,000
Motor vehicles		22,000
Office equipment		5,500
Computer equipment		8,000
Goodwill		23,900
		101,400
Current assets		
Stock	8,000	
Debtors	10,500	
	18,500	
Creditors	2,600	
Bank overdraft	4,300	
	6,900	11,600
		113,000
Share capital		65,000
Share premium		10,000
Profit and loss account		38,000
		113,000

28.13.4 Self-test

Highway Connections Ltd

(a) (i)

Calculation of Purchase price for Wessex Quarries Limited	
Buildings	160
Machinery	380
Furniture	37
Vehicles	145
Stock	25
Debtors	22
Bank	12
Cash	2
Goodwill	30
Creditors	(72)
Purchase Price	741

(ii) Purchase Price £741,000/£1.50 = 494,000 shares

(b) (i)

Highway Connections – Realisation Account			
Buildings	200	Creditors	46
Machinery	950		
Furniture	70	Roadworks	2,202
Vehicles	550	(Purchase Consideration)	
Stock	58		
Debtors	22		
Bank	36		
Cash	21		
Sundry Shareholders			
(Profit on Realisation)	341		
	2,248		2,248

(ii)

Highway Connections Sundry Shareholders Account			
Roadworks	2,202	Share Capital	800
(Purchase Consideration		Share Premium	200
1,468 shares at £1.50 each)		Profit & Loss Account	861
		Realisation Account	
		(Profit on Realisation)	341
	2,202		2,202

(c)

Balance sheet of Roadworks Limited as at 1 April 2007

Buildings	440	
Machinery	1,330	
Furniture	97	
Vehicles	695	
Goodwill	304	
Fixed Assets Total		2,866
Stock	80	
Debtors	44	
Bank	48	
Cash	23	
Current Assets Total	195	
Creditors	118	
Working capital		77
Net Assets		2,943
Ordinary Shares of £1 each	1,962	
Share Premium @ 50p share	981	
Capital Employed		2,943

(d) **For Merger**

Shareholders in Highway Connections "receive a profit" on realisation of £341,000 also Goodwill valuation of £274,000

New company should enjoy benefits of vertical integration as in same line of business

New company could enjoy economies of scale e.g. bulk buying of machinery

Or enjoy managerial economies of scale or marketing economies of scale

Larger company could enjoy financial benefits e.g. easier to get bank loans at a lower interest rate

Against Merger

Dilution of ownership and voting power

Wessex Quarries do not appear to be in a healthy financial state e.g. negative profit & loss reserve

Original Wessex balance sheet appears to have many assets overvalued e.g. machinery overvalued by £100,000

Also liquidity position of Wessex is worrying as they appear to have low working capital ratio/negative working capital

Wessex may be a drain on the liquid resources of the new company, especially with the large amount of creditors to pay

28.13.5 Self test

(a) In the books of Sun Ltd

Realisation Account

Jan 1	Buildings	70,000	Creditors	4,600
	Machinery	20,000	SunLand Ltd (PP)	148,000
	Stock	2,300		
	Debtors	1,500		
	Bank	18,800		
	Sundry Shareholders	40,000		
		152,600		152,600

Sundry Shareholders Account

Jan 1	SunLand Ltd	148,000	Share Capital	100,000
			Profit/loss	8,000
			Realisation (Profit)	40,000
		148,000		148,000

(b) Calculation of Purchase Price

	Sun Ltd	Land Ltd
Goodwill	20,000	14,000
Buildings	90,000	
Machinery	20,000	80,000
Vehicles (£40,000 − £3,800)		36,200
Stock	2,300	21,000
Debtors	1,500	14,050
Bank (£12,000 + £3,000)	18,800	15,000
	152,600	180,250
Less Creditors	4,600	3,450
PURCHASE PRICE	148,000	176,800
Shares issued at 50p each	296,000	353,600

Total shares = 649,600

Chapter 29

29.2.3 Self-test

Larnaca Limited

(a)   **Profit and loss account for year ended 31 March 2006**

Turnover		900,000
Cost of sales*		560,751
Gross profit		339,249
Administrative expenses* W1	145,100	
Selling and distribution costs	68,000	213,100
		126,149
Interest payable* W2		2,800
Profit on ordinary activities before tax		123,349
Corporation tax		11,000
Profit on ordinary activities after tax		112,349
Dividends		10,000
Retained profit for the year		102,349
Retained earnings brought forward		19,000
Retained earnings for the year		102,349
Retained earnings carried forward		121,349

Workings
W1
Admin Expenses

Audit fees	800
Directors fees	32,000
Office Expenses	74,800
Depr on Premises	12,000
Depr on Machinery	25,500
	145,100

W2
Interest payable

Int on Loan stock	800
Int on Debentures	2,000
	2,800

Balance Sheet at 31 March 2006

Fixed Assets			
Tangible			
Leasehold workshop*		108,000	
Machinery*		<u>117,500</u>	225,500
Current Assets			
Stock	86,000		
Prepaid expenses	700		
Debtors	95,200		
Cash at bank	<u>25,789</u>	207,689	
Creditors – amounts falling due within 1 year			
Creditors		<u>76,840</u>	
Net current assets			130,849
Total assets less current liabilities			356,349
Creditors – amounts falling due after more than 1 year			
8% Debenture stock		25,000	
8% Loan stock		<u>10,000</u>	<u>35,000</u>
			<u>321,349</u>
Financed by:			
Capital and reserves:			
Share capital		200,000	
Retained earnings		<u>121,349</u>	<u>321,349</u>

W3	
Shop at cost	180,000
– provision for depreciation	72,000
	108,000
W4	
Machinery	160,000
+ additions	10,000
– provision for depreciation	–52,500
	117,500
W5	
Creditors	50,500
Accruals	5,340
Corp Tax	11,000
Prop Dividend	10,000
	76,840

29.2.4 Self-test

Lister Ltd

Profit and loss account for the year ended 30 June 2009

Sales		210,625
Less cost of sales		
Opening stock	13,400	
Purchases	124,000	
Closing stock	15,500	121,900
Gross profit		88,725
Less expenses		
Carriage outwards	3,000	
Directors' salary	5,500	
Electricity and gas	2,800	
Insurance	1,400	
Office expenses	4,900	
Rent and rates	7,750	
Wages and salaries	35,800	
Depreciation – plant and machinery	5,360	
Depreciation – motor vehicles	1,000	
Provision for bad debts	840	68,350
Net profit		20,375
Dividend – interim	625	
Dividend – final	625	1,250
Retained profit for the year		19,125

Balance sheet as at 30 June 2009

	Cost	Acc depr	NBV
Fixed assets			
Plant and machinery	42,000	20,560	21,440
Motor vehicles	8,000	5,000	3,000
	50,000	25,560	24,440
Current assets			
Stock		15,500	
Trade debtors	32,800		
Less: provision for bad debts	1,640	31,160	
Prepayment		300	
Bank		700	
		47,660	
Current liabilities			
Trade creditors	13,900		
Accruals:			
Rent and Rates	250		
Dividend	625	14,775	
Net current assets			32,885
Net assets			57,325
Financed by:			
Authorised share capital			
200,000 Ordinary Shares of 50p		100,000	
Issued share capital			
50,000 Ordinary Shares of 50p each, fully paid		25,000	
Profit and loss account (13,200 + 19,125)		32,325	57,325

29.2.5 Self-test

Allied Holdings Ltd

Trading, profit and loss account for the year ended 31 December 2009

Sales			503,000
Less cost of sales			
Stock	43,000		
Add purchases	191,000	234,000	
Less stock		18,900	215,100
Gross profit			287,900
Less expenses			
Audit fees		3,500	
Directors' remuneration		48,000	
Motor expenses		6,300	
Salaries		93,600	
Provision for bad debts		2,730	
Bad debts		12,100	
Depreciation – plant and equipment		14,300	
Depreciation – motor vehicles		3,140	
Depreciation – fixtures and fittings		1,200	184,870
Net profit for the year			103,030
Less appropriations			
Dividend preference shares		4,800	
Dividend ordinary shares – interim		12,000	
Dividend ordinary shares – final		20,000	36,800
			66,230
Add balance at 1/1/09			62,000
Balance of undistributed profit at 31/12/09			128,230

Allied Holdings Ltd – Balance sheet as at 31 December 2009

	Cost	Accumulated depreciation	Book value
Fixed assets			
Land and buildings	1,950,000		1,950,000
Plant and equipment	143,000	28,300	114,700
Motor vehicle	25,000	12,440	12,560
Fixtures and fittings	12,000	2,300	9,700
	2,130,000	43,040	2,086,960
Current assets			
Stock	18,900		
Debtors	34,470		
Cash in bank	11,100	64,470	
Less current liabilities			
Creditors	19,600		
Proposed dividends	24,800	44,400	
Working capital			20,070
			2,107,030
Long-term liability			
Debentures			78,800
			2,028,230
Financed by:			
Authorised share capital			
800,000 6% preference shares of £1 each			800,000
4,400,000 ordinary shares of 50p each			2,200,000
			3,000,000
Issued share capital			
800,000 6% preference shares of £1 each, fully paid		800,000	
2,000,000 ordinary shares of 50p each, fully paid		1,000,000	
Add reserves			
Share premium account		100,000	
Profit and loss account balance		128,230	
Shareholders' funds			2,028,230

29.2.6 Self-test

Delta Furnishing Ltd

Trading, profit and loss account for the year ended 31 December 2009

Sales			199,000
Less cost of sales			
Stock	18,800		
Add purchases	80,200	99,000	
Less stock		34,000	65,000
Gross profit			134,000
Reduction in provision for bad debts			50
			134,050
Less expenses			
Rates and insurance		1,300	
Carriage outwards		9,240	
Wages and salaries		46,500	
Office expenses		12,400	
Debenture interest		1,800	
Directors' remuneration		2,000	
Bad debts		700	
Advertising		12,940	
Depreciation – Furniture and fittings		2,400	89,280
Net profit before taxation			44,770
Less:			
Ordinary dividend			2,700
Balance of undistributed profit for the year			42,070

Delta Furnishing Ltd Balance sheet as at 31 December 2009

	Cost	Accumulated depreciation	Book value
Fixed assets			
Freehold property	180,850		180,850
Furniture and fittings	24,000	21,400	2,600
	204,850	21,400	183,450
Current assets			
Stock	34,000		
Debtors	4,800		
Prepaid expenses	460		
Cash in bank	400		
Cash in hand	300	39,960	
Less current liabilities			
Creditors	24,640		
Proposed dividend	2,700		
Accrued expenses	3,000	30,340	
Working capital			9,620
			193,070
Less: Long-term liabilities			
10% debentures			18,000
			175,070
Financed by:			
Authorised share capital			
20,000 6% preference shares of £1 each			20,000
180,000 ordinary shares of £1 each			180,000
			200,000
Issued share capital			
10,000 6% preference shares of £1 each			
100,000 ordinary shares of £1 each		90,000	
Add reserves			
Profit and loss account (43,000 + 42,070)		85,070	
Shareholders' funds			175,070

29.2.7 Self-test

Hilmor Ltd

Trading, profit and loss account for the year ended 31 December 2009

Sales			451,000
Less cost of sales			
Stock	17,460		
Add purchases	280,020	297,480	
Less stock		46,500	250,980
Gross profit			200,020
Less expenses			
Rates and insurance		1,700	
Motor expenses		4,700	
Audit fees		1,300	
Wages and salaries		122,000	
Directors' remuneration		29,000	
Bad debts		2,600	
Provision for bad debts		820	
Advertising		17,400	
Depreciation – plant and equipment		2,200	
Depreciation – furniture and fittings		600	
Depreciation – motor vehicles		3,000	185,320
Net profit for the year			14,700
Add opening balance			12,400
Closing balance at year end			27,100
Less appropriations			
Preference dividends		1,200	
Ordinary dividend		10,000	11,200
Balance of undistributed profit			15,900

Hilmor Ltd Balance sheet as at 31 December 2009

	Cost	Accumulated depreciation	Book value
Fixed assets			
Freehold land	100,000		100,000
Plant and equipment	22,000	8,200	13,800
Motor vehicles	15,000	9,700	5,300
Furniture and fittings	6,000	1,600	4,400
	143,000	19,500	123,500
Current assets			
Stock	46,500		
Debtors	12,780		
Cash in bank	6,420		
		65,700	
Less current liabilities			
Creditors	17,700		
Proposed dividend	10,600	28,300	
Working capital			37,400
			160,900
Financed by:			
Authorised share capital			
20,000 6% preference shares of £1	20,000		
180,000 £1 ordinary shares	180,000		
	200,000		
Issued share capital			
20,000 6% preference shares of £1	20,000		
100,000 £1 ordinary shares	100,000	120,000	
Add reserves			
Profit and loss account	15,900		
General reserve	15,000		
Share premium	10,000	40,900	
Shareholders' funds			160,900

29.2.8 Self-test

Washer Trading Ltd

Trading, profit and loss account for the year ended 31 December 2010

Sales		975,000
Less cost of sales		
Stock 1/1/10	325,000	
Purchases	481,000	
	806,000	
Stock 31/12/10	216,000	590,000
Gross profit		385,000
Office expenses	98,200	
Selling expenses	26,000	
Bank interest	5,200	
Depreciation: Office fittings	78,000	
Depreciation: Motor vehicles	109,200	
Audit fees	14,000	
Consultation fees	28,000	
Provision doubtful debt increase	7,800	366,400
Net profit for the year		18,600
Add balance 1/1/10		486,200
Balance at 31/12/10		504,800

Balance sheet as at 31 December 2010

	At cost	Acc depr	Net BV
Fixed assets			
Land and buildings	520,000		520,000
Office fittings	390,000	156,000	234,000
Motor vehicles	520,000	265,200	254,800
	1,430,000	421,200	1,008,800
Current assets			
Stock	216,000		
Debtors	234,000		
Prepayment	24,000	474,000	
Current liabilities			
Creditors	195,000		
Overdraft	78,000		
Accruals	42,000	315,000	
Net current assets			159,000
Net assets			1,167,800
Financed by:			
Authorised share capital			
500,000 £1 ordinary shares			500,000
Issued share capital			
416,000 £1 ordinary shares fully paid		416,000	
Share premium account		156,000	
Revaluation reserve		91,000	
Profit and loss		504,800	1,167,800

29.2.9 Self-test

Nuwaste Trading Ltd

Trading, profit and loss account for the year ended 31 December 2010

Sales		1,800,000
Less cost of sales		
Stock 1/1/10	600,000	
Purchases	888,000	
	1,488,000	
Stock 31/12/10	398,000	1,090,000
Gross profit		710,000
Selling commission and rent	181,600	
Office expenses	48,000	
Debenture interest	14,400	
Depreciation: Fixtures and fittings	144,000	
Depreciation: Motor vehicles	201,600	
Audit fees	20,000	
Consulting fees	38,000	
Increase in bad debts provision	14,400	662,000
Net profit for the year		48,000
Add balance 1/1/10		897,600
Balance at 31/12/10		945,600

Balance sheet as at 31 December 2010

	At cost	Acc depr	Net BV
Fixed assets			
Freehold land and buildings	960,000		960,000
Fixtures and fittings	720,000	288,000	432,000
Motor vehicles	960,000	489,600	470,400
	2,640,000	777,600	1,862,400
Current assets			
Stock	398,000		
Debtors	432,000		
Prepayment	44,000	874,000	
Current liabilities			
Creditors	360,000		
Overdraft	144,000		
Accruals	62,800	566,800	
Net current assets			307,200
			2,169,600
Long-term liabilities			
Debentures			288,000
Net assets			1,881,600
Financed by:			
Authorised share capital			
1,500,000 £1 ordinary shares			1,500,000
Issued share capital			
768,000 £1 ordinary shares fully paid		768,000	
Revaluation reserve		168,000	
Profit and loss		945,600	1,881,600

29.2.10 Self-test

Camden Trading Ltd

Profit and loss account for the year ended 31 December 2010

Sales		375,000
Less cost of sales		
Stock 1 Jan 2010	125,000	
Purchases	185,000	
	310,000	
Stock 31 Dec 2010	175,000	135,000
Gross profit		240,000
Administration expenses	35,000	
Selling and distribution expenses	10,000	
Debenture interest	3,000	
Consulting fees	15,000	
Depreciation: Fixtures and fittings	30,000	
Depreciation: Motor vehicles	42,000	
Audit fees	12,000	
Provision for doubtful debt increase	3,000	150,000
Net profit for the year		90,000
Add balance 1 Jan 2010		187,000
Balance at 31 Dec 2010		277,000

Balance sheet as at 31 December 2010

	At cost	Acc depr	Net BV
Fixed assets			
Land and buildings	200,000		200,000
Fixtures and fittings	150,000	60,000	90,000
Motor vehicles	200,000	102,000	98,000
	550,000	162,000	388,000
Current assets			
Stock	175,000		
Debtors	90,000		
Prepayment	12,000	277,000	
Current liabilities			
Creditors	75,000		
Overdraft	30,000		
Accruals	28,000	133,000	
Net current assets			144,000
			532,000
Long-term liabilities			
Debentures			60,000
Net assets			472,000
Financed by:			
Authorised share capital			
200,000 £1 ordinary shares			200,000
Issued share capital			
160,000 £1 ordinary shares fully paid		160,000	
Revaluation reserve		35,000	
Profit and loss		277,000	
			472,000

Chapter 30

30.1.1 Self-test

Kitt Ltd

6 months insurance prepaid = 6/12 of £8,000	4,000
Accountancy fees to be accrued	2,000
Bad debts must be deducted from debtors	40,000
Debenture interest 7% to be accrued	14,000
Depreciation	
Delivery vehicles = 20% on cost	40,000
Machinery = 15% on cost	36,000
Commission to sales agents to be accrued	12,000

Profit and loss account for the year ended 31 December 2009

Sales		1,494,000
Less cost of sales		
Opening stock	400,000	
Purchases	700,000	
Closing stock	360,000	740,000
Gross profit		754,000
Less expenses		
Administration expenses	404,000	
Bad debts	40,000	
Depreciation	76,000	
Selling and distribution costs	32,000	
Debenture interest	14,000	
Interest paid	10,000	576,000
Net profit		178,000

Balance sheet as at 31 December 2009

	Cost	Acc depr	Net BV
Fixed assets			
Buildings	460,000		460,000
Machinery	240,000	136,000	104,000
Delivery vehicles	200,000	160,000	40,000
	900,000	296,000	604,000
Current assets			
Stock	360,000		
Debtors	348,000		
Prepayments	4,000		
	712,000		
Current liabilities			
Creditors	400,000		
Bank overdraft	10,000		
Accruals	28,000		
	438,000		
Net current assets			274,000
			878,000
Long-term liabilities			
7% debentures			200,000
Net assets			678,000
Financed by:			
Share capital			
Ordinary shares		100,000	
7% preference shares		100,000	
Share premium account		110,000	
Profit and loss account (190,000 + 178,000)		368,000	678,000

30.1.2 Self-test

Muddle Ltd

Profit and loss account for the year ended 31 December 2008

Sales		2,150,400
Less cost of sales		
Opening stock	640,000	
Purchases	1,080,000	
Closing stock	493,000	1,227,000
Gross profit		923,400
Less expenses		
Administration expenses	654,600	
Provision for doubtful debts	18,624	
Depreciation (48,000 + 11,200 + 5,200)	64,400	
Selling and distribution costs	110,600	
Debenture interest	28,800	
Interest paid	46,000	923,024
Net profit		376

Balance sheet as at 31 December 2008

	Cost	Acc depr	Net BV
Fixed assets			
Fixtures and fittings	436,000	389,200	46,800
Office equipment	384,000	171,200	212,800
Motor vehicles	320,000	240,000	80,000
	1,140,000	800,400	339,600
Current assets			
Stock	493,000		
Debtors	602,176		
Cash at bank	68,000		
	1,163,176		
Current liabilities			
Creditors	540,000		
Accruals (28,800 + 5,000 + 8,600)	42,400		
	582,400		
Net current assets			580,776
			920,376
Long-term liabilities			
9% debentures			320,000
Net assets			600,376
Financed by:			
Share capital		220,000	
Profit and loss account		380,376	600,376
			600,376

30.1.3 Self-test

Allie Ltd

Profit and loss account for year ended 30 June 2009

Sales		2,056,290
Less cost of sales		
Opening stock	126,900	
Purchases	1,203,980	
	1,330,880	
Closing stock	195,000	1,135,880
Gross profit		920,410
Investment income	4,240	
Commission received	5,700	
Discount received	12,340	22,280
		942,690
Less expenses		
Advertising	30,130	
Debenture interest	7,000	
Directors' salary	55,000	
Discount allowed	51,430	
Electricity	22,134	
Insurance	17,890	
Office expenses	43,210	
Machine repairs	8,000	
Rent and rates	67,210	
Wages and salaries	321,900	
Depreciation:		
Machine	48,284	
Vehicles	8,035	
Provision for bad debts	6,572	686,795
Net profit		255,895
Dividend paid		4,400
Retained profit for the year		251,495
Add balance at 1.7.08		121,300
Balance at 30.6.09		372,795

Note: In this example both the discount received and discount allowed are shown in the profit and loss account. It could be argued that the discount received reduces the cost of purchases and therefore should be shown as a deduction from purchases.

Balance sheet as at 30 June 2009

	Cost	Acc depr	NBV
Fixed assets			
Machinery	410,320	217,184	193,136
Motor vehicles	83,240	59,135	24,105
Investments	28,500		28,500
	522,060	276,319	245,741
Current assets			
Stock	195,000		
Debtors	286,368		
Bank	19,900		
	501,268		
Current liabilities			
Creditors	69,214		
Accruals	8,000		
Debenture interest	7,000		
	84,214		
Net current assets			417,054
			662,795
Long-term liabilities			
Debentures 10%			70,000
Net assets			592,795
Financed by:			
Ordinary share capital		220,000	
Profit and loss account		372,795	
			592,795

30.1.4 Self-test

Sunnie Ltd

Profit and loss account or year ended 30 June 2009

Sales		2,109,580
Less cost of sales		
Opening stock	341,570	
Purchases	1,672,230	
	2,013,800	
Closing stock	443,100	1,570,700
Gross profit		538,880
Discount received	2,483	
Investment Income	8,135	
Commission received	11,330	21,948
		560,828
Less expenses		
Telephone and postages	12,032	
Debenture interest	24,000	
Directors' salary	165,000	
Discount allowed	10,874	
Electricity and gas	26,780	
Insurance and rates	12,114	
Office salaries and commissions	12,322	
Machine repairs	11,300	
Rent and rates	86,200	
Bank charges	2,314	
Depreciation:		
Plant and machinery	22,496	
Delivery vehicles	28,272	
Loose tools	3,760	
Provision for bad debts	11,395	428,859
Net profit		131,969
Interim dividend		6,000
Retained profit for the year		125,969
Add balance at 1.7.08		187,600
Balance at 30.6.09		313,569

Balance sheet as at 30 June 2009

	Cost	Acc depr	NBV
Fixed assets			
Plant and machinery	246,880	156,896	89,984
Delivery vehicles	113,087	96,079	17,008
Loose tools	29,760	3,760	26,000
	389,727	256,735	132,992
Current assets			
Stock	443,100		
Debtors	429,695		
Bank	19,870		
	892,665		
Current liabilities			
Creditors	236,788		
Accruals	11,300		
Debenture interest	24,000		
	272,088		
Net current assets			620,577
			753,569
Long-term liabilities			
12% debentures			200,000
Net assets			553,569
Financed by:			
Ordinary share capital		240,000	
Profit and loss account		313,569	
			553,569

30.1.5 Self-test

Terry Ltd

Profit and loss account for the year ended 30 June 2008

Sales		316,800
Less cost of sales		214,200
Gross profit		102,600
Add:		
Interest received	1,011	
Discount received	3,879	4,890
		107,490
Less:		
Selling and distribution costs*	4,512	
Administrative expenses**	5,871	10,383
Net profit before interest and tax		97,107
Less interest payable***		9,008
Profit on ordinary activities before tax		88,099
Taxation		2,430
Profit on ordinary activities after tax		85,669
Less dividends to shareholders		5,700
Retained profit for the year		79,969
Retained earnings brought forward		20,008
Retained earnings at 30.6.08		99,977

* Selling and distribution costs = Depreciation
** Administrative expenses = Bad debts + Bank charges + Office expenses
*** Interest payable = Interest on loans + Debenture interest

Balance sheet for the year ending 30 June 2008

Fixed assets		
Intangible:		
Goodwill		40,000
Tangible:		
Machinery	123,420	
Office equipment	11,800	135,220
		175,220
Current assets		
Stock	5,900	
Debtors	5,890	
Prepayments	2,970	
Cash at bank	1,003	
	15,763	
Current liabilities		
Creditors	5,662	
Taxation	4,142	
Dividends due	5,700	
Accruals	1,772	
	17,276	
Net current assets		−1,513
		173,707
Long-term liabilities		
Loan due 2012	12,900	
Debentures	6,000	−18,900
Net assets		154,807
Financed by:		
Ordinary shares		30,000
Preference shares		19,000
Share premium		5,830
Retained earnings		99,977
		154,807

30.1.6 Self-test

Sarah and Mary

As we do not have a balanced trial balance we need to construct a statement showing the assets and liabilities of the partnership. Any missing figure will be the profit for the year.

Assets and liabilities of the partnership at 31 December 2008

Plant and machinery	82,000	
Office equipment	7,448	89,448
Stock	3,859	
Debtors	8,177	
Cash at bank	1,942	
Cash on hand	106	14,084
		103,532
Creditors		2,314
		101,218
Drawings – Sarah	28,900	
Drawings – Mary	34,600	63,500
		164,718
Less: Capital accounts		100,000
Profit for the year		64,718

Profit and loss appropriation account for year ended 31 December 2008

Net profit			64,718
Interest on capital:			
Sarah	3,500		
Mary	3,500	7,000	
Salaries:			
Sarah	28,000		
Mary	28,000	56,000	
Share of profit:			
Sarah	859		
Mary	859	1,718	64,718

Partners' current accounts at 31 December 2008

	Sarah	Mary		Sarah	Mary
Drawings	28,900	34,600	Interest on capital	3,500	3,500
Balance c/d	3,459		Salary	28,000	28,000
			Profit share	859	859
			Balance c/d		2,241
	32,359	34,600		32,359	34,600
Balance b/d		2,241	Balance b/d	3,459	

30.1.7 Self-test

NuDeal Ltd

Trading and profit and loss account for the year ended 31 December 2010

Sales			796,000
Less cost of sales			
Opening stock	75,200		
Add purchases	320,800		
Add carriage inwards	2,960	398,960	
Less closing stock		123,500	275,460
Gross profit			520,540
Add:			
Reversal of provision for doubtful debts			260
			520,800
Less expenses			
Rates		5,790	
Bad debts		2,800	
Wages and salaries		194,600	
Carriage outwards		34,000	
Office expenses		49,600	
Debenture interest		7,200	
Advertising		51,760	
Depreciation – Equipment		9,600	355,350
Net profit before taxation			165,450
Taxation			33,090
Net profit after taxation			132,360
Less ordinary dividends			28,800
Profit for the year			103,560
Add balance carried forward			172,000
Balance of undistributed profit			275,560

Nudeal Ltd Balance sheet as at 31 December 2010

	Cost	Less depreciation	Book value
Fixed assets			
Equipment	96,000	85,600	10,400
Land and buildings	723,400		723,400
	819,400	85,600	733,800
Current assets			
Stock	123,500		
Debtors	19,260		
Rates prepaid	1,250		
Cash in bank	1,600		
Cash in hand	1,200	146,810	
Less current liabilities			
Creditors	98,560		
Provision for taxation	33,090		
Accruals	12,600		
Proposed dividend	28,800	173,050	
Working capital			−26,240
			707,560
Long-term liabilities			
10% debentures			72,000
			635,560
Financed by:			
Authorised share capital			
2,000,000 ordinary shares of 50p each		1,000,000	
Issued share capital			
720,000 ordinary shares of 50p each			360,000
Profit and loss account balance			275,560
Shareholders' funds			635,560

30.1.8 Self-test

James Ltd

Trading and profit and loss account for the year ended 31 December 2010

Sales		451,000
Less cost of sales		
Opening stock	17,460	
Add purchases	280,020	
	297,480	
Less closing stock	86,500	210,980
Gross profit		240,020
Less expenses		
Audit fees	1,300	
Bad debts	2,600	
Wages and salaries	122,000	
Rates and office expenses	1,700	
Directors remuneration	29,000	
Motor expenses	4,700	
Depreciation – Plant and equipment	2,200	
Depreciation – Furniture and fittings	500	
Depreciation – Motor vehicles	3,000	
Commission	17,400	
Provision for bad debts	820	185,220
Net profit before taxation		54,800
Taxation		16,440
Net profit after taxation		38,360
Less appropriations		
Preference dividends – paid	600	
Preference dividends – proposed	600	
Ordinary dividend – proposed	5,000	6,200
Net profit for the year		32,160
Balance at 1.1.10		12,400
Balance of undistributed profit		44,560

Balance sheet as at 31 December 2010

	Cost	Less depreciation	Book value
Fixed assets			
Plant and equipment	22,000	8,200	13,800
Furniture and fittings	6,000	1,500	4,500
Motor vehicle	15,000	9,700	5,300
Land and buildings	100,000		100,000
	143,000	19,400	123,600
Current assets			
Stock	86,500		
Debtors	12,780		
Cash in bank	6,420	105,700	
Less current liabilities			
Creditors	17,700		
Provision for tax	16,440		
Proposed dividends	5,600	39,740	
Working capital			65,960
			189,560
Financed by:			
Authorised share capital			
360,000 ordinary shares of 50p each			180,000
20,000 6% preference shares of £1 each			20,000
			200,000
Issued share capital			
200,000 ordinary shares of 50p each			100,000
20,000 6% preference shares of £1 each			20,000
Add reserves			
Share premium account		10,000	
General reserve		15,000	
Profit and loss account		44,560	69,560
Shareholders' funds			189,560

30.1.9 Self-test

Aye Ltd

Issued capital is 120,000 shares of £1 each = £120,000.
The dividend is calculated at 8 per cent of the amount issued = £9,600.

30.1.10 Self-test

Only a rights issue (b) will introduce further cash into the company.

30.1.11 Self-test

Top Ltd

Net assets acquired	£27,300
Goodwill	2,700
Purchase price	£30,000
Shares	27,000
Cash	£3,000

Combined balance sheet of Top Ltd

Goodwill		2,700
Equipment	47,000	
Motor vehicles	23,000	
Office fixtures	3,000	73,000
		75,700
Current assets		
Stock	9,000	
Debtors	8,300	
Cash at bank	6,800	
	24,100	
Creditors	8,800	15,300
		91,000
Ordinary shares	77,000	
Revenue reserves	14,000	91,000

30.1.12 Self-test

Top Ltd

Assets acquired	£24,300
Goodwill	95,700
Purchase price	£120,000
Shares	80,000
Share premium	32,000
Cash	£8,000

Balance sheet of Top Ltd after acquisition

Goodwill		95,700
Equipment	44,000	
Motor vehicles	22,000	
Office fixtures	3,000	69,000
		164,700
Current assets		
Stock	8,400	
Debtors	8,100	
Cash at bank	1,800	
	18,300	
Creditors	7,000	11,300
		176,000
Ordinary shares	130,000	
Share premium account	32,000	
Revenue reserves	14,000	
		176,000

30.1.13 Self-test

Robin and Ann

Profit and loss account for the year ended 30 June 2009

Sales		197,000
Stock	7,320	
Purchases	21,008	
	28,328	
Closing stock	9,820	18,508
Gross profit		178,492
Depreciation – plant and machinery	12,700	
Depreciation – motor vehicles	8,420	
Salary and wages	7,120	
Postage and telephone	4,930	
Printing and stationery	2,460	
Rates and taxes	5,922	
Bad debts	425	
Interest on loan	2,940	
Electricity	3,649	
Selling expenses	2,086	
Provision for bad debts	314	50,966
		127,526
Interest on drawings (160 + 475)		635
		128,161
Interest on capital (18,000 + 11,000)	29,000	
Salaries (36,000 + 24,000)	60,000	89,000
Profit for partners		39,161
Robin	19,581	
Ann	19,580	39,161

Robin – current account

1/7/08	Balance b/d	1,021	30/6/09	Salary	36,000
1/3/09	Drawings	8,000		Interest	18,000
30/6/09	Interest	160		Profit share	19,581
	Balance c/d	64,400			
		73,581			73,581
			1/7/09	Balance b/d	64,400

Ann – current account

1/7/08	Balance b/d	14,060	30/6/09	Salary	24,000
1/10/09	Drawings	9,500		Interest	11,000
30/6/09	Interest	475		Profit share	19,580
	Balance c/d	30,545			
		54,580			54,580
			1/7/09	Balance b/d	30,545

Balance sheet as at 30 June 2009

	Cost	Accumulated depreciation	NBV
Fixed assets			
Land and building	316,734		316,734
Motor vehicles	42,100	30,900	11,200
Plant and machinery	127,000	37,500	89,500
	485,834	68,400	417,434
Current assets			
Stock	9,820		
Debtors	3,525		
Prepayments	98		
Cash at bank	8,103	21,546	
Current liabilities			
Creditors	8,960		
Accruals	3,075		
Loan*	42,000	54,035	−32,489
			384,945
Capital – Robin		180,000	
Capital – Ann		110,000	290,000
Current accounts:			
Robin		64,400	
Ann		30,545	94,945
			384,945

* Note: As the loan is repayable on 1 July it is shown as a current liability.

30.1.14 Self-test

Monica, Cyril and Gene

Profit and loss account for the year ended 31 December 2010

Sales less returns		285,400
Stock	44,970	
Purchases less returns	82,470	
	127,440	
Closing stock	31,000	96,440
Gross profit		188,960
Provision for bad debts reversed		1,602
Investment income		1,420
		191,982
Depreciation – motor vehicles	4,000	
Salary and wages	17,080	
Bank charges	370	
Printing and stationery	1,870	
Rates and taxes	12,990	
Bad debts	2,000	
Interest on loan	5,390	
Office expenses	2,210	
Motor expenses	3,340	49,250
		142,732
Interest on capital – Monica	4,950	
Interest on capital – Cyril	3,150	
Interest on capital – Gene	1,350	
	9,450	
Salaries – Monica	19,000	
Salaries – Gene	23,000	
	42,000	51,450
Profit for partners		91,282
– Monica	36,513	
– Cyril	36,513	
– Gene	18,256	91,282

Monica – current account

1/01/10	Balance b/d	8,600	31/12/10	Salary	19,000
31/12/10	Balance c/d	51,863		Interest	4,950
				Profit share	36,513
		60,463			60,463
			1/1/11	Balance b/d	51,863

Cyril – current account

1/01/10	Balance b/d	3,800	31/12/10	Interest	3,150
31/12/10	Balance c/d	35,863		Profit share	36,513
		39,663			39,663
			1/1/11	Balance b/d	35,863

Gene – current account

1/1/10	Balance b/d	4,800	31/12/10	Salary		23,000
31/12/10	Balance c/d	37,806		Interest		1,350
				Profit share		18,256
		42,606				42,606
			1/1/11	Balance b/d		37,806

Balance sheet as at 31 December 2010

	Cost	Acc depr	NBV
Fixed assets			
Goodwill	19,800		19,800
Land and building	211,590		211,590
Delivery vehicles	40,000	34,210	5,790
	271,390	34,210	237,180
Current assets			
Stock	31,000		
Debtors	24,402		
Prepayments	160		
Other debtors *(investment income)*	320		
Cash at bank	13,050	68,932	
Current liabilities			
Creditors	22,850		
Accruals (240 + 3,490)	3,730	26,580	42,352
			279,532
Long-term loan			49,000
			230,532
Capital – Monica	55,000		
Capital – Cyril	35,000		
Capital – Gene	15,000	105,000	
Current accounts:			
Monica	51,863		
Cyril	35,863		
Gene	37,806	125,532	
			230,532

30.1.15 Self-test

K, L and M

Trading account for the year ending 31.12.09

Sales		401,800
Stock 1 January 2009	16,000	
Purchases	198,300	
	214,300	
Stock 31 December 2009	5,000	209,300
Gross profit		192,500

Profit and loss account for the period

	1.1. to 30.6.09		1.7. to 31.12.09		Total	
Gross profit		96,250		96,250		192,500
Wages to staff	41,050		41,050		82,100	
Office expenses	7,450		7,450		14,900	
Depreciation:						
Vehicles	4,600		4,600		9,200	
Office computers	525		525		1,050	
Interest on loan			750		750	
		53,625		54,375		108,000
Net profit		42,625		41,875		84,500
Salary						
K	8,000		8,000		16,000	
M			6,000		6,000	
Interest on capital						
K	650		650		1,300	
L	450				450	
M	350		350		700	
		9,450		15,000		24,450
Profit for partners		33,175		26,875		60,050
Share of profit						
K	16,588		13,437			30,025
L	8,294					8,294
M	8,293		13,438			21,731
		33,175		26,875		60,050

Balance sheet as at 31.12.09

	Cost	Depr	NBV
Fixed assets			
Delivery vehicles	46,000	20,200	25,800
Office computers	11,000	5,050	5,950
	57,000	25,250	31,750
Current assets			
Stock	5,000		
Debtors	14,000		
Cash at bank	41,356	60,356	
Current liabilities			
Creditors	4,600		
Accrual *(loan interest)*	750	5,350	55,006
			86,756
Less loan from L			15,000
			71,756
Capital accounts			
K	18,000		
M	10,000	28,000	
Current accounts			
K	27,325		
M	16,431		
		43,756	
			71,756

Capital accounts	K	L	M		K	L	M
Goodwill	8,000		4,000	Balance 1.1.09	26,000	18,000	14,000
				Goodwill		12,000	
Transfer to loan		15,000					
Bank		15,000					
Balance 30.6.09	18,000		10,000				
	26,000	30,000	14,000		26,000	30,000	14,000
				Balance 1.7.09	18,000		10,000

Current accounts	K	L	M		K	L	M
Drawings	11,000	8,000	6,000	Balance 1.1.09 b/d	4,000	3,000	3,000
Bank		3,744		Profit to 30 June	16,588	8,294	8,293
				Salary	8,000		
Balance 30.6.09 c/d	18,238		5,643	Interest on capital	650	450	350
	29,238	11,744	11,643		29,238	11,744	11,643
Drawings	13,000		9,000	Balance 1.7.09 b/d	18,238		5,643
				Profit to 31.12.09	13,437		13,438
Balance 31.12.09 c/d	27,325		16,431	Salary	8,000		6,000
				Interest on capital	650		350
	40,325		25,431		40,325		25,431
				Balance 1.1.10 b/d	27,325		16,431

30.1.16 Self-test

Rush and Aldridge

(a)

	DR £	CR £
Land – cost	120,000	
Fixtures and fittings	70,000	
Fixtures and fittings – depr		20,000
Creditors		17,000
Debtors	21,000	
Balance at bank		7,500
Bank loan		20,000
Provision for bad debts		1,000
Sales		98,000
Purchases	39,000	
Stock – 1-12-04	11,000	
Rent and rates	3,000	
Insurance	1,500	
Salaries and wages	13,700	
Office expenses	2,800	
Heating and lighting	1,750	
Advertising	900	
Capital – Rush		80,000
Capital – Aldridge		50,000
Current – Rush		3,850
Current – Aldridge	2,000	
Drawings -Rush	3,700	
Drawings – Aldridge	7,000	
Total	297,350	297,350

(b)

Rush and Aldridge

Trading and Profit and Loss Account for the period ended 30.11.05

Sales		98,000
Opening stock	11,000	
Purchases	39,000	
	50,000	
Closing stock	(13,800)	
Cost of goods sold		(36,200)
Gross profit		61,800
less: expenses		
Rent and rates	3,500	
Insurance	1,420	
Salaries and wages	14,820	
Office expenses	2,800	
Heat and light	1,750	
Advertising	900	
Increased provision for		
bad debts	150	
Interest	2,000	
Depreciation – fix/fittings	5,000	
		(32,340)
Net profit for appropriation		29,460
Interest on capital		
Rush	8,000	
Aldridge	5,000	
Salaries		
Rush	8,000	
Aldridge	2,000	
Profit share		
Rush	3,876	
Aldridge	2,584	
		(29,460)

Rush and Aldridge
Balance Sheet as at 30.11.05

Fixed Assets			
Land		120,000	
Fixtures and fittings	70,000		
Less: depreciation	(25,000)	45,000	165,000
Current Assets			
Stock		13,800	
Debtors	21,000		
Less: provision for bad debts	(1,150)	19,850	
Prepayments		80	
		33,730	
Current liabilities			
Creditors	17,000		
Accruals	3,620		
Bank overdraft	7,500	(28,120)	
Working Capital			5,610
			170,610
less: long-term liabilities			
Bank Loan			(20,000)
Net Assets			150,610
Financed by:			
Capital accounts			
Rush		80,000	
Aldridge		50,000	130,000
Current accounts			
Rush		20,026	
Aldridge		584	20,610
			150,610

30.1.17 Self-test

Dixon and Phillips

(a) **Trading, profit and loss and appropriation account for the year ended 31 March 2009**

Sales		78,600
Opening stock	2,100	
Add: purchases	31,700	
Less: closing stock	(4,240)	
Cost of Goods sold		(29,560)
Gross profit		49,040
Less : expenses		
Rent (1,120 + 400)	1,520	
Rates	2,360	
Insurance (3,540 − 720)	2,820	
Heating	8,020	
Salaries and wages	14,290	
Depreciation − buildings (126,000 × 0.25)	3,150	
− fixtures 0.20 × (8,000 − 1,600)	1,280	(33,440)
Net profit (available for appropriation)		15,600
Interest on capital		
− Dixon (150,000 × 0.05)	(7,500)	
− Phillips (75,000 × 0.05)	(3,750)	(11,250)
Salaries		
− Dixon	(2,000)	
− Phillips	(500)	(2,500)
Profit share		1,850
− Dixon (1,850 × 2/3)	(1,233)	
− Phillips (1,850 × 1/3)	(617)	(1,850)
		−

Dixon and Phillips
Balance Sheet at 31 March 2009

	£	£	
Fixed Assets			
– Land	100,000		100,000
– Buildings	126,000	(12,600)	113,400
– Fixtures	8,000	(2,880)	5,120
	234,000	(15,480)	218,520
Current assets			
Stock		4,240	
Debtors		4,900	
Prepayments		720	
		9,860	
Current liabilities			
Creditors	1,300		
Accruals	400		
Bank overdraft	840	(2,540)	
Working capital			7,320
Net assets			225,840
Financed by			
Capital accounts			
Dixon		150,000	
Phillips		75,000	225,000
Current accounts			
Dixon		4,803	
Phillips		(3,963)	840
			225,840

Current accounts *

	Dixon	Phillips
Opening balance	(1,750)	(2,650)
Interest on capital	7,500	3,750
Salaries	2,000	500
Profit share	1,233	617
Drawings	(4,180)	(6,180)
Closing balance	4,803	(3,963)

30.1.18 Self-test

Filling and Kap

(a)   **Profit and Loss Account for year ended 31 March 2006**

Opening stock	2,000			Fees received	42,000
Materials	22,000				
Less drawings	500				
Less closing stock	640	22,860			
Wages		40,000			
Admin Expenses		8,500			
Advertising		840			
Interest on loan (Filling)		500			
Insurance owing		900			
Provision for depr fittings		6,000			
			79,600		
Net Profit			340,400		
			420,000		420,000

(b)   **Appropriation Account for year ended 31 March 2006**

Interest on Capital				Net Profit	340,400
Filling	5,000			Interest on Drawings	
Kap	2,500	7,500		Filling	1,000
Salaries				Kap	950
Filling	80,000				
Kap	80,000	160,000	167,500		
Share of Profit					
Filling	104,910				
Kap	69,940		174,850		
			342,350		342,350

Current Accounts of Filling and Kap

	Filling	Kap		Filling	Kap
Balance b/d		15,000	Balance b/d	5,000	
Drawings	100,500	95,000	Interest on Capital	5,000	2,500
Interest on drawings	1,000	950	Share of Profit	104,910	69,940
Balance c/d	93,910	41,490	Salary	80,000	80,000
			Interest on Loan	500	
	195,410	152,440		195,410	152,440

(d)   **Balance sheet at 31 March 2006**

Fixed Assets			
Premises		255,300	
Fixtures & Fittings	60,000		
Less provision for depreciation	24,000	36,000	291,300
Current Assets			
Stock	640		
Bank	7,500		
Cash	275	8,415	
Less Current Liabilities			
Insurance owing	900		
Creditors	3,415	4,315	
Working Capital			4,100
			295,400
Capital Accounts			
Filling	100,000		
Kap	50,000	150,000	
Current Accounts			
Filling	93,910		
Kap	41,490	135,400	285,400
Loan from Filling			10,000
			295,400

30.1.19 Self-test

Sylett Cricket

Subscription account

April 1	Balance b/d	250	April 1	Balance b/d	100
Mar 31	Inc/Exp	50,000	Mar 31	Bank/R & P	50,250
Mar 31	Balance c/d	150	Mar 31	Balance c/d	50
		50,400			50,400
Apr 1	Balance b/d	50	Apr 1	Balance b/d	150

Income and Expenditure Account of Sylett Cricket Club for year ended 31 March 2006

Rent	1,600		Subscriptions	50,000
Less prepaid	120	1,480	Competition receipts	800
Wages	8,500			
Add accrued	140	8,640		
Repairs		320		
Competition fees		350		
Deprn on Equip		2,500		
Loss on sales equipment		36	13,650	
SURPLUS			37,150	
			50,800	50,800

30.1.20 Self-test

Charford Social club

Income and Expenditure account of the Charford Social Club for year ended 31 December 2002					
Expenditure			**Income**		
Rent		500	Subscriptions	4,200	
Wages		5,200	Less last years	80	
Light and heat	1,870		Less next years	120	
Add electricity owing	100	1,970	Add in arrears	90	4,090
Draw prizes		400	Sale of draw tickets		900
Dance expenses		340	Sale of dance tickets		1,000
Refreshments	1,500		Sale of refreshments		4,000
Add owing	600		Deficit		640
Less last years	500	1,600			
Depreciation on furniture		620			
		10,630			10,630

30.1.21 Self-test

Bromsgrove High School

(a)   **Income and Expenditure Account of Bromsgrove High School Camp 2002**

Maps		420	Fees/Subs	30,000
Coaches		7,500	Maps	300
Site fees	6,000			
Add owing	225	6,225		
Food and drink	4,000			
Less closing stock	40	3 600		
Bad debts		320		
Depreciation		1,800		
Mountain rescue		280		
Ambulance fees		150		
Staff travel		2,300		
Total Expenditure		22,595		
SURPLUS		7,705		
		30,300		30,300

(b) At 1 August 2001 the Accumulated fund was £26,980 and was made up of

Tents	20,000
Cash at bank	6,200
Pots and pans	460
Debtors	320

(c) Decrease: because the camp is running at a surplus of £7,705. There is some £10,970 at the bank even though the stock of tents has been increased. It should, therefore be possible to charge students less for Camp next year.

Increase: even though the camp is running at a surplus and there is money in the bank, it may be that the tents/pots and pans are very old and need replacing. Increasing the amount that students must pay may mean they have more modern equipment.

Chapter 31

31.3.1 Self-test

Transaction	Effects on profit	Effects on cash flow
Issue of new shares	No effect	Increase
Bad debt written off	Decrease	No effect
Goods bought for cash	No effect	Decrease
Bonus share issue	No effect	No effect
Dividend paid to shareholders	No effect	Decrease
Goods purchased for credit	No effect	No effect
Delivery van purchased for cash	No effect	Decrease

31.5.3 Self-test

	A	B	C
Change in stock	+2	−50	+70
Change in debtors	+30	−15	−10
Change in creditors	+5	+55	−18
Depreciation	15	20	25
Operating profit (after depreciation)	+100	−80	+40
Cash – opening balance	+200	−160	−23
Cash – closing balance	+288	−100	−10

31.5.4 Self-test

Increase in debtors	4,250
Sales	23,751
Bad debts written off	170
Cash received	19,331
Increase in creditors	3,320
Purchases	17,192
Cash paid	13,872

31.7.2 Self-test

J J Motors Ltd

Net cash flow from operating activities		
Net profit		30,600
Depreciation	720	
Increase in creditors	720	
Increase in stock	(10,080)	
Decrease in debtors	1,800	(6,840)
Net cash inflow		23,760

Cash flow statement for the year ended 31 December 2009

Net cash inflow	23,760
Returns on investment and servicing of finance	
Payment for fixed assets	(10,800)
Financing	
Share capital repaid	(21,600)
Decrease (outflow) in cash	(8,640)
Changes in cash during the year	
Opening bank balance	5,400
Net cash outflow during the year	(8,640)
Overdraft at year end	(3,240)

The cash flow statement shows that although the company earned a profit of £30,600 during the year, cash resources were depleted by carrying a higher stock, purchasing additional fixed assets and repaying £21,600 of share capital.

31.7.3 Self-test

Maxwell & Co. Ltd

Cash flow statement for the year ended 31 December 2009

Net cash flow from operating activities		
Net profit		63,325
Depreciation	1,490	
Increase in creditors	1,490	
Increase in stock	−20,860	
Decrease in debtors	3,725	−14,155
Net cash flow from operating activities		49,170
Net cash flow from operating activities		49,170
Returns on investment and servicing of finance		
Payment for fixed assets		−22,350
Financing		
Share capital repaid		−44,700
Decrease (outflow) in cash		−17,880
Changes in cash during the year		
Opening balance		11,175
Net cash outflow		−17,880
Balance (overdraft) at year end		−6,705

31.7.4 Self-test

Hilmar Trading Ltd

Cash flow statement for the year ended 31 December 2009

Cash flow from operating activities (Note 1)		1,152
Returns on investments and servicing of finance		
Interest Paid		−60
Taxation (W1)		−230
Capital expenditure		−165
Purchase of fixed assets (W3)	−191	
Sale of fixed assets (W3)	26	
Equity Dividends paid (W2)		−144
Cash inflow before financing		553
Financing		−570
Issue of ordinary shares	68	
Repayment of loans	−638	
Decrease in cash in period		−17

Reconciliation of net cash flow to movement in net debt

Decrease in cash in period	−17	
Repayment of long-term loan	638	
Change in net debt (Note 2)		621
Net debt at 1 January 2009		−944
Net debt at 31 December 2009		−323

Notes to cash flow statement

Note 1

Reconciliation of operating profit to operating cash flows

Operating profit	893
Depreciation (W4)	251
Loss on sale of fixed assets (W5)	38
Increase in stock	−9
Increase in debtors	−34
Increase in creditors	13
Net cash inflow from operating activities	1,152

Note 2

Analysis of changes in net debt	1.1.06	Cash flows	31.12.06
Cash at bank	119	−17	102
Loan	−1,063	638	−425
Total	−944	621	−323

Workings

W1

Taxation					
Cash		230	1/01/09	Balance b/d	183
31/12/09	Balance c/d	217	31/12/09	Profit and loss	264
		447			447

W2

Dividends					
Cash		144		Balance b/d	34
31/12/09	Balance c/d	43	31/12/09	Profit and loss	153
		187			187

W3

Fixed assets					
Balance b/d		3,315	Sale		115
Add		191	31/12/09	Balance c/d	3,391
		3,506			3,506

W4

Depreciation					
Depreciation on disposal		51	1/01/09	Balance b/d	476
31/12/09	Balance c/d	676	31/12/09	Profit and loss	251
		727			727

W5

Disposals					
Cost fixed asset		115		Depreciation	51
			31/12/09	Loss on sale	38
				Cash	26
		115			115

31.7.5 Self-test

Peter Paul plc

Operating profit		68
Add back:		
Depreciation	36	
Loss on sale	2	38
		106
Decrease in stock	2	
Increase in debtors	(26)	
Increase in creditors	16	(8)
Cash flow from operating activities		98
Net cash flow from operating activities		98
Returns on investment and servicing of finance		
Interest paid	(8)	
Interest received	4	(4)
Taxation (W1)		
Corporation tax paid		(30)
Capital expenditure and financial investment		
Purchase of fixed assets (W2)	(50)	
Receipts from sale of fixed assets (W3)	8	(42)
Equity dividends paid (W4)		(24)
Management of liquid resources (investments)		(30)
Cash outflow before financing		(32)
Financing		
Issue of debentures		40
Increase in cash		8

Workings

W1

Taxation ledger account					
Cash	30	1/7/08	Balance b/d		30
30/6/09 Balance c/d	24	30/6/09	Profit and loss		24
	54				54

W2

Fixed assets at year end (260 + 160)	420	
Add cost of assets sold in year	30	450
Less cost at beginning of year		400
Assets purchased during year		£50

W3

Asset sold – at cost (*per note*)	30	
Accumulated depreciation	20	10
Cash received on sale		8
Loss on sale		2

W4

Dividend ledger account					
Cash		24	1/7/08	Balance b/d	24
30/6/09	Balance c/d	28	30/6/09	Profit and loss	28
		52			52

31.7.6 Self-test

Calculation of net profit before taxation	
Retained profit	−25,300
Increase in general reserve	14,000
Proposed dividend	68,000
Provision for taxation	51,000
Debenture interest	40,000
Net profit before interest and taxation	£147,700

31.7.7 Self-test

Interest receivable = 70,000 + 180,000 − 84,000 = £166,000.

31.7.8 Self-test

Plant at cost					
1.1.09	Balance b/d	274,000	1.1.09	Disposal a/c	46,000
31.12.09	Purchases	96,000	31.12.09	Balance c/d	324,000
		370,000			370,000

Accumulated depreciation – plant					
1.1.09	Disposal account	28,000	1.1.09	Balance b/d	48,800
31.12.09	Balance c/d	52,300	31.12.09	P&L	31,500
		80,300			80,300

Disposal account					
1.1.09	Plant – cost	46,000	1.1.09	Depreciation	28,000
			1.1.09	Sale	11,000
			1.1.09	Loss on sale	7,000
		46,000			46,000

Motor vehicles at cost					
1.1.09	Balance b/d	31,200	1.1.09	Sale	12,000
31.12.09	Purchases	34,000	31.12.09	Balance c/d	53,200
		65,200			65,200

Accumulated Depreciation – motor vehicles

1.1.09	Disposal	7,500	1.1.09	Balance b/d	9,100
31.12.09	Balance c/d	14,300	31.12.09	P&L	12,700
		21,800			21,800

Disposal account

1.1.09	Motor vehicle	12,000	1.1.09	Depreciation	7,500
31.12.09	Profit on sale	2,500	1.1.09	Cash	7,000
		14,500			14,500

Operating activities

Depreciation for the year		
Plant	31,500	
Motor vehicles	12,700	44,200
Loss on sale	7,000	
Less profit on sale	2,500	4,500
Investing activities		
Purchase plant	−96,000	
Purchase motor vehicles	−34,000	
Sale of fixed assets (11,000 + 12,000)	23,000	−107,000

Note: The £230,000 increase in the premises is not because of a further purchase but rather because of a revaluation. This can be seen from the asset revaluation account of £230,000. As such, it does not appear in the cash flow statement.

31.7.9 Self-test

Taxation

31.12.09	Bal c/d	932,000	31.12.08	Bal b/d	764,000
	Tax paid	648,000		P&L	816,000
		1,580,000			1,580,000
			1.1.10	Bal b/d	932,000

Tax paid amounts to £648,000 and this figure is shown in the cash flow statement.

31.7.10 Self-test

		Dividend account			
31.12.09	Bal c/d	257,000	31.12.08	Bal b/d	186,000
	Div paid	278,000		P&L	349,000
		535,000			535,000
			1.1.10	Bal b/d	257,000

The dividend paid during the year was therefore £278,000 and this is the amount to be shown in the cash flow statement. It consists of the final dividend for 2008 plus the interim dividend of 2009.

Chapter 32

32.4.3 Self-test

Calculator Ltd

Profitability ratios	2008	2009
Gross profit margin	8,900 ÷ 44,800 × 100 = 19.86%	11,180 ÷ 52,620 × 100 = 21.25%
Net profit margin	4,345 + 480 ÷ 44,800 × 100 = 10.77%	5,464 + 130 ÷ 52,620 × 100 = 10.63%
ROCE	4,345 + 480 ÷ 16,400 × 100 = 29.42%	5,464 + 130 ÷ 17,000 × 100 = 32.91%

32.4.6 Self-test

Calculator Ltd

Liquidity ratios	2008	2009
Working capital ratio	11,470 : 4,720 = 2.43:1	12,424 : 4,954 = 2.51:1
Acid test	11,470 − 6,000 : 4,720 = 1.16:1	12,424 − 7,400 : 4,954 = 1.01:1

32.4.10 Self-test

Calculator Ltd

Gearing ratios	2008	2009
Gearing	6,000 ÷ 16,400 × 100 = 36.59%	1,200 ÷ 17,000 × 100 = 7.06%
Interest cover	4,345 + 480 ÷ 480 = 10.05 times	5,464 + 130 ÷ 130 = 43.03 times

32.4.15 Self-test

(i)

	John Ltd	James Ltd
Operating profit	60,000	60,000
less Debenture interest		(32,000)
Net profit before tax	60,000	28,000
Corporation tax (20%)	(12,000)	(5,600)
Net profit after tax	48,000	22,400

Earnings per share $\dfrac{48,000}{500,000} = 9.6$ pence $\qquad \dfrac{22,400}{100,000} = 22.4$ pence

(ii)

	John Ltd	James Ltd
Operating profit	800,000	800,000
less Debenture interest		(32,000)
Net profit before tax	800,000	768,000
Corporation tax (20%)	(160,000)	(153,600)
Net profit after tax	640,000	614,400

Earnings per share $\dfrac{640,000}{500,000} = £1.28 \qquad \dfrac{614,400}{100,000} = £6.14$

The above example shows that the smaller number of ordinary shareholders gain when profits increase.

32.4.16 Self-test

Calculator Ltd

Investment ratios	2008	2009
EPS	4,224 ÷ 11,400 = 0.37p	5,312 ÷ 12,056 = 0.44p
PE ratio	2.50 ÷ 0.37 = 6.76 times	3.50 ÷ 0.44 = 7.95 times
Dividend payout	180 ÷ 4,224 × 100 = 4.26%	240 ÷ 5,312 × 100 = 4.52%
Dividend cover	24.66 times	23.16 times

32.4.19 Self-test

Calculator Ltd

Efficiency ratios	2008	2009
Stock turnover	35,900 ÷ 5,410 = 6.6 times	41,440 ÷ 6,700 = 6.2 times
Debtors' turnover	4,800 ÷ 44,800 × 365 = 39.1 days	4,200 ÷ 52,620 × 365 = 29.1 days
Creditors' payment	4,420 ÷ 37,080 × 365 = 43.5 days	4,562 ÷ 42,840 × 365 = 38.9 days
Asset turnover	44,800 ÷ 16,400 × 100 = 273.2%	52,620 ÷ 17,000 × 100 = 309.5%

32.4.20 Self-test

Valued Ltd	2008	2009
Working capital ratio	$\dfrac{270,000}{259,950} = 1.04 : 1$	$\dfrac{478,800}{264,960} = 1.81 : 1$
Acid test	$\dfrac{270,000 - 60,000}{259,950} = 0.81 : 1$	$\dfrac{478,800 - 36,000}{264,960} = 1.67 : 1$
Debtors' collection	$\dfrac{165,000}{1,350,000} \times 365 = 44.61$ days	$\dfrac{189,000}{1,800,000} \times 365 = 38.33$ days
Creditors' payment	$\dfrac{72,000}{750,000} \times 365 = 35.04$ days	$\dfrac{108,000}{1,080,000} \times 365 = 36.5$ days
Gross profit %	$\dfrac{570,000}{1,350,000} = 42.22\%$	$\dfrac{684,000}{1,800,000} = 38\%$
Operating profit %	$\dfrac{237,450 + 24,000 - 135,000}{1,350,000} = 9.37\%$	$\dfrac{177,300 + 36,000 - 72,000}{1,800,000} = 7.85\%$
Earnings per share	$\dfrac{165,450}{1,350,000} = 12.26$ p	$\dfrac{132,300}{1,620,000} = 8.17$ p
Dividend cover	$\dfrac{165,450}{112,500} = 1.47$ times	$\dfrac{132,300}{108,000} = 1.23$ times

32.4.21 Self-test

Rekon Ltd

Workings

Net profit before tax	11,107
Plus interest payable	3,058
PBIT	14,165

Capital employed = 45,031 + 19,082 = 64,113

Note that short-term liabilities can also be included. In this case an additional £16,290 will be added.

Gross profit margin = 43,192 ÷ 312,524 × 100 = 13.82%

Mark-up = gross profit on cost of sales = 43,192 ÷ 269,332 × 100 = 16.04%

Net profit margin = PBIT/turnover = 14,165 ÷ 312,524 × 100 = 4.53%
Note the difference between mark-up and margin.

Return on capital = PBIT/capital employed = 14,165 ÷ 64,113 × 100 = 22.09%

32.4.22 Self-test

November plc	2009	2010
Working capital ratio	$\dfrac{839}{380} = 2.21:1$	$\dfrac{936}{428} = 2.19:1$
Acid test	$\dfrac{839 - 520}{380} = 0.84:1$	$\dfrac{936 - 670}{428} = 0.62:1$
Debtors' collection	$\dfrac{280}{2,340} \times 365 = 43.67$ days	$\dfrac{219}{2,984} \times 365 = 26.79$ days
Creditors' payment	$\dfrac{229}{1,986} \times 365 = 42.09$ days	$\dfrac{247}{2,563} \times 365 = 35.18$ days
Gross profit %	$\dfrac{433}{2,340} = 18.50\%$	$\dfrac{571}{2,984} = 19.14\%$
Net profit %	$\dfrac{327 + 30}{2,340} = 15.26\%$	$\dfrac{394 + 10}{2,984} = 13.54\%$
ROCE	$\dfrac{327 + 30}{938 + 300} = 28.84\%$	$\dfrac{394 + 10}{1,151 + 100} = 32.29\%$
Earnings per share	$\dfrac{224}{680} = 32.94$p	$\dfrac{285}{680} = 41.91$p
Gearing	$\dfrac{300}{938} = 31.98\%$	$\dfrac{100}{1,151} = 8.69\%$
Interest cover	$\dfrac{327 + 30}{30} = 11.9$ times	$\dfrac{394 + 10}{10} = 40.4$ times
Stock turnover	$\dfrac{1,907}{(441 + 520/2)} = 3.97$ times	$\dfrac{2,413}{(520 + 670/2)} = 4.06$ times

32.4.23 Self-test

Traveller Ltd

(i) $460,000 \div 1,000,000 = 46$ pence per share
     Note: Share premium account cannot be used to pay a dividend.
(ii) Market price = £1.80 per share. Dividend paid = £460,000
     Dividend yield = £460,000 ÷ £1.80 = 25.56%
(iii) Gearing ratio:
     Debt ÷ Capital equity = 480,000 ÷ (1,500,000 + 220,000 + 480,000) = 21.82%
     or
     Debt ÷ equity = 480,000 ÷ (1,500,000 + 220,000) = 27.91%
     Note: The profit and loss amount of £460,000 was paid out as a dividend on 1 January 2009.

Chapter 33

33.3.11 Self-test

Multi Ltd

In order to advise management, we change the cost structure of each hairdryer to absorb the total fixed costs. This now results in the hairdryer having fixed costs of £17.50 per unit. Using this information we can calculate the following costing:

		Hairdryer
Selling price		35
Unit cost:		
materials	14	
labour	9	
other variable costs	2	
fixed costs	17.5	
Total cost		42.5
(Loss)/Profit per unit		(7.5)
Units produced	1,000	
(Loss) /Profit on product:	(7,500)	

This result is clearly far worse than when producing both products, and arises because the total fixed costs must now be borne by a single product – what has been lost is the contribution towards those fixed costs that had originally been made by the hair curlers.

We now re-examine the original situation by showing the contribution per unit from both products.

	Hair curler		Hairdryer	
Selling price per unit		25		35
Unit cost:				
materials	10		14	
labour	7		9	
other variable costs	3.5		2	
Total variable costs		20.5		25
Contribution per unit		4.5		10
Units		2,500		1,000
Contribution per product		£11,250		£10,000
Total contribution		21,250		
less Total fixed costs		17,500		
Profit		£3,750		

This shows what each product is actually contributing to the business. It also enables us to see what will happen if the firm stops producing hair curlers – the loss of the £11,250 contribution on the hair curlers turns an overall £3,750 profit into a £7,500 loss.

We see from this example that any product with a positive contribution will help us maximise our profits.

The fixed costs are not specific to either product. This is not always the case. Although fixed costs are supposed to remain constant in the short term, regardless of the volume of production or sales, certain costs, such as maintenance of machinery or managers' salaries, could well disappear if the manufacture of one product ceased.

The assumptions made here using the contribution approach for the two products need to be looked at in more detail. The firm may be able to sell more dryers, in which case the greater contribution per unit gained from selling each dryer could build up a sufficient total contribution to absorb the fixed costs, and the production capacity used for the curlers could perhaps be diverted to the dryers.

Normally a firm concentrates on a product that has the highest contribution per unit, provided that there is sufficient demand and no shortage of resources.

In this example, the firm must continue to manufacture both products. Should there be an upsurge in demand for the hair curler, the loss per unit that it is currently making could be turned into a profit, provided that fixed costs remain unchanged.

33.3.12 Self-test

Jason Ltd

	Normal production	Special order
Selling price per unit	40	36
Total variable costs per unit	(30)	(30)
Contribution per unit	10	6
Units demanded	5,000	1,000
Fixed costs	£40,000	

For normal production, total contribution is £50,000 (£10 × 5,000 units), so profit will be £10,000 after deducting fixed costs. Although the special order has a lower selling price, the variable costs have not risen per unit. This results in an extra contribution of £6,000 and, as the fixed costs are already covered, this extra amount is all profit.

When a customer wants a special order, extra costs may be incurred. These costs could be for special packaging or delivery costs. The company must ensure that there is a positive contribution, and that it cannot use the spare capacity more profitably.

In this example Jason Ltd would not want to end up with all the units for sale at £36, as this would give a contribution of only £36,000 (£6 × 6,000 units). This would result in a loss of £4,000.

33.3.13 Self-test

Cindy & Co.

Our answer to the question of ranking would be calculated as follows:

	A	B	C
Selling price	25	20	23
Variable costs	10	8	12
Contribution	15	12	11
Machine hours	4	3	4
Contribution per machine hour	3.75	4.00	2.75
Ranking order	2	1	3

Based on the above calculations we can produce 20 units of B × 3 = 60 hours and 22 units of A × 4 = 88 hours. This makes use of the total hours available.

We cannot produce the remaining 3 units of A, nor the 30 units of C.

33.3.14 Self-test

Bertha & Co.

	A	B	C
Selling price per unit	50	40	65
Variable costs per unit	25	19	29
Contribution	25	21	36
Hours of labour per unit	5	3	6
Contribution per labour hour	5	7	6
Ranking	3	1	2

Therefore product B should be produced first and then C. If any labour hours remain they can be used for producing product A, which has the lowest contribution per labour hour.

33.3.15 Self-test

Erin & Co.

The Gold service has the highest contribution followed by the Bronze service and finally the Silver service. This would produce the following results.

	Gold	Silver	Bronze
Hours of skilled service work	80,000	22,200	42,000
Services performed	2,000	740	1,200
Contribution per service	£800	£540	£600
Total contribution per service	1,600,000	399,600	720,000
Total contribution	2,719,600		
less Fixed costs	£400,000		
Profit	£2,319,600		

Note that there are only 22,200 hours left for Silver service. Therefore only 740 units of this service can be offered.

We must also examine the contribution per service per hour of skilled employee time, and use the ranking produced from that to find a profit figure for Erin & Co.

Contribution per service	£800	£540	£600
Contribution per service per hour	20	18	17.14

The above table indicates that although Erin & Co should still place the Gold service first, the Silver service should be ranked before the Bronze service.

We now need to calculate the profit using this fact.

Hours of skilled service work	80,000	60,000	4,200
Services performed	2,000	2,000	120
Total contribution per service	£1,600,000	£1,080,000	72,000

Total contribution	£2,752,000
less Fixed costs	£400,000
Profit	£2,352,000

If the ranking for the contribution per scarce factor were identical to that for the contribution per service, the result would be the same. As this is not the case, we find the maximum possible profit by taking into consideration not just the differences between revenues and variable costs, but also how economical the usages are of the limiting factor.

The Silver service requires less of the scarce skilled employee time than the Bronze service, even though it had a lower contribution per service.

Note: While this method indicates the highest profit obtainable, a firm may have reasons, such as competition, for choosing a different combination.

33.3.16 Self-test

Pat Fabrics

$$\text{Contribution} = £28 - (7 + 2 + 3 + 2) = £14 \text{ per tie.}$$

New SP – VC = 18 – 14 = £4 contribution. Additional fixed costs are 2 months at £300 p.m. = £600.

Therefore the contribution from this order = 400 ties @ £4 per tie = £1,600. The extra fixed costs incurred for this order = £600 additional rent. This results in a positive contribution of £1,000 so the order should be accepted.

New designs:

	Style 1	Style 2	Style 3
Material	£4	£3	£5
Trimmings	£2	£1	£2
Wages	£3	£3	£3
Packaging	£1	£1	£1
Total VC	10	8	11
Selling Price	£25	£20	£31
Contribution	£15	£12	£20

	Style 1	Style 2	Style 3
Machine hours per tie	5	3	4
Contribution per hour	£3	£4	£5
Ranking	3rd	2nd	1st
Demand in units p.m.	20	15	25
Production in hours	55	45	100
Production in units	11	15	25

Only style 1 has a limit placed on production. Although there is a demand for 20 units only 11 can be produced because of machine-hour limitation.

33.3.18 Self-test

Able & Co.		Marginal cost		Absorption cost
Sales		6,000		6,000
Material	60p	−1,200	60p	−1,200
Labour	40p	−800	40p	−800
Contribution		4,000		
Factory rent	£1,000	−1,000	£1,000	−1,000
Salary	£2,000	−2,000	£2,000	−2,000
Profit				1,000

33.3.19 Self-test

Myco Ltd

	Small	Medium	Large
Selling price (per unit)	100	140	200
Total variable costs	68	92	128
Contribution	32	48	72
Contribution per machine hour	£8	£6	£12
Ranking:	2	3	1

Myco Ltd will therefore elect to produce Large first, followed by Small. Should there be any machine hours still available after that then they will be used to produce Medium. In this case 2,000 units of Medium can be manufactured.

	Small	Medium	Large
Machine hours needed	160,000	16,000	120,000
Products made	40,000	2,000	20,000
Contribution per unit	32	48	72
Total contribution	1,280,000	96,000	1,440,000
Total contribution	2,816,000		
less Fixed costs	330,000		
Profit	£2,486,000		

33.3.20 Self-test

Paula Ltd		UK	Spain
Selling price per unit		£150	£150
Variable costs:			
Materials		60	66
Labour		30	31.5
Variable factory cost		10	10
Variable selling cost		15	12
Contribution		35	30.5
Total contribution		(35 × 20,000)	(30.5 × 5,000)
		700,000	152,500
less Fixed costs		330,000	16,000
Profit		370,000	136,500
Total profit		£506,500	

Paula Ltd would increase its profit by accepting the order. However, it will have incurred additional fixed costs of £16,000 per annum and if the Spanish order is not repeated the following year, profit will be reduced by this additional fixed cost of £16,000 per annum.

The decision will, therefore, depend on how anxious the company is to sell to another market and whether it has any idea if the order is likely to be repeated.

33.3.21 Self-test

The present profit/loss situation, based on full cost, is as follows.

Norman Ltd	Trumpets	Saxophone
Sales revenue	750,000	540,000
Total cost	657,000	546,000
Profit/loss	£93,000	–£6,000

Total profit for Norman Ltd is therefore £87,000.

If the factory producing saxophones were to be closed, £66,000 of the fixed costs still remain to be paid. As there would be no revenue coming from saxophone production, this £66,000 would have to be deducted from the profit of the trumpets, leaving a profit of only £27,000.

33.3.22 Self-test

Nathan Ltd

Contribution = Selling price	23.50
less Variable costs	9.30
Contribution	£14.20
Total contribution (30,000 @ £14.2 per unit)	426,000
less Fixed costs	63,750
Profit	21,250

You were told that the directors require a minimum return on capital employed of 16 per cent. The above costing statement shows a return of 16.35 per cent. Therefore, the directors will agree that the selling price can be held at the lower level of £23.50.

33.3.23 Self-test

Clothes & Co.

At first glance, we might decide that we should stop making ties and jackets, as each of these products has a negative contribution towards fixed costs, and obviously is non-profit-making. However, we also know that customers buy shirts and ties so, if production of ties is discontinued, we should also lose our market for shirts.

In order to arrive at a well-formed opinion we need to summarise the various alternatives.

Discontinue jackets only

Total contribution:	Shirts	216,000
	Ties	−12,000
	Pants	312,000
		516,000
	Fixed costs	180,000
	Profit	336,000

Discontinue jackets and ties and lose market for shirts

Total contribution:	Pants	312,000
	Fixed costs	180,000
	Profit	132,000

Although ties have a negative contribution (£12,000), they are bought jointly with shirts, which have a positive contribution. Therefore, the firm should continue to produce and sell ties and, in so doing, should also be able to sell shirts. This would maximise profits at £336,000.

Clothes & Co. should, of course, try to find ways of reducing the variable costs relating to ties in order to raise profits further.

The volume of sales determines profit. For example, if the firm's sales of pants had been identical to those for shirts and ties (i.e. 40,000 units) then the contribution from pants would be only £156,000.

Therefore, although we look for items that give us a positive contribution per unit, it is the amount we are then able to sell which is important. Where there are products that have a joint demand (such as above), we must consider the options very carefully.

33.3.24 Self-test

Total contribution:	Shirts	216,000
	Ties	−12,000
		204,000
	Fixed costs	180,000
	Profit	24,000

In addition the firm can sell 80,000 units of pants at a profit of £3.80 each. The profit of £304,000 is added to the £24,000, as above, giving a total profit of £328,000. This is still £8,000 less than if the firm manufactured all three products itself.

Unless Clothes & Co. can use the spare capacity that it now has (because of no manufacturing of pants) and that output produces a greater contribution per unit, it could find that its profits are smaller. It still has to cover its fixed costs and no longer has the contribution of £3.90 per pair of pants. All it now has is the difference between the price it pays for the pants from Dress Ltd and the selling price, i.e. £3.80. Only if the contract price were less than Clothes & Co.'s variable costs would it become a proposition.

Chapter 34

34.3.3 Self-test

Bob Ltd

The break-even point in units will be:

$$\frac{160,000}{8} = 20,000 \text{ units}$$

Now let us consider independently:

Selling price increases to £40 per unit:

$$\text{BEP} = \frac{160,000}{40 - 30} = 16,000 \text{ units}$$

Fixed costs increase to £180,000 and the selling price remains at £38:

$$\text{BEP} = \frac{180,000}{8} = 22,500 \text{ units}$$

Variable costs increase to £36 per unit; the selling price remains at £38:

$$\text{BEP} = \frac{160,000}{38 - 36} = 80,000 \text{ units}$$

Conclusions:

(a) The effect of an increased selling price is to reduce the level at which the firm will break even.
(b) When either fixed or variable costs increase, the break-even point rises.

Therefore, the break-even point moves in the same direction as cost changes, but in the opposite direction to changes in selling price.

34.3.6 Self-test

Excel Toys

To calculate the break-even point we first need to know what the contribution is per unit.

Variable costs = £18 + (£6 + £9) + £14 = £47
Contribution per unit = £90 − £47 = £43

(a) BEP in units = $\dfrac{\text{Fixed costs}}{\text{Contribution per unit}} = \dfrac{430,000}{43} = 10,000$ units

(b) Margin of safety

$$\dfrac{\text{Estimated turnover}}{\text{SP per unit}} = \dfrac{945,000}{90} = 10,500 \text{ units}$$

MOS = Estimated sales in units less BEP = 10,500 − 10,000 = 500 units

(c) Calculation using marginal costing

Sales (10,500 @ £90)	945,000
less Variable costs	(493,500)
Total contribution	451,500
less Total fixed costs	430,000
Anticipated profit	21,500

(d) To allow for the target profit of £215,000 we need to add that amount to the fixed costs.

We now have a total of 430,000 + 215,000 that must be covered through the contribution that each unit makes.

i.e. $\dfrac{430,000 + 215,000}{43} = 15,000$ units

Profit calculation for each of the alternatives:

(i) SP £90 − 30% = £63
Volume/Sales units 10,500 + 50% = 15,750

Sales 15,750 units @ £63	£992,250
Variable costs 15,750 @ £43	(677,250)
Total contribution	315,000
less Fixed costs	(430,000)
Net loss	(115,000)

(ii) Sales 10,500 + 60% = 16,800 units
Variable o/h £14 + 50% = £21
Variable costs now = £18 + (£6 + £9) + 21 = £54

Sales 16,800 @ £63	1,058,400
Variable costs (£54)	(907,200)
Contribution	151,200
less Fixed costs	(430,000)
Net loss	(278,800)

(iii) Variable costs are now increased because of the additional cost of a free toy.
£43 + £15 = £58
Sales 10,500 + 120% = 23,100

Profit statement

Sales 23,100 @ £90	2,079,000
Variable costs (£58)	(1,339,800)
Contribution	739,200
less Fixed costs	(430,000)
Profit	£309,200

The best option is (iii), above.

34.3.8 Self-test

Howard Ltd

Present contribution per unit is £8 less (2 + 2.50 + 0.60) = £2.90.

Future contribution per unit should be £7.80 less (1.60 + 2.50 + 0.60) = £3.10.

Present break-even point in units $= \dfrac{£96,000}{2.90} = 33,103$ units.

Present break-even point in £s = 33,103 × £8 = £264,824.

Future break-even point in units $= \dfrac{£96,000}{3.10} = 30,967$ units.

Future break-even point in £s = 30,967 × £7.80 = £241,543.

Margin of safety = 36,000 units – 30,967 units = 5,033 units.

34.3.9 Self-test

Pat Fabrics

Break-even point = FC/Contribution = 3,000 ÷ 14 = 215 ties.
Revised break-even = FC + profit = 3,700 + 4,000 = £7,700.
Contribution is SP – VC = 21 – 14 = 7.
Therefore, ties to be sold = 7,700 ÷ 7 = 1,100 ties.

34.3.10 Self-test

Design Ltd

Sales (9,000 units @ £65)		585,000
Less:		
Direct materials	156,600	
Direct labour	256,500	
Variable production overhead	21,600	
Variable admin overheads	10,800	445,500
Total contribution		139,500
Fixed production overhead	54,000	
Other fixed costs	27,000	81,000
Net profit		58,500

Calculation: £139,500 ÷ 9,000 = £15.5 per unit

Break-even:

Fixed costs	£81,000
Contribution per unit	£15.50
Break-even (units)	5,226 units
Break-even (£s)	£339,690

Margin of safety (units) = 9,000 – 5,226 = 3,774 units
Margin of safety (£s)   £245,310

Sales (13,000 units @ £57)		741,000
Less:		
Direct materials	226,200	
Direct labour	305,500	
Variable production overhead	31,200	
Variable admin overheads	15,600	578,500
Total contribution		162,500
Fixed production overhead	99,000	
Other fixed costs	27,000	126,000
Net profit		36,500

Contribution per unit £12.50
Fixed costs   £126,000

Break-even (units) = 126,000 ÷ 12.5 = 10,080 units

34.3.11 Self-test

Rocky Ltd

(a) Contribution per unit = 60,000 ÷ 15,000 = £4
    BEP = Fixed costs/Contribution = 30,000 ÷ 4 = 7,500 units
(b) Sales price = 10 + 20% = £12
    Variable costs per unit = £6 + 50% = £9
    Contribution = £3
    Therefore BEP = £30,000 ÷ 3 = 10,000 units

34.3.12 Self-test

First Aid Ltd

Fixed costs:
Depreciation $10\% \times 26,000 = £2,600$
Rent $= 36,000$
Total annual fixed costs $= 38,600$

	Bandages	Dressings
Direct material	0.30	0.45
Direct labour	0.28	0.52
Overheads	0.09	0.24
Total variable costs	0.67	1.21
Selling price	1.00	1.40
Contribution	0.33	0.19
Fixed costs	$7 \div 10 \times 38,600 = 27,020$	$3 \div 10 \times 38,600 = 11,580$

Break-even point:
Bandages $27,020 \div 0.33 = 81,878$ units p.a.
Dressings $11,580 \div 0.19 = 60,947$ units p.a.

Budgeted profit and loss account for the year ending 31 December 2011

Sales	Bandages	Dressings		Total
– Units	82,800	64,800		
– £	82,800	90,720		173,520
Material costs	24,840	29,160	54,000	
Labour costs	23,184	33,696	56,880	
Overheads	7,452	15,552	23,004	133,884
Contribution				39,636
Fixed overheads				38,600
Budgeted profit				£1,036

34.3.13 Self-test

X Ltd

Total variable costs $= £3,100$.
This is equal to $3,100 \div 200 = £15.50$ per box.
The contribution based on a selling price of £20 per box is $4.50 \times 200 = £900$.
BEP $= 700 \div 4.50 = 156$ boxes.

At a selling price of £18 the contribution $= 2.50 \times 450 = £1,125$.
BEP $= 700 \div 2.50 = 280$ boxes.

At £17 the contribution $= 1.50 \times 600 = £900$.
BEP $= 700 \div 1.50 = 467$ units.

This means that the company should reduce its selling price to £18 and achieve a profit of £425 per month. This assumes that the company is able to achieve budgeted sales and that fixed overheads remain constant.

Chapter 35

35.7.5 Self-test

Rainbow Ltd

Flexible Budget

Production	6,600
Direct Materials	21,120
Direct Labour	54,780
Fixed Overheads	2,300
Total Cost of Production	78,200

35.8.1 Self-test

Daniel

(a) Sales budget

	Tables		Chairs		Total	
	No. of units	Value	No. of units	Value	No. of units	Value
Sales	40	£20,000	100	£14,000	140	£34,000

(b) Production budget

	Tables No. of units	Chairs No. of units
Sales	40	100
Less opening stock	(20)	(40)
Plus closing stock*	6	15
Units required	26	75

* You calculate the closing stock by taking 15 per cent of the number of units sold in April. Once you know that then the difference equals the number of units that Daniel is required to manufacture in April.

(c) Materials usage budget

	No. of units	Material kg	Price per kg	Total in £
Tables	26	312	£14	4,368
Chairs	75	375	£14	5,250
Total material cost				£9,618

(d) Labour usage budget

	No. of units	Hours	Price per hr	Total in £
Tables	26	286	£9	£2,574
Chairs	75	450	£9	£4,050
Total labour cost				£6,624

(e) Budgeted profit and loss

	Tables	Chairs	Total
Sales	20,000	14,000	34,000
Material cost	4,368	5,250	9,618
Labour cost	2,574	4,050	6,624
Contribution	13,058	4,700	17,758
Administration, selling and distribution overheads**	350	550	900
Profit	£12,708	£4,150	£16,858

** The administration, selling and distribution costs are apportioned on the basis of hours taken in production.

35.8.2 Self-test

Jetset Ltd

Cash budget for the 3 months ending 30 June 2009

	April	May	June
Cash receipts/inflows			
Cash sales	124,000	120,000	96,000
Credit sales	60,000	64,000	58,000
Tax rebate			50,000
Total cash inflows	184,000	184,000	204,000
less Cash payments/outflows			
Purchases	76,000	86,000	90,000
Wages	24,000	24,000	24,000
Overheads	36,000	36,000	36,000
Loan	70,000		
VAT		23,000	
Total			
Cash outflows	206,000	169,000	150,000
Net cash surplus/deficit	(22,000)	15,000	54,000
Opening cash balance	15,000	(7,000)	8,000
Closing cash balance	(7,000)	8,000	62,000

A deficit in cash could be overcome by increasing the capital of the company or by arranging overdraft facilities or other form of loan.

There are ways in which a deficit can be prevented. These include:

(a) negotiate better credit terms with suppliers;
(b) reduce the time allowed and taken by debtors to pay for credit sales;
(c) hold lower stocks which allows for a reduction in monthly purchases;
(d) encourage cash sales by offering special discounts; and
(e) reduce monthly expenditure wherever possible.

35.8.3 Self-test

Outdoor Shopping

2010 budget (£000):

Cash inflows	March	April	May	June	July	Aug
Cash sales	10	8	8	12	10	8
60% credit	48	24	19.2	19.2	28.8	24
40% credit	25.6	32	16	12.8	12.8	19.2
	83.6	64	43.2	44	51.6	51.2

Cash outflows	March	April	May	June	July	Aug
Purchases	40	10	60	10	30	20
Wages	10	14	18	18	14	10
Rent	2.8	2.8	2.8	2.8	2.8	2.8
Loan interest		12			12	
Office equip			14			
	52.8	38.8	94.8	30.8	58.8	32.8

Net surplus	March	April	May	June	July	Aug
(deficit)	30.8	25.2	(51.6)	13.2	(7.2)	18.4
Opening balance	5.9	36.7	61.9	10.3	23.5	16.3
Closing balance	36.7	61.9	10.3	23.5	16.3	34.7

35.8.4 Self-test

Rose Fashions Ltd

Cash inflows	Jul	Aug	Sept
Cash sales	70,000	45,000	80,000
Credit sales	65,000	75,000	70,000
	135,000	120,000	150,000

Cash outflows	Jul	Aug	Sept
Purchases	65,000	50,000	90,000
Overheads	10,000	7,000	11,000
Wages	35,000	35,000	35,000
Rent	18,000		
Taxation		10,000	
Computer		50,000	
	128,000	152,000	136,000

Net surplus	Jul	Aug	Sept
Opening balance	5,000	12,000	(20,000)
Surplus/deficit	7,000	(32,000)	14,000
Closing balance	12,000	(20,000)	(6,000)

35.8.5 Self-test

Jack Ltd

Finished goods stock budget:

Month	January	February	March	April
Opening stock	46	84	112	128
Production*	232	238	296	352
	278	322	408	480
Less sales	194	210	280	320
Closing stock	84	112	128	160

Raw material budget:

Month	January	February	March
Opening stock	140	214	266
Purchases of raw material*	422	409	494
	562	623	760
Less production usage	348	357	444
Closing stock	214	266	316

* Note that these figures are the balancing figures.

35.8.6 Self-test

One-one Ltd

Receipts	Sep	Oct	Nov	Total
Cash	21,609	12,965	17,287	51,861
Debtors	32,340	26,950	16,170	75,460
	53,949	39,915	33,457	127,321
Payments				
Credit purchases	8,400	11,200	15,400	35,000
Labour	9,000	5,400	7,200	21,600
Other variable	6,000	3,600	4,800	14,400
Fixed costs	5,850	5,850	5,850	17,550
	29,250	26,050	33,250	88,550
Net surplus/deficit	24,699	13,865	207	38,771
Opening balance	11,800	36,499	50,364	11,800
Closing balance	£36,499	£50,364	£50,571	£50,571

35.9.1 Self-test

Wood Products Ltd

Sales budget for July–December 2010

	July	Aug	Sept	Oct	Nov	Dec	Total
UK	700	700	700	700	700	700	4,200
USA	300	300	300	500	500	575	2,475
Totals	1,000	1,000	1,000	1,200	1,200	1,275	6,675

Budgets are prepared in the following order:

(a) Sales – this is the key budget for all the others.
(b) Stock – this ensures sufficient quantity of raw material at all times.
(c) Production – prepared to meet sales and stock levels.
(d) Cash – the budget is derived from production and sales budgets.

Chapter 36

36.5.3 Self-test

Rainbow Ltd

(i) Materials Price variance = (Standard Price – Actual price) × Actual Quantity = (0.80 – 0.78) × 26,400 = £528 Favourable
(ii) Labour Rate variance = (Standard Rate – Actual Rate) × Actual Hours = (4.15 – 4.24) × 13,200 = £1,188 Adverse

Possible causes of favourable material price variance:
Purchasing department/buyers negotiated strongly.
World price of material/cotton was lower than expected after budget was prepared.
Supplier offered us unexpected discount as part of sales drive.
New supplier in the market offered a lower price to gain customers.
Supply in market was high due to good harvest/weather/new firm etc.
Poor quality materials were supplied.

Evaluate how well the budget has been set:

Well set budget:
Overall variance is only £660 Adverse out of total of £78,200. Therefore it is fairly accurate – less than 1% error rate.
Variance of only £528 favourable on materials – accurate – 3% error rate.
Variance of only £1,188 adverse on labour – accurate – 2.6% error rate.
No variance on fixed overheads, material usage, or labour efficiency.

Poorly set:
Production was 20% more than planned – so not well set.
Before flexing the budget, the variances are large.

36.5.6 Self-test

Ralph & Co.

We need to flex the budget, which will show the effect on profit and the output volume differences. We cannot compare budget and actual cost where the output does not coincide. In this example we increase the budget to a 1,900 unit output.

Flexed budget		1,600 units		1,900 units	
Sales			32,000		38,000
Direct materials:	Plastic £25/kg	6,000		7,125	
	Colourants £10/litre	8,000		9,500	
Direct labour	Skilled £2.5 per hour	2,000		2,375	
	Unskilled £2 per hour	5,000		5,938	
Fixed overheads		6,000	27,000	6,000	30,938
Budgeted profit			5,000		7,062

Usage for 1,600 units	Usage for 1,900 units	Actual usage/cost
Material usage 240 kg	Material usage 285 kg	Material usage 155 kg
Price £25/kg	£25/kg	£49/kg
Colourants 800 litre	Colourants 950 litre	Colourants 460 litre
£10/litre	£10/litre	£20/litre
Skilled 800 hour	Skilled 950 hour	Skilled 845 hour
£2.5 per hour	£2.5 per hour	£2.6 per hour
Unskilled 2,500 hour	Unskilled 2,969 hour	Unskilled 2,375 hour
£2 per hour	£2 per hour	£2.2 per hour
Fixed costs	£6,000	£5,980

Sales variance = Budgeted selling price − Actual selling price = £1,500 (A)

Material usage (Actual − Standard usage) × Standard price = 130 kg @ 25 = 3,250 (F)
Material price (Actual − Standard price) × Actual usage = (49 − 25) × 155 kg = 3,720 (A)
Colourant usage = (460 − 950) = 490 litres @ 10 = 4,900 (F)
Colourant price (20 − 10) × 460 litres = 4,600 (A)

Skilled labour hours (Actual hours − Standard hours) × Standard rate = (845 − 950) × £2.50 = 105 hours × £2.50 = £262.50 (F)
Skilled labour rate (Actual rate − Standard rate) × Actual hours = (£2.60 − £2.50) × 845 = £84.50 (A)

Unskilled labour hours (2,375 − 2,969) × £2 = 594 hours @ 2 = 1,188 (F)
Unskilled labour rate (£2 − £2.20) × 2,375 hours = £475 (A)

Fixed costs usage = Actual overhead expenditure − Budgeted overhead expenditure = £5,980 − £6,000 = £20 (F)

Variances	F	A
Sales		1,500
Materials	3,250	3,720
Colourants	4,900	4,600
Skilled labour	262.50	84.50
Unskilled	1,188	475
Fixed overheads	20	
Totals	9,620.50	10,379.50

Difference between flexed budget and actual results = £7,062 − £6,303 = £759 (A)

Actual profit and loss account

Sales			36,500
Direct materials:	Plastic	7,595	
	Colourants	9,200	
Direct labour	Skilled	2,197	
	Unskilled	5,225	
Fixed overheads		5,980	30,197
Actual profit			6,303

The difference between the favourable and unfavourable variances = £759. This is the difference between the budgeted and actual results.

36.5.7 Self-test

Mervyn & Co.

	Budget	Flexed budget	Actual
Number of units	**2,200**	**2,300**	**2,300**
Direct material	88,000	92,000	92,600
Direct labour	44,000	46,000	46,400
Fixed overheads	40,000	40,000	38,600
Profit	48,000	52,000	49,400
Sales	220,000	230,000	227,000
Material used	88,000 kg	92,000 kg	92,600 kg
Labour	5,500 hours	5,750 hours	5,920 hours

Original profit minus flexed profit = 48,000 − 52,000 = £4,000 (F)

This is favourable because we sold more than in the original budget. You must note that this is the only time that we use any information from the original budget for comparison.

All the remaining variances are calculations between the actual results and the flexed budget.

Sales price variance:

$$£230,000 - £227,000 = £3,000 \text{ (A)}$$

Material usage variance:

We take the excess in kg used at the budget price = 600 × £1 = £600 (A)

Material price variance:

92,600 − (92,600 × £1) = 0. There is no variance here as the cost price paid for the actual usage was the same price as per the budget.

Labour efficiency variance:

5,920 − 5,750 = £170 additional hours taken for the production. This amount is then multiplied by the budgeted hourly rate of £8 and we achieve an amount of £1,360 (A)

Labour rate variance:

$$(5,920 × 8) − 46,400 = £960 \text{ (F)}$$

Fixed overhead variance:

$$40,000 − 38,600 = £1,400 \text{ (F)}$$

Reconciliation:

Profit per original budget		48,000
Add favourable variances:		
Sales volume	4,000	
Labour rate	960	
Overhead	1,400	6,360
		54,360
Less adverse variances:		
Sales price	3,000	
Material usage	600	
Labour efficiency	1,360	4,960
Actual profit		49,400

36.5.8 Self-test

Francis & Co.

Sales volume variance:

Production was 200 units less which resulted in a loss of £8,000 (A)

Sales price variance:

£4,000 (F)

Material usage variance:

2,000 m extra at £1 per metre = £2,000 (A)

Material price variance:

We take the actual metres used at the budget price = 74,000 × £1 = 74,000. From this we deduct the actual amount paid of £73,800. This results in a £200 (F) variance.

Labour efficiency variance:

$$4,300 \text{ hours} - 4,500 \text{ actual hours} \times £8 = £1,600 \text{ (F)}$$

Labour rate variance:

$$4,300 \text{ hours} \times £8 = 34,400 - 35,000 = £600 \text{ (A)}$$

Fixed overhead variance:

More was spent than allowed in the budget: £1,400 (A)

Reconcilation

Profit per original budget		40,000
Add favourable variances:		
Sales price	4,000	
Material price	200	
Labour efficiency	1,600	5,800
		45,800
Less adverse variances:		
Sales volume	8,000	
Material usage	2,000	
Labour rate	600	
Fixed overheads	1,400	12,000
Actual profit		33,800

36.5.9 Self-test

Marcel Ltd

	Original budget	Flexed budget	Actual
Units	1,400	1,700	1,700
Material usage	2,800	3,400	3,672
Material price	£145,600	£176,800	£264,384
Labour hours	4,200	5,100	5,440
Labour rate	£85,400	£103,700	£136,000
Fixed overheads	£12,600	£12,600	£18,000
Sales	£366,800	£445,400	£579,020
Profit	£123,200	£152,300	£160,636

Variances
Sales volume = 123,200 − 152,300 = 29,100 (F)
Sales price = 579,020 − 445,400 = 133,620 (F)
Material usage = 3,672 − 3,400 = 272 × 52 = 14,144 (A)
Material price = 264,384 − (3,672 × 52) = 73,440 (A)
Labour rate = 136,000 − (5,440 × 61/3) = 25,386,(A)
Labour efficiency = 5,440 − 5,100 = 340 × 61/3 − 6,914 (A)
Overheads = 18,000 − 12,600 = 5,400 (A)

Original profit		123,200
Add favourable variances:		
Sales volume	29,100	
Sales price	133,620	162,720
		285,920
Less adverse variances:		
Material usage	14,144	
Material price	73,440	
Labour rate	25,386	
Labour efficiency	6,914	
Overheads	5,400	125,284
Actual profit		160,636

36.5.10 Self-test

Vera Ltd

(a) Standard hours $(15 \times 5 \times 8) \times 4 = 2,400$

(b) Actual hours $2,400 + (2 \times 15 \times 5 \times 3) = 2,850$

(c) Labour efficiency variance $2,400 - 2,850 \times £6.40 = £2,880$ (A)

(d) Total standard wages $2,400 \times 6.40 = £15,360$

(e) Total actual wages $15,360 + (450 \times £10) = £19,860$

(f) Wage rate variance $15,360 - 19,860 = £4,500$ (A)

(g) Actual wage rate $19,860/2,850 = £6.968$ per hour

(h) Wage rate variance $6.968 - 6.40 = 0.568 \times 2,950 = £1,618.80$ (A)

Chapter 37

37.1.1 Self-test

1. (a)
2. (c)
3. (a)
4. (d)

37.1.2 Self-test

Musical Ltd

1. (a)
2. (c)
3. (c)
4. (b)
5. (d)

37.1.3 Self-test

Esef Ltd

1. (a)
2. (a)
3. (a)
4. (a)
5. (c)

37.1.4 Self-test

Master Ltd

	Increases gearing	Reduces gearing
Issuing new debentures	✓	
Issuing new ordinary shares		✓
Issuing new preference shares	✓	
Redeeming ordinary shares	✓	
Redeeming debentures		✓

37.1.5 Self-test

Mushtaq and Hasan

(a)

Cash budget	Month 1	Month 2	Month 3	Month 4
Income				
Share capital	20,000			
Bank loan	20,000			
Sales – cash	10,500	12,600	15,120	18,144
Sales – credit		3,500	4,200	5,040
Total income	50,500	16,100	19,320	23,184
Expenditure				
Shop premium	12,500			
Fixtures and fittings	13,000			
Purchases	22,000	7,000	8,400	10,080
Expenses	4,000	4,000	4,000	4,000
Directors' drawings	3,200	3,200	3,200	3,200
Total expenditure	54,700	14,200	15,600	17,280
Monthly balance	−4,200	1,900	3,720	5,904
Opening balance	0	−4,200	−2,300	1,420
Closing balance	−4,200	−2,300	1,420	7,324

(b)

Debtors' budget	Month 1	Month 2	Month 3	Month 4
	3,500	4,200	5,040	6,048

37.1.6 Self-test

Milly & Co.

(a) $\text{BEP} = \dfrac{\text{Fixed cost}}{\text{Contribution}}$

$$\text{BEP} = \frac{430,000}{£50 - £27}$$

BEP = 18,696 units

Calculation of profit

Total contribution	80,000 × £23	1,840,000
less Fixed costs		430,000
Profit		1,410,000

(b) **Plan 1.** Sales needed to maintain profits at £1,410,000.
Selling price reduced to £45, so contribution reduced to £18 (23 − 5).
To maintain profit level, total contribution needs to stay at £1,840,000.
So £1,840,000 divided by £18 gives the number of units that must be sold:

$$\frac{1,840,000}{18} = 102,223 \text{ units}$$

Plan 2. Sales needed to maintain profits at £1,410,000.
Selling price increased to £56, so contribution increased to £29.
To maintain profits, total contribution needs to stay at £1,840,000.
So £1,840,000 divided by £29 gives the number of units that must be sold:

$$\frac{1,840,000}{29} = 63,449 \text{ units}$$

Plan 3. Sales needed to maintain profits at £1,410,000.
Fixed costs reduced by £85,000 means contribution only needs to be 1,840,000 − 85,000 = £1,755,000.
But variable costs increased by £5 per unit, so new contribution is £18 per unit.
So £1,755,000 divided by £18 gives the number of units that must be sold:

$$\frac{1,755,000}{18} = 97,500 \text{ units}$$

(c) BEP for Plan 3

$$\text{BEP} = \frac{\text{Fixed cost}}{\text{Contribution}}$$

$$\text{BEP} = \frac{345,000(430,000 - 85,000)}{£50 - £32}$$

BEP = 19,167 units

The BEP for Plan 3 is lower than the original situation.

(d) Plan 2 would be the easiest to achieve because fewer items need to be sold to reach the required profit level.

The most telling limitation is the reliance on actually selling this quantity at the raised price. Break-even analysis assumes this and it may not be realistic. We really would need to know about the demand for the product before proceeding with a definite solution.

37.1.7 Self-test

Seahow Ltd

Cash budget for 2 months ended 31 December 2010

	November	December
Sales	61,800	43,600
Interest received	600	600
Total receipts	62,400	44,200
Purchases	48,750	31,250
Wages	4,800	5,200
Expenses	5,000	4,800
Total expenses	58,550	41,250
Balance b/d	3,200	7,050
Receipts less payments	3,850	2,950
Balance c/d	7,050	10,000

Seahow Ltd will not be in a position to pay the entire loan back because if it does so it will be overdrawn by £15,000. It can, however, elect to repay part of the loan up to a maximum of £10,000.

37.1.8 Self-test

Kayla Ltd

(a)

Product	1	2	3
Sales	250,000	600,000	750,000
Variable costs	120,000	270,000	350,000
Labour	40,000	120,000	200,000
Contribution	90,000	210,000	200,000
Unit contribution	9	7	4

(b) Total contribution £500,000

(c) Total profit = 500,000 − 400,000 = £100,000

(d) ROA 10%

37.1.9 Self-test

Ices Ltd

	Marginal cost		Absorption cost	
Sales		21,000		21,000
Direct material	4,800		4,800	
Direct labour	8,400		8,400	
Variable overheads	3,600		3,600	
	16,800		16,800	
Fixed overheads	3,000		3,000	
	19,800		19,800	
Closing stock	2,800	17,000	3,300	16,500
Profit		4,000		4,500

Closing stock valuation:
Price per cake:

$$\text{Marginal } £14 = 16,800/1,200 = £14 \text{ per cake} = 14 \times 200 = £2,800$$
$$\text{Absorption } £16.5 = 19,800/1,200 = £16.5 \text{ per cake} = 16.5 \times 200 = £3,300$$

As marginal costs of £14 are covered by a £16 selling price, Ices Ltd could accept the price for a limited period. This must be a short-term decline in price otherwise the fixed costs will not be met over the financial year.

37.1.10 Self-test

Kings Ltd

Product	1	2	3	4
Selling price	60	40	70	80
Variable costs	33	20	40	38
Contribution	27	20	30	42
Machine hours	3	5	6	7
Contribution per machine hour	9	4	5	6
Ranking	1	4	3	2
Demand	1,800	1,900	1,400	1,100
Machine hours needed	5,400	9,500	8,400	7,700
Optimum hours	5,400	400	8,400	7,700
Production	1,800	80	1,400	1,100
Contribution	48,600	1,600	42,000	46,200

Total contribution = £138,400
Fixed overheads = £62,000
Monthly profit = £76,400

37.1.11 Self-test

	Own staff	Contract	Difference
Food stuff	700		700
Contract fee		18,000	−18,000
Wages	11,000		11,000
Hire of equipment	1,440	1,440	−
	13,140	19,440	−6,300

The company would be better off if it hired its own staff to provide the canteen facilities.

37.1.12 Self-test

	Own staff	Contract	Difference
Purchase trimmings	2,600		2,600
Outside pleaters		35,500	−35,500
Own staff	16,400		16,400
Hire pleating machines	44,400	44,400	−
	63,400	79,900	−16,500

The company would save £16,500 by hiring its own staff to undertake the pleating.

37.1.13 Self-test

	Own staff	Contract	Difference
Purchase tools	13,200		13,200
Outside firm		74,000	−74,000
Own staff	52,500		52,500
Hire lathes	12,000		12,000
	77,700	74,000	3,700

It would be more advantageous to contract outside as the saving is £3,700 per annum.

37.1.14 Self-test

Machine hours	98	90	82
Contribution	280,100	359,400	260,780
Contribution per hour	2,858	3,993	3,180
Ranking per contribution	2	1	3
Ranking per machine hour	3	1	2

To achieve the above Company X requires 270 hours which is not available. It must therefore reduce the hours by 20 from the style that gives the lowest contribution per hour – style A.

The company needs to manufacture all of style B and C but will only be able to use 78 hours in the manufacture of style A.

37.1.15 Self-test

Hat manufacturer

Skilled labour hours	25	31	47
Contribution	52,000	41,000	89,900
Contribution per hour	2,080	1,323	1,913
Ranking per contribution	2	3	1
Ranking per labour hour	1	3	2

As skilled labour is the scarce factor we need reduce the hours on the manufacture of style B from the required number (31) to the available number of hours left after manufacturing styles A and C. This means that we only have 8 hours available for manufacturing style B.

37.1.16 Self-test

Eezysnooze Limited

(a) (i) Purchases Budget – £

Month 1	Month 2	Month 3
£9,600	£9,600	£9,600

(ii) Purchases Budget – Units

Month 1	Month 2	Month 3
240	240	240

(iii) Production Budget – Units

Month 1	Month 2	Month 3
180	240	240

(iv) Sales Budget – Units

Month 1	Month 2	Month 3
110	220	220

(v) Stock Budget – Units

	Month 1	Month 2	Month 3
To Stock each month	70	20	20
Total in Stock	70	90	110

(vi) Creditors Budget – £

Month 1	Month 2	Month 3
£7,200	£7,200	£7,200

(vii) Debtors Budget – £

Month 1	Month 2	Month 3
£33,000	£66,000	£66,000

(b) **For Decision**

Makes full use of factory i.e. capacity utilisation is 100%, no wastage.

Sales may be more than 55 units a week. Able to meet this demand from production or stock.

In the event of production breakdown customers orders can be met – this will maintain customer loyalty.

Beds kept in stock do not deteriorate/perish so money is not lost.

Against Decision

Stock is building up continually, and this involves a number of costs e.g. rent and insurance. This ties up working capital.

Eventually will run out of storage space, so must find alternative premises or reduce production.

It is possible that beds could deteriorate in stock e.g. due to dampness.

Possible that tastes change and firm left with stock that they cannot sell.

37.1.17 Self-test

DEF Ltd

(a)

	January	February	March	April
Sales units	5,000	2,000	2,500	6,000
Closing stock (10% of sales)	500	200	250	600
	5,500	2,200	2,750	6,600
Less: Opening stock	1,000	500	200	250
Units to produce	4,500	1,700	2,550	6,350

(b)

Receipts	January	February	March	April
Sales units × £150				
Current (60%)	450,000	180,000	225,000	540,000
1 month (35%)	113,750	262,500	105,000	131,250
	563,750	442,500	330,000	671,250
Payments				
Materials (units × £60)	270,000	102,000	153,000	381,000
Labour (units × £30)	135,000	51,000	76,500	190,500
Fixed overheads	60,000	60,000	60,000	60,000
Machinery			200,000	
Tax				150,000
Dividend				75,000
Overdraft interest (1%)	2,000	1,033	0	343
	467,000	214,033	489,500	856,843
Net cash flow	96,750	228,467	−159,500	−185,593
Opening balance	−200,000	−103,250	125,217	−34,283
Closing balance	−103,250	125,217	−34,283	−219,876

(c) The cash position has worsened over the four month period by nearly £20,000.

Implications:
The future for the company appears good.
Without the purchase of equipment, the company would have generated a positive cash flow.

37.1.18 Self-test

Solar Chocolates plc

(a)

Sales Budget for 6 months July to December

	July	August	September	October	November	December
Jupiter	3	3	3	3	6	12
Neptune	2	2	2	2	4	8
Saturn	4	4	4	4	6	9
Total	9	9	9	9	16	29

(b)

Production Budget for 6 months July to December

	July	August	September	October	November	December
Jupiter	3	6	6	6	6	3
Neptune	2	2	4	5	5	2
Saturn	4	5	6	6	6	4
Total	9	13	16	17	17	9

(c)

Stock Budget for Chocolate Crumb for 6 months July to December

	July	August	September	October	November	December
Total	18	26	32	34	34	18

(d) **For**

Reduces costs of holding stock – e.g. rent, security, electricity, insurance.

Helps cash flow situation as little cash tied up in stock.

Unwanted stock may deteriorate or go past sell by date etc or stays fresh.

Against

Possibility of running out of stock which may mean sales are lost.

Profit and/or production has to stop if only part or component.

Increases in demand may mean firm does not have enough stock to meet demand.

37.1.19 Self-test

Gleaston

(i)	Gross profit	$13,685/28,980 \times 100 = 47.22\%$
(ii)	Net profit	$9,900/28,980 \times 100 = 34.16\%$
(iii)	Current ratio	$22,970/11,610 = 1.98:1$
(iv)	Acid test	$9,110/11,610 = 0.78:1$
(v)	Debtors' collection	$8,030/28,980 \times 365 = 101.14$ days
(vi)	Creditors' payment	$4,650/12,608 \times 365 = 134.62$ days

37.1.20 Self-test

Sharma

(a) (i) Acid test ratio = Current assets – Stock/Current liabilities

   (ii) Gross margin = Gross profit × 100/Sales

   (iii) Rate of stock turnover = Cost of sales/Average stock

(b) Answer could include any acceptable strategy to improve profit, e.g. advertising campaign to boost sales, reduce costs by finding a cheaper supplier, etc.

(c) Answer could include any acceptable strategy to improve liquidity, e.g. offer cash discount to encourage quicker payment by debtors, reduce prices to turn stock into cash, sell off surplus fixed assets, etc.

37.1.21 Self-test

(a) (i) Earnings per share = Net profit attributable to ordinary shareholders ÷ Number of ordinary shares issued = £1,136 – £360 ÷ 16,000 = 4.85p

   (ii) Price earnings ratio = Market price ÷ Earnings per share = 64p ÷ 4.85p = 13.2

   (iii) Dividend yield = Dividend per share ÷ Market price per share = £800/16,000 (or 5p) ÷ 64p = 7.8%

   (iv) Gearing = Prior charge capital ÷ Total capital = £9,000 × 100 ÷ £19,060 = 47.2%

(b) Make appropriate comment on each of the 3 elements and a decision based on the comments.

For example:

P/E Ratio

The p/e ratio shows that investors have more confidence in the management and prospects of Athena plc. The chances are, therefore, that this confidence will translate into more improvement in the price of shares in Athena plc.

Dividend policy

Athena plc is pursuing a more prudent and sustainable dividend policy. While earning 6.4p per share, it is paying a dividend of only 4.5p per share. As the dividend cover ratio shows, it will be able to maintain this level of dividend. Thessaloniki plc on the other hand is earning 4.85p per share and paying a dividend of 5p per share. Even at current levels of earnings its dividend policy is not sustainable.

Gearing

Athena plc is not geared at all. Thessaloniki plc is significantly geared (though not highly geared). Any downturn in performance will, therefore, have a more than proportionate impact on the amounts available to ordinary shareholders in Thessaloniki plc.

Chapter 38

38.4.3 Self test

Why Ltd

	Machine A	Machine B	Machine C
Investment	(150,000)	(180,000)	(165,000)
Year 1 cash flow	45,000	36,000	30,000
	(105,000)	(144,000)	(135,000)
Year 2	45,000	42,000	39,000
	(60,000)	(102,000)	(96,000)
Year 3	45,000	90,000	39,000
	(15,000)	(12,000)	(57,000)
Year 4	30,000	60,000	75,000
	15,000	48,000	18,000
Year 5	24,000	45,000	75,000
	39,000	93,000	93,000
Payback time	3.5 years	3.2 years	3.8 years

Based on the time taken to recover the cost of the new machine, Why Ltd should select machine B.

38.6.1 Self-test

Why Ltd	Year	Discount factor	A	B	C
Initial investment	0	1	(150,000)	(180,000)	(165,000)
Net cash inflows:	1	0.893	40,185	32,148	26,790
	2	0.797	35,865	33,474	31,083
	3	0.712	32,040	64,080	27,768
	4	0.636	19,080	38,160	47,700
	5	0.567	13,608	25,515	42,525
Net present value			**(9,222)**	**13,377**	**10,866**

This would indicate that B should be chosen.

38.7.3 Self-test

Martin & Co.

Printing press
Annual cash flows: 500,000 – 50,000 (wages) – 100,000 (material) = £350,000

Payback year	Cash flow	Cumulative cash flow
0	–400,000	–400,000
1	350,000	–50,000
2	350,000	300,000

The payback period is longer than 1 year but less than 2 years.

$$1 \text{ year} + (52 \text{ weeks} \times 50,000 \div 350,000) = 1 \text{ year } 7.4 \text{ weeks}$$

(a) Net present value

Year	Cash flow	Factor	NPV
0	–400,000	1	–400,000
1	350,000	0.8333	291,655
2	350,000	0.6944	243,040
3	350,000	0.5787	202,545
4	350,000	0.4823	168,805
	1,000,000		506,045

The positive NPV satisfies the company's investment criteria.

(b) Accounting rate of return

Annual net profits = sales – wages – materials – depreciation (400,000/4)
$$= 500,000 - 50,000 - 100,000 - 100,000 = £250,000$$
Average capital employed = 400,000 ÷ 2 = £200,000
ARR = average annual profit ÷ average capital employed × 100%
250,000 ÷ 200,000 × 100 = 125%

Card cutting machine

Annual cost savings = savings 325,000 – 100,000 (annual cost of new machine)

= £225,000

(a)

Payback year	Cash flow	Cumulative cash flow
0	–300,000	–300,000
1	225,000	–75,000
2	225,000	150,000

Payback period is longer than 1 year but less than 2.

$$1 \text{ year} + 75{,}000/(225{,}000/12) = 1 \text{ year} + 4 \text{ months}$$

(b) Net present value

Year	Cash flow	Factor	Net PV
0	–300,000	1	–300,000
1	225,000	0.8333	187,493
2	225,000	0.6944	156,240
3	225,000	0.5787	130,208
4	225,000	0.4823	108,518
	600,000		282,459

The result shows a positive NPV.

(c) ARR

Annual profit improvement = cutting revenue – running cost – depreciation.

$$325{,}000 - 100{,}000 - \left(\frac{300{,}000}{4} \right) = 150{,}000$$

$$\text{Average capital employed} = \frac{300{,}000}{2} = 150{,}000$$

$$\text{ARR} \ \frac{150{,}000}{150{,}000} = 100\%$$

The new printing press gives the best return. Although the card cutting machine also gives a good return (100 per cent) the printing press shows a shorter payback period.

38.7.4 Self-test

Art Ltd

NPV

Year	Discount factor	P.V.
1	0.909	(9,090)
2	0.826	49,560
3	0.751	71,345
4	0.683	51,225
		163,040
Initial investment		100,000
NPV		63,040

Investment worthwhile because positive NPV.

IRR

Year	PV 20%	PV 25%	PV 30%
1	(8,333)	(8,000)	(7,690)
2	41,640	38,400	35,520
3	55,005	48,640	43,225
4	36,150	30,750	26,250
	124,462	109,790	97,305
Investment	100,000	100,000	100,000

IRR is between 25% and 30%.

38.7.5 Self-test

Fred Ltd

(a) Net cash flows resulting from the replacement machine

	Cash inflow	Cash outflow	Net cash flow
2011	365,000	200,000	165,000
2012	557,600	295,800	261,800
2013	702,000	374,400	327,600

(b) Net present value of the replacement machine

Year	Net cash flow	Discount factor	Present value
2011	−400,000	1.000	−400,000
2011	165,000	0.909	149,985
2012	261,800	0.826	216,247
2013	327,600	0.751	246,027
Net present value			212,259

(c) The payback period is the amount of time it takes to recover or receive in cash the income required to match the amount spent on the investment.

   The accounting rate of return is the average profit (expressed as a percentage) of the capital invested in the project.

(d) From the financial point of view the net present value indicates a return on investment significantly in excess of the 10 per cent cost of capital faced by the company. There may be non-financial factors to take into account, e.g. reduction of the labour force. Overall it would depend on company policy and how this decision fitted in with its overall strategy.

(e) If the net present value were 0 instead of £212,259 then the exact return on the investment would have equalled the chosen discount rate (10 per cent). The exact rate is known as IRR. Since NPV is higher than 0 the IRR must be higher than 10 per cent. It is possible to estimate the IRR by deciding how much above 0 the return is and expressing this as a percentage.

(f) The internal rate of return is more valuable than the net present value because it is more precise.

38.7.6 Self-test

Helico Ltd

Workings:
Income calculation
Years 1 & 2 = 300 days × £690 = £207,000
Year 3 = (320 days × 2) × £690 = £441,600
Years 4, 5 & 6 = (320 days × 2) × £828 = £529,920

Depreciation = £900,000/6 = £150,000 p.a.
Monthly expenses £315,000 for years 1 & 2
Years 3, 4 & 5 = £355,000
Year 6 = £381,000

(i) Payback period

Year	Cash inflow	Cash outflow	Net cash flow
0		(950,000)	(950,000)
1	207,000	(165,000)	42,000
2	207,000	(165,000)	42,000
3	441,600	(205,000)	236,600
4	529,920	(205,000)	324,920
5	529,920	(205,000)	324,920
6	529,920	(231,000)	298,920

At the end of year 5 £970,440 is paid back as calculated in the above cash flow statement. Payback is after 4 years and (20,440/324,920) × 365 days = 4 years 23 days.

   Using the payback method and the fixed criteria of the company we would not invest as the period is greater than 4 years (only 23 days excess).

(ii) Net present value

Year	Net cash flow	Discount factor	Disc cash flow
0	(950,000)	1.000	(950,000)
1	42,000	0.870	36,540
2	42,000	0.756	31,752
3	236,600	0.658	155,683
4	324,920	0.572	185,854
5	324,920	0.497	161,485
6	298,920	0.432	129,133
NPV			(249,553)

NPV shows that the company should not invest.

(iii) Average rate of return
Total surplus of project £1,269,360 – 950,000 = £319,360

$$\text{Average annual return} = \frac{£319,360}{6 \text{ years}} = £53,227 \text{ per year}$$

$$\text{Accounting rate of return} = \frac{£53,227}{£950,000} \times 100 = 5.60\%$$

As the company only invests where an average of 10 per cent return is shown, it should not invest in this project.

Recommendations

In considering this project there are many things to be taken into account. These include:

(a) Accuracy of predictions.
(b) Chance of renewal of contract after the initial 6 years.
(c) Other possible investment projects available.
(d) Does the project identify with other objectives and/or strategy of the company?

Chapter 39

39.1.1 Self-test

Walter & Co.

	Sales – original estimate	Sales – revised estimate
2010	£1,500,000	£1,500,000
2011	£2,000,000	£2,100,000
2012	£2,500,000	£2,625,000
2013	£3,000,000	£3,150,000

	Costs – original estimate	Costs – revised estimate
2010	£1,000,000	£1,000,000
2011	£1,000,000	£1,030,000
2012	£1,120,000	£1,153,600
2013	£1,500,000	£1,545,000

(a) Revised cash flow

	Income	Costs	Net cash flow
2010	£1,500,000	£1,000,000	£500,000
2011	£2,100,000	£1,030,000	£1,070,000
2012	£2,625,000	£1,153,600	£1,471,400
2013	£3,150,000	£1,545,000	£1,605,000

(b) NPV

Year	Discount factor	Cash flow £	Discounted cash flow
0	1.000	(2,000,000)	(2,000,000)
1	0.909	500,000	454,500
2	0.826	1,070,000	883,820
3	0.751	1,471,400	1,105,021
4	0.683	1,605,000	1,096,215
NPV			1,539,556

39.1.2 Self-test

Gems Ltd

	Present costs and income	Remaining 25%
Sales 600,000 @ £12	7,200,000	
200,000 @ £9		1,800,000
Variable costs @ £7.20	4,320,000	1,440,000
Fixed costs	1,300,000	
Profit	1,580,000	360,000

By accepting the offer, Gems Ltd increases its profits by £360,000.

Extra fixed costs of £280,000 and a 5 per cent loss of existing sales (30,000 brooches):

Loss of contribution = 30,000 × £4.80 per brooch = £144,000
Total loss of income = 280,000 + 144,000 = £424,000

As this is greater than the profit achieved by the offer, it should be declined.

39.1.3 Self-test

Healthy Products

Product	A	B	C
Selling price £	6	8	12
Variable cost £	4	5	7
Contribution	2	3	5
WX234 kilo per unit	0.5	1	2
Contribution per kilo used	4	3	2.5
Ranking	1	2	3
Budget sales	24,000	15,000	30,000
Kilo of WX234 required	12,000	15,000	60,000

The need is greater than the 34,500 kilo available. Therefore, the raw material is the limiting factor. Product C, which has the lowest ranking contribution, will therefore not be able to be produced in full and sales will be limited to 3,750 units requiring 7,500 kilo.

Maximum profit

Product	Quantity	WX234	Unit contribution	Total contribution
A	24,000	12,000	2	48,000
B	15,000	15,000	3	45,000
C	3,750	7,500	5	18,750
		34,500		111,750
Fixed costs				45,000
Profit				66,750

39.1.4 Self-test

Motorman Ltd

Receipts	Sept	Oct	Nov	Total
Cash (30%)	67,500	75,000	66,000	208,500
Credit (70%)	133,000	157,500	175,000	465,500
	200,500	232,500	241,000	674,000

Payments	Sept	Oct	Nov	Total
Purchases*	152,000	180,000	200,000	532,000
Wages	16,000	18,000	18,000	52,000
Expenses less depreciation	13,750	6,400	15,150	35,300
Tax	38,500			38,500
Delivery van			25,000	25,000
	220,250	204,400	258,150	682,800

* Purchases are equal to 80 per cent of the sales to provide the mark up of 25 per cent.

	Sept	Oct	Nov	Total
Opening balance	25,000	5,250	33,350	25,000
Surplus/deficit	−19,750	28,100	−17,150	−8,800
Closing balance	5,250	33,350	16,200	16,200

39.1.5 Self-test

Alex Ltd

Product X	Budget based on 40,000 units	Budget based on 45,000 units	Budget based on 30,000 units
Variable costs £18 per unit	720,000	810,000	540,000
Repairs	16,000	16,750	14,500
Indirect wages	32,000	35,750	24,500
Fixed costs	8,000	8,000	8,000
Total costs	776,000	870,500	587,000

Chapter 40

40.4.2 Self-test

Answers can be taken from sections 40.2.2 and 40.2.3.

40.4.3 Self-test

Spreadsheets can be used in the ways described in section 40.3.1. In addition they are invaluable when we have to combine companies (consolidation) or where we have a number of branches, each with their own trading accounts.

Another common use for spreadsheets is their use in converting pounds sterling to euros or dollars for purposes of combining results of foreign branches or companies.

Chapter 41

41.7.1 Self-test

- There are a large number of different national standards. This imposes additional costs on the capital markets. Some of that cost is direct and borne by companies that must meet multiple standards if they seek to raise capital in different markets.
- No individual standard setter has a monopoly on the best solutions to accounting problems. It is argued that US GAAP is the most detailed and comprehensive in the world. This does not mean that every individual US standard is the best. The goal of IASB is to identify the best in standards from around the world.
- There are many areas of financial reporting in which a national standard setter finds it difficult to act alone. A tough standard would put local companies at a competitive

disadvantage relative to companies outside their jurisdiction. An international standard setter can establish financial reporting standards that would apply to all companies in all jurisdictions, thus eliminating any possible disadvantages.

41.7.2 Self-test

Dividends are shown in (d) Statement of changes in equity and also in (c) Statement of cash flows.

41.7.3 Self-test

The statement of cash flows shows dividends paid and also the proceeds of a rights issue. Both involve the flow of cash.

41.7.4 Self-test

Income statement for Camden Trading Ltd for the year ended 31 December 2010

Turnover		375,000
Cost of sales		135,000
Gross Profit		240,000
Administration expenses	95,000	
Selling & distribution expenses	52,000	
Financial expenses	3,000	150,000
Profit for the year attributable to equity holders		90,000

Statement of financial position as at 31 December 2010

Assets		
Non-current assets		
Tangible		388,000
Current Assets		
Inventory	175,000	
Trade receivables	90,000	
Other receivables	12,000	277,000
Total assets		665,000
Equity and liabilities		
Equity		
Ordinary shares	160,000	
Revaluation reserve	35,000	
Retained earnings	277,000	472,000
Liabilities		
Non-current liabilities		
Debentures		60,000
Current liabilities		
Trade payables	75,000	
Overdraft	30,000	
Other payables	28,000	133,000
Total equity and liabilities		665,000

41.7.5 Self-test

Income statement for Hilmor Ltd for the year ended 31 December 2009

Turnover		451,000
Cost of sales		250,980
Gross profit		200,020
Distribution costs	7,700	
Administration expenses	177,620	185,320
Profit before tax*		14,700
Preference dividends		1,200
Profit for the year attributable to equity holders		13,500
Ordinary dividend		10,000
Balance of undistributed profit for the year		3,500

* The question does not provide for tax therefore the profit before tax and after tax is the same.

Statement of financial position of Hilmor Ltd as at 31 December 2009

Non-current assets			
Tangible assets			123,500
Current Assets			
Inventory	46,500		
Trade receivables	12,780		
Bank	6,420		65,700
Total Assets			189,200
Equity and liabilities			
Equity			
6% preference shares	20,000		
Ordinary shares	100,000	120,000	
Retained earnings	15,900		
General reserve	15,000		
Share premium	10,000	40,900	160,900
Liabilities			
Current liabilities			
Trade payables		17,700	
Other payables		10,600	28,300
Total equity and liabilities			189,200

Statement of changes in equity

Balance 1 January 2009	12,400
Profit for the year	13,500
	25,900
Ordinary dividends paid	10,000
Balance at 31 December 2009	15,900

Appendix 2

Present value table

Present value of £1, that is $(1 + r)^{-n}$ where r = interest rate; n = number of periods until payment or receipt.

Periods (n)	Interest rates (r)									
	1%	2%	3%	4%	5%	6%	7%	8%	9%	10%
1	0.990	0.980	0.971	0.962	0.952	0.943	0.935	0.926	0.917	0.909
2	0.980	0.961	0.943	0.925	0.907	0.890	0.873	0.857	0.842	0.826
3	0.971	0.942	0.915	0.889	0.864	0.840	0.816	0.794	0.772	0.751
4	0.961	0.924	0.888	0.855	0.823	0.792	0.763	0.735	0.708	0.683
5	0.951	0.906	0.863	0.822	0.784	0.747	0.713	0.681	0.650	0.621
6	0.942	0.888	0.837	0.790	0.746	0.705	0.666	0.630	0.596	0.564
7	0.933	0.871	0.813	0.760	0.711	0.665	0.623	0.583	0.547	0.513
8	0.923	0.853	0.789	0.731	0.677	0.627	0.582	0.540	0.502	0.467
9	0.914	0.837	0.766	0.703	0.645	0.592	0.544	0.500	0.460	0.424
10	0.905	0.820	0.744	0.676	0.614	0.558	0.508	0.463	0.422	0.386
11	0.896	0.804	0.722	0.650	0.585	0.527	0.475	0.429	0.388	0.350
12	0.887	0.788	0.701	0.625	0.557	0.497	0.444	0.397	0.356	0.319
13	0.879	0.773	0.681	0.601	0.530	0.469	0.415	0.368	0.326	0.290
14	0.870	0.758	0.661	0.577	0.505	0.442	0.388	0.340	0.299	0.263
15	0.861	0.743	0.642	0.555	0.481	0.417	0.362	0.315	0.275	0.239
16	0.853	0.728	0.623	0.534	0.458	0.394	0.339	0.292	0.252	0.218
17	0.844	0.714	0.605	0.513	0.436	0.371	0.317	0.270	0.231	0.198
18	0.836	0.700	0.587	0.494	0.416	0.350	0.296	0.250	0.212	0.180
19	0.828	0.686	0.570	0.475	0.396	0.331	0.277	0.232	0.194	0.164
20	0.820	0.673	0.554	0.456	0.377	0.312	0.258	0.215	0.178	0.149

Periods (n)	Interest rates (r)									
	11%	12%	13%	14%	15%	16%	17%	18%	19%	20%
1	0.901	0.893	0.885	0.877	0.870	0.862	0.855	0.847	0.840	0.833
2	0.812	0.797	0.783	0.769	0.756	0.743	0.731	0.718	0.706	0.694
3	0.731	0.712	0.693	0.675	0.658	0.641	0.624	0.609	0.593	0.579
4	0.659	0.636	0.613	0.592	0.572	0.552	0.534	0.516	0.499	0.482
5	0.593	0.567	0.543	0.519	0.497	0.476	0.456	0.437	0.419	0.402
6	0.535	0.507	0.480	0.456	0.432	0.410	0.390	0.370	0.352	0.335
7	0.482	0.452	0.425	0.400	0.376	0.354	0.333	0.314	0.296	0.279
8	0.434	0.404	0.376	0.351	0.327	0.305	0.285	0.266	0.249	0.233
9	0.391	0.361	0.333	0.308	0.284	0.263	0.243	0.225	0.209	0.194
10	0.352	0.322	0.295	0.270	0.247	0.227	0.208	0.191	0.176	0.162
11	0.317	0.287	0.261	0.237	0.215	0.195	0.178	0.162	0.148	0.135
12	0.286	0.257	0.231	0.208	0.187	0.168	0.152	0.137	0.124	0.112
13	0.258	0.229	0.204	0.182	0.163	0.145	0.130	0.116	0.104	0.093
14	0.232	0.205	0.181	0.160	0.141	0.125	0.111	0.099	0.088	0.078
15	0.209	0.183	0.160	0.140	0.123	0.108	0.095	0.084	0.079	0.065
16	0.188	0.163	0.141	0.123	0.107	0.093	0.081	0.071	0.062	0.054
17	0.170	0.146	0.125	0.108	0.093	0.080	0.069	0.060	0.052	0.045
18	0.153	0.130	0.111	0.095	0.081	0.069	0.059	0.051	0.044	0.038
19	0.138	0.116	0.098	0.083	0.070	0.060	0.051	0.043	0.037	0.031
20	0.124	0.104	0.087	0.073	0.061	0.051	0.043	0.037	0.031	0.026

Index

Note: Figures are indicated (in this index) by *italic numbers*, and footnotes by suffix 'n'.